BUILDING A
CISCO NETWORK
FOR WINDOWS 2000

SYNGRESS®

KEY	SERIAL NUMBER
001	9TRR52MDSE
002	XPSTEH7TC4
003	CLNBC28FV7
004	DC128N4RL6
005	Z745Q25DBR
006	PF62R2DXMB
007	DT88A5ZX44
008	XRCJ743RTG
009	6532M92L8S
010	SMYR8PS2RN

PUBLISHED BY
Syngress Media, Inc.
800 Hingham Street
Rockland, MA 02370

Building a Cisco Network for Windows 2000

Printed in the United States of America

1 2 3 4 5 6 7 8 9 0

ISBN: 1-928994-00-8

Copy edit by: Adrienne Rebello
Technical edit by: Stace Cunningham
Index by: Robert Saigh
Project Editor: Katharine Glennon

Proofreading by: Nancy Adams
Page Layout and Art by: Shannon Tozier
and Katharine Glennon
Co-Publisher: Richard Kristof

Distributed by Publishers Group West

Acknowledgments

We would like to acknowledge the following people for their kindness and support in making this book possible.

Richard Kristof, Duncan Anderson, Jennifer Gould, Robert Woodruff, Kevin Murray, Dale Leatherwood, Rhonda Harmon, and Robert Sanregret of Global Knowledge, for their generous access to the IT industry's best courses, instructors and training facilities.

Ralph Troupe and the team at Callisma for their invaluable insight into the challenges of designing, deploying and supporting world-class enterprise networks.

Karen Cross, Kim Wylie, Harry Kirchner, John Hays, Bill Richter, Kevin Votel, Brittin Clark, Sarah Schaffer, Ellen Lafferty and Sarah MacLachlan of Publishers Group West for sharing their incredible marketing experience and expertise.

Mary Ging, Caroline Hird, and Simon Beale of Harcourt International for making certain that our vision remains worldwide in scope.

Annabel Dent, Anneka Baeten, Clare MacKenzie, and Laurie Giles of Harcourt Australia for all their help.

David Buckland, Wendi Wong, David Loh, Marie Chieng, Lucy Chong, Leslie Lim, Audrey Gan, and Joseph Chan of Transquest Publishers for the enthusiasm with which they receive our books.

Kwon Sung June at Acorn Publishing for his support.

Ethan Atkin at Cranbury International for his help in expanding the Syngress program.

Special thanks to the professionals at Osborne with whom we are proud to publish the best-selling Global Knowledge Certification Press series.

From Global Knowledge

At Global Knowledge we strive to support the multiplicity of learning styles required by our students to achieve success as technical professionals. As the world's largest IT training company, Global Knowledge is uniquely positioned to offer these books. The expertise gained each year from providing instructor-led training to hundreds of thousands of students worldwide has been captured in book form to enhance your learning experience. We hope that the quality of these books demonstrates our commitment to your lifelong learning success. Whether you choose to learn through the written word, computer based training, Web delivery, or instructor-led training, Global Knowledge is committed to providing you with the very best in each of these categories. For those of you who know Global Knowledge, or those of you who have just found us for the first time, our goal is to be your lifelong competency partner.

Thank your for the opportunity to serve you. We look forward to serving your needs again in the future.

Warmest regards,

Duncan Anderson
President and Chief Executive Officer, Global Knowledge

Contributors

Russell Brown (CCNP, MCSE+I, A+) is an independent consultant in Minneapolis, MN. He focuses on networking and security, specializing primarily in integrating Microsoft products with Cisco Routing. He has over three years of computer consulting experience but still finds time to play the guitar in several bands around the Twin Cities. Some of the projects Russ has worked on include LAN/WAN troubleshooting for small companies, Firewall and Proxy design and implementation, designing procedures for desktop rollouts, and various routing and switching implementations. Russ lives in Minneapolis, MN and can be reached at brown@isd.net. His website is http://ruebarb.tripod.com.

Melissa Craft (CCNA, MCSE, Network+, CNE-5, CNE-3, CNE-4, CNE-GW, MCNE, Citrix CCA) designs business computing solutions using technology to automate processes, and using business process reengineering techniques. Melissa has successfully designed, implemented and integrated networks ranging in size from a few nodes to over 100,000 nodes. Her consulting experience has incorporated extensive project management, needs-analysis, LAN and WAN design, deployment and operational turnover. Currently, Melissa is Director of e-Business Offering Development for MicroAge Technology Services, a global systems integrator that provides IT design, project management, and support for distributed computing systems. Melissa holds a bachelor's degree from the University of Michigan, and is a member of the IEEE, the Society of Women Engineers and American MENSA, Ltd. Melissa currently resides in Glendale, Arizona with her family, Dan, Justine, and Taylor, and her two Great Danes (a.k.a Mobile Defense Units), Marmaduke and Apollo and her Golden Retriever (a.k.a. Mobile Alarm Unit) Pooka. Melissa can be contacted via e-mail at mmcraft@compuserve.com.

Elliot Lewis (CCNA, CCDA, MCSE, CCSE, MCP+I, MCT) is the Director of Solution Architecture at EngineX Networks, a leading infrastructure design firm that specializes in designing and implementing industry-leading networking technologies. Specialties include Voice over technologies, High Availability Infrastructure, IP Video/Audio Conferencing, IP

Telephony, Wireless, and Content Networking. Elliot has over 13 years of experience in the design, implementation, and troubleshooting of large mission critical networks. He authored *Configuring Cisco Voice Over IP* with Syngress Media. He lives in Pleasanton, CA with his wife Meg and two sons, James and Zachary.

Elliot Lewis contributed to the technical editing.

Sean Thurston (CCNA, CCDA, MCP+I, MCSE) is a Solution Architect for EngineX Networks, a San Francisco-based Voice over IP/QoS network design and implementation company. Sean has extensive network design and implementation experience in complex LAN and WAN environments. He lives in Renton, WA with his fiancée Kerry.

Technical Editor

Stace Cunningham (CCNA, MCSE, CLSE, COS/2E, CLSI, COS/2I, CLSA, MCPS, A+) is a Systems Engineer with SDC Consulting located in Biloxi, MS. SDC Consulting specializes in the design, engineering, and installation of networks. Stace is also certified as an IBM Certified LAN Server Engineer, IBM Certified OS/2 Engineer, IBM Certified LAN Server Administrator, IBM Certified LAN Server Instructor, IBM Certified OS/2 Instructor. Stace has participated as a Technical Contributor for the IIS 3.0 exam, SMS 1.2 exam, Proxy Server 1.0 exam, Exchange Server 5.0 and 5.5 exams, Proxy Server 2.0 exam, IIS 4.0 exam, IEAK exam, and the revised Windows 95 exam.

In addition, he has coauthored or technical edited about 30 books published by Microsoft Press, Osborne/McGraw-Hill, and Syngress Media as well as contributed to publications from The SANS Institute and Internet Security Advisor magazine.

His wife Martha and daughter Marissa are very supportive of the time he spends with his computers, routers, and firewalls in the "lab" of their house. Without their love and support he would not be able to accomplish the goals he has set for himself.

Stace Cunningham authored a chapter in addition to acting as technical director for the book.

Contents

Chapter 10—Implementing the Cisco Switches   391

Preface

The leading edge, the bleeding edge, the latest, the hottest, the coolest developments, the newest advances...how many of these descriptions have you heard applied to technology? How about to Microsoft's or Cisco's products? The fact is that both these companies are developing useful new networking technologies with advances made at a frantic pace.

Leading technologies, like Microsoft's and Cisco's, remind me of a comment my mother once made on the fact that today's society is completely different from that of her parents. Technology today, she said, gives people opportunities that they never would have had in the past. People use technology to provide themselves with things that they would have had to work extremely hard for, or would simply have done without, in even the most recent history.

To my mother's point: my grandfather, Arthur Conat, drove a carriage with horses when he was a teenager. He didn't have a TV, or a telephone, or a car, or a refrigerator, or a washing machine, or running water aside from that at a hand-pumped well. By the time he was my age (mid-30s), he had entered a lifelong career at the Bell Telephone Company, which is today AT&T. He lived through two world wars, and entered the military with pride to serve his country. Communications were his game, and they were a critical contributing factor in winning World War II. Did communications win the war? No—they contributed. The technology for communications made it easier for information to be sent to vital units about events happening around them, and obstacles they might encounter. Thus, they were able to make better decisions about how to proceed.

Communications, or telecommunications in electronic format, with the encryption and speed available today, are far more advanced than any the world has seen before our lifetimes. The Internet has been around for only a mere speck of time in documented history. (You can read the Internet history in Chapter 1, by the way.) Although the Internet's popularity has made it indispensable to many businesses, it has barely begun to pervade our existence. But it has become such an enabler, such a contributing factor, to the way people and businesses win their own wars, so to speak, that it has grown to nearly overtake everything that people can do—from global positioning systems in cars, to cell phones with Web browsers. And the technology keeps developing.

There are countless companies vying for the chief ranking in the techno-race. From software development corporations to hardware manufacturers to Internet startups (e.g., the "dot-coms"), they are all trying to gain the majority market share of dollars spent on technology—apparently hoping that their version of the technology will be the one that consumers want to spend money on. You will find a lot of crossover with the technology out there—an Application Service Provider (ASP) can provide much the same services as some software and hardware by original equipment manufacturers (OEMs) out there. People have the choice of outsourcing their business needs to an ASP, purchasing software from developers, or buying hardware from OEMs.

Who will win the techno-race? Winning would presume that there would be an end to technology research and development. I mean, do you think people will stop learning, changing, and trying new things? Well, would you stop learning, changing, and trying new things? I doubt it. I believe that there will be an ever-evolving mixture of technologies gaining the edge on the market, and new types of technologies to explore in the future. At any point in time, you will see a different leader. Even now, you can look back over the past two decades and see the evolution. At one time, Apple was in the lead (or it was IBM, or Novell, or Microsoft), and recently Cisco made the news as having edged out Microsoft as the leading capitalized technology giant. Microsoft edged Cisco back the next day, of course, but the statement was made—there are changes in the way people invest in technology and those changes are happening today. So rather than "who will win?" we need to think about "who is it today?" and "who will be next?".

Who is it today? The answer is that there are two top technology companies—Microsoft and Cisco. Microsoft, as a software development corporation, provides operating systems and applications for both business and personal use. Cisco, as a hardware original equipment manufacturer, produces internetwork equipment and the internetwork operating systems that move data from one point in an internetwork to another point. Internetworks are primarily business-based. However, the Internet (the world's largest internetwork) has unlocked internetworking for personal use, enabling individual consumers to interact with businesses for various transactions across it.

With the advent of the Internet, the need for moving data across internetworks has grown to immense proportions. Businesses and people alike are attached to the Internet. Currently, the United States has connected the largest percentage of people to the Internet, but other countries are catching up quickly. Both Cisco and Microsoft have strong Internet integration strategies for their respective products. Their strategies encompass a wide spectrum of services that Internet users will want, for both business and personal reasons. Both Cisco and Microsoft support the Internet Protocol (IP) natively, and therefore sustain Internet connectivity.

Users are increasingly accessing the Internet for personal entertainment purposes. Businesses are providing entertainment services and products. The Internet entertainment list keeps growing—you can find any of the following and much more on the Internet:

- Retransmitted televisions shows

- Movies on demand

- Audio music files to be downloaded

Because of its multimedia components, entertainment services require high bandwidth and streaming data to perform well. One of the technologies that can be used to guarantee higher bandwidth and uninterrupted data streams is Quality of Service (QoS). Both Cisco's Internetwork Operating System (IOS) and Microsoft's Windows 2000 have the ability to provide QoS, which we discuss in a couple of chapters in this book.

Users are also using the Internet for voice communications. There are personal "Net Phones," and there are PBX and voicemail applications for businesses. Voice communications is an area in which the Internet provides cost reductions by removing long distance costs from all, or a percentage, of the calls made. Generally, a person or business saves because they can use their local connection to the Internet in the place of a long distance telephone call placed over the public service telephone network. Voice-over Internet Protocol (VoIP) and telephony applications for Cisco's IOS and Microsoft's Windows 2000, both used to provide voice communications over the Internet, are both discussed in this book.

What would the Internet be without the World Wide Web? The majority of Internet usage is downloading HyperText Markup Language (HTML) pages and their contents. Before HTML, the Internet was used mostly for electronic mail, file transfers, or network news. All of these services are provided by Windows 2000 and can be managed effectively with Cisco IOS. You will learn about these throughout this book.

While users are pushing the limits of Internet bandwidth consumption and technology, businesses have a new problem—managing the users. Not only does a business have to manage the users who work for them, but there is also an escalating challenge with managing the data that attaches to the visitors of their Web sites. When visitors log on to a Web site, businesses realize that they will return more often if visitors receive personalized data. To track that data, a directory service can store users' information, preferences, and interests. Windows 2000 provides an LDAP-compliant directory service called Active Directory. It is accessible over any TCP/IP based internetwork, including the Internet. Directory services are expected to expand in the future to contain information about all sorts of network systems, resources, and information. As such, the Active Directory is the foundation of this book.

This book is unique in that it explores the technologies of Cisco and Microsoft both separately and together. If you have a network that uses either Cisco equipment or Microsoft Windows 2000, you will find the book useful. If you have a network that uses both Cisco equipment and Microsoft Windows 2000, you will find the book invaluable.

We wrote the book for the advanced systems administrator. There are concepts within it that require some existing knowledge of networking, Windows NT, and routing of data. To provide a basis, we've added a primer in Chapter 1. (If you are comfortable with your knowledge of networking, you can skip the primer, or just browse it to give yourself an update.)

In addition to the general knowledge of what the technology is, why it can be beneficial, and how to implement it, there's an additional section at the end of a majority of the chapters called "Case Studies." This section discusses two different companies, along with their business requirements and their existing networks, and then the case study applies the concepts discussed in that particular chapter to each company. The same two fictional companies are used throughout the Case Studies sections. These sections should provide the real-world translation from concept to usage for the Cisco and Windows 2000 technologies. Not only do they run through the implementation of the technology, but they also discuss the design of the internetworks for each.

At the end of the book, you will find a chapter named "Fast Track." This chapter will encapsulate the major concepts found throughout the book. If you want to get an overview of everything before you start, flip to the back and read "Fast Track" first. If you read through the book and you don't really care for a review, then the only part of "Fast Track" that will be of value is the section that discusses some of the up and coming technologies for Cisco and Microsoft.

I hope you find value in this book, and that you are able to use it to help design, implement, and manage a Cisco/Microsoft network.

Chapter 1

Developing a Windows 2000 and Cisco Internetwork

Solutions in this chapter:

- Directory Enabled Network (DEN)

- Windows 2000 overview

- Cisco IOS overview

- Networking basics

- OSI reference model

Introduction

Microsoft and Cisco are two of the largest technology vendors in the information technology industry today. Microsoft's Windows 2000 is its latest network operating system (NOS), and Cisco is pushing the limits for routing and switching voice, video, and data across internetworks. Beyond this, Microsoft and Cisco have partnered in order to integrate their respective systems using directory enabled networking (DEN). By merging their technologies, Microsoft and Cisco are placing their bets that DEN will lead the future of global internetworking. Now, any organization can take advantage of the benefits that DEN offers through the implementation of a combination Microsoft/Cisco internetwork, using their directory software products.

Directory Enabled Network

DEN is the brainchild of the Cisco and Microsoft relationship. They developed the basis for its specifications and presented it to the Distributed Management Task Force (DMTF) and the Internet Engineering Task Force (IETF) for standardization.

Why did Cisco and Microsoft develop the DEN concept? They discovered that, although most network operating systems and applications supported a directory service, most were proprietary. Take Novell's NetWare, for example. A legacy NetWare server holds its own directory service, called a *bindery*, on each server separately. User account information must be entered into every server that the user needed to access.

It was difficult, if not impossible, to ensure that the user account information and password, and even the account name itself, was synchronized among the various servers. Novell realized this was an issue, and in the mid-1990s released Novell Directory Services (NDS), which was branded NetWare Directory Services at the time. NDS is a proprietary directory service that multiple NetWare services and NetWare applications can all access. A user account needs to be entered into the directory only one time for the user to be granted access to any server or resource existing in the NDS directory.

For a directory service to work well in an organization, it must be nonproprietary, and capable of being accessed by different operating systems that participate on the network. If a directory service is nonproprietary, as the DEN standard presents, then the directory service can contain rules about how a user account is allowed to access any number of systems. The result is a greatly reduced administrative cost to the network. Users would be required to learn only a single user ID and password. Administrators would only be required to maintain information in a single directory.

Internetworks are becoming increasingly complex. With network operating systems providing Web services, with changes in technology, and with databases being integrated to create new e-business systems, the internetwork has grown to include new media types, multiple protocols, many different types of devices, and a large number of services. Organizations are running into a conflict between business unit managers who need new functionality for providing new e-business services and Information Technology (IT) groups who are tasked with reducing the total cost of owning the technology on the network. IT groups are also faced with management applications that are proprietary and database systems that are unable to interoperate; both situations hinder the addition of new network services or result in increased integration costs. This divided system is shown in Figure 1.1.

Figure 1.1 Separate application-specific databases limit interoperability.

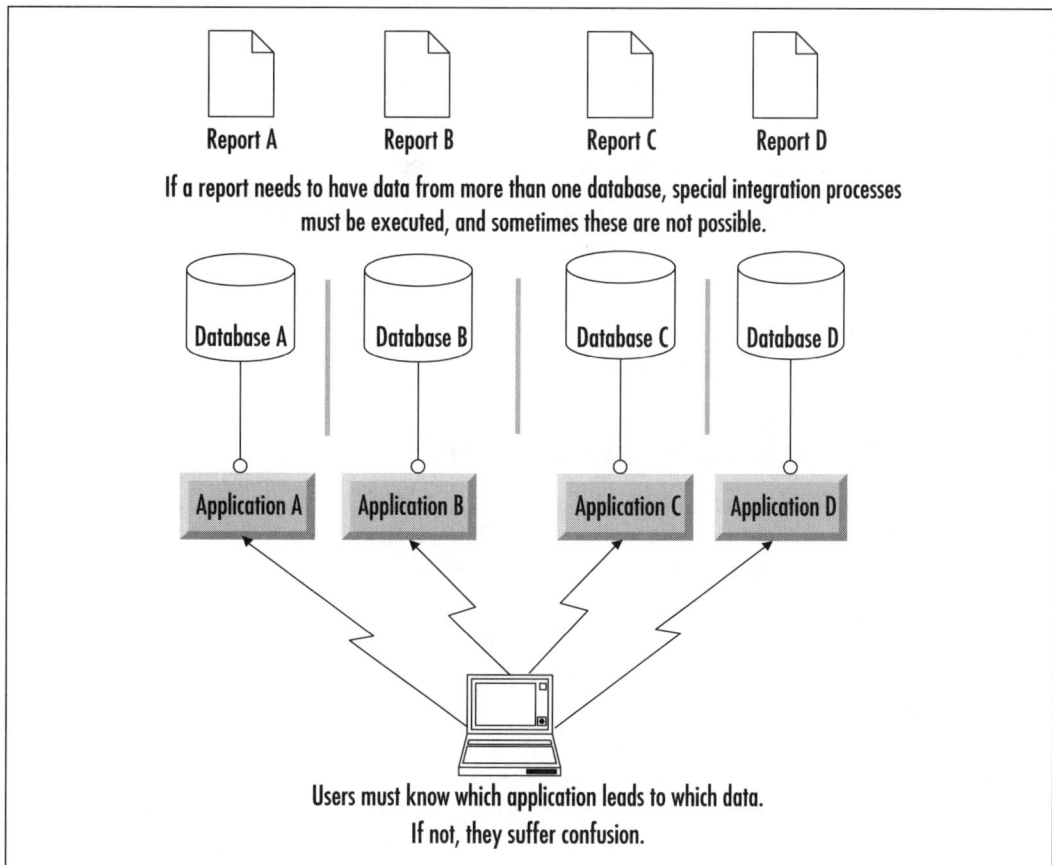

The DEN Solution

DEN is a solution to several challenges from which both enterprise administrators and software vendors suffer. Administrators and vendors are faced with the following issues:

- How to integrate new e-business systems

- How to incorporate service level agreements for specific users

- How to apply and manage policies

- How to integrate management "islands" (i.e., separate network administration units and separate network management systems)

- How to get interoperability from systems right out of the box

- How to achieve advanced services that are applicable network-wide

DEN solves these issues with the definition of a directory service, shown in Figure 1.2, which can manage:

- Integration of e-business systems, media, devices, and protocols

- Incorporation of service levels into the management of users and applications

- Application and management of policies

- Integration of extensible management applications into the directory to centralize the network management

- Utilization of common protocols, common application programming interfaces (APIs), and a common repository for information to ensure interoperability

- Advanced services from configuration, access control, security, and provisioning of Quality of Service (QoS)

As a result, DEN harnesses the power of a database to centralize and manage network systems and services. DEN defines a common schema for network units and services, and enables interoperability between them. DEN specifies an object-oriented information model, called a *directory*, for networked units. A networked unit is defined within the directory as a *class*. The network units, or classes, are not limited to devices or user accounts, but encompass every possible application or system that can participate on the network. Classes are composed of *objects* that share the same basis of attributes. Any single network element (a user account, server, policy, etc.) represents some individual entity (Joe User, Server1, or SecurityPolicyA, and so on) on the network. Each object contains a set of

Figure 1.2 Directory-enabled networking architecture.

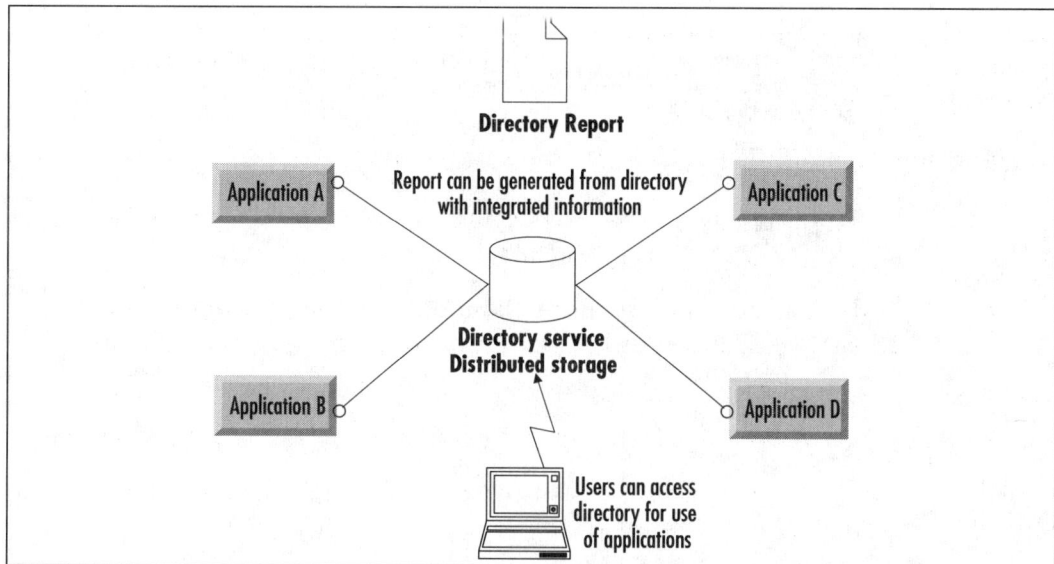

attributes that describe its properties. For example, an attribute for a user account may be the user's telephone number.

DEN does not define a management protocol like Simple Network Management Protocol (SNMP), even though it enables network management at a new level. It does not define a network protocol like Lightweight Directory Access Protocol (LDAP), although new directory services will likely integrate LDAP. It does not define a new type of schema for a database. DEN is not a product in and by itself.

DEN is a definition of the foundational elements required for building a directory enabled network service or application. It defines a standard hierarchy for a directory service, but opposes limitations by defining extensibility. When DEN is used, multiple vendors will not experience conflicts between their schemas, and network device configuration and management can be performed through the use of the directory service.

In the DEN policy server model, network devices will use standard protocols to access the network, such as Domain Name System (DNS) and Dynamic Host Configuration Protocol (DHCP). The network devices will access servers or hosts to attempt a network transaction, which will check the directory service (whether it is stored locally, or on other servers) for any policies that may apply.

If a policy does apply to the network transaction, the policy is applied and the transaction is permitted with whatever alterations the policy requires, or denied based on the policy, as shown in Figure 1.3.

Figure 1.3 Policy server model.

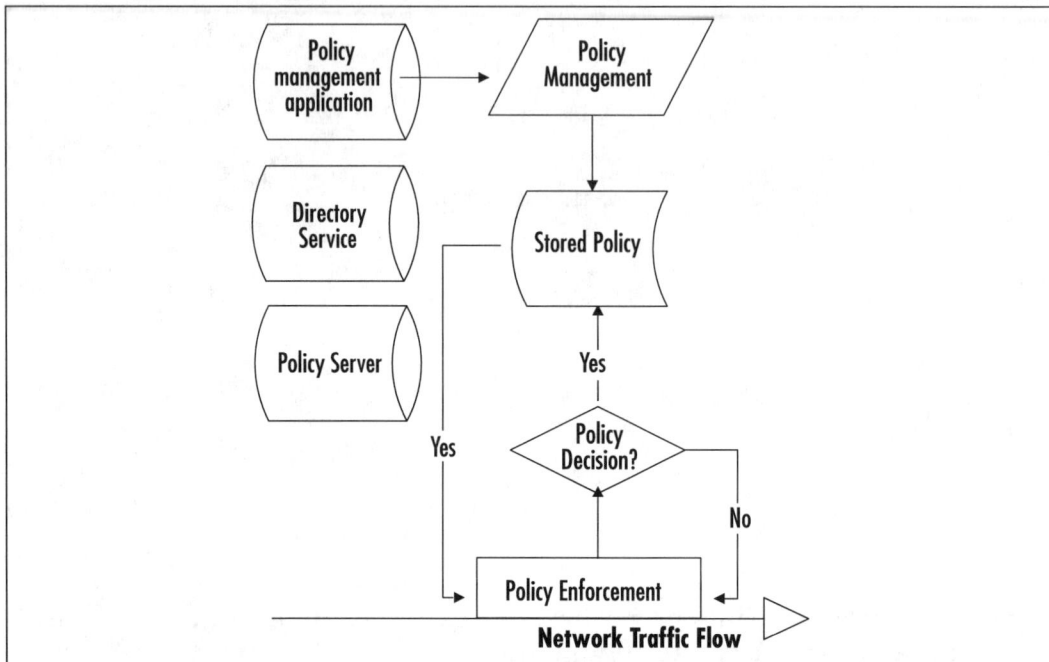

QoS is a way of establishing a priority (or lack of priority) for a specific type of traffic depending on when it is sent, what type of traffic it is, where it is going, or from where it is coming.

Look at an example where it is assumed that a corporate executive videoconferences with direct reports over the internetwork on a monthly basis. This executive travels from one location to another and can be any-where when he or she holds the videoconference. As a result, the executive is never using the same computer or the same Internet Protocol (IP) address when videoconferencing. Many QoS products will mark a type of traffic with priority based on its physical or Media Access Control (MAC) address, which is determined from either the IP address or host name of the computer using Address Resolution Protocol (ARP). If the executive wants the videoconference to be granted priority over other network ser-vices, then the network administrator will need to know what IP address or host name the executive is using at the time the videoconference is held. Not only that, but the administrator will need to find out that same infor-mation each and every time the executive holds a videoconference. Without a network administrator manually configuring the videoconference to have priority through QoS, the videoconference will suffer, and as a result, this type of QoS usage will result in an excessive amount of administrative overhead. If the executive holds a spontaneous videoconference without notifying the administrator, then he or she will not receive the expected performance and will be disappointed that the business objective was not met by the QoS product. All of this is a recipe for failure.

The type of network environment in which a QoS product using IP addresses for policy definition will work well is a static environment in which the IP addresses, host names, and traffic types rarely change. With the rate of change of technology today, this type of network is rare.

A DEN-based QoS product can resolve this issue. A DEN-based QoS product potentially can attach a user's account dynamically to his or her computer's IP address at logon, and statically attach the QoS policy to the user's account. Going back to our videoconferencing executive, he or she would log on to the network and would already have a VideoConference QoS policy attached to his or her user account (the policy having been created by the administrator and assigned to the user account). At logon, this policy would dynamically be assigned to the IP address the executive had at that moment. The administrator never needs to be involved except for the initial definition of the QoS policy, and the executive always receives the QoS needed for his or her videoconferences, regardless of where he or she logs on to the network.

TIP

Whitepapers and other information about QoS and policy-based networking can be found on the Internet at the following addresses:
www.qosforum.com/tech_resources.htm
www.xedia.com/products/demystify/htm
www.packeteer.com/technology/tcp.htm
www.netreference.com/PublishedArchive/WhitePapers/WPIndex.html
www.lsiinc.com/warp/public/732/net_enabled/qos_management.html
www.stardust.com/iband3/whitepaper
www.whatis.com/qos.htm
www.internet2.edu/qos/wg/calendar/Feb98ChicagoWGMtg/qos3/tsld001.htm

About Microsoft's Windows 2000 and Cisco's IOS

Microsoft's Windows 2000 and Cisco's Internetwork Operating System (IOS) combine to provide the power of a DEN model. These operating systems are described briefly in the following section, and in much more detail in Chapter 2, "A Tour of Windows 2000," and Chapter 3, "Cisco Hardware and IOS Basics."

Cisco's IOS and Software Products

Cisco develops a great deal of software products to work with their hardware products. The Cisco IOS is a platform that provides network services to an internetwork. It supports both local area network (LAN) and wide area network (WAN) environments, although actual configuration for an environment must also be supported by the Cisco hardware. The IOS can scale to multiple interfaces on a single piece of hardware, and with multiple routers in an internetwork, the IOS proves to be versatile in addition to being scalable from small offices to large enterprise internetworks. IOS supports standard network protocol stacks and media types, including (but not nearly limited to):

- Transmission Control Protocol/Internet Protocol (TCP/IP)
- Internetwork Packet Exchange/Sequenced Packet Exchange (IPX/SPX)
- AppleTalk
- Ethernet
- Token Ring
- Frame Relay
- Integrated Services Digital Network (ISDN)
- Asynchronous Transfer Mode (ATM)

Cisco's IOS is the operating system that Cisco routers, switches, and access servers use to boot up. To enhance access services, routing, and bridging, the IOS supports a full set of security features—encryption, authentication, access control, packet filtering, and firewall services. The IOS is upgradeable as Cisco releases new versions. Each version includes new capabilities and network services. These new services meet enterprises' business requirements for new technology. The IOS can support and grow with an organization's needs.

In the grand tradition of UNIX enthusiasts, the IOS is command-line friendly. Although Cisco routers do not come equipped with monitors, they can be accessed over the network, or through a terminal connection. The Command Line Interface (CLI) appears as a simple text-based screen with a prompt, somewhat similar to a DOS prompt. Newer versions of the IOS can be configured using HTML pages and a Web browser.

Cisco ConfigMaker

Designing an internetwork is not an easy job. It takes knowledge of protocols, hardware, software capabilities, and how to place and configure them to achieve the optimal

- Performance
- Reliability
- Availability
- Security
- Scalability
- Manageability

These must meet the client's business requirements, and some are in conflict with others. For example, a highly secure internetwork placed in an environment where usability of the network is the highest priority for a business requirement may not be easily achieved. To the organization, usability may mean granting users short passwords that are identical from system to system and that never change, whereas a highly secure network would absolutely require lengthy passwords that change on a frequent basis. A designer must be aware of these types of issues and be prepared to make decisions based on business requirements. The network designer should make recommendations that are sensible for the environment, even if the organization might want something a little different. In the security versus usability requirements, for example, the network designer could recommend using DEN-compliant systems where all user account information was held in a single database for the entire internetwork, thus requiring users to need only a single password. Then again, the designer could recommend that the users are trained on having longer passwords using numbers and characters (rather than alphabet-only), and suggest that a policy be put in place to force the users to change the passwords on a 60- or 90-day basis. This may not be the most usable system, but it is a fair compromise!

Cisco provides a free tool (yes, FREE!) called Cisco ConfigMaker that a network designer can use when designing an internetwork. Cisco

ConfigMaker which is an application that runs on Windows 95, Windows 98, Windows NT, or Windows 2000 (on Windows 2000, you should install the Windows NT version). ConfigMaker is downloadable from www.cisco.com/go/configmaker, and is shown in Figure 1.4.

ConfigMaker is straightforward, allowing the network designer to configure a small- to medium-size network, or begin the basic design for an enterprise wide area network, or a section of a large network that does not utilize the enterprise 7x00 series routers that are not listed within the ConfigMaker tool. Each new version adds new equipment and features, but the latest version 2.4 supports Cisco routers from the 800 through the 4000 series, switches, hubs, voice equipment, modems, ISDN, and other network devices.

Figure 1.4 Cisco ConfigMaker.

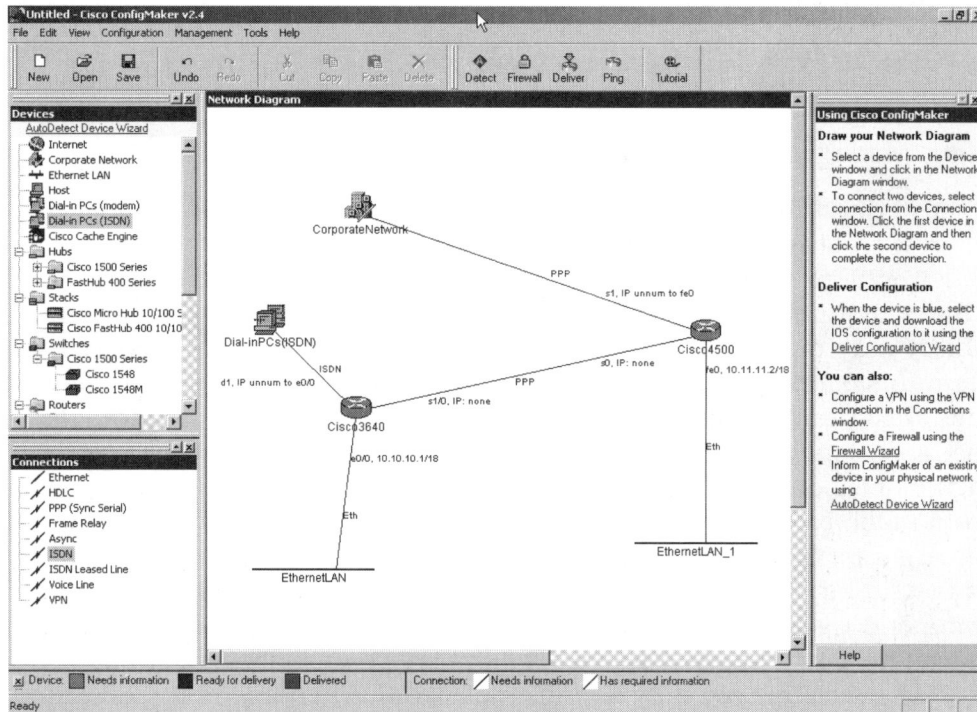

Even though the ConfigMaker tool looks similar to other design applications in which you simply drag a network component to the design window and create the connections, it has a couple of additional features. ConfigMaker forces the designer to make critical design decisions while building the design. It will not allow a connection to be created between two routers if either does not have a port available for that connection. It

Figure 1.5 ConfigMaker router slot configuration.

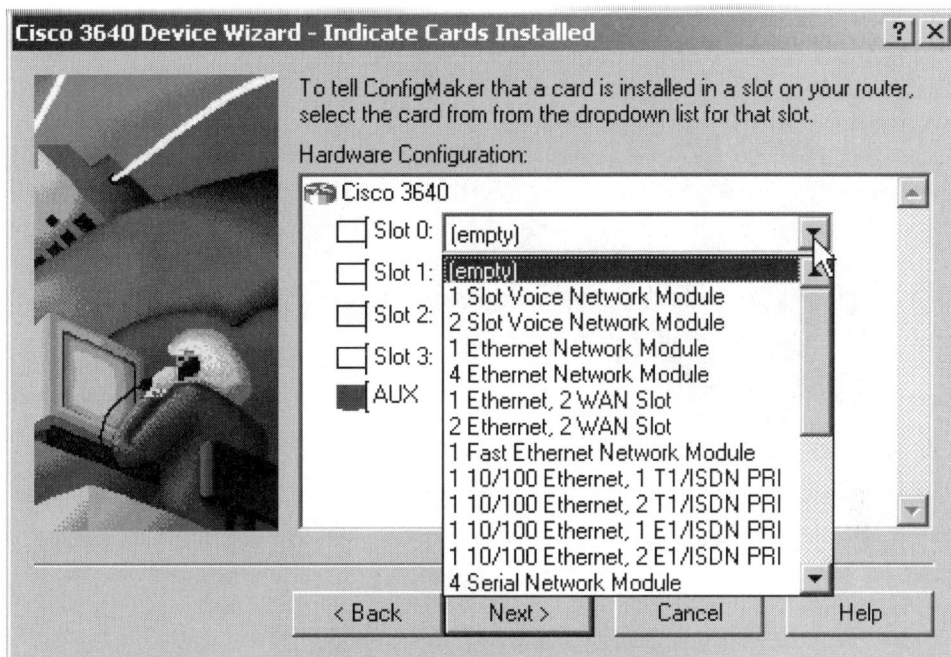

requires you to state the IP addresses of the interfaces, and warns you if you have selected an IP address that is assigned to another network segment. It forces you to apply passwords to the routing equipment. A typical router configuration dialog, illustrated in Figure 1.5, shows how ConfigMaker includes the interfaces available for the slots in a router (in drop-down boxes) so that you can select each interface as you build the router, and do not accidentally select an interface that is not available for that particular device.

ConfigMaker can also collect information about a Cisco device on your network, read which interfaces are installed within it, and then put that information into your network design. In addition, ConfigMaker can write configuration files to routers. It can greatly reduce the time and effort it takes to diagram an existing internetwork. The AutoDetect Device Wizard is shown in Figure 1.6.

Cisco FastStep

Cisco provides another tool, also for use on Windows 95, 98, and NT (or 2000), for configuration of Cisco series 700, 800, 1600 routers and dialup 2500 series access servers. It is called FastStep. This tool is available as a free download at www.cisco.com/go/faststep.

Figure 1.6 AutoDetect Device Wizard can assist in diagramming a network.

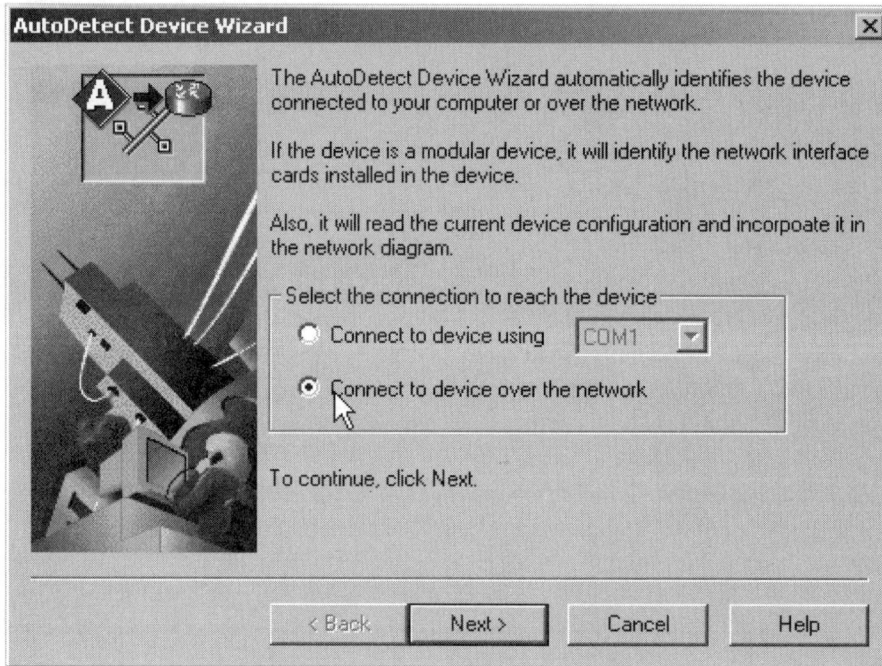

Figure 1.7 Fast Step for 800 series routers.

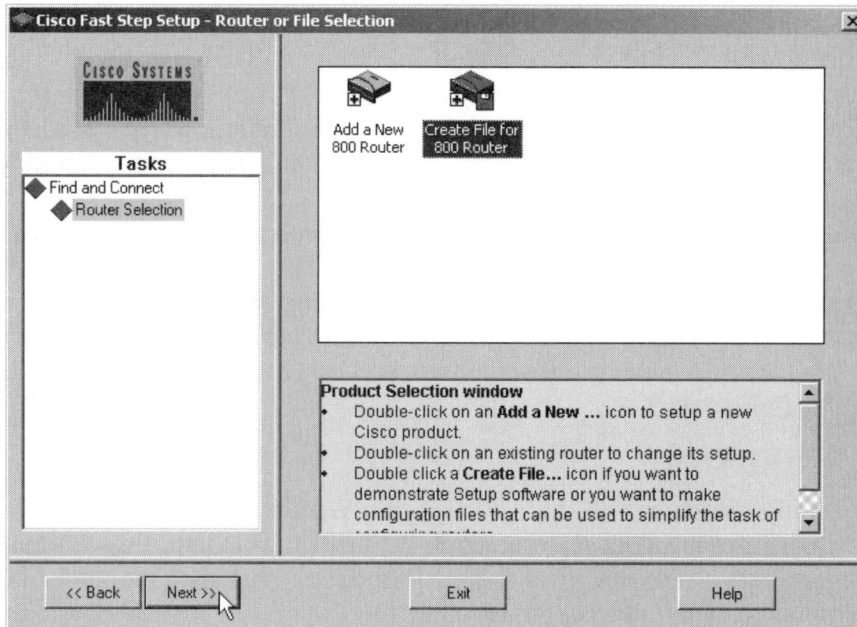

Figure 1.8 Router and option selection in Fast Step.

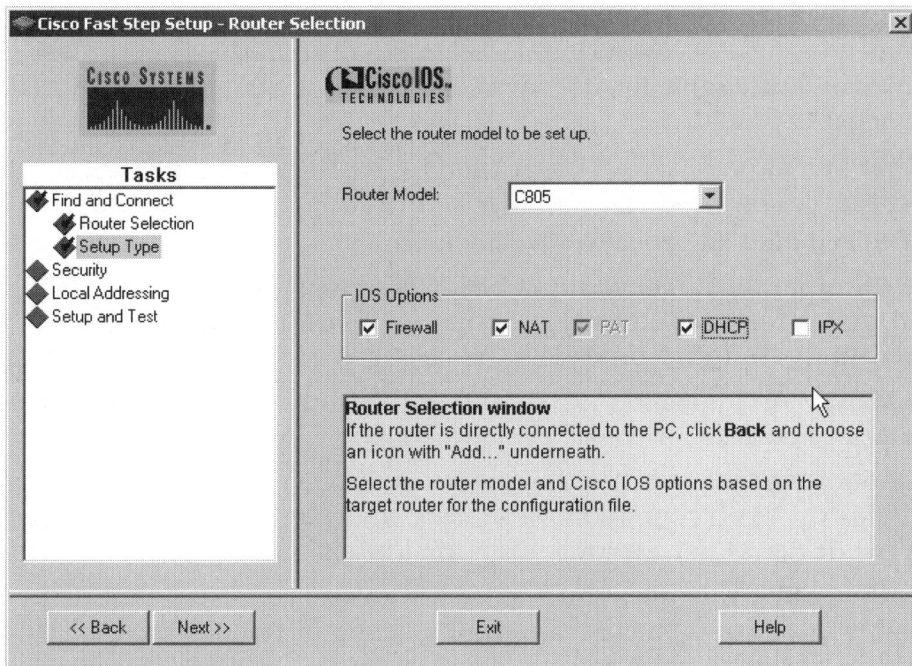

The FastStep application guides an administrator using a "wizard-like" sequence of dialog boxes, such as those shown in Figure 1.7. Each dialog box adds new information towards building a configuration and then applying it to a router.

FastStep allows the administrator to select the specific router model and the types of options that the IOS should support on the router. The dialog that illustrates this selection is shown in Figure 1.8.

When you complete a router configuration with FastStep, the application will save your options in a file. This file will be the name you give your router concatenated with the suffix .cfg. So, if you run the FastStep application and name your router MyRouter, the file will be called MyRouter.cfg. A sample of this file is available in Appendix A.

CiscoWorks 2000

Once a router or switch is up and running, the administrator's next task is to manage it. A network consisting of only one or two routers or switches that is used only during standard business hours (Monday through Friday, 8:00 AM to 5:00 PM) is a simple system and fairly easy to manage on a manual basis. However, if you have a complex internetwork, or one that must be online and available 24 hours a day, seven days a week, then you need to look at the manageability features and management applications.

CiscoWorks is one such application for network management. Cisco recommends that CiscoWorks be used in small to medium networks. CiscoWorks is available for use on UNIX, and there is a version available for Windows.

There are several components within the CiscoWorks application:

CiscoView A graphical view of back and front panels of the Cisco devices, provided remotely in order to simplify monitoring and configuring devices.

Show Commands A translator of the IOS command-line language to displayed router system and protocol data, facilitating a novice administrator's ability to understand how the router is configured and working

StackMaker An application that an administrator can use to create a virtual stack of devices for easier visual management

Threshold Manager A remote monitoring (RMON) application that can set thresholds on Cisco routers and switches in order to alert an administrator when the device is not working at optimal levels

WhatsUp Gold An application licensed from Ipswitch, Inc. that delivers the ability to discover the internetwork's configuration and to map it, as well as the ability to monitor and track alarms.

NOTE

More about the Cisco IOS and other Cisco products can be found in Chapter 3.

Microsoft's Windows 2000

Microsoft developed Windows 2000 in answer to a number of challenges. Some of the challenges were from the latest business requirements for Microsoft customers. Other challenges were from technology drivers of the Information Technology industry. And finally, some challenges were posed by the previous Microsoft Windows NT technology—feedback from customers and critics exhorted Microsoft to transform some of the less usable features of Windows NT.

Business drivers are always changing. Organizations need to be competitive in order to be of value, and as a result, they are always pushing the envelope of technology to assist them in gaining competitive advantages. Increasingly, business is being done on the Internet, so much so that it is called e-business. Organizations no longer use their Web site as solely a marketing message, but they also utilize it to:

- Enhance their customer relationships by enabling customers to self-manage their data in Customer Relationship Management (CRM) applications
- Sell products and services through e-commerce applications
- Demonstrate products through remote control applications that run over IP
- Streamline accounting, logistics, and other processes between their own organization, vendors, and clients using business-to-business (B2B) applications

The Internet delivers a critical requirement for security to businesses. The Internet is the world's most publicly accessible data interchange. Any network resource or service that is attached to it, any user that sends data across it, is subject to the possibility of being endangered by someone (who for reasons of malice, idleness, challenge, or pure insanity, decided to attack that resource, service, or data). Depending on the use of the resource, service, or data, there are various levels of security that a business may wish to apply. A network administrator may wish to protect a Web site page used for marketing the company from being altered while it sits on the Web server, but that network administrator would probably not need to encrypt that page while it travels across the Internet. It's marketing, why hide it? However, when creating a B2B system between a vendor and the organization for the streamlining of accounting information, the network administrator would probably want the data to be encrypted while it crosses the Internet. And for servers that store development data for a small group of internal developers, the network administrator may not wish that server to be available on the Internet at all.

Another challenge that businesses face is the increasing need for mobility in end-users. These users must be able to move from one location to another, and to carry their data and the ability to work along with them. Not only do users move about from one office to another within large enterprises, but there is an escalating requirement for businesses to support telecommuting. Laptops, once a small or nonexistent percentage of equipment attached to a network, are rising to become greater than 30 percent of networked clients in many organizations.

Technology is constantly changing. New developments that are becoming more accepted by businesses include:

- Data/voice/video convergence
- Quality of Service
- Virtual private networking (VPN) in the forms of IP Security (IPSec) and Layer 2 Tunneling Protocol (L2TP)
- Digital Subscriber Line (DSL)
- Policy-based networking

Not only does an operating system need to look forward at new technologies, being able to adapt to them quickly, but it also needs to be able to work within an existing infrastructure. New media and old media, new protocols and old protocols, new hardware and old hardware must all be supported.

Critics of Microsoft's Windows NT bemoaned its lack of reliability. They created an acronym, BSOD, for the Blue Screen of Death, describing the blue screen with a nearly indecipherable error message for the problem that caused the NT machine to fail. BSODs were common. What was just as bad, however, was the need to reboot ... all the time. Whenever you made a change to the NT machine, especially involving a change to the system itself or the addition of a new application, you were forced to reboot it. If it was a server you were configuring, you then needed to ask all the users to log out of the server while it rebooted so that any files that they were using would not be lost or damaged due to a sudden disconnection. For those organizations who were familiar with Windows NT's need for rebooting, they created a policy that configuration changes could be completed only after business hours, or during slow periods (if they had extended business hours).

In addition to reliability issues, Windows NT was simply not user- or laptop-friendly. It did not detect hardware—instead the hardware had to be configured with special Windows NT drivers. Installing the Windows NT operating system seemed easy enough, unless some component did not have an NT driver. It did not easily connect to the Internet through its remote access client application. If an NT File System (NTFS) partition somehow became corrupted, or a system file within an NTFS partition became corrupted, there was no way (without a third-party utility) to access the NTFS partition and make those system file replacements. The power management capabilities (absolute requirements on laptops) were nonexistent, again depending on the vendor of the hardware to provide any power utilities. Users became frustrated when faced with these challenges.

Microsoft created Windows 2000 with solutions to these types of challenges. They made absolutely certain that the new Windows 2000 operating system included the following:

- Support for e-business through the incorporation of Internet services, World Wide Web (WWW), File Transfer Protocol (FTP), Network News Transport Protocol (NNTP), and more. (In contrast to Windows 2000's standard inclusion of these features, Microsoft made these features available in Windows NT v4.0 as an Option pack; the standard operating system did not include them.)

- Security mechanisms and new technologies such as QoS, IPSec, L2TP, and DSL.

- Data/voice/video, using standards-based protocols for its Telephony Application Programming Interface (TAPI) version 3.0 Call Control and Media Services, and support for multicast forwarding.

- Policy-based networking capabilities within the new Active Directory services.

- Answers to users' issues with reliability, usability, and laptop-friendliness. There are very few reasons why a Windows 2000 machine requires rebooting. The BSOD is much more rare than it was in Windows NT. Installation is uncomplicated, since the Windows 2000 will detect hardware and install Plug and Play standard hardware. The user interface (UI) is simplified and the operating system supports power management standards.

Active Directory

The Windows 2000 Active Directory is a tremendous enhancement to Windows 2000. This is a feature that can be installed only as part of the Windows 2000 Server line. There are four products:

Windows 2000 Professional Meant to be installed on workstations and PCs for end-user usage, and is considered the upgrade for Windows NT Workstation v4.0.

Windows 2000 Server Intended for small or workgroup servers, and is considered the upgrade version of Windows NT Server v4.0.

Windows 2000 Advanced Server Intended for enterprise servers through support for additional processors and network load balancing clusters, and is considered the upgrade for Windows NT Server v4.0 Enterprise Edition.

Windows 2000 DataCenter Server ntended for the highest-end servers, supporting up to 32 processors, and released only through Original Equipment Manufacturers (OEMs), it is customized for that manufacturer's high-end server equipment. This is not considered an upgrade for any Windows NT version.

Figure 1.9 Active Directory policy-based networking.

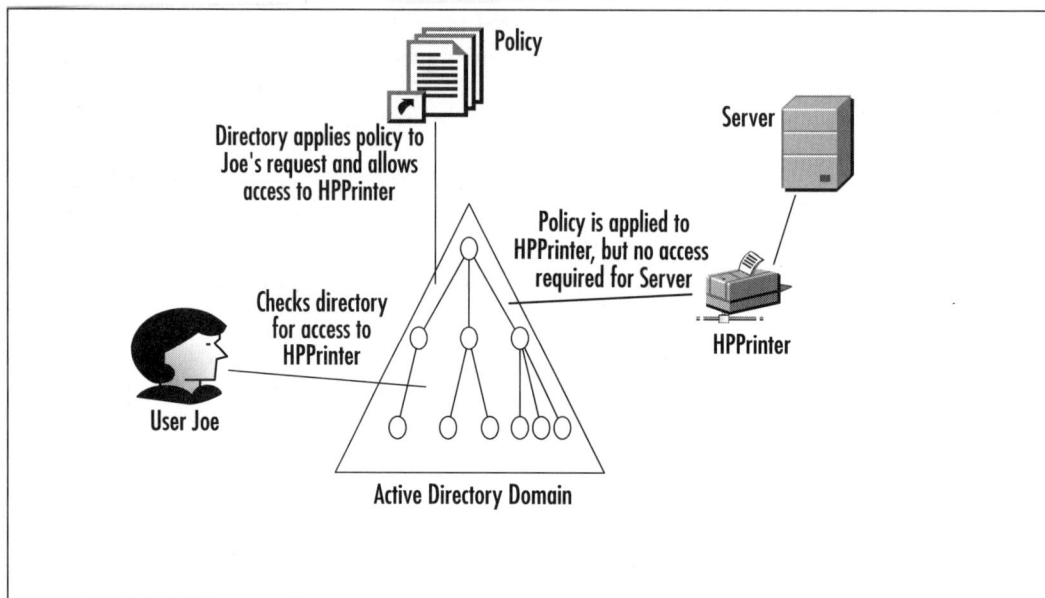

Three products, Windows 2000 Server, Windows 2000 Advanced Server, and Windows 2000 DataCenter Server, can become Active Directory domain controllers (DC). A DC is a server that stores a replica of an Active Directory partition on its storage system. The Active Directory itself is a database, using a structured schema of classes, objects, and attributes (just like the DEN specification) that store data about user accounts, network services or applications, and network resources or equipment. In addition, the Active Directory stores policies about each of these components such that relationships between the objects (individual users, services, and resources) can be managed. For example, a policy can be created that states a User named Joe can access administrative level components of a resource named HPPrinter, thus enabling Joe to manage the print jobs that are sent to that printer by other users, but not requiring him to have administrative access to the server that provides HPPrinter services to the network, as shown in Figure 1.9.

The Active Directory incorporates all of the features shown in Table 1.1.

Table 1.1 Active Directory Features

Feature	Description
Active Directory Services Interface (ADSI)	The Active Directory Services Interface (ADSI) is an API for programming and scripting Active Directory applications.
Domain Name System (DNS) integration	The Active Directory is integrated with DNS, using it as the mechanism for locating services on the internetwork.
Extensible schema	The Active Directory schema can be extended with new objects, classes, and attributes to support new technologies and capabilities.
Group Policy	Centralized policy management is provided through Group Policy integrated with the Active Directory. Group Policy provides predefined policies for customizing network activity.
Hierarchical architecture	The Active Directory database is organized into a tree, or hierarchy. Each single Active Directory domain can be subdivided through the creation of Organizational Units (OUs). An OU can contain other objects, including other OUs, thus resulting in a structure much like a file system's directory structure.
Hierarchical namespace	Each Active Directory domain is created as its own DNS namespace, and is connected through hierarchy of DNS naming. For example, if syngress.com were the root domain, a subdomain could be named media.syngress.com.
Kerberos	The Active Directory uses Kerberos security as its authentication method.
LDAP integration	The Active Directory is compliant with Lightweight Directory Access Protocol (LDAP) version 3, so that it will be able to interoperate with other LDAP-compliant applications and services.
Multimaster replication	The Active Directory is capable of storing multiple replicas of the same partition of its database on different servers. To ensure synchronization between all the replicas, each partition is considered a master and uses an algorithm to resolve any conflicts when the updates to the database are replicated between servers.
Scalability	Because the Active Directory uses the hierarchy of domains, it can support multiple partitions and can scale up to millions of users, resources, and services.

NOTE

More about Microsoft Windows 2000 can be found in Chapter 2.

Merging together with Cisco Networking Services for Active Directory

The Microsoft and Cisco partnership, and their DEN initiative, has resulted in Cisco Networking Services for Active Directory (CNS/AD). CNS/AD extends the schema of the Active Directory to include new object classes for Cisco equipment, as well as new attributes for existing Active Directory objects.

By extending the schema with this software, policies can be applied to users from within the Active Directory itself. The simple Windows 2000 user interface enables a point-and-click system for defining some complex administrative tasks.

When CNS/AD is installed, new objects exist for the administrator. Routers can be added using their specific version object. Users can also be added as user accounts. Policies can be added to the Active Directory to guide how the user's traffic will interact with the router.

When the router comes online, it recognizes an Active Directory domain controller as its policy server storage. At the time that traffic comes from a source, the router checks the Active Directory for the policy. If the policy includes instructions on handling the traffic, the router follows those instructions.

Best Practices for Implementing a Network

When you are ready to start planning your Cisco and Microsoft internetwork, you can use the following best practices to ensure a swift, undisruptive deployment.

The first phase of your deployment will be to gather information about the existing network. Most enterprises already have a network of some type. You will need to discover and assess:

- Cabling media
- Existing servers, peripherals, and desktop hardware
- Operating systems being used
- Applications in use

- Protocols being deployed

- Integration with mainframe and other network resources

- Security requirements and methods currently used

The second phase of your deployment will be to designate the teams for your project. Not only should you use technology experts in each team, but also decision makers and business unit leaders. Although the decision makers may have little to offer in the discussion of the technology, they will have far more insight into how that technology must be able to support their existing business processes.

The third phase is to create a vision of the future network. This is the goal of your project. In many cases, it is a good idea to go ahead and put the impossible down as a goal when a team member suggests a technology need. Sometimes that so-called "impossible" feat is actually available as a feature of a technology already available. Other times, the requirement that drives that goal can be met by configuration changes or other technology implementation. When you reject the goal outright, you can miss the opportunity to improve the enterprise. When you discuss your vision, make sure to include the following:

- Business requirements

- Proposed hardware and software

- Needs for Internet integration

- Configuration requirements

- Future changes in media, servers, desktops, or peripherals

- Security requirements

In most large businesses, you will then need to ensure that you have executive sponsorship and a budget for moving forward with the project. And after that, you will use the vision to guide the internetwork design, which absolutely requires a network designer who is familiar with the protocols, hardware, software, operating systems, and applications.

The designer will need to determine what other network components are required, where they should be placed, how they are interrelated, and how they should be configured. Each design decision should be justified, especially when it is one that will affect the budget for your project. The network design should be business-requirement driven, and should include the following elements:

- Desktop environment design

- Server environment design

- Directory service designs (directory services may require several elements to their design)

- Hubs, switches, and LAN design

- Routers and WAN design

- Strategies for supporting mobile users, Internet, IP Addressing, network management, and network security

The network designer should be able to leverage the existing infrastructure as much as possible and design the resulting network structure for a flexible administration. The architecture of the new network should eliminate any existing single points of failure and resist bringing any new single points of failure into the internetwork. It should also provide a capacity projection for network bandwidth, router storage, router memory, server storage, server memory, and standard desktop storage and memory.

Once the teams and executive sponsors accept the design, the project can begin with providing proof of concept. This is done through a lab. Each design element is tested and developed such that the deployment of the design can be performed with the least risk and the most efficiency. This may result in changes to the design.

When the lab team is satisfied that the processes and design are ready for production, the project can begin a pilot. The pilot is basically a mini-project performed for a small subdivision of users, services, and resources on the internetwork. If the pilot is unsuccessful, the team should return to the lab and work out the problems.

Once the pilot is successful, however, the project can be fully deployed across the rest of the internetwork. Sometimes, this final deployment is best done in phases consisting of multiple pilots and deployments until everything has been completed. All in all, when deploying a project that involves every section within the internetwork, best practices dictate that the enterprise backbone is completed first, the server and secured access portion of the internetwork is completed next, and the desktops and peripherals are completed last.

Networking Basics

A solid knowledge of networking basics is required for understanding the concepts in this book. If you need a refresher course, just browse through the OSI Protocol Reference Model, Internet History, and IP Networking Primer sections. Otherwise, if you are confident with your networking basics knowledge, just skip to the Case Studies section and then on to the rest of the book!

For IT Professionals

Resolving Network Bottlenecks

Network bottlenecks are sometimes encountered during a lab, but most often are encountered after the network has been in use for some time and users have become comfortable in using it, hence causing more internetwork traffic. The typical causes for a network bottleneck are:

- Over-utilized servers, either in memory or storage
- High-bandwidth utilization on network media, usually only on a portion of the internetwork
- Loss of network integrity

You can resolve many bottlenecks by following these best practices:

- Balance network traffic to a server by using multiple network adapters and network load balancing.
- Use media and protocols that enable the highest bandwidth available. If you have Category 5 cabling and are using shared Ethernet 10BaseT, consider changing to a switched Ethernet configuration or Ethernet 100BaseT, or even both!
- Whenever possible, use interfaces that can offload functions from the machine's CPU, such as IPSec offloading or checksum offloading.
- Reduce the number of protocols that you are using on your internetwork.
- Use routers, bridges, or switches to segment broadcast domains.

OSI Protocol Reference Model

In the Information Technology industry, you will run into some oddball ways of doing things. The Open System Interconnection (OSI) Protocol reference model represents one of the strange phenomena that persists in this industry—standards follow usage. You would think that a standard would be created and then it would be put to use. However, to meet the demand for new technology capabilities, to gain a competitive edge, and in keeping with the counterculture attitude of Silicon Valley, a lot of technology is put to use first. If a practice works, if it meets a real technology need, and if it is used by a significant number of people, it eventually is accepted as a standard. Since this type of technology is used in fact, it is called a de facto standard. If the technology need is truly great, being required on many different manufacturers' equipment or software, then a standard is developed by a standards organization (called a *de jure* standard) and published for use by all vendors.

The OSI Protocol reference model is one such standard. The International Organization for Standardization (ISO) developed and released the OSI Protocol reference model in 1984. They used the following principles to determine what protocol layers were required in a protocol stack.

1. Create a new layer whenever differentiation is apparent.

2. Ensure that each layer provides a specific purpose.

3. Select each layer's function with international standards in mind.

4. Select boundaries between the layers to minimize the information needed to flow between them.

5. Ensure that the number of layers in the model provide flexibility but are not too complex.

This OSI model is a standard that is not implemented with one-to-one correlation in any extant protocol stack, excepting the rarely used OSI protocol stack. This fact begs the question, why would anyone need the OSI model anyway?

The answer is that the OSI model provides vendors a common entity to which they can refer when describing the workings of their products with other products. In this way, the OSI reference model provides a learning tool, a common orientation, and a method to encourage interoperability. If you want to be able to describe networking, the OSI model simplifies your task.

The OSI model consists of seven layers. Each layer is given a name, but many of them are referred to as a number. For example, Layer 1 is the physical layer, and Layer 3 is the network layer. Figure 1.10 illustrates each layer and its commonly used number.

Each layer contributes to the communication of networked devices. Even though there are seven separate layers, they are frequently implemented in combination. For example, Ethernet defines the physical and data-link layer communications. These first two layers specify movement of data across a physical medium. The middle two layers specify movement of data between separate physical segments. The upper three layers specify the movement of data between services.

When two hosts transmit data across a network, the data goes through a system of encapsulation. At the sending host, the data starts from the

Figure 1.10 OSI Protocol reference model.

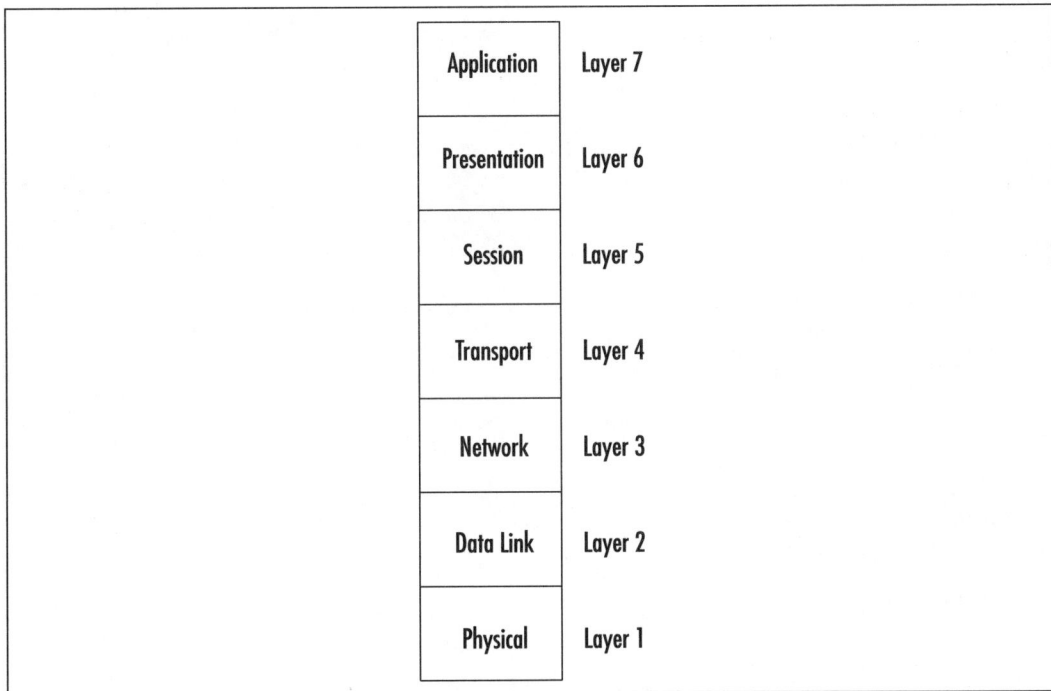

Application	Layer 7
Presentation	Layer 6
Session	Layer 5
Transport	Layer 4
Network	Layer 3
Data Link	Layer 2
Physical	Layer 1

application layer, where it is placed within a header that includes information about how to handle the data at the application layer. The data is then passed to the presentation layer, where it endures the same process. This is repeated for each layer through the stack until the data reaches the physical layer. Some layers, however, do break the data into somewhat smaller packets in order to make them more manageable. At the physical layer, the data is changed into a bitstream and transmitted across the network medium. When the receiving host accepts the bitstream, the physical layer reassembles the bits into the packets that the data-link layer will understand, dropping any additional bits that it used for control information. The data-link layer drops the data-link header information and assembles the data into the network layer packets. And so the data travels through the protocol stack, dropping headers like a rocket dropping unnecessary parts as it travels through the atmosphere, until the data is received by the application in a format that it understands. Because of the way that data is sent, each layer communicates with the peer layer on the other host. This process is illustrated in Figure 1.11.

Figure 1.11 Data transmission viewed from the OSI model's perspective.

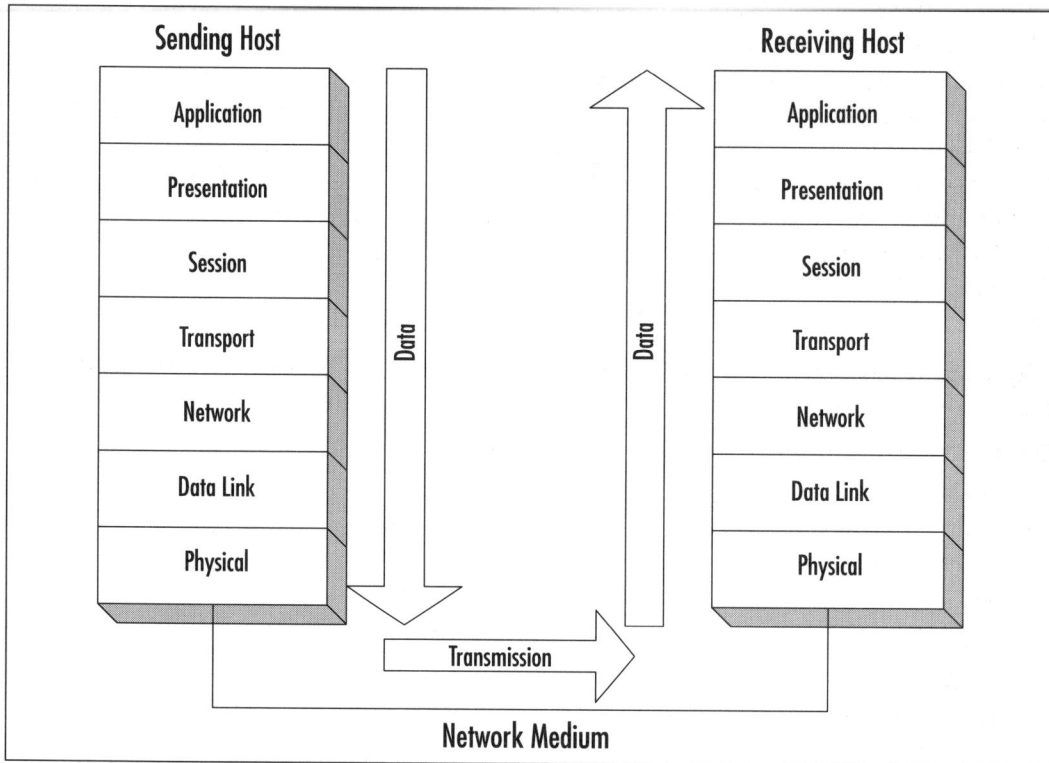

Physical Layer

Layer 1, the physical layer, is responsible for raw data transmission in the form of a bitstream. The specifications for this layer contain:

Media type Wireless or cabling-type baseband transmission, where the data utilizes the entire bandwidth of the cable; or broadband transmission, where the data is segmented into channels, enabling a different signal on each channel.

Media interface Pin arrangements required to access the media.

Signaling methods The arrangement, frequency, and amplitude of signals that are then understood as 1 or 0 bits.

Physical topology The shape of a single physical network segment, such as a star, bus, cellular, or ring configuration.

Data-Link Layer

Layer 2, the data-link layer, is responsible for assembling frames of data. The data-link consists of two sublayers, the MAC layer and the Logical Link Control (LLC) layer. The MAC layer is the lower portion of the data-link layer and handles much of its functions. The Institute of Electrical and Electronics Engineers (IEEE) specified the LLC upper portion for the 802 protocol definition series. The LLC provides a common interface for upper layer protocols, which enables a protocol stack such as TCP/IP or IPX/SPX to run over Ethernet (IEEE 802.3) just the same as Token Ring (IEEE 802.5), without having to include those specifications within its own protocol stack. The data-link layer specifies the following:

Physical addressing of hardware interfaces This address is also called a MAC address.

Error and flow control These are provided through the header control information.

Logical topology Whereas the physical topology describes the shape that you can see of the actual cabling and media equipment, the logical topology describes the shape of the path that the data travels around the segment. The two logical topologies are bus and ring.

Method of media access This is the logical way that data transmits across the media. There are three types of media access: contention, token-passing, and polling. Contention is used in Ethernet and is the method whereby all hosts attempt to access the media when they need to transmit. Token-passing is used in Token Ring and is the method whereby a special frame called a token is passed from host to host until one needs to send data and accepts the token. Polling is a rarely used method in which a central controlling station polls the remaining network hosts to determine whether any needs to send data.

Network Layer

Layer 3, or the network layer, provides for data passage between two physical segments that do not necessarily use the same media or lower layer protocols. The device used for moving the data is generally called a router or Layer 3 switch. The network layer specifies:

Network segment addressing Each segment is given a different address so that the data can be labeled with a segment address in the network layer header and then forwarded to the appropriate segment based on that header address information.

Logical node addressing Each network node is assigned a logical node address. In the case of Internetwork Packet Exchange, the MAC address is used as the logical node address, whereas in the case of IP, a specific address is applied to the node. Each node address must be unique.

Datagrams The frames received from the data-link layer are organized into datagrams at the network layer. The datagram includes a header for the network layer addressing information.

Routing The data can be moved from one segment to another through a path, or route, defined in the network. Routers must decide how to switch the data as it comes in from one interface onto an outgoing interface.

Transport Layer

Layer 4, or the transport layer, provides an interface from upper layers into the network layer. The transport layer is responsible for the following:

Identifying upper layer processes with service addressing The transport layer will identify an upper layer process with a port or socket number placed in the header of the message. For example, an e-mail message would use TCP Port 25 in its header if Simple Mail Transport Protocol (SMTP) sent it.

Data segmentation and multiplexing To enable multiple processes to utilize the same Internet connection, the transport layer segments the messages and can interleave them with their identifying port numbers before sending them onto the network layer at the sending host. On the receiving host, the transport layer performs the opposite task of unraveling the data messages and sending them to the appropriate processes identified by their port numbers.

Sending data reliably A transport layer protocol can be connectionless where data is not sent reliably, or it can be connection-oriented where data is sent reliably. A reliable, connection-oriented transmission uses acknowledgement (ACK) packets to determine whether data is received correctly at the other end, and whether or not it needs to be retransmitted. Note that neither connection-oriented nor connectionless protocols will guarantee delivery.

The Session Layer

Layer 5, or the session layer, is responsible for establishing, maintaining, and terminating dialogs, or sessions, between two devices. The session layer specifies:

Network-independent data conversations The session layer will establish and maintain a dialog between two devices regardless of the path(s) that the data travels throughout the internetwork.

Session types The dialog that is established can be simplex (one-way communication), half-duplex (each participant takes turns communicating), or duplex (bidirectional, simultaneous communication).

The Presentation Layer

Layer 6, or the presentation layer, sets up the presentation of data, literally. This layer is responsible for how the data will look. It is responsible for data presentation options such as:

Compression and expansion Data is compressed for more efficient transmissions and then expanded at the receiving host so that it can be understood by upper layers.

Encryption and decryption Encryption, where data is disguised to not be readable, is generally set at the presentation layer. Decryption is the process of decoding the encrypted data. Note that encryption can be handled at other layers.

Data translation Data is translated into a mutually agreed upon syntax. This format may be in bit order (whether to read each byte from the first bit received or last bit received), or byte order (whether to read from the first byte received or last byte received).

The Application Layer

Layer 7, or the application layer, provides the interface of the network to the application and user. There are three ways that applications can access the network:

1. Client/server collaboration. Both the client and the server interact with the application and share processing.

2. Operating System (OS) Call Interception. The network protocol stack on the host intercepts application calls, and if they are really intended to be sent to the network, then the application call is redirected. Otherwise, it is processed in the normal fashion.

3. Remote Control. The application connects to another host and remotely controls the console on that host by passing along keyboard and mouse clicks to the host and returning the video image to the client.

Internet History

The history of the Internet is fascinating testimony to the swift development of technology, increasing at an almost geometric pace. The story begins in the 1960s. The RAND Corporation researched how communication networks could be used in the United States military in 1962. They made a significant decision after recognizing that a central model for a network would become an easy target and could cause chaos if it became compromised. A central authority was rejected and a distributed model, one in which all links were considered unreliable—therefore created to be redundant—was developed. Paths through the internetwork would be independent of the sending and receiving hosts, so that any path could be selected depending on current network conditions. With this model, the network could not be compromised by any section's failure.

In 1968, the National Physical Laboratory in Great Britain set up a distributed, packet-switched test network based on these assumptions, and on other concepts developed by RAND, along with MIT and UCLA. Afterward, the Advanced Research Projects Agency (ARPA) funded a larger project in the United States, which became ARPANET. The first node was installed at UCLA in 1969, and by December of that year there were four nodes.

ARPANET was intended for the use of sharing radar data, but was unintentionally altered into a news- and message-sharing system on top of the data that was transmitted. Electronic mail had made its debut by 1971. List services soon followed, and one of the first large mailing lists was for science fiction fans, rather than collaborative computations.

In 1977, smaller networks started connecting to the ARPANET via TCP/IP. But by 1983, part of the network segmented off to become MILNET. MILNET was dedicated to the military.

The 1980s and early 1990s saw the incredible expansion of personal computers into nearly every social stratum. By adding network interfaces and TCP/IP (a public domain protocol stack), these computers could hook up to the ever-expanding network now being called the Internet.

DNS was developed in 1984 when the number of hosts outnumbered 1000, and Internet domains were established for various geographical locations, in addition to the .gov (government), .mil (military), .edu (educational), .com (commercial), .org (nonprofit organizations), and .net (backbone Internet gateways) domains.

In 1986, the National Science Foundation (NSF) decided to invest in a huge internetwork linking five computing locations. They wanted to hook up to the various educational facilities, but could not afford to do so separately. Instead, NSF hooked up one site to ARPANET, which was hooked up to the educational facilities.

The first serious security threat occurred in 1988, when the Internet Worm disabled 10 percent of the hosts on it. The Computer Emergency Response Team (CERT) was formed to counteract future attacks. In 1989, the ARPANET was officially retired. The remaining extant network was then global.

The years 1989 through 1991 brought about the World Wide Web, with the development of hypertext by Tim Berners-Lee. From that initiative, Marc Andreesen, along with some other programmers, developed Mosaic, the first Web browser, which became available in 1993. Traffic and participation on the Internet immediately exploded.

In 1995, NSFNET left the Internet in commercial ownership. By 1996 there were over ten million hosts online.

Today, the Internet is undergoing yet another transformation … e-business. Businesses are taking advantage of the reductions in costs that they can take by becoming as distributed, decentralized, redundant, and location-independent as the Internet itself. They are developing processes to enhance their customers' services and products, as well as to decrease their costs in working with vendors. Reverse auctions online are common today. But in 1962? It was inconceivable that this could exist!

IP Networking Primer

The Internet Protocol is one of several protocols within the TCP/IP protocol stack. The protocol stack originated from the Department of Defense (DoD), and has become the default protocol stack used on the Internet. The fundamental layers of the DoD model are the network access layer, internetwork layer, host-to-host transport layer, and the application layer. The way that these layers relate to the seven-layer OSI model is illustrated in Figure 1.12.

The DoD protocol layers consist of the services described in Table 1.2. You will soon see that these layers include many of the same functions that the OSI Protocol reference model specifies in the mapped layers. For example, the Internetwork layer of the DoD Model provides the identical functions that the OSI network layer provides.

Figure 1.12 OSI model mapped to the DoD model.

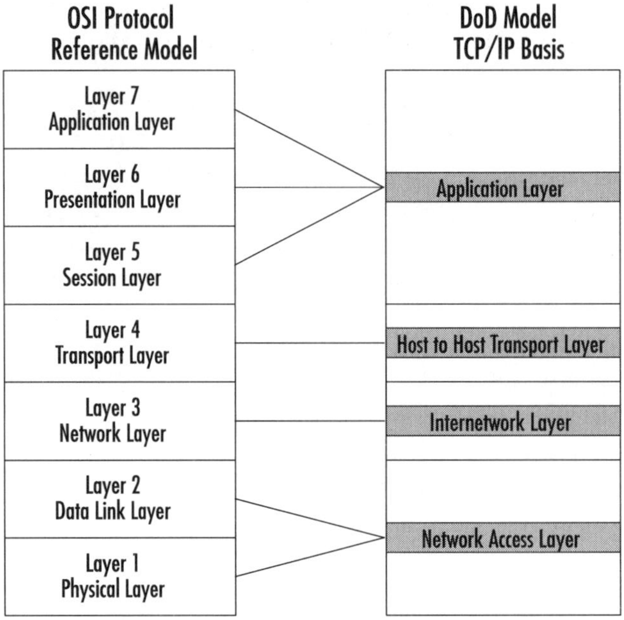

Table 1.2 DoD Model Layer Functions

DoD Model Layer	Mapped to OSI Layer(s)	Function
Network Access	Physical Data Link	Defines frames and bitstream format for data. Transmission of data across physical media. Specifies the physical address for the network interface.
Internetwork	Network	Routes messages through the internetwork. Packages data into datagrams. Provides logical network segment and node addressing.
Host to Host Transport	Transport	Provides end-to-end data integrity through reliable, connection-oriented connections. Handles multiplexing and data segmentation.
Application	Session Presentation Application	Provides user interface functions and application services. Provides data encryption, decryption, compression, and expansion. Manages sessions between two hosts.

Deciphering IP Addresses

The most common use of IP is version 4. The addressing scheme described here is IP v4. IP addresses were designed to be 32 bits in length, represented as four octets separated by dots. An IP address at the bit level would look like:

```
10110011.10100011.00010011.10111011
```

However, series of ones and zeroes are difficult to remember, so the address is translated into decimal format. Each bit represents a value within its own octet, from left to right, of 2^7 to 2^0 or 128 to 1. When an octet is completed with all 1 bits, its value is 255. Translating this address, the result is 179.163.19.187. To reach the result, you would add up the value of each octet. In the case of these octets, you would add the following:

```
128 + 0 + 32 + 16 + 0 + 0 + 2 + 1 = 179
128 + 0 + 32 +  0 + 0 + 0 + 2 + 1 = 163
  0 + 0 +  0 + 16 + 0 + 0 + 2 + 1 =  19
128 + 0 + 32 + 16 + 8 + 0 + 2 + 1 = 187
```

The IP address represents both a network number and a host address. There are three common classes of IP addresses:

Class A The first octet identifies the network, and the first bit must be zero. The network numbers range from 1–126. (Network number 127 is reserved as a loopback address for testing.) The remaining octets represent the host address. Although there are only 126 networks, each class A network can have over 16 million hosts. For IP address 53.1.3.88, the network number is 53, and the host is 1.3.88.

Class B Both the first and second octets are used to identify the network number, and the first two bits must be 1 and 0. This means that the first octet of network numbers range from 128–191. There are 16,382 class B network numbers. Each class B network can have 65,534 hosts. For IP address 143.12.44.55, the network number is 143.12, and the host is 44.55.

Class C The first, second, and third octets are used to identify the network number, and the first three bits must be 1 1 0. This means that the first octet of network numbers range from 192–223. There are over two million Class C networks. Each class C network has 254 hosts. For IP address 199.5.5.88, the network number is 199.5.5 and the host address is 88.

NOTE

To connect to the Internet, you will need to have a registered IP address for your network. Some organizations, however, require far more addresses than they have available in their registered address set. To get around this issue, Request for Comments (RFC) 1918 provides unregistered addresses. To use them and still connect to the Internet, the organization must translate between a registered IP address that is applied to an interface connected to the Internet, and the unregistered IP addresses that are applied to the hosts on the internal network. This process is called network address translation (NAT). RFC 1918 reserves the following addresses:

Class A–10.x.x.x
Class B–172.16.x.x to 172.31.x.x
Class C–192.168.1.x to 192.168.254.x
RFC 1918 is available at ftp://www.arin.net/rfc/rfc1918.txt.

The remaining addresses from 224 through 239 are reserved for class D, or multicasting. From 240 through 255, the addresses are considered class E or experimental. No matter what address a host is assigned, it must be unique on the internetwork.

IP addressing and routing can be performed without the use of classes. This is called Classless InterDomain Routing (CIDR). Each distinct route on the network is not advertised separately. Instead, it is aggregated with multiple destinations. One benefit of using CIDR is to reduce the size of the routing tables.

Each address must have a way of separating the network's IP address from the host's IP address. This is achieved with a mask. When you "subtract" the mask from the full address, the result separates the two. Each class of addresses has its own default mask. A class A address has the default mask of 255.0.0.0. As you see, the first octet is masked, enabling the IP address portion to remain. The default mask for class B is 255.255.0.0, and the default mask for class C is 255.255.255.0.

When a network administrator wants to apply a network address to two different network segments, the IP address must be subnetted. Subnetting is the process of shifting the boundary from the network portion into part of the host portion. This creates multiple subnets that can be applied to physically distinct network segments.

For Managers

Dynamic Host Configuration Protocol for IP Address Management

Until Dynamic Host Configuration Protocol (DHCP) arrived, IP address management was the bane of many a network administrator's existence. Each host was matched up with an IP address that had to be unique from all other IP addresses. In addition, the IP address uses a mask to determine on which network segment the host is located; to do so, all hosts on the same segment had to have the same mask. Errors in IP addressing, such as duplicate IP addresses and wrong subnet masks, were common. In addition, there tended to be an inefficient assignment of IP addresses. If a user went on vacation, his or her workstation's IP address went unused during that time. If a workstation was replaced, it may have been assigned a new IP address and the old one remained assigned to a computer that was no more than a ghost on the network. With a dearth of IP addresses available, network administrators needed to reclaim any unused IP addresses that they could. DHCP was helpful because it could allocate an IP address automatically, as it was needed, and configuration of the mask was performed a single time for a group of IP addresses. Above all, DHCP assigned IP addresses through a leasing system that reclaimed an IP address after the lease expired.

Subnets are achieved by adding more 1 bits to the default mask. For instance, a subnet mask for a class A address could be 255.192.0.0 instead of 255.0.0.0. The addition of two 1 bits changed the mask.

If you add two 1 bits to a class C subnet mask, you create two subnets, each with a possible 62 hosts available to it. If you add three 1 bits, you create six subnets, each with a possible 30 hosts.

Case Studies

Throughout this book, various chapters will include discussions about implementing the technology for two fictional companies.

ABC Chemical Company

The ABC Chemical Company has the following characteristics. It is a large industrial chemical company involved in the manufacturing of pharmaceuticals, household products, and raw chemical supplies for clientele. The company is housed in one large area—a campus environment—with the exception of two distribution warehouses: one on the east coast, one on the west coast.

The main campus consists of three large complex buildings that house the company's five main departments: Research and Development, Executive Management, Sales and Marketing, Distribution, and IT/e-commerce.

There are 1100 employees; the breakdown per department is as follows:

Research and Development: 500

Sales and Marketing: 250

Distribution: 150

Executive Management: 25

IT/e-commerce: 75

Warehouse East: 50

Warehouse West: 50

The ABC Chemical Company currently is running on a Windows NT network on the main campus with each of the warehouses dialing in to report to executive management. The network was designated originally for the Management and Sales divisions only, but over the years the network has evolved into a mainstay tool of the company. The immediate decision to upgrade to Windows 2000 and Active Directory is being considered in order to stay within FDA and government requirements for Internet and company security. Secondary objectives are to increase productivity and collaboration between the departments. There is also a desire to gain a strategic advantage over competition by utilizing video and audio conferencing over the Internet for sales and communication with clients. Finally, the IT department intends to cut costs of administrating the internetwork.

To accommodate the networking needs of the LAN environment on a campus backbone design, the company is investigating whether to deploy a "hub and spoke" switch-intensive design. The three main buildings at the main campus would be linked in a triangular fiber gigabit configuration to allow for redundant backbone functionality while providing the best possible speed between the campus buildings. The switched network is proposed to be configured with two gigabit switches at the core, equipped with dual Route Switch Modules (RSM) and Supervisor cards. One of the gigabit switches may be configured as an online backup to the other gigabit switch utilizing Hot Standby Routing Protocol (HSRP) to allow for a completely redundant network core. The RSM modules will be programmed to route between the department virtual local area networks (VLANs) (see later) and outlying company resources.

Department switches are proposed to run into the core switches via fiber gigabit links to allow for connectivity to the user community. Each set of department switches will be configured with their own VLAN, thus allowing for better network performance within the departments and for tighter physical network security for data-sensitive areas such as Human Resources (a subsection of the Executive Management department) and Research and Development.

The IT department is considering setting up its own VLANs, to be used exclusively for the corporate server farm and server backup systems. The IT department also houses two routers that it intends to keep: one for the Internet and voice communications systems and another to allow access via frame relay to the warehouse facilities.

West Coast Accounting, L.L.C.

West Coast Accounting, Limited Liability Corporation, is a medium-sized accounting firm with offices in key cities up and down the west coast. There are offices in Seattle, Los Angeles, Portland, and Phoenix, with the main headquarters in San Francisco. The San Francisco office has 100 employees, including Executive Management, Human Resources, Accounting, and IT departments. The IT department handles all connectivity to the Internet, e-commerce, and Web-hosting tasks, as well as thin-client server management and remote dial-in systems. Each of the branch offices house 50 employees, including accountants and support staff. There are a total of 300 employees.

The company has grown over time via acquisition of smaller individual companies. This caused a scenario in which IT has had to support multiple network operating systems and configurations including peer-to-peer Windows sharing, Windows NT server/client architecture, and Novell NetWare architecture, as each acquisition was incorporated into the network. All interoffice collaboration was done via phone, fax, or individual Internet e-mail accounts.

The decision to install a Microsoft Windows 2000 and Cisco environment is being considered due to West Coast's need to consolidate the company onto one cohesive networking system. This would allow data access to all offices and the Internet via one network in order to reduce overall communications, network administration costs, and to integrate the e-mail systems to one MS Exchange system for interoffice collaboration. Secondary objectives are to create an Internet presence for the entire company under one Internet domain and to replace the old analog dial-in systems with a more secure and dynamic virtual private network (VPN) access system. Finally, there is a desire to implement Voice over IP (VoIP) in the future to eliminate the long distance phone bills inherent in the operations of the multicity company.

Under consideration is a new WAN design in which a new Cisco-routed architecture will be implemented over Frame Relay connections. The main site will have a switched core for the user community and central server farm running Windows Terminal Server (for centralized applications for billing and reporting) and will be linked to the remote offices using redundant core Cisco 3640 routers linked over Frame Relay to Cisco 2610s out at the offices. The Internet will be connected at the main site using a 2610 router equipped with the IP Plus feature set to allow for NAT translation and Cisco PIX Firewall capability.

Summary

Directory enabled networking (DEN) is a new technology specification that was originally developed by Microsoft and Cisco. The two companies then presented their specification to the Distributed Management Task Force (DMTF) and the Internet Engineering Task Force (IETF) for standardization.

DEN specifies a directory service, which has a common schema. The schema is the list of classes, or types of objects that can exist within the directory. It also describes the attributes, or values, of the objects. Objects represent the services, resources, or user accounts that can participate on the network. The directory service can specify the policies that manage how these objects relate to each other.

DEN's value is in becoming a standard. If directory services developed by different vendors all meet DEN requirements, then different vendors' directories can be integrated. The fewer directory services there are, the less administrative overhead will be utilized. This can free up a traditional information technology staff for more interesting projects than managing multiple user accounts in multiple directories.

One of the opportunities for DEN is to enable policy-based networking such that a user's account can be granted various capabilities on the internetwork through the application of a policy. The alternative to policy-based networking is to micromanage the granting of capabilities when necessary—for the IP address or host name of the user's computer.

Windows 2000 is the latest operating system released by Microsoft. This operating system has four versions:

Windows 2000 Professional The workstation version, also considered the upgrade for Windows NT Workstation v4.0.

Windows 2000 Server The workgroup server version, considered the upgrade for Windows NT Server v4.0.

Windows 2000 Advanced Server The enterprise server version, considered the upgrade for Windows NT Server v4.0 Enterprise Edition.

Windows 2000 DataCenter Server A special original equipment manufacturer (OEM) release for high-performance server equipment.

Microsoft has released Windows 2000 with a new feature called Active Directory. Active Directory is a directory service that provides a hierarchical management of the Microsoft network resources, services, and user accounts. The Active Directory is an implementation that closely resembles the DEN specification.

Cisco develops routing and switching equipment. Cisco routers run the Cisco Internetwork Operating System (IOS). The IOS has the capability of scaling from small workgroup networks to global, wide area networks. Cisco produces not only the equipment and its operating system, but also several applications. Some of the tools available for designing and managing a Cisco internetwork include:

Cisco ConfigMaker A free design tool that runs on Windows PCs.

Cisco FastStep A free configuration tool for some of the Cisco routers and access servers, which also runs on Windows PCs.

CiscoWorks A suite of management applications that has versions available for UNIX and for Windows.

Cisco and Microsoft converge their technologies with the Cisco Networking Services for Active Directory (CNS/AD). This technology enables true policy-based networking extended to the routing and infrastructure equipment on the internetwork.

Networking basics apply to understanding the Microsoft and Cisco technologies. These include the Open Systems Interconnection (OSI) protocol reference model developed by the International Organization for Standardization (ISO). The OSI model encompasses seven layers:

Application layer (Layer 7) Provides the user interface and application interface to the network.

Presentation layer (Layer 6) Provides data format services such as encryption and compression.

Session layer (Layer 5) Establishes, maintains, and terminates end-to-end sessions between two network hosts.

Transport layer (Layer 4) Provides data multiplexing, segmentation, and end-to-end reliability services.

Network layer (Layer 3) Specifies the logical network segment and logical network node addressing, and provides routing of data between distinct physical segments.

Data-link layer (Layer 2) Composed of two sublayers—the Media Access Control and the Logical Link Control layers. Provides the physical, or hardware address; also known as the MAC address.

Physical layer (Layer 1) Specifies the data signaling and physical cabling in order to provide the raw bitstream of data over media.

The Department of Defense (DoD) created a model for the TCP/IP protocol stack. This is a four-layer model consisting of these layers.

Application layer Handles application interface, data formatting, and end-to-end session services.

Host to Host Transport layer Handles data multiplexing and segmentation services; also enables reliability services.

Internetwork layer Specifies the logical network and node addressing, and the routing of the data throughout the internetwork.

Network Access layer Specifies the media access, hardware addressing, and the raw bitstream and frame format for data.

In addition to understanding these models, you will need to understand the workings of Internet Protocol addressing. IP version 4 addressing is the most commonly used scheme on the Internet. It uses a 32-bit address and is commonly denoted in a dotted decimal format. Each byte is translated to a decimal by adding the binary value of the 8 bits, and then it is separated by a dot. The IP address of 01100111111100001010101100010011 is translated to 103.240.171.19 for dotted decimal format.

There are three commonly used classes of IP addresses:

Class A All networks with the first octet from 1 through 126 (network 127.x.x.x is reserved for loopback). The default subnet mask is 255.0.0.0.

Class B All networks with the first octet from 128 through 191. The default subnet mask is 255.255.0.0.

Class C All networks with the first octet from 192 through 223. The default subnet mask is 255.255.255.0.

FAQs

Q: What are the advantages of directory enabled servers?

A: A suite of directory enabled server applications can share information. Another advantage is that network devices don't need to be compatible with multiple schemas; they only need to speak a standard protocol.

Q: Does DEN replace SNMP?

A: No. DEN is not a protocol like SNMP, it is a storage system that can store policies.

Chapter 2

A Tour of Windows 2000

Solutions in this chapter:

- Windows 2000 overview

- Understanding the changes since Windows NT 4

- The Active Directory architecture

- Migrating an NT network to Windows 2000

Introduction

Fasten your seatbelt! We are going to take a turbo-ride of Windows 2000. This is one-half of the technology that will guide how your network works. The other half is, of course, your Cisco infrastructure. This chapter will give you an overview of the Windows 2000 features that you will be implementing in your environment. As you read further chapters, it will be like peeling back the layers of an onion; each one will give you more information until you finally understand the whole architecture.

What's New Since Windows NT 4

Although Windows 2000 does not mention "NT," it is still built on that technology. In fact, Windows 2000 was originally named "Windows NT 5.0." There are four versions of Windows 2000:

- **Windows 2000 Professional** This 32-bit desktop operating system has the capability of sharing files in a workgroup environment. Enterprise workstations are typically consumers of information, rather than providers. Windows 2000 Professional is the upgrade to Windows NT Workstation v4.0.

- **Windows 2000 Server** Windows 2000 Server is the first level of 32-bit network operating systems in the Windows 2000 family and is meant for the business server. It supports up to four processors, Terminal Services, Active Directory, security features such as IP Security and Kerberos authentication. This is the upgraded version of Windows NT Server v4.0.

- **Windows 2000 Advanced Server** A higher-end level of Windows 2000, Windows 2000 Advanced Server builds upon the features of Windows 2000 Server. It supports up to eight processors, up to 8GB of RAM, two-node clusters, and network load balancing. This version is upgraded from Windows NT Server 4.0 Enterprise Edition.

- **Windows 2000 DataCenter Server** DataCenter Server will only be released by Original Equipment Manufacturers (OEMs) as a network operating system that is customized for an extremely high-end server. It supports up to 32 processors and four nodes within a cluster. DataCenter Server is new, not an upgrade from Windows NT.

Active Directory

Active Directory is the directory service that organizes all Windows 2000 user accounts, group accounts, servers, domains, domain controllers, and security policies together into a hierarchical or tree structure. The directory service is actually an Extensible Storage Engine (ESE) database that is distributed across multiple domain controllers. Distribution of the database means that it must be synchronized whenever a change is made. This is done through multimaster replication. All domain controllers are masters of their own database portion. This means that, unlike Windows NT, there is no primary domain controller (PDC) that owns all the changes and copies them to backups. Instead, each domain controller can have a change made on it, and that change is then replicated to all other domain controllers to synchronize them.

The Active Directory is a key differentiator between Windows 2000 and Windows NT. It enables central management of the Windows 2000 network. Even though there still exists a domain architecture for Windows 2000 domain controllers, Active Directory provides the Global Catalog (GC), which holds partial information about all user accounts and network resources from every participating Active Directory domain, to make them available network-wide.

Group policies can be distributed through the Active Directory domains, sites, and organizational units (OUs) to define and control the environments of users and desktops. These policies are a major portion of Intellimirror desktop management and automated software distribution.

From an administrative point of view, Active Directory's hierarchical structure lets an administrator delegate specific rights and privileges to other administrators. For example, an administrator can be given only the right to change passwords for a group of users, but not for others. The common way to manage users is through the Active Directory Users and Computers Console shown in Figure 2.1.

Installation Options

For those of you who have deployed Windows NT Workstation in an enterprise environment, the enhancements made to Windows 2000 Professional installation features will be deeply appreciated. There are three ways to deploy Windows 2000:

- SYSPREP
- Remote Installation Service
- Unattended

Figure 2.1 A view of the Active Directory Users and Computers snap-in.

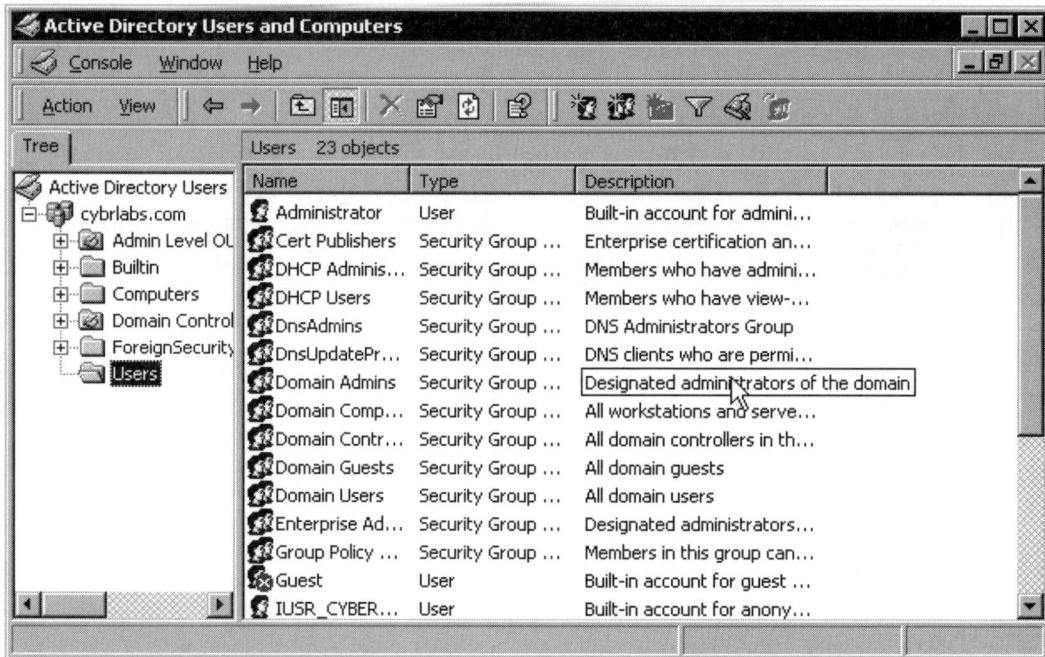

SYSPREP is a method of copying an entire image from one workstation and using it on another with a nearly identical set of hardware. You should use SYSPREP when you have few different types of hardware, and a standard image with identical applications. SYSPREP does not offer much in the way of customization of the image during installation; it is only while creating the image that you will be able to select the applications and configure the machine, or after you have "splatted" the image onto the workstation. This method is used for fresh installations, not upgrades.

Remote Installation Services (RIS) offers the shortest time for installing Windows 2000 and begins with an application called RIPREP, which is similar to SYSPREP. RIS requires that all the workstations have a Pre-boot-Execution-Environment (PXE)-capable Beginning Input Output System (BIOS) or network interface card (NIC). You will also need a Windows 2000 Server to provide the RIS. A PXE-capable NIC from some manufacturers, like 3Com, may come with management software. If not, there may be management software available from the manufacturer, so that the workstation (through the NIC) can be "awakened" and installed or configured remotely without any need for someone's presence at the other end. The disadvantage to RIPREP, however, is the same as the SYSPREP issue in that the image is established for a rigid set of hardware and applications

Figure 2.2 Remote Installation Service.

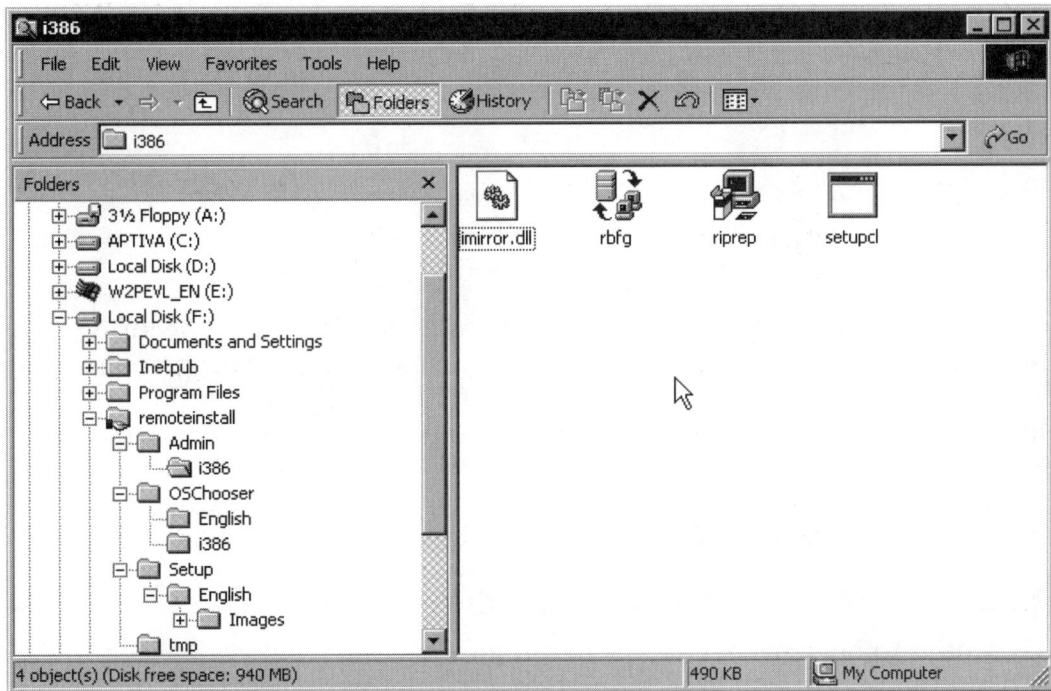

and is only used for fresh installations. Figure 2.2 shows the location of the RIS.

An unattended installation using a file called unattend.txt is the legacy installation method from Windows NT 4. It does take longer to install a workstation using unattend.txt because each application and the entire operating system are installed from scratch. One thing about the unattended installation is that you can use a different unattend.txt for different types of hardware. However, the base set of installation files is identical, which offers significant savings in storage and flexibility for hardware types. You can use unattend.txt files for upgrades and complete format and reinstallations. It takes much more time to configure an unattend.txt install project in the lab, but the flexibility of it saves time at the desktop.

Security Options

Windows 2000 comes with a host of new security features.

- IP Security (IPSec), which is a way of encrypting traffic that passes on the network.

- Layer 2 Tunneling Protocol (L2TP) for an industry standard virtual private network (VPN) over the Internet.

- Kerberos authentication for the Active Directory.

- The Encrypting File System, which allows users to encrypt data on their local hard drive.

- The Server version has a service for certification authority that can pass out certificates for security purposes.

- It implements Public Key Infrastructure (PKI) using a system of digital certificates provided by Certificate Authority servers.

Besides these security options, Windows 2000 uses legacy security methods from Windows NT for backward compatibility. When installed as a standalone server, legacy NTLM (Windows NT Challenge/Response authentication) security is used to authenticate users. When using remote access services, the server implements protocols like Point-to-Point Tunneling Protocol (PPTP) for virtual private networking, and Microsoft Challenge Authentication Protocol (MS-CHAP) for authentication.

Internet Information Services

What used to be delivered as a separate product for Windows NT is now available as part of Windows 2000. Internet Information Services provides a production quality Web server. It also provides File Transfer Protocol (FTP) services, and fulfills other ancillary needs as well.

Terminal Services

The history of Terminal Server is an interesting one. Back during the days of Windows NT 3.5, a company named Citrix licensed Windows NT from Microsoft and extended it to enable remote control of separate console sessions by multiple, simultaneous users in an architecture called Multiwin. Users could run these remote sessions from DOS, Windows 3.1, and other operating systems that might not support 32-bit Windows applications through a client application using a low-bandwidth protocol called Independent Computing Architecture (ICA). Citrix named this product WinFrame.

When Windows NT 4 was introduced, Microsoft announced that it would develop a similar functionality for Windows NT 4. After that, Microsoft and Citrix worked out an agreement to license back the Multiwin portion of the Citrix architecture. Microsoft then introduced Windows NT 4 Terminal Server Edition based on this technology with their own client for 32-bit Windows. Citrix retained the ICA portion as an add-on product to

Figure 2.3 Terminal Services.

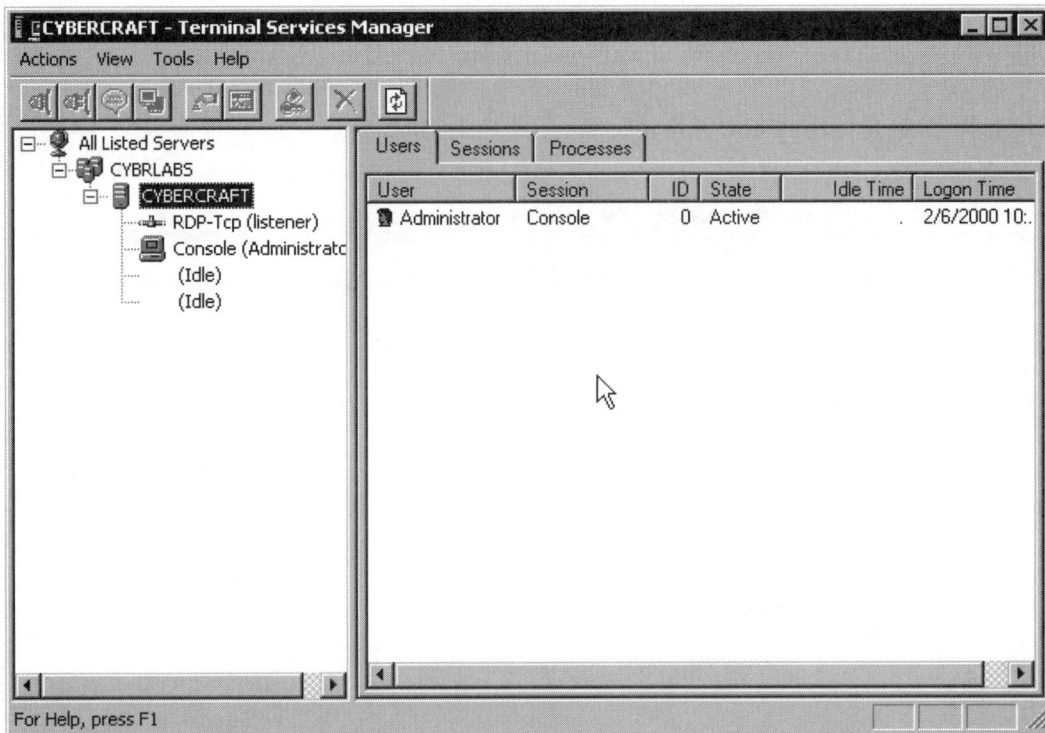

Terminal Server called MetaFrame, which supports clients with both 32-bit Windows and other operating systems. Terminal Services are now included in the Windows 2000 Server family (see Figure 2.3).

As administrators of Novell's NetWare servers know, one of the drawbacks of managing Windows NT servers was the lack of a remote control function for the server (such as NetWare's RCONSOLE). Now, with Terminal Services for Windows 2000, remote control makes managing a Windows 2000 server easy—even across a phone line. The benefits of using Terminal Services for management have been realized by Microsoft, and there is now a way to install Terminal Services with licensing meant just for management of the server.

Remote Access Protocols

Remote access protocols have improved. Besides a standard Point-to-Point Protocol (PPP) connection over a phone line, a user can connect remotely to a network via the PPTP and L2TP/IPSec. PPTP and L2TP/IPSec provide a VPN through the Internet. The value of L2TP/IPSec is that the data is encrypted while traveling across the wire. For example, if a user connects with L2TP/IPSec and runs an e-mail application, that user's e-mail messages would not be readable if a packet sniffer picked them up. The Routing and Remote Access Console is illustrated in Figure 2.4.

Figure 2.4 Routing and Remote Access Console.

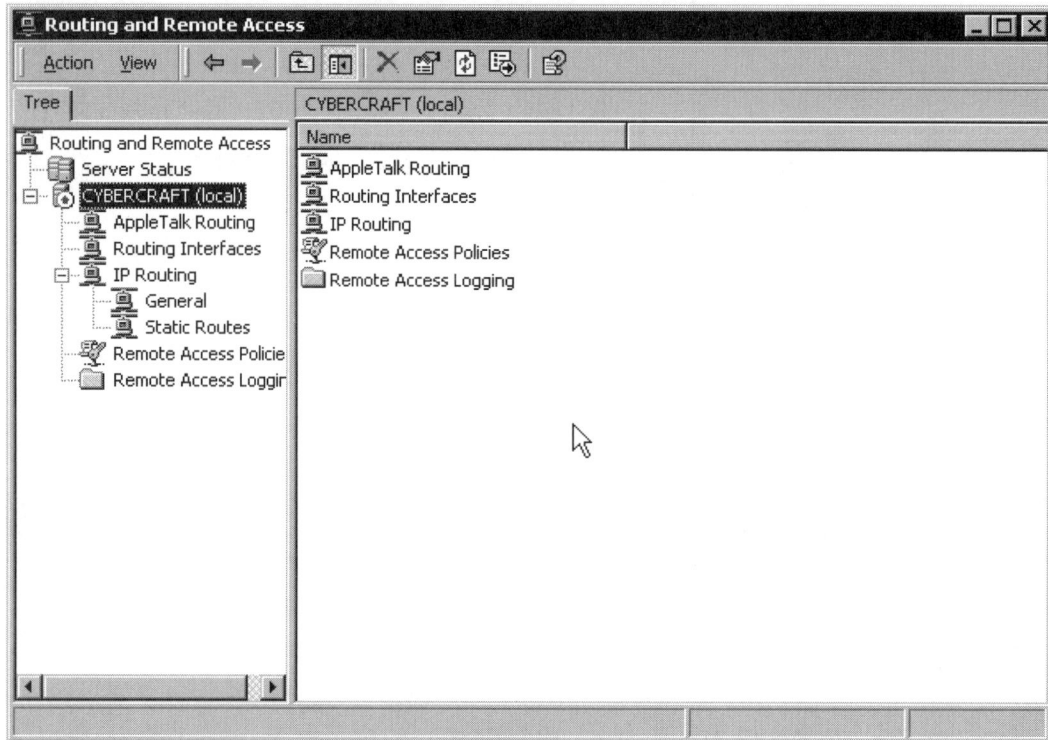

Network Load Balancing

Network load balancing is only available for Windows 2000 Advanced Server and DataCenter Server versions. When implemented, clients perceive that there is a single server responding to their requests, when in fact, there are multiple servers providing the same service. For example, in Figure 2.5 a workstation tries to access a Web site called www.domain.com. This Web site is replicated on three different servers. When the client makes the request, it is directed to the server that is the least busy. Network load balancing can ensure that a Web site is highly available and provides a high performance level.

Both of these are requirements for an Internet Web server, since time-outs and Server Not Found errors can cause a business to lose money and have irreparable damage to their brand name. Windows 2000 implements network load balancing as part of cluster services. This pairing of services effectively takes a highly reliable solution (clustering) and turns it into a highly available solution (clustering with network load balancing).

Figure 2.5 Network load balancing

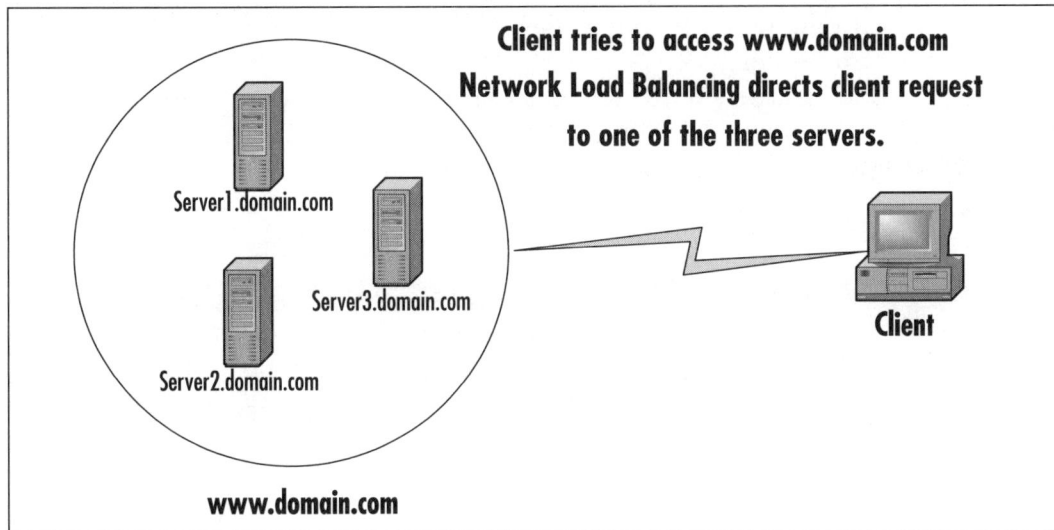

NOTE

Alternatives to network load balancing from Cisco: Allowing Windows 2000 Server to manage network load balancing may not be the best option, since it will require some processing power of the server itself. Cisco offers a hardware-based alternative that does not have this draw-back: the Cisco Local Director. This box will direct traffic to designated servers that host a replicated service. The Local Director box expects to find these servers on the same local network. However, Cisco has a box called a Global Director that can perform this same request redirection to servers located anywhere in the world. The Global Director can even determine whether a client is located closer to one of the global servers and redirect its request to the closest one.

What Happened to WINS?

Windows Internet Naming Service (WINS) still exists in Windows 2000 if you choose to deploy it. WINS cross references a NetBIOS name for a host with its IP address. In Windows 2000, you can choose to deploy Domain Name System (DNS) without WINS, and servers will still be able to be located. However, some enterprises may choose to retain WINS, especially if they maintain a mixed NT/2000 environment for any period of time.

The new version of WINS in Windows 2000 comes with some extra features. One is a new WINS Manager (see Figure 2.6) in which both dynamic and records can be deleted.

Connections between WINS servers can be marked as persistent to ensure that there is less overhead in opening and terminating a connection. Persistent connections also speed replication.

Figure 2.6 WINS Manager.

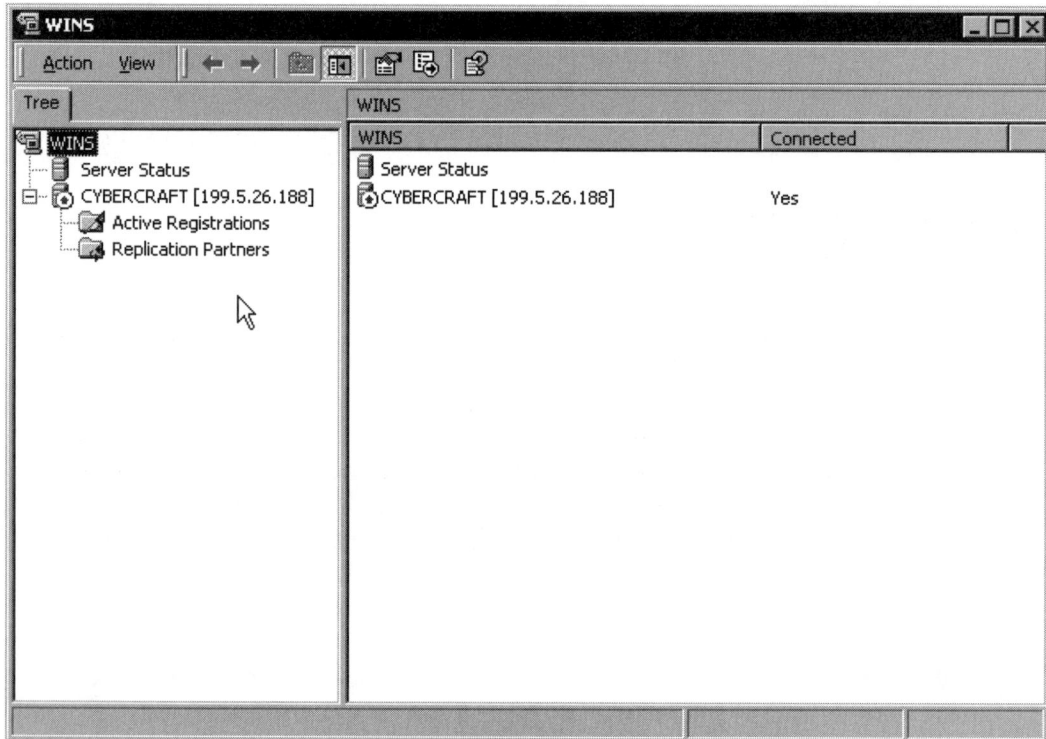

DNS Support

DNS is a requirement to run Windows 2000 Active Directory. Active Directory uses it as the locator service for domain controllers to communicate with other domain controllers, and for workstations to locate a domain controller and to log on to the network. While Windows NT did have a DNS service within it, Windows 2000's DNS has several new features (Figure 2.7).

Integration with Active Directory DNS zones, which are portions of the DNS database, can be integrated into several Active Directory domain controllers, thus gaining those zones the benefits of multimaster replication.

Service Resource Records (SRV RRs) To support Active Directory, all DNS servers must support SRV RRs, because they are the type of DNS record that provides location of services.

Dynamic Updates DNS administrators should rally and cheer for dynamic updates—they are better than sliced bread. Dynamic updates allow DNS clients to update their own resource records on a DNS server. Without this functionality, a DNS administrator must manually edit IP addresses and host names on the DNS server—a tedious and time-consuming task.

Aging and scavenging Another task for a DNS administrator is to remove stale records from the DNS database. Windows 2000 DNS has the ability to age records and remove them (scavenge) if they are not renewed.

Incremental zone transfers DNS servers can be either primary or secondary servers for a zone. Secondary servers periodically refresh their records by downloading the latest information from the primary server (called a *zone transfer*). In large DNS zones, this zone transfer can use up quite a bit of bandwidth. Incremental zone transfers reduce the bandwidth usage because they only download the changes that were made to the zone. In a fairly static environment, the bandwidth consumption is greatly reduced with this feature.

Figure 2.7 Windows 2000 DNS Console.

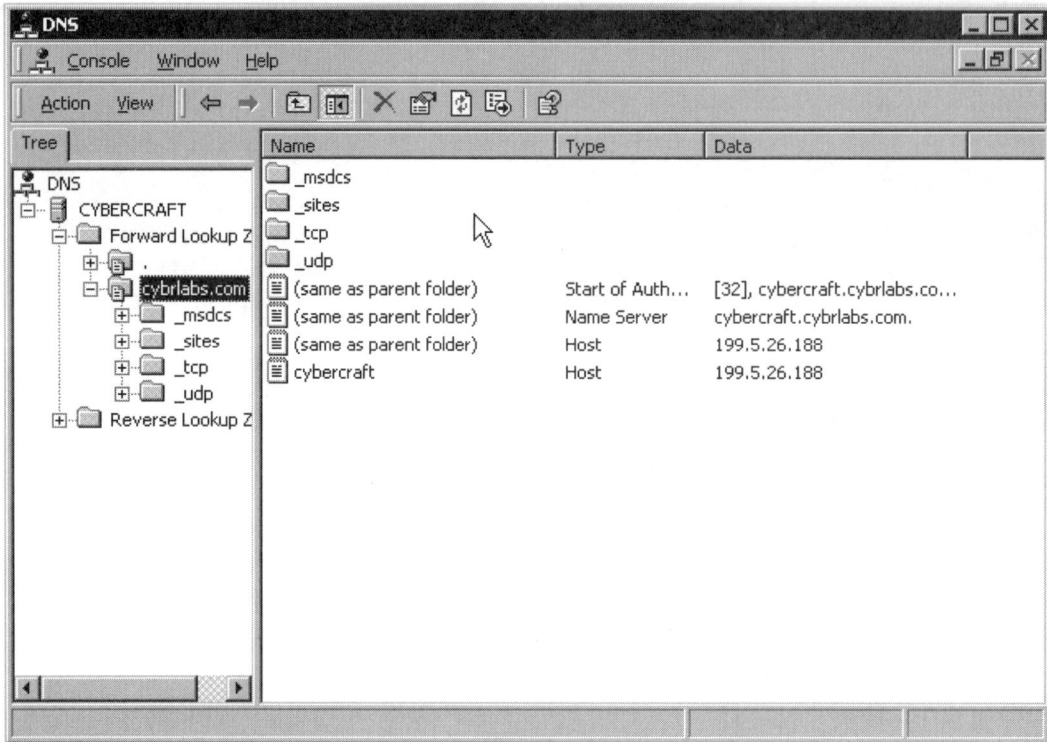

DNS Management during an Upgrade

DNS was not required for Windows NT; in fact, neither was TCP/IP. If you did deploy TCP/IP, WINS was the required service to map NetBIOS names to IP addresses. WINS is more self-sufficient than a traditional DNS system—not requiring every host to be manually entered as DNS requires. So how do you handle the transition from a WINS system to DNS when you upgrade to Windows 2000?

First, you're not going to be able to migrate a WINS database to a DNS database without more work than it would take to simply enter in DNS resource records. Second, you're going to need WINS to be online for awhile—you can't just flip the switch one day and change from WINS to DNS.

What you will need is an understanding of your DNS system.

Continued

- Do you have an existing DNS server? If not, you will need to install a compliant DNS server. Because you are already installing Windows 2000 servers, you should consider installing the Windows 2000 DNS service rather than looking elsewhere for a compliant DNS service.

- If you have an existing DNS server, does it meet the minimum requirements for Windows 2000? If not, you will need to upgrade or replace that server with a compliant DNS server, or add a compliant DNS server to manage the Windows 2000 network.

- If you have a compliant DNS system, does it already have the domain names for your Windows 2000 domains registered as zones within it? If not, you will need to register the zones in your system and add in all the A (Address) resource records for each of your Windows 2000 servers.

- If you have a compliant DNS system, do you have enough DNS servers to provide redundancy and high performance for queries and authentication? If not, you will need to install DNS servers with secondary zones in each designated location. You can install the Windows 2000 DNS service and configure a secondary zone to an existing DNS server.

- If you wish to have as self-managing a system as possible, you should turn on dynamic updates for DNS. This will ensure that each host registers its domain name and IP address in the DNS database, and your work is greatly reduced.

You will also need to determine your phase-out plan for WINS.

- Do you have any systems that are dependent on WINS? If you do, you will need to upgrade, replace, or retire those systems in order to phase out WINS.

- Will you be using mixed domains, both Windows NT and Windows 2000? If so, you should keep WINS until your domains are entirely Windows 2000.

- Will you be upgrading your existing WINS servers to Windows 2000? If you are, you will need to upgrade the WINS service as well. If not, you will need to plan a date for retiring the WINS servers.

Continued

The general plan for changing over from DNS to WINS is simple. Install DNS servers on the network. Enable all clients to act as DNS clients. Upgrade WINS servers if they will be used as Windows 2000 servers in the future. Upgrade or replace all systems that require WINS (such as Windows NT servers). Set a date to retire the WINS service. Establish a back-out plan. Back up the WINS servers—twice. Disable the WINS service on each WINS server. Be prepared for WINS errors. If there are any, reenable the WINS service and then troubleshoot the system that had a WINS error. If not, wait for two weeks or longer before uninstalling WINS.

Recovery Console

The Recovery Console for Windows 2000 is not installed by default. Instead, it is accessible through the Windows 2000 installation CD-ROM, or it can be installed after the server is functional by executing WINNT32 /CMDCONS from a command prompt. The Recovery Console makes recovery of a Windows 2000 computer much faster and easier to perform than it was in Windows NT. For example, in Windows NT, a DOS diskette was used to boot the server to recover it, but an NTFS partition could not be accessed and repaired without the use of a third-party tool. Under Windows 2000, the Recovery Console is able to access an NTFS partition so that failed drivers or corrupt files can be replaced from a source such as the Windows 2000 installation CD-ROM.

Quality of Service

Windows 2000 supports Quality of Service (QoS) in both the server and client versions. QoS is a method of marking packets with a priority so that they are allowed to consume a dedicated portion of network bandwidth. For this reason, all nodes, whether they are the end nodes or the routers and switches in the middle, must support QoS. One of the main reasons that an enterprise implements QoS is for multimedia—video, audio, and telephony. These types of traffic suffer when they are interrupted, but perform well when QoS provides them with a dedicated channel of bandwidth. QoS does not change the bandwidth available on the network. Instead, it makes more efficient use of that bandwidth by being able to place priority on mission-critical traffic.

File System Changes and Disk Support

Windows 2000, by default, supports NT File System (NTFS), File Allocation Table (FAT), and 32-bit File Allocation Table (FAT32). In addition, Windows

2000 supports Compact Disc File System (CDFS) for CD-ROMs. The new NTFS v5.0 is an upgraded version of Windows NT NTFS. It has been enhanced to support disk quotas, defragmentation while online, and compressed network I/O. NTFS is required for all domain controllers, because Active Directory files cannot be stored on any other file systems. The CONVERT.EXE command is used to update a disk partition to NTFS. All domain controllers must be running NTFS before the Active Directory can be installed. The CONVERT/FS:NTFS command must be run with a switch to indicate the file system. FAT and FAT32 enable dual-booting and access to local drives.

In addition to the file system support, there are other enhancements to Windows 2000:

- Encrypting File System (EFS)
- Distributed file system (Dfs)
- File Replication Services (FRS)

When Windows NT came out with NTFS, the file system itself was deemed a form of security. Without the password and ID to access the NT operating system, no one could access the files on the hard drive. However, once third-party tools (such as NTFSDOS) were introduced that could access an NTFS formatted partition from a DOS prompt, the files were no longer secure. In Windows 2000, EFS solves this security issue by enabling a user to encrypt files or folders on the local hard drive. EFS only works on local NTFS formatted disk drives. The user can see his own files, but no one else will be able to read them. EFS automatically decrypts the file to be used and re-encrypts it when it is saved. Because EFS is built into the file system, it is transparent to the user and difficult for hackers to attack. This is an ideal technology for laptops; it adds extra protection in the event a laptop is lost or stolen.

EFS uses public and private key pair encryption technique. The user who encrypts a file is the only person assigned the private key. The public key is distributed from a PKI service. The public key encrypts the key, and the private key decrypts it. That means that the user must log on to the network in order to read encrypted files.

Most enterprises have multiple servers that are accessed by multiple users. It is not uncommon to see a user with several mapped drives to different servers in order to perform daily duties. If the administrator does not map drives in a logon script, the user is left to search out data on his own. If shared volumes have cryptic names or names that have little to do with their contents, it will take far longer for a user to find the data he needs to perform his job, which, unfortunately, leads to a form of "productive downtime." Dfs can resolve this dilemma.

Dfs is a logical namespace. It enables an administrator to assign other names to shares, names that more closely reflect the contents of the share. Dfs also allows an administrator to map multiple shared volumes as subfolders of a single logical name—very handy when pushing the limitations of the alphabet for drive mappings.

Dfs consists of both a client and a server component, whose console is shown in Figure 2.8. The server component can be implemented as either a single machine Dfs, or as an Active Directory domain integrated Dfs. The machine Dfs stores the topology in the registry of the Dfs server. The Active Directory domain Dfs stores the topology in the Active Directory and further supports replication via FRS.

FRS replicates data between domain controllers and requires NTFS. It automatically is installed to support the replication of the NetLogon component of the Active Directory domain controllers. Only changes to data are replicated between the multimaster domain controllers. My recommendation for the maximum data to be replicated during a 24-hour period is 1GB.

Figure 2.8 DFS Console.

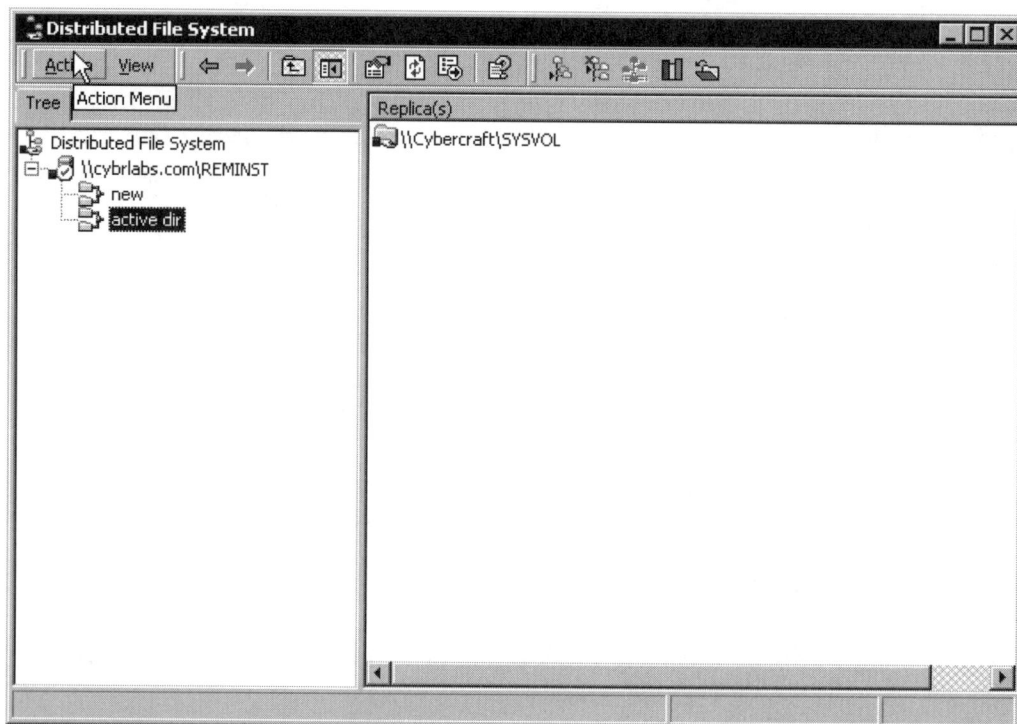

Active Directory Architecture

Because the Active Directory will influence much of the traffic on the network, you need to understand its architecture. In general, Active Directory traffic can be subdivided into three types:

- **Query traffic** A user performs a search on the Active Directory contents.

- **Authentication traffic** A user logs on to the network via the Active Directory.

- **Replication traffic** Data is synchronized between domain controllers with updates to the Active Directory database and to the contents of the FRS folder structure.

Domain Architecture Changes

Like Windows NT, Windows 2000 Active Directory still implements domains. However, these domains are now organized in a different structure. In Windows NT, a domain was the single topmost component of a group of servers. In Windows 2000, the topmost component is the forest.

Forest

The forest is a group of domain trees as shown in Figure 2.9. All the domains within the forest share a schema, configuration, and Global Catalog (explained later in the chapter). The domain trees do not share a single namespace within a forest. For example, one domain tree may have TREE.COM as its namespace, while a second domain tree uses ROOT.COM as its namespace. Both of these domains are part of the same forest. However, only one of the domain trees can contain the root domain. The root domain of the forest is the first domain installed into the forest.

Domain Tree

A domain tree is a group of domains that all share a common namespace, schema, configuration, and Global Catalog. Note that namespaces cannot cross outside a domain tree or a forest. An example of a domain tree is the group of root.com domains shown in Figure 2.9 enclosed by an oval. The namespace shared is root.com, while the schema, configuration, and Global Catalog are shared by all forest-wide domains.

Figure 2.9 An example of a forest and domain tree.

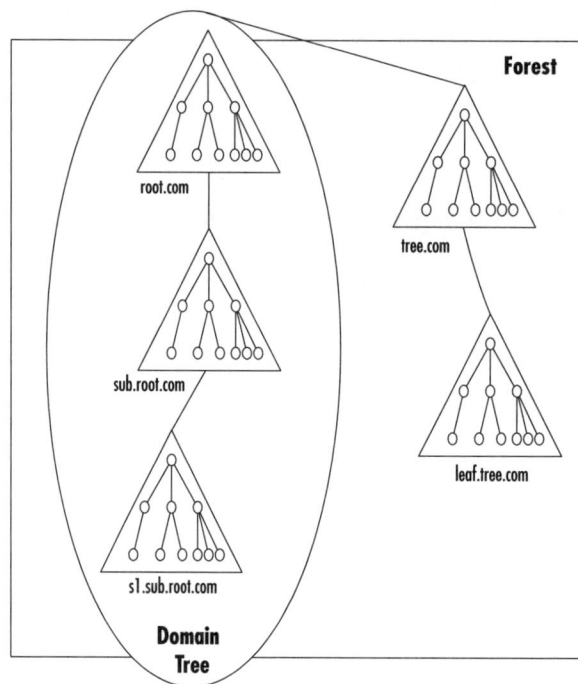

Domain

The Windows 2000 Active Directory domain is a group of domain controllers, much the same as it was in Windows NT. Each Active Directory domain is assigned a domain name, such as DOMAIN.COM, as well as a backward-compatible NetBIOS name, such as DOMAIN.

Another of the differences is that there is no longer a primary domain controller or backup domain controllers (BDC) in the domain. Instead, all domain controllers are equal. The domain information is stored in a strict partition of the Active Directory, and each domain is a separate partition. For example, Server1.root.com will have the same domain information stored within its Active Directory files as Server2.root.com, but will *not* have the same domain information as Host.tree.com. The fact that each domain holds a separate partition of the Active Directory plays a part in how replication of data affects your infrastructure. Balancing network utilization with user-perceived performance will play a part in deciding what the infrastructure looks like, as well as the Active Directory design.

One of the difficulties in managing a Windows NT domain was that a member server could not easily be updated to a domain controller or demoted. In Windows 2000, a server can easily be promoted to a domain controller and then demoted. This is done with the Active Directory wizard, which is the executable DCPROMO.EXE.

Sites

Sites are defined as a group of well-connected IP subnets. Whether links are considered to be "well-connected" between those IP subnets is going to be a subjective decision. Aside from that issue, a site is used to control the way query, authentication, and replication traffic is sent across the network. For example, when a user logs on to the network, the workstation attempts to log on to a domain controller that is located within its own site. When replication occurs within a site, it uses uncompressed Remote Procedure Call (RPC) based traffic. However, when replication occurs between sites, it uses compressed RPC-based traffic, but only on a scheduled basis. If replication occurs between sites and those sites do not share the same domain (meaning only Global Catalog, schema, and configuration data is exchanged), then the replication can be configured to use only Simple Mail Transfer Protocol (SMTP). As you can see, sites are the key to managing the Windows 2000 Active Directory traffic.

Organizational Units

If you are familiar with Novell's Directory Service (NDS) or with the directory service standard called X.500, then you can guess what organizational units (OUs) are. OUs perform the same function in the Active Directory. An OU is contained within a domain and is used as a container for accounts and network resources. OUs can be nested within each other, and as such, are able to create a hierarchical structure. The OU forms the basis for delegation of administration for groups of users within a domain. An example of an OU structure is shown in Figure 2.10.

User Accounts

Users are represented within the Active Directory as user accounts. Each user account is a separate object within the Active Directory database. User accounts provide end users with their logon IDs, and provide administrators with a method of providing access to network resources to those end users, and organizing information about the end users. Figure 2.11 illustrates how a user account is seen in the Active Directory.

Figure 2.10 An OU hierarchy.

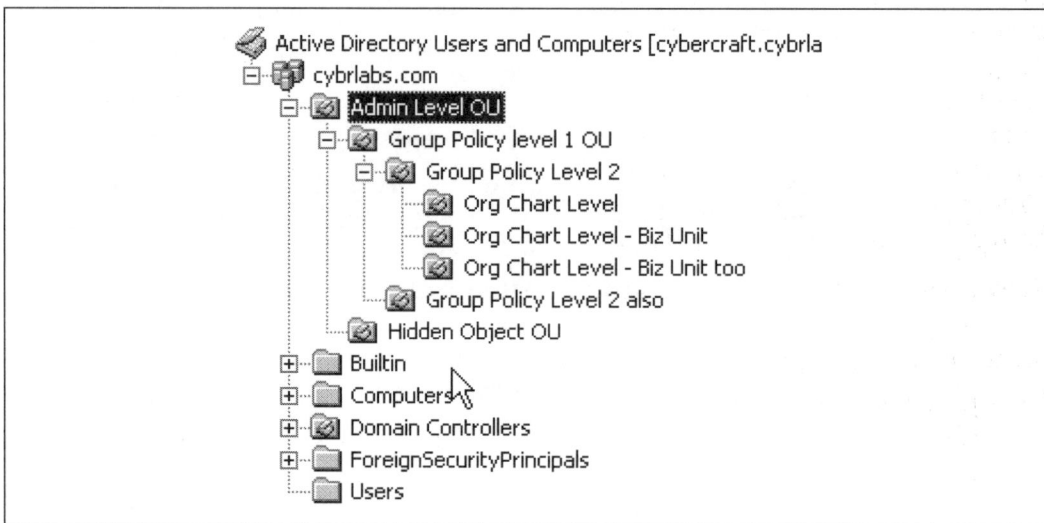

Figure 2.11 User account.

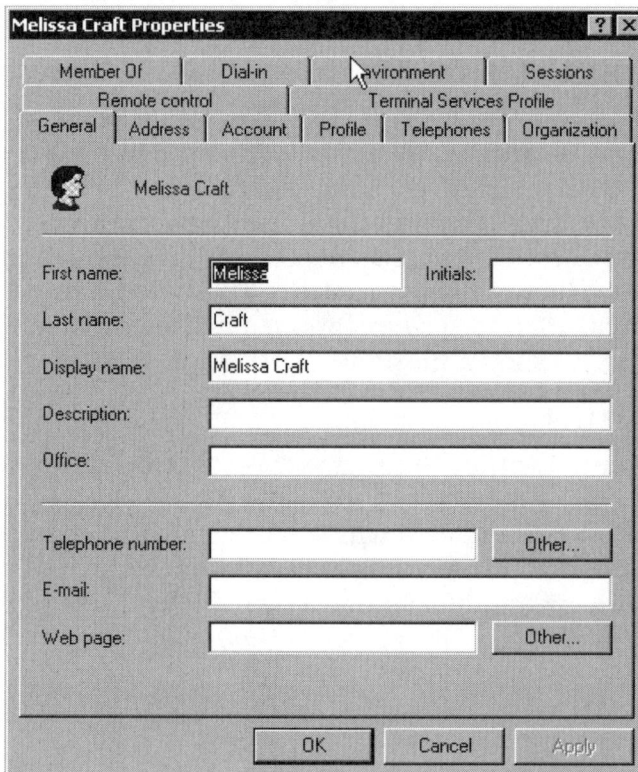

Groups

Groups are a form of an account within the Active Directory that logically arranges a set of accounts into a single unit. An administrator can grant the group rights and privileges to network resources one time, and the members will receive those rights and privileges. Groups are a time saver when the same rights and privileges must be assigned to multiple users— especially hundreds or thousands of users. While groups did exist in Windows NT, they have somewhat different rights under Windows 2000 Active Directory. Groups can be classified in two ways:

Group types There are two group types: security and distribution. A security group type is one that can be granted rights and privileges. A distribution group type is used solely for e-mail.

Group scope There are three group scopes: domain local, global, and universal. The group scope will act slightly differently depending on whether the domain is in native mode or mixed mode. Native mode is when the domain supports only Windows 2000 domain controllers. Mixed mode is the default state for a new domain, and is backward compatible to Windows NT backup domain controllers. For example, a domain local group can contain only user and global groups from any domain in mixed mode. In native mode, however, the domain local group can also contain universal groups from any domain and domain local groups from the local domain. Therefore, in native mode, groups can be nested. The one thing that group scope will affect network bandwidth utilization in, however, is the universal group. A universal group is only available as a security group in native mode. It replicates each member to the Global Catalog, which is replicated between domains across a forest. When there is a large universal group (with up to thousands of members), it can make replication much larger than it has to be. The fix for this is to only make other groups members of universal groups; that will cut down the membership and resulting replication traffic issues.

FSMOs

FSMO stands for Flexible Single Master of Operations. *Flexible* means that the role can be moved from one server to another. *Single* means that there is only one of the servers within either a domain or a forest, depending on which FSMO it was. Active Directory has five FSMOs:

RID Master There is one RID master per forest. It provides the relative ID (RID) portion of SIDs (Security IDs that are applied to machines) to domain controllers to prevent conflicts within the forest.

PDC Emulator There is one PDC Emulator per domain. This computer acts as a PDC for Windows NT BDCs when a domain is in mixed mode. In native mode, the PDC Emulator remains to handle password changes and hold authority over the domain's time settings.

Infrastructure Master There is one Infrastructure master per domain. This domain controller manages group-to-user references so that users are able to access network resources.

Domain Naming Master There is one domain naming master per forest. This FSMO assures that each domain added to the forest is given a unique name. This domain must also be a Global Catalog server.

Schema Master There is only one schema in a forest, and therefore only one Schema Master in a forest. The Schema master is the one domain controller on which the schema can be changed.

Global Catalog

There is only one Global Catalog (GC) in any forest. The implication is that if you have multiple forests, you will have multiple GCs. A GC is an Active Directory database partition that contains a partial copy of user, group, and network resource objects from every domain in the forest. For example, user objects will have certain properties copied to the GC, but not other, less common properties. This allows a user to perform searches for resources on the network regardless of the domain in which they reside. Because the GC only contains a portion of the properties, the GC is not excessively large. And, because you can select which servers are GC servers, the replication of the GC database partition can be managed somewhat by GC server placement.

Configuration

The configuration is the information about site placement and replication information, and is copied to each domain controller. This is a small amount of information contained in its own database partition. Once a configuration is set, replication of this partition occurs when changes are made to sites, including the site link definitions or IP subnet allocations to sites.

Schema

Databases usually contain some form of definition file that determines what types of objects can exist within the database. In the Active Directory, this is the schema. It contains the list of objects that can be created, and their types and properties. The schema can be extended if the Schema

Administrator (a user who is a member of the Schema Administrators group) adds a new object type or property to an existing object type.

LDAP

Lightweight Directory Access Protocol (LDAP) is a standard protocol created for accessing X.500 directories. The X.500 client was very network intensive or *heavy*, so LDAP was created to provide the same directory access but not overwhelm the network—hence the name *lightweight*. Active Directory supports both LDAP and the X.500 naming model so that it can work with other LDAP-compliant directories.

So, You Want to Migrate?

When faced with a new technology and being able to use that technology for reducing costs or a competitive advantage, enterprises will migrate to that technology. If no advantage is seen in changing the technology from the one being used currently, then there is no reason to migrate at all. Business reasons should always drive the technology decisions made in a migration project. For example, if a business wanted to use Windows 2000 for file and print services, it would be foolish to install the Internet Information Service (that takes processing power away from the file and print services) just because it was a service that was new and interesting to the installer.

Quick! Plan Your Project

Best practices dictate that you need to know the business requirements for your project before you even begin planning. Gathering these requirements in a large enterprise can be considered a project by itself. With multiple business units and their resultant goals for the new environment, your project team will then be tasked with determining which are in conflict with each other, and then establishing which requirements should receive priority by working with the business units. Beyond this, your team will need to look at other business requirements even if a business unit does not request them. These include:

- Administration requirements and delegation
- International functionality
- Security
- Network protocol strategy
- Policies and desktop environment requirements

- Roaming users, VPN, extranet, and remote access needs
- Additional Windows 2000 Services, such as Terminal Services, Internet Information Server, etc.
- Applications

You will also need to gather information about your organization. This information will help determine the details of your technology deployment. For example, two of the most critical lists you will have are the inventories of the hardware and software. These inventories need to be compared to the compatibility lists for hardware and applications. Those computers and applications on the inventories that do not have approval through the compatibility list will probably not work in the final deployment. These items will need to be retired or replaced. Some of the information that you will need to gather includes:

- TCP/IP information, especially DNS and Dynamic Host Control Protocol (DHCP) configuration
- Current network infrastructure plan, including both wide area network (WAN) and local area network (LAN) links
- Protocols used
- Network operating systems, those that currently exist and those that will be in place after the migration is complete
- Desktop operating systems
- Services that will be migrated, such as Web services and file and print services
- Hardware inventory
- Software inventory
- Applications used

Planning the directory structure will be the next process. This will occur hand in hand with planning the infrastructure. There may be an intent to use the existing infrastructure without making any changes to it when deploying Windows 2000. You may find that this is not the case when you size up your needs for an infrastructure, so keep your options open. This process consists of several final plans:

- Active Directory forest plan
- Active Directory domain and DNS plan, including the naming strategy

- Active Directory organizational unit hierarchy for each domain
- Infrastructure strategy
- Active Directory site topology based on the infrastructure

The next phase for your project will be testing. This phase is sometimes glossed over or not given much time in a migration project. Don't make the same mistake. Testing is a critical function in deciding how to deploy Windows 2000. The lab environment should be a reflection of the actual environment in which Windows 2000 is deployed. The hardware should be the same, and all hardware needs to be tested. The applications should also be tested. The DNS server should be the same version and service as is used in the production environment. You will want to test the bandwidth utilization of various types of traffic in the lab so that you can determine the size for your WAN and LAN links. This means that you need to have similar types of WAN and LAN equipment in the lab as well.

The lab period will be complete when all the objectives for Windows 2000 are tested and acceptable, and a pilot group has been deployed successfully. After that, deployment will begin. This is typically rolled out in three phases, each which may have subphases of its own. The first phase is to upgrade and deploy infrastructure equipment. This may include changing the Cisco IOS parameters to support different types of traffic requirements. The second phase is to upgrade and deploy servers, starting with supporting services such as DNS and ending with the Windows 2000 domain controllers and member servers. The third and final phase will be to deploy the workstations and peripherals—whether they will be upgraded or changed in order to access the new Active Directory, and whether you will implement a new desktop management system.

Windows 2000 Case Studies

Windows 2000 has a lot to offer as a network operating system. Since its various versions can be deployed on both servers and workstations, it offers a synergistic networking model. A pure Windows 2000 network on which both workstations and servers only run Windows 2000 requires less administrative overhead because there is only one type of operating system to manage. We will examine how to design these networks and services for Windows 2000 in Chapter 6, "Designing the Windows 2000 Network."

ABC Chemical Company

The ABC Chemical Company has a complex switched internetwork using Windows NT servers to provide file and print services. To review, the business requirements for ABC are:

- Meet FDA and government requirements for security, both Internet and corporate

- Increase productivity and collaboration between departments

- Utilize video/audio conferencing over the Internet as a method of customer relationship management to gain a competitive advantage

- Cut costs of administration

Windows 2000 can assist in meeting these objectives.

- For Internet and corporate security it offers IPSec to encrypt data across the wire and L2TP for virtual private networking over the Internet. In addition, it uses Kerberos for Active Directory authentication and EFS for local data encryption.

- For increased productivity and collaboration, the Active Directory can provide published resources that can be searched for using natural language. In addition, the Active Directory stores user accounts that enable easy location of others, whether they are within the same domain or in another.

- To support the audio and video conferencing future needs, Windows 2000 utilizes both Telephony Application Programming Interface (TAPI) and QoS.

- To cut administrative costs, the ABC Chemical Company can implement Windows 2000 at both the server and the workstation for a single operating system to support.

West Coast Accounting, L.L.C.

West Coast Accounting relies on routers to move data between its many branches. The network that they plan to build with Windows 2000 must provide them with the following business requirements:

- Thin-client system support

- An Internet presence under a single Internet domain

- Reduction of operating systems to a single type

- Data access to all offices and the Internet
- Replace dial-in remote access with VPN access to reduce costs
- Implement Voice over IP (VoIP)—a form of telephony—to reduce long distance costs

Windows 2000 has the capabilities to provide all of West Coast Accounting's business requirements.

- Windows 2000 includes Terminal Services, which is a thin-client application server package. Existing thin-client services can be migrated to the Windows 2000 Terminal Service.

- Windows 2000 includes Internet Information Services, which enables Windows 2000 to become a Web and FTP server. This can provide West Coast Accounting with a Web presence.

- West Coast Accounting and ABC Chemical Company have the same requirement to reduce administrative costs by reducing the operating system to a single type. Since Windows 2000 can be deployed on both workstations and servers, it can reduce the operating systems on the network to one.

- Windows 2000 has native support for TCP/IP (Transmission Control Protocol/Internet Protocol). TCP/IP is a routable protocol stack that can move data throughout a network and the Internet. The TCP/IP stack in Windows 2000 will allow data access throughout West Coast Accounting's offices and beyond to the Internet.

- Windows 2000 Routing and Remote Access works with both direct dial-in access to the network and with virtual private networking capabilities using L2TP or backward compatibility with PPTP. This will provide West Coast Accounting with the remote access support using VPN, as well as provide the capability for direct dial-in access while phasing users from one method to the other.

- Windows 2000 supports telephony using TAPI, and even includes a telephone dialer application for executing voice calls over a network, as is required by West Coast Accounting.

Summary

Windows 2000 is a network operating system that can be deployed on servers and workstations. There are several versions available:

- **Windows 2000 Professional** Developed for workstations

- **Windows 2000 Server** Supports workgroup and medium-sized servers

- **Windows 2000 Advanced Server** Supports medium- to enterprise-sized servers, including clustering, network load balancing, and more processors in a symmetrical multiple processor solution

- **Windows 2000 DataCenter Server** Released only as an OEM operating system, DataCenter Server can support extensive enterprise-level server equipment

Active Directory is one of the main reasons that large enterprises will implement Windows 2000 on its servers. The Active Directory provides a directory service for user accounts and network resources in which these objects are organized in a hierarchy. As a directory service, there is a single point of administration for the Windows 2000 network.

Installation options in Windows 2000 are greatly improved from previous versions of Windows NT. Windows 2000 can be installed using an unattended method (unattend.txt file to script an installation), or through disk duplication methods. Disk duplication methods include SYSPREP and RIPREP. Whereas SYSPREP is used with a boot disk, RIPREP is used with Remote Installation Services and does not need to have a person attend the installation.

Security protocols and capabilities are updated in Windows 2000. They include virtual private networking using L2TP, Kerberos authentication, the encrypting file system, IPSec, and PKI with Certificate Authority services. These represent several different types of security capabilities; some are authentication focused, while others are encryption focused.

Routing and Remote Access Services provide a native ability for direct dial in to the network, and for virtual private networking services through the Internet. Remote users can log on to the network and run applications as though they were connected locally to the network.

Internet Information Services in Windows 2000 provides a Web server and FTP server that can be run internally as an intranet server, or externally as an Internet server.

Terminal Services provide thin-client capability on Windows 2000. An application installed on a Windows 2000 server running Terminal Services can be used via remote control of the Windows 2000 server. The remote control is established with a terminal emulation program. The low-bandwidth utilization properties of Terminal Services make Windows 2000 an ideal application server for remote users.

File System Support includes three different file systems: FAT, FAT32, and NTFS. FAT and NTFS support is inherited from Windows NT, but FAT32 support is new. Now, disk partitions formatted with FAT32 can be accessed from a Windows 2000 computer. File storage is further enhanced with the new capabilities of Distributed File System (Dfs) and the Encrypting File System (EFS). Dfs can create a single file structure from multiple servers. Dfs can even be made redundant by distributing the files via the Active Directory. EFS is the ability to encrypt files locally on a hard drive. Users can encrypt their own files and, when they leave their desk or laptop, they can be assured that the files are not readable on the hard drive.

FAQs

Q: What is Windows 2000?

A: Windows 2000 is the next version of Windows NT. There are four versions: Windows 2000 Professional, Windows 2000 Server, Windows 2000 Advanced Server, and Windows 2000 DataCenter Server. These versions can be used for desktop workstations, laptops, small branch office servers, mid-sized network servers, and enterprise-level servers.

Q: How do I install the Recovery Console?

A: The Recovery Console is a method of being able to access the Windows 2000 NTFS hard drive and manipulate files and services. Many times the ability to replace a corrupted file or stop a service will recover a server. The way to install the Recovery Console so that it is always available is to run WINNT32/CMDCONS.

Q: How do I promote a Windows 2000 Server to a domain controller?

A: Use the DCPROMO.EXE command to promote a Windows 2000 server to a domain controller. This same command can demote a domain controller to a member server.

Q: My server will not let me run the DCPROMO utility to update it to a domain controller because it does not have NTFS. How do I change the FAT disk partition to NTFS?

A: You can run CONVERT/FS:NTFS to change a disk partition to NTFS.

Chapter 3

Cisco Hardware and IOS Basics

Solutions in this chapter:

- Networking basics: the difference between routers and switches

- Switching overview and application

- Routing overview and application

- Cisco IOS

- QoS functionality and how it works on the switches and routers

Introduction

How do you know what Cisco equipment you should use for your Windows 2000 network infrastructure in order to support features such as Active Directory/Directory Enabled Network (DEN), Quality of Service (QoS), and security? It's not easy to know, considering the vast quantity of infra-structure equipment available from Cisco. In this chapter, we hope to alleviate some of the frustration of deciding what Cisco equipment is available for what purpose by discussing the differences between routers and switches and when it is appropriate to use one or the other. We also discuss the features of these switches and routers as well as the different wide area network (WAN) technologies available. We also discuss the Cisco Internetwork Operating System (IOS) and how to navigate around it. We conclude the chapter with a look at Quality of Service.

Let's start by discussing the differences between routers and switches.

Networking Basics: The Difference between Routers and Switches

Why do we have both routers and switches available for our use? Why not just have one or the other? The answer is that both routers and switches have their own place in your Windows 2000 network infrastructure. First let's look at which layer of the Open System Interconnection (OSI) each of these types of equipment operate. Routers operate at Layer 3, the network layer, and switches typically operate at Layer 2, the data-link layer. Since routers and switches operate at different layers of the OSI model, they pass packets and frames, respectively. The packets passed through routers depend on the Layer 3 destination address, or networking address, whereas the frames passed by Layer 2 switches depend on the Media Access Control (MAC) address, or physical address. Another difference between routers and switches is that routers are protocol dependent but switches are not. Routers are used to connect different networks and separate broadcast domains, whereas switches are used to separate collision domains since each port is seen as its own network segment.

NOTE

Switches can operate at multiple layers of the OSI model (discussed later in this chapter), but for the majority of our discussions in this chapter we will concern ourselves with only traditional switches that operate at Layer 2.

Hierarchical Design Model

Cisco believes in designing internetworks in layers. They believe that by designing your internetwork in this manner, you can easily make changes as the network grows—in other words, changes will have to be made to only a portion of the network instead of to the entire network.

Changing a small portion of your network infrastructure can be very costly, but imagine the cost if you had to replace your entire network infrastructure! Cisco recognizes a Hierarchical Design Model that consists of the following three layers:

- Core layer (also known as the backbone layer)
- Distribution layer
- Access layer

The purpose of the core layer is to move packets as fast as possible. Since you want packets to be moved quickly at this layer you should ensure that nothing is slowing down the packets, such as performing any sort of filtering on the packets or using any other sort of access list on the routers used in this layer. Since the distribution layer is situated between the core and access layers it acts as a demarcation point. This provides boundary definition for the other two layers. In other words, the demarcation point is the point at which one layer changes from one entity to another. For example, we discussed that no filtering is done on the routers at the core layer; however, filtering of packets is allowed (and should be done) in the distribution layer. Keep this in mind as you design your Windows 2000 network infrastructure. There are several functions that can take place within the distribution layer; a few of these are:

- Defining the broadcast domain
- Routing of virtual local area networks (VLANs)
- Performing media transitions
- Performing remote site access to the network

The purpose of the access layer is, as its name states, the access point that users are permitted on the network. This can be via leased lines, Frame Relay, and other wide area network means for users at remote locations, or it can be via the organization's local area network. Access lists and other filtering on routers can also take place at this layer, just as it can at the distribution layer. Some of the functions accomplished at this layer include:

- Microsegmentation
- Switched bandwidth
- Shared bandwidth

Think of the three layers as being wrapped around each other, with the core layer in the middle, the distribution layer wrapped around it, and then the access layer encompassing the distribution layer, as shown in Figure 3.1.

Figure 3.1 The Hierarchical Design Model.

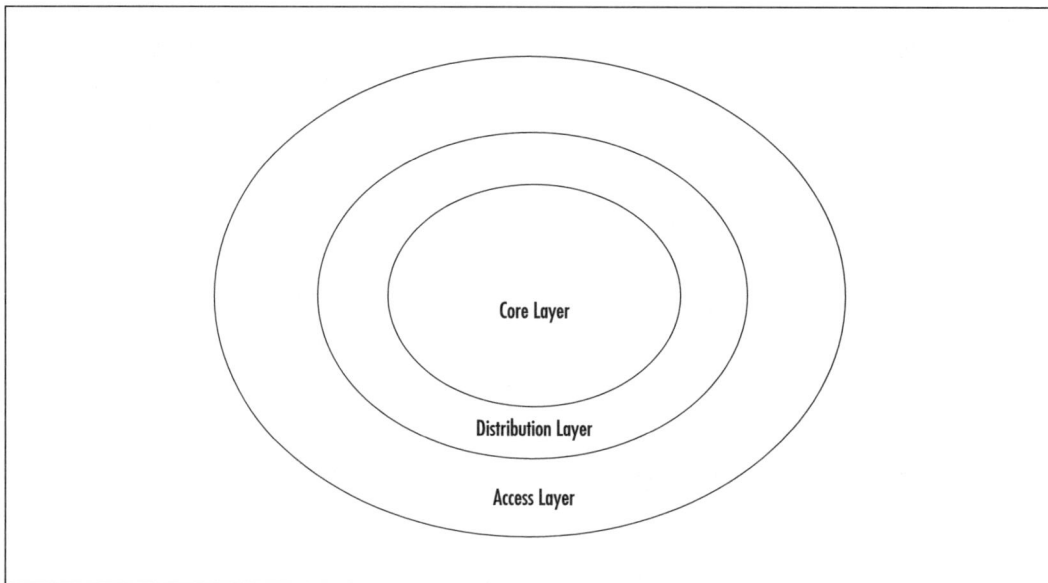

When Is It Appropriate to Use Routers?

At what layer(s) of the Hierarchical Design Model do you think you would use a router in your Windows 2000 network infrastructure? All three layers are suitable for using routers. Earlier, we discussed at which layer of the model you would use access lists or other filtering when you use routers in your infrastructure. The routers you use at the core layer should not have any filtering done on them at all, and they need to be as heavy duty as possible so they can efficiently move the packets as fast as possible. Routers used in the distribution layer and the access layer can have filtering done to meet your needs.

A function that routers have (that switches do not) is that they allow you to optimize the path for the traffic. This is done using various routing protocols such as Open Shortest Path First (OSPF), Enhanced Interior Gateway Routing Protocol (EIGRP), and Border Gateway Protocol (BGP).

There are several other functions provided by routers (but not switches), such as providing load balancing, providing alternative paths when link failures occur, filtering, media translation, network segmentation, and the prioritization of traffic flow. Cisco routers support various queuing techniques that are discussed later in this chapter.

When Is It Appropriate to Use Switches?

Based on the earlier discussion about when it is appropriate to use routers, you may be thinking that you could just use a router for everything and not worry about using any switches in your Windows 2000 network infrastructure—however, this is very far from the truth. Switches can also be used in all three layers. However, not all switches are meant to be used at the core layer, so do not think you can buy a low-end switch for your backbone!

One of the benefits to using switches is that each switch port provides dedicated bandwidth. This can greatly enhance the productivity for the enduser of a switch used in the access layer. In essence, each switch port is its own network segment. Other benefits of using switches in your Windows 2000 network infrastructure is the ability to create VLANs and the capability of the switch to translate one frame format to another frame format automatically. We discuss VLANs later in the chapter.

Switching Overview and Application

Now that you have learned the benefits of using routers and switches in your network infrastructure, let's take a closer look at some of the switches available from Cisco.

Cisco Switch Models

Not all switches are created equal—some switches are better suited for certain parts of your network infrastructure than others. Let's take a quick look at some of the switches available from Cisco and where they are best suited for use in a network infrastructure.

Catalyst 6500 Series

The Catalyst 6500 series of switches is part of the Catalyst 6000 family and was first introduced in January 1999. The 6500 series is available in a six- or nine-slot chassis (6506 and 6509), supports redundant power supplies, and has a switching capacity of 256 Gbps when used as a traditional

Layer 2 switch. The 6500 series provides a switching capacity of 150 Mbps when operating as a multilayer switch. Figure 3.2 shows the 6509 switch.

The port capacity of the 6500 series varies depending on the interface type. For example, the 6509 supports up to 384 10/100 Ethernet, or up to 192 100FX Fast Ethernet, or up to 130 Gigabit Ethernet ports.

The 6500 series is designed for use in backbones as well as in the distribution layer. The 6500 series provides support for multimedia and multicast applications running on your intranet by using several different protocols including Internet Group Management Protocol (IGMP), Cisco Group Management Protocol (CGMP), and Protocol Independent Multicast (PIM).

Figure 3.2 Nine-slot Catalyst 6500 Series switch (6509) with a single power supply.

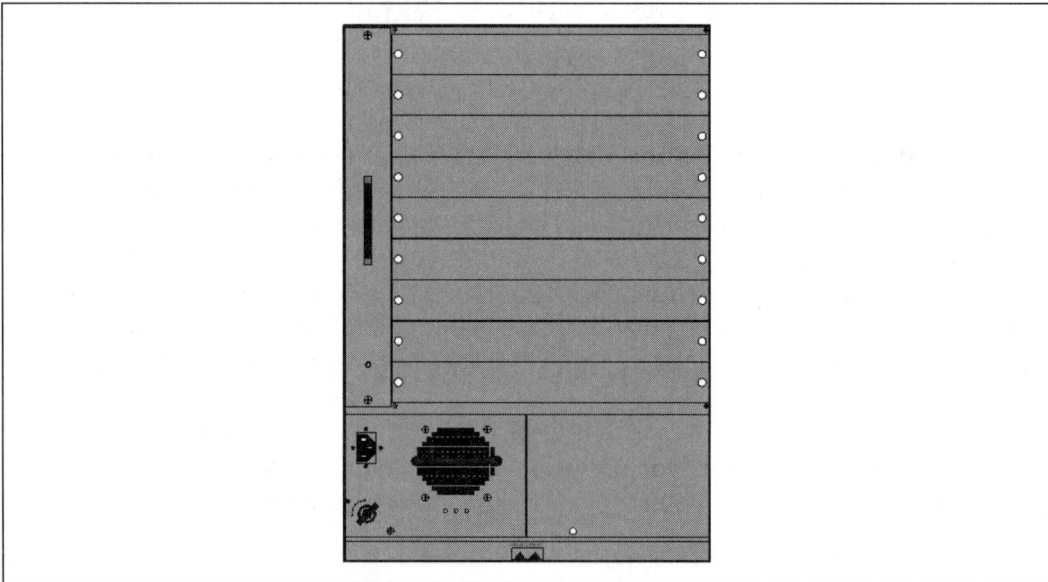

Catalyst 5000 Series

The 5000 family of switches consists of the 5505, which has five slots (shown in Figure 3.3); the 5500, which has 13 slots; and the 5509, which has nine slots. There are also the older 5000 and 5002 models, which are not widely used anymore in lieu of the 4000 series switches. A variety of modules can be used in the 5000 series switch line including the Supervisor Engine, Ethernet, Fast Ethernet, Token Ring, Asynchronous Transfer Mode (ATM), and Fiber Distributed Data Interface (FDDI). The Supervisor Engine is a mandatory device that is used in every chassis switch to control access to the switching backplane.

Figure 3.3 The front and rear view of the Catalyst 5505.

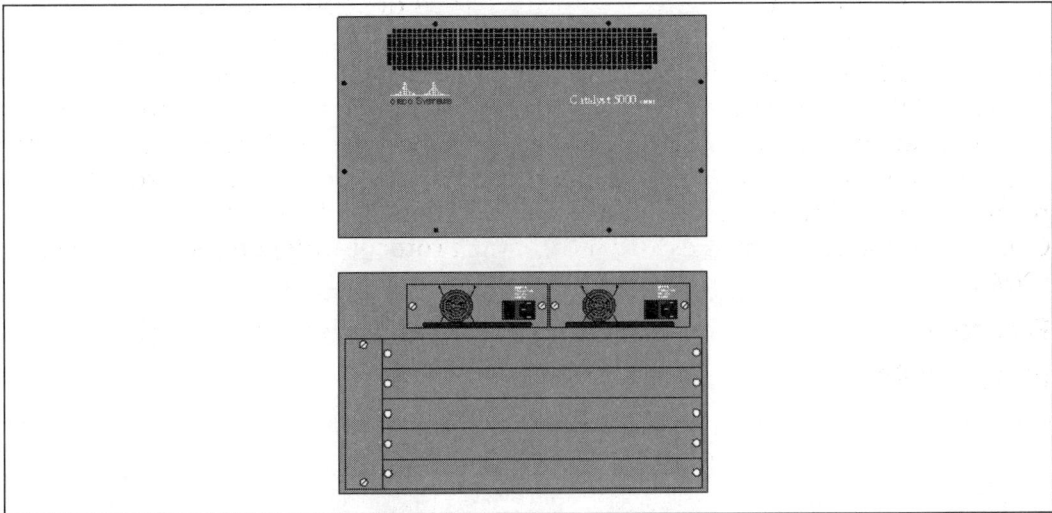

Since it was first introduced, organizations rolled out the 5000 series within their wiring closets as well as for their small to midsize campus backbones. Cisco has introduced new functionality for the 5000 series over the years so the investments that organizations have made in the 5000 series do not have to start over by replacing their 5000 series infrastructures with totally new equipment. For example, in May 1999 Cisco announced new Supervisor Engines that allowed multicast switching, gigabit connectivity, and 24-port 10Base-FL modules.

The 5000 series allows you to replace the hubs in your wiring closets with switch capability so that dedicated bandwidth is provided to each of your end users. The 5000 series is also good to use for segmenting your backbone.

Catalyst 3500 Series XL

The Catalyst 3500 series XL switches were first available in May 1999. The role of this switch is to provide scalable 10/100 Ethernet and Gigabit Ethernet capability to the desktop so it works great within your wiring closets. The models available in the 3500 series XL family include the 3512 XL, 3524 XL, and 3508G XL. The 3524 XL switch is shown in Figure 3.4.

The switching fabric contained within the Catalyst 3500 series XL is capable of supporting 10 Gbps. This switch is available in two editions, Standard and Enterprise. The Enterprise edition adds several features such as 802.1Q and ISL VLAN support (discussed later in the chapter), fault tolerance, and Terminal Access Controller Access Control System Plus (TACACS+) security.

Clustering of Catalyst 3500 series XL switches is accomplished using Cisco Switch Clustering technology. What is neat about the clustering of these switches is that they do not have to be geographically next to each other. Up to 16 switches can be clustered using a single Internet Protocol (IP) address. The cluster is managed using a standard Web browser.

Figure 3.4 The Catalyst 3524 XL switch.

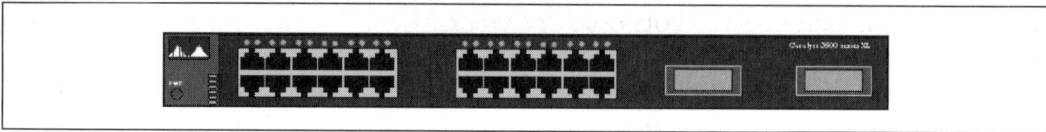

Gigastack Capabilities

The Catalyst 3500 series XL switch allows flexibility for growth within workgroups since it is stackable. Up to nine Catalyst 3500 series XL (or modular Catalyst 2900 series XL) switches can be stacked using the Gigastack Gigabit Interface Converter (GBIC) when you are using a half-duplex configuration. In a half-duplex cascade, configuration performance is 1 Gbps, and in a full-duplex point-to-point configuration, performance is 2 Gbps. Figure 3.4 shows the two GBIC slots located on the right side of the switch.

NOTE

The GBIC slots can also be used for standard GBICs to supply standard uplink connections.

Catalyst 2900 Series XL

The Catalyst 2900 series XL switches were first introduced in January 1998. The Catalyst 2900 series XL features 10/100 autosensing and comes in a variety of models. In January 1999, Cisco enhanced its line of 2900 series switches to include five new models that are available in a variety of configurations including 12- and 24-port densities using different media. For example, you may have 22 RJ45 ports and two fiber optic ports. Recently, Cisco introduced the Catalyst 2948G 48-port Gigabit switch. The Catalyst 2900 series XL is great for providing 10 Mbps or 100 Mbps to your end users. The Catalyst 2900 series XL also includes models that are modular so that a variety of expansion capabilities, such as GBIC, exist to meet your needs. Figure 3.5 shows a nonmodular 24-port Catalyst 2900 series XL switch.

This series of switches is available in both Standard and Enterprise editions. The main difference between the two editions is that the Enterprise edition provides support for VLANs. There used to be a price difference between the Standard and Enterprise editions but recently I have noticed that both editions are available for the same price. If this is the case in your area, you may as well get the enhanced capability of the Enterprise edition, even if you don't plan on using VLANs, since the function of the switch may change later on.

The Catalyst 2900 series XL is equipped with a mode switch that provides different statistics about the switch including bandwidth utilization, redundant power supply, and the system.

Figure 3.5 The Catalyst 2924 switch.

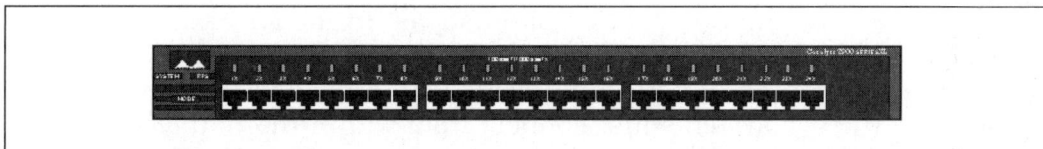

GBIC Technologies

As previously mentioned in the discussion on the 3500 series and 2900 series Catalyst switches, you have the capability of using GBIC technology. However, the use of GBIC technology is not limited to only those two series of switches. There are multiple GBICs available including the aforementioned Gigastack GBIC for use with the 3500 and 2900 series, as well as a model that links the Gigabit Ethernet port of Catalyst 5000 and 6000 series switches to the fiber optic network. The models of GBICs available for the 5000 and 6000 series includes short wavelength (1000BaseSX), long wavelength/long haul (1000BaseLX/LH), and extended distance (1000BaseZX).

The GBIC are hot-swappable, but static- and dust-sensitive. When inserting or removing a GBIC, take the proper anti-static precautions and ensure you do not leave the cable openings exposed to dust when cables are not plugged in.

NOTE

GBICs are keyed so they cannot be inserted incorrectly.

VLANs and How They Function

Throughout our discussion on switches we have identified VLANs. What exactly is a virtual LAN? Simply put, a VLAN can be thought of as being equivalent to a *broadcast domain*. Okay, then what is a broadcast domain? A broadcast domain consist of a group of nodes that receive the Layer 2 broadcasts sent by other members of the same group. Typically, broadcast domains have been separated by creating additional network segments or by adding a router.

Let's look at an example of using VLANs. Consider that you have an Engineering section consisting of 14 nodes and a Research section consisting of eight nodes, all on the same physical subnet. Users typically communicate only with other systems within their respective section. Both sections share an Enterprise edition Catalyst 2924 XL switch. To diminish the size of the necessary broadcast domain for each section, you can create two VLANs, one for the Engineering section and one for the Research section. After creating the two VLANs, all broadcast traffic for each section will be isolated to its respective VLAN. But what happens when a node in the Engineering section needs to communicate with a node in the Research section? Do the two systems just connect from within the Catalyst 2924 XL switch? No, this cannot occur since the two sections have been set up on two different virtual LANs. In order for traffic to be passed between VLANs (even when they are on the same switch) a router must be used.

Trunking Technologies

Cisco switches support a number of trunking technologies for VLANs that you can utilize within your Windows 2000 network infrastructure. A trunk is defined as a point-to-point link from one switch to another switch. The purpose of a trunk is to carry the traffic of multiple VLANs over a single link. The two trunking technologies supported in Cisco switches are Inter-Switch Link (ISL) and IEEE (Institute of Electrical and Electronics Engineers) 802.1Q.

NOTE

Trunking capabilities are IOS dependent so you need to verify the capabilities of your Cisco switches.

ISL

Inter-Switch Link (ISL) is Cisco's proprietary protocol for trunking VLANs over Fast Ethernet and Gigabit Ethernet. When using ISL, an Ethernet frame is encapsulated with a header that maintains VLAN IDs between switches. A 30-byte header is prepended to the Ethernet frame, and it contains a two-byte VLAN ID. This multiplexing protocol allows a single link to carry traffic for multiple VLANs between switches throughout your entire network since each frame carries its VLAN ID.

IEEE 802.1Q

Another trunking technology is the IEEE 802.1Q. This is an industry standard that was finalized in December 1998. 802.1Q differs from ISL because it uses an internal tagging mechanism in place of the encapsulation used by ISL. A tag is actually inserted within the frames of each VLAN in all cases except for one. The only time a VLAN does not have a tag inserted is when it is configured to be the *native VLAN*. A native VLAN is configured the same on both sides of the trunk. That way, it can deduce which VLAN a frame belongs to when it receives a frame with no tag.

The tag consists of four bytes, which include a 12-bit VLAN-ID, and three bits that are reserved for 802.1p priority tagging. After the tag is inserted, the Frame Check Sequence (FCS) is recalculated.

VTP Servers and Clients

The VLAN Trunk Protocol (VTP) allows you to centrally manage the configuration of the switches within your network. This is important because manageability could easily get out of hand when you have dozens of switches and they are running a mixture of ISL and IEEE 802.1Q. For example, imagine you are configuring your switches manually when you decide that you want to assign some ports on a few switches to a VLAN that had not yet been defined. First you have to define the VLAN, and then you would have to define the name. After that you would have to make sure the network type matched and then assign an uplink to carry the VLAN's traffic. After that, if anything ever changed you would manually have to find and update all of the switches that had that VLAN on them. As you can see, this could become quite burdensome.

VTP is a messaging protocol that maintains VLAN configuration consistency by managing the addition, deletion, and renaming of VLANs throughout your network. So how does VTP work? First you must establish one of your switches to be the VTP server. When a switch is configured as the VTP server you can change the VLAN configuration and have it propagate throughout the network to all of the VTP clients. When a switch is configured as a VTP client then you cannot physically change the VLAN configuration on that switch. The only way to change the VLAN configuration in this instance is when the VTP client switch receives VTP updates from its VTP server.

But what happens if you want to have multiple VTP servers managing different VTP clients? When you configure VTP on your switches you must specify a VTP domain. This allows you the flexibility to have several different VTP servers and clients, each distinct group within its own respective domain.

> **NOTE**
>
> There are two versions of VTP, version 1 and version 2. These two versions cannot be mixed. If you have a choice of either version, Cisco suggests you use version 2.

Layer 3 Switching

Our discussion on switches up to this point has concentrated on switches that typically operate at Layer 2, the data-link layer. However, Cisco has made some of their switches capable of operating at Layer 3, the network layer. As you are already aware, this is the layer that routers function at. The key item to look at in regard to Layer 3 switching is the manner in which it differs from a traditional router. After all, this is the reason why Layer 3 switching exists in the first place. Performance is that key item. Today, it is possible for a Layer 3 switch to have a throughput in the millions of packets per second whereas routers typically range to approximately a million packets per second. Why do Layer 3 switches have such a higher throughput? It boils down to the hardware used in each respective item. Routers typically use microprocessor-based engines to conduct their packet switching and switches perform their packet switching using application specific integrated circuits (ASICs).

Layer 3 switching can use *route caching* or *forwarding information base*. Route caching uses a table that is built based on the traffic flow coming into the switch. This type of switching is also known as flow-based or demand-based. Forwarding information base prepopulates the route cache with information from the routing table. This allows lookups to happen quickly since it is not necessary for the traffic to have already flowed into the switch.

Onboard Layer 3 Options

Several Cisco switches do support Layer 3 switching. Two of the switches we have discussed previously support a Layer 3 onboard option for switching, the 6500 series and the 5000 series.

6500 Series and the MSFC

The Catalyst 6500 series of switches provides support for the Multilayer Switch Feature Card (MSFC). The MSFC provides Layer 3 route switching and acts as a router directly tied to the backplane of the switch. The interfaces of the MSFC correspond to the active VLANs defined on the switch and allow for router configurations per VLAN. InterVLAN routing can be provided in a Catalyst 6500 switch by using the virtual interfaces of the MSFC.

NOTE

The newest version of the card is the Multilayer Switch Feature Card 2 (MSFC2). This card is integrated with the Policy Feature Card (PFC) into the Supervisor Engine IA and provides IP, IPX, and IP Multicast switching at 15 Mbps.

5000 Series and the RSM

The Catalyst 5000 series of switches provide support for the Route Switch Module (RSM). The RSM runs Cisco IOS software and connects directly into the Catalyst 5000 switch backplane. The Catalyst 5000 sees the RSM as a module with a single trunk port with a single MAC address. However, this MAC address does not have any attributes (such as media type or speed) that other modules do.

The RSM allows interVLAN routing capability to this series of switches. Each VLAN that is routed by the RSM is seen as a separate virtual interface. The RSM supports two channels, 0 and 1. By default, the RSM uses VLAN 0, on channel 0, to communicate to the Catalyst 5000 switch and is not accessible to the user. The RSM uses VLAN 1, on channel 1, to communicate to the default VLAN on the switch. However, you are not limited to only these two VLANs. As you create new VLANs they are toggled between the two channels. You may also map a VLAN to a specific channel if you want to balance the load on each channel.

NOTE

The RSM can support routing for up to 256 VLANs.

The front panel of the RSM contains more items (see Figure 3.6) than the MSM used by the Catalyst 6000 series switches that we just discussed. The items on the front panel include the following:

- PCMCIA (Personal Computer Memory Card International Association) slots
- Reset button
- Auxiliary port
- Console port
- Status LED
- CPU Halt LED
- Enabled LED
- PCMCIA Slot LEDs
- Transmit and Receive LEDs for each channel

Figure 3.6 Route Switch Module for the Catalyst 5000 switch.

NOTE

The RSM also provides support for the optional Versatile Interface Processor 2 (VIP2) module. This module allows the RSM to emulate a Cisco 7500 series router.

Routing Overview and Application

Let's turn our attention away from switches and turn instead to Cisco routers that you can use in your Windows 2000 network infrastructure. However, before we delve into particular models of Cisco routers, let's begin with an overview of the LAN/WAN technologies that you may encounter when dealing with Cisco routers.

General Overview of LAN/WAN Technologies

Various technologies are used when passing traffic between routers. For example, it is not unusual for a router to be configured with Ethernet, Token Ring, and serial ports. Let's review a few of the existing LAN/WAN technologies that are in use in today's networks.

Ethernet

Ethernet is a network technology that is commonly used today in the majority of LANs. It currently is available in 10MB, 100MB (Fast Ethernet), and 1000MB (Gigabit Ethernet). Ethernet uses a carrier sense multiple access collision detect (CSMA/CD) method.

In the CSMA/CD network, nodes can access the network any time they have data to send. Before a node transmits data, it checks to see if the network is busy. If the network is not busy, it transmits data; then the node waits. Collisions occur if two nodes listen, hear nothing, and then transmit simultaneously. This ruins both transmissions and both nodes have to try a second time. A *backoff algorithm* creates a random wait time for retransmissions so that a second collision will not occur. Ethernet is a broadcast system so that all nodes see all data frames (unless switches are being utilized).

Token Ring

Token Ring networks were originally a proprietary network specification created by IBM in the 1970s. Token Ring networks are available in only 4MB and 16MB and they have faded from popularity over the last several years. The main concept of token ring is described in its name. It is a token-passing network that connects nodes in a logical ring topology. Token passing uses a small, specially formatted frame, called a token, which is passed from node to node on the ring. When a node possesses the token, it is granted transmission rights. If there is nothing to transmit, the node sends the token on to the next node. When a node does have information to transmit, it flips one bit of the token and turns it into a start-of-frame field, appends the data, and forwards it on. Unless *early token release* is used, the node retains the token until the data frame travels around the ring back to the sender. The data follows the ring until it reaches the destination node, which copies the data. The data frame goes back to the sending node, where the originator can check whether the data transmission was successful.

HDLC

High-level Data Link Control (HDLC) was derived from Synchronous Data Link Control (SDLC). Although commonly referred to as a protocol, HDLC isn't a protocol at all. It's actually a data-link layer bit-stuffing algorithm that specifies a data encapsulation method for synchronous serial links.

HDLC is used primarily in a peer-to-peer environment; one node is designated to be the primary and the others become secondary. A session can use one of the following connection modes, which determines how the primary and secondary node interact:

- Normal unbalanced
- Asynchronous
- Asynchronous balanced

Normal unbalanced occurs when the secondary node responds only to the primary node. Asynchronous occurs when the secondary node initiates the message, and asynchronous balanced occurs when both nodes send and/or receive over part of a duplex line.

Frame Relay

Frame Relay is a widely used packet-switched WAN protocol. Frame Relay relies on the physical and data-link layer interface between Data Terminal Equipment (DTE) and Data Communications Equipment (DCE) devices. The key benefit of Frame Relay is the capability to connect with multiple WAN sites through a single link. This makes Frame Relay much cheaper than point-to-point circuits for large WANs.

Frame Relay uses a virtual circuit, either permanent (PVC) or switched (SVC) between the source and destination, and uses statistical multiplexing for managing multiple data streams. SVCs are temporary links best used in networks with sporadic data transmission. PVCs are permanently established links and are the most common implementation.

Frame Relay uses the Data Link Connection Identifier (DLCI). The DLCI is a number used locally by a DTE and assigned by the Frame Relay provider. It refers to the connection between two DTEs in the Frame Relay network. Because it is a local identifier, each DTE may use a different number to identify the link.

PPP

Point-to-Point Protocol (PPP) is the replacement for the Serial Line Internet Protocol (SLIP) physical layer protocol commonly found in the UNIX world. The purpose of both protocols is to provide serial connections between two networks, or between a network and a remote node.

PPP was designed to address the shortcomings of SLIP and the need for a standard Internet encapsulation protocol. PPP works at both the physical and data-link layers. PPP includes enhancements such as encryption, error control, security, dynamic IP addressing, multiple protocol support, and automatic connection negotiation. PPP works over serial lines, Integrated Services Digital Network (ISDN), and high-speed WAN links.

Routing Models

When the name Cisco is mentioned, normally the first thing that comes to people's minds are their routers. Cisco has routers ranging all the way from the high end, which are placed in the core of multinational organizations, to the low end, which provide routing capability between offices. In this section we examine a few of Cisco's routers and their capabilities so you are aware of what is available for use in your Windows 2000 network infrastructure.

7500 Series

The 7500 series consists of the 7505, 7507 (shown in Figure 3.7), 7513, and 7576. This router series provides a high-end platform for not only data, but also voice and video. Each model in the 7500 series utilizes a high-speed Cisco Extended Bus, also called a CyBus. Some models feature multiple CyBuses. This series of routers supports any combination of interfaces including Ethernet, Fast Ethernet, Gigabit Ethernet, Token Ring, ATM, T1, channelized T3, FDDI, synchronous serial, Packet OC-3, and others.

The 7500 series uses the Route Switch Processor (RSP) card as the main system processor, thus each model must contain at least one RSP. The RSP2 is the base module for the Cisco 7505, Cisco 7507, and Cisco 7513. The RSP4 is the base module for the Cisco 7576 and is an option for the Cisco 7507 and Cisco 7513. Table 3.1 illustrates the number of slots available for RSPs and interface cards for the different models in the 7500 series.

As you can see from Table 3.1, the Cisco 7576 router is a bit different than the other models available in the 7500 series. The 7576 actually contains two routers in a single Cisco 7513 chassis footprint. Obviously the backplane between the two models is different even though the chassis and power supplies are the same.

Table 3.1 RSP and Interface Slots Availability for the 7500 Series Routers

Model	RSP Slots	Interface Card Slots
7505	1	4
7507	2	5
7513	2	11
7576	Router "A" 1	6
	Router "B" 1	5

The 7500 series is designed for heavy-duty use, and as such is an outstanding choice for the core layer of your mission-critical Windows 2000 network.

Figure 3.7 The front and rear view of a Cisco 7507 router.

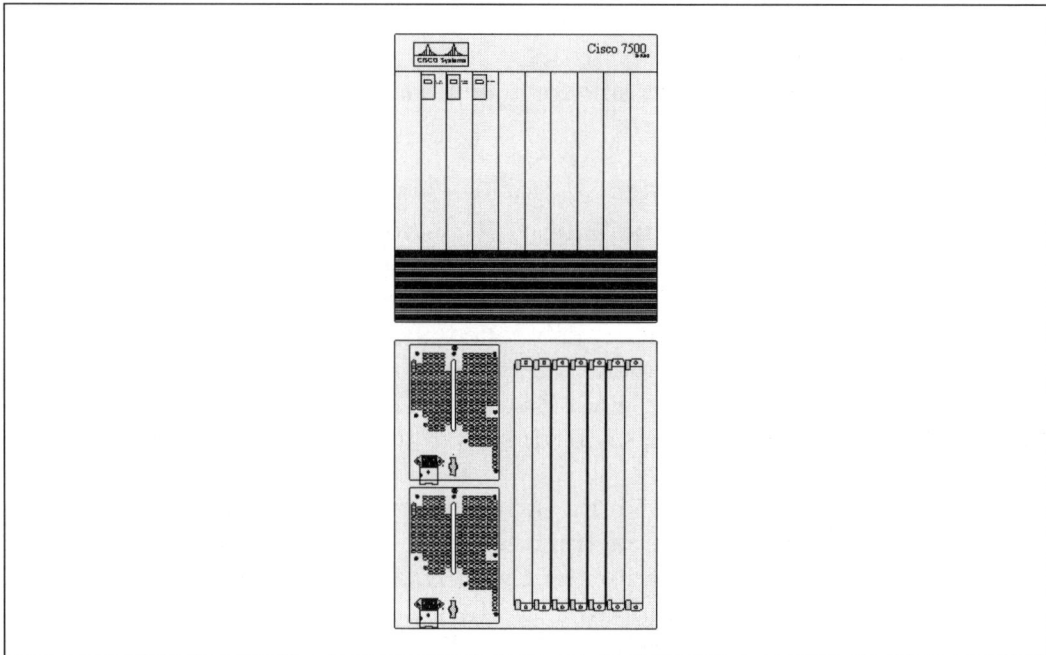

7200 Series

The 7200 series consists of the 7204VXR (shown in Figure 3.8), 7206, and 7206VXR. Don't let its small size (in comparison to the 7500 series) fool you. This router series can support OC-3, DS-3, Fast Ethernet, and

Gigabit Ethernet to name just a few. The 7200 series is a good solution if you need to provide fast WAN connections at remote regional offices. This series of routers provides support for Online Insertion and Removal (OIR), dual hot-swappable load sharing power supplies, and environmental monitoring and reporting functions.

Figure 3.8 The front of a Cisco 7204VXR router.

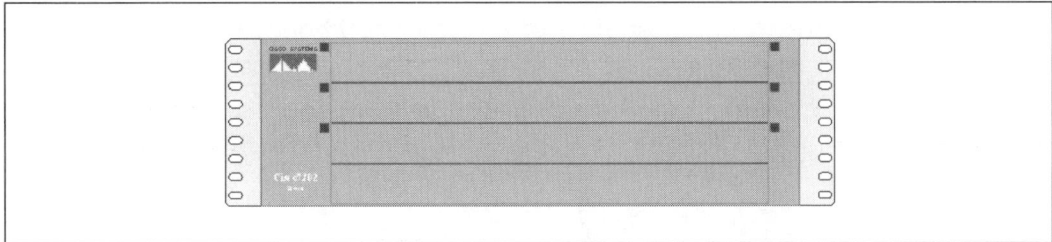

3600 Series

The 3600 series consists of the 3620, 3640 (shown in Figure 3.9), and 3660. This modular series of routers is designed for medium and large-sized offices. It supports the integration of data, voice, and video in the same unit. This series of routers supports a variety of WAN interface cards including ISDN Basic Rate Interface (BRI), serial, T1, and E1, to name only a few.

The modular design of the 3600 series provides great flexibility for configuration options when compared to models such as the 2500 series and other built-in hardware designs. If the nature of your network changes then it may be possible simply to change the network module, WAN interface card, or Voice interface card instead of replacing the whole router.

Figure 3.9 The front and rear view of a Cisco 3640 router.

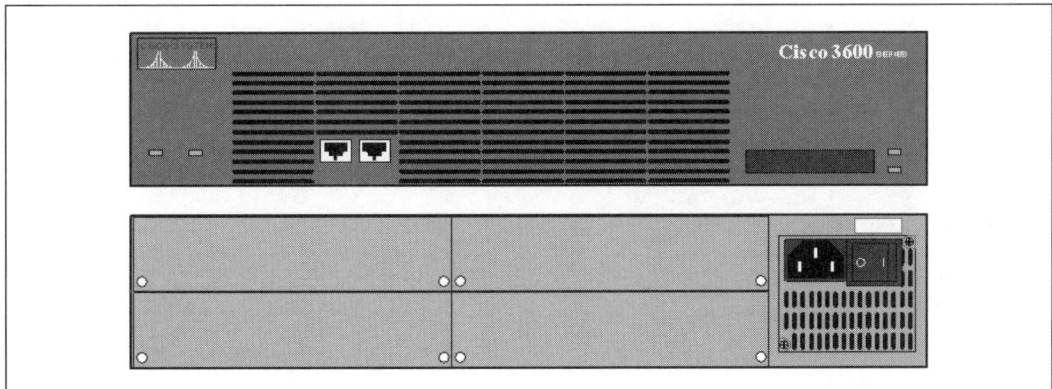

1700 Series

The 1700 series (shown in Figure 3.10) consists of two routers, the 1720 and the 1750. The 1750 is available in three models: the 1750, 1750-2V, and 1750-4V. The difference in the three 1750 models is that the 2V and 4V models contain all the features, memory, and Digital Signal Processing (DSP) necessary to support voice and fax. The 2V provides support for two analog voice ports and the 4V provides support for four analog voice ports.

Figure 3.10 The front and rear view of a Cisco 1700 Series router.

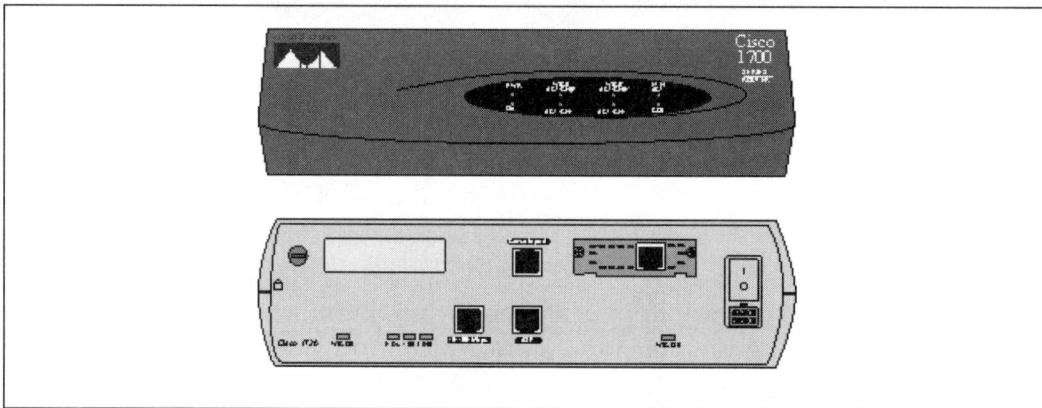

This series of routers is modular and is designed for small branch offices as well as small- and medium-sized businesses. The 1720 is equipped with a single 10/100 Fast Ethernet port, two modular WAN interface card slots (which can utilize the same WAN cards that are available for the 3600 series), an auxiliary port, a console port, and an internal expansion slot for the virtual private network (VPN) hardware encryption module. The 1750 is equipped with the same items but adds a Voice interface card slot.

The VPN module, which fits inside the 1700 series, encrypts data using the Data Encryption Standard (DES) and triple DES (3DES). This allows the possibility of having up to 100 encrypted tunnels for concurrent sessions with other sites or even mobile users. This allows you to provide office-to-office encryption for traffic going between two 1700 series routers.

1600 Series

The 1600 series (shown in Figure 3.11) consists of the 1601 R, 1602 R, 1603 R, 1604 R, and 1605 R (the R stands for "Run from RAM"). This series of routers is a good choice to provide data access for small branch offices as well as small businesses. Table 3.2 illustrates the differences in the five basic models in the 1600 series.

The 1600 series provides support for a variety of security measures including standard and extended Access Control Lists (ACLs), and various authentication, authorization, and accounting (AAA) methods such as Password Authentication Protocol (PAP), Challenge Handshake Authentication Protocol (CHAP), Terminal Access Controller Access Control System Plus (TACACS+), and Remote Authentication Dial-In User Service (RADIUS).

Figure 3.11 The front of a Cisco 1600 Series router.

Table 3.2 Port Configurations of the Cisco 1600 Series Routers

Model	Ports	Comments
1601 R	1 Ethernet 1 Serial 1 WAN interface card slot	The serial port can be used to support asynchronous serial connections of up to 115.2 Kbps. It also provides support for synchronous serial connections (Frame Relay, Switched 56, Switched Multimegabit Data Service (SMDS), and X.25) of up to 2.048 Mbps. The WAN interface cards available for the WAN interface slot include Serial (asynchronous and synchronous), T1/Fractional T1 CSU/DSU, 56/64 Kbps four-wire CSU/DSU, ISDN BRI with S/T interface, and ISDN BRI with integrated NT1, U interface.

Continued

Table 3.2 Continued

Model	Ports	Comments
1602 R	1 Ethernet 1 Serial w/integrated 56 Kbps CSU/DSU (Channel Service Unit/Data Service Unit) 1 WAN interface card slot	The serial port can be used to support asynchronous serial connections of up to 115.2 Kbps. It also provides support for synchronous serial connections (Frame Relay, Switched 56, and X.25) of up to 2.048 Mbps. The WAN interface cards available for the WAN interface slot include Serial (asynchronous and synchronous), T1/Fractional T1 CSU/DSU, 56/64 Kbps four-wire CSU/DSU, ISDN BRI with S/T interface, and ISDN BRI with integrated NT1, U interface.
1603 R	1 Ethernet 1 ISDN BRI (S/T interface) 1 WAN interface card slot	The WAN interface cards available for the WAN interface slot include Serial (asynchronous and synchronous), T1/Fractional T1 CSU/DSU, 56/64 Kbps four-wire CSU/DSU, ISDN BRI leased line.
1604 R	1 Ethernet 1 ISDN BRI with integrated NT1 (U interface) 1 S-bus port for ISDN phones 1 WAN interface card slot	The WAN interface cards available for the WAN interface slot include Serial (asynchronous and synchronous), T1/Fractional T1 CSU/DSU, 56/64 Kbps four-wire CSU/DSU, ISDN BRI leased line.
1605 R	2 Ethernet 1 WAN interface card slot	The WAN interface cards available for the WAN interface slot include: Serial (asynchronous and synchronous), T1/Fractional T1 CSU/DSU, 56/64 Kbps four-wire CSU/DSU, ISDN BRI with S/T interface, and ISDN BRI with integrated NT1, U interface.

800 Series

The 800 series (shown in Figure 3.12) consists of 11 different models including the 801, 801 CAPI, 802, 802 IDSL, 803, 803 CAPI, 804, 804 IDSL, 805, 827, and 827-4V. This series of routers is designed for small offices as well as telecommuters. The 800 series provides integrated voice and data support as well as security with VPNs. It can be confusing trying to compare the differences in the different models within the 800 series so Table 3.3 logically illustrates the differences.

Figure 3.12 The front of a Cisco 800 Series router

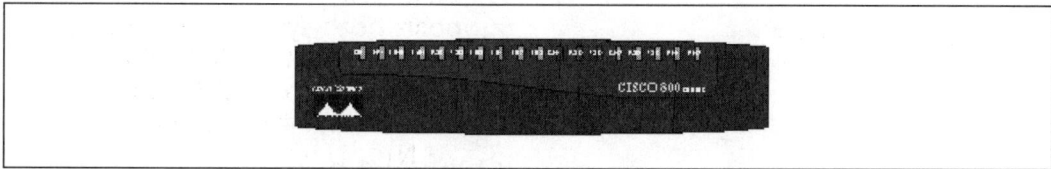

Table 3.3 Port Configurations of the Cisco 800 Series Routers

Model	Ports	Comments
801	1 Ethernet 1 IDSN BRI (S/T interface)	
801 CAPI	1 Ethernet 1 IDSN BRI (S/T interface)	Provides support for European ISDN and the Common Application Programming Interface (CAPI).
802	1 Ethernet 1 IDSN BRI with integrated NT1 (U interface)	
802 IDSL	1 Ethernet 1 IDSL (ISDN Digital Subscriber Line) with integrated NT1 (U interface)	Supports line rates up to 144 Kbps.
803	4-port Ethernet hub 1 IDSN BRI (S/T interface) 2 Analog RJ-11	Supports call waiting, call-waiting cancel, call hold, call retrieve, three-way conferencing, and call transfer.
803 CAPI	4-port Ethernet hub 1 IDSN BRI (S/T interface) 2 Analog RJ-11	Provides support for European ISDN and the Common Application Programming Interface (CAPI).

Continued

Table 3.3 Continued

Model	Ports	Comments
804	4-port Ethernet hub 1 IDSN BRI with integrated NT1 (U interface) 2 Analog RJ-11	Supports call waiting, call-waiting cancel, call hold, call retrieve, three-way conferencing, and call transfer.
804 IDSL	4-port Ethernet hub 1 IDSL with integrated NT1 (U interface)	Supports line rates up to 144 Kbps.
805	1 Ethernet 1 Serial	Supports both synchronous serial (Frame Relay, leased line, and X.25) connections up to 512 Kbps and asynchronous dial-up connections.
827	1 Ethernet 1 ADSL (Asymmetric Digital Subscriber Line)	Ideal for up to 20 users in a small office.
827-4V	1 Ethernet 1 ADSL 4 Analog RJ-11	Ideal for up to 20 users in a small office.

Cisco IOS

The "brains" of both Cisco switches and Cisco routers is the Internetwork Operating System (IOS). Without the IOS the hardware might as well be used as boat anchors. The IOS is responsible for everything from allowing the configuration of interfaces, to security using ACLs, and everything in between.

Differences in Switch and Router IOSs

The term *Internetwork Operating System* can be misleading—you may think that all IOSs are created equally. In reality, there is a difference in the IOSs used by switches and routers. Switch IOSs can support the configuration of VLANs, VTP, and items unique to switches, whereas router IOSs provide configuration support for various WAN configurations. The IOSs do have some commonality as they are used to configure Ethernet (and other) interfaces that can be present on both types of equipment.

Router Feature Sets

Not only are there differences in switch and router IOSs, but there are even different feature sets among the router IOSs geared toward different functions. The decisions don't stop after you decide on the routers for your Windows 2000 network infrastructure. You need to determine which IOS feature set meets the needs for the routers in question since each feature set contains a specific set of Cisco IOS features. Let's examine some of the different feature sets that you need to be aware of.

Enterprise

The Enterprise feature set provides the widest range of features available in the IOS. Some of the features normally found within the Enterprise feature set, which can vary depending on the hardware platform, are support for Apollo Domain, Banyan VINES, Frame Relay SVC support, Intermediate System-to-Intermediate System (IS-IS), Kerberos V client support, and other items normally seen in the enterprise environment.

IP/IPX/IBM

The IP/IPX/IBM feature set provides support for adding IP, IPX, and IBM routing support to the router. The IBM features include support for Systems Network Architecture (SNA) bisync, caching and filtering, NetView Native Service Point, as well as numerous other items.

IP Plus

The IP Plus feature set adds items related to the Internet Protocol. Some of the items present in the IP Plus feature set include Network Address Translation (NAT), Hot Standby Router Protocol (HSRP), Voice-over IP (VoIP), and ATM LAN Emulation (LANE). Of course these features can vary and are dependent on the hardware on which the IOS is running.

Firewall Feature Set

The Firewall feature set provides additional security functionality to the routers on which it is running. It provides not only firewall features such as stateful, application-based filtering, but also intrusion detection. Alerts can be configured to provide reporting in real-time. The Firewall feature set can be combined with IP Security (IPSec) and Layer 2 Tunneling Protocol to provide a complete virtual private network environment.

Memory Requirements

The amount of memory required for your router depends in part on the feature set you plan to use. For example, on a 3620 router with the

Enterprise feature set you need a minimum of 16MB of flash memory and 64MB of dynamic random access memory (DRAM). If you decide instead to use the IP/H323 feature set, the router requires a minimum of 8MB of flash memory and 48MB of DRAM. Of course these are just the minimum requirements for the feature set and you may require more memory depending on the use of the router within your Windows 2000 network infrastructure.

Command Line Interface (CLI)

The most common method of interacting with the router is through the command line interface provided by the Cisco IOS software. Every Cisco router has a console port that can be directly connected to a PC or terminal so that you can type commands at the keyboard and receive output on a terminal screen. The part of the Cisco IOS software that provides the user interface and interprets the commands you type is called the command executive, or EXEC.

For IT Professionals

Enhanced Editing Keys

Some of the commands you will type in the CLI can be very long. Cisco has been thoughtful enough to include a series of keystrokes that you can use to navigate around on the command line. This feature is known as *enhanced editing*, and for those of you familiar with UNIX, you will recognize the following keystrokes as the EMACS editing keystrokes.

CTRL-A   Go to the beginning of the line
CTRL-E   Go to the end of the line
ESC-B   Go back to the beginning of the previous word
ESC-F   Go forward to the beginning of the next word
CTRL-B   Go back one character
CTRL-F   Go forward one character

These are not the only keys available to you in the IOS; I encourage you to research the documentation that came with your router for other time-saving keystrokes.

How to Get Around in the IOS

Moving around the IOS is similar to typing at an MS-DOS prompt on a PC. You don't change directories as you do on a PC, but you can change the mode you are operating in as well as various configuration settings.

The IOS has a context-sensitive Help feature built in. This is a feature you will learn to depend on as you work with the command line interface. To enter the Help system all you need to do is type a **?**. The screen will show the commands that are available to you. This list changes depending on the mode you are in within the IOS as well as on where you are in the IOS when you enter the help system. You can also enter the help system if you forget the syntax for a command. All you have to do is type the part of the command you remember and then a **?**. The help system will display the options available to you at that point.

While in the IOS you do not have to type the full command name. You can abbreviate commands to the point that it is unique so that the IOS knows what you want to do. Look at the following example from a Catalyst 2924 switch in which the command **show running-config** has been abbreviated to **sh ru**. The IOS understands what you want to accomplish but you have saved yourself a lot of typing!

```
2924Outside#sh ru

Building configuration...


Current configuration:

!

version 11.2

no service pad

no service udp-small-servers

no service tcp-small-servers

!

hostname 2924Outside

!

enable secret 5 $1$.LeN$Cjuf.cxxxxxxxxxxyu9YTKgU/

!

username kesnet privilege 15 password 7 xxxxxxxxx 0 9

!

!

clock timezone Central 0
```

```
!
interface VLAN1
 ip address 10.10.14.150 255.255.255.0
 no ip route-cache
!
interface FastEthernet0/1
 switchport access vlan 2
interface FastEthernet0/2
 switchport access vlan 2
!
interface FastEthernet0/3
 switchport access vlan 2
!
interface FastEthernet0/4
 switchport access vlan 2
!
interface FastEthernet0/5
 switchport access vlan 2
!
interface FastEthernet0/6
 switchport access vlan 2
!
interface FastEthernet0/7
 switchport access vlan 2
!
interface FastEthernet0/8
 switchport access vlan 2
!
interface FastEthernet0/9
 switchport access vlan 3
!
interface FastEthernet0/10
 switchport access vlan 3
!
```

```
interface FastEthernet0/11
 switchport access vlan 3
!
interface FastEthernet0/12
 switchport access vlan 3
!
interface FastEthernet0/13
 switchport access vlan 3
!
interface FastEthernet0/14
 switchport access vlan 3
!
interface FastEthernet0/15
 switchport access vlan 3
!
interface FastEthernet0/16
 switchport access vlan 3
!
interface FastEthernet0/17
 switchport access vlan 3
!
interface FastEthernet0/18
 switchport access vlan 3
!
interface FastEthernet0/19
 switchport access vlan 3
!
interface FastEthernet0/20
 switchport access vlan 3
!
interface FastEthernet0/21
 switchport access vlan 3
!
interface FastEthernet0/22
```

```
  switchport access vlan 3
 !
interface FastEthernet0/23
  switchport access vlan 2
 !
interface FastEthernet0/24
  switchport access vlan 3
  ip default-gateway 10.10.14.1
snmp-server community XXXX RW
snmp-server chassis-id 0x0F
banner motd ^C
Access permitted to XXXXXXX personnel only...all others must disconnect
immediately!!!
^C
 !
line con 0
  stopbits 1
line vty 0 4
  access-class 100 in
  password XXXXXXXX
  login local
line vty 5 15
  access-class 100 in
  password XXXXXXXX
  login local
 !
end
```

Enable Mode

The IOS supports multiple modes. When you first log into a router you are in *user EXEC mode*. This mode is the lowest level of access to the router, and allows you to examine the status of most of the router's configurable components, see the contents of routing tables, and do basic nondisruptive network troubleshooting. You cannot change the router's configuration while in user EXEC mode, nor can you view the contents of the router's configuration files. To do these things you must be in *privileged EXEC mode*. This mode is sometimes called the *enable mode*, since that is the command you use to get this level of access. You can verify that you are in enable mode by the # sign shown after the router name. At this level you have full access to the router so you can do anything from viewing configuration files to disrupting network traffic by rebooting the router.

ROMMON Mode

The ROM monitor (ROMMON) mode is used to boot the router or perform diagnostic tests. There are two instances in which you enter ROMMON mode: if the router does not find a valid system image, and if you purposely interrupt the boot sequence by first using the *reload* command and then pressing the Break key within 60 seconds of booting. Once in ROMMON mode you can load an image from a Trivial File Transfer Protocol (TFTP) server, perform a stack trace, as well as other actions. When you want to exit ROMMON mode, simply type **continue**. This places you in user EXEC mode. If you want to initialize the router, enter the command **i**. This command causes the bootstrap program to reinitialize the router, clear the memory, and boot the system.

Normally the item everyone deals with when in ROMMON mode is the configuration register. The configuration register is 16-bit and is modified using the **confreg** command while in ROMMON mode. You may specify the hexadecimal address of the item you want to change as a value of the confreg command or type **confreg** by itself to be prompted for each bit. For example, the lowest four bits of the configuration register are used for the boot field. This field determines whether the router boots from the network, from Flash memory, manually, or from ROM.

Global vs Interface Mode on the CLI

To configure the router you must be in the correct mode. First you must enter enable mode as all configurations are done from the privileged EXEC mode. Once you are in privileged EXEC mode you may enter *global configuration mode*. Use this mode to accomplish tasks such as naming your router and configuring a banner message for users logging into the router. Any configuration command that affects the operation of the entire router would be entered in global configuration mode. To enter global configuration mode, use the command **configure terminal**.

Of course not all of the router configuration can be done in global configuration mode. To configure an interface you must go into the interface configuration mode for the correct interface you want to configure. It is easy to tell what configuration mode you are in as the router displays special prompts. When you are in global configuration mode you will see the following prompt:

```
RouterName (config)#
```

To move to the interface configuration mode you type *interface <interface id>* at the config prompt as shown in the following example:

```
RouterName (config)# interface eth0
```

When you are in interface configuration mode you will see the following prompt:

```
RouterName (config-if)#
```

QoS Functionality and How it Works on Switches and Routers

Windows 2000 provides support for Quality of Service (QoS). But what exactly is Quality of Service? QoS is a combination of mechanisms that provide a specific level of traffic across disparate networks. This type of service provides organizations with the following three benefits:

- Lower network delays

- Delays the need for additional bandwidth

- Greater level of control over the network for the network administrator

Some of the components involved with QoS relate to the network infrastructure, such as switches and routers, as well as a method for classifying network traffic and determining priority based upon predefined policies. QoS as it relates to Windows 2000 focuses on the Resource Reservation Protocol (RSVP).

RSVP

Resource Reservation Protocol is the host-to-host communication/negotiation of the QoS requirements. Network devices, such as Cisco switches and routers, will listen to the RSVP signaling between two hosts and determine whether the user requesting service, quantity of resources, or type of service being requested falls within the pre-established policies of the network. Other networking devices do not listen to the RSVP signaling and just let the traffic pass. Because RSVP is based upon host-to-host communication, there is some concern about its ability to scale sufficiently. RSVP is covered in greater detail in Chapter 9.

Queuing Techniques

RSVP is not the only way that Quality of Service is implemented within Cisco routers. Various queuing techniques can be used so that when the amount of traffic going through a particular interface is greater than the interface's bandwidth, the packets are queued. The priority of traffic depends on the policy in place. Let's examine the different queuing techniques implemented in Cisco routers.

Weighted Fair Queuing

Weighted Fair Queuing is used primarily to manage low-bandwidth and high-bandwidth traffic streams. Its queuing algorithm simultaneously schedules low-bandwidth traffic to the front of the queue, and shares the remaining bandwidth between high-bandwidth traffic streams. This is necessary because some high-bandwidth traffic streams have a tendency to act as a shuttle train by disallowing low-bandwidth data traffic its due bandwidth. This scenario can often facilitate increased response time on low-bandwidth networks, causing noticeable latency.

Priority Queuing

Priority Queuing was designed to support a very specific need. For some applications, it is imperative that data is delivered on time and that bandwidth is available, requiring a traffic prioritization scheme. Priority Queuing is by far the most discriminating of the queuing services. Priority Queuing can ensure correct delivery using a structure of four queues designated as *high*, *medium*, *normal*, and *low*. The queues apply the specified traffic hierarchy and route packets toward designated queues. Of the four queues available in Priority Queuing, the high queue has priority and is always emptied first. If there is a packet in the high queue, it is sent immediately. If there are no more packets in the high queue, then a packet is sent from the medium queue. Before a second packet is sent from the medium queue, the high queue is checked again. If there is data to be sent in the high queue, the entire queue is emptied before the medium queue is revisited. As you can see, lower-priority traffic may have problems getting any transmit time, especially if higher priority queues are always full. The main concept to remember here is queue priority. Higher priority queues have precedence over all lower queues. This is the most important concept to understand when deciding to use Priority Queuing. Priority Queuing should be used only when certain types of traffic must have guaranteed bandwidth over other types of traffic.

Custom Queuing

With Custom Queuing, by controlling the bandwidth that each of 16 custom queues use, you remove the potential for dropping low-priority traffic with priority queuing. In Custom Queuing, a round-robin dispatching scheme sequentially services each of 16 queues. Each queue is serviced until either the queue is emptied, or a queue threshold is reached. Each queue can be sized differently to fine-tune additional control on traffic flow. More specifically, the sizing of the queue is used to define the byte-count allowed for transmission before the next queue gets a chance to send its packets. The larger the queue, the more packets transmitted during a cycle. A system queue is predefined by the Cisco IOS; it uses queue 0. High-priority packets, such as keep-alives, use the system queue.

Class-based Weighted Fair Queuing

You can think of Class-based Weighted Fair Queuing as using the strongest characteristics of two queuing techniques we have already discussed, Weighted Fair Queuing and Custom Queuing. Class-based Weighted Fair Queuing gives higher weight to high-priority traffic just as Weighted Fair Queuing does, but it determines the weight based upon the classes that have been created on the interface. In this regard, the classes are comparable to Custom Queues. Each interface can have up to 64 classes and each class is policy-based, in which you identify certain characteristics of the traffic, such as the protocol, and allocate a portion of the interface's bandwidth for the traffic flow.

Traffic Shaping Techniques

Traffic shaping differs from the queuing methods we just discussed since it is accomplished through policies defined within ACLs. Policies can be based on a variety of characteristics such as the type of traffic, its source address, its destination address, and other items. Another difference between traffic shaping and queuing is that traffic flow is always affected when traffic-shaping policies are used, even when the flow of traffic is not packed. This is unlike queuing that is used when traffic is packed on an interface.

Summary

In this chapter we examined network basics with regard to the differences between switches and routers. We learned that switches typically operate at the data-link layer (Layer 2) and routers operate at the network layer (Layer 3). We also examined the Hierarchical Design Model that consists of the core, distribution, and access layers. We determined when it is appropriate to use switches and routers within your Windows 2000 network infrastructure.

Next we examined a variety of switches available from Cisco including the Catalyst 6500 series, Catalyst 5000 series, Catalyst 3500 series, and Catalyst 2900 series. We saw that VLANs can break down the size of broadcast domains. VLANs can utilize different trunking technologies, including ISL and IEEE 802.1Q. The VLAN Trunk Protocol (VTP) allows you to manage the configuration of the switches centrally within your network by setting up a VTP server and VTP clients. We also identified that some switches can operate at Layer 3 including the Catalyst 6000 series, which uses the MSFC, and the Catalyst 5000 series, which uses the RSM.

Next we turned our attention to the routers that are available from Cisco including the 7500 series, 7200 series, 3600 series, 1700 series, 1600 series, and 800 series. In this section we also reviewed different LAN/WAN technologies.

The Cisco IOS, which is used by both switches and routers, was discussed next. We looked at some of the differences between switch and router IOSs as well as different feature sets available within the IOS. We learned how to navigate within the CLI and the purpose of the enable, ROMMON, global, and interface modes.

We finished out the chapter with an examination of Quality of Service where we determined that Windows 2000 and Cisco routers provide support for RSVP. Other methods of providing Quality of Service include various methods of queuing as well as traffic shaping techniques. Traffic shaping differs from queuing because it is always applied, even if traffic flow is not packed.

FAQs

Q: My organization has several small branch offices consisting of between 10 and 15 people in each office. What router should I use to provide network connectivity to the organizations network?

A: In this instance I suggest using either the 1600 or 1700 series (if VPN is desired) routers using a serial WIC (WAN interface card). The 1x00 series that you use should be connected on the organization's side into a 3600 series to handle the capacity load.

Q: What router do we need if we want to have OC-3 connectivity?

A: The 7200 series is the minimum that you could use for OC-3 connectivity. You could also use the 7500 series if you want.

Q: We want to use multiplayer switches within our environment so that we can route the VLANs without having to use an external router. What switch models can we use for this purpose?

A: We discussed two switch series that can support Layer 3, the 6500 series and the 5000 series. The 6500 series uses the Multilayer Switch Feature Card and the 5000 series uses the Route Switch Module. If you use one of these series with the appropriate module then you will not need an external router in order to route between your VLANs.

Chapter 4

Protocols and Networking Concepts

Solutions in this chapter:

- Understand the TCP/IP protocol stack

- Set TCP/IP parameters on Windows 2000 and Cisco routers

- Use the Domain Name System

- Review other protocols and stacks

- Look at multiservices over IP

Introduction

Networking is dependent solely on how a protocol is configured. An administrator can control how a computer interacts with the network by the way a protocol is selected, set up, and monitored on that computer.

Since the Internet has pervaded networks globally, the Transmission Control Protocol/Internet Protocol (TCP/IP) stack is one of the main protocol stacks installed on internetworks. However, since the Windows 2000 Active Directory requires TCP/IP, administrators will be installing it on all Windows 2000 Active Directory networks.

The TCP/IP Protocol Stack

TCP/IP has four functional layers according to the common Department of Defense (DoD) model. When compared to the Open System Interconnection (OSI) Protocol reference model, the functions translate according to Figure 4.1.

Figure 4.1 OSI reference model mapped to the TCP/IP model.

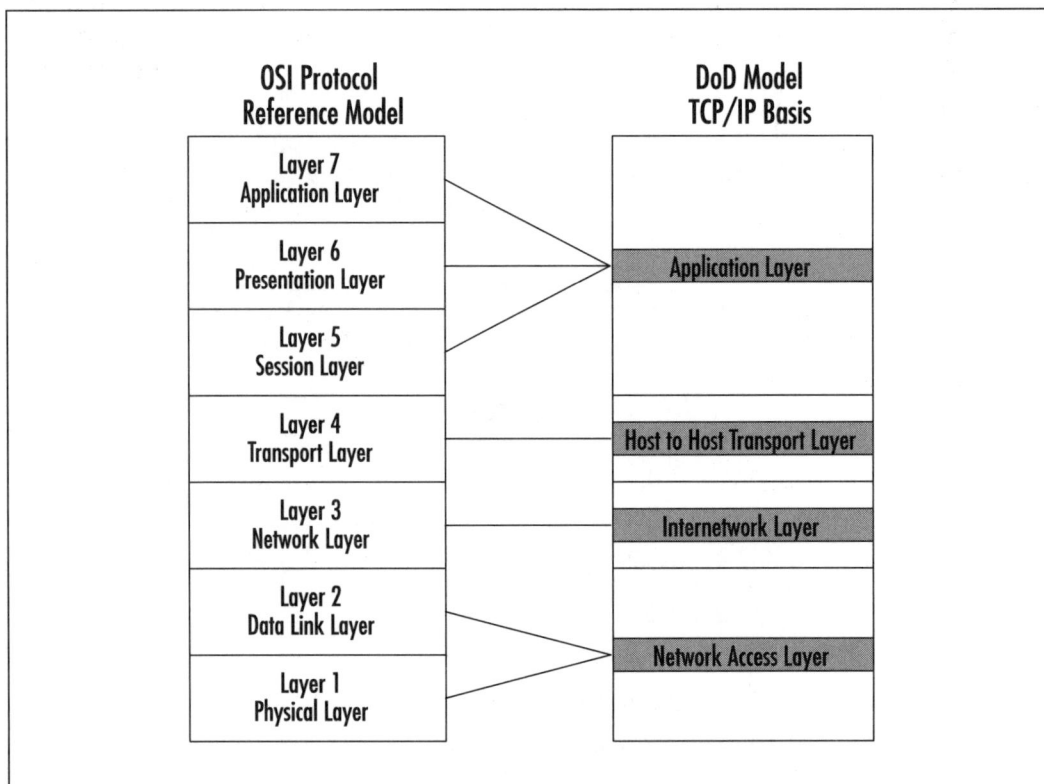

In these models, each layer defines a data communication function that can be performed by one or more protocols. For example, TCP or User Datagram Protocol (UDP) can act as the host-to-host transport layer protocol depending on the network application used. Each layer on the sending host communicates with the same layer on the receiving host. This peer-level communication still depends on the intermediary layers to pass the data through the internetwork. At each layer, there is a header, and sometimes a trailer, of control information including addressing, routing controls, and error checking. As the data travels through the protocol stack at the sending host, each layer's header wraps it. This is called encapsulation. When the data is received, each layer is processed and the header/trailer is dropped off, somewhat like the pieces of a rocket after it has blasted into space.

The way that this encapsulated data interacts with a router is somewhat different than how it interacts with a server. A router does not need to know much more than how to get data to its destination, and to do so with the most efficiency; it does not need to process layers above the network layer, which includes the network address, since that is the minimum amount of information needed to move the data.

A server needs to use an application to manage the data it received. For this reason, the client and the server typically communicate through each layer of the protocol stack. Broken down into protocol layers, the difference is illustrated in Figure 4.2.

Figure 4.2 Routers process packets only up to the layer with network address information, illustrated here with OSI reference model layers.

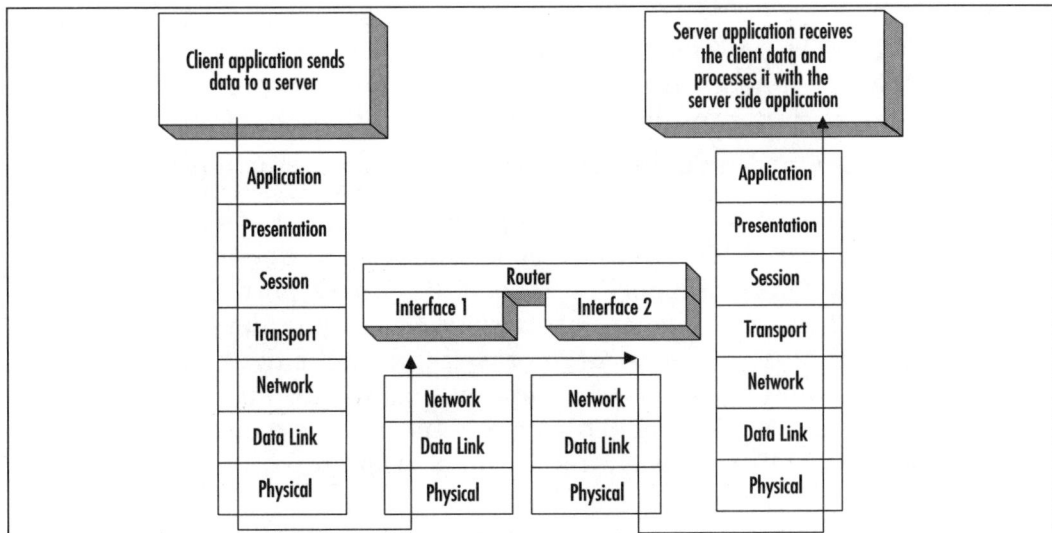

In the TCP/IP protocol stack, the Internet Protocol (IP) is responsible for network layer addressing. IP provides a logical host address and a logical network segment address. The IP address is used to identify each device within the internetwork. Address Resolution Protocol (ARP) maps each IP address to its host's physical address so that the data can be delivered to the host. Each IP address must be unique on the entire internetwork to prevent data from being delivered to the wrong host. The physical address is also known as the MAC address; MAC refers to the Media Access Control portion of the data-link layer, which is the protocol that carries the address.

Furthermore, IP is used in every data transmission using the TCP/IP protocol stack. There is no other network layer protocol that assigns a logical address for routing. It is absolutely critical for IP addressing to work correctly.

The way that IP works on a router is this:

1. IP checks the destination IP address in the network layer header.

2. If the destination IP address exists on that segment, the packet is sent directly to it.

3. If the destination IP address does not exist on the local segment, a routing decision is made that determines to which router the packet is sent. If there is a default gateway set with no other routers attached to that segment, then there is only one place to forward the packet.

4. The router reassembles the data into an IP packet. The IP packet includes the destination physical address of the next router in the path and is forwarded to it.

5. At the next router, another decision is made either to send the packet to a node on a directly attached segment, or to send it to the next router in the path to the destination host.

6. At each stop, the data is repackaged to represent that next hop.

When IP sends data to the transport layer—either to TCP or UDP—it uses a port number to identify the application that has sent the data. For example, Simple Mail Transport Protocol (SMTP) uses port 25, and Telnet uses port 23. These well-known ports are universally understood. Applications can use ports that are not well known for their own purposes. When an application should not be allowed through a router, it can be blocked using its port number. This type of blocking is called a packet-level filter. Packet-level filters must translate data through the transport layer.

The Internet Control Message Protocol (ICMP) is a protocol that exists at the network layer. ICMP uses an echo response to determine whether a route to the destination host exists. It also assists with flow control by being able to send source quench messages to hosts that are transmitting data too quickly. It can redirect traffic by sending a message to use a different router. ICMP functions as an informational management system for IP addressing.

More about IP addressing is discussed in Chapter 1.

Setting an IP Address on Windows 2000

Configuring the IP address for Windows 2000 is executed in the Network and Dial-Up Connections applet found in Control Panel. You can also access this by right-clicking on the My Network Places icon on the desktop and selecting Properties from the pop-up menu.

1. Double-click the connection for which you are configuring an IP address. You will see the dialog shown in Figure 4.3.

Figure 4.3 Connection properties dialog.

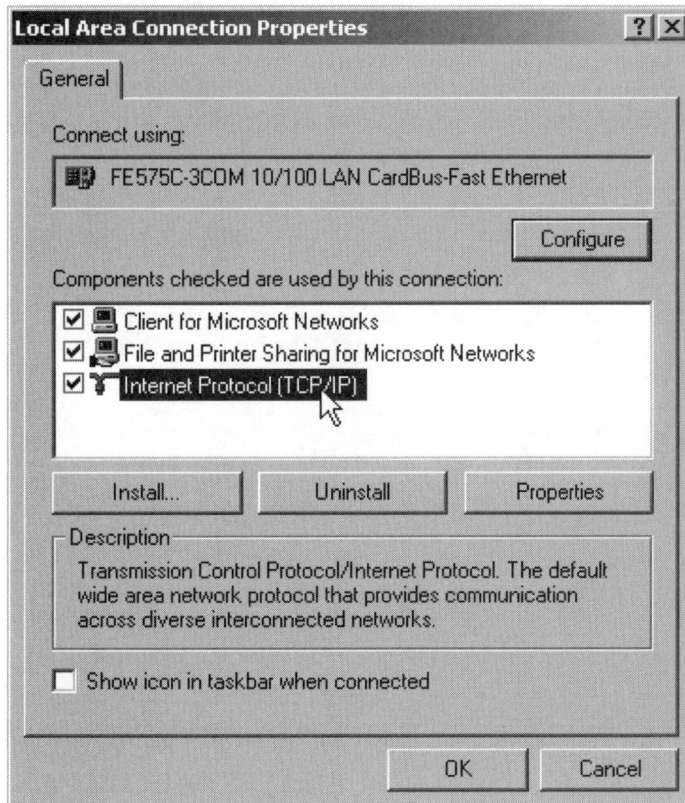

2. Click on the Internet Protocol (TCP/IP) item. (If it does not exist, then click the Install button, select Protocol, click the Add button, and select Internet Protocol (TCP/IP).)

3. Click the Properties button.

4. Select Use the following IP address.

5. Type the IP address and subnet mask in the appropriate spaces.

6. Click OK.

7. Click OK once more to close the Network and Dial-up Connections properties.

Establishing the Default Router

In the Internet Protocol (TCP/IP) Properties dialog, the space below the subnet mask is specified for the default gateway, also known as the default router. Simply type the correct address of the router connected to the segment that leads outside to the main internetwork. This is shown in Figure 4.4.

Figure 4.4 Configuring the Default gateway for Windows 2000.

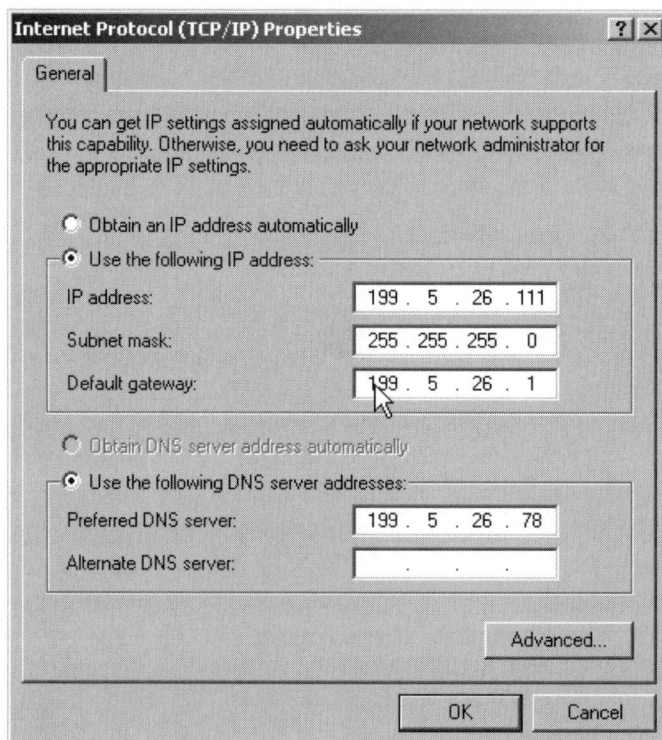

Testing IP with ICMP on Windows 2000

Packet Internet Groper (PING) is an application that uses the ICMP protocol to determine whether a host exists on the internetwork based on its IP address. PING is a command-line application. To use it, start a command prompt and type PING *ip_address* to determine that address's existence. There are additional command parameters that can be used on Windows 2000, as depicted in Figure 4.5.

Figure 4.5 PING on Windows 2000.

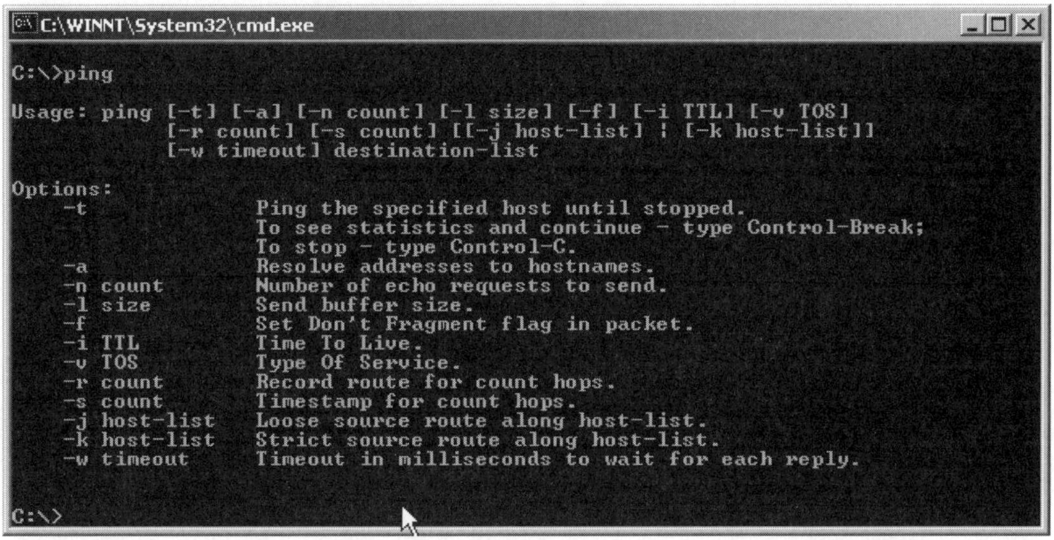

```
C:\WINNT\System32\cmd.exe

C:\>ping

Usage: ping [-t] [-a] [-n count] [-l size] [-f] [-i TTL] [-v TOS]
            [-r count] [-s count] [[-j host-list] ¦ [-k host-list]]
            [-w timeout] destination-list

Options:
    -t             Ping the specified host until stopped.
                   To see statistics and continue - type Control-Break;
                   To stop - type Control-C.
    -a             Resolve addresses to hostnames.
    -n count       Number of echo requests to send.
    -l size        Send buffer size.
    -f             Set Don't Fragment flag in packet.
    -i TTL         Time To Live.
    -v TOS         Type Of Service.
    -r count       Record route for count hops.
    -s count       Timestamp for count hops.
    -j host-list   Loose source route along host-list.
    -k host-list   Strict source route along host-list.
    -w timeout     Timeout in milliseconds to wait for each reply.

C:\>
```

Setting an IP Address on a Cisco Router

When running a client or server, there is typically only a single network interface. The host requires only a single IP address. That single IP address is sometimes misconstrued as the equivalent of the host's name, but it is only the identification of the interface. When there is a router, there are multiple network interfaces. Each interface requires its own IP address, which must exist as part of the IP subnet assigned to that network segment.

To assign an IP address to a router interface:

1. Enter Privileged EXEC mode by typing **enable** at the prompt and providing the password when prompted.

2. Enter Interface Configuration mode by typing **interface *ethernet0*** where *ethernet0* represents the name of the interface being configured. Then press Enter.

3. Type **ip address *ip_address subnet_mask*** and press Enter.

Establishing the Default Route

The default route on Cisco routers is established for the entire router in global configuration mode. To set the default route type:

```
Ip default-network [network-number]
```

where `network-number` represents the IP subnet address of the network segment where packets should be directed; for example, 200.12.34.0 represents a class C subnet address.

Testing IP with ICMP on a Cisco Router

Cisco routers are equipped with PING. In user mode, PING is a simple command executed as:

```
Ping [ip-address]
```

The command returns the results of five packets to that address. The results can be understood via their symbols, shown in Table 4.1.

Table 4.1 PING Results

Resulting symbol	What it means
!	Successful echo reply
.	There was a time out waiting for an echo reply
U	The destination address is unreachable
&	The Time To Live (TTL) was exceeded

If PING is executed in Privileged EXEC mode, it has extended capabilities. Extended PING is an interactive command rather than a command line. It prompts for a configuration by giving options and waiting for selections before executing a PING command. To view the extended options, type **ping ?** at the EXEC prompt and press Enter. The extended command mode for PING permits you to specify the supported IP header options. This allows the router to perform an extensive range of testing options. To enter PING extended command mode, enter **yes** when prompted for extended PING.

DNS

The Domain Name System (DNS) maps hostnames to IP addresses using a hierarchical system. DNS provides a way for multiple servers to work together in providing name-to-address mapping on the Internet. The DNS database is logically distributed among servers and is unlimited in its growth potential. Each server maintains a separate physical DNS database, and each DNS database includes references to both subordinate and parent DNS servers. In this way, DNS is a hierarchy and can grow to any size that is required.

DNS names form a hierarchical tree structure, which is termed a domain namespace. Each domain name consists of labels separated by periods. A fully qualified domain name (FQDN) identifies each host uniquely, as well as provides its position within the DNS database. For example, in Figure 4.6, you can follow the name of the host monet.art.cybercraft.org back to the root of the DNS namespace as well as the host monet.syngress.com. Although each host uses the same initial label, the DNS name is unique.

The root of the DNS hierarchy is represented as a dot. The domains directly below the root are used for specific types of organizations. Each organization will select and register a name within its appropriate domain, listed in Table 4.2, unless that organization is in a country other than the United States. It then uses an abbreviation for the country, such as .uk for the United Kingdom.

Figure 4.6 DNS hierarchy.

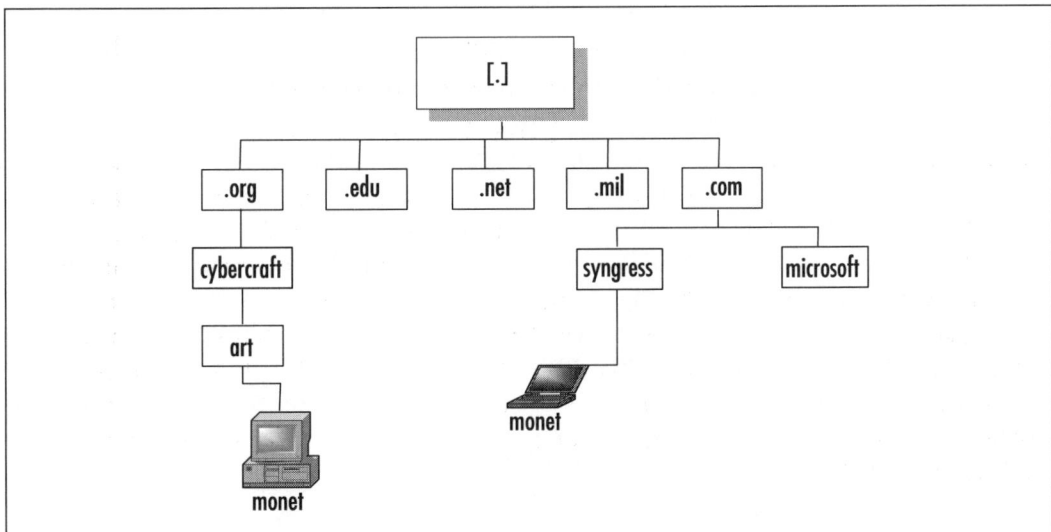

Table 4.2 DNS Top-Level Domains

Domain Name	Organization type
.com	Commercial organizations
.edu	Educational institutions
.gov	U.S. nonmilitary government units
.mil	U.S. military government units
.net	Network backbones for the Internet
.org	Nonprofit organizations

Each DNS domain has a partition of the database known as a zone. Subdomains can be delegated to other servers. For example, a zone for the domain named mydomain.com could be placed on the server dns1.mydomain.com. The zone for a subdomain named sub.mydomain.com could be placed on the server dns2.sub.mydomain.com. Both servers would know of the other server's existence and role within the hierarchy so that they can refer to the other server to find a name for IP address mapping that does not exist within its own zone. DNS servers can host more than one zone. When a server is primary, it is authoritative for the zone and all updates to the zone are made on it. A server can also be secondary, where it contains a read-only copy of the zone and is available only for lookups, but not for changes.

TIP

If you install Windows 2000 DNS, you can store a zone in the Active Directory database by creating an Active-Directory-Integrated zone on that DNS server. When you create this type of zone, it becomes part of the Active Directory domain partition. The zone is stored on each domain controller within that same domain. Although you do not need to create a secondary zone since the Active Directory database provides redundancy, you can still create secondary zone servers on non-Windows 2000 DNS servers in a mixed DNS environment. An additional benefit of using Active-Directory-Integrated zones is the use of Secure DNS Updates. Once a zone is placed in the Active Directory, users and groups must be granted access to modify the zone.

The way that servers know of each other and the way that host names are mapped to IP addresses is done through resource records (RRs). The RR specifies each resource within the zone and its usage. Table 4.3 describes some RR examples.

Table 4.3 Resource Record Examples

Resource Record	Type	Purpose
A	Address	Specifies the hostname and address
NS	Name Server	Identifies a DNS server
SRV	Service locator	Specifies services in the zone
MX	Mail Exchange	Specifies a mail exchange server
CNAME	Canonical Name	Identifies an alias name
SOA	Start of authority	Identifies the primary DNS server for the zone
PTR	Pointer	Resolves IP addresses when given a host name in a reverse lookup zone

When a primary zone updates a secondary zone, it conducts a zone transfer. Originally zone transfers consisted of copying the entire zone file from the primary server to the secondary. Newer versions of DNS, including the Windows 2000 DNS service, provide incremental zone transfers that consist of the latest updates to the zone, but not the entire file.

A client (called a *resolver*) or a DNS server can make two different types of queries (requests for RRs) to DNS servers:

Recursive query The query is made to a DNS server, which must refer the query to other DNS servers to resolve the request. The response is returned to the DNS server, which in turn forwards the response to the resolver. Eventually a recursive query may be sent to a root server. A cache file with root server information can be downloaded from ftp://rs.internic.net/domain/named.cache.

Iterative query The query is made to a DNS server, which is expected to have the answer within its local zone or cache files. This type of DNS server never forwards an iterative query.

DNS was originally established as a file that had to be updated manually by a DNS administrator. Using a manual update method is both prone to error and time consuming. In today's quick-changing networks where "Internet Time" requires that a change be made nearly instantaneously, there is a real need to automate these types of administrative functions.

Request for Comments (RFC) 2136 came to the rescue with its Dynamic Updates architecture, also known as Dynamic DNS (DDNS).

DDNS provides a way for a client to update the DNS database without any manual editing. This is how it works:

1. The DNS client locates the primary DNS server with a Start of Authority (SOA) query.

2. The client verifies whether it is already registered in the database.

3. If the client is not registered, it sends a dynamic update package to register itself in the database.

4. The client registers A (address) and PTR (pointer) records.

If using Windows 2000 Dynamic Host Configuration Protocol (DHCP), the DHCP server can update the DNS server dynamically on behalf of the client. With the dynamic nature of both the IP address and the DNS resource records, the Windows 2000 DNS service provides a way to age and scavenge the database. Aging is a method of checking with the DNS client to determine whether it is still active on the internetwork. When the client has not been active for longer than the aging period, which is called the *refresh interval*, it is considered stale. A stale record is deleted automatically through the scavenging algorithm. Scavenging can be configured to occur periodically.

Setting up DNS Services on Windows 2000

Windows 2000 Server versions provide the DNS service, but Windows 2000 Professional does not. The DNS service starts when the server is configured using the DNS console in the Administrative Tools menu. To configure the server:

1. Select the server that will be configured.

2. Click the Action menu.

3. Select the option to Configure this server.

4. The Configure this Server wizard starts. Click Next.

5. Select whether this is the first DNS server on the network or not, then click Next. If there are other DNS servers, type the IP address.

6. You are then prompted to create a forward lookup zone. You do not need to create the zone at this point; you can add it later. If you are configuring a domain controller, you will have the option of creating an Active-Directory-Integrated zone, as shown in Figure 4.7.

7. When complete, click Finish.

Figure 4.7 Configuring an Active-Directory-Integrated zone.

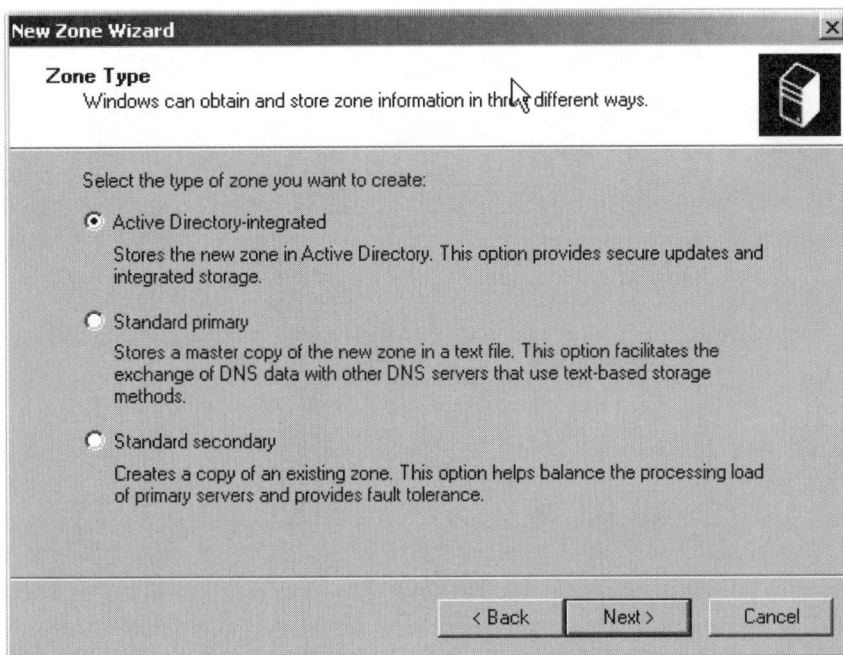

You can add a new zone by selecting either the Forward lookup zone container or the Reverse lookup zone container, then clicking the Action menu and selecting New zone. You can change the type of zone by right-clicking on a zone and selecting Properties from the pop-up menu. On the General tab, click the Change button, as shown in Figure 4.8. You will be allowed to select any of the three types of zones—primary, secondary, or Active-Directory-Integrated.

Dynamic updates are configured only on the Primary DNS server for that zone. On the primary DNS server, right-click the zone in the DNS console and select Properties from the pop-up menu. On the General tab you will see the drop-down box for Allow Dynamic Updates. Select Yes from the two options, as shown in Figure 4.9.

Aging and scavenging is also configured on the primary DNS server. On the primary DNS server, right-click the zone in the DNS console and select Properties from the pop-up menu. On the General tab, click the Aging button to see the dialog for setting the zone's aging and scavenging proper-ties, as depicted in Figure 4.10. You can set aging and scavenging for every zone hosted on your server by right-clicking the server object in the DNS console and selecting Set Aging/Scavenging for all zones from the pop-up menu. If you open the properties of the DNS server and select the Advanced

Figure 4.8 Changing the zone type.

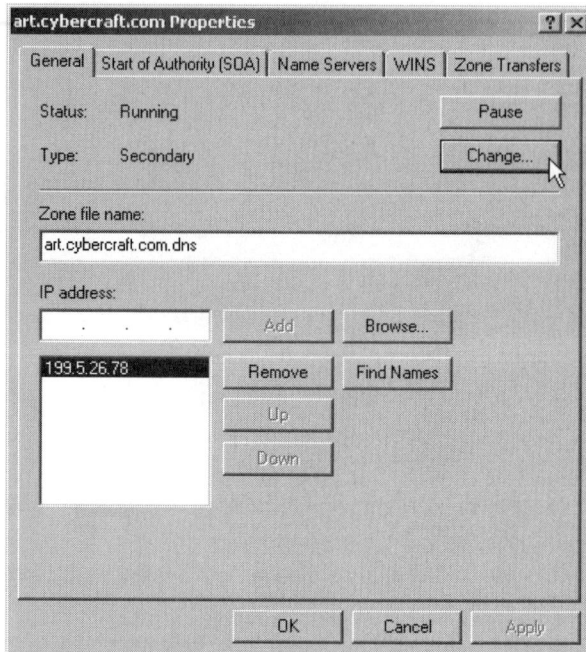

Figure 4.9 Configuring dynamic updates.

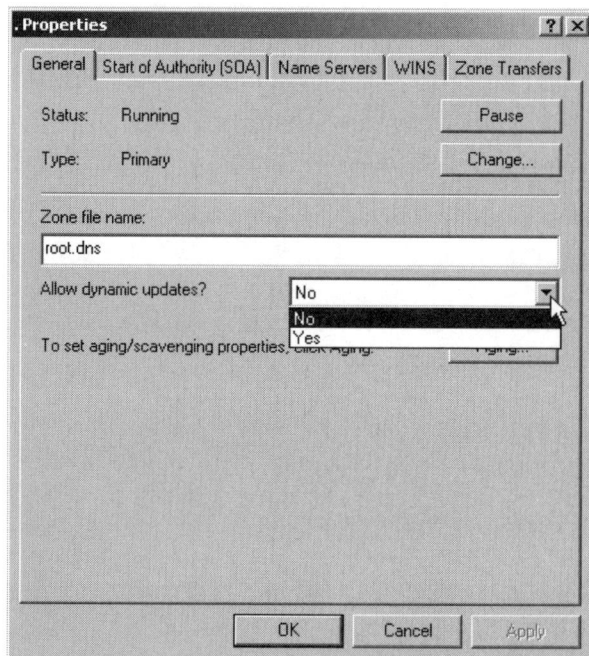

Figure 4.10 Aging and scavenging properties.

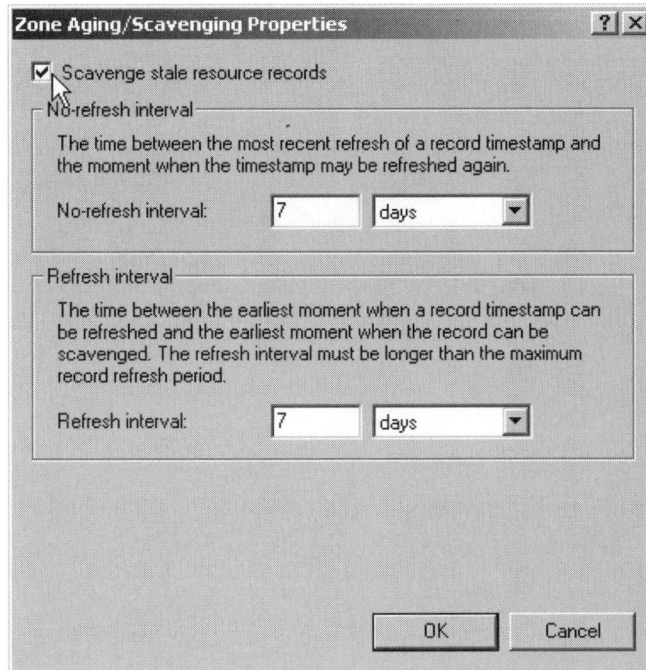

tab you can enable automatic scavenging of stale records by checking that box and then setting the scavenging period.

Setting Up DNS Clients on Windows 2000

Setting up the DNS client on Windows 2000 is done through the same dialog as the assignment of the IP address.

1. Open the Network and Dial-up Connections applet in Control Panel.

2. Double-click the connection icon for which you are configuring a DNS server.

3. Select the Internet Protocol (TCP/IP) item.

4. Click the Properties button.

5. In the Use the following DNS server addresses boxes, type the IP addresses for two of the DNS servers on the network. You should always have at least two DNS servers for the network to provide redundancy if one of the DNS servers should fail.

6. The DNS addresses should look similar to Figure 4.11.

Figure 4.11 Setting the DNS server addresses on a Windows 2000 computer.

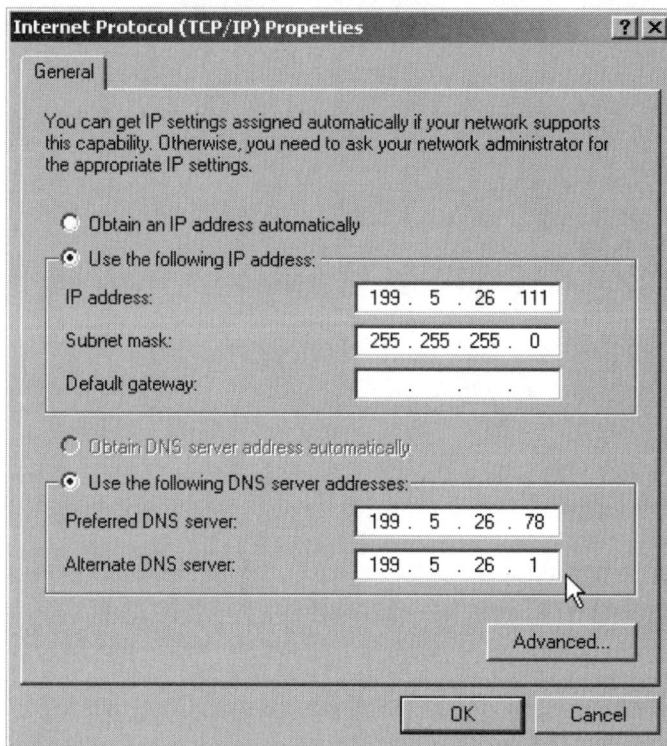

Setting Up DNS Addresses on a Cisco Router

On Cisco routers, using DNS lookups is automatically enabled. To disable it, use the global configuration command:

```
no ip domain-lookup
```

If you wish to reenable it, use the command:

```
ip domain-lookup
```

Even though DNS lookups are enabled, the router still needs to know how to contact a DNS server. Unlike a Windows 2000 DNS client, a Cisco router can use up to six DNS servers for redundancy. To add these DNS server addresses, use the command:

```
ip name-server server_ip_address_1
[server_ip_address_2]…[server_ip_address_6]
```

When the router forwards a DNS lookup request, it sometimes will receive host names that are not fully qualified domain names. The router can concatenate a domain name suffix to complete the FQDN before sending the request onto a DNS server. To set the default domain name that the router appends to a host name lookup, use the following command but substitute your desired domain name for mydomain.com.

```
ip domain-name mydomain.com
```

If you have multiple default domain names to use, you would use the command:

```
ip domain-list domainname
```

For Managers

Cisco's DNS/DHCP Manager

The Cisco DNS/DHCP Manager is an application suite that can provide DNS and DHCP management, Trivial File Transfer Protocol (TFTP) and Network Time Protocol (NTP) services, and a SYSLOG server for error logging. This application suite is installed on UNIX versions from Sun Solaris (v2.4), HP-UX (v10.0), and IBM's AIX (v4.1.3). A version is also available for Windows NT.

So, should you use the Windows 2000 services? Or should you purchase and install the Cisco application suite on a UNIX or NT server? If you have a pure Windows 2000 server network, there are a few reasons to use the Windows 2000 versions of DNS and DHCP:

- The Windows 2000 DNS service is known to be compatible with the Windows 2000 Active Directory, which depends on DNS to work properly.

- They are included as part of the Windows 2000 Server operating system and won't cause any incremental costs.

- You do not need to install a non-Windows 2000 server.

If you have a network that includes several different types of operating systems, or if you already use the Cisco DNS/DHCP Manager suite, then a combination DNS strategy would work well. In this type of system, you can configure one of the DNS servers to provide secondary zone services.

Dynamic Host Configuration Protocol (DHCP)

DHCP replaces the error-prone and cumbersome method of manually assigning IP addresses to each host on the internetwork. DHCP is an updated form of the Bootstrap Protocol (BOOTP), which provided remote boot capabilities to hosts based on UDP broadcasts. DHCP servers respond to DHCP client requests for IP addresses. There are a couple of ways of offering an address through a DHCP server:

Dynamically assigned A pool of IP addresses, called a *scope*, is established for a subnet. Each DHCP client receives an IP address that is available for a temporary period of time, called a *lease*. At the lease expiration, the client can reestablish a new lease for the same address, or if the lease expired before the client started up again on the network, it can lease a new address.

Reservation IP addresses are set aside for individual hosts, so that when the client starts up on the network it always receives the same IP address.

Windows 2000 DHCP supports multicast IP addresses, as well as standard IP addresses. It is available as part of the Windows 2000 Server operating system.

The Windows 2000 DHCP client has a new capability compared to older Windows DHCP clients. The Windows 2000 DHCP client can automatically self-configure its own IP address and subnet mask even if there is no DHCP server available on the network. The IP address is selected from the class B network 169.254.0.0 using a subnet mask of 255.255.0.0. The DHCP client will check the network to see if the IP address exists. If so, the client tries another address. Even though the client autoconfigures this way, it will continue to test the network for a DHCP server. If a DHCP server is found, the autoconfigured addressing is discarded, and new DHCP addressing information is requested from the DHCP server. This functionality is called Automatic Private IP Addressing (APIPA).

Configuring Windows 2000 DHCP Services

Windows 2000 DHCP service is available as part of the server operating system. The Windows 2000 DHCP service prevents unauthorized DHCP servers from popping up on the network by requiring each DHCP server to be configured and then authorized. When an unauthorized server appears on the internetwork, it is ignored. To begin configuring a DHCP server:

1. Start the DHCP console in the Administrative Tools menu.
2. Click the Action menu and select New Scope.

3. The new scope wizard will start; click Next to bypass the Welcome dialog.

4. Type a name and description for the scope and click Next.

5. Type the Start IP address and the End IP address, and then verify the subnet mask, as shown in Figure 4.12. Click Next.

6. Type any excluded IP addresses and click Next.

7. Establish your lease duration. The default is 8 days. Use a longer lease if you have a static network and plenty of IP addresses. Use a shorter lease if people move around the network, if the scope is for dial-up users, or if you have very few IP addresses to share. Click Next.

8. The next screen will prompt to configure DHCP options. To add items such as the DNS servers to be passed to the client when it obtains an address, select Yes and click Next.

9. For the DHCP options, you will be prompted for a Default Gateway address, the domain name and DNS servers on the network, and WINS servers addresses.

10. You will be prompted to activate the scope. Click Next.

11. Click Finish.

Figure 4.12 Configuring the scope address range.

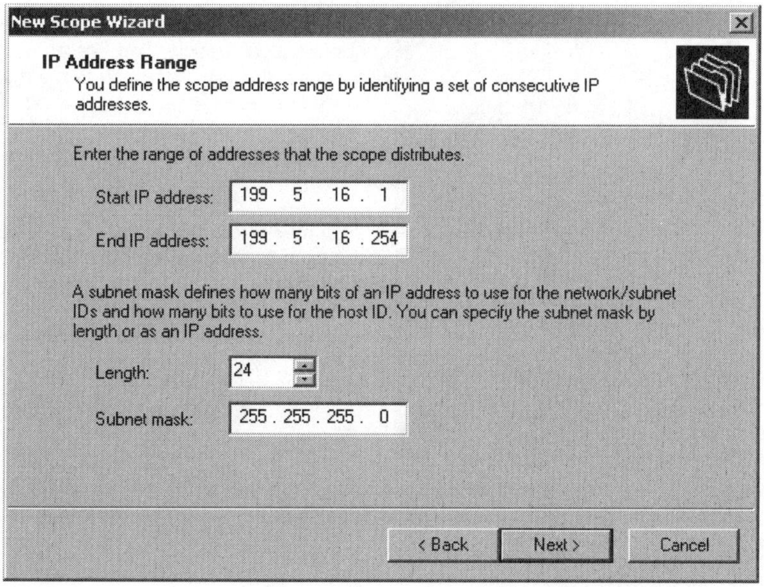

To authorize a DHCP server, select the DHCP server and right-click on it. From the pop-up menu shown in Figure 4.13, select Authorize.

Once you have created a DHCP scope, you can change it. Select the scope in the DHCP console and expand it to see the objects contained within it. You should see the Address Pool, Address Leases, Reservations, and Scope Options. To change any of these items, you can right-click them and select items from the pop-up menu. You can also right-click on the scope and select Properties. This will bring up the main scope components as shown in Figure 4.14. You can change any of the items within the scope except the subnet mask. To change the subnet mask, you will need to delete the scope and create a new one to replace it.

Configuring Windows 2000 DHCP Clients

Windows 2000 client interfaces can either be configured with static IP addresses or DHCP, but not both. Because this is an either/or option, it is configured in the same place as the IP address. The default configuration

Figure 4.13 Authorizing a DHCP server.

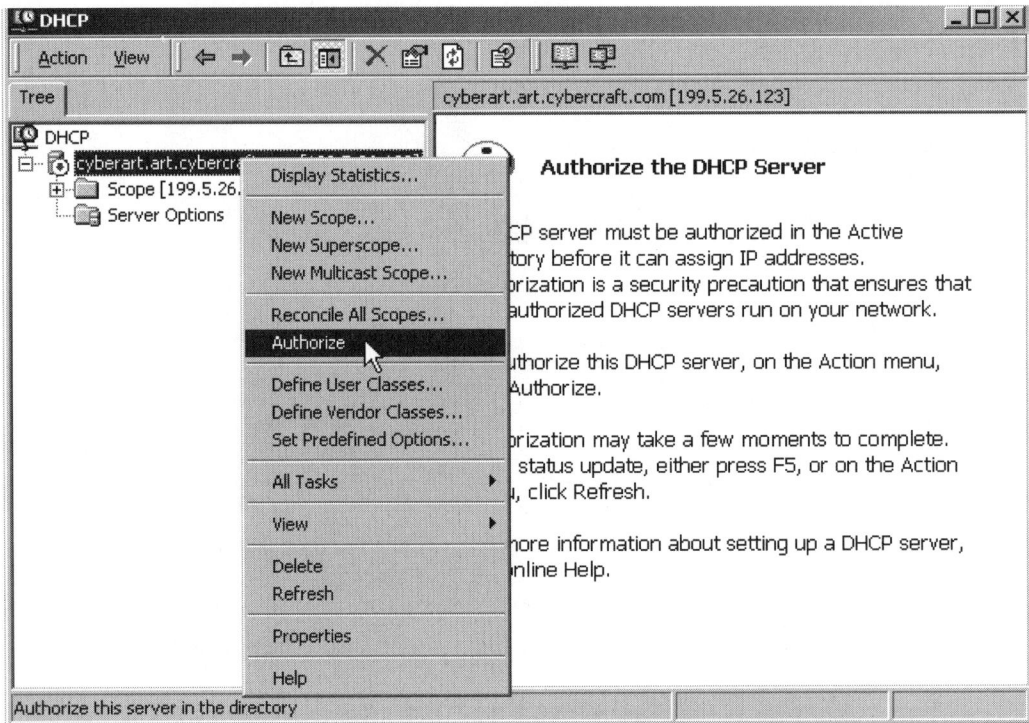

for a network interface that uses the IP protocol is as a DHCP client. If an IP address has been statically configured, you can change the configuration as follows:

1. Start the Network and Dial-up Connections applet in the Control Panel.

2. Double-click the connection for which you are configuring DHCP.

3. Select the Internet Protocol (TCP/IP) option.

4. Click the Properties button.

5. Select the radio button for Obtain an IP address automatically.

6. If your DHCP server provides a DNS server address as optional information, you should also select the radio button for Obtain DNS server address automatically, as shown in Figure 4.15.

Figure 4.14 Scope properties.

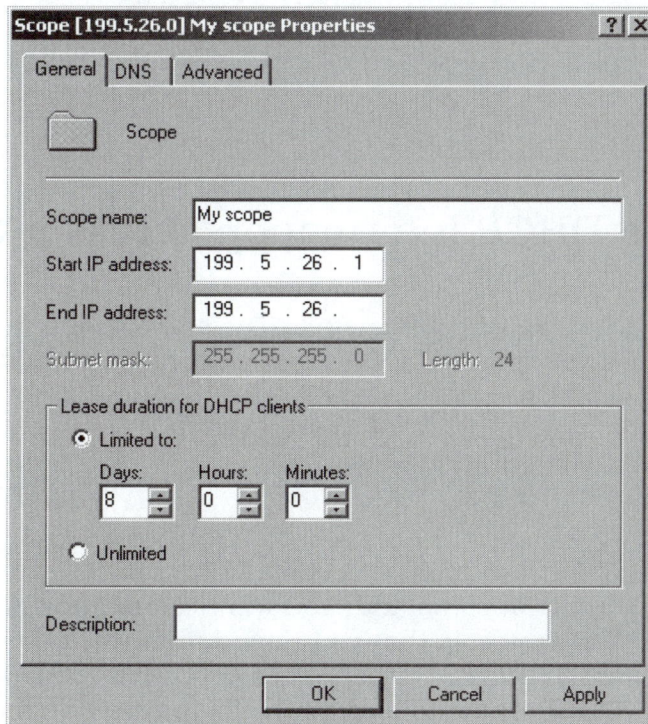

Figure 4.15 Configuring the Windows 2000 DHCP client.

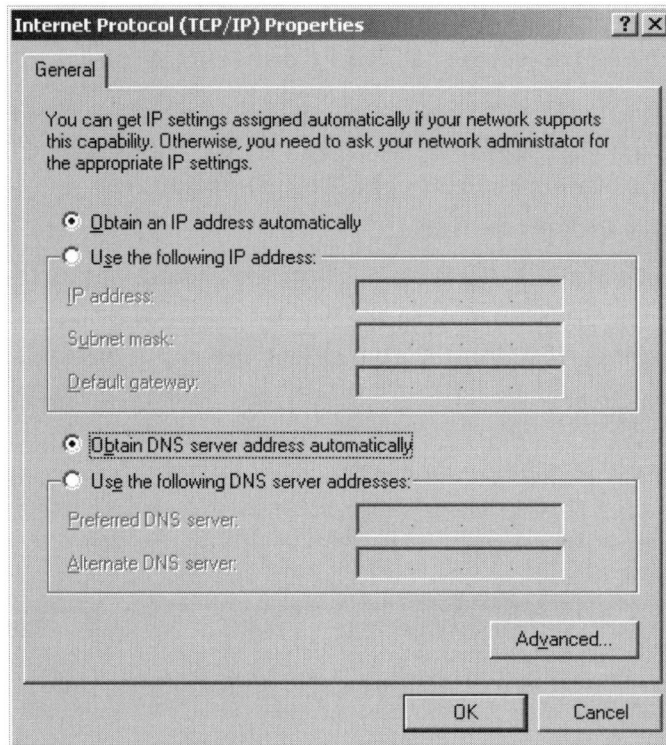

Forwarding DHCP Information across a Cisco Router

DHCP is a broadcast-based traffic using UDP, and as such is not automatically forwarded. If you have a DHCP server that provides IP addresses to a subnet residing across a router, you will need to forward that traffic. To forward DHCP information, you can invoke the IP HELPER-ADDRESS command in interface configuration mode:

```
ip helper-address ip_address
```

If you intend to forward more than just DHCP traffic, you can use the IP FORWARD-PROTOCOL command. You will need to know which port numbers of the UDP protocols that you intend to forward. For example, if you want to forward TFTP traffic that is based on UDP, you would use port 69. However, for DHCP traffic to be forwarded, you need to forward both of the BOOTP ports—67 and 68—as shown here:

```
ip forward-protocol udp 67
ip forward-protocol udp 68
```

File Transfer Protocol (FTP)

FTP, based on RFC 959, is a common protocol used to manipulate files on remote hosts on an IP network. File operations supported by FTP include:

- Listing the contents of a directory
- Creating, moving, and deleting directories
- Transferring files between local and remote hosts
- Creating, renaming, and deleting files

FTP can be configured with basic security options to prevent users' access to some file manipulation commands, such as deleting or renaming files and directories. Limits can be placed on the number of users as well as on which hosts can be allowed to connect to the FTP server.

FTP requires two connections between the ftp client and server. One connection is used by the client to establish the ftp session. The second connection is established for any file operations.

Setting Up Windows 2000 FTP Services

FTP services are part of the Internet Information Services (IIS) for Windows 2000. IIS is installed by default as part of Windows 2000 Server (all versions) but must be added as an optional component for Windows 2000 Professional. To configure the FTP services:

1. Start the Internet Services Manager console, which is located in the Administrative Tools menu.

2. The FTP service should start with the default share of the Phone Book Service. To create a new FTP share, right-click the server and select New.

3. From the New submenu, select FTP Site.

4. The FTP Site Creation wizard will start. Click Next.

5. Type the description for the FTP site you are creating. Click Next.

6. Select the IP address to use for the FTP site from the drop-down box. If you are planning to create an ultra-secure FTP site, you should also change the port from the well-known port of 21 to a registered or private port. This dialog is shown in Figure 4.16. Click Next.

7. Type or Browse for the path of the new FTP directory. Click Next.

8. Select the permissions for the FTP site—you can select Read, Write, or both by checking the boxes. Click Next.

9. Click Finish.

Figure 4.16 FTP site addressing.

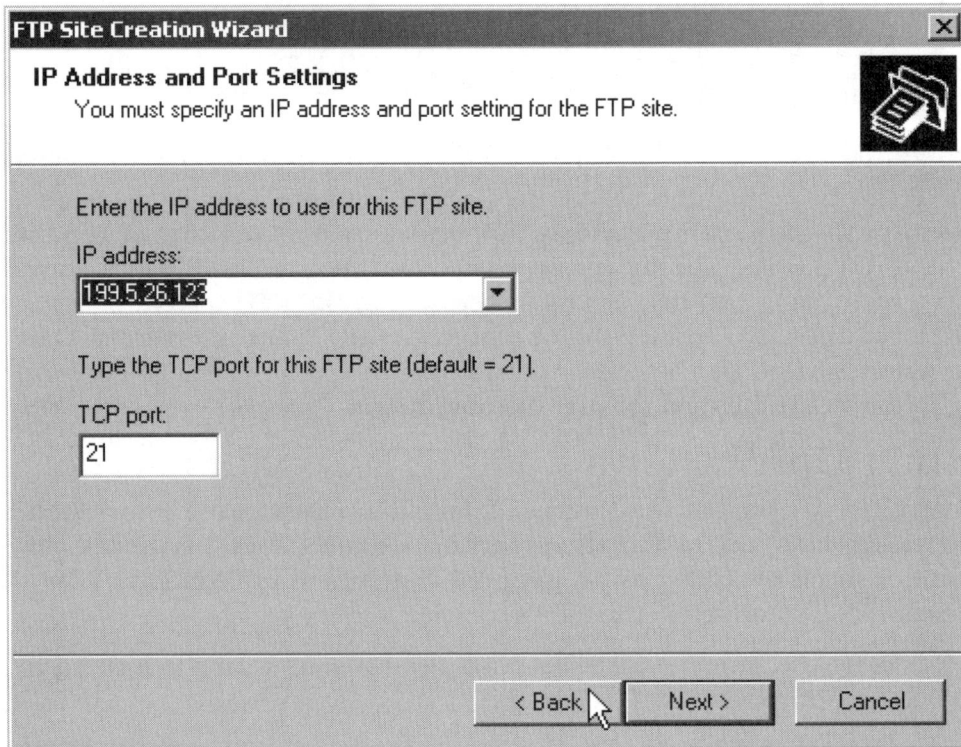

Setting up the FTP site is just the first step towards configuration. There are many more options available within the properties of the FTP site. To change the options, right-click on the new FTP site and select Properties from the pop-up menu. Then make the changes to the FTP site in order to customize it for your purposes.

For example, if you wished to create a highly secure FTP server, you can do the following to the FTP site properties.

FTP Site tab Change the TCP port to a port number that is not well known, then limit the connection numbers to the maximum you would ever expect to connect at one time. Reduce the connection timeout to 300

For IT Professionals

Port Assignments

TCP port numbers are divided into three ranges:

- Well-Known Ports, ranging from port 0 to port 1023
- Registered Ports, ranging from port 1024 to port 49151
- Private Ports (also called Dynamic Ports), ranging from 49152 to 65535

Well-Known Port numbers are assigned by Internet Assigned Numbers Authority (IANA). Most systems can use Well-Known Ports only for system processes, but in some cases they can be used by administrative-level users.

TCP uses ports to name the processes at the ends of logical connections. When an unknown system requests services, it can still receive those services by using a predetermined, standard port number. Well-Known Ports constitute a list of these types of ports for commonly used services. As much as possible, these same port assignments are used with the User Datagram Protocol (UDP).

IANA also lists Registered Ports, which can be used by ordinary processes or nonadministrative users. Manufacturers can register ports with IANA; generally, these are intended to be used with a program that the manufacturer has developed. After a port is registered, developers can create programs to use the registered port and to access the original manufacturer's program over the Internet. However, there is nothing preventing a person from using a port that is registered, or a port that is in the Registered Ports range, for some other purpose.

You can visit IANA's Web site at www.iana.org. The Internet Corporation for Assigned Names and Numbers (ICANN) has taken over much of IANA's responsibilities. You can visit ICANN at www.icann.org. You can look up port numbers at support.kcfishnet.com/scripts/fishnet/portnumbers/portnumbers2.asp.

seconds (which is five minutes). Make certain that logging is enabled, and select the Properties button to increase what is logged. From the extended logging properties page, select items to monitor such as bytes sent and received, the protocol version, and the host.

Security accounts tab Uncheck the box for Allow Anonymous Connections. Remove the Administrators group from the FTP Site Operators and add in a specific group to manage this site.

Message tab Type a security message that announces that the user has connected to your site and some wording to the effect that the site is secure and you will be logging and tracking any unauthorized users.

Home Directory tab Uncheck the box for Write, so that users can only Read files, not change them.

Directory Security tab Select the Denied Access radio button and then click the Add button to enable only specific IP addresses to access the FTP site.

You can add virtual directories to the FTP site. These virtual directories will appear as subdirectories of the FTP site. They can be located on the local server or on other servers around your network. When an FTP user connects to the site, he or she will see the directory as though it were physically part of the FTP Site directory structure.

Running an FTP Client Session on Windows 2000

FTP is a command-line utility found on Windows 2000. You start a command prompt and then type FTP and the IP address or host name of the FTP server. The FTP commands are similar to MS-DOS file commands, such as **cd** to change to a different directory. To access the FTP help, you can start the FTP client in the command line by typing FTP and pressing Enter. Then you type a question mark (?) to see the commands available to you. To find out what each command means, type the command and follow it with the question mark.

Blocking FTP Traffic from Crossing a Cisco Router

FTP sites can be risky to run on your network. If you don't intend to provide FTP services, you should Stop or Delete the default FTP site from each Windows 2000 server on the network. If you do want to provide FTP services, there may be some circumstances in which you do not want FTP traffic to be transmitted over your router.

Figure 4.17 Example network for blocking traffic.

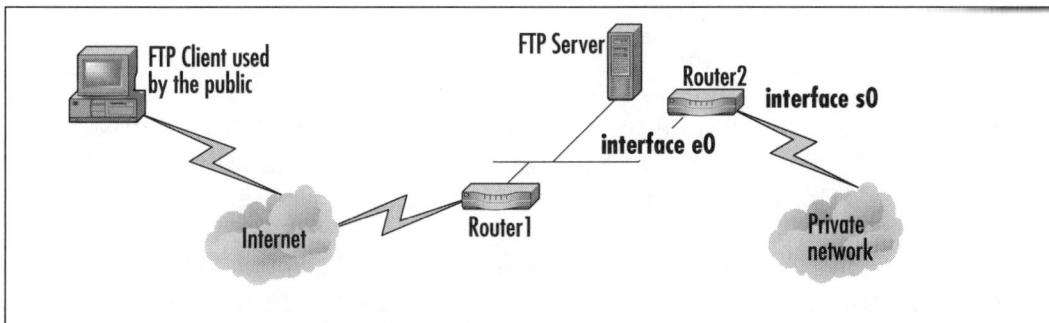

For example, if you have a network in which an FTP server is provided to the public and that server sits outside the private network, you will want to block FTP traffic from coming into the private network router from the public network. Figure 4.17 shows this configuration.

In this network, the FTP traffic must travel freely to and from the FTP client. This will go through Router1. However, you do not want the FTP client's traffic to go through Router2 into the private network, or any other network that might be connected to Router2 in the future. To do this, you will want to configure an access list that blocks FTP traffic incoming to interface e0 on Router2.

Telnet

Telnet, based on RFC 854, is used extensively on Cisco routers, which are configured automatically as Telnet servers. Telnet is a virtual terminal protocol providing sessions to remote users. Administrators use Telnet to remotely manage Cisco routers. Windows 2000 servers can be configured as Telnet servers, but the need to do so is small since Windows 2000 also provides graphical Terminal Services that are much easier to use and do not consume much in the way of bandwidth.

Setting Up Telnet on a Windows 2000 Server

Setting up Telnet on a Windows 2000 server means using the Telnet Server Administration console found in the Administrative Tools menu. This is a text-based console, unlike the others that Windows 2000 provides. However, being text-based, a Telnet server can be administered from any terminal in the network.

First you must start the Telnet service by selecting option 4 from the initial Telnet Server Administration menu. To configure the options for the server, select option 3 from the initial menu. You can then manage the domains that can access the server, the login script, the Telnet port, and others.

Running a Telnet Session on a Windows 2000 Client

You can run a Telnet session from the HyperTerminal application in the Accessories menu of Windows 2000. To set up the session for a host on the network, you will change the Connect Using box to TCP/IP (Winsock) as shown in Figure 4.18. Even if you are connecting to a Cisco router to manage it via Telnet, these are the settings that you would select, unless the port number was changed.

If you're a diehard command-line user, you can start a Telnet session from the command prompt with the command **telnet**. Then you type OPEN and the IP address of the server to which you are connecting.

Figure 4.18 Telnet over IP.

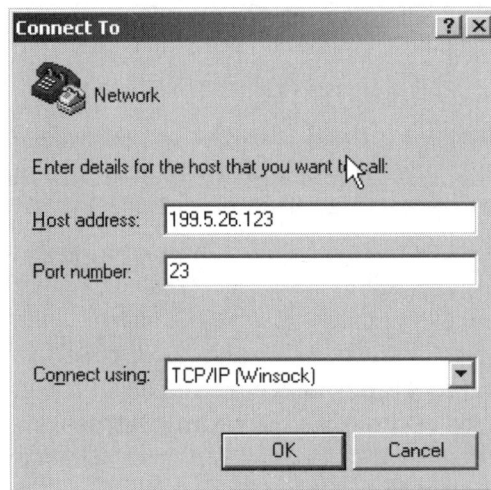

HyperText Transfer Protocol (HTTP)

HTTP (HTTP version 1.1 is based on RFC 2068) is the protocol that powers the World Wide Web with a low-bandwidth-overhead transport of files based on text, but which includes graphics. These files use the HyperText Markup Language (HTML) to control how the client interprets the file. HTTP is a connection-oriented protocol based on TCP and uses port 80. Even though the protocol is connection-oriented, the connection only lasts for as long as it takes to load an HTML page or other HTTP-based objects for downloads into a client's Web browser. Once the page, file, or object is downloaded, there is no reason to maintain the connection so it is closed, making the HTTP protocol very efficient. Windows 2000 includes the Internet Information Service (IIS) to support HTTP.

Setting Up HTTP Support on Windows 2000

IIS is installed by default on Windows 2000 Server versions, unless the installer customized the installation. To add IIS for HTTP support:

1. Use the Add/Remove Programs applet in the Control Panel.
2. Select Add/Remove Windows Components.
3. Click the Components button.
4. Select Internet Information Services.
5. Click the Details button to add or remove the options for IIS, and ensure that World Wide Web Server is checked.
6. Click OK.
7. Click Next.
8. Click Finish.

Once the service is installed, you can set up a Web site using the Internet Services Manager found in the Administrative Tools menu. To set up a new Web site on the server:

1. In the Internet Services Manager console, expand the server by clicking the plus (+) sign to the left of it.
2. Right-click on Default Web Site.
3. Select Site from the pop-up menu.
4. The Web Site Creation Wizard will start. Click Next to bypass the welcome dialog.
5. Type the description of the Web site you are adding.
6. Click Next.
7. Select the IP address for the Web site, accept the default TCP port (80) or change it to a custom port to secure the Web site, and type in the host header or leave it blank. Click Next.
8. Type or browse for the path to the Web site's home directory where you will be posting all the HTML documents and other content. This directory must already exist on your hard drive. Check the box for anonymous access if the Web site will be made public. Do not check this box if people must authenticate before accessing your Web site. Click Next.

Figure 4.19 Web Site Creation Wizard permissions page.

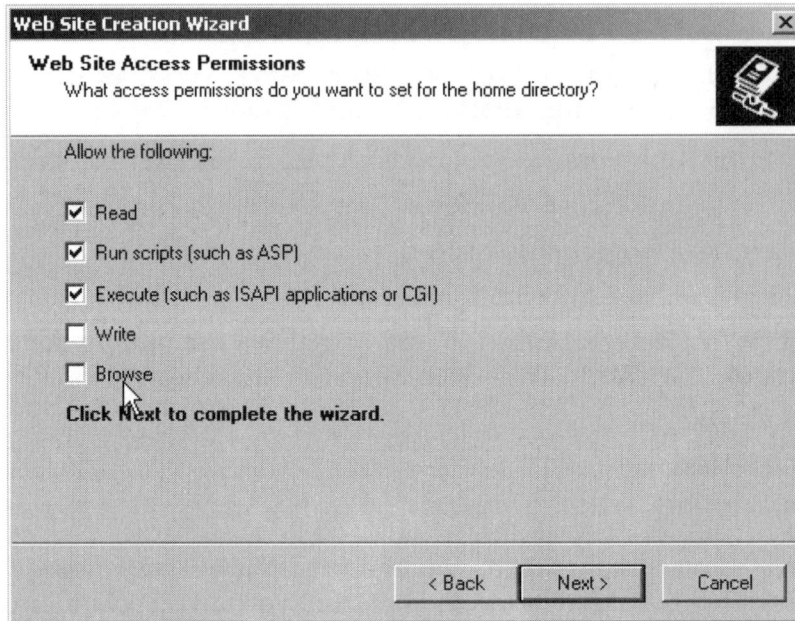

9. Select the permissions for the Web site, which are shown in Figure 4.19.

10. Click Next and then click Finish.

The options for Web site permissions are:

Read Be able to read HTML documents from the Web site.

Run Scripts (such as ASP). Be able to run Active Server Pages and other types of scripts.

Execute (such as ISAPI applications or CGI). Be able to run an application from the Web site.

Write Be able to edit or add HTML documents to the Web site.

Browse Be able to list the Web site directory contents.

Monitoring a Cisco Router from a Web Interface

You can both configure and monitor a Cisco router using a Web browser. The router must be using Cisco Internetwork Operating System (IOS) version 11.2 or later. Before you do so, however, you must enable the router to provide HTTP services using the following global configuration command:

```
ip http server
```

This same command preceded by the word "no" will turn off the HTTP server.

Once you have enabled the HTTP server, you can open the files using the IP address of the router from a Web browser. For example, if your router's IP address is 10.10.10.88, then you can enter http://10.10.10.88 from a Web browser to start the HTML configuration page.

Network News Transport Protocol (NNTP)

NNTP is a standard Internet protocol used for Usenet newsgroups. Multiple distributed servers on the Internet, which are configured with NNTP, provide Usenet newsgroup services in the form of discussion groups. A server with a configured newsgroup can replicate that newsgroup to other servers. This is done through a push (the main server transmits updates to the other servers) or a pull (the other servers request updates from the main server) system. This is called a *newsfeed*.

Discussion groups allow people to read and participate in conversations on a variety of topics. Each newsgroup is dedicated to a single topic or particular set of topics. Tens of thousands of these newsgroups are available. A newsreader client is used for accessing newsgroups.

Configuring NNTP in Windows 2000

Although NNTP is installed as part of IIS, it is not one of the default IIS components. You must add NNTP if you've installed the server with a default configuration. To add NNTP:

1. Use the Add/Remove Programs applet in the Control Panel.
2. Select Add/Remove Windows Components.
3. Click the Components button.
4. Select Internet Information Services.
5. Click the Details button to add or remove the options for IIS, and ensure that NNTP Service is checked.
6. Click OK.
7. Click Next.
8. Click Finish.

Configuring Outlook Express to Access a Newsgroup

Windows 2000 includes an application called Outlook Express, an e-mail and newsgroup reader application. To configure Outlook Express to read a newsgroup:

1. Start Outlook Express from the Programs menu.

2. Click the Tools menu.

3. Select Accounts.

4. Click the Add button.

5. Select News… from the submenu.

6. Type a name that will be seen when a message is posted to the newsgroup and click Next.

7. Type the e-mail address for where the responses should be sent directly, and click Next.

8. Type the name of the news server and select whether you are required to logon. Click Next.

9. If you must log on to the news server and you checked that box, you are prompted for the name and password and type of authentication in the next dialog. Click Next.

10. Click Finish.

11. Click Close and you will be prompted to view the newsgroups available on the specified server.

12. Once the newsgroups have been viewed, you can subscribe to the ones with topics you prefer.

Simple Network Management Protocol (SNMP)

SNMP is a protocol used to collect messages regarding device management from networked hosts. To use SNMP, you will need two components:

■ Management Information Base (MIB), which is a set of objects representing information about the network configuration.

■ The protocol, SNMP, which is a standard based on UDP, defining the way that information is communicated between SNMP devices.

Network hosts can be managed from a central SNMP host that runs an SNMP Manager software. The SNMP clients that this central host manages are called *SNMP agents*. The information that SNMP provides the central host can be used to monitor network throughput, configure information for receipt by remote hosts, and detect network faults or errors—the most common usage for SNMP.

Windows 2000 supports SNMP versions 1 and 2C. Note that SNMP v1 suffered some security problems, so whenever possible, you should implement later versions. The Windows 2000 SNMP service provides SNMP agents for Windows 2000 Server and Professional, as well as some Windows NT services. A third-party SNMP management software must be used to manage the agents. It does not need to run on the Windows 2000 server. The SNMP management system requests information from network hosts. The SNMP agent on that host responds with the requested information retrieved from its MIBs. The SNMP agent will also send the information from the MIBs when a trap event occurs. Traps are configured to send information to a specific destination host when an event occurs. An event could be a reboot or other action that occurred on the server.

SNMP services can be configured to exchange information with only a specified group of computers. This is done through the configuration of a community. The community is a named list of hosts that typically are administered together, although it is considered a form of a password because you must know the community name in order to share the community data. To reduce your security risks, you should change the SNMP community from the default "public" community.

Configuring the Windows 2000 SNMP Agent

The Windows 2000 SNMP service must be added to the Windows 2000 computer before it can be used to provide messaging:

1. Open the Add/Remove Programs icon in the Control Panel.
2. Select Add/Remove Windows Components.
3. Check the box for Management and Monitoring Tools.
4. Click Next and then Finish.

The way to configure the SNMP agent is to open Computer Management in the Administrative Tools menu. Click on Services and then select SNMP Service. Click the Action menu and then select Properties. You can configure the community name and traps for the service.

Remote Procedure Call (RPC)

RPCs make an application that is running on a remote computer appear as though it is running locally. It is considered the heart of client/server computing by some, and is used extensively in the Windows 2000 Active Directory communications with clients and domain controllers.

In the RPC model of an application, a portion of an application resides on a client and the remainder resides on a server. Passing the application from the client to the server is via a stub procedure. The client calls a stub procedure that refers to the code that resides on the server. The server code returns data to a server stub that converts the data in output form for the client computer. When the application executes, both the client and the server provide processing power toward the result.

Windows 2000 RPCs traffic between domain controllers for replication traffic. They are also used between clients and domain controllers for Active Directory queries and authentication. RPCs cannot be replaced with another protocol for these activities except in the case of replication between two Active Directory sites that do not share a domain. Then, SMTP can be used instead.

Simple Mail Transport Protocol (SMTP)

The Active Directory uses Simple Mail Transport Protocol (SMTP) for replication between sites that do not share a domain partition. SMTP is not a replacement for RPCs. Normally it is used for communication between electronic mail systems on the Internet. SMTP uses the following process:

1. A user SMTP process connects to a server with SMTP over TCP port 25.

2. The server SMTP process listens for that TCP connection on port 25.

3. Once connected, the user and server SMTP processes dialog using an SMTP request/response.

4. The user process transmits the e-mail addresses of the message's originator and recipient(s).

5. The server process must accept the addresses before the user process transmits the message, which is formatted with a header according to RFC 822.

Within Windows 2000, SMTP is used for intersite replication between sites that are not spanned by a domain. This is further discussed in Chapter 6, "Routing and Remote Access." For now, remember that SMTP's asynchronous nature is appropriate for replication traffic over slow, wide area network (WAN) links.

Configuring a Site Link to Use SMTP

To configure a site link with SMTP:

1. Open the Active Directory Sites and Services console.

2. Navigate to the Transports container, and below that to the SMTP container.

3. Right-click the container and select New Site Link.

4. Add the sites to the link and click OK.

Internetwork Packet Exchange (IPX)

Novell developed the Internetwork Packet Exchange (IPX) protocol stack based on the Xerox Network Systems (XNS) protocol. Like TCP/IP, Novell's IPX is a stack of multiple protocols that are arranged in layers. The IPX protocol stack defines the five upper layer functions of the OSI protocol stack, and can run over virtually any data-link/physical protocol such as Token Ring or Ethernet.

The IPX protocol works at the network layer (Layer 3) and defines the logical addressing of the network segments and nodes, which is the basis of routing data. The IPX network addresses must be unique. They are represented typically in hexadecimal format. The network number is 32 bits in length; the node number is usually adopted from the MAC address, which is 48 bits in length. Since IPX uses the MAC address as a node address, it can direct packets directly to the destination computer. (Compare this to IP, in which you need to use Address Resolution Protocol to discover the MAC address from the logical IP node address.)

The interesting thing about IPX is that there are multiple encapsulations possible. Remember, an encapsulation is the header and sometimes a trailer placed around data packets. This creates a "frame" around the data, which explains why Novell documentation calls the encapsulation a Frame Type. Table 4.4 shows the correlation of Cisco Encapsulation names to Novell Frame Type names.

Table 4.4 Encapsulation and Frame Type Names

Topology	Cisco Encapsulation name	Novell Frame Type name
Ethernet	Sap	Ethernet_802.2
Ethernet	Novell-ether	Ethernet_802.3
Ethernet	Arpa	Ethernet_II
Ethernet	Snap	Ethernet_SNAP
Token Ring	Sap	Token-Ring
Token Ring	Snap	Token-Ring_SNAP
Fiber Distributed Data Interface (FDDI)	Snap	FDDI_SNAP
Fiber Distributed Data Interface (FDDI)	Sap	FDDI_802.2
Fiber Distributed Data Interface (FDDI)	Novell-fddi	FDDI_RAW

The IPX protocol stack uses the Service Advertisement Protocol (SAP) to collect information about services available on the network and to advertise them. SAP is the single most aggravating protocol in the IPX stack. SAP uses a tremendous amount of overhead, which increases with each server and its shared services. SAP sends out updates every 60 seconds in an attempt to synchronize all servers' lists of network services. Both routers and servers listen to SAPs and build a table of the services and their network addresses. Each update identifies the type of service being shared by the server, such as 7 for a print server.

For Novell NetWare servers using IPX, you cannot contact a server without ensuring that SAP is getting through the internetwork. Like most bandwidth-intensive protocols, SAP makes life easy for network users. Looking for a service on the network can be done with a query to the nearest router or server's SAP database. Then, the client has the address of the service and can contact the server directly. The end-user doesn't know this, but when he double-clicks the Network Neighborhood in his Windows desktop, that's what is going on behind the scenes. Of course, a user can double-click Network Neighborhood with a total IP solution, but someone had to configure DNS or WINS (or both) for the Network Neighborhood to be able to locate services on the internetwork. SAP, on the other hand, is automatic.

SAP is no longer necessary for the newest versions of NetWare. Not only can clients use Novell Directory Services (NDS) clients over IPX to locate service, but they also can use a pure IP option to contact NDS. In the pure IP configuration, there never will be a need for SAPs.

Sequenced packet exchange (SPX) is the transport layer protocol that performs roughly the same types of services that TCP performs in the IP protocol stack. Like TCP, SPX is a reliable, connection-oriented protocol.

There are several upper layers of the IPX protocol stack. But the most important protocols for Novell NetWare clients are the NetWare shell and the NetWare Core Protocol (NCP). The NetWare shell runs on clients, and intercepts calls from applications and redirects them to the network as needed. NCP satisfies application requests coming from the NetWare shell.

Configuring Windows 2000 to Use IPX

You can configure Windows 2000 to use IPX for a specific network interface. It can be used with the Client for Microsoft Networks and with the Client Services for Novell networks. To add IPX to an interface:

1. Right-click the My Network Places icon on the desktop.

2. Select Properties from the pop-up menu.

3. The Network and Dial-up Connections window will open. Select the connection to which you will be adding IPX and double-click it.

4. Click the Install button.

5. Select Protocol and click the Add button.

6. Select NWLink IPX/SPX/NetBIOS Compatible Transport Protocol and click OK.

Managing SAP on a Cisco Router

Because of the frequency (every 60 seconds) and bandwidth utilization that SAPs tend to have, being able to manage whether SAPs are sent or how often can reduce overhead costs. Filtering out SAPs is the easiest way to conserve bandwidth. To filter out SAPs from traveling across a network link, you can create an access list.

To create the access list for IPX SAP, you need to define a numbered access list in the range of 1000 to 1099. The access list can be an input or an output filter on the router. The command to use when defining the SAP filter for SAPs coming into the interface is:

```
ipx input-sap-filter 1001
```

For an output filter, it is:

```
Ipx output-sap-filter 1002
```

After defining the filter, the next task is to add the filter statements to it. These statements tell which SAPs to deny or let pass through the router. Always end an access list with a permit –1 statement so that anything that is not explicitly denied will be allowed to pass through the router. The following statements filter out all SAP traffic for any network (represented by the –1) and any services (represented by the 0) from server1, and permit all other SAP traffic.

```
Access-list 1001 deny -1 0 server1
Access-list 1001 permit -1
```

NetBEUI

One of the protocols with which legacy Windows NT used to communicate was NetBIOS Extended User Interface (NetBEUI). NetBIOS is a session-layer protocol Application Programming Interface (API). NetBEUI is a protocol stack that uses NetBIOS as well as its broadcast-based name to 802.x address translation. IBM developed it for use in local area networks, and it is commonly found in LAN Manager, LAN Server, Windows for Workgroups, and Windows NT systems. Windows NT uses Server Message Blocks (SMBs) as the application layer protocol used for NT networking, but was able to use SMBs over different protocol stacks.

The NetBEUI protocol stack does not include a network layer. This means that it is not a routable protocol. Even so, the NetBIOS Frames Control Protocol (NBFCP) can be used by a NetBEUI application to transfer packets across a PPP connection through a Remote Access Server.

Configuring NetBEUI on Windows 2000

The NetBEUI protocol is enabled on a per-interface basis in Windows 2000. You can enable NetBEUI by:

1. Right-clicking the My Network Places icon on the desktop.
2. Double-click the connection to which you will be adding the NetBEUI protocol.
3. Click the Install button.
4. Select Protocol and click the Add button.
5. Select the NetBEUI Protocol as shown in Figure 4.20, and click OK.

Figure 4.20 Adding the NetBEUI protocol.

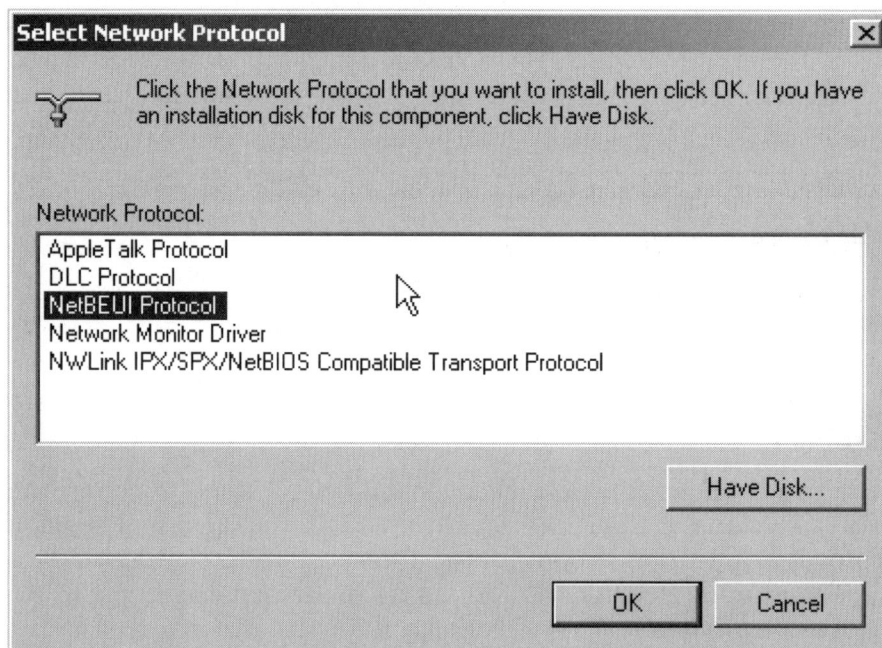

Supporting NetBEUI on Cisco Routers

One of the Cisco router capabilities is to support NetBEUI remote clients over a Point-to-Point Protocol (PPP) connection. To configure a remote access interface to provide NetBEUI services you can use the commands in Table 4.5.

Table 4.5 Cisco NetBIOS and NetBEUI Commands

Command	Configuration Mode	Function
NetBIOS nbf	Interface configuration	Configures the remote access router interface to enable NBFCP. This should be done for each side of the NetBEUI link.
Show nbf sessions	EXEC	View NetBEUI connections information.
Show nbf cache	EXEC	Displays NetBIOS name cache.
Multilink-group	Global configuration	Enables NetBIOS Frames (NBF) on the router.
NetBIOS name-cache	EXEC	Defines static name cache entries for NetBIOS names. Each entry maps the defined NetBIOS-name to a MAC address and states whether the server is locally available through the specified interface, or remotely available through a ring group-number.

Miscellaneous Protocols and Multiservices

The IP protocol stack does not stop at the routing of data between network segments. It enables multiple services and protocols to run on top of the network layer protocols. Services, such as voice or fax, can run on top of an IP network (instead of analog network); and protocols at the session, presentation, and application layers provide further user-interaction with the network. User-interaction is the reason that these protocols are implemented. People want to take advantage of the network that they have in front of them for more than file sharing. The following are the types of protocols that you may encounter when deploying your Windows 2000/Cisco network.

Remote Desktop Protocol

The Remote Desktop Protocol (RDP) is the key protocol component of the Microsoft Terminal Services client and for Microsoft's NetMeeting product. RDP is based on the T.120 protocol, developed by the International Telecommunications Union (ITU-T). The T.120 protocol is an international standard used for multichannel transmissions, enabling separate virtual channels for sessions. RDP currently runs over TCP/IP and provides up to 64,000 separate channels for data transmission.

Four key components of RDP are:

- Multipoint Communication Service (MCSMUX)

- WDTSHARE.SYS

- TDTCP.SYS

- Generic Conference Control (GCC)

MCSMUX consists of the T.122 standard that defines multipoint services and T.125 that defines the data transmission protocol. This essentially assigns channels through multiplexing data into predefined virtual channels.

WDTSHARE.SYS is the RDP driver that transfers the User Interface (UI), and that compresses, encrypts, and frames data. TDTCP.SYS is the transport driver that packages the data to sit on top of TCP/IP. GCC manages the multiple channels onto which MCSMUX multiplexes data. Terminal Services uses GCC to create and delete session connections.

H.323

H.323 is a specification developed by the ITU-T for voice, video, and data traffic transmission across a LAN. H.323 can run across many types of protocol stacks, including TCP/IP. There are four components to H.323 to consider:

- H.323 terminals, which carry voice, but video and data transmissions are optional

- H.323 multimedia communication units (MCUs), which carry multimedia transmissions

- H.323 gateways, which act as gates between IP and voice networks (including speech terminals)

- H.323 gatekeepers, which perform address translation, access control, bandwidth, and zone management

Cisco's AS5300 Universal Access Server voice service provider is an H.323 gateway for Voice-over IP (VoIP) applications. In addition, the Cisco 2500 and 3600 series routers can both be configured with H.323 for VoIP support by adding a one- or two-slot voice module.

To configure a 3600 series router as an H.323 gateway, you would first complete the voice port configuration, which is discussed in the VoIP section. Once that is complete, you then enable the gateway from global configuration mode with the command **gateway**. Next, you define the H.323 gateway ID on the interface that will service the H.323 gateway with the interface configuration mode commands **h323-gateway voip interface** and **h323-gateway voip id GK01.syngress.com ipaddr 10.10.10.1**. After this, the gateway can define technical prefixes for gateways with the commands **h323-gateway voip h323-id gw02@syngress.com** and **h323-gateway voip tech-prefix 2#**.

Voice-over IP (VoIP)

There are various options for implementing Voice-over IP:

VoIP gateway A system that receives a voice transmission from a PBX, converts it to IP, then transfers it across a network to another VoIP gateway which converts the data from IP to a voice transmission that can be understood by the destination telephone system. This is usually a router with a voice card or a Windows 2000 Server with software and voice cards.

IP PBX A complete phone system with IP telephony applications, which is usually based on a Windows NT/Windows 2000 Server with telephony software and voice cards. There are also new IP PBXs produced as standalone systems with proprietary hardware and software.

Custom configurations New systems are being developed for combining IP data networks with voice networks.

To deploy VoIP on a Cisco router, you should have an IP network, voice interface cards installed in the routers, a telephone network, and a plan to integrate them. Then you need to configure the IP network to support real-time voice transmissions, which involves supporting extension numbers through number expansion, specifying dial peers, and configuring voice ports.

Figure 4.21 NetMeeting application.

Using Microsoft NetMeeting on a VoIP Network

Microsoft NetMeeting is a conferencing software product that provides a shared video, audio, chat, whiteboard, and applications. NetMeeting is shown in Figure 4.21.

NetMeeting can be used on a VoIP network when the router is configured as a voice gateway. This is done by creating a VoIP dial peer with the session target being the IP address of the NetMeeting host. The CODEC for the dial peer should be either g711ulaw or g711alaw.

NetMeeting must also be configured to work with VoIP using the following steps:

1. Start NetMeeting.

2. Click the Tools menu.

3. Select Options.

4. Click Advanced Calling....

5. Select Use a gateway to call telephones and videoconferencing systems. (If you have a gatekeeper, you can use that option for Use a gatekeeper to place calls instead.)

6. Type the IP address of the gateway. (If using a gatekeeper, type a logon name or phone number as necessary.)

7. Click OK.

8. Click the Audio tab.

9. Click the Advanced... button.

10. Check the box for Manually configured compression settings.

11. Under the preferred codec drop-down box, select CCITT u-Law 8.000kHz, 8 Bit, Mono.

12. Click OK.

13. Click OK to exit to the main NetMeeting window.

You can now place a call from NetMeeting using the Place a Call button.

Fax-over IP

One type of service that is commonly found in networks is faxing. A legacy configuration for network faxing is a fax modem in a server that is shared as a printer to client machines. The clients print to the printer, and it is translated to a fax at the server and transmitted over the PSTN. When transmitted, the fax connects to the remote fax machine using the T.30 (formats nonpage data) and T.4 (formats the page image) protocols developed by the ITU-T. Each page is negotiated separately between the two fax machines.

Fax-over IP in a packet network does not work quite this way. Instead, the fax travels across a network towards a fax peer on the same IP network. The fax can be sent either in real time or in a store and forward mode. Real-time transmission requires the routers to spool the fax so that the fax machine can receive the fax in its normal negotiated method. Store and forward mode incorporates a delay and does not require the Cisco router to spool the fax. Not all Cisco routers support Fax-over IP. Table 4.6 lists the commands used to configure fax services for Cisco routers that support Fax-over IP (Cisco's AS5300 software, for example).

Table 4.6 Fax-over IP Commands

Command	Configuration Mode	Function
Fax-rate	Dial-peer configuration mode	Establishes the rate at which a fax is sent to the dial peer. The options for the command are fax-rate (1200|2400|4800|7200|9600|14400|disable|voice) bytes. The numbers (1200, 2400, etc.) each are a different bit per second. *Disable* disables faxing. Voice is the highest speed allowed. Bytes forward DMTF tones using H.245 protocol so that faxes can be forwarded to different destinations.
Dial-peer Codec	EXEC mode Dial peer config-	Enters dial-peer configuration mode. States the voice coder rate of speech for the uration mode dial peer.
Fax receive called-subscriber	Global configuration mode	Sets the phone number for the sending fax machine—which is typically seen in a liquid crystal display of the receiving fax machine. The full command is **fax receive called-subscriber (d|string)**, in which *d* specifies that the information is captured from the configured destination pattern, or is the string parameter, used to specify the destination telephone number. This command is used for store and forward fax.
Fax send center-header	Global configuration mode	Specifies the data that appears in the center of the fax header. The command is **fax send center-header (a|d|p|s|t|string)** where *a* adds a date, *d* inserts the destination fax, *p* gives the page count, *s* inserts the sender fax address, *t* gives the transmission time, and *string* is whatever text information is desired within the header. This command is used for store and forward fax.

Continued

Table 4.6 Continued

Command	Configuration Mode	Function
Fax send left-header	Global configuration mode	Specifies data appearing in the left portion of the fax header. See fax send center-header for parameters.
Fax send right-header	Global configuration mode	Specifies data appearing in the right portion of the fax header. See fax send center-header for parameters.
Fax send coverpage comment	Global configuration mode	Defines the title for a fax cover page by following this command with a string of text.
Fax send coverpage e-mail-controllable	Global configuration mode	Overrides the fax send coverpage comment command if an e-mail header is sent with the fax information, and generates a fax coversheet itself.
Fax send coverpage enable	Global configuration mode	Generates fax coversheets from e-mail messages.
Fax send coverpage show detail	Global configuration mode	Includes all of the e-mail header information to generate the fax coversheet.
Fax send max-speed	Global configuration mode	Specifies the maximum rate at which a fax will be sent outbound from the router. The options are **fax send max-speed (12000| 14400|9600|7200|4800|2400)** where each number represents the bit per second rate of transmission.
Fax send transmitting-subscriber	Global configuration mode	Defines the transmitting subscriber identifier (TSI) for the fax. The command is **fax send transmitting-subscriber (s|string),** where *s* inserts a sender name from the captured header information, and where *string* specifies the telephone number.

Summary

The language spoken by each computer is a binary system of ones and zeros. The protocol stack is the syntax of that language when it travels between computers. When you look at a protocol stack, you should use the OSI reference model to relate to how that protocol works with the other protocols in the stack.

Transmission Control Protocol/Internet Protocol (TCP/IP) is the protocol stack used by the Internet. It is the protocol that is closest to being implemented universally on networks worldwide. The protocol stack works over most media, wide area network (WAN) protocols, and the IEEE (Institute of Electrical and Electronics Engineers) 802 series physical and data-link layer protocols, which includes Ethernet (IEEE 802.3) and Token Ring (IEEE 802.5) as well as many others. The network layer protocol, IP (Internet Protocol), provides the addressing for network nodes and segments. The transport layer protocols, TCP (Transmission Control Protocol) and UDP (User Datagram Protocol), provide connection-oriented and connectionless connectivity, respectively.

Each interface in a server or router is given its own IP address. On Windows 2000, the IP address is set in the Network and Dial-up connections applet found in the Control Panel. On a Cisco router, the IP address is set in interface configuration mode.

DNS (Domain Name System) is important for mapping host names to IP addresses. DNS is required for Windows 2000 Active Directory. It is the mechanism by which servers discover each other to exchange information, and by which clients discover servers in order to authenticate and query the Active Directory database. DNS services can be installed on Windows 2000, or Windows 2000 can be configured to use other DNS servers.

DNS is a hierarchical system that includes root servers on the Internet. DNS lookups that cannot be resolved on a DNS server can be passed through the hierarchy until an answer is found. DNS uses a zone for each segment of its hierarchy. A DNS server can have a primary zone, for which it is the sole authoritative server, or a secondary zone, which is a copy of a primary zone on a different server. A Windows 2000 DNS server can also use an Active-Directory-Integrated zone to take advantage of the redundancy found within the Active Directory.

DHCP (Dynamic Host Configuration Protocol) is used for assigning IP addresses to hosts. A scope is created on a DHCP server. The scope consists of a pool of IP addresses that can be assigned to clients. When a client requests an address, the DHCP server assigns either an address reserved for it, or one from within a pool of available addresses. DHCP services can be installed on Windows 2000, or Windows 2000 can be configured as a DHCP client. DHCP is based on BOOTP (Boot Protocol), which uses UDP (User Datagram Protocol). UDP packets are broadcast-based and not typically forwarded beyond the current network segment. In a routed environment, routers must be configured to forward UDP packets in order for a DHCP server to provide its services to segments to which it is not directly connected. This is usually accomplished by configuring an IP helper address on the router.

FTP (File Transfer Protocol) is an application layer protocol used for manipulating files on remote servers. Windows 2000 can be configured as an FTP server through the installation and configuration of the Internet Information Services. If FTP services are not to be provided across a router, the router can be configured to filter the FTP protocol with an access control list.

Telnet is an application layer protocol used to provide terminal sessions. Cisco routers are automatically Telnet servers, providing sessions for remote control of the routers from which an administrator can configure the routers. Windows 2000 can be configured as a Telnet server, and can include two types of Telnet clients—telnet.exe and HyperTerminal.

HTTP (HyperText Transfer Protocol) is an application layer protocol used for downloading HTML (HyperText Markup Language) documents. HTTP is the basis of the World Wide Web. Windows 2000 can be installed with Internet Information Services and configured to provide Web services.

NNTP (Network News Transport Protocol) is an application layer protocol used for Usenet newsgroups. Windows 2000 can be configured to provide newsgroup services from its Internet Information Services application.

RPCs (Remote Procedure Calls) are a session layer API (Application Programming Interface) that can make remote procedures appear to be happening locally. Windows 2000 Active Directory depends on RPCs for its replication traffic both within sites and between sites.

SMTP (Simple Mail Transport Protocol) is a protocol typically used for transferring electronic messages over TCP/IP. Windows 2000 Active Directory can use SMTP for replication between sites that do not share a domain. This is done through specific configuration of a site link in the Active Directory Sites and Services console.

IPX (Internetwork Packet Exchange) is usually associated with Novell NetWare servers. Windows NT and Windows 2000 servers also use it as a mode of network transport. If you install the Active Directory, you must have TCP/IP as the network protocol stack. However, in multiprotocol networks or for standalone servers, IPX is optional. Cisco router interfaces can be configured with IPX in interface configuration mode.

RDP (Remote Desktop Protocol) is a protocol used by Terminal Services on Windows 2000, and runs on top of TCP/IP. RDP provides the client interface as a terminal session.

H.323 is a multiservices support protocol. It provides voice, video, and data transmissions. Four components are available in H.323 networks: H.323 terminals, H.323 MCUs (Multimedia Communication Units), H.323 gateways, and H.323 gatekeepers. Voice-over IP (VoIP) and Fax-over IP use H.323.

FAQs

Q: Is it possible to convert an Active-Directory-Integrated DNS zone to primary?

A: Yes. You can convert any type of DNS zone (primary, secondary, or Active-Directory-Integrated) to any other type on a Windows 2000 DNS server. When you convert an Active-Directory-Integrated zone to a primary zone, the DNS server becomes the single primary for that zone. The Active Directory information must be deleted from all the domain controllers' domain partitions after the conversion to prevent errors.

Q: Can I filter out RDP communications between two computers located on the same network segment?

A: No, you cannot filter out a protocol on a segment without placing some filtering device between them. Filters are access control lists placed on Cisco routers that specify which protocols can or cannot be permitted through an interface. This effectively would create a firewall at the protocol level between two segments. An IP access control list can be used specifying the TCP port number used for RDP to filter it out between the two segments.

Q: What is the difference between Fax-over IP and Voice-over IP?

A: The difference between Fax- and Voice-over IP is not that great. Fax-over IP is an H.323 Voice-over IP system with faxing "extras." For example, in a store and forward fax Cisco router configuration, the difference is that the router must be configured to support fax information such as the fax header information. In real time fax Cisco router configuration, the router must be configured to support the queuing of faxes so that fax devices experience the delays they normally would experience in standard faxing, in which pages are negotiated between fax machines on a page-by-page basis.

Chapter 5

Routing and Remote Access

Solutions in this chapter:

- Understanding remote access protocols
- Understanding routing protocols
- Enabling routing on a Windows 2000 server
- Securing a network through virtual private networking

Introduction

One of the interesting things about a Cisco and Microsoft Windows 2000 network is that both Cisco routers and Windows 2000 servers can perform routing. In order to route, each needs to have at least two interfaces, and needs to be configured to route data from one network segment to another. So if both will support this feature, why not just use Windows 2000 to do it all—file, print, Web, and routing services? This is the kind of question that you may run across from time to time. Engineers instinctively veer away from running everything on a single machine, but it makes little sense to nontechnical people to spread the processing around the network if it can all be done in a single place. In projects where each expense must be justified, you can use the following reasons to explain your network design.

- Performance and availability on the network is decreased when a combination server and router is used, thus increasing downtime, which affects the productivity of network users.

- Single points of failure cause excessive downtime if there is a failure. A Windows 2000 server that also acts as a router is a single point of failure on the network.

- Using separate hosts (a Cisco router as a router, and a Windows 2000 server as a server, for instance) for different functions on the network will increase the security on the network—a hacker must breach both the router and the server in order to access the network.

- Using separate routers and servers vastly increases the scalability of the network.

Because remote access servers utilize modems in the same way as a network interface they are, effectively, routers. That is why remote access and routing are generally grouped together.

Remote Access Protocols

Legacy remote access protocols were simply those that worked across the plain old telephone system (POTS). They were required to convert digital data to analog, travel across a serial line, and then be converted back at the receiving station. Though analog lines are still used to connect to remote access servers today, alternate means of communications are now available.

ISDN

The Integrated Services Digital Network (ISDN) is sometimes referred to as the "I Still Don't kNow" acronym. The reason for this sarcastic description is based on the fact that ISDN was not available immediately, even though it was broadly discussed. ISDN was an exciting option for remote access since it provided increased bandwidth, reduced latency, faster call establishment, and less noise interference with the signal.

ISDN is a digital call switching service that is provided in two forms:

- Basic Rate Interface (BRI)
- Primary Rate Interface (PRI)

Both types of interfaces are available in most areas where legacy analog Public Switched Telephone Network (PSTN) equipment has been updated with digital equipment. The new digital switches can support both ISDN and POTS.

BRI provides two B (bearer) channels and one D (data) channel. The B channels provide 64 Kbps bandwidth each and are used for bearer services (voice or data), and the D channel, at 16 Kbps, is used for signaling and control. The D channel is used for building, maintaining, and releasing the bearer service connections over the B channels. BRI's bandwidth is therefore 128 Kbps over the B channels. BRI can be provided over legacy analog phone service local loops. ISDN local loop length is limited to approximately 18,000 feet.

PRI provides 23 B channels at 64 Kbps and 1 D channel at 64 Kbps. The B channels still provide bearer services and the D channel provides signaling and control in the same way as it does for BRI. PRI services are provided over T1 lines. PRI's bandwidth is 1.472 Mbps over those 23 B channels. (PRI services also can be provided over E1 leased lines with 30 64Kbps B channels and a single 64Kbps D channel.)

ISDN Equipment Types

The components used in ISDN networks include several types:

Terminal Adapter (TA) An adapter that is used with legacy equipment or non-ISDN-capable equipment in order to connect to the ISDN network. This is used for BRI rates.

Terminal Equipment Type 1 (TE1) A device that can connect directly to an ISDN network and has ISDN capabilities built in.

Terminal Equipment Type 2 (TE2) A device that requires a TA to connect to the ISDN network.

Network Termination Type 1 (NT1) A device that sends and receives signals to the service provider's ISDN switch. The ISDN U interface is used by an NT1. U interfaces are used in the United States to provide full-duplex data transmission over a single pair of wires. A U interface can connect only to a single NT1. An S/T interface supports full-duplex data transmission over two pair of wires. The S/T interface can support up to seven NT1s.

Network Termination Type 2 (NT2) A device that concentrates ISDN switching services at the client's site. NT2 devices connect to NT1 devices in order to access the service provider's ISDN network.

Local Exchange (LE) An ISDN switch providing both switching and termination services for ISDN traffic, located at the service provider's network.

It is possible to have TA and TE1 devices with NT2 devices built in, or with both NT1 and NT2 devices built in. It is common in Europe to have only a built-in NT2 device since service providers provide NT1 services. In the United States, however, both NT1 and NT2 devices are required. When configuring ISDN routing, each TE1, TE2, NT1, or NT2 device must be configured with the correct type of LE switch.

ISDN Protocol

When a connection between two hosts over an ISDN B channel link is created, it is encapsulated in Point-to-Point Protocol (PPP), High-level Data Link Control (HDLC), or X.25 or V.120 protocols. Both ISDN routers must be configured with the same encapsulation in order for data to transmit properly. The majority of ISDN implementations encapsulate with PPP. D channels use Link Access Protocol D (LAPD) for signaling between terminal equipment and the ISDN switch. Within a service provider's ISDN network, the ISDN switches use Signaling System 7 (SS7) Protocol.

ISDN operates at the physical, data-link, and network layers of the OSI protocol reference model. The LE provides clocking for the physical layer's synchronous bitstream of ISDN data. Data-link layer addressing assigns a unique physical address called a Terminal Endpoint Identifier (TEI) to each ISDN interface. At the network layer, ISDN services on each device are assigned logical addresses.

When either a TE1 or TE2 comes online, it requests a TEI from the service provider's LE. The LE assigns a unique TEI for traffic identification. The switch assigns a Service Profile Identifier (SPID)—a logical address—to each B channel. The SPID is used like a telephone number to build the circuit connection between ISDN devices. A Service Access Point Identifier (SAPI) is assigned to each separate service performed by the ISDN device. SAPIs are used to prioritize data.

Dial-on-Demand Routing

Dial-on-demand routing (DDR) can provide seamless connectivity between networks. An ISDN router receives a packet destined for the other network and establishes the connection. After a configured time period of no routing to that network, the ISDN router disconnects. One use of ISDN DDR is as a redundant backup link for a network connection.

DDR is useful in containing ISDN costs since there is no need for full-time data connectivity over leased lines. ISDN data services are charged on per-minute rates regardless of whether they are long distance or local calls. In addition, users must invest in ISDN equipment in order to use the ISDN services, such as an ISDN telephone or terminal adapter for use with their existing analog telephones. These costs are prohibitive for a casual ISDN user, but as a backup link, ISDN is a cost-effective option.

Configuring BRI on a Cisco Router

To configure BRI, you will need the type of ISDN switch used by the service provider. The ISDN switch types, all of which are used within the United States, use different signaling:

- AT&T 5ESS
- Northern DMS-100
- National ISDN-1

The command to identify the ISDN switch is entered in global configuration mode. The command follows, and Table 5.1 lists the switch options.

```
isdn switch-type switchtype
```

If you are using a Cisco 700 router, the set switch command is used, and only the three switches for the United States are options in the U.S. software image. The Cisco 700 router command is

```
Set switch [5ess | dms | ni-1 | perm64 | perm128]
```

After configuring the switch type, you then enter the SPIDs for a BRI. SPIDs are not required for PRI. These commands are entered in BRI interface configuration mode. The 5ess interface will allow up to eight SPIDs for each B channel, whereas the DMS-100 and National ISDN-1 interfaces allow two SPIDs for each B channel. To enter into this mode and then configure the SPIDs, type the following commands:

```
router>enable
router#conf t
```

Table 5.1 BRI Switch Types

LE Switch Equipment	Country in which the Switch Is Used	Command Identifier for Switch Type
1TR6	Germany	basic-1tr6
AT&T 5ESS	United States	basic-5ess
Northern DMS-100	United States	basic-dms100
NET3	U.K. and Europe	basic-net3
National ISDN-1	United States	basic-ni1
NET3	Norway	basic-nwnet3
NET3	New Zealand	basic-nznet3
TS013	Australia	basic-ts013
NTT	Japan	ntt
VN2	France	vn2
VN3 and VN4	France	vn3

```
router(config)#interface bri0
router(config-I)#isdn spid1 0828828201 8288282
router(config-I)#isdn spid2 0828828401 8288284
```

On the Cisco 700 Series, the SPID configuration again uses set commands, as follows:

```
Set 1 spid 51282882820101
Set 1 directorynumber 8288282
Set phone1 = 8288282
Set 2 spid 51282882840101
```

To verify your BRI configuration, use the following command in EXEC mode:

```
Show isdn status
```

On the Cisco 700 Series router, you use the following command instead:

```
Show status
```

Configuring PRI on a Cisco Router

PRI is configured on Multichannel Interface Processor (MIP) cards. MIP cards support channelized T1/E1 or PRI. There are PRI cards for Cisco 4x00, 36x0, 5x00, and 7x00 Series routers. To configure the ISDN switch type use the **isdn switch type** global configuration command as follows, along with the switches shown in Table 5.2:

```
Isdn switch-type switchtype
```

Table 5.2 PRI Switch Types

LE Switch Equipment	Country in which the Switch Is Used	Command Identifier for Switch Type
AT&T 4ESS	United States	primary-4ess
AT&T 5ESS	United States	primary-5ess
Northern Telecom	United States	primary-dms100
NET5	Europe	primary-net5
NTT	Japan	primary-ntt
TS014	Australia	primary-ts014

Configuring the T1 or E1 controllers enables PRI services. The PRI B channels are numbered 0 through 23, but are mapped to primary-group timeslots numbered 1 through 24, as shown in the following router configuration:

```
Controller t1 0
Framing esf
Clock source line primary
Linecode b8zs
Pri-group timeslots 1-24
```

The D channel must be configured with the ISDN configuration commands. The D channel for a T1 line is interface serial0:23.

```
Interface serial0:23
Dialer rotary-group 1
Interface dialer 1
Ip unnumbered ethernet0
```

```
Encapsulation ppp

Per default ip address pool default

Dialer in-band

Dialer idle-timeout 120

Dialer-group 1

No fair-queue

No cdp enable

Ppp authentication pap chap

Ppp multilink
```

Configuring an ISDN Interface on Windows 2000

Windows 2000 uses an ISDN line the same way that it uses a modem and analog line. It is considered a dial-up network connection and is configured in the Network and Dial-up Connections icon found in the Control Panel. You can implement a complex advanced routing system using Windows 2000 and multiple ISDN adapters with multiple dialing profiles and multi-link PPP (a system in which multiple PPP links are added to create a higher bandwidth connection overall).

The first thing you need to do is install the ISDN interface adapter into the computer. Then you need to power up the computer so that the ISDN ports are detected by the hardware detection mechanism within Windows 2000. Use the Device Manager to configure the switch type for the ISDN adapter: to access the Device Manager, right-click on My Computer and select Properties from the pop-up menu. Then click the Hardware tab and click the Device Manager button, which is shown in Figure 5.1.

As with the Cisco routers, a Windows 2000 computer needs to know to which ISDN switch (LE) the ISDN adapter is connecting. The AT&T 5ESS (ATT), the National ISDN-1 (NI-1), and Northern Telecom (NTI) switches are all common options. Once the switch is identified, use the following instructions to configure the ISDN connection:

1. Right-click on My Network Places.

2. Select Properties. The Network and Dial-up Connections window will appear.

3. Right-click on the connection that uses the ISDN device. (If Windows 2000 did not automatically detect your ISDN interface, you will not show this connection. You should verify that the ISDN interface is compatible with Windows 2000 first. If so, you can attempt to add the connection manually by double-clicking the Make New Connection icon and following the dialog boxes and making selections for your device.)

Figure 5.1 Accessing the Device Manager.

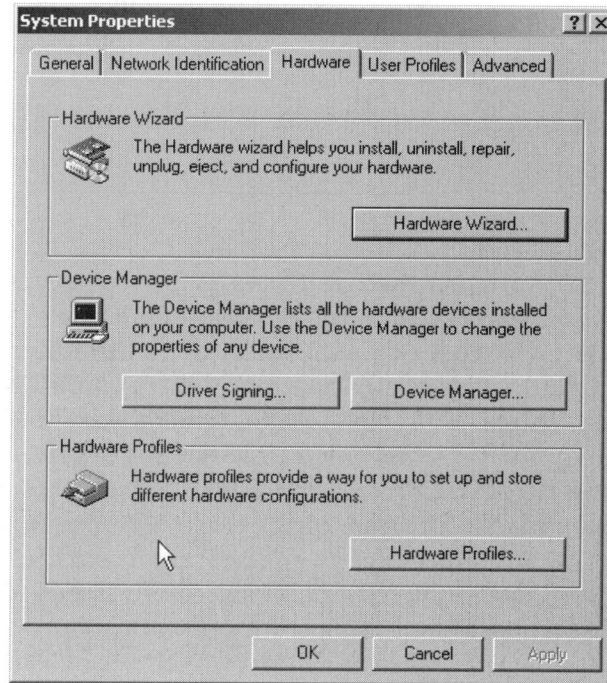

4. Select Properties from the pop-up menu.

5. Click the ISDN device in the Connect using box on the General tab.

6. Click Configure.

7. Select the line type or check the box whether to negotiate the line type.

8. Click OK to exit.

Digital Subscriber Line (DSL)

The Digital Subscriber Line (DSL) technology utilizes the same twisted-pair copper wires that telephones use for high-bandwidth data transmissions. xDSL describes different types of DSL technology, such as High-bit-rate Digital Subscriber Line (HDSL), Very-high-bit-rate Digital Subscriber Line (VDSL), and Asymmetric Digital Subscriber Line (ADSL), and even G.Lite, which is a specific implementation of ADSL. Because xDSL services provide dedicated point-to-point connections over the last mile (the twisted-pair copper wiring on the telephone company's local loop) with minimal changes to the service provider's network, it draws significant attention as a new technology.

HDSL

HDSL provides high-speed wideband digital transmissions over existing copper lines. There is an equal amount of data transmitted for uploads as for downloads, which means it is symmetrical. HDSL is intended to be used for transmission within an office between the DSL provider and a customer.

ADSL

ADSL provides high-speed data transmission over standard telephone wiring, enabling telephone companies to realize more profits from their existing copper infrastructure. The term *asymmetric* refers to the fact that the upstream and downstream transmission rates are different. ADSL offers up to 9 Mbps downloading capability and up to 640 Kbps uploading capability. Note the usage of "up to"—ADSL speeds vary based on the quality of the copper wire and distance to service provider's network.

ADSL's asymmetric speed system matches the usage of users who tend to consume Internet media, downloading HTML Web pages along with multimedia components, and who tend to upload much smaller data amounts in the form of e-mail and small file transfers. ADSL is not as appropriate for businesses that transmit equal amounts of data to and from the Internet. Nor is it appropriate for an Internet Web server since a Web server tends to upload data to users through the Internet rather than download from them.

ADSL does not digitize the voice line. Instead, ADSL transmits standard analog voice service. Whereas the voice service uses a dial-up number, the data service doesn't. A portion of the analog line's bandwidth that is not utilized by voice transmission is used for data. This enables a simultaneous voice and data transmission. A splitter is placed on the telephone jack to filter out ADSL signaling and to ensure the quality of the line.

ADSL equipment divides the available bandwidth of the telephone line using one of the following methods:

Frequency division multiplexing (FDM). Assigns one frequency band for upstream data and another band for downstream data. The downstream path is divided using time division multiplexing (TDM) into high- and low-speed channels. The upstream path is divided using TDM into corresponding low-speed channels so that each upstream and downstream channel is a pair.

Echo cancellation. Assigns the upstream band to overlap the downstream band, then separates the bands with a local mechanism that is also used in V.32 and V.34 modems.

Regardless of how the bandwidth is divided, ADSL dedicates a 4 kHz region for the telephone voice service.

ADSL and Cisco Routers

Small offices can utilize Cisco routers (for example, the Cisco model 677 ADSL router with 10/100 Ethernet and ADSL ports) for ADSL connectivity to the Internet. Figure 5.2 demonstrates how a small local area network (LAN) could connect using this router. Note that ADSL is appropriate only for offices that will experience heavy downloads from the Internet and minor uploads to the Internet.

Figure 5.2 Small LAN connected to the Internet via a Cisco router and ADSL.

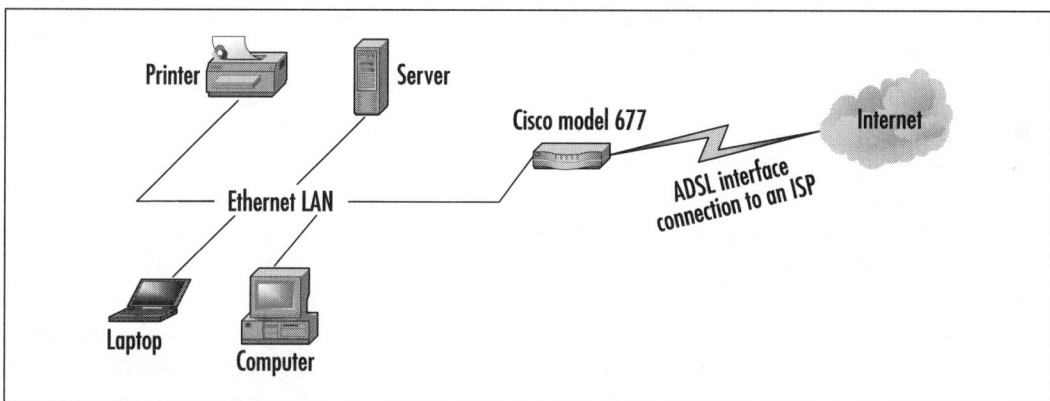

Using ADSL on a Windows 2000 Computer

To use a Windows 2000 computer with an ADSL line, you first need a special DSL adapter. You first install the DSL adapter physically into the computer, and then when the computer powers online, you install the drivers so that the adapter is recognized as a network adapter. The connection is then displayed in Network and Dial-up Connections, which is found in the Control Panel.

TIP

Many corporations will be looking into DSL for their telecommuting end-users. This will provide a high-speed connection for them. When they install DSL in their homes, they will need filters for their telephone jacks to work appropriately. These filters enable the voice traffic to flow through to the telephone without data interrupting it.

G.Lite

One specific implementation of ADSL is called, informally, G.Lite. G.Lite allows asymmetric connectivity over standard telephone lines. G.Lite's speeds (about 384 Kbps downstream, and 128 Kbps upstream) are much faster than analog modem services, but are still somewhat slower than the full range of speeds offered by all the implementations of ADSL.

VDSL

VDSL technology depends on the upcoming technology of Fiber to the Neighborhood (FTTN), in which fiber optic media is installed to reach optical network units that feed large buildings and neighborhoods. From the optical network units, short drops of copper wiring service the building and the neighborhood. This is where VDSL comes in. Because fiber optic media provides services for the majority of the distance, vastly increased speeds are available on the copper media. The speeds are dependent upon the length of the wiring. Over short distances of 1000 feet, downloads may be as fast as 50 to 55 Mbps, whereas a 4000 feet distance would enable about 13 Mbps download speed.

VDSL currently is being defined and discussed, and is not ready for implementation except with a small number of preliminary products. It is likely that VDSL will incorporate slower upload speeds using echo cancellation except in the shortest distances where it may be only slightly slower or equivalent to the download speed. VDSL is clearly an appropriate technology for an enterprise network to use in connecting to the Internet.

SLIP and PPP

Serial Line Internet Protocol (SLIP) and PPP are well-known remote access protocols. Each of these protocols defines methods of sending IP packets over standard analog lines. PPP supports Internetwork Packet Exchange (IPX) and AppleTalk as well. Dial-up connections to a corporate network can be a cost-effective method for connectivity for remote users or even for remote sites. A dial-up connection is also appropriate as a backup link upon the occasion that a main wide area network (WAN) link fails.

SLIP encapsulation was first introduced in UNIX computers. PPP followed SLIP and provided services beyond those of SLIP's, such as greater security mechanisms. However, SLIP is required in some implementations to provide remote access services to legacy UNIX computers that do not support PPP.

Configuring IP over a SLIP Link for Cisco Routers

There are three steps to configuring IP over a SLIP connection for Cisco routers. The first step is enabling IP routing on a serial interface. Two interface configuration commands will do this:

```
Ip address ip-address mask [secondary]
```

```
Ip unnumbered type number
```

The first command assigns an IP address to the interface and essentially enables IP routing. The second command can be used in place of the first. It configures IP unnumbered routing for a serial interface.

The second step enables the SLIP encapsulation to take place over the serial connection. This is an interface configuration command.

```
Encapsulation slip
```

The third step is meant to enable interactive mode on the asynchronous interface via an interface configuration command.

```
Async mode interactive
```

To connect to a remote node from the Cisco router over a SLIP link, you can use the following EXEC mode command.

```
slip [/default]{remote-ip-address | remote-name}[@tacacs-server]
[/routing][/compressed]
```

Configuring IP over a PPP Link for Cisco Routers

The first step to configuring IP over a PPP link is enabling IP routing on a serial interface of the Cisco router. Two interface configuration commands will do this:

```
Ip address ip-address mask [secondary]
```

```
Ip unnumbered type number
```

The first command assigns an IP address to the interface and essentially enables IP routing. The second command can be used in place of the first. It configures IP unnumbered routing for a serial interface.

The second step is to create the encapsulation of PPP on the serial interface. This is done with the following interface configuration command:

```
Encapsulation ppp
```

The third and final step to enabling IP over a PPP link is to allow an asynchronous interactive mode. This, again, is an interface configuration command as follows:

```
Async mode interactive
```

To connect to a remote node from the Cisco router over a PPP link, you can use the following EXEC mode command.

```
Ppp {/default | {remote-ip-address | remote-name} [@tacacs-server]}
[/routing]
```

Using TCP Header Compression

When you compress the headers of the TCP/IP packets, the result is a reduction in size and increased performance. You should use header compression when you have a large percentage of small packets that use Transport Control Protocol (TCP) instead of User Datagram Protocol (UDP). The reason for compressing TCP headers and not UDP headers is that TCP headers are so much larger due to the extra information included to provide connection-oriented services. TCP header compression is supported with PPP encapsulation, but must be enabled at both ends of the connection.

To enable TCP header compression, use the following interface configuration command:

```
Ip tcp header-compression
```

Then specify the number of header compression connections that can exist on the interface using the following interface configuration command. The number of connections can be anywhere from 3 to 1000. The default is 32 connections:

```
Ip tcp compression-connections number
```

Configuring a Banner Message for SLIP and PPP Connections

The Cisco IOS includes a banner message command to create a custom message for SLIP or PPP connections. The message can supply custom connection strings for legacy client applications as well as a simple message. To configure the banner message for both SLIP and PPP connections, use the following command in global configuration mode. The ^ symbol in this command represents a delimiter that you specify.

```
Banner slip-ppp ^message^
```

Configuring PPP and SLIP in Windows 2000

Both PPP and SLIP are available in Windows 2000 for connecting to networks. The default dial-up connection in Windows 2000 is configured with PPP, due to its prevalence and preferred usage in Windows 2000 remote access servers. This procedure assumes that you have already installed a modem on your computer. To configure a SLIP connection:

1. Right-click My Network Places.

2. Select Properties. The Network and Dial-up Connections window will appear.

3. Double-click the Make New Connection icon. The wizard will start.

4. Click Next.

5. Select Dial-up to Private Network and click Next.

6. Type the phone number and check the box if you prefer using the dialing rules. Click Next.

7. Select whether this connection is for all users, or for the current logged in user. Click Next. (If you are configuring a connection for all users, you will be prompted for Internet Connection Sharing as an additional step. If you will be enabling this connection for all users on the network to share, then make that selection.)

Figure 5.3 Configuring a SLIP dial-up connection.

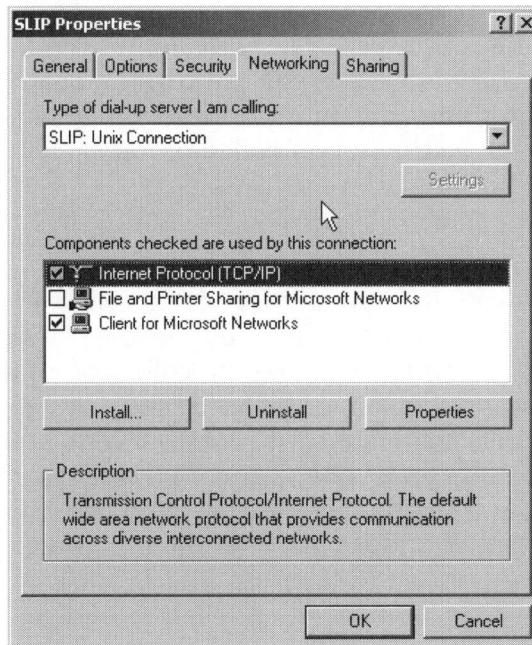

8. Type a name for the connection and click Finish. The connection will show up in the Network and Dial-up Connections window. This is, by default, a PPP connection at this point.

9. Right-click your new connection and select properties.

10. Click the Networking tab.

11. Click the drop-down arrow for the box entitled "Type of dial-up server I am calling:" and select SLIP: Unix Connection. This is illustrated in Figure 5.3.

12. Click OK to finish.

Routing Protocols

Routing is the process of moving data from one network segment to another. A protocol must be able to identify the network segment, as well as the host, in order to route data to it. Network segment addressing is handled at the network layer. A router is the computer connected to two or more segments via two or more interfaces, which identifies the network segments and forwards data received from a segment to another segment. A router needs to determine the path, ideally the best path, to the destination host before forwarding the packet.

When a router receives a packet, it checks to see if it has a listing in its routing table for the destination network, which is called *path determination*. If it does, it forwards the packet to that segment, which is called *packet switching*. If the router is not directly connected to the segment, it may know which segment is next in the path to the destination and forwards the packet onto that segment. Each router that a packet passes through from source to destination is called a *hop*.

NOTE

A network can be defined in many ways: It is called a local area network (LAN); it can be an IP subnet, defined by the Class A, Class B, or Class C address (and subnet mask); it can be the collection of all the computers on a single broadcast domain; or it can be the point-to-point link between two routers that connect to create a wide area network (WAN).

A network is made up of one or more physical segments. The easiest way to think about a segment is the collection of all hosts on media bounded by routers or bridges. An internetwork is a collection of networks.

A routing table can have static routes, default routes, or dynamic routes defined. Static routes are simply manual entries made by the network administrator. Static routes become increasingly difficult to manage as an internetwork grows in size. Default routes are like a static route in that they are configured manually. However, a default route is the place that the router is told to send any packet for which it does not have a specific listing in its routing table. Default routes are useful in stub networks that have only one outlet to the rest of an enterprise internetwork. In Figure 5.4, the stub network represented by the Token Ring network 10.10.10.0 is only connected to the rest of the network via router1. The default route for Router1 for any packets originating from that network would be to Router2. In addition, Router4 automatically can forward all packets originating from stub network 10.10.15.0 towards Router3.

Routing protocols are responsible for creating and destroying routes within a router's routing table. These are dynamic routes, so named because they change along with the internetwork's changing topology. If a link goes down or is taken off the network for some reason, a routing protocol will detect the change and make the appropriate changes to the

Figure 5.4 Stub networks.

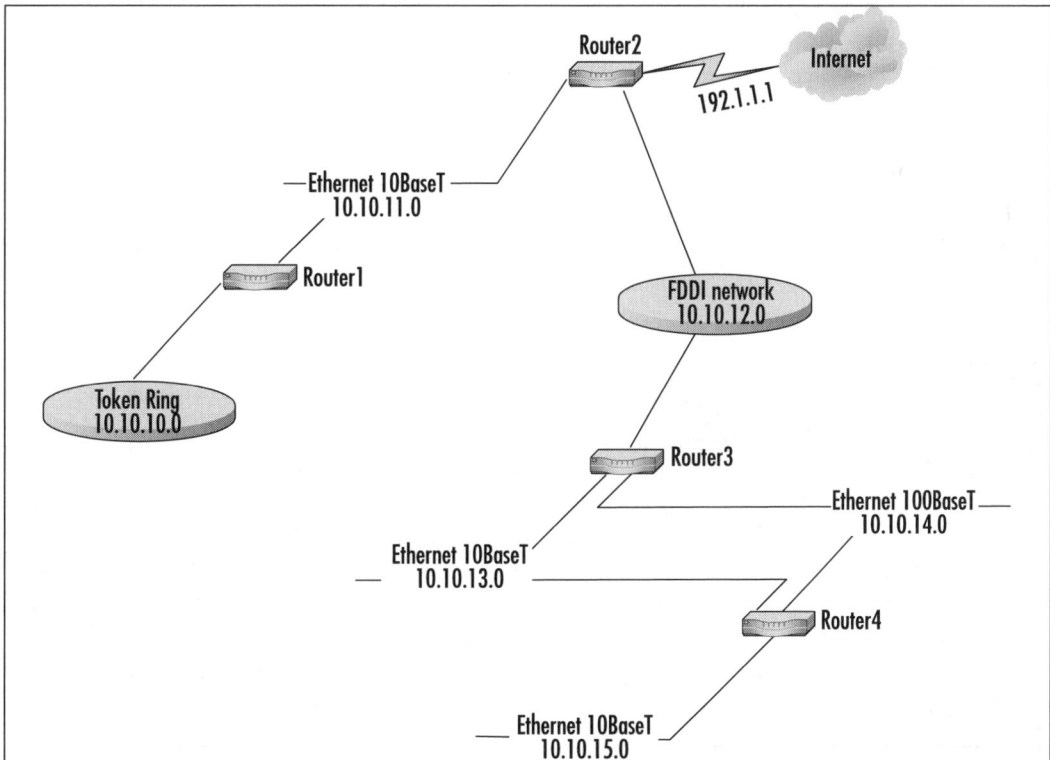

routing table based on its route detection mechanisms. The time it takes for a routing change to propagate throughout an internetwork is called its *convergence time*. Dynamic routes save administrators a great deal of time and effort when compared to static routes.

WARNING

Once you learn about routing protocols, it is difficult to imagine that anyone would configure a router to function without one. But it is not necessary to have any routing protocols running on a router in order for routing of data to occur. Routing protocols do not route data, they dynamically establish route listings in the routing table.

RIP

Routing Information Protocol (RIP) is a dynamic distance vector routing protocol. Distance means that the routing protocol detects the distance, usually in number of hops, to a destination network. Vector means that the routing protocol determines the direction, in the form of which network, in which the packet needs to be sent. RIP is sometimes confusing because both the IP stack and the IPX stack have a RIP distance vector protocol. These are not the same protocol, but are similar in nature and perform the same function. IP RIP simply performs it for IP packets, and IPX RIP performs it for IPX packets. IP RIP has been developed in two forms—RIP 1 and RIP 2. RIP 2 includes more information in RIP packets and enables authentication.

NOTE

You can learn more about RIP in Request for Comments (RFCs) on the Internet. IP RIP is described in RFC 1058 and 1723. You can find these at www.cis.ohio-state.edu/hypertext/information/rfc.html.

Updating the Routing Table

RIP uses a single metric value for measuring the distance between the sending and receiving hosts. This is called the hop count, and measures the number of routers on the path between the two hosts. RIP considers all hop counts above 15 to be "infinity," or unreachable.

RIP updates the routing table by sending routing-update messages at regular intervals (every 30 seconds). It also sends routing-update messages when the network topology changes. When one of the routing updates includes a change from the receiving router's routing table entries, the router updates its routing table to reflect the new route, incrementing the metric value for the number of hops by one. Then the router broadcasts the new route to its neighbors. The only time the router does not broadcast a new route is when that route is more than 15 hops away.

Routing Loops

A routing loop is caused when a packet travels back and forth over the same network paths. This can happen when the network topology changes, especially since routers depend on information received from their neighbors.

In Figure 5.5, for example, if the link between RTR3 and RTR4 were to go down, RTR3 would send out an update that it no longer had a route to Network C. But RTR1 would hear from RTR2 that it had a route to Network C, not knowing that it too was through RTR3, and would change its routing table to send all packets bound for Network C through RTR2. RTR3 would hear from RTR1 that it had the new route to Network C and would update all its packets to go to RTR1 that are bound for Network C. By then, RTR3 would tell RTR2 that it had a new route and RTR2 would update its routing table with the new hop count. RTR1 would hear about the new route and update its routing table. The network flood of RIP packets would continue until the hop count finally reached 16. For all intents and purposes, the network has been flooded with useless information. This process can create a denial of service condition.

Figure 5.5 Network example for routing loops.

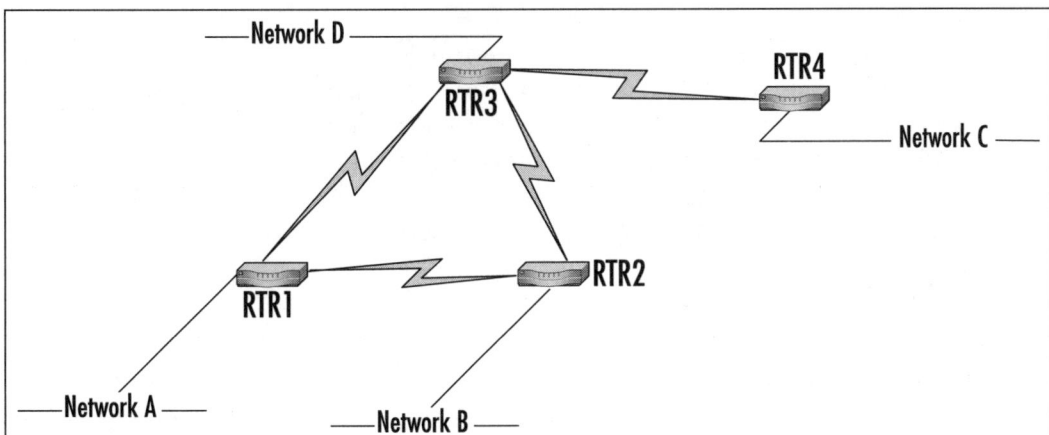

To counteract routing loops, RIP includes a split horizon algorithm and hold-down timers. Split horizon is a mechanism in which a router does not broadcast routing information back along the path from which that information was received. Poison reverse is a variation of split horizon, in which the router does broadcast the routes back, but attaches an unreachable hop count to them so that the effect is the same. For example, in Figure 5.5, RTR2 would not send a route that it heard from RTR1 back to RTR1, or vice versa. The hold-down timers do not allow a topology change to be updated until a period of time has passed, thus enabling all routers to converge with the knowledge that a route is unavailable before an invalid route can be broadcast.

Cisco routers use RIP timers to regulate the way that RIP performs on the network.

Routing update timer The interval between periodic updates can be changed from the default of 30 seconds.

Route timeout The timeout for each routing table entry. If the routing table entry is not updated within this period, it is marked invalid in the routing table.

Route-flush timeout The route table entry that is marked invalid will wait this amount of time before the router flushes the route completely from its table.

Configuring RIP on a Cisco Router

When you enable a routing protocol on a Cisco router, it is enabled for all interfaces. For that reason, the routing protocol commands are performed in global configuration mode. To enable RIP, use the following global configuration command:

```
Router rip
```

To limit the networks to which the router should send its routing updates, you can follow the router **rip** command with the following global configuration command, replacing the *network-ip-address* with the range of networks to which you wanted to forward RIP updates. For example, if you wanted to send routing updates to 199.5.1.0 through 199.5.255.0, you would replace the *network-ip-address* parameter with 199.5.0.0, which would encompass all of them:

```
Network network-ip-address
```

Configuring RIP on a Windows 2000 Server

Routing via RIP must be enabled on a Windows 2000 Server only when it has more than one network interface card. To add RIP 2 for IP:

1. Begin in the Routing and Remote Access console, which is found in the Administrative Tools menu. (For this procedure to work, you should already have completed the Routing and Remote Access Server Setup Wizard for this Windows 2000 Server.)

2. Add the server by right-clicking the Routing and Remote Access root, as shown in Figure 5.6, and selecting Add Server.

Figure 5.6 Adding a server in the Routing and Remote Access console.

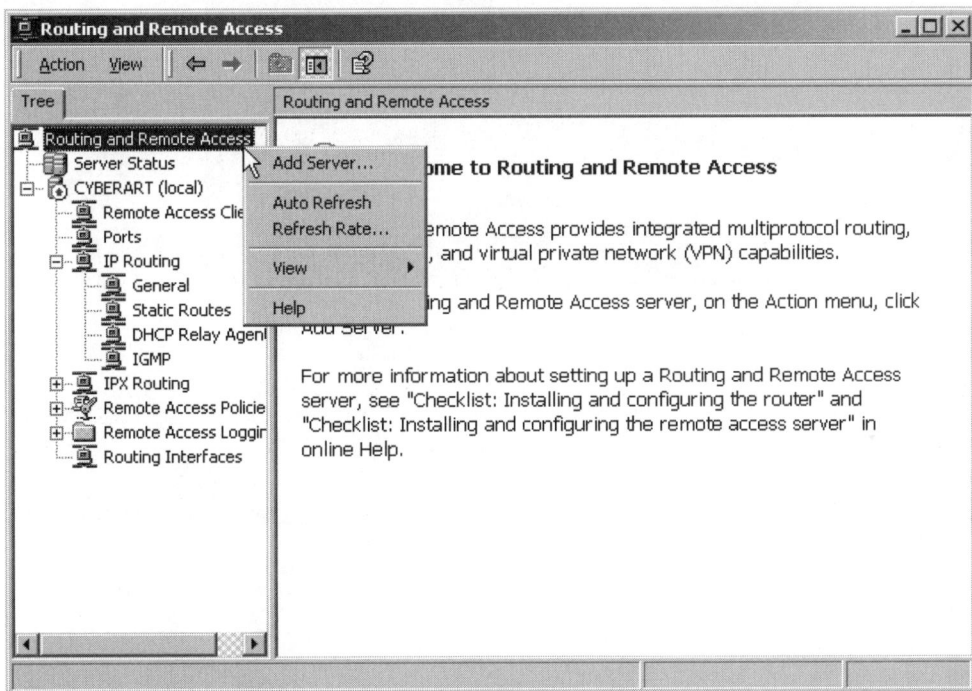

3. Enable routing on the server by right-clicking the server you just added.

4. Select Properties from the pop-up menu. The General tab should appear, as shown in Figure 5.7.

5. Make certain to check the box next to Router and select whether this will be for the LAN or for both the LAN and remote access connections using demand dial routing.

Figure 5.7 Enabling Routing on a server.

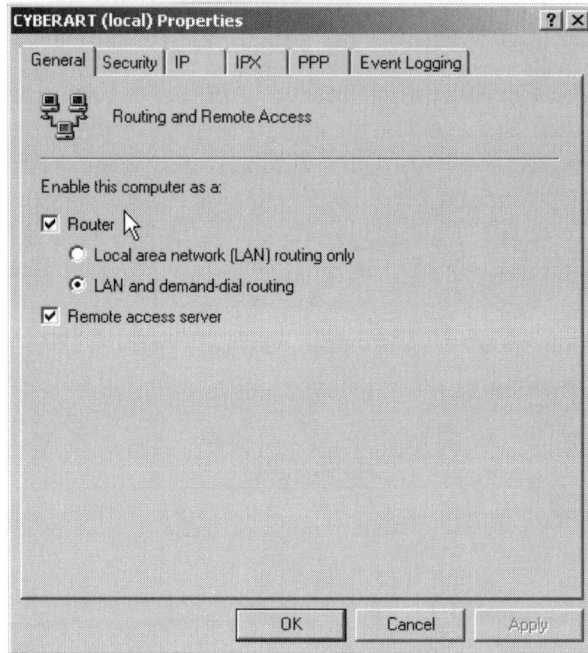

Figure 5.8 Adding RIP.

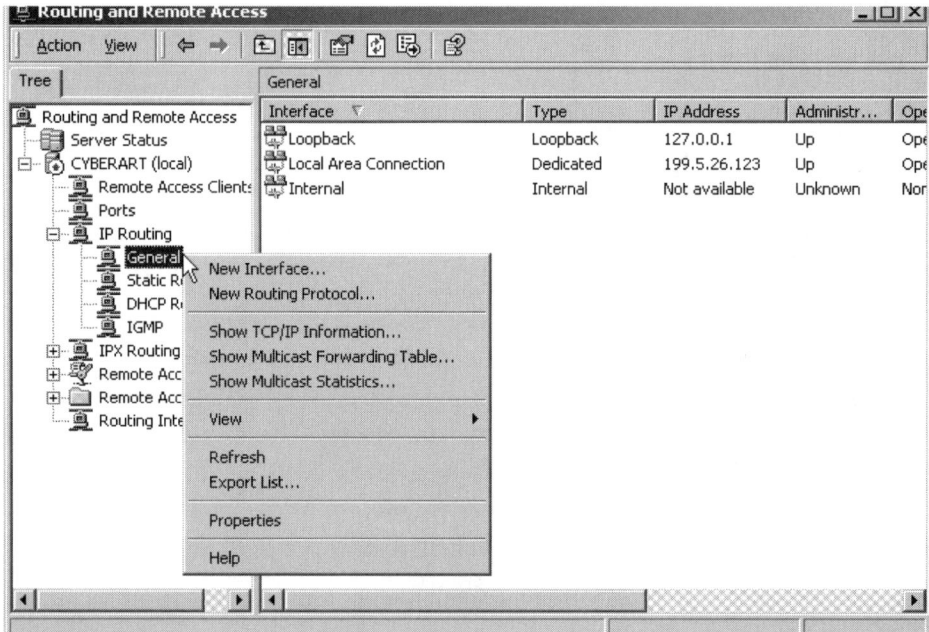

6. Click the IP tab and make certain the Enable IP Routing check box is checked.

7. Add RIP as the routing protocol by expanding the items below the server in the left-hand frame of the RRAS Console window. Below the server, you should see an IP Routing item. This, too, needs to be expanded.

8. Right-click the General item as shown in Figure 5.8.

9. Select New Routing Protocol from the pop-up menu. The New Routing Protocol dialog will appear.

10. Select RIP Version 2 for Internet Protocol and click the OK button. RIP will appear as a new item below IP Routing in the RRAS Console hierarchy.

11. Add the interfaces to the RIP Routing by right-clicking on RIP as shown in Figure 5.9.

12. Select New Interface.

13. Choose the interface that will be using RIP.

14. Click the OK button.

Figure 5.9 Adding a RIP Interface.

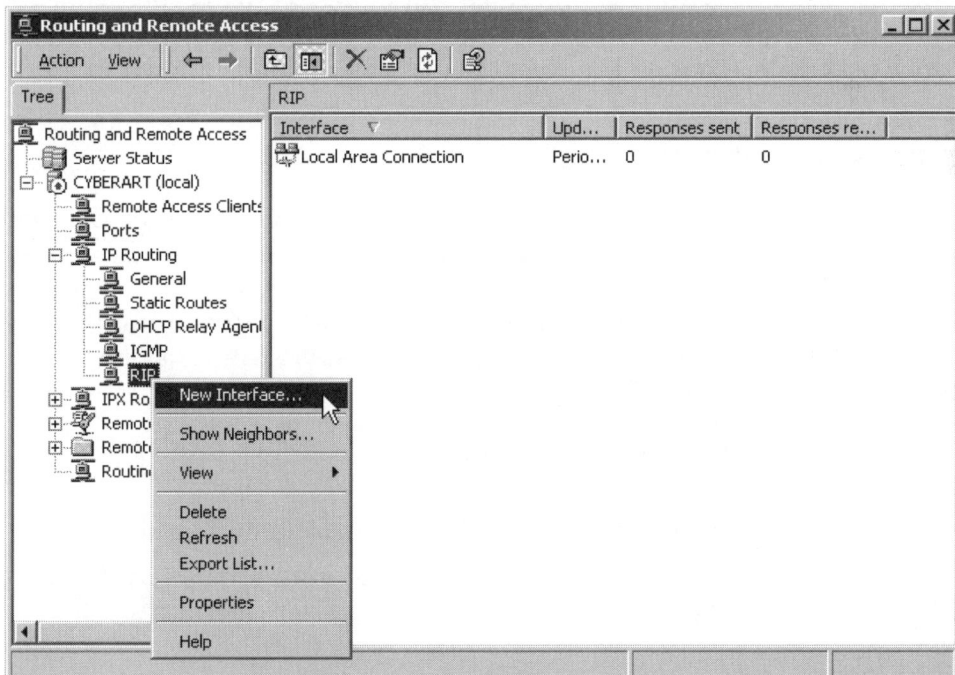

Figure 5.10 Configuring RIP properties.

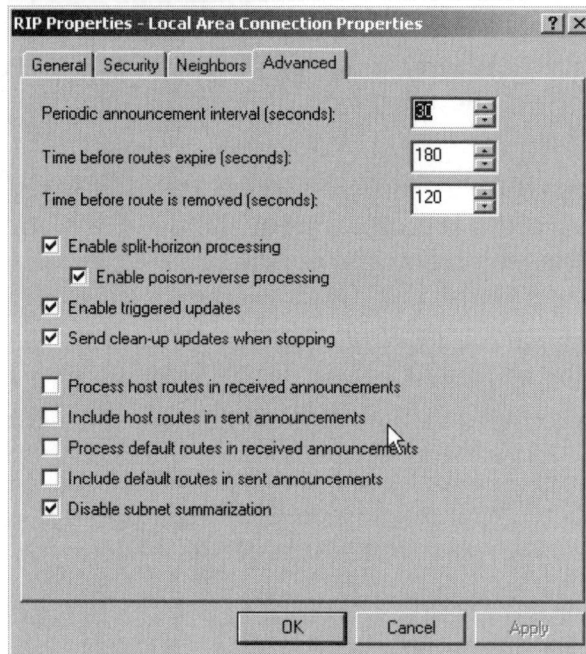

The RIP properties for that interface will appear. This is the dialog for configuring RIP options. On the Advanced tab, you can select whether to use split horizon or change the RIP timers. This dialog is shown in Figure 5.10.

IGRP and EIGRP

Interior Gateway Routing Protocol (IGRP) and Enhanced Interior Gateway Routing Protocol (EIGRP) are not available in Windows 2000. These are distance vector routing protocols created by Cisco. If you use both Cisco routers and Windows 2000 routing in your network, you will not be able to use IGRP or EIGRP to handle routing table updates on both systems.

IGRP advertises three kinds of routes:

- Interior, routes between subnets in the network attached to a router interface

- System, routes to networks within an autonomous system (AS)

- Exterior, routes to networks outside the autonomous system, typically used for default routes

> **NOTE**
>
> Many routing protocols will define areas within an enterprise network in order to "divide and conquer" the issues with routing. These areas are called autonomous systems, and are generally a set of routers that all connect to each other and are all managed by the same administrative unit. Sometimes autonomous systems are defined for routers with similar routing policies.

IGRP sends update broadcasts every 90 seconds. A route table entry is considered unreachable if it is not updated within three update periods. After seven update periods, the route is flushed from the routing table. IGRP speeds up the convergence time of the network by using flash updates, which send an update sooner than the periodic update interval, and poison reverse updates, which defeat routing loops by placing a route in a hold-down mode when it is being removed so that new routing information cannot be used until the hold-down is released.

Configuring IGRP on a Cisco Router

There are several steps to configuring IGRP on a Cisco router. The first step is to enable it for the autonomous system of which the router will be a part. This is done with the global configuration mode command:

```
Router igrp autonomous-system-number
```

The next step is to add the networks with which the router will exchange IGRP information. This is a global configuration command that should follow the router **igrp** command.

```
Network network-number
```

If you have a router that must exchange IGRP routing updates with a nonbroadcast network, then the neighboring router must be defined with the following global configuration command:

```
Neighbor ip-address
```

To adjust the IGRP timers and enhance the performance of the IGRP routing updates, you can use the timers' basic command in global configuration mode. This command has several parameters:

update Changes the periodic interval in seconds at which routing updates are transmitted.

invalid Changes the time in seconds during which a route remains invalid before being flushed.

holddown Changes the amount of time in seconds for which no new information about a routing path is used after the old route entry was declared invalid.

flush Changes the interval before a route is flushed from the routing table.

sleeptime Specifies the time that you can suspend routing updates.

The command is simply:

```
Timers basic update invalid holddown flush [sleeptime]
```

EIGRP

EIGRP is just what it sounds like—an upgraded version of IGRP. It uses the Diffusing Update Algorithm (DUAL) to reduce a complex internetwork's convergence time to five seconds or less. It supports variable-length subnet masks (VLSMs) and unequal load balancing across multiple networks. To add EIGRP to a router, use the following commands in global configuration mode. The EIGRP commands are nearly identical to IGRP commands.

```
Router eigrp autonomous-system
Network network-ip-address
```

OSPF

Open Shortest Path First (OSPF) is a link state protocol. Like RIP, both Windows 2000 routers and Cisco routers support OSPF routing updates. Cisco OSPF routers can redistribute routes that it has learned via RIP or IGRP to other OSPF routers. OSPF can be configured as

- Area border routers (ABRs), which are connected to multiple areas
- Autonomous System Boundary Routers (ASBRs), which are connected to an autonomous system and an external network

Configuring OSPF on a Cisco Router

The first step to setting up OSPF on a Cisco router is to enable it. Then you need to associate the network address range and area ID for the OSPF routing protocol. This is done in global configuration mode. These commands are:

```
Router ospf process-id
Network ip-address wildcard-mask area area-id
```

Once OSPF is enabled on the router you can configure parameters that are specific to each interface. This is necessary since, in the cases of ABRs and ASBRs, the router will have an interface connected to one area or autonomous system, and another interface connected to a different area, autonomous system, or external network. You can use these parameters to enhance the performance of OSPF on the network, although using the defaults is usually fine:

Ip ospf cost *cost* Defines a custom cost for transmitting packets.

Ip ospf retransmit-interval *seconds* States the number of seconds between link-state acknowledgement (LSA) packet retransmissions.

Ip ospf transmit-delay *seconds* States the number of seconds to send a Link-State Update (LSU) packet.

Ip ospf priority *number* Sets a priority so that OSPF can determine which router is the Designated Router (DR) for the network.

Ip ospf hello-interval *seconds* Sets the time between hello packets for OSPF to send out.

Ip ospf dead-interval *seconds* Sets the time that a router does not see a hello packet before the router declares the neighboring router down.

Ip ospf authentication-key *key* Defines a password that must be used by neighboring OSPF routers when using OSPF simple passwords.

Ip ospf message-digest-key *key-id* **md5** *key* Enables the MD5 form of authentication. *key-id* and *key* parameters must match those specified for all OSPF routers connected to the same network segment.

When you configure the OSPF areas, you can use the following commands. Note that stub areas must use default routing, because external route information is not transmitted within the stub area. Instead the routers point to a default route outside of the stub area.

Area *area-id* **authentication** Specifies that authentication is going to be used in the area.

Area *area-id* **authentication message-digest** Sets authentication to use MD5.

Area *area-id* **stub [no-summary]** Defines an area to be a stub.

Area *area-id* **default-cost** *cost* Assigns the cost for the default route used in the stub area.

Configuring OSPF on a Windows 2000 Computer

OSPF is configured in the same Routing and Remote Access Console in which RIP is configured. Nearly identical steps can be used to configure OSPF:

1. Open the Routing and Remote Access Console from the Administrative Tools menu. You should already have completed the Routing and Remote Access Server Setup Wizard before starting this series of steps.

2. If the server is not added as a RRAS server, right-click the Routing and Remote Access root.

3. Select Add Server from the pop-up menu.

4. Right-click the server.

5. Select Properties from the pop-up menu.

6. Check the box next to Router on the General tab and select whether it is a LAN or LAN plus remote access connections using Demand Dial Routing.

7. Click the IP tab.

8. Check the Enable IP Routing checkbox.

9. Expand the IP Routing item below the server.

10. Right-click on General below IP Routing.

11. Select New Routing Protocol from the pop-up menu.

12. In the New Routing Protocol dialog, select OSPF and click OK.

VPN

Virtual private networks (VPNs) leverage the Internet to provide access to private networks for remote users. A VPN is a tunnel from a remote client through a public network to a private network, creating a connection that emulates a direct connection to the private network. Data that travels across the VPN connection is encrypted.

A VPN requires the following components:

VPN Server Provides VPN connections to remote access clients or routers.

VPN Clients Hosts—either client computers or routers—that initiate VPN connections to the VPN server.

Encapsulation Private data is encapsulated with a header allowing data to traverse the public internetwork.

Tunnel The path that the data travels.

Encryption Private data is encrypted at the sending VPN host (either client or server) and decrypted at the receiving end.

Authentication The VPN server verifies that the VPN client has appropriate permissions for access to the private network.

IPSec

Internet Protocol Security (IPSec) enables VPN protocols to create secure tunnels between devices by providing secure transmission of data across a public network, provides authentication mechanisms, and enables confidentiality of data. IPSec components include the following:

- IPSec tunnels use the Authentication Header (AH) protocol to encapsulate the original IP packet in another IP packet with a new IP header—the AH header. AH can authenticate the data source, but the AH header does not provide data confidentiality.

- IPSec tunnels use the Encapsulating Security Payload (ESP) protocol to provide data confidentiality by encrypting the original IP packet and attaching an ESP header with an IP header, plus an ESP trailer. ESP also enables data source authentication through an authenticator, which can be turned off by setting it to null.

IPSec tunnels may use AH with ESP, or ESP alone, to provide a fully confidential tunnel. Two components are used for encryption within IPSec—a cipher and a secret key. The cipher is an algorithm that converts data to an encrypted form. The cipher uses the secret key to decrypt the data. IPSec supports Data Encryption Standard (DES) and Triple Data Encryption Standard (3DES). In DES, a single secret key is used to encrypt data and to decrypt it. In 3DES, three secret keys are used. The first key is used to encrypt, the second key is used to partially decrypt, and the third key is used to encrypt again. IPSec encryption is applied to packets at Layer 3, the network layer in the OSI Reference model.

Configuring IPSec on Cisco Routers

When configuring IPSec on Cisco routers, you will use crypto map sets. Crypto maps originally were supported under Cisco IOS v11.2; however, the commands were enhanced in IOS v11.3 T and later versions with additional keywords, as shown next. A crypto map set maps its entries to access lists that permit or deny access, and then to tag a packet that is permitted by the access list as a certain type. Crypto map entries are similar to access lists in that they are searched in order. When an entry tags the packet as ipsec-isakmp or ipsec-manual, then IPSec is being used (isakmp stands for Internet Security Association and Key Management Protocol). The difference between ipsec-isakmp and ipsec-manual is that ipsec-isakmp will use Internet Key Exchange protocol (IKE) to protect the traffic that has no security association, whereas ipsec-manual will drop traffic that has no security association. Crypto maps can transform unsecured traffic that is received by a router; otherwise that unsecured traffic (i.e., any packets that are not using IPSec) is dropped.

When configuring IPSec on a router, you will need to ascertain whether existing access lists are IPSec compatible, as well as create access lists that are specifically compatible with IPSec. Because IPSec ESP and AH protocols use TCP ports 50 and 51, and IKE uses UDP port 500, you will need to ensure that these ports are not blocked for all interfaces that use IPSec. The following process is used to configure IPSec on Cisco routers:

1. In global configuration mode, set the timed lifetime and traffic-volume lifetime for security associations. The default is 3600 seconds for the timed lifetime and 4,608,000 kilobytes for the traffic-volume lifetime. (If you wish to change lifetimes after you have already created security associations, you will need to use the **clear crypto sa** command first.) To change the timed lifetime, type **crypto ipsec security-association lifetime seconds** *number*, where *number* is the new number of seconds before the security association times out. To change the traffic-volume lifetime, type **crypto ipsec security-association lifetime kilobytes** *number*, where *number* is the new number of kilobytes to use IPSec in a tunnel before the security association times out.

2. Create crypto access lists in global configuration mode. Cisco recommends that each peer is given a mirror image access list to ensure that data is easily secured. Type the command access-list access-list-number {deny | permit} protocol source source-wildcard destination destination-wildcard [precedence precedence] [tos tos] [log]. Using the permit statement means that you will be protecting the data.

3. Your next task is to define transform sets. The command to do this is **crypto ipsec transform-set** *transform-set-name transform1 [transform2] [transform3]*. You can use only one of the following transforms for AH protocol: *ah-md5-hmac*, *ah-sha-hmac*, and *ah-rfc1828*. You can use either *esp-des* or *esp-rfc1829* for ESP encryption protocol. If you select the esp-des transform, you can also use either *esp-md5-hmac* or *esp-sha-hmac* for ESP authentication protocol.

4. With the crypto access lists ready and the transforms selected, you can now specify the entries for the crypto map set. Create crypto map entries with the same crypto map name, but with different crypto map sequence numbers to group them into a crypto map set. Only one crypto map set can be applied to a single interface, but can include both Cisco Encryption Technology (CET) and IPSec entries. To create the entries for IPSec in manual mode, use the global configuration command **crypto map** *map-name map-number* **ipsec-manual**. (To use IPSec with IKE, replace the parameter ipsec-manual with ipsec-isakmp.) This command will place you in crypto map configuration mode. Follow up this command with **match address** *access-list-identifier* to specify the access list. Then use the command **set peer** *[hostname | ip-address]* to specify the IPSec peer where the secured traffic will be forwarded. The crypto map needs to select a transform, so then use the command **set transform-set** *transform-set-name*. If the transform uses AH, then you must use the **set session-key inbound ah** *spi hex-key-data* and **set session-key outbound ah** *spi hex-key-data* commands to establish the security parameter indices (SPI) and the keys (in hexadecimal format). If the transform uses ESP, then you must use the **set session-key inbound esp** *spi* **cipher** *hex-key-data* **[authenticator** *hex-key-data]* and **set session-key outbound esp** *spi* **cipher** *hex-key-data* **[authenticator** *hex-key-data]* commands. Use the **exit** command to go back to global configuration mode.

5. Now you must apply the crypto map set to the interface to which it belongs. This is done with a single command in interface configuration mode: **crypto map** *map-name*.

Configuring IPSec on Windows 2000

To configure IPSec, you will need to use the Microsoft Management Console (MMC) for IP Security Policy Management.

1. Click Start.
2. Click Run.
3. Type MMC and click OK.
4. Select the Console menu and choose Add/Remove Snap-in.
5. Click Add.
6. Double-click IP Security Policy Management. If the computer is a domain controller or member of a domain, you may select whether

the scope of the IPSec Policy Management will be for the local computer, another computer, the local domain, or another domain.

7. Click Close and then OK.

8. To save the console to be used again, select the Console menu and choose Save.

9. Type a title for the console and click Save. The console will now appear in Administrative Tools.

To configure a workstation to use IPSec and to use a specific IP Security Policy, do the following:

1. Right-click My Network Places on the desktop.

2. Select Properties from the pop-up menu. The Network and Dial-up Connections window will open.

3. Right-click the connection that will use IPSec, and select Properties from the pop-up menu.

4. Click Internet Protocol (TCP/IP) as indicated in Figure 5.11, then click the Properties button.

Figure 5.11 Connection Properties dialog.

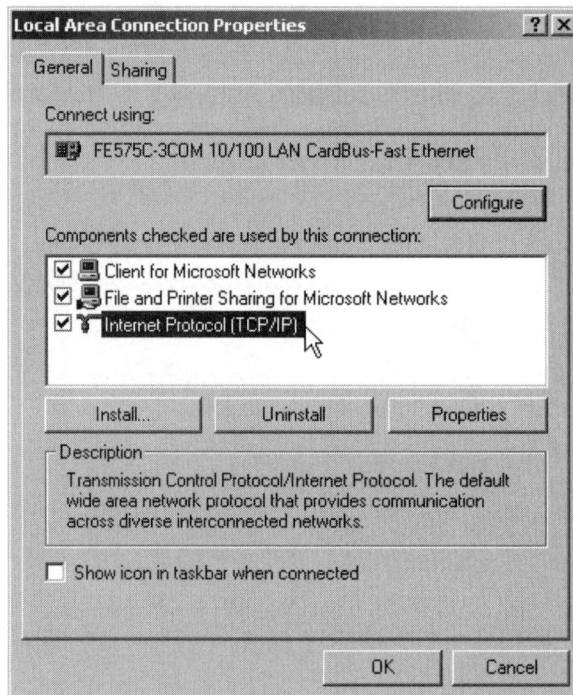

Figure 5.12 IP Security Policy selection.

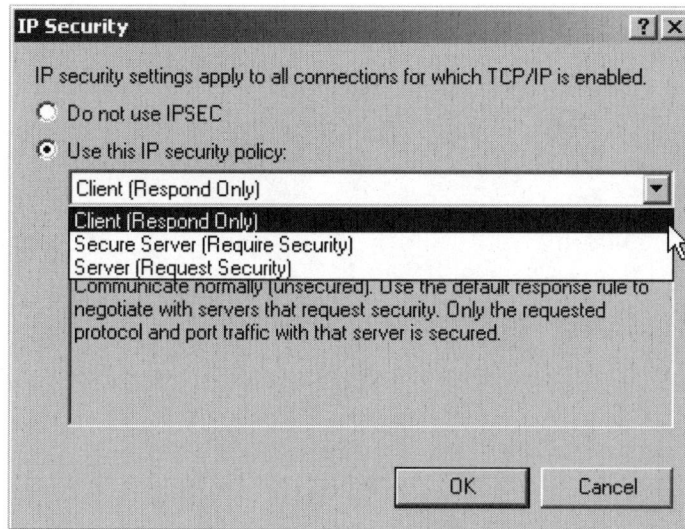

5. Click the Advanced button.

6. Click the Options tab.

7. Select IP security and then click the Properties button.

8. Click the radio button to use IP Security and then choose the security policy from the drop-down box as shown in Figure 5.12. There are three options available: the Client security policy, which is only for IPSec response; the Secure Server policy, which requires IPSec to be used; and the Server policy, which will request IPSec to be used.

L2TP

The Layer 2 Tunneling Protocol (L2TP) is an Internet Engineering Task Force (IETF) standard that extends the Point-to-Point Protocol. L2TP supports multiple protocols, due to its PPP relation, as well as private IP addressing over the Internet. L2TP can be used with remote access infrastructure, including modems, ISDN, and DSL technology. Figure 5.13 illustrates the L2TP tunnel.

Figure 5.13 L2TP tunnel.

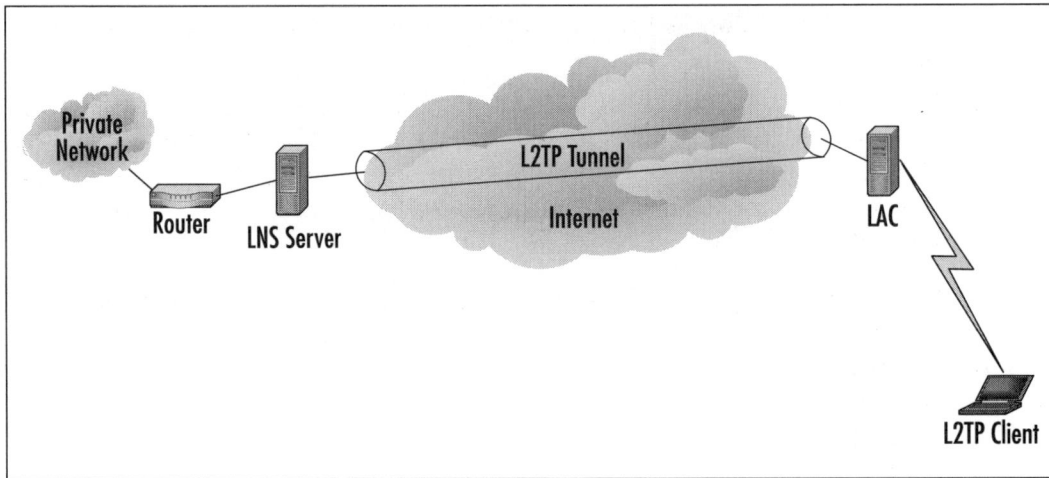

Two components of the L2TP tunnel are:

- L2TP access concentrator (LAC), a device to which a client connects directly as a network access server. From here, PPP frames are tunneled to the L2TP network server (LNS).

- L2TP Network Server (LNS), the server at the end of the L2TP tunnel that accepts L2TP/PPP frames and passes them to higher layer protocols.

L2TP creates the concept of the virtual access interface. This concept provides that each client connecting via L2TP is assigned an instance of a virtual interface, unique on the server. A virtual template interface can be created for the basis of all virtual access interfaces, providing common configurations. The LAC exchanges PPP messages with remote users, while exchanging L2TP requests and responses with the LNS at the other side of each L2TP tunnel created with a virtual access interface for the remote users. Connecting via L2TP works in the following sequence:

1. A remote user dials up to ISP and creates a PPP connection with the ISP's LAC.

2. The LAC partially authenticates the remote user with Challenge Handshake Authentication Protocol (CHAP) or Password Authentication Protocol (PAP). The LAC determines if the user can be connected to the LNS and if so, does so.

3. The LAC authenticates the LNS and vice versa. Then a tunnel is created.

4. The L2TP session is initiated for the remote user between the LAC and LNS.

5. The LAC forwards the CHAP or PAP information to the LNS, which forwards it directly to the virtual access interface for the session. If the information is correct, the session negotiation is completed and the session is established. If incorrect, the remote user is disconnected.

L2TP tunneled data is processed through a series of headers. When a header is processed, it is read for its information, acted on, and then dropped off the packet and discarded. An L2TP server receiving an L2TP packet will process the Data Link header and trailer first. The IP header is processed next. Then the IPSec ESP Auth Trailer is processed for authentication of the IPSec ESP Header and remaining data. The IPSec ESP Header is processed next, and the encrypted packet data is decrypted. The UDP header is processed and the L2TP header is reviewed for the Tunnel ID and Call ID to specify the L2TP tunnel. Then the PPP Header is processed to access the remaining data and to process it at the upper protocol layers. The L2TP packet structure is illustrated in Figure 5.14.

Figure 5.14 L2TP packet structure.

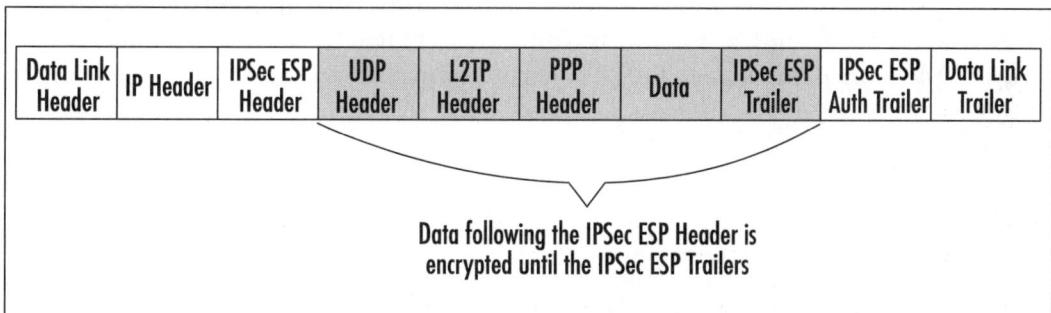

Data following the IPSec ESP Header is encrypted until the IPSec ESP Trailers

Configuring L2TP on a Cisco Router

You will need to configure L2TP on the LAC as well as the LNS. To configure the LAC, use the following commands:

```
Aaa new-model
Aaa authentication ppp default local
Username myname password l2tp1234
```

```
Vpdn enable
Vpdn group group-number
Request dialin [l2tp|l2f] ip ip-address {domain domain-name|
dnis dialed-number}
```

These commands will accomplish the following:

- Enable authentication globally
- Enable authentication for PPP
- Define a username as "myname" and password as "l2tp1234"
- Enable vpdn to look for tunnel definitions
- Define the local group number
- Let the router request a dial-in tunnel to an IP address

To configure the LNS, use the following commands. Note that these are nearly identical to the LAC, except for the final command, which configures the LNS to accept dial-in requests from a LAC and assigns the virtual template to use for access interfaces.

```
Aaa new-model
Aaa authentication ppp default local
Username myname password l2tp1234
```

Here, the LNS needs to have additional commands applied. These are all geared to creating the virtual template interface. To configure the virtual template interface, use the following commands:

```
Interface virtual-template number
Ip unnumbered ethernet 0
Encapsulation ppp
Ppp authentication pap|chap
```

Complete the LNS configuration with the same commands used on the LAC:

```
Vpdn enable
Vpdn group group-number
Accept dialin [l2tp|l2f|any] virtual-template virtual-template-number
remote remote-peer-name
```

Windows 2000 and L2TP

L2TP uses UDP to send packets of tunneled data as well as tunnel maintenance control. Windows 2000 clients are L2TP compliant, and do not
require the LAC to create the L2TP tunnel; instead, the client creates the
L2TP tunnel by interacting with the LNS. Both the Windows 2000 L2TP
client and a Windows 2000 L2TP server (LNS) use UDP port 1701, although
the server can be configured to use another port as well. Windows 2000
L2TP clients use IPSec's ESP for encryption.

To create an L2TP VPN connection in Windows 2000, you begin with
the Network and Dial-up Connections dialog found in the Control Panel.
You can also access this dialog by right-clicking the My Network Places
icon on the desktop and selecting Properties from the pop-up menu.

1. Double-click the Make New Connection icon.

2. Click Next.

3. Select Connect to a private network through the Internet .

4. Click Next.

5. You can select an existing dial-up connection, or if you are already
   connected to the Internet, select Do not dial the initial connection.

6. Click Next.

7. Type the IP address or hostname of the LNS.

8. Click Next.

9. Select whether this is a connection to be made available for all
   users or just for the currently logged on user. (If you are enabling
   the connection for all users, you will be prompted for Internet
   Connection Sharing. If you wish to make this connection available
   to other users on the local area network, then make the selection.)

10. Click Next.

11. Type a name for the connection.

12. Click Finish.

To ensure that this connection will connect only to L2TP servers, you
can configure the connection's properties. Right-click the new icon in the
Network and Dial-up Connections window and select Properties from the
pop-up menu. Click the Networking tab. Drop down the box for Type of
VPN server I am calling and select Layer-2 Tunneling Protocol (L2TP) as
shown in Figure 5.15.

You may need to change the authentication settings for the connection.
To do so, click the Security tab. Select the Advanced (Custom Settings)
radio button and click the Settings button. Figure 5.16 shows the available
authentication options.

Figure 5.15 Configuring a connection for L2TP.

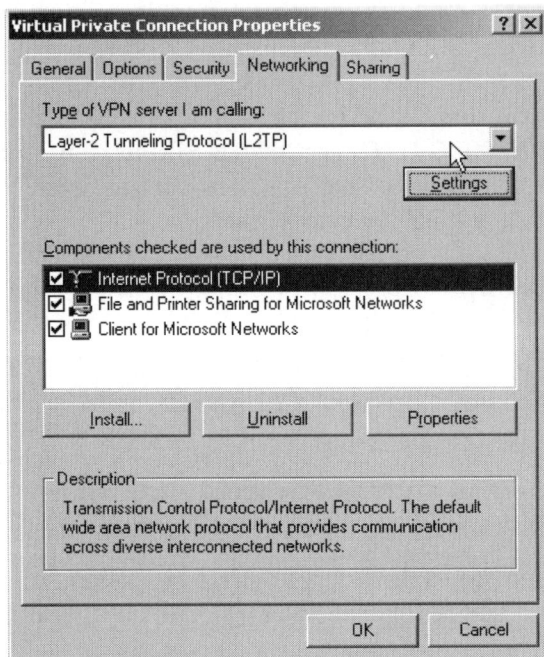

Figure 5.16 Advanced security options for a connection.

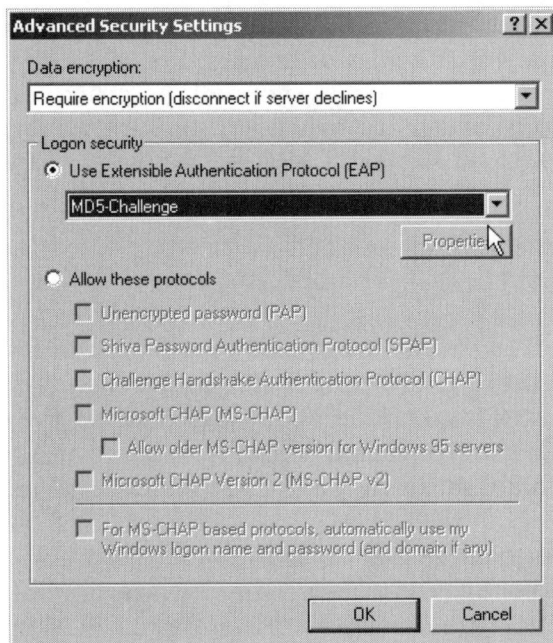

PPTP

The Point-to-Point Tunneling Protocol (PPTP) provides a method of tunneling PPP frames within IP datagrams to connect securely over the Internet. Microsoft developed PPTP to create, maintain, and terminate tunnels using encapsulated PPP frames.

NOTE

L2TP is based partially on Microsoft's PPTP. It is also based partially on Cisco's Layer 2 Forwarding (L2F) Protocol. Whereas both PPTP and L2F are proprietary VPN protocols, L2TP is an open standard. Many NT networks may be using PPTP as the VPN system. When upgrading to Windows 2000, it can be tempting simply to leave the existing PPTP system in place. However, it is recommended that an upgrade of the PPTP system to L2TP be considered, especially with the security concerns about PPTP. An analysis of the security concerns can be found at www.counterpane.com/pptp.html.

PPTP uses TCP port 1723. PPTP Control Connection packets provide PPTP tunnel maintenance. PPTP packets provide tunneled data, and their structure is illustrated in Figure 5.17. Note that the PPP frame is encapsulated with a Generic Routing Encapsulation (GRE) header. GRE is covered in RFCs 1701 and 2784.

Some Internet service providers configure their routers to filter out GRE packets because they use GRE packets for routing information. This can cause PPTP tunneled data not to be forwarded across the Internet, but can be remedied by removing the GRE filters or changing to L2TP.

Figure 5.17 PPTP Tunneled Data Packet structure.

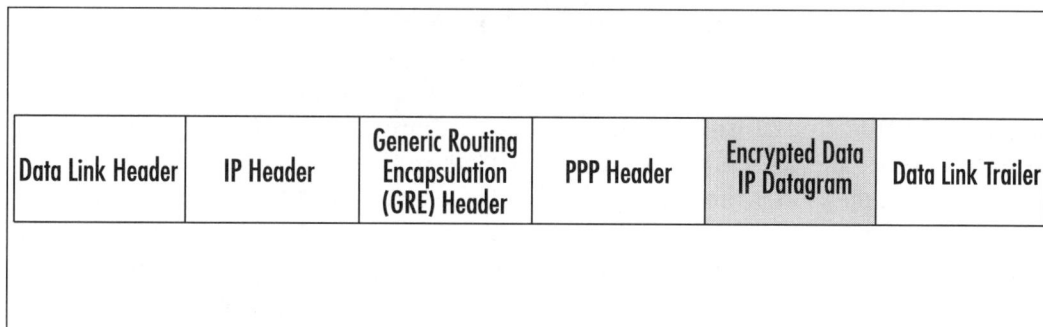

Data Link Header	IP Header	Generic Routing Encapsulation (GRE) Header	PPP Header	Encrypted Data IP Datagram	Data Link Trailer

Configuring Windows 2000 PPTP Connection

A nearly identical process is used to create a PPTP connection in Windows 2000 as that used to create an L2TP connection. Start with the Network and Dial-up Connections dialog found in the Control Panel.

1. Double-click the Make New Connection icon.
2. Click Next.
3. Select Connect to a private network through the Internet.
4. Click Next.
5. You can select an existing dial-up connection, or if you are already connected to the Internet, select Do not dial the initial connection.
6. Click Next.
7. Type the IP address or host name of the PPTP server .
8. Click Next.
9. Select whether this is a connection to be made available for all users or just for the currently logged on user. (If you are enabling the connection for all users, you will be prompted for Internet Connection Sharing. If you wish to make this connection available to other users on the local area network, then make the selection.)
10. Click Next.
11. Type a name for the connection.
12. Click Finish. The connection will be defaulted to automatic. To specify PPTP, you should right-click the new connection icon and select properties from the pop-up menu. Then click the Networking tab and choose PPTP from the drop-down box.

Summary

Remote access and routing are tightly integrated functions. A remote access server is, essentially, a router. When a remote user dials into a remote access server, access to the rest of the network must be granted by routing the remote user's requests to the various requested resources. Because of this tight integration, it is not uncommon to see routing and remote access services combined on a single network component.

Remote access services are provided for clients that have access to analog lines and modems, and are also provided for Digital Subscriber Line (DSL) and Integrated Services Digital Network (ISDN) clients. The most widely available remote access method is the usage of analog lines and modems. Users dial up to remote access servers over these modems using either Serial Line Internet Protocol (SLIP) or Point-to-Point Protocol (PPP).

ISDN and DSL are digital access methods over copper telephone lines. ISDN offers identical upload and download speeds for one of two configurations. Basic Rate Interface (BRI) offers 128 Kbps using two bearer (B) channels at 64 Kbps each, and one data (D) channel at 16 Kbps. BRI can run over standard telephone lines. Primary Rate Interface (PRI) offers 1.472 Mbps using 23 B channels at 64 Kbps and 1 D channel at 64 Kbps. PRI must run across a T1 line.

DSL is most commonly implemented as an Asymmetric Digital Subscriber Line (ADSL), although other configurations are emerging, such as Very High Data Rate Digital Subscriber Line (VDSL). ADSL is considered asymmetric because the upload and download rates are different. The upload rate is much slower than the download rate. These rates vary based on the length of the wire from the local office, but typically are up to 9 Mbps for downloads, and up to 640 Kbps for uploads. ADSL is appropriate for remote users or remote offices.

SLIP is a legacy protocol created for UNIX machines to dial into a network over an analog line and modem. SLIP is the precursor of PPP. PPP is far more commonly used. Users can run PPP over ISDN, DSL, and analog lines.

Routing protocols are used not to route the data from one network segment to another, but to dynamically discover and maintain routes in a router's routing table. A routing protocol can greatly reduce the administrative overhead of a network.

Routing Information Protocol (RIP) is a distance vector routing protocol for TCP/IP. Actually, RIP-2, a newer version of RIP, is most often the version that is implemented. As a distance vector protocol, RIP logs the distance, in number of hops, to the destination network as well as the direction, or vector, to that destination. This information is maintained in a routing table that is broadcast periodically to the router's neighboring routers.

RIP is susceptible to routing loops in which a router's broadcast of a route is returned to itself as though it were a new route, at which point the router updates its routing table and rebroadcasts the route. This type of situation can cause denial-of-service conditions. To counteract it, RIP uses split horizon, a system in which a router does not broadcast routes back to a neighboring router from whom the router learned of the route. RIP can also use poison reverse, which is a variation of split horizon. Instead of not broadcasting the routes, poison reverse will broadcast the routes back to the router from whom the route was learned, but it will broadcast them as having a hop count of 16, which ensures that the routes are considered unreachable. RIP can be implemented on Cisco routers, as well as on Windows 2000 Routing and Remote Access Servers.

Cisco routers can implement Interior Gateway Routing Protocol (IGRP) or Enhanced Interior Gateway Routing Protocol (EIGRP), both distance vector protocols, to route IP traffic across an internetwork. When using IGRP or EIGRP, the Cisco routers cannot work in concert with Windows 2000 Routing and Remote Access Servers, because IGRP and EIGRP are not supported on Windows 2000.

Open Shortest Path First (OSPF) is a link state protocol that can route IP traffic across an internetwork. Both Windows 2000 Routing and Remote Access Servers and Cisco routers can implement OSPF.

Virtual private networking (VPN) is the ability to encrypt and encapsulate data packets so that they can access a private network, even though they are traveling across a public network. A VPN is regarded as a tunnel through the public network in which the private data can safely travel. VPN protocols include Layer 2 Tunneling Protocol (L2TP) and Point-to-Point Tunneling Protocol (PPTP), which both can work in conjunction with IP Security (IPSec).

FAQs

Q: Can I upgrade my PPTP VPN from Windows NT to a PPTP VPN over Windows 2000?

A: Yes. This type of upgrade should be easy to implement since the clients will not need to be changed. However, you should consider upgrading to L2TP VPN instead of PPTP because of the increased interoperability that L2TP has due to being a standard protocol, and because of the security concerns with PPTP.

Q: We have the choice of implementing a Windows 2000 Server with two network interface cards to act as a router as well as a file and print server, or implementing a Cisco Router plus the Windows 2000 Server with a single network interface card. Which would be the optimal solution?

A: Optimal depends on your business objectives. If your objectives are to select the cheapest solution regardless of the functionality, then the obvious choice is to implement a Windows 2000 Server that also acts as a router. Be aware that this type of solution probably will not perform well. It is far more optimal, from a performance and reliability standpoint, to implement both the Cisco router and the Windows 2000 server. The use of a separate router and server will enable the router to perform much faster routing of data, and the server to perform faster file and print services. Using a separate router will reduce the impact of a downed server on the network, clients would still be able to access the remaining network even if the server went down, so it would no longer be a single point of failure.

Q: When I configure a VPN connection on my Windows 2000 client, it still connects to the L2TP LNS, even though I didn't change the properties to select L2TP. Why is that?

A: The VPN connection on Windows 2000 uses an automatic detection system, in which it attempts to connect to either a PPTP or L2TP server to create a VPN tunnel. This means that the default configuration of the VPN connection will work with either a PPTP or L2TP server. If you have difficulty accessing a L2TP LNS, you may need to change the properties of the VPN connection to L2TP as a troubleshooting process.

Chapter 6

Designing the Windows 2000 Network

Solutions in this chapter:

- Understanding the elements of the Active Directory

- Designing an Active Directory forest

- Creating a naming strategy for your DNS domains

- Establishing the site topology

- Creating an organizational unit hierarchy

- Designing other Windows 2000 services

Introduction

If Windows 2000 is based on existing NT technology, then why is the Active Directory so important? Good question. The Active Directory is not part of the traditional NT technology—it is brand new. Not only that, but it is directly responsible for the communication that occurs between the domain controllers and workstations that participate within it.

This type of communication is different from what traditional NT domain controllers shared. In the legacy NT domain, there is a single primary domain controller (PDC) and any number of backup domain controllers (BDC). When a change was made to a user account, a machine account, or any security item, it was made solely on the PDC. The PDC then communicated the change out to the BDCs at regular intervals. Without a BDC or PDC nearby, a user's logon or query had to travel across WAN links, and the response was usually very slow. This method had a few other drawbacks. The PDC was a single point of failure. If it failed, no changes could be made until it was up and running, or a BDC was promoted to take its place. The PDC was also a center of traffic, a hub with all BDCs as spokes, which caused further bandwidth consumption. All BDCs had to be able to contact that one PDC in order to function, and if the network infrastructure did not mirror the hub and spoke structure, then traffic to replicate the PDC's database was doubled, tripled, or worse on links that were in a serial progression, as shown in Figure 6.1.

Figure 6.1 Infrastructure and server placement in NT domain affects traffic patterns.

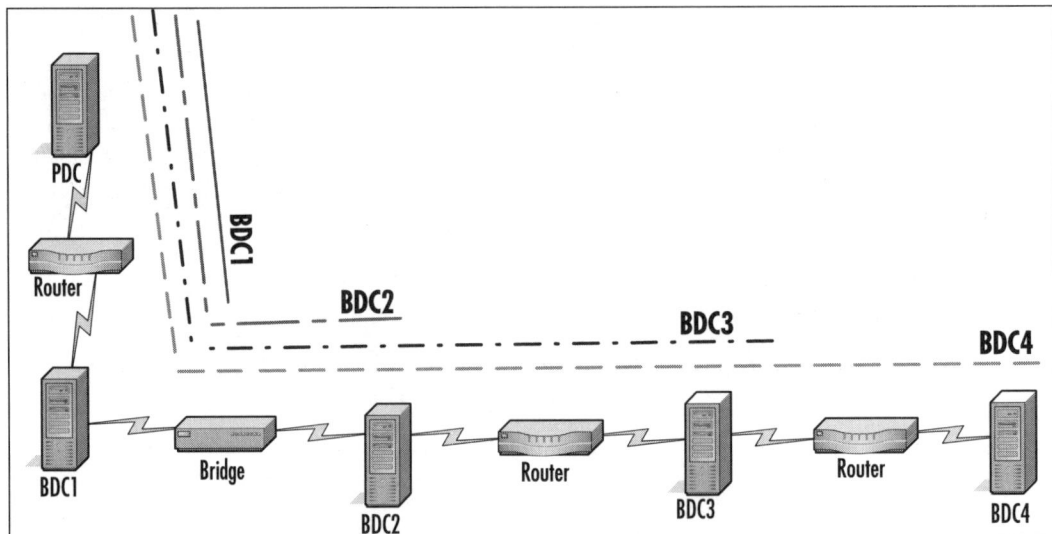

These weren't the only problems with NT domains. However, since administrators placed multiple BDCs in remote locations to speed up users' perceived logon performance, the infrastructure tended to suffer higher utilization rates.

The Active Directory was designed to ensure that these problems will not be experienced in a Windows 2000 network. As flexible as the Active Directory will prove to be, you will find that you need to carefully consider how you lay out the Active Directory. The Active Directory design will both affect and be affected by the infrastructure that you design along with it.

Design Planning

The Active Directory is a logical architecture that is situated on top of the physical infrastructure. This architecture is flexible enough to reflect most enterprises, and both the design of the infrastructure and that of the Active Directory will determine:

- Fault tolerance
- Availability of the directory
- Bandwidth utilization characteristics between domain controllers
- Network usage by directory clients
- Scalability

Best practices, as listed next, for a design project should be followed during this process. That means that you will be interviewing members of every business unit and adding key personnel to the design team. Then your team will decide what business processes will change when the Active Directory is in place. As you design the various structures, you will need to make your decisions carefully if those structures are difficult to change in the future (for example, domains and forests). Other structures, such as sites or organizational units (OUs) that are easy to change, should still be designed carefully, but they can also be redesigned to optimize network performance as the enterprise grows and changes.

- Document the acceptance criteria for the design before you start the project.
- Keep the design as simple as possible; this will make the network easier to manage in the long run.
- Build in scalability to the design. This will ensure that the network can grow and change as your business does.

- If your first design does not succeed, design, design again. Although this sounds trite, it is very true. Test your design and make sure it meets your acceptance criteria before you deploy it in your production network.

- Create four design documents for the Active Directory: the Forest plan, your Domain and Domain Name System (DNS) plan, your Organizational Unit hierarchy, and your Site Topology.

- Create a fifth design for the infrastructure to support the Active Directory forest and the services you will have on the network. How to create a Cisco infrastructure design is discussed in Chapter 8, "Deciding the Cisco Infrastructure Design."

- Document the design and make certain that all parties have a copy of the design and agree to its principles.

Forest Plan

The first plan you will need to document is your forest plan. A forest is the largest unit of an Active Directory, and consists of all participating domains, which share the configuration, schema, and Global Catalog (GC).

One of the reasons that you need to have a forest plan is simply this: You can create several on a single network. In fact, if you so desired, you could create a new forest with each server you install. Of course, if you did so, the forests would not consist of very much, and the value you would receive from the Active Directory would be very little indeed.

Having multiple forests running on a single network will bring incremental traffic and additional administrative overhead to your network. A forest's architecture is completely separate from all other forests. The result is that the overhead involved in replication traffic is duplicated for each forest that spans a network link.

The type of data that is replicated throughout a forest includes:

- The **schema**, which is replicated between each domain controller in the forest. The schema specifies which types of objects and their properties can exist in the Active Directory database. These object types are defined as *object classes*, and properties are defined as *attributes*. The schema administrators group manages it.

- The **configuration**, which is replicated between each domain controller in the forest. The Active Directory configuration container stores information from directory-aware applications. In fact, the configuration container holds the data about the underlying network, such as the sites and their assigned IP subnets, as well as site links, site link bridges, and connection objects. The enterprise administrators group manages the configuration.

- The **Global Catalog**, which is replicated between designated Global Catalog (GC) servers throughout the forest. The Global Catalog is a partition of the Active Directory database that contains a partial copy of each object from every domain that participates in the forest. The fact that only a portion of the attributes is copied from the domain partitions ensures that the size of the Global Catalog is kept to a reasonable size. The Global Catalog exists to facilitate searching for objects in the Active Directory by providing an index of all the objects regardless of the domain to which the objects belong.

You need to be aware of two other factors when designing the Active Directory:

- Bidirectional, transitive trust relationships (Kerberos trusts) are created automatically between all the domains within the forest. The domains within the forest are then in a complete trust model, as shown in Figure 6.2.

Figure 6.2 Complete trusts within a forest.

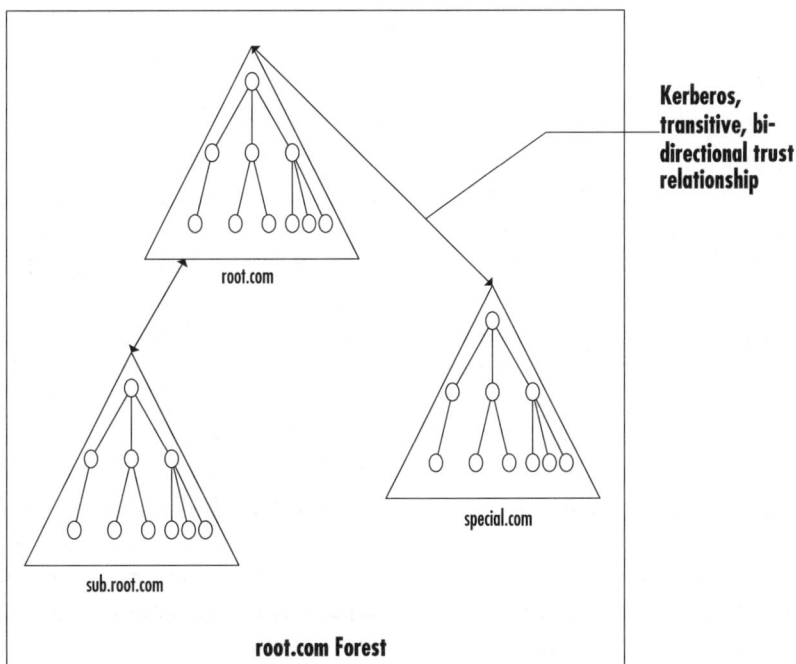

Kerberos, transitive, bi-directional trust relationship

root.com

sub.root.com

special.com

root.com Forest

- User Principle Names (UPNs) can be implemented to simplify the logon process. In the forest, each domain can have an entirely different namespace, but users may not know to which domain they belong, and may have difficulty selecting one from a list. However, using a UPN name, the users can use an account name that is identical to an Internet e-mail address format, *user@domain.com.* This is a familiar format that users find easy to remember. Within a single forest, all users can use their UPN name, and no longer need to select any domain.

Forest Plan Objectives

The objectives of a forest plan are fairly simple. You will want to specify the number of forests that will exist on the network. You will want to specify which domain is the root of each forest, and that domain's DNS name. In addition, you will want to set the policies for the forest—both those that affect the trusts with domains outside the forest, and those that affect change management for the forest.

Before you start the plan, gather the following information:

- Current NT domain configuration, if one exists
- Network infrastructure

You will also want to meet with network administrators and various business unit heads to determine if there will be a need for more than one schema or Global Catalog.

Establishing the Number of Forests

If possible, you should not create more than a single forest on your network. One of the advantages of the Active Directory is the ability to use a single hierarchical tree for managing users and network resources, yet still be able to delegate specific administrative privileges to specific users. This means that, in contrast to Windows NT, there is no need to create additional domains or forests in order to define a separation in administrative dominion. Since control over a set of users or resources was one of the main reasons that separate NT domains were created in the past, you need not let this issue concern you regarding the number of forests on your network.

There are some situations, however, that do call for multiple forests. These situations occur when you need to have more than one Global Catalog or more than one schema. A lab network is a perfect example of needing to separate both the Global Catalog and the schema from the production network's forest. The Global Catalog is the list of all users and resources on the network. You would not want users to perform searches on resources and user accounts that existed on the lab network, or lab engineers to perform searches (or tests!) on those that were part of the production network. In addition to separate Global Catalogs, you would also want to design separate schemas. This will ensure that you can test a schema change in the lab without it affecting those in the production network. The only way to do this is to have a separate lab forest.

Another situation that might call for two separate Global Catalogs is when implementing the Active Directory for a private network and a public network such as the Internet. By combining these global catalogs into a single directory, there is a small security risk, since someone could search the private network user accounts on the public network. That person would only need to figure out the password in order to access the private network. In addition, it would be confusing for the private network users to encounter user accounts that existed for use on the public network.

When an organization is divided into discrete businesses, the businesses may require that the administration, global catalog, and schema all remain completely divided. In this case, separate forests are a requirement. Maintaining separate forests is a must in any case where a subsidiary or partner venture is likely to be sold or spun off as a separate business. Your final forest plan should look something like Figure 6.3.

Figure 6.3 Forest plan.

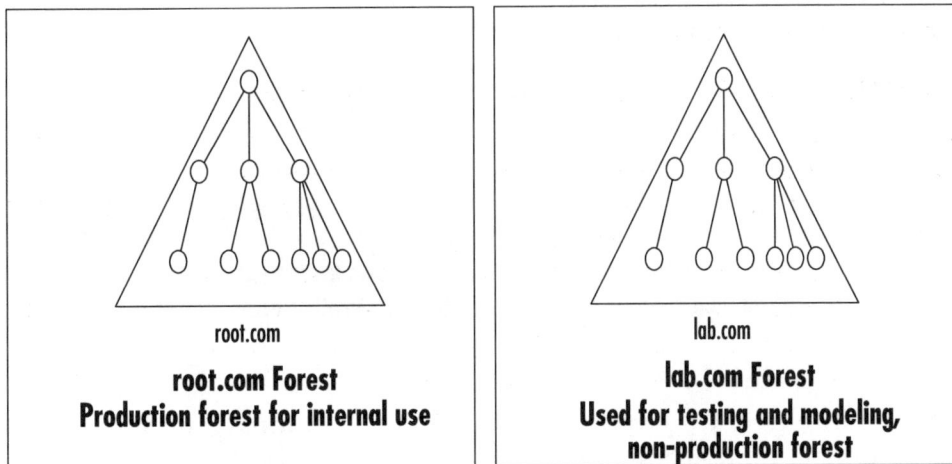

root.com

root.com Forest
Production forest for internal use

lab.com

lab.com Forest
Used for testing and modeling,
non-production forest

Overhead Involved with Multiple Forests

There is an added cost involved when you have multiple forests within a single organization. Before you add a new forest to your forest plan, you should be aware of this overhead.

- Each forest will require completely separate administration of the schema, global catalog, and configuration. To access resources from a domain in one forest when your domain exists in another forest, a trust relationship must exist as shown in Figure 6.4, or you must have a separate logon ID and password for each forest. The administration of either trust relationships or multiple user IDs per user is additional overhead that could be avoided by having a single forest.

Figure 6.4 Trust relationships between separate forests.

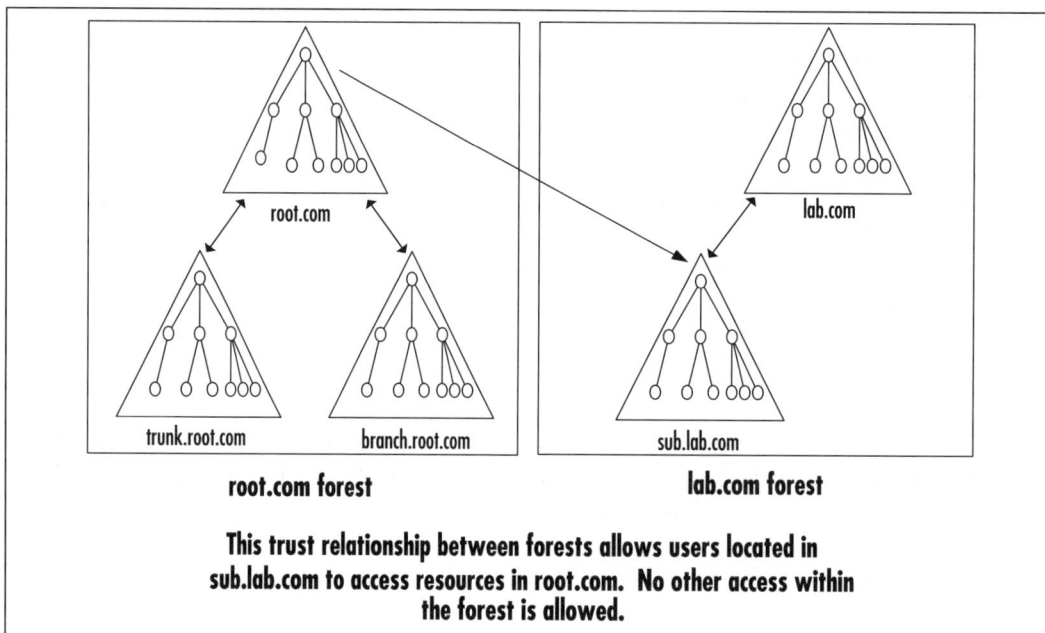

root.com

lab.com

trunk.root.com   branch.root.com

sub.lab.com

root.com forest   **lab.com forest**

This trust relationship between forests allows users located in sub.lab.com to access resources in root.com. No other access within the forest is allowed.

- Each forest will require separate sites, site links, site link bridges, connection objects, and IP subnets allocated to the sites. As a result, the administration is separate, but the replication traffic overhead is duplicated for each forest.

- Users who are located in one forest must know the location of the resources in another forest in order to access them. This is in contrast to the ease of querying the global catalog of their own forest.

- You cannot move user accounts or groups between forests. Instead, you must use a utility to clone the user accounts or groups.

DNS/Domain Plan

A DNS and domain plan must be created for each forest that is specified. (If you've decided to create more than one forest, then you will already realize the extra work that goes into having multiple forests with this step.) The DNS plan is an absolute must for the Active Directory, and because of its naming implications, it is tied to the domain plan. While not as influential as your site topology, which you will plan later, the domain plan that you create will be a critical factor in the traffic characteristics of replication and queries.

A forest, at its simplest configuration, consists of a single domain. However, you can create multiple domains and include all of them within the same forest, if multiple domains are required. Each additional domain adds incremental traffic and management overhead to your network, so only add domains when it is absolutely required.

DNS Plan

DNS, the Domain Name System, is a TCP/IP service that maps host names to IP addresses.

This system is used globally with root DNS servers existing on the Internet. DNS is a hierarchical system and consists of domains that are nested within other domains, as illustrated in Figure 6.5. The names of domains indicate the path to the root of the DNS system, with each nested domain name separated by a dot (.). For example, a fictitious domain named faery.tale.grimms.com represents the domain named "faery," which is a subdomain of "tale," which in turn is a subdomain of "grimms," and which is a commercial subdomain of "com," which exists below the root domain (.).

A DNS plan will consist of the following items:

- Naming strategy for domains
- DNS service type
- DNS options

The DNS naming strategy lists the domain names that are used for the domains. You will need to determine whether you will use an existing domain name or add a new one. If the new namespace is not one that is registered with InterNIC (the Internet Network Information Center), then you will need to register the name. You can use multiple namespaces within the same forest. For example, ACME has two subsidiaries—Alpha and Omega—that act separately but are willing to share a forest, since a single administrative group manages all three businesses' network infrastructure, but otherwise require separate domains. The three domains can be named acme.com, alpha.com, and omega.com. If Omega had never registered the domain name, then the administrative group should register it with InterNIC.

Figure 6.5 DNS hierarchy.

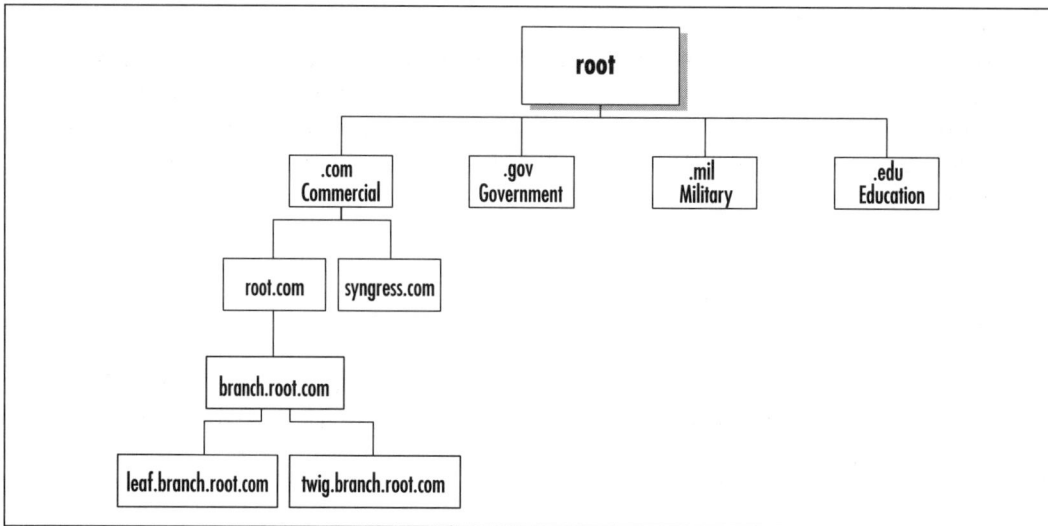

TIP

In order to ensure that there are no conflicts with domain names, all domain names must be registered with InterNIC. InterNIC will only accept unique names. Once registered, the domain name can be used on the Internet. InterNIC has a list of approved registrars on their Web site at rs.internic.net, as well as a whois utility to determine whether a domain name has already been registered to another. Once a unique name is located, you can go to one of the approved registrar's Web sites and register the name.

There are some rules for DNS names. This partially depends on the DNS service that you use. When you implement the Windows 2000 DNS service, you can use Unicode characters. The Unicode character set is based on 16 bits, rather than the standard 7- or 8-bit ASCII (American Standard Code for Information Interchange developed by the American National Standards Institute), or 8-bit EBCDIC (Extended Binary Coded Decimal Interchange Code developed by IBM), which have 128 or 256 characters. This means that the Unicode character set can have up to 65,536 characters. As such, Unicode encompasses most of the world's languages in one set of characters. However, using Unicode characters in your DNS names may cause some issues. If you connect the Windows 2000 DNS service to a network that uses a different vendor's DNS and try to implement a zone transfer, the Unicode characters will not be understood. In that case, use the following rules to ensure that names will be compatible regardless of the changes that may occur to DNS in the future. You can validate your DNS naming strategy with RFC 1123 (http://freesoft.org/CIE/RFC/1123/).

1. Use the characters a–z.

2. Use the numerals 0–9.

3. Use the dash (-) symbol.

4. Only create unique names, but do not create unique names by changing the letter case. Many systems interpret ACME and acme to be identical.

5. Do not use any of the following characters: !@#$%^&*() -_?<>'";::[]{}\|/.,

6. Do not use a blank space.

7. Keep your domain name to 64 characters or less. For example, the total "subdomain.domain.com" name could exceed 64 characters, but any portion of it, such as "subdomain," cannot. Windows 2000, rather than DNS' naming conventions enforce this requirement.

Legacy Windows NT did not require that an organization implement TCP/IP. Instead, it could have used NetBEUI or NWLink. Many organizations have implemented TCP/IP as a standard protocol, however, because of Internet connectivity needs. There may be an existing DNS server already on the network, and it may not be compatible with Windows 2000's DNS. Windows 2000 requires that DNS servers support service resource records (SRV RRs). One of the popular DNS servers is Unix BIND. It is recommended that you use BIND version 8.2.2 patch level 5 or better.

TIP

Although it is not necessary to use a short name, it is easier for everyone. Because of the hierarchical nature of DNS, long names can grow to extremely cumbersome lengths. If you had a domain name of myfirstandonlydnsdomainname.com for your root domain, and then named a subdomain as wouldntyouknowiusedaseconddomain.myfirstandonlydnsdomainname.com, there would be a tremendous opportunity for spelling errors when typing out either of the names. When performing administrative tasks, this can simply add to the time it takes to manage and troubleshoot the network.

Regardless of which DNS server you use, you will want to look at the other options it provides. Two recommended options are dynamic updates and incremental zone transfers. When dynamic updates are implemented, DNS clients will register their host name and IP address with the DNS server, automatically creating resource records in their zone. This saves administrators an enormous amount of time and effort. When incremental zone transfers are implemented, a DNS zone transfer will only send out the changes that have occurred within the zone. This is in contrast to a standard zone transfer in which the entire contents of the zone are sent from the zone's primary server to every DNS server that hosts its secondary zone. The result is a reduction in network bandwidth consumption. Another plus with using Windows 2000 DNS is the ability to create an Active-Directory-Integrated zone. When the zone is integrated into Active Directory, zone transfers occur as a part of replication; it uses the security inherent in Active Directory and only sends zone transfers on an incremental basis.

Domain Plan

You will be creating the DNS plan simultaneously with your domain plan because the naming of the domains is intertwined in both of the plans. It follows that if you make a change in one of the plans, you will probably need to make sure it works with the other plan. The domain plan is the specification of the number of the domains, their purpose, and membership. You will need to have the following information before beginning the domain planning:

For IT Professionals

How a DNS Query Takes Place

The process that takes place when a client workstation queries the DNS server is as follows:

1. The client.root.com sends a query to its local DNS server, dns.root.com. If the client is configured for multiple DNS servers, it will start with the primary DNS server. If it does not receive a response, it will use the secondary DNS server, and so on until the last DNS server has been queried with no response.

2. Let's assume that the client is looking for the address for server.tree.com. The DNS server, dns.root.com, will query any one of the root DNS servers (a.root-servers.net through m.root-servers.net) to find the location of a DNS server that is authoritative for tree.com.

3. The root server responds to dns.root.com with the address of a DNS server for tree.com—dns.tree.com.

4. dns.root.com then queries dns.tree.com directly for the address of server.tree.com.

5. dns.tree.com responds to dns.root.com with the IP address of server.tree.com—10.10.10.10.

6. dns.root.com returns the IP address of server.tree.com to client.root.com.

7. client.root.com then uses the IP address to contact server.tree.com.

- Current Windows NT domain configuration
- Current DNS server types and DNS configuration
- Network infrastructure design

In large enterprises, typically one group will manage the DNS system while another will manage the Windows NT servers. For Windows 2000 domain planning, you will need to bring both of these groups into the planning conference.

When you determine the number of domains for the forest, begin with a single domain model and grow from there. Although it is recommended that you have complete documentation of the existing Windows NT domain configuration, you will want to set that configuration aside while you design the Windows 2000 Active Directory. Many legacy NT domains were created for reasons that are no longer applicable to Windows 2000. For example, the Windows NT domain SAM database was limited to 40,000 objects, while Windows 2000 Active Directory domains in native mode can have up to a million objects or more. Another reason that organizations created additional domains was for the purpose of separation or delegation of administrative duties. With Windows 2000 Active Directory, administration can now be delegated within the organizational unit hierarchy, so this reason is also no longer valid.

Each domain created will cause some additional traffic on the network. However, since there is no longer a PDC that requires high availability to all other BDCs, the network infrastructure does not have to provide high availability to any single Windows 2000 domain controller (DC). Except for where you need granular control over replication, you can completely ignore physical infrastructure when you create domains. The following are the reasons that may prompt you to create additional domains within your forest.

Separate organizations If an enterprise has one or more subsidiaries or partnership ventures, they each may require a separate domain, especially if they each will require separate namespaces.

Domain security policy The domain level security policy that exists for each domain is applicable only to a domain unit. For example, if one group needs to have passwords changed every 60 days, and another group requires passwords to be changed every 15 days, then they must belong to separate domains.

Highly sensitive resource security If a business unit worked on extremely sensitive data, it would add a level of security to provide that unit a separate domain with its own administration.

Granular control over replication Each domain is a physical partition of the Active Directory database. The objects within a domain are only replicated to other DCs in that domain. Take, for example, an organization that has two campuses located in two different countries. Each campus contains 5000 or more users and has its own administrative group. If this organization had a single domain, then any change made on any DC would be replicated to the DCs in both countries. If this organization created a domain for each country, then changes made to an object in one country would only be replicated within that country. (Note that this does not reduce the replication of attributes that are copied to the global catalog.)

The first thing to do is create a logical design for your domains. Each domain should have a known set of users and a function associated with it. The next thing to do is to apply this design to the physical network. This does not have to be an exact microscopic representation of each user and relation to the network. However, it does have to depict the wide area network (WAN) or low-speed links that a domain will span, as well as any virtual private network (VPN) links, and will resemble Figure 6.6. What you are looking for is a set of two or more domains that span the same link, or for any domain with more than 10,000 objects that spans a WAN link. To estimate the number of objects in a domain, multiply the number of users by four. Once you identify these domains, you need to decide whether the available bandwidth should be enough to handle the intra-domain traffic, whether to upgrade the links, or whether to split the domain into smaller ones. You must create two domains for a logical unit that is separated by a link that allows only Simple Mail Transport Protocol (SMTP) traffic across it. You will also want to create two domains when the logical unit spans a "pay per bit" link, even if it is a high-speed, reliable connection. You may prefer to change or upgrade the link if the original logical domain contains a sizeable number of roaming users. If these roaming users are in a single domain, they will have access to network resources regardless of the location where they log on.

Figure 6.6 Logical domain structure applied to physical network.

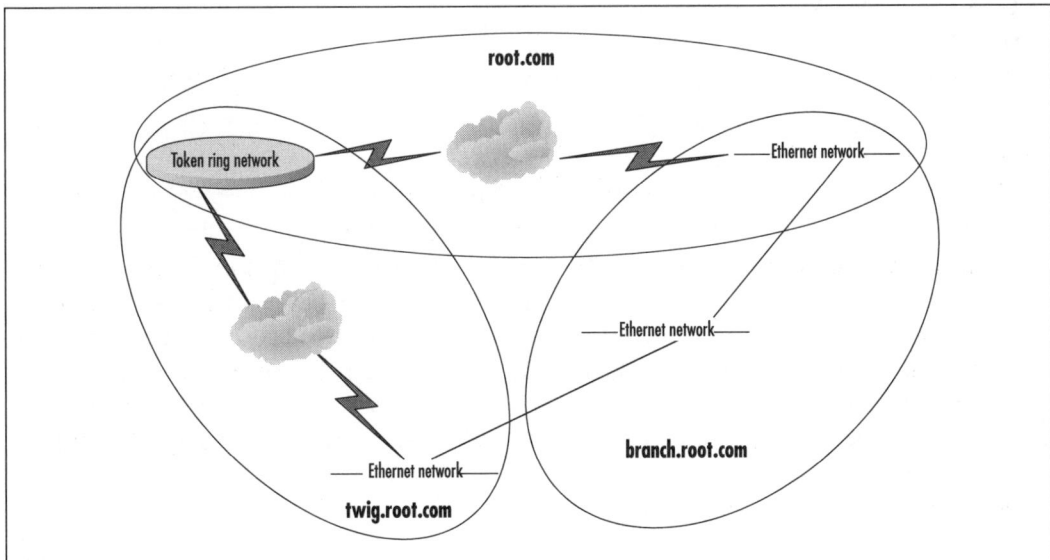

You should have selected the root domain of the forest in your forest plan. This domain will be the first domain installed for that forest. This domain is critical because its loss (the loss of all of its DCs) can affect all other domains in the forest; in addition, it can only be restored from backup and cannot be reinstalled as a root. For this reason, you will want the root domain to have at least one or more DCs located in different geographic locations to ensure the domain is always available.

The next thing to do is to logically organize the domains into a tree structure and then apply DNS names to them. You should already know how many namespaces you will need, and what they are, from the DNS plan. You should also have as many logical domains as you have namespaces, or more domains than namespaces. For example, Acme has three namespaces, acme.com, omega.com, and alpha.com. Acme.com has been selected as the root domain for the forest. Acme's domain plan lists four domains, one for the Acme business, one for Omega and one for Alpha. In addition, another domain was specified for Human Resources (HR) at Acme because of the highly sensitive resources on that network. HR is located in its own physically secure building in New York and does not share space or administration with any other Acme business unit. The only domain that would remain unnamed from a namespace point of view is HR's domain. Logically, because HR is within the Acme business, its domain should be a subdomain of Acme.com. The name could reflect the unit or its location, or another name that makes sense to the group. Possible names include hr.acme.com, ny.acme.com, or something else that HR may select. The final DNS/domain plan would look something like Figure 6.7.

NOTE

Even if you upgrade an existing Windows NT domain system to Windows 2000, you will need to establish new DNS names for each domain. If you have fewer namespaces than you have domains, then you will also logically organize these domains into nested subdomains. Legacy Windows NT domains used the NetBIOS Name System (NBNS) to assign names and locate domains on the network. NBNS was a flat naming system with no hierarchical organization to the system whatsoever. In addition, NBNS is not a global system (whereas DNS is)—you cannot log on to a public network and use NBNS to access resources. NetBIOS names still exist in Windows 2000 as *downlevel names* for backward compatibility, but the focal names for the domains are the DNS names in the format of subdomain.domain.com.

Figure 6.7 Sample DNS/domain plan for Acme.

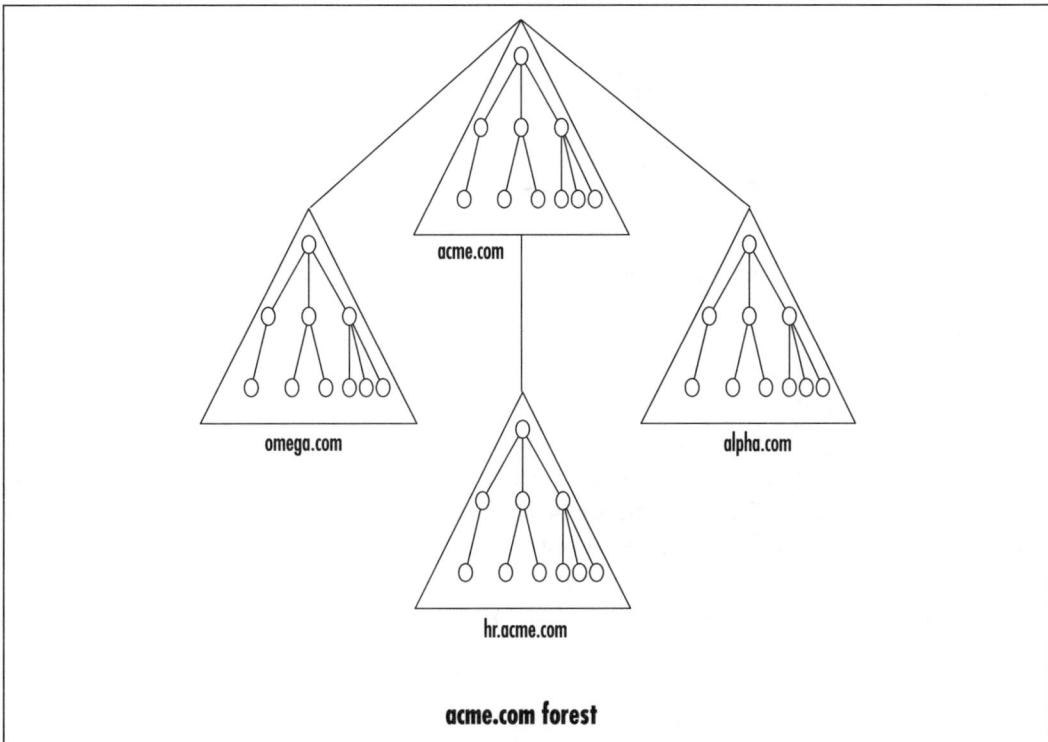

acme.com forest

Kerberos

The trusts within a forest are all based on Kerberos, a network authentication service developed for use on client/server networks and has since been applied to use over the Internet.

Active Directory uses Kerberos to verify the identity of users, services, resources, and domains. Kerberos does not rely on Windows 2000 or on specific IP addresses to validate an identity. Kerberos uses credentials for identity verification.

Windows NT trusts differ from the way that Kerberos trusts work. For example, in a legacy Windows NT domain system, if the Zeus domain trusted Hera domain, then it did *not* follow that Hera trusted Zeus. Instead, a separate trust relationship had to be created for Hera to trust Zeus. If we add in a third domain, Hercules, and Zeus trusts Hera and Hera trusts Hercules, then in the legacy Windows NT world, Zeus did *not* trust Hercules. This is illustrated in Figure 6.8.

Figure 6.8 Nontransitive, unidirectional, legacy Windows NT trusts.

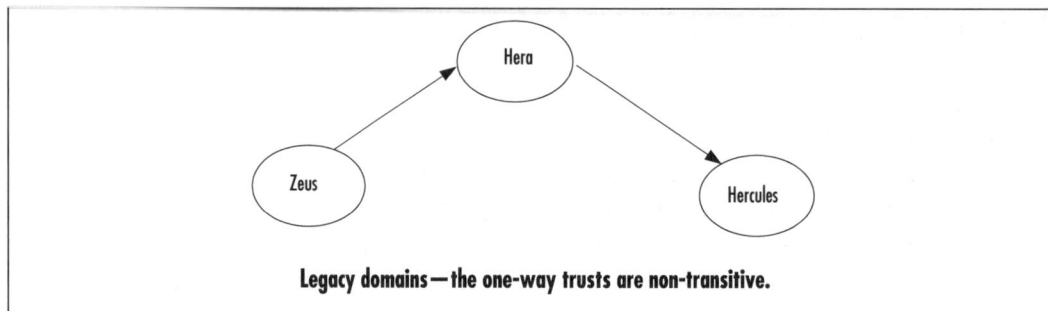

Legacy domains—the one-way trusts are non-transitive.

Kerberos trusts are both transitive and bidirectional, and they are automatically created upon the installation of a domain into a forest. For example, if Olympus.com were created and zeus.Olympus.com was installed next, then zeus.Olympus.com would trust Olympus.com and Olympus.com would trust zeus.Olympus.com. In addition, if hera.Olympus.com were installed, then not only would it trust Olympus.com and vice versa, but the trust relationship would flow through to zeus.Olympus.com, and hera.Olympus.com would trust zeus.Olympus.com. This is illustrated in Figure 6.9.

Figure 6.9 Transitive, bidirectional, Kerberos trusts.

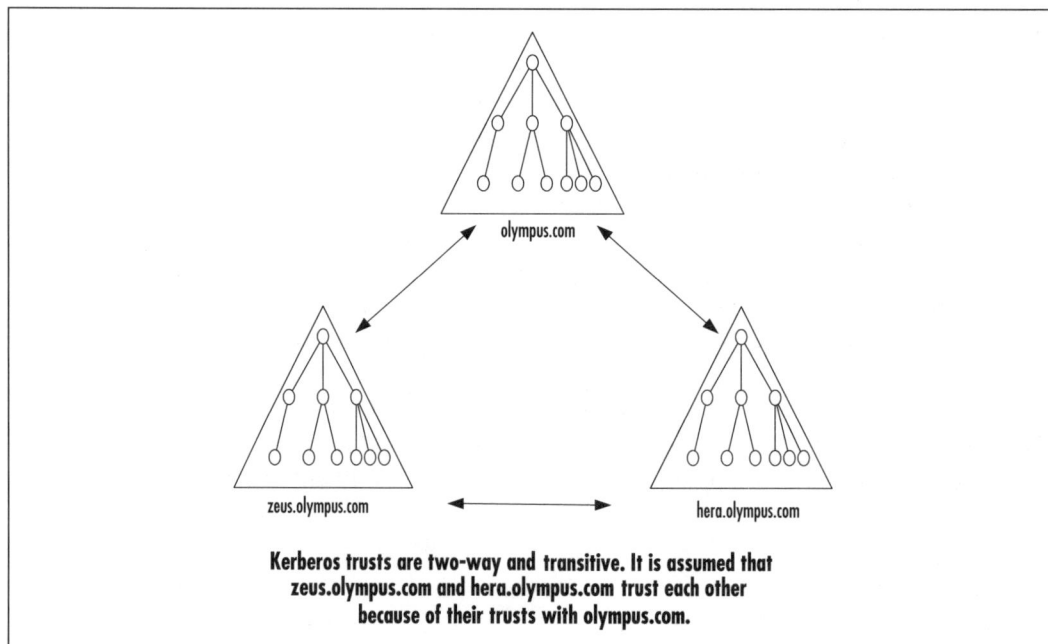

olympus.com

zeus.olympus.com   hera.olympus.com

Kerberos trusts are two-way and transitive. It is assumed that
zeus.olympus.com and hera.olympus.com trust each other
because of their trusts with olympus.com.

Since Kerberos trusts are created automatically upon installation, you do not need to do too much in the way of administration of them. However, when you are planning access to resources, you do need to know how they work.

Site Topology

The site topology is the formative basis for your infrastructure needs. Like DNS and domains, however, your existing infrastructure is also the formative basis for your site topology. It is somewhat like the chicken and the egg debate (which came first?), except that you are given an infrastructure to start with and can change it after you establish the site topology—which, once you change the infrastructure, may lead to changing the site topology again. Take heart, though, the site topology, while critical, can be adjusted at any point in time for any reason, and is done so in a fairly straightforward manner.

The site topology represents the physical infrastructure in a logical manner. There is only one site topology per forest. Sites are defined as a set of well-connected IP subnets, which means that you really don't want to select an IP subnet out of a building in Germany, another from a building in France, a third from a building in Australia, and then consider that a site. Instead, you would define the IP subnets within the building in Germany as one site, the IP subnets in France as another site, and the Australian IP subnets as a third.

An interesting feature about sites is that they are not domain-centric. A site can span a domain, or a domain can span a site. For example, there can be two users who have computers on the same IP subnet, and so by definition belong to the same site, as illustrated in Figure 6.10 where a computer belongs to root.com and another belongs to domain.com. Each computer belongs to a different domain, but the IP subnet only belongs to a single site—this is an example of a site spanning domains. Likewise, two users who have computers on different IP subnets in different sites can both belong to the same domain—this is an example of a domain spanning sites. This is also illustrated in Figure 6.10, since computers belonging to the root.com domain exist in both Site 1 and Site 2.

Intrasite Replication Characteristics

Intrasite replication is the replication traffic that occurs within a single site. This site may contain DCs from one domain or DCs from multiple domains. The site may contain global catalog servers, or it may not have any. The replication within the site will consist of updates to at least one domain's partition, the schema, and the configuration. More complex sites will also have replication of additional domains and the global catalog.

Figure 6.10 Domains and sites can span each other.

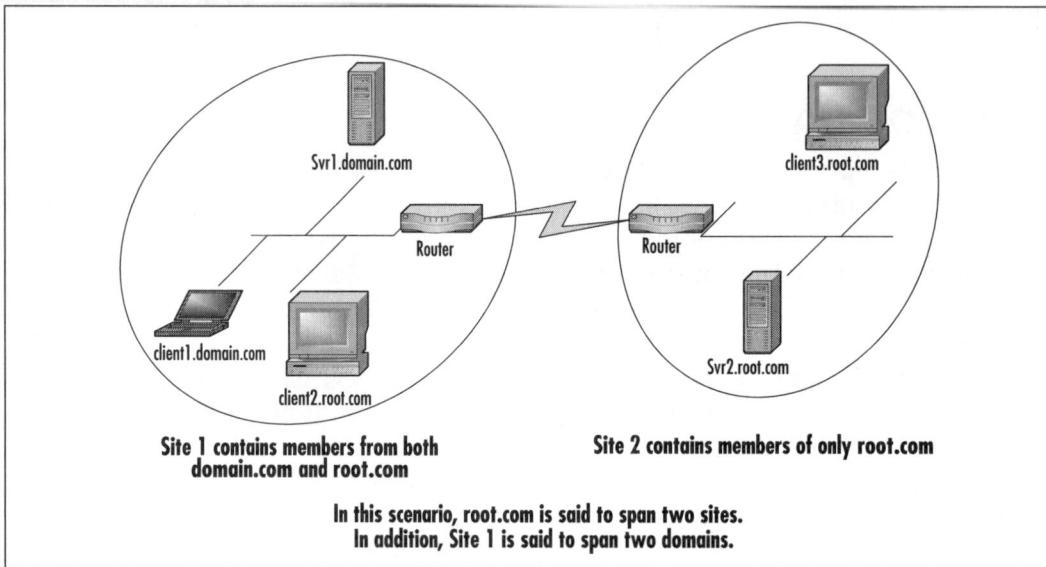

Site 1 contains members from both domain.com and root.com

Site 2 contains members of only root.com

In this scenario, root.com is said to span two sites.
In addition, Site 1 is said to span two domains.

The traffic for this replication will be solely based on Remote Procedure Calls (RPCs) running over TCP/IP. RPCs are session layer Application Programming Interfaces (APIs) that make remote applications appear to be running locally. Not only will this traffic use RPCs, but it will be uncompressed traffic that transmits whenever a change is made on a DC. In actuality, the traffic transmits any changes that were recently made every few minutes, as shown in Figure 6.11.

Figure 6.11 Intrasite traffic transmission interval.

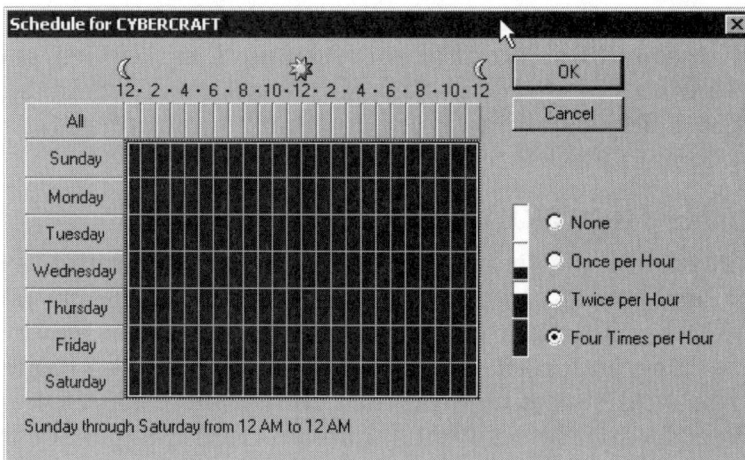

Connection objects handle the replication within the site. A connection object is unidirectional and located on a DC. If one DC has a connection object pointing to another DC, it does not need to be reciprocated, although it often is. The connection objects create a ring that has no more than three hops back to the originating DC, which ensures that synchronization within a site is always completed within 15 minutes. Replication traffic follows the direction of the connection object ring, also known as the intrasite replication topology.

The Knowledge Consistency Checker (KCC), which is a service that runs on every DC, creates connection objects on the destination DC, or an administrator can create them manually. The connection objects that the KCC creates are generally sufficient for replication within a site. If there is a significant amount of latency, an administrator may decide to create a connection object to reduce it. The KCC will not delete any of the manually created objects. The KCC will run every 15 minutes to reconfigure the intrasite replication topology to make certain that replication occurs even if there is a failure in the network.

Intersite Replication Characteristics

Between sites, replication is highly manageable, but the contents of the replication traffic can be extensive. At the most basic, intersite replication must include global catalog, schema, and configuration traffic. However, a site can transmit updates to multiple domain partitions, to the global catalog, to the schema, and configuration to another site—even if the receiving site does not contain those domain partitions or a global catalog server. This situation takes place if the receiving site happens to be located between two sites that contain other domain partitions and global catalog servers. This "location" is not necessarily a physical location, but a logical location dependent largely on the design of the site topology.

The traffic for intersite replication is normally based on RPCs running over TCP/IP. This traffic is compressed—unlike intrasite replication traffic. In addition, sites that will only be sending global catalog, schema, and replication traffic (e.g., those that are not spanned by a domain) can connect via SMTP. SMTP can never be used to connect sites that share a domain, and is meant only for those sites that are separated from the rest of the network by a link that cannot support RPC traffic.

Intersite replication is highly manageable in that you can set an availability period for a link. For example, you can state that the link between Site A and Site B is only "open" for replication transmission between certain hours, such as 10 P.M. to 3 A.M. In addition, the frequency of replication transmissions can be controlled. You can set replication to take place as often or as seldom as you need.

Unlike intrasite replication, the topology between sites must be created manually. The KCC will not do this for you. Not only will the administrator need to create the connection objects between DCs, but also the site links between sites, site link bridges between site links, and designated bridge-head servers.

Establishing the Sites

The site topology should, in the majority of cases, reflect the physical network. Sites should include IP subnets that are located within a close physical proximity and have a significant bandwidth available to them. The boundaries of sites should be the IP subnets that do not have significant bandwidth, which are generally WAN links. There are only two situations in which you may wish to include a WAN link as part of a site:

- The WAN link is a high-speed link with a lot of available bandwidth.

- The WAN link connects to a location that has a small number of users, and no DCs will be placed there.

When a high-speed WAN link exists, it meets the criteria of a well-connected IP subnet. As such, a site can span this link and allow replication to flow as needed. However, let's face facts: Not everyone has an OC-48 fiber optic network to hook up their offices around the world. Most WAN links are not capable of supporting the replication traffic of thousands of users with the intrasite replication model. The only way to make these links function as you need them to is to control traffic. And the only way that you can truly control traffic is by separating the network into sites with the WAN link as the boundary.

There is one situation, though, in which you may decide to allow a site to span a slow WAN link. If you have a branch office with a few users and do not intend to place a DC at that site, you can make it a part of the site to which its WAN link connects. In this way, users will log on to the DCs located directly across the WAN link, and there will be no replication traffic going across the WAN link. (No DCs means no need to replicate.) You do not need to create a site for any branch office with about 50 or fewer users. However, if there is a significant degradation in performance, you may wish to create a site for that office and place a DC/global catalog server at that site to enhance performance.

When you create a site link between two sites, you will want to establish the following parameters to model your replication traffic:

Transport This is the protocol that will transmit the replication traffic between the sites. It should be set to RPC unless there is some limitation to the link that prevents RPC traffic and allows only SMTP traffic.

Replication interval This is the frequency of the replication transmission—so that if you want replication to occur every four hours, you will set it to happen here.

Replication schedule This institutes the availability of the link. You can state that the link is not available during certain hours of the day so that replication traffic does not interrupt business-critical traffic.

Cost Cost lets you place a priority on the site link. Many businesses create backup network links to ensure that the network can run when the primary link has failed. It is not uncommon to find a WAN link backed up by a modem connection. To ensure that the replication traffic will still take place even if the main link fails, a second site link must be created. However, you don't want the backup site link representing the modem to transmit the replication traffic if the main site link is available. That's when you assign a cost to the link. You should assign a low cost for the main link and a high cost for the backup link, as shown in Figure 6.12.

Figure 6.12 Establishing a cost on a redundant link.

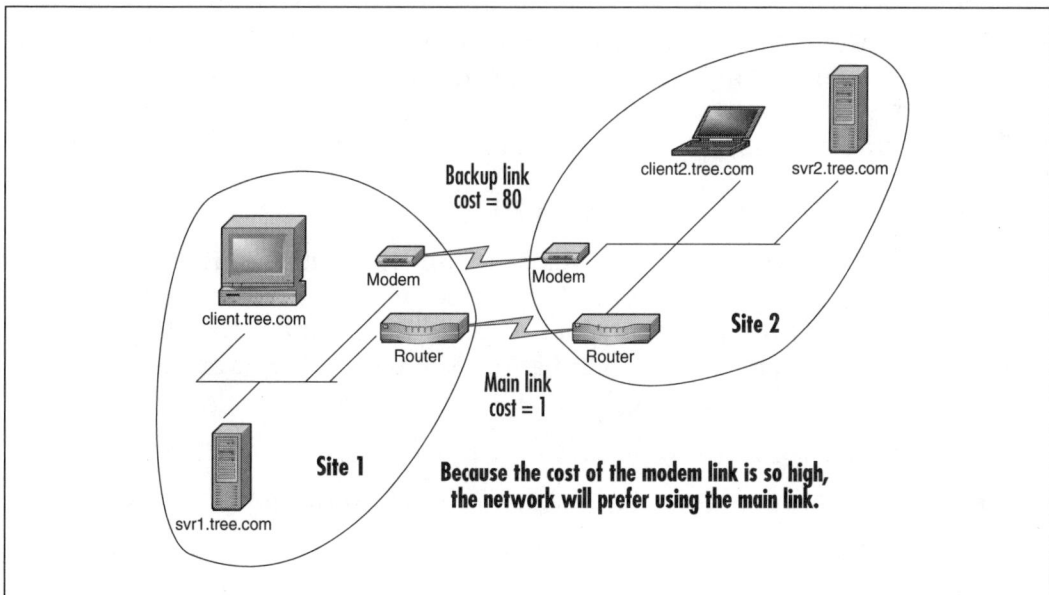

The site topology plan is the first step. As the network grows and changes, the site topology plan will change. In addition, as users change their work habits, there will be differing usage rates on the network. You will want to tune the network performance, and the most effective change you can make to performance is adjusting the site topology.

Even though you will change the site topology, you will want to start out with a documented plan for it before implementing Windows 2000. This will include the following elements:

- Network infrastructure diagram of the WAN links and LAN locations.

- Depiction of which areas will be sites, and what site links will exist between them, including whether the links are based on RPC or SMTP.

- Site links should have documentation of the link speed, reliability, and utilization percentage.

Authentication and Queries in the Site Topology

The site topology affects more than just the replication traffic in the network; it also affects the query and authentication traffic. When the client workstation begins communicating on the network for the very first time, it sends a message to any DC of the domain in which the client is a member. The DC uses the client's IP address to resolve which site the client belongs to. The client stores that information and uses it to find a DC in its own site from then on for authentication and for queries. Sites are used to localize all types of traffic: query, authentication, and replication.

Organizational Unit Hierarchy

An organizational unit (OU) is an object within the Active Directory database that can contain other objects such as user accounts or even other OUs. The OU hierarchy is a set of nested containers that is located within a domain. Each domain will have a separate OU hierarchy.

There are several reasons to use OUs:

- Organize user accounts and network resources
- Apply group policy to certain users or computers
- Hide objects
- Delegate administration

Organization of the user accounts and network resources is a huge improvement over the flat file domain structure offered by legacy Windows NT. One thing to remember, though, is that the OU structure is not an org chart. It is not intended to be navigated by end users on a search for resources—they will find it easier to locate resources using the Find utility. The OU structure should be created to provide a function for administration, whether it's group policy application, delegation of administration, or hidden objects.

To organize the OUs to provide a truly functional system, start at the top of the tree. The top of the tree is the largest administrative division. Administrators allowed to manage from this level will have the largest scope of the domain. If there is a clear division of who manages what, you will want to create multiple administrative OUs at the root of the domain. Only the highest level of administrative authority should be placed at the top of the tree. Lesser authority can be granted at the OU levels below that.

The next level of OUs is best used to hide objects. The administrator can hide objects by creating a top-level OU in his own hierarchy, then limit the ability of other users to see the objects in that OU by removing the List Contents right for the OU. This can be accomplished through the Active Directory Users and Computers console by changing the Security on the Properties for the OU.

One of the more intriguing aspects of OUs is the ability to apply group policy to them. A group policy is a grown-up version of Windows 9x and NT System Policies. They are a key component of Intellimirror that lets you manage desktop and user environment. The new group policies in conjunction with the tree structure of OUs can create an enterprise user and desktop environment structure that filters through the OUs, beginning with general enterprisewide policies and adding more specific policies to the OUs below. When the group policies are applied to the end user and client workstation, they develop a complete environment, as illustrated in Figure 6.13.

Designing Other Services

The Active Directory for Windows 2000 is a single service. Windows 2000 Servers provide many other services beyond the directory service. These other services can enhance the way that administrators manage a network, or enhance the capabilities of the network for end users. However, the way that some of these services act on the network can affect network bandwidth utilization, or worse, can change the expected paths of data, which in turn can create a bottleneck.

Figure 6.13 Group policy application in an OU hierarchy.

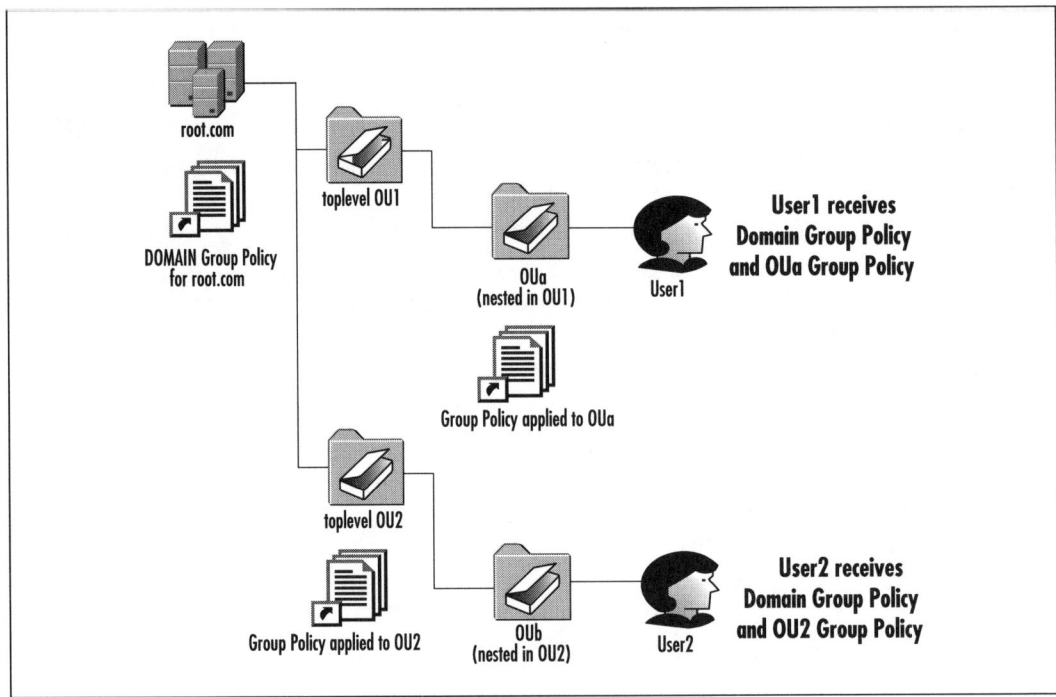

DHCP Servers

Dynamic Host Configuration Protocol (DHCP) is an open IETF standard that allocates IP addresses to computers. Using DHCP, administration of IP addresses is greatly reduced when compared to assigning IP addresses manually. DHCP enables the pooling of IP addresses to support a larger number of workstations than there are IP addresses available. When compared to a manually applied IP address, DHCP is much easier to manage. In a manual system, each machine is assigned a unique address whether or not it is online, which means that IP addresses can be taken even if they are not being used.

With DHCP, a computer's IP address is reclaimed if it is not online and its lease has expired. DHCP can save so much time and effort in network management that it is used in the majority of IP environments. Most DHCP servers will work with most DHCP clients, even if the client was developed by a different vendor than the DHCP server.

This is how DHCP works:

1. A client sends a DHCP request on the network.

2. The DHCP request remains on the same segment until it locates a server or a router that is able to forward the request. DHCP requests are based on Uses Datagram Protocol (UDP) traffic—port 67 when sending to the server, so they are not automatically routed. Routers must be configured with IP Helper addresses to forward the UDP traffic.

3. The DHCP server has a database of IP address ranges called scopes. The scopes also include additional information such as DNS servers, subnet mask, default gateway, and other variables.

4. The server assigns, or leases, an address that is free from a scope, or it renews the lease of an IP address already assigned to that client. Then the server sends the DHCP lease out via UDP port 68.

For IT Professionals

DHCP Terminology

Scope A group of consecutive IP address ranges that can service all DHCP clients on a physical subnet. Each subnet will receive its own scope.

Address pool A range of available IP addresses within a scope minus the ranges of IP addresses that are excluded.

Exclusion range A sequence of IP addresses that are within the range of a scope, but which are designated to *never* be assigned to clients by the DHCP server.

Reservation An IP address that is permanently leased to a particular DHCP client so that the client always receives the same IP address. Reservations are best used for servers, printers, and other systems that are accessed by multiple users. A reservation is assigned to a specific Media Access Control (MAC) address. Since MAC addresses are unique, only the system with that MAC address will receive the IP address.

Superscope A group of separate scopes that are managed as a single entity.

Lease The length of time that an address is assigned to a DHCP client. At the midpoint of the lease, the client will attempt to contact the server to renew the lease.

5. The client receives the lease and retains the IP address for the duration of the lease.

When you place DHCP servers, you will want to make certain that IP addresses are available in every major site. This design issue is based on the fact that, if a scope has too short of a lease and there is a lengthy outage of a WAN link that connects a site to its only DHCP server, then clients cannot connect to the network. Multiple DHCP servers can service the same scope. When you design your DHCP system, build redundancy into your plan.

In order to determine the number of DHCP servers, you need to understand the following aspects of your network:

- Location of routers and whether a DHCP server is required on each side of the router.

- Location of WAN links and their transmission speeds. If the link is slow, performance of DHCP requests and responses may not be acceptable.

- Remote access servers' locations and requirements for DHCP.

- DHCP server configuration including disk capacity and CPU speed to determine the server's performance.

Using Windows 2000 DHCP Services

Windows 2000 provides DHCP services with extended capabilities.

- **DHCP is integrated with DNS.** The DHCP server registers the IP address and host name with the DNS service if it is configured for dynamic updates.

- **Supports both vendor-specific and class ID options.** You can configure the server to look at what type of client is making the DHCP request. Then you can have the DHCP server send out different options, such as a longer lease to a desktop and a shorter lease to a laptop.

- **Detects rogue DHCP servers.** The DHCP server can discover another DHCP server that was not authorized to be installed. This will prevent duplicate address errors and assist in management of the network. This functionality is integrated into the Active Directory. The Active Directory stores the addresses of valid DHCP servers for comparison to any detected DHCP servers.

- **Allocates multicast addresses.** The DHCP server can assign multicast addresses the same way that unicast addresses are, thus leveraging the existing infrastructure for audio and video conferencing.

For Managers

How to Detect Unauthorized DHCP Servers with Windows 2000

When Active Directory stores records of authorized DHCP servers, it also validates the status of any Windows 2000 DHCP servers on the network. First, the administrator uses the DHCP manager utility to authorize DHCP servers. In addition, the administrator can assign access rights to this configuration data so that others cannot change the servers listed as "approved."

Once a DHCP server comes online, it checks the directory to determine its domain location, and then if it is an authorized DHCP server in that domain. If the server is authorized, it sends out a DHCPINFORM request to discover if it is valid in other domains as well. The server will respond to client requests if it is valid in the directory. The Windows 2000 DHCP server does not respond to client requests if any of the following occur:

- It cannot contact the Active Directory.
- It does not find itself in the authorized list of DHCP servers.

A DHCP server that is not a DC or member server in an Active Directory domain, but is a standalone server, uses a different startup sequence. First, the server broadcasts the DHCPINFORM request. Other Active Directory DCs and member servers answer with a DHCPACK response including the name of the Active Directory domain in which they participate. If the stand-alone server detects another DHCP server on the network that belongs to the Active Directory, it does not respond to client requests. If it does not detect any other servers, it will respond to client requests, but will periodically repeat this sequence until it does detect an Active Directory DHCP server.

Internet Information Services

Internet Information Services (IIS) is a Web server program that is offered as an enterprise service on Windows 2000. IIS offers multiple types of TCP/IP services for the network, including a HyperText Transfer Protocol (HTTP) server and a File Transfer Protocol (FTP) server. IIS appears to be a simple Web server, but that is deceptive. In reality, this service is an enterprise-level server for the Internet. It can scale a single site on multiple servers using content replication services, or support multiple Web sites on a single server. Such flexibility requires a complex application. To provide some of its flexibility, IIS takes advantage of the Windows 2000 operating system's capabilities, such as:

- IIS installation is integrated into the Windows 2000 Server installation process.

- IIS can take advantage of Microsoft Cluster Services to add to the Web site's fault tolerance.

- IIS can use Windows 2000's Network Load Balancing to scale Web sites across multiple servers.

- IIS utilizes the security features of Windows 2000 and its Active Directory.

The design of IIS servers must be based on the business requirements for the Web site. For example, a small intranet established to distribute occasionally accessed public information for a small business unit would not need to be installed on a cluster, nor take advantage of network load balancing or security features. By contrast, a large Web site that provides an e-commerce application on the Internet must be able to take advantage of all these features because it would need the scalability, reliability, availability, and security that they offer.

Installation

IIS is not only included as a service in Windows 2000, it is installed by default on each Windows 2000 Server. (It is not installed by default on Windows 2000 Professional workstations. It must be installed later through the Add/Remove Programs Optional Components Manager.) If a server requires IIS because it will be an FTP server or a Web server, then this behavior is desirable. However, installing a feature that is not required is simply a waste of server resources. You should take careful note of the role a server should play, and if IIS is not required, then be certain to not install it.

Cluster Services

Clustering is a method of linking more than one computer together so that the additional computers act as backup machines ready to pick up the server role should the primary server fail. This is called *failover*. Windows 2000 Advance Server and Windows 2000 DataCenter Server have the cluster service available for installation on hardware that supports this feature. Using cluster services will increase a Web site's fault tolerance. This functionality is required when a Web site cannot go down. E-commerce servers are examples of those that cause the company a loss of income when the server goes down. Those, as well as other mission-critical Web sites, should take advantage of the reliability that cluster services offer.

What happens in a cluster is fairly simple. In a basic cluster of two servers (called *nodes*), each node has a separate hard drive storage that contains information specific to that node. But then, each node shares a common hard drive storage. Only one node can access the resources on the common hard drive at a single time. If the node that is primary fails, the secondary node takes over as a primary node and controls access to the common hard drive. When the other node restarts, it synchronizes and again can take over as the primary node.

While many applications are not designed to take advantage of clustered servers, IIS is designed to use cluster services. There is a command-line utility called IISSYNC.EXE to replicate settings and content from one node to another. In addition, the Content Deployment Service from Microsoft Site Server can replicate the same information automatically.

Security and Active Directory

IIS takes full advantage of Windows 2000 security features. These include open standard protocols that assure interoperability with other systems:

Basic Authentication for HTTP v1.0 Basic authentication is used for transmitting passwords across the Internet using Base64 encoding. However, this method does not encrypt passwords.

Digest Authentication for HTTP v1.1 Digest authentication, which is based on basic authentication, will transmit the passwords through a hashing algorithm so that the password cannot be deciphered from the hash.

Secure Sockets Layer v3.0 (SSL) SSL ensures authentication and confidentiality of the transmission through the use of certificates.

Transport Layer Security (TLS) TLS, which is based on SSL, provides user authentication and encryption framework. TLS improves performance by reducing the amount of traffic that must transverse the network, and includes a caching mechanism.

Fortezza Fortezza is a U.S. government security standard that uses a cryptographic mechanism to encrypt network transmissions and ensure their integrity. It requires both the server and browser software to support it, as well as a PC card.

PKCS #7 and PKCS #10 These public key protocols define the format of digital signatures and requests for certificates, respectively. Both are implemented in the IIS certificates.

Kerberos v5 Kerberos v5 is the primary security protocol for access to Windows 2000 domain resources.

Windows CryptoAPI Certificate storage is integrated with the Windows CryptoAPI storage for a single place for administrators to manage. Certificates are X.509 v3.

For IT Professionals

Security Terminology

Access control Protecting the network from intruders while enabling authorized users to access it. IIS uses both Web permissions and NTFS file.

Auditing Monitoring the network's usage and access to ensure that security has been maintained.

Authentication A method of verifying the user's identity.

Certificates An electronic form (X.509 v3) used to send and receive identity information. Certificates are distributed through a certification authority (CA) that is mutually trusted by the client and the server. Windows 2000 uses a CA that can either be used with the Active Directory, or without.

Encryption A method of changing the data so that it is unreadable by any except the intended recipient of that data. Encryption is typically defined in number of bits. The largest number of bits results in the most difficult to decode encryption. Typical encryption is in 40-bit, 56-bit, and 128-bit encryption. Export restrictions disallow 128-bit encryption outside the United States and Canada.

Applications can integrate with both the Active Directory and IIS by using the Active Directory Service Interface (ADSI). This capability allows an application to utilize the Active Directory objects and namespace structure, even adding custom objects and attributes to it. IIS includes an ADSI provider to facilitate access.

When you are designing your IIS Web sites, security and availability are of utmost importance. You will need to determine the following:

- Where the certification authority server(s) should be located.

- Whether to use SSL or TLS to secure transmissions, and how to ensure that the infrastructure will support various security methods and protocols.

- For high availability Web sites, whether to use cluster services or network load balancing.

In addition, you will want to look at the traffic that is shared with the Web traffic on the connection to the Internet. If that traffic is business-critical and has a high priority compared to the Web traffic, then you will want to throttle the Web site's bandwidth consumption at the network interface card (NIC). IIS allows you to regulate the bandwidth consumption for HTML files, as illustrated in Figure 6.14.

Figure 6.14 Per Web site bandwidth throttling.

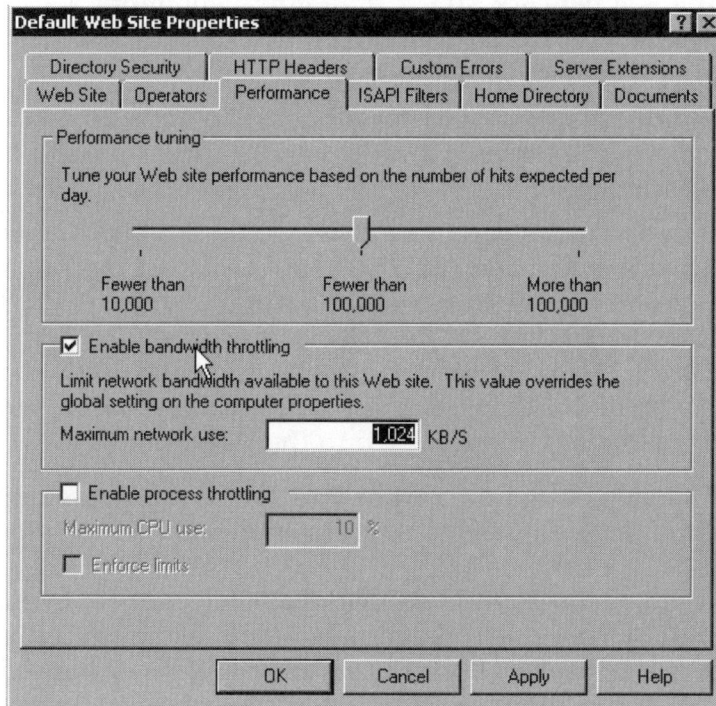

If your Web site is used as an e-commerce solution, it is more likely that you will consider the Web site's traffic to be more critical than other business traffic to the Internet, such as e-mail or Web browsing. A better solution is to place the Web site on a separate connection to the Internet than that used by the business traffic.

Yet another solution to making better use of your available bandwidth is to incorporate HTTP compression where you can. HTTP compression will work only with compatible browsers. Using it can increase the performance of the Web site for end users. It will also decrease the amount of traffic that traverses the Internet.

IPSecurity

IP Security (IPSec) is an open-standard, network layer encryption and authentication method. IPSec can protect against various network attacks by ensuring that the data transmitted across the wire cannot be read or decrypted. IPSec not only handles encryption, but also certificates and authentication of devices. IPSec has the goal of protecting IP packets and defending against network attacks.

Eavesdropping is a network attack that simply monitors network traffic and reads the unencrypted communications. This can also lead to modifying the data and transmitting the new version.

IP address spoofing is the ability for a hacker to make his data appear to be coming from an IP address that is trusted, rather than the IP address his station is assigned.

Denial-of-service attacks can cause damage by not allowing any users to access the network or the servers. This can be caused by transmission of data that causes a server to suffer an abnormal end, or by the flooding of data on the network so that nothing else can access it, or by blocking of data transmission. Denial-of-service attacks interrupt production business during the attack, and if they occur on an e-commerce Web site, they can further cause customers to not return to the Web site.

IPSec can be deployed on a LAN or WAN between clients and servers, between routers, between gateways, and for Internet access from a private network.

IPSec uses an encapsulating security payload protocol to encrypt IP packets. Then IPSec uses a cryptographic key to establish a digital checksum for the IP packet. Both the sending and receiving computers must share this key so that they can determine whether the IP packet has been modified. IPSec also uses authentication between systems. Furthermore, IPSec filters IP packets to determine whether communication is allowed or blocked depending on various parameters: IP address, protocol, or port.

When you design IPSec, you need to evaluate the amount of security that each server and client, router and gateway, and remote users and remote networks will require. The results of that evaluation should help you define which systems will need to use IPSec, and which will not. You may also define which level of IPSec should be applied to the systems.

Windows 2000 contains several predefined policies for IPSec that you can view in the group policies, as shown in Figure 6.15. In addition, you can create a custom IPSec policy for one or more computers.

Figure 6.15 Predefined policies for IPSec.

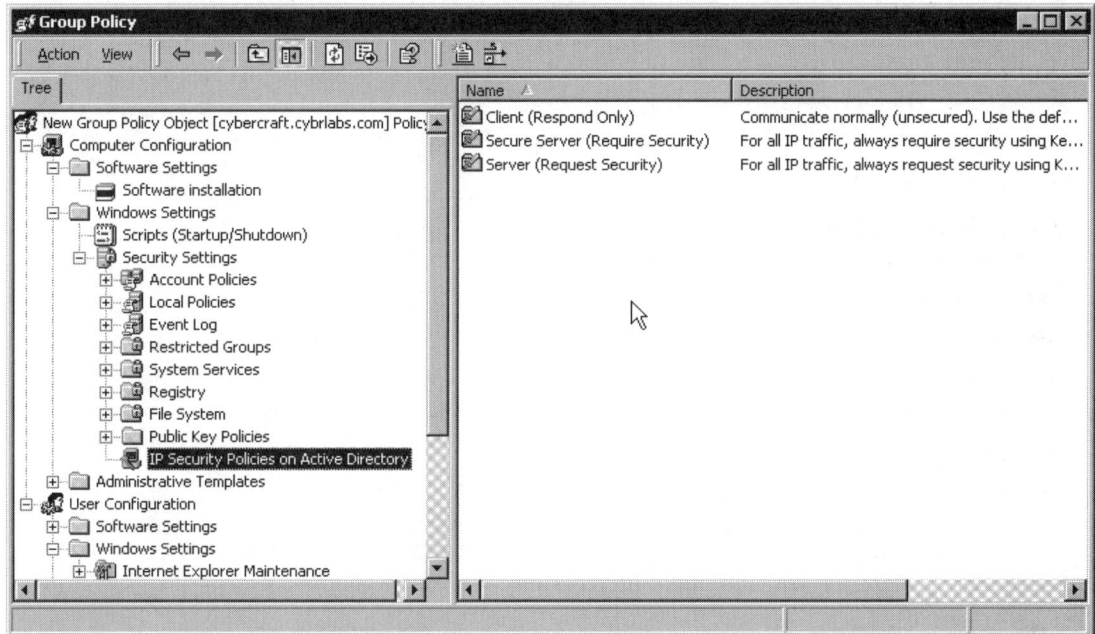

Public Key Infrastructure and Certification Authorities

Public Key Infrastructure (PKI) is a security method based on certificates. As the name implies, there is a public key in this encryption mechanism, but there is also a private key that is paired up with it. A public key is used to encrypt a message to send to a certain destination. Only the destination user knows the private key and can use it to unlock messages received that were encrypted with the public key.

The certification authority issues the certificate with a public key to a trusted user. The CA can distribute the public key to anyone. When the trusted user sends a message to the destination user, the public key is used to encrypt the message. When the destination user receives the message, he can unencrypt the message using his private key.

Another use for public key cryptography is to ensure that data was sent from a specific person. To do this, a user encrypts a message with his private key and sends it to a user on the network. The destination user must contact the CA to gain the public key. The public key is used to unencrypt the message and ensures that the message was received from the holder of the private key. This is called a *digital signature*.

PKI is usually used as a method of securing e-mail messages and for secure Web communications. IPSec, Smart Cards, and the Windows 2000 Encrypting File System use PKI, as well.

If you are planning to implement PKI, then you will need to decide the design of the CA servers. Many times, an existing file and print server or a domain controller may be applicable as a CA server. Other times, you may wish to have a stand-alone server provide the certificate services. The CA is a required service for users to be able to read encrypted messages, or to send them. Therefore, if a CA fails and there are no other CA servers, then users may not be able to perform their duties. In addition, the CA server will not perform well if using a long key or a complex algorithm. Both reliability and performance are issues for large enterprises, or organizations with extensive numbers of certificate users. For this reason, you should deploy CA servers in a hierarchy or with redundant hardware. In addition, you should make certain that the processing capabilities of the CA server are capable of performing at a high level, incorporating both the current usage rates and the future growth of the organization.

More about deploying CA servers in a hierarchy will be discussed in Chapter 7, "Sizing the Infrastructure for Windows 2000."

Terminal Services

Windows 2000 Terminal Services provides applications to users in a very similar way that a mainframe does. The Windows 2000 Server is a central delivery mechanism for multiple simultaneous users. They each receive remote control of an application on the Windows 2000 Server at their desktop. The data traveling across the wire consists of compressed draw commands, and mouse and keyboard responses over TCP/IP. All of the application, its execution, its data and storage are run on the server. The client executes terminal emulation software.

All Windows 2000 Server versions include Terminal Services as an optional component. When Terminal Services are deployed in a network, you need to consider the applications that the Terminal Server will be providing to end users. When an application requires access to another server, such as a database client application, the Terminal Server needs to be placed in close proximity to that other server. This means that the two servers should be placed on the same network segment whenever possible.

The reason for doing this boils down to performance. The terminal emulation client uses a minute amount of bandwidth, so a Terminal Server does not need to be placed close to clients. The application client that runs on the Terminal Server will gain the greatest performance boost by being placed close to the application's server. When that Terminal Server is running multiple sessions of the application client, then the amount of bandwidth utilization between those servers will increase arithmetically for each simultaneous session.

WINS

Windows Internet Naming Service (WINS) is used to map IP addresses to NetBIOS names. The WINS database is needed only when using Windows NT on the network. If you are using a Windows 2000 network, you can rely completely on DNS to provide host name to IP address mapping.

Designing with Media Integration

Media consists of the wiring or cable plant that supports the network traffic. Windows 2000 supports new types of media and integration with other types of traffic that runs on that media. Some of these technologies include:

- Telephony
- Remote Access
- Quality of Service (QoS)
- Network Load Balancing
- Asynchronous Transfer Mode (ATM)

Telephony

Windows 2000 implements telephony support through the Telephony Application Programming Interface (TAPI). TAPI can integrate information running on a telephone system, including caller ID, speed dialing, call transfer, video conferencing, and IP telephony. TAPI can work with hardware-based systems using an interface card, or it can work through a software IP telephony application deployed on Windows 2000.

On Windows 2000, TAPI is an interface. Windows 2000 also provides a TAPI application called Phone Dialer. The Phone Dialer application can perform both audio and video conferencing through the TAPI function calls.

You can start Phone Dialer by clicking the Start menu | Programs | Accessories | Communications, and you will see the screen illustrated in Figure 6.16.

Figure 6.16 TAPI Phone Dialer application.

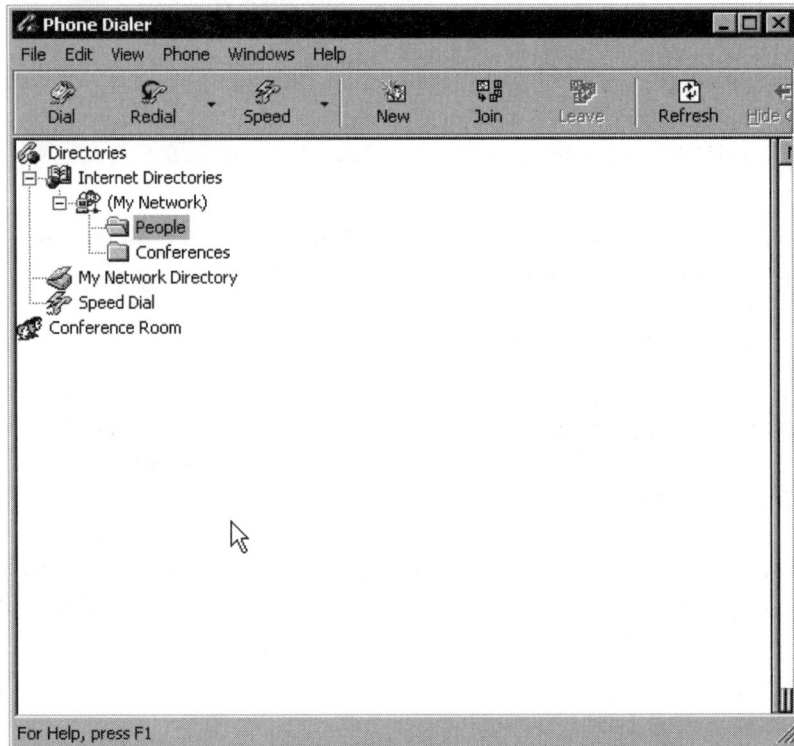

When deploying TAPI-integrated applications on Windows 2000, you should select ones that utilize IP multicast. When using multicast, the large bandwidth usage of audio/video data is reduced to a great degree. Not only does multicast create a single data stream that can be joined by multiple users, but it also uses a spanning tree algorithm to minimize network traffic. Without this architecture, there are separate data streams for each of the users.

Remote Access

Remote Access is a service that Windows 2000 inherited from Windows NT. Remote Access is a simple matter of connecting to the network from a remote location and being able to act as though the computer is locally connected to the network. This is typically a point-to-point connection either directly through a modem, or indirectly via the Internet over a virtual private network (VPN) connection.

The Remote Access server design will need to take into account the following factors:

Data storage for user accounts Will remote users need access to other servers? Where are these other servers located in relation to the remote access server?

Address assignment Will remote users require IP addresses? Will they require access through the network to an outside IP network (such as the Internet)? If DHCP addresses are used, how long should the DHCP lease be assigned?

Security Which users will be allowed to connect to the network remotely? How are users authenticated? Will accounts be locked out if there are too many invalid connection attempts? Will the remote access activity be recorded and audited? Is encryption required for remote connections?

When designing Remote Access servers, you need to pay attention to the protocols that remote users utilize to access the network. Will they be using the industry-standard Point-to-Point Protocol (PPP)? Or do they use a legacy UNIX system that requires Serial Line Internet Protocol (SLIP) or a legacy DOS, Windows for WorkGroups, LAN Manager, or Windows NT 3.1 system that requires Asynchronous NetBEUI (AsyBEUI)? It is generally safe to assume that PPP will be used for direct connections, but these considerations must be accounted for.

Quality of Service

Quality of Service is becoming more popular as a way of policy-based networking. When implementing QoS, an administrator can set policies for various computers, applications, users, or protocols on the network such that traffic for these items receive priority over other types of network traffic. An administrator may wish to prioritize video traffic, due to its streaming qualities, over something like a file transfer, which can withstand pauses in delivery without any loss of quality to the resulting file. As a result of implementing QoS, a network should have the most efficient use of its bandwidth, and high-priority applications will not suffer when network traffic is high.

Implementing QoS successfully requires both end nodes between a transaction, as well as any routers and switches between the end nodes, to support QoS. In Windows 2000, the QoS architecture uses the Resource Reservation Protocol (RSVP) Service to carry QoS requests with priority bandwidth requirements throughout the network. RSVP is a signaling protocol defined by the IETF in RFC 2205. The RSVP protocol is independent of the media, so that QoS is possible between each of the end nodes. So, whereas IP will route the data throughout the network, RSVP configures a reservation for data flowing along the route that IP has determined for the packet. To implement a policy-based QoS for end users, RSVP identifies the user's IP address and then communicates with a domain controller that holds the user account to obtain the policy for QoS. Packets are then marked so that network devices can provide the QoS.

When designing QoS on the Windows 2000 network, the main issue is ensuring that all devices on the network support QoS. Each server and each client should be able to support QoS, as well as all routers and switches.

Network Load Balancing

Network Load Balancing is a method of balancing incoming network traffic between various servers or clustered servers. When using Network Load Balancing, a user requests a network service. That request is directed to the first available of multiple servers. This way, if one server is busy, another will respond, and the availability of the service is maintained. One of the most common uses of Network Load Balancing is in Web services.

Windows 2000 implements Network Load Balancing as part of multinode clusters. This method will ensure that the workload is distributed among servers. When you design Network Load Balancing into your network, you may select only clustered servers that require high availability. You will want to ensure that servers with mission-critical applications and that serve a high number of simultaneous users will use clusters with Network Load Balancing. For example, a Web server providing an e-commerce application to customers on the Internet would be a good candidate for this type of service. By contrast, a small workgroup server providing file and print services would not.

ATM

Asynchronous Transfer Mode (ATM) is a protocol stack that can support high speeds over multiple types of media. It uses a fixed-length 53-byte *cell*, which is the name selected to describe this very small portion of data. Because the cells use a fixed length, each ATM host and router can easily determine the quality of the cell, and can process and switch it through the internetwork quickly. The short cell length means that the data can be switched in and out of memory without being written to hard disk storage, which is much slower than random access memory (RAM).

One of the most typical implementations of ATM is establishing it as a backbone networking protocol, and then routing the data to other dissimilar network types before it reaches servers or workstations. ATM does have the capability of traveling all the way to the end node, but for various reasons, is not typically configured to do so. Various reasons usually includes the fact that workstations and servers would need new network interfaces, and all the switching and routing hardware would need to be changed. This can be a prohibitive cost, and many organizations have chosen to implement ATM at the backbone to obtain at least a portion of the speed enhancements that it offers. Another reason for not implementing ATM is the lack of support for ATM within desktop operating systems. A third-party protocol may be implemented, but the overhead in administering network using third-party drivers is costly as well.

Windows 2000 does support ATM natively at the desktop. For those organizations that have waited to deploy ATM all the way to the end node, they can now upgrade their networks when implementing Windows 2000. The support in Windows 2000 includes:

- LAN emulation for ATM (LANE)
- IP over ATM
- PPP over ATM
- TAPI and Direct Show
- Direct streaming and other services
- Network Driver Interface Specification (NDIS)

When designing ATM into the Windows 2000 network, you will need to determine whether ATM will be implemented at the desktop, at the server, or only at the backbone. If ATM already exists on the backbone, you may wish to deploy ATM to the servers and route from the server access area of the network to the desktop access subnets, or you may wish to deploy ATM all the way to the desktops. Your decision will be based on several factors, including the costs involved, the current network performance, and how ATM would be utilized over the long term.

Case Studies

Designing a Windows 2000 network is a complex and involved process. Like all things worth doing well, the thought process into designing the network will reap the rewards of a highly performing, reliable network.

ABC Chemical Company

The ABC Chemical Company has many considerations in their network, from the Active Directory to the use of media in the network.

The first plan to create for an Active Directory is the forest plan. Even though it is large, ABC Chemical Company is physically located on a single campus. The company has three main manufacturing areas—pharmaceuticals, household products and raw chemical supplies—but the responsibilities for supporting these products are shared by five main departments: R&D, Executives, Sales & Marketing, Distribution, and IT/e-commerce. The Forest plan must decide how many forests are required, and what the root domain will be for each. In this case, ABC Chemical Company will need two production forests. One will provide Internet services outside the firewall, and the other will provide internal production services inside the firewall. The reason that these are two separate forests is that ABC requires FDA security standards, and to do that, their internal and external networks must remain both physically and logically separated. ABC Chemical Company elects to add a third forest for their IT Lab so that the IT group can test changes to the schema without affecting the production network. The root domain for each of the forests will be:

- Production internal forest—ABCChem.com
- Production e-commerce forest—ABC.com
- IT Lab forest—ABCLab.com

The next step in the Active Directory design is to determine the DNS/Domain plan. The number of domains must be determined for each forest and then DNS names applied to them. The ABC company decides that both the production internal forest and the e-commerce forest only require a single domain each. Since the forest domain plan designated the root domain name already, the work for these domains is complete. However, the ABC IT Group wants to model both a single domain plan in the lab, and add other domains later to model possible configurations for use later on. The lab forest, however, will be at a single domain for the near term, so the initial plan will only designate a single domain within it. Note that ABC made their DNS/Domain plans without consideration for their existing Windows NT domains. ABC wanted to have a best-case plan when they finished the Active Directory design, so they did not consider whether they should migrate existing domains into a final structure.

As for the DNS options, ABC has decided to migrate their existing DNS services running on Windows NT 4 to the Windows 2000 DNS service. This decision is based on their desire to implement dynamic updates, Active-Directory-Integrated zones, and the required SRV RRs.

The organizational unit (OU) hierarchy will be different for the e-commerce and the internal domains because of their different requirements. Since the IT Lab forest is created for "bashing and building" various models, the ABC group will not decide an OU hierarchy for the IT Lab domain. The guiding principals for OU hierarchies are to create the Administrative separations first, then divide out the hidden object folders below that, next reflect the group policy inheritance flow that is desired, and finally, only if needed, reflect the business org chart. The OU hierarchy is fairly simple and easy to change, so ABC is interested in a simplistic plan to begin with, which will change in the future. ABC decides to do the following:

E-commerce root domain—ABC.com—will have a single administrative-level OU because it is centrally managed by a single group. Below that, there will be a single OU for hidden objects from Internet users, and a single OU for group policy application. Further below the Group Policy OU there will be three OUs for more specific group policies. Each of these three represent the three types of products that an Internet user might purchase or work with—pharmaceuticals, household products, and raw chemicals. There is no need for any organization beyond that, because there is no org chart for Internet users, so the final OU hierarchy is illustrated in Figure 6.17.

Figure 6.17 OU hierarchy for ABC e-commerce domain.

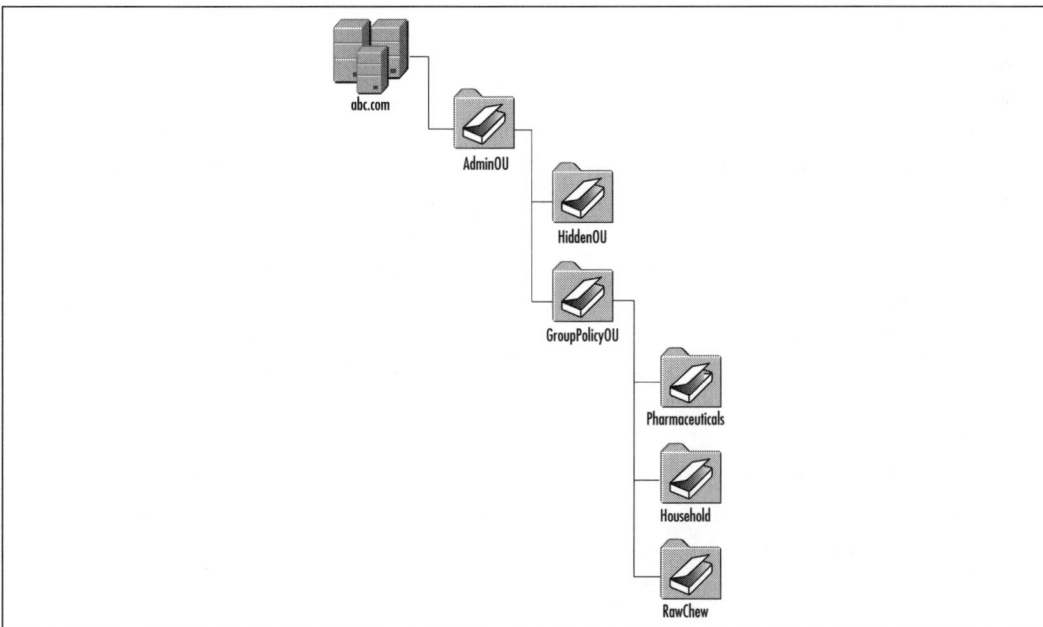

The internal production forest's root domain—ABCChem.com—will be somewhat different. Because each of the five business units has a separate administrator, there will be a top-level administrative OU (for the CIO) and five sub-OUs representing the business units. The need for hidden objects exists only within the R&D group, so that OU will have two sub-OUs, one for hidden objects and one for public objects. The group policies were planned to be applied by business unit, so there is no need for additional OUs. The ABC IT group did not see the need to create any organizational OUs since they plan to train end users to use searches for resources, rather than browsing. The resultant OU hierarchy is displayed in Figure 6.18.

Figure 6.18 OU hierarchy for ABC Internal Production domain.

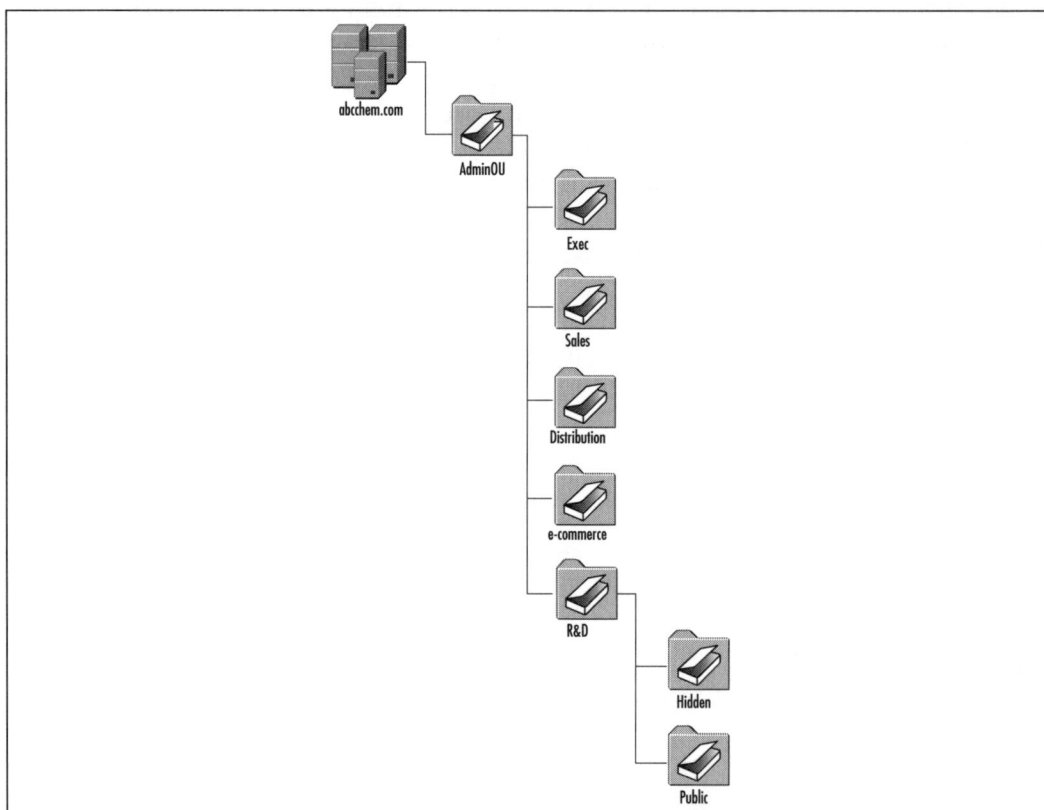

The site topology plan for ABC is an interesting matter. There are two possibilities for this company, since the site topology reflects the physical network. The first possibility is to create a single site to represent the campus, and one to represent each of the warehouses that are connected via Frame Relay. The second possibility is to create a single site to represent each building on the campus so that there are three sites and, because the warehouses do not have many users, to consider each part of the site in which the IT Group resides. The ABC IT Group decides to use the first option of two sites for the Internal Production network. However, for the e-commerce forest, they decide to use a single site in total—mainly because all the e-commerce servers are located in the server farm in one building and are routed directly to the Internet.

DHCP is a must for the ABC Chemical Company. Because they have decided to implement Windows 2000 DNS with dynamic updates enabled, they decide to take advantage of the Windows 2000 DHCP service that can register DNS names on behalf of clients. This will further enable departments such as the Research and Development unit to collaborate on a peer-to-peer basis.

The ABC e-commerce forest will be deployed completely on the Windows 2000 operating system. The e-commerce servers will all run the Internet Information Services (IIS). However, the ABC Group has decided to not install IIS on any server that is not, nor is currently designated as a future participant in the Internet or intranet. This decision means that the installation of ABC's servers will need to remove or avoid IIS because it is installed by default.

With the need for a highly secured network, ABC has decided to deploy the following Windows 2000 security options:

- Certificate Authority servers to provide trusted certificates to clients and servers as part of PKI.

- Kerberos authentication as part of the Active Directory (this is default).

- IPSec for encrypted data on the network wire.

The IT Group has decided that Terminal Services are not required for ABC Chemical Company production users. However, they have determined that they would like to reduce the costs of administration by being able to remotely control the Windows 2000 servers. Therefore, ABC will deploy Terminal Services in administrative mode only.

WINS is required for the existing Windows NT network. However, once the Windows 2000 servers and clients are completely in place, the WINS service will no longer be required. ABC plans to use WINS during the time that they have a mixed NT/2000 network, and then to remove the service completely once the network has been completely migrated to Windows 2000.

Telephony is one of ABC's main business requirements of audio conferencing, so the ABC Chemical Company plans to deploy the telephony applications on the Windows 2000 servers and clients. Remote Access services are not required for ABC Chemical Company. Quality of Service will be implemented to provide a better quality of video and audio conferencing across the network. Clusters and Network Load Balancing will be used for the Internet Information Servers to provide a highly reliable and available solution. ATM is not a media that will be implemented in this internetwork, so the Windows 2000 servers and clients do not need to support it.

West Coast Accounting, L.L.C.

West Coast Accounting is also going to deploy Windows 2000 on both clients and servers in their environment. The same decision-making process will be used in the West Coast Accounting design, but as you will see, the results will be much different!

West Coast Accounting has several sites, but only 300 end users. They perform some e-commerce and Internet Web hosting, but do not have to face stringent security limitations. One of the main business objectives for West Coast Accounting is to consolidate the management of the network through a single operating system in an effort to reduce administrative costs. Since additional forests cause incremental costs in administration, it is decided that West Coast Accounting will create a single forest with the root domain being westcoast.com.

The DNS/Domain plan for West Coast Accounting's forest needs to provide an e-commerce/Internet Web host domain, and an internal production domain. It is decided that the two domains need to be in separate namespaces. It is further decided that the root domain will be the internal production domain, while the namespace for the Internet domain will be wcacctg.com. The resulting DNS/Domain plan is illustrated in Figure 6.19. West Coast Accounting decides to implement the Windows 2000 DNS services, because the existing DNS server does not meet the minimum requirements of providing SRV RRs. They also decide to deploy dynamic updates and incremental zone transfers.

There are two organizational unit hierarchies that need to be created, one for each domain within the forest. The westcoast.com domain begins with a single administrative OU at the top level for the main network administrators. Below that, there are administrative OUs for each of the offices in Seattle, Phoenix, Los Angeles, San Francisco, and Portland. Only San Francisco creates a sub-OU for use in hiding objects. Since there are no plans for differing group policies applied at any site, and since the administrators do not want to create org chart OUs, no further sub-OUs are created. The Internet domain wcacctg.com is created with a single administrative OU and a single hidden object OU below that. There are no further OUs created for either group policy or for organizational purposes, although it is acknowledged that West Coast may create subdivisions in the OU hierarchy later on.

Figure 6.19 West Coast Accounting's DNS/Domain plan.

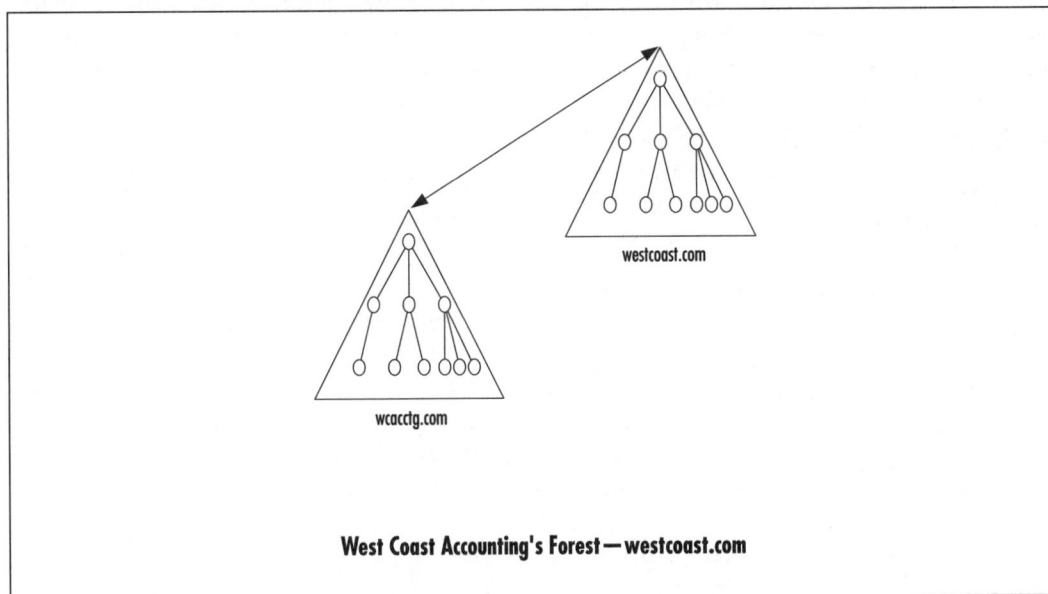

West Coast Accounting's Forest—westcoast.com

The site topology is created for the forest as a reflection of its physical structure. Each office—Seattle, Phoenix, Los Angeles, San Francisco, and Portland—is designated as a separate site. This is because each office is separated from the others via one or more WAN links, and each office will have at least two servers located within it. One consideration that West Coast Accounting gave to the site topology was to create a single site for the entire network. Because there were only 50 users in each location barring San Francisco, the need for creating separate sites based on user queries and authentication is small. However, when West Coast Accounting considered the traffic patterns when domain controllers were placed in each site, it became apparent that a single site would enable a person in Seattle to log on to a server in Phoenix, after passing through two WAN links and the San Francisco office. This traffic pattern was not desirable, so the design of separate sites was the final decision.

West Coast Accounting decides to implement DHCP services for Windows 2000. They consider a single DHCP server at the San Francisco site, but are concerned over the single point of failure aspect. Their final consideration is to have at least two DHCP servers in at least two different sites to provide redundancy.

West Coast Accounting will implement Windows 2000's Internet Information Services on the servers located in the wcacctg.com domain. They do not wish to implement IIS on production servers not providing e-commerce applications.

West Coast Accounting uses several accounting packages whose clients are bandwidth intensive. Because of the distributed nature of the offices, they decide to implement Terminal Services to provide the accounting applications over the WAN to every office. This will reduce the bandwidth consumption on the network, and reduce the administrative overhead. West Coast also decides to implement the Terminal Services option for administrative purposes for all other domain controllers, but not for member servers, since the local administrative team will be able to manage local member servers.

WINS is a required service for the existing Windows NT network, but not for Windows 2000. West Coast Accounting has a goal of a pure Windows 2000 network, so the WINS service will not be required after the network is completely migrated.

Since West Coast Accounting is going to deploy Voice-over IP, they plan to implement the telephony capabilities of Windows 2000. They also plan to deploy Routing and Remote Access with L2TP and IP Security as their virtual private network through the Internet. Quality of Service is tied to the implementation of Voice-over IP, but not for any other applications because of the use of Terminal Services to provide those mission-critical applications over the WAN. Clusters and Network Load Balancing are considered as a requirement for the servers that provide the mission-critical accounting applications even more so than they are required for the Internet e-commerce servers. ATM is not required for the network, and so it will not be deployed on the Windows 2000 servers or workstations.

Summary

The core of Windows 2000 design planning is the plan for the Active Directory. This is complex planning process that is intended to create a design meeting many factors:

- Fault tolerance
- Availability of the directory
- Bandwidth utilization characteristics between domain controllers
- Network usage by directory clients
- Scalability

The Active Directory consists of four different plans:

Forest plan The number of forests to deploy on the network and the designation of a root domain for the forest.

DNS/Domain plan The number of domains organized into a hierarchy using a DNS namespace, their DNS names, and the functions for each domain need to be designated in this plan.

Organizational unit hierarchy The organization of containers within each domain, beginning at the top with administrative containers and hidden object containers, then following with containers for the application of group policies, and after that, any OUs reflecting the organization chart.

Site topology The number of sites and locations for them, noting that this configuration will affect the traffic traversing the WAN.

Windows 2000 deployments do not consist solely of an Active Directory. They also consist of other services that need to be selected based on the enterprise's business objectives. DHCP is a service that can reduce network administration costs. While it is not necessary to deploy a Windows 2000 DHCP server to reduce the administrative costs, if deploying the Windows 2000 DNS service (determined in the DNS/Domain plan), it can further reduce administrative costs through its ability to register IP addresses on behalf of DHCP clients with the Windows 2000 DNS service running dynamic updates.

One of the default services that Windows 2000 comes with is Internet Information Services (IIS). Many organizations are deploying Web servers and FTP servers as part of an e-business reengineering effort. IIS is automatically deployed with every Windows 2000 server, but that may not be desirable for some servers and should then be removed as a Windows 2000 service.

Security options for Windows 2000 are another reason that Windows 2000 is deployed. It supports IP Security, Certificate Authority services, PKI, virtual private networking, and Kerberos authentication within the Active Directory.

One of the new Windows 2000 components is Terminal Services. This service provides a remote control capability of a Windows 2000 server in which multiple simultaneous users can take remote control of separate sessions of a single server. They can run different applications, and their sessions never overlap.

Windows 2000 includes some backward-compatible services, one of them being WINS. WINS provides a NetBIOS name to IP address mapping service. WINS is required for legacy Windows networks, but not for pure Windows 2000 networks.

Windows 2000 supports telephony applications through the implementation of TAPI. It also provides the ability to dial in directly to a network or tunnel through the Internet with its Routing and Remote Access service.

FAQs

Q: How can I limit the bandwidth utilized by a noncritical Web server?

A: IIS provides a per-Web-site Bandwidth Throttling option on the properties of a Web site to reduce the amount of network bandwidth that a Web site consumes. Because this is a per-Web-site option, that means that a noncritical Web site can be throttled, while a critical Web site provided by the same server can be left unchecked.

Q: What type of data will not be sent across the wire if I'm replicating two different domains within the same forest in two separate sites?

A: Since the domains are in the same forest, they will have the global catalog, schema, and configuration traffic to exchange. However, because they do not share domain namespace, they will not be exchanging data from either domain's partition. This is one of the more efficient designs, since it reduces bandwidth consumption to only the minimum required within a forest.

Q: How do I enable TAPI support in Windows 2000?

A: Telephony support offered through TAPI is enabled automatically in Windows 2000. This is not true of Windows NT 4, however, since TAPI was introduced as part of Service Pack 4 and required additional installation steps.

Chapter 7

Sizing the Infrastructure for Windows 2000

Solutions in this chapter:

- **Exploring sites**

- **Understanding the File Replication Service (FRS)**

- **Understanding replication of the Active Directory database**

- **Utilizing Simple Mail Transport Protocol (SMTP) or Remote Procedure Call protocols appropriately for replication**

- **Optimizing network traffic through strategic server placement**

- **Determining the right size for the infrastructure**

Introduction

In an enterprise network, changes are made every day. Each time a change is made in the Active Directory, the domain controller that the change was made upon must synchronize its database with the rest of the domain controllers in its domain. Also, if the change affected the Global Catalog (GC), then all of the GC servers would also require the update.

Users need the network to perform well for logging onto the network, searching for resources, and for their network applications. The key to ensuring that your infrastructure has enough bandwidth to provide the performance required by users is to understand the network bandwidth utilization of all these types of traffic—most importantly of the traffic generated by Active Directory replication.

Active Directory Replication Topology

There are several elements to the Active Directory replication; the enablers are:

- Connection objects
- Sites
- Site links
- Site link bridges
- IP subnets
- Bridgehead servers
- Replication protocols

These elements eventually create a topology, or path, throughout the internetwork that enables synchronization of each portion of the Active Directory. These elements make up the Active Directory traffic that is replicated:

- Global Catalog
- Domain partitions
- Schema
- Configuration

The Path for Replication Traffic

The replication topology is the path that replication traffic follows when it traverses the network. The topology consists of several components, listed in Table 7.1.

Table 7.1 Replication Components

Component	Role	Description
Connection objects	Replication enabler	Objects placed below NTDS Settings objects that belong to the domain controllers receiving traffic. Connection objects represent unidirectional flow of traffic between domain controllers. (NTDS stands for NT Directory Service. Each domain controller has an NTDS Settings object.)
Sites	Replication enabler	Collections of well-connected Internet Protocol (IP) subnets. They typically represent local area networks (LANs) and do not span wide area network (WAN) links.
Site links	Replication enabler	Logical connections between sites, which are connected directly by a physical link. Site links enable replication to take place between different sites.
Site link bridges	Replication enabler	Site link bridges are connections between site links that share a common site. This enables replication to take place between sites that are not connected directly by a physical link.
IP subnets	Replication enabler	IP subnets are objects created to represent a Transport Control Protocol/Internet Protocol (TCP/IP) subnet applied to a physical local area network segment.
Bridgehead servers	Replication enabler	Designated servers within a site that deliver traffic between sites. These servers can be used to control the flow of traffic.
Replication protocols	Replication enabler	Both RPC over TCP/IP and SMTP protocols.
Global catalog	Replicated traffic	Global catalog servers all carry a copy of the global catalog partition of the Active Directory, but standard domain controllers don't. Changes to the global catalog must be replicated to all global catalog servers.

Continued

Table 7.1 Continued

Component	Role	Description
Domain partition	Replicated traffic	Each domain controller has a copy of its own domain's partition of the Active Directory, but does not carry a copy of any other domain partition. Updates to the domain are replicated only to domain controllers that belong to the same domain.
Schema	Replicated traffic	The schema updates are replicated to every domain controller in the forest.
Configuration	Replicated traffic	The configuration updates are replicated to every domain controller in the forest.

Sites are the main building blocks of the replication topology. Since sites represent physical portions of the network, they have been developed to be flexible—they can easily be changed, added, or deleted from the replication topology. When designing a replication topology, there are rules to follow that can make the topology more effective for your network:

1. The physical network should be reflected in the replication topology.

2. Every individual site should have at least one dedicated domain controller.

3. Sites are independent of domains—a domain can span sites or a site can span domains. Figure 7.1 illustrates how a domain can span sites, and Figure 7.2 illustrates how a site can span domains.

4. Each site should be considered for at least one Global Catalog server, which can be the same server as its domain controller.

5. No site should span a slow, unreliable link. WAN links tend to be either slow or unreliable.

6. Remote access users do not need a separate site.

Figure 7.1 Domain spans multiple sites.

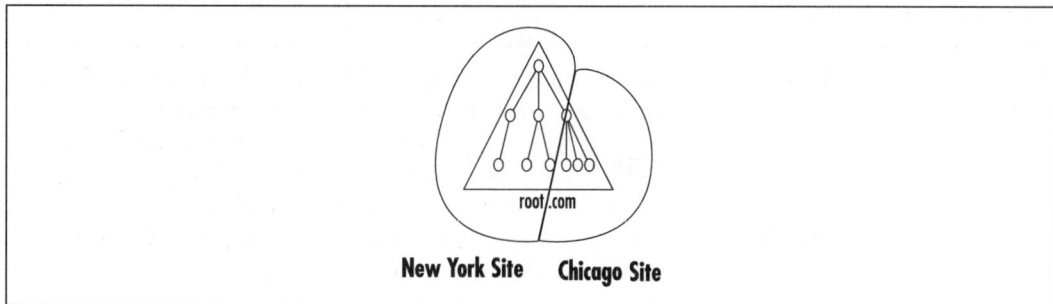

New York Site   Chicago Site

Figure 7.2 Site spans multiple domains.

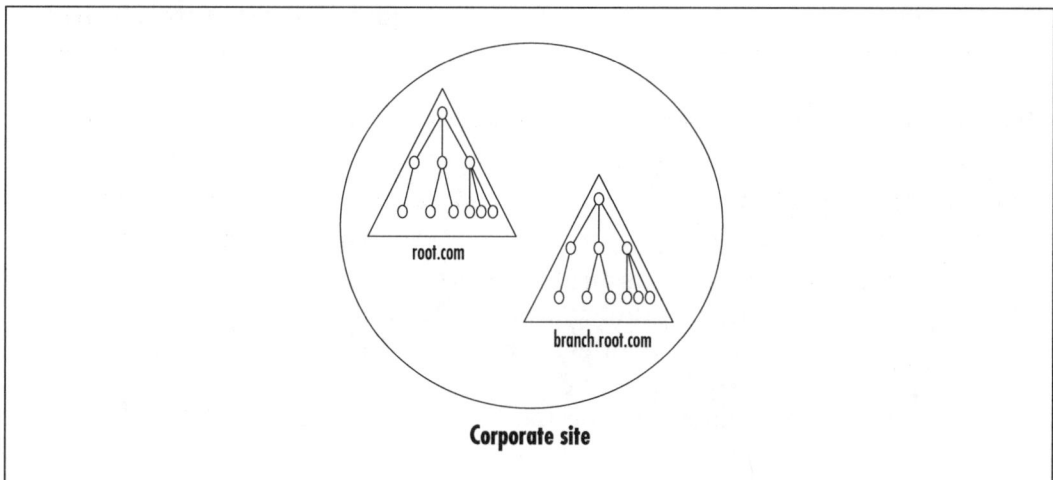

Corporate site

TIP

Sites play a role in the query and authentication traffic management as well. Sites determine the proximity of networked computers to Active Directory domain controllers. As such, they are not part of the domain namespace, but sites can locate a nearby domain controller within their geographic boundaries. When a user logs on to the Active Directory, the IP address of that computer is used to identify the user's location—that is, the IP subnet and the site. From then on all the user's authentication and query traffic are directed to a domain controller within the same site.

Default-First-Site-Name

The first site within the replication topology is created automatically. It has an obvious name—the Default-First-Site-Name. Whenever a domain controller (DC) is installed, it automatically is placed within the Default-First-Site-Name site, unless one of the following events has occurred:

1. A different site has been designated as the default site for the forest.

2. The name of the Default-First-Site-Name is changed. This can be done in the Active Directory Sites and Services console by right-clicking on Default-First-Site-Name, selecting Rename from the pop-up menu, and typing the new name.

3. The IP subnet on which the new domain controller has been installed is already designated as part of a different site. In this case, the new domain controller would join that different site automatically.

Partitions within the Active Directory

There are several partitions in the Active Directory. Updates to each partition of the Active Directory must be replicated only to the domain controllers that hold that same partition. Some domain controllers are used as conduits for the traffic, such as bridgehead servers. The trick to reducing network bandwidth consumption is understanding which partitions must be replicated across various connections and designing the Active Directory partitions and sites in such a way that reduces the amount of traffic.

The Global Catalog is one of the most important partitions of the Active Directory when there are multiple domains in the Active Directory forest. It contains a partial copy of each object in the forest so that a user can search for resources in any domain in the Active Directory. In a way, the GC glues the domains together so that they work as a single directory service. The network administrator can designate any domain controller as a Global Catalog server. It is recommended that every site have at least one Global Catalog server so that users' query traffic is contained within the site. The only time when you may not need a GC server at every site is when you have only a single domain:

- All users share the same context in a single domain so there is no need for User Principal Names (UPNs).

- There is no need to re-index all the resources that exist in the domain.

- Universal groups are not required to group objects that exist in multiple domains.

One of the things to watch out for with the Global Catalog is how many objects and attributes you place in the GC. Universal groups are particularly an issue since the contents of the universal group are copied individually to the GC. If you place a thousand user objects in a universal group, then you have added a thousand user objects to the GC. However, if you place a thousand user objects in a global group, and then place the single global group within the universal group, then you have added a single global group object to the GC.

You can designate any server as a GC server. To do so:

1. Open the Active Directory Sites and Services console.

2. Expand the Sites container by clicking the plus sign (+) to the left of it.

3. Expand the site that contains the server you wish to make a GC server.

4. Expand the Servers container.

5. Expand your future GC server.

6. Right-click on the NTDS Settings object below that server.

7. Select Properties from the pop-up menu.

8. Check the box to make this server a Global Catalog server.

Domain controllers from different domains do not share domain partition traffic. Each domain is a separate partition of the Active Directory. Only domain controllers that belong to the same domain will replicate that domain's partition traffic. What can be inferred from this is that when a domain does not span sites, then no domain partition update traffic will pass over the site boundary, as illustrated in Figure 7.3. A domain controller will hold only the partition for its own domain, and you cannot place more than one domain partition on a single DC.

The schema and configuration containers are both replicated to every DC in the forest. Both of these containers hold a very stable partition of the Active Directory. The schema is a listing of the types of objects and attributes that are allowed to exist in the Active Directory. Changes to the schema are rare, but when a change occurs, all DCs must have a copy of the new schema in order for those new objects and attributes that are created to be recognized and usable. The configuration is the physical placement of Active Directory partitions, including the entire site arrangement. Only when changes are made to the configuration will there need to be updates replicated to other DCs.

Figure 7.3 Domain updates are not replicated across site boundaries when domains do not span the sites.

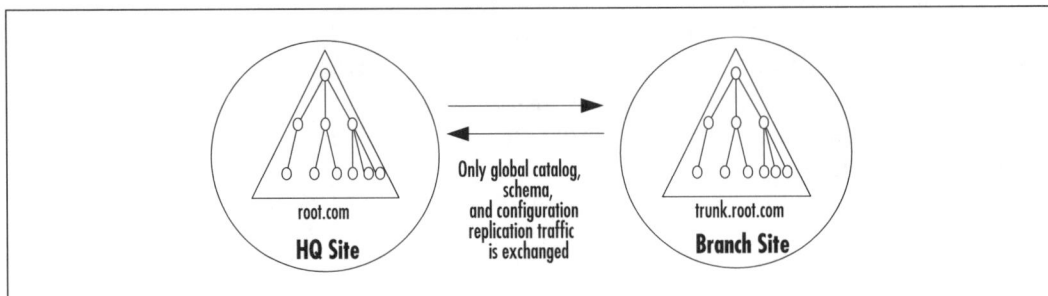

Only global catalog, schema, and configuration replication traffic is exchanged

root.com
HQ Site

trunk.root.com
Branch Site

Site Plan

Sites are sets of well-connected IP subnets. These network segments are able to transmit traffic to each other at a speed that generally is equated with a LAN. Bandwidth is generally available at 4 Mbps or better between well-connected IP subnets, but this is not set in stone. Designating an IP subnet as part of a site is a decision that you make depending on your needs for directing traffic.

Knowledge Consistency Checker (KCC)

The KCC is a key component to intrasite replication. It is a process that runs on each DC to ensure that the replication traffic generated on that DC reaches its destinations (for example, all other DCs within that same site) in a timely fashion.

The KCC automatically generates connection objects within a site. This is not a one-time act, though; the KCC persistently checks the site and reconfigures connection objects to ensure that the replication ring of DCs is always no more than three hops, as shown in Figure 7.4, and that latency is not suffered in the ring. If there is excessive latency, the KCC will create additional connection objects to create what amounts to a shortcut between DCs inside the site.

The goal of intrasite replication is to achieve replication around a ring in 15 minutes. The default five-minute interval of the replication within a site combined with the maximum of three hops in a ring meets this goal. Replication traffic is not generated without any updates. Instead, it is triggered whenever a change is made to the DC's database. A priority change will not wait for a five-minute interval—it will trigger replication immediately within the site. (Priority changes include password changes, account lockouts, and policy changes for passwords and account lockouts, as well as Relative Identification (RID) changes for domain naming of the Security Identifier (SID) for security principal objects such as users and groups.)

Figure 7.4 Replication ring.

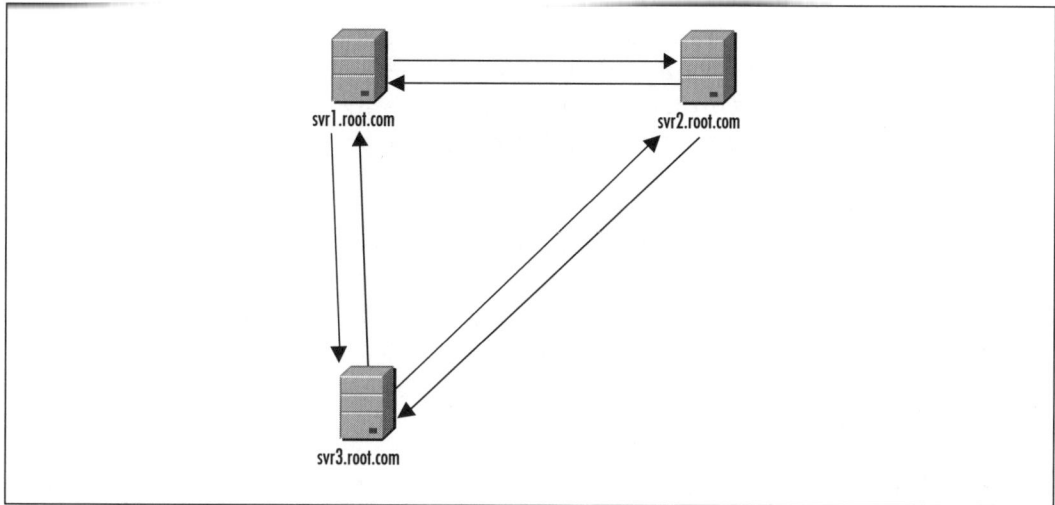

The KCC creates connection objects *only* for intrasite replication. The KCC does not create connection objects or site links or any other objects for replication between sites (intersite replication). An administrator must create all intersite replication objects.

Connection Objects

A connection object directs traffic to a target DC. The connection object exists as an object in the Active Directory Sites and Services console, below the NTDS Settings for the target DC. It represents a unidirectional flow of traffic. When two DCs exchange replication traffic with each other, they each must have a connection object.

WARNING

Be careful when you move a server from one site to another. When you move the server, its connection objects are moved along with it. If you don't want intersite replication to occur between whatever servers for which the KCC generated connection objects in the old site, then you will need to delete the connection objects *on the DCs in both sites*. After that, you will need to determine where the traffic needs to be sent and to create the connection objects on DCs in both sites. If you intend to use bridgehead servers, you will simply want to direct traffic to the DC's site bridgehead server. The bridgehead servers will need to have connection objects pointing at each other to ensure that data is transmitted between the two sites.

Site Links and Site Link Bridges

Site links exist solely for intersite replication. Not only does intersite replication require connection objects, but it requires site links between sites
that are connected physically by at least one network link. A site link is a
logical conduit of communication between two sites. Communication will
not happen unless there are connection objects between DCs in each of
the connected sites.

Communication can take place over a site link using either RPC or
SMTP traffic. You can use SMTP communication only between sites that
are not spanned by the same domain because the SMTP protocol will not
transport domain updates, only GC, schema, and configuration traffic.
RPCs over TCP/IP are the default intersite replication traffic; SMTP is used
where traffic is configured between sites that are not spanned by domains,
as illustrated in Figure 7.5.

Figure 7.5 SMTP replication between sites does not transmit domain updates.

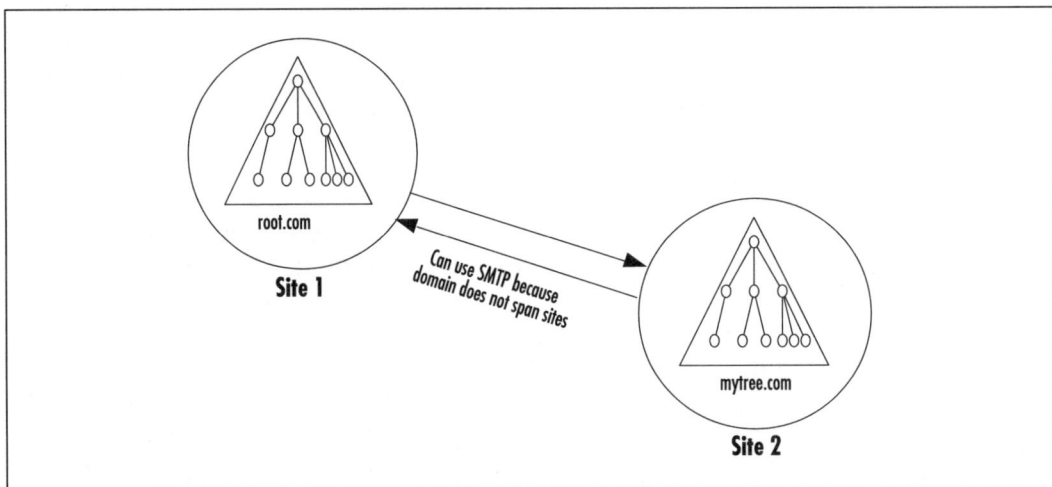

A site link can contain more than two sites, if that physical link is
attached to more than two sites. WAN "clouds" such as Frame Relay or
X.25 networks are examples of this type of site link. Any site attached
directly to the cloud can be part of the site link.

You can configure information about the site, such as:

- Cost, a parameter stating the logical expense of using this site link
  as opposed to another site link that could lead to the same destination.

- Schedule of availability, allowing the site link to be active for replication during certain periods of time.

- Replication frequency, the periodic basis for the replication traffic.

A site link bridge connects site links together. It creates a forwarding system using intermediate sites shared by two or more different site links so that the nonadjacent sites can exchange replication traffic. Figure 7.6 illustrates this system.

Figure 7.6 How a site link bridge works.

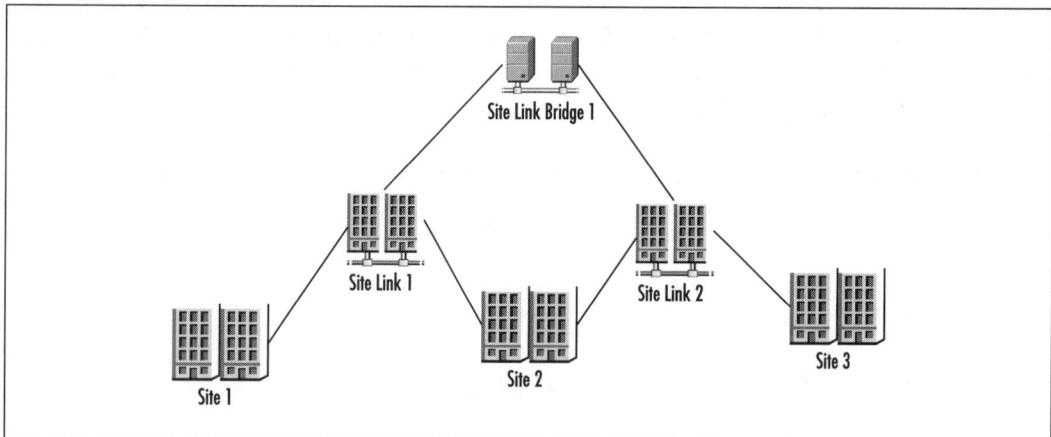

Bridgehead Servers

A bridgehead server is designated for its site as the main (or one of the main) domain controller to send replication traffic over a site link. You can use a bridgehead server to manage the flow of traffic between various sites. Some campus networks are large and complex, but still would work best as a single site. In these networks, the domain controllers located closest to the routers leading to other sites should be designated as bridgehead servers. That will ensure that the data going across the site link is filtered through one or a very few servers, rather than from any server located anywhere within the site, as depicted in Figure 7.7.

Figure 7.7 Bridgehead servers in a complex network.

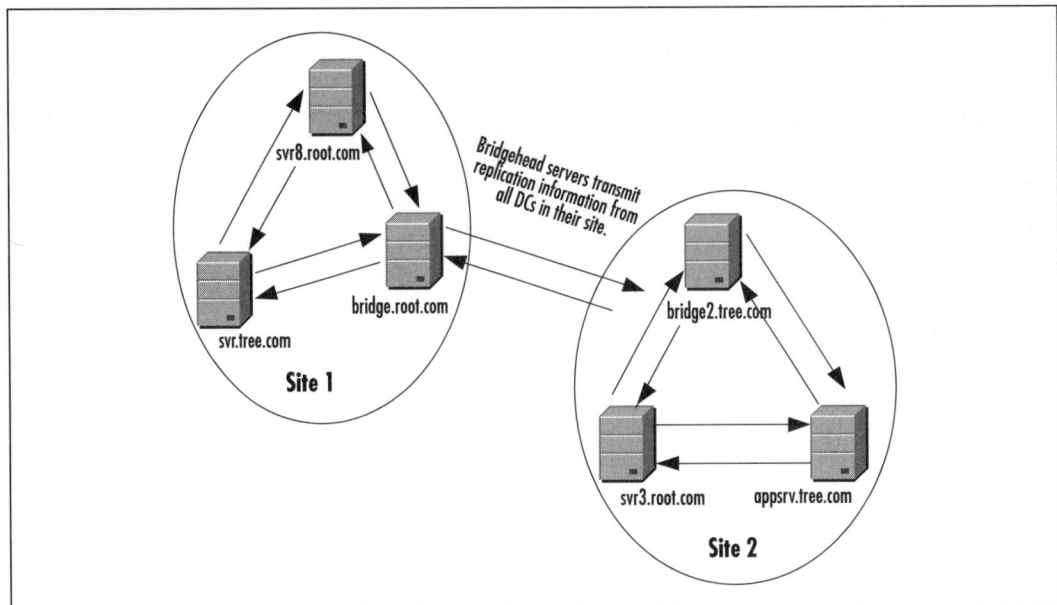

Planning the Site Topology

Your site topology plan will reflect your network. If you are planning on making changes to your network infrastructure before deploying Windows 2000, you will want to make your site topology plan based on the future network infrastructure.

Now this is where it gets complicated … Not only may you intend to make decisions about the Windows 2000 site plan based on your network infrastructure, but you also may wish to make changes to your network infrastructure *because* of Windows 2000. So, how does this affect your site topology plan the next go-round? The answer is not simple. You may adjust each plan more than once based on the changes you had made to the other plan. Since each plan is directly related to the other, optimization of Windows 2000 and the network infrastructure will be a system of cause and effect.

When you are planning your site topology, you will need to decide whether a single site will suffice or whether you need more. You should designate separate sites for those network areas that are geographically independent. When you do this, your network will receive the following benefits:

- Within each site, query and authentication traffic is localized.

- Within each site, replication traffic occurs freely and frequently (It is uncompressed and sent by default every five minutes if updates are available) so users will see updates on local network resources within a short period of time.

- Users perceive higher response performance when authenticating to the network or querying for resources because their request is maintained within the local site.

- WAN links that exist between two sites experience reduced traffic because replication traffic is compressed and can be scheduled by the administrator.

There are situations in which you have two distinct LANs separated by a WAN link, where you may decide *not* to create a separate site for each LAN. This will happen if you have a location that will not have a dedicated domain controller, or that simply does not have many users and would not create a large amount of query or authentication traffic. You should always have a domain controller in each site. So if you do not intend to place a domain controller somewhere, do not create a separate site for it. For how many users in a location separated from the rest of the network should you provide with a domain controller and a separate site?

This will have to be something that you analyze and optimize over time. A guideline that I generally recommend would be to dedicate a domain controller and site when you have around 50 to 75 or more users in a LAN.

Planning Time Synchronization

When domain controllers replicate the Active Directory database updates to each other, they use a method to make certain that conflicts do not occur. A decision to resolve an Active Directory conflict is based on version, timestamping, and globally unique IDs. Time synchronization plays a great deal of importance in all distributed databases. Most of them use the timestamp at some stage in determining which conflicting update is the last update made to the Active Directory, and therefore wins the right to update the database.

For example, if the network administrator in Detroit, Michigan makes a change to the phone number for the user account George Jones at 2:22 PM, and the network administrator in Seattle, Washington makes a change to George Jones' phone number at 11:21 AM, then the change made in Detroit would win. (The different time zones resolve to show that the Detroit change was made one minute later than the Seattle change.) Time synchronization is critical to this process. If the time was set even two minutes earlier in Detroit (at 2:20 PM), then the Seattle change would win—and time is not self-correcting; it could be set minutes, hours, days, months, or even years apart from one system to the next if it is not managed. When time is managed, a common time is agreed upon by all systems and they periodically check with designated time services to ensure that the common time is synchronized among all of those systems.

The Active Directory process for resolving a conflict is a three-tiered check and balance process. First, the version number of the updated attribute is checked. Whichever of the two changes has the highest version number will win this conflict. If the version numbers are equal, then the timestamps of the conflicting updates are compared. The latest timestamp wins. If the timestamps are equal, then the Globally Unique Ids (GUIDs) of the originating Directory Service Agent (DSA) that wrote the change are evaluated.

The Windows 2000 W32TIME service manages time synchronization. It is implemented as the Simple Network Time Protocol (SNTP) defined in RFC 1769 and updated in RFC 2030, and can be started with the NET START W32TIME command.

There are both time servers and time clients. The first DC installed acts as the primary SNTP server. Subsequent DCs act as time servers for all member servers and workstations, which are time clients. Time servers will resolve the common time with the primary SNTP server.

Time clients contact time servers at logon, and every eight hours thereafter until the client logs off the network. Time servers grant time clients a two-minute time variance. If the time variance is greater than two seconds, then the time client adjusts its time to match that of the time server, and then the time client contacts the time server every four hours.

FRS

FRS is the File Replication Service. It exists on each domain controller in the Active Directory forest, but it is not a form of Active Directory replication. FRS is not as bandwidth-sensitive as Active Directory replication. It does not simply replicate the latest update to other servers; instead it replicates the entire file.

FRS uses the SYSVOL directory as the repository for a file directory structure that is replicated. SYSVOL is a directory that exists on each domain controller in the Active Directory. The NETLOGON share, group policies, system policies, and logon/logoff scripts all exist within the SYSVOL directory.

When any of the contents of the SYSVOL directory structure are modified, added, or deleted, the rest of the domain controllers are synchronized to match. FRS uses the same sites, site links, connection objects, and schedule as that used for Active Directory replication. Therefore, when the Active Directory is synchronized, you can expect FRS changes to be synchronized.

FRS is basically a redundant set of folders on domain controllers with a designated NTFS folder. FRS is multimaster, providing multiple distribution paths between replicas in a replica set. Dampening logic is used to prevent a file being replicated to the same server twice during the same replication cycle.

When a file is updated on server 1, then FRS attempts to update the same file on server 2. If the file on server 2 was changed more than the default time period later than the file on server 1, then the update is rejected. The default time period is 30 minutes. If the file on server 2 was last updated more than 30 minutes earlier, then the update is accepted immediately and the file on server 1 is copied to server 2.

If the file on server 1 is updated within the default 30 minutes of the last time the file on server 2 was updated, then the version numbers are checked. The file with the greater version number wins and is updated to the other server.

If the versions are equal, the event time is checked to see which of the files was changed last. The file that was changed last wins and is updated to the other server. What happens next is this:

1. Once a change has been made to a file, NTFS enters the change into the NTFS change journal.

2. FRS monitors its own files by reviewing the NTFS change journal and using file and folder filters to check for closed files that are updated. A three-second delay mechanism, called the aging cache, prevents FRS from replicating files that are undergoing rapid changes.

3. The updated file is logged in the inbound log as a change order.

4. A copy of the updated file is placed in the local staging directory—a temporary storage area used prior to copying data across the network that ensures file copying can take place if there is some reason that the original file is inaccessible.

5. The outbound log is updated with the change order.

6. A change notification about the updated file is sent to replica partners.

7. The replica partners determine whether to accept or reject the update. If it is accepted, the partners write the change to the inbound logs.

8. The file is copied from the staging directory on the originating server to the staging directory of the replica partners.

9. The replica partners write the change to the outbound log.

10. The file is moved from the staging directory to the ultimate directory on the replication partners.

Dfs

Dfs is the Distributed file system. It can exist either on standalone member servers or Active Directory domain controllers. Because Dfs can be on standalone servers, automatic file replication must be enabled on standalone servers. This is done by:

1. Opening the Dfs console (Start | Programs | Administrative Tools | Dfs).

2. Right-clicking the Dfs link in the replica set. (These steps are given for a Dfs server in which the Dfs root has already been created.)

3. Selecting Replication Policy from the pop-up menu.

4. Clicking Enable in the replication policy dialog.

After this, the Dfs replication occurs as though it were a part of FRS replication, except in certain cases. In the following cases, Dfs folders will not be replicated:

- Replication is not enabled on the computer hosting the shared folder.

- The disk partition hosting the Dfs shared folder is formatted with an older version of NTFS.

- The computer hosting the Dfs shared folder does not belong to a Windows 2000 domain.

TIP

FRS is new to Windows 2000. Windows NT 4 used a different method of replication called LMRepl. When you have a domain that is mixed—with both NT 4 backup domain controllers and Windows 2000 domain controllers—then you need to bridge the FRS to LMRepl in order to ensure that files are copied across from Windows 2000 to NT4. To do this, you will need to copy files from the Windows 2000 FRS directories manually to the Windows NT 4 LMRepl directories. You can also do this through a batch file script that you load as a scheduled service on a designated Windows 2000 domain controller. Your batch file will include a line that is similar to:

xcopy \\mydomain.com\sysvol\domain.com\scripts \\nt4server\export\ scripts /s /D

This command will copy only the newest files in the entire subdirectory structure to the NT4 server. The batch file can be scheduled using the Windows 2000 scheduler. Note that this batch file will only push files to the NT4 server, but will not pull any files from it. If a user makes a change to a file on the NT4 server, the file will be overwritten by any updated files that are pushed down from the Windows 2000 FRS.

Preparing the Infrastructure for Windows 2000

Before you start making changes to your network, you will need to have a complete set of documentation for it. This is a long and involved set of documents that will describe every detail of the network. These documents will guide you, not only on your needs for upgrading or replacing non-Windows-2000-compliant hardware and software, but also with making decisions on your network infrastructure planning. You will need, at a minimum, an inventory of the following network elements:

- Server hardware, operating systems, and applications
- Router hardware and operating system versions
- Switches and their operating system versions
- Server roles—file servers, web servers, print servers, etc.
- Mission-critical applications
- Existing and future directory service design
- Security requirements, policies, and applications

Many enterprises maintain an inventory on their network equipment, whether they create a manual inventory or use an asset management software system. The importance of this asset inventory is highlighted during any network upgrade—whether that applies to servers, clients, or other infrastructure equipment. The items you should include on this inventory are:

- Computer and peripheral hardware, manufacturer, model, type, Beginning Input Output System (BIOS) versions, and other differentiating factors such as drivers and configuration specifics (such as two disks being mirrored or three disks running Redundant Array of Inexpensive Disks (RAID) 5, and so on).

- Network operating systems and desktop operating systems, including versions, hotfixes, and service packs applied.

- Software, both Commercial Off The Shelf (COTS) and line of business (typically home-grown) applications, including versions and any applied hotfixes.

- Infrastructure equipment, including manufacturer, model, type, Cisco's Internetwork Operating System (IOS) version, and any other differentiating factors.

These inventories will give you a good idea of what equipment and software on your network is compatible with Windows 2000, since you can compare them to the Windows 2000 Hardware Compatibility List and Application compatibility list. (Windows 2000 HCL is located at www.microsoft.com/hcl, and the application compatibility can be found at www.microsoft.com/windows.) A hardware and software inventory will provide you with only part of the story. To truly understand your network environment, you need to look at the language those computers speak—their protocols:

- Are all the computers on the network running TCP/IP?

- Are some running another protocol—Network Beginning Input Output System (NetBIOS), Internetwork Packet Exchange (IPX), Systems Network Architecture (SNA), Digital Equipment Corporation Networking (DECNet), AppleTalk, and so on?

- What types of remote access protocols are being used? Are users dialing directly to a Remote Access Service (RAS) server? Do the connections use Serial Line Interface Protocol (SLIP), Point-to-Point Protocol (PPP), or something else? What type of remote authentication is required?

- Is encryption commonly used? What type?

- Is there a virtual private network (VPN)? Does it use Layer 2 Transport Protocol (L2TP), Point-to-Point Tunneling Protocol (PPTP), IP Security (IPSec), or another proprietary protocol?

- Does a firewall separate the network from the Internet? What type of firewall is it? Does it filter protocols, filter IP addresses, or provide proxy services?

- Are some protocols used on some LANs, whereas other protocols are used on other LANs?

- Is there a Dynamic Host Configuration Protocol (DHCP) server? What about Windows Internet Naming Service (WINS)? Domain Name Service (DNS)?

You will need to create a graphical representation of your network at a high level—basically depicting the WAN links and large networks in the enterprise, if you have a very large internetwork. You will also need to create more detailed network maps of each portion of the network in order to ensure that you've examined all of it. In your map, you should note which networks are running what protocols and where the servers, routers, and switches are located. An example is shown in Figure 7.8.

Figure 7.8 An example of a network diagram.

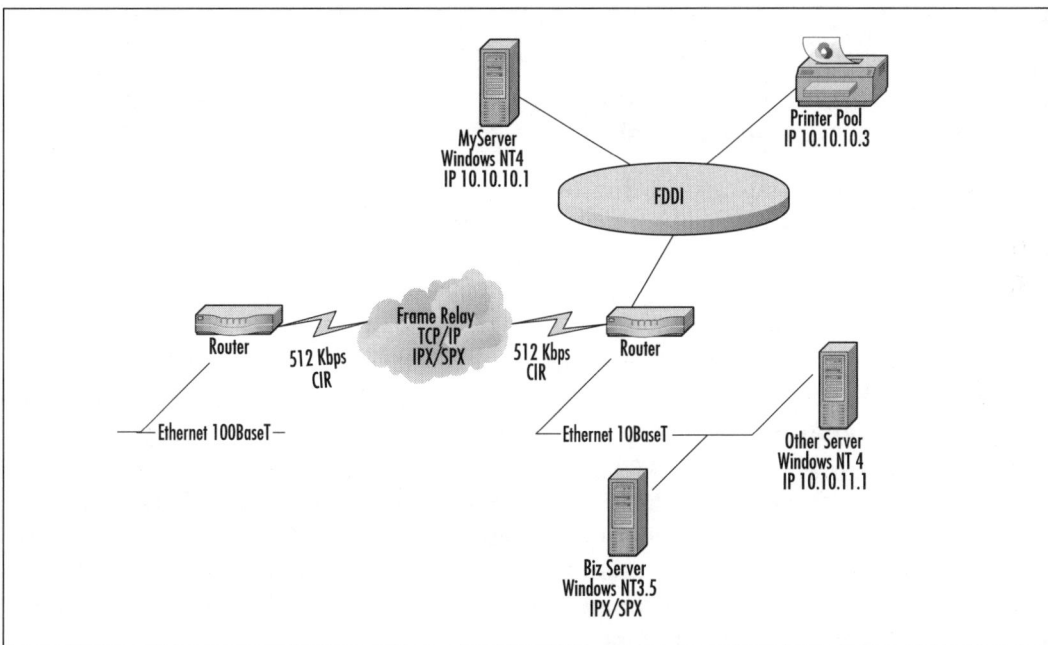

One advantage to mapping the network is that you can use it to visually see the problem areas of your network. For example, if you have a stub network where the users complain of long delays in accessing their e-mail, you may find that the traffic is being routed through several other networks before it reaches the e-mail server, *or* that the users in that network are running a graphics application and sending huge print jobs across the wire, glutting the network with excessive low-priority traffic. A single symptom can represent different problems. A bottleneck needs to be identified before it can be fixed.

The network map you create should include the following information:

Physical wiring Cable lengths and grades, paths in and out of the wiring closet.

Remote access Integrated Services Digital Network (ISDN), analog, and VPN accesses to the network.

Routers Name, IP addresses of interfaces, IOS versions, access list names, protocols used, special services provided (if any).

Servers Host name, IP address, protocols used, special services provided such as DNS.

Switches, bridges, and hubs Name, IP addresses of interfaces, Virtual Local Area Networks (VLANs) (if any).

WAN links Type of WAN link, bandwidth provided, bandwidth available (provided bandwidth minus any used bandwidth).

Usage Number of users at each site, peak number of simultaneous users at any site that runs multiple shifts, web server locations with usage rates.

Another useful diagram is the logical representation of your NT domain architecture. This is a simple picture showing each domain, the trusts that it may have with other domains, and any servers playing primary domain controller or backup domain controller (PDC/BDC) roles or other special service roles within it, as shown in Figure 7.9. While you create this diagram, be aware that it will be ancient history once you finish upgrading to Windows 2000. You will need to have your future diagrams of your Windows 2000 forest, domains/DNS, and site topology for a future view of your network.

If you already use TCP/IP, then you will need to document how you have implemented it on the network. If you don't use TCP/IP, you will want to decide how you will want to use it in the future since it is required by Windows 2000. (With the pervasiveness of the Internet, it is not likely that many non-TCP/IP networks exist.)

- Do you use DHCP? What are your rules around DHCP leases for network clients or remote network clients?

- What addresses are statically assigned to servers? Do you have addresses statically assigned to other network hosts? Which ones, and why?

- What are the default gateways for each network segment?

- What subnet system are you using, if any?

- Are there any reserved IP addresses in the DHCP configuration?

Figure 7.9 NT domain architecture diagram.

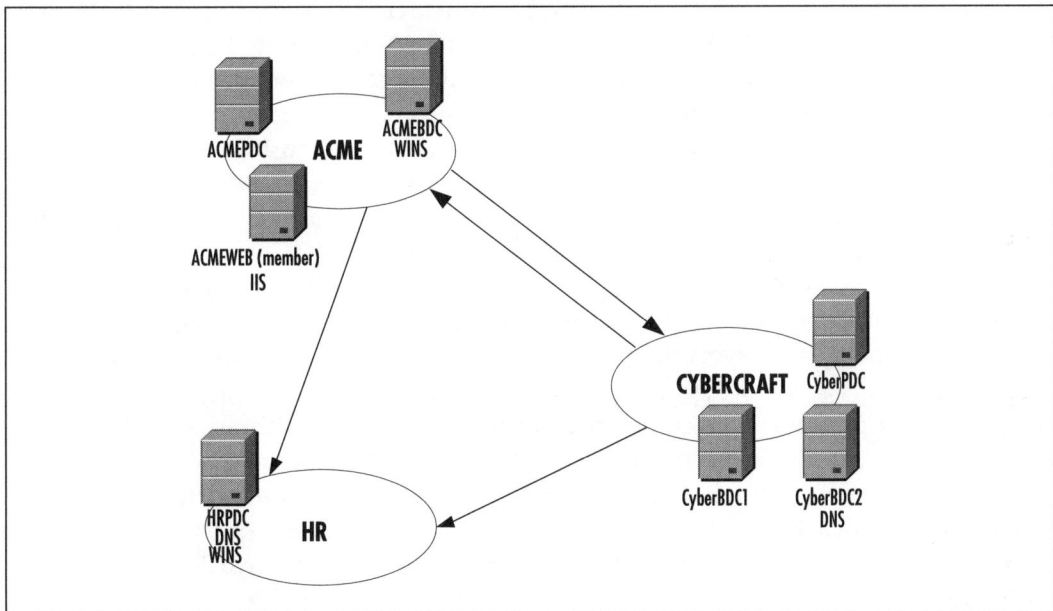

Security is critical to the ongoing health of your network. Security may need to be reevaluated, though, since Windows 2000 supports many security features natively that previously were supported only with third-party software. You should review the existing security that is implemented, your organization's security requirements, and any security policies that have been set. Make certain to look at the following security features:

- Password and account lockout policies

- User and desktop environment policies and profiles

- Group security access to network resources

- Administrative roles
- Secure protocols
- VPN rules
- Remote access policies

Internetwork Considerations

The path that data travels throughout the internetwork is one of the things that you need to analyze when determining the infrastructure component needs for migration as well as for daily computing needs. For example, if you place a Windows 2000 Web server on a LAN segment that is two or more hops distant from the segment leading to the Internet, then traffic will suffer performance problems due to the path that it is forced to take. Likewise, during the migration of client workstations to Windows 2000, if you place a source server at a site located across a slow WAN link, then the WAN link will be glutted with traffic as the Windows 2000 images are transferred to workstations from the source server.

A second consideration for the internetwork is the quality of the wiring and infrastructure devices. Bad wiring can cause excessive lost packets, data corruption, and even data loss. Infrastructure devices may have excessive latency, or delay, in transmitting data from one physical segment to another. Although this may not be an issue during slow-use periods, it may become an issue during peak periods. With Windows 2000 being able to support more collaborative applications, the chances are that there will be more network traffic traversing the wire. This means that you will need to ensure that the infrastructure supports an increased traffic amount, not just the amount of data traffic generated by current usage patterns.

One of the simplest changes you can make to the network to enhance the network performance is to change from a shared network to a switched network. Let's examine the difference between changing from 10 Mbps shared Ethernet to 100 Mbps shared, and 10 Mbps shared to 10 Mbps switched, in which each user receives a full port on the switch. When you change from a 10 Mbps shared segment to 100 Mbps shared, the network segment users will get about 30 to 40 percent maximum throughput—or 40 Mbps to be shared by all the users on the segment. If you have 20 users, they each receive 2 Mbps during a peak period while all are online. When you change from 10 Mbps shared to 10 Mbps switched, however, each individual user receives a full 10 Mbps. This is five times more effective than using 100 Mbps shared. Seems somewhat backward, doesn't it? But then again, if you truly want to get the most performance out of either 10 Mbps or 100 Mbps Ethernet, then you will change to 100 Mbps switched—which gives each user a full 100 Mbps pipe if they each receive a full port on the switch.

The services that your network provides to each client workstation must be examined as well. There is a cost for using voice and video on the same network that supports your data. Even so, it may be preferable to combine these networks since the administration is reduced to a single network. One of the options you have with voice and video is to utilize Quality of Service to mark various network packets as priority over others. Due to the streaming nature of voice and video, you should mark those types of data packets with priority over data transmissions like file transfers.

Measuring Replication Traffic

Windows 2000 offers three tools with which to measure replication traffic. Once it is measured, you can make changes to the way that sites are arranged and scheduled and then adjust it.

- Performance monitor
- Replication monitor
- Network monitor

The Performance monitor is used to measure an individual server's activity in many areas. This includes replication traffic for that server, as shown in Figure 7.10. The replication counter you can use to look at all the replication traffic coming into a server is DRA Inbound Bytes Total. To look at the replication traffic sent to other servers within the site, use the DRA Outbound Bytes Not Compressed counter. You can explore several other counters for replication traffic when measuring its affect on a server.

The Replication monitor, illustrated in Figure 7.11, is provided specifically to view replication traffic between servers within a site, as well as between sites. The replication monitor can graphically display the replication topology, as well as when replication fails, and can even enable an administrator to synchronize the Active Directory between two servers.

The Network monitor, depicted in Figure 7.12, is a utility that looks at the traffic traversing a network segment. It can track all incoming and outgoing packets from the server's perspective. If you have the opportunity to use the Network monitor (NetMon) application that is included in Microsoft's System Management Server (SMS) v2, you will be able to capture additional traffic traveling across the network.

Figure 7.10 Performance monitor for replication traffic.

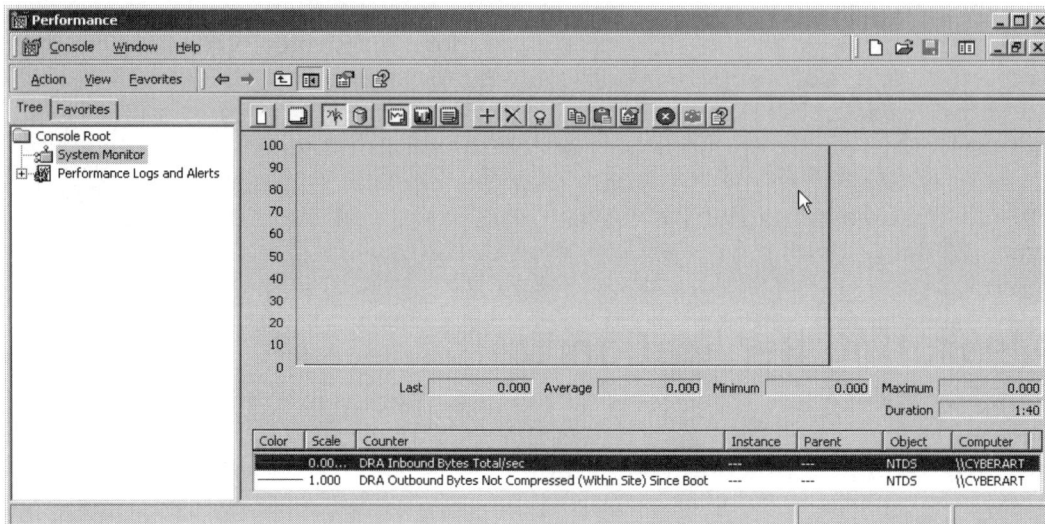

Figure 7.11 Replication monitor.

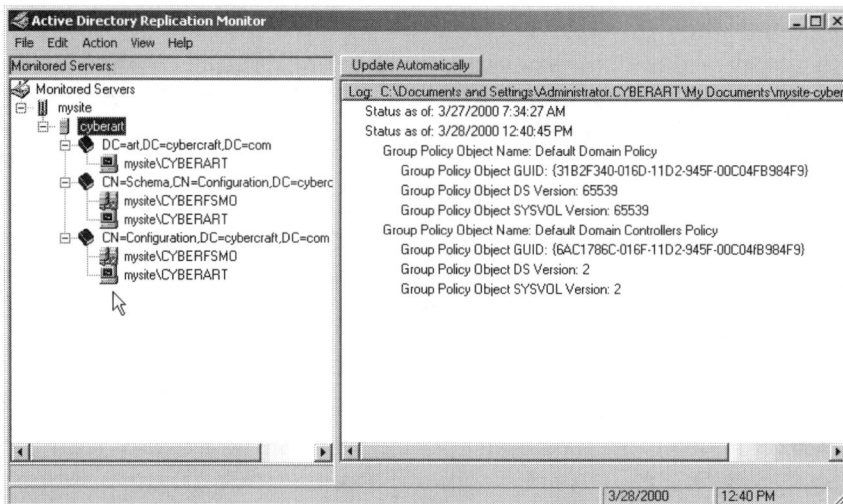

Figure 7.12 Network monitor.

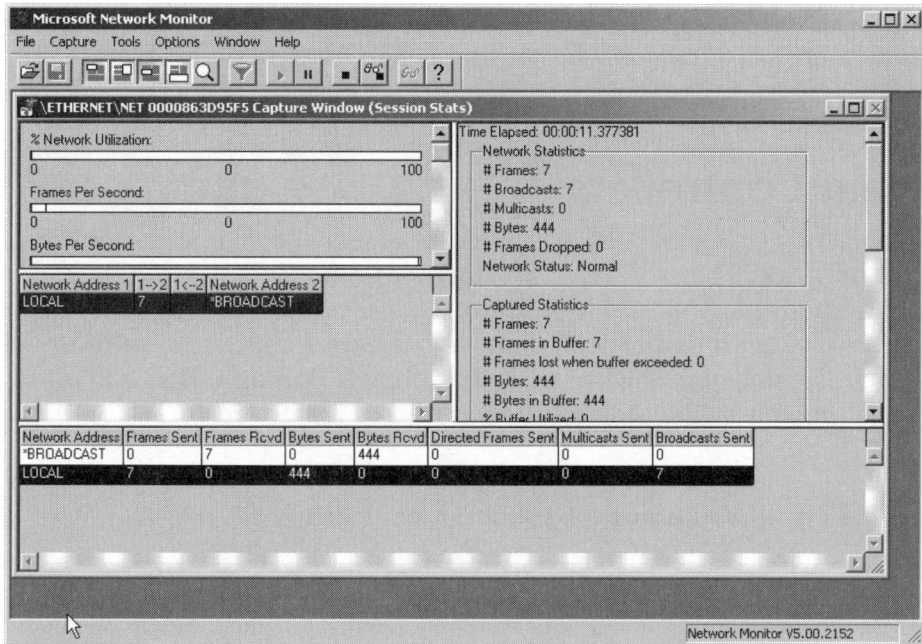

The problem with using the Network monitor lies in the fact that it captures every packet, and does not filter at the capture level according to the packet type. What you can do, however, is to set a port for RPC traffic by configuring the registry key at HKLM\System\CurrentControlSet\Services\NTDS\Parameters\TCP/IP Port.

Once the port for this is set, you can start the Network monitor. Next you will need to force replication by opening the Active Directory Sites and Services console, then right-clicking on the NTDS Settings objects below each domain controller object and selecting "Replicate Now." Once replication has completed, you can review the captured packets for those with the port number you configured. Those will represent the RPC traffic. If you have configured a site link to use SMTP traffic, you should also look for packets using port 25.

Server Placement

Which servers do you place into which sites? Do they have to be domain controllers? Do they have to be Global Catalog servers? Which sites need DNS servers or DHCP servers? Where do you put a RAS server for dial up? Where do you put a RAS server for VPN? What about a branch office with

30 users—do they need a domain controller or just a file and print server? Now server placement seems to be a dilemma—but it is one that is easily solved.

First, there definitely will be an impact on your network traffic when you place servers in various sites. The availability of the Active Directory is directly affected by the placement of various types of servers as well.

Domain Controllers

When you start this exercise, you should already have a site topology plan for your network. This will be your starting point for determining the placement of domain controllers. In addition to the site topology plan, you should have your domain/DNS plan, and an understanding of the physical location of the end-users who will exist in each domain. This will allow you to determine which domains span which sites, and vice versa, as shown in Figure 7.13.

Figure 7.13 Domains and sites spanning each other.

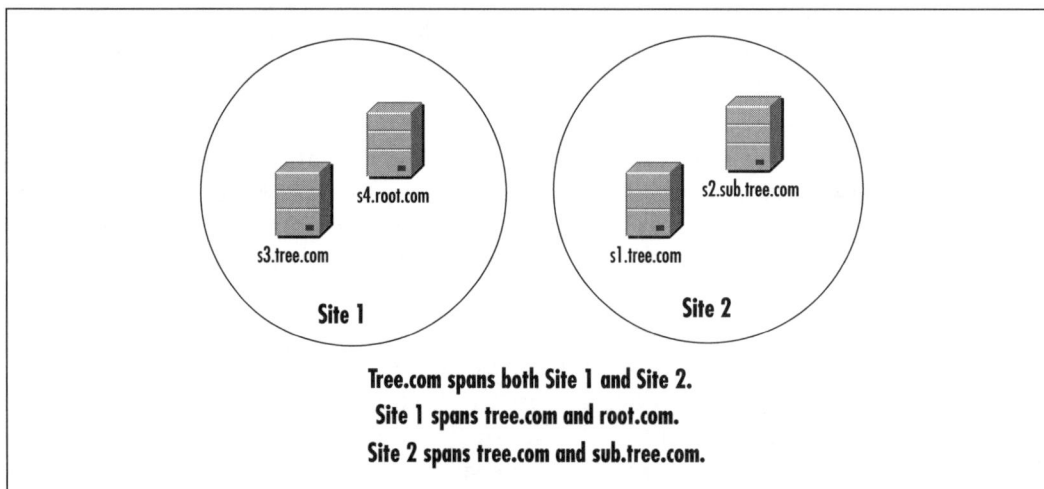

Tree.com spans both Site 1 and Site 2.
Site 1 spans tree.com and root.com.
Site 2 spans tree.com and sub.tree.com.

It is highly recommended that, for each domain existing within a site, you also place a domain controller for that domain. There are some exceptions to this recommendation—if you have a set of 10 users in a site for DOMAIN.COM, and you have 287 users in that same site belonging to ROOT.COM, then you will not need a DC for DOMAIN.COM in that site. However, if you have 100 users for DOMAIN.COM and 287 users for ROOT.COM, then you will probably want to include a DC from both domains.

Imagine if you have a large campus network with five domains in a single site. You would want to put five different DCs in that single site simply to support authentication traffic. As you can see, the more domains that exist in a site, the more separate servers you will need. And this is not counting whether you need separate Global Catalog, DNS, DHCP, or other servers running in those sites yet.

Once you've decided which sites will receive at least one domain controller from the domains in your plan, you need to determine how many domain controllers total you will want for that domain. This decision will be based partially on the number of sites that you deem require a domain controller, and partially on the size and power of the server hardware that will support the domain controllers. A single-processor Pentium PC with a 4GB hard drive will not support even a fifth as many users as a four-processor Pentium III server-class machine with a 40GB RAID array. But you don't want to max out your server to start with either; you need to plan to leave room for growth. You will want to take into account whether your domain controller will provide other services such as DNS, DHCP, or file and print services because these services will reduce the capacity of the domain controller to support the Active Directory services.

So, there is no magic formula regarding the number of users a domain controller will support. But there is a way of figuring out how many *your domain controller* will support. The first thing to do is to look at some statistics such as those in Table 7.2, and estimate what size servers you will need for today and for the future. Note that these are averages, and that there may be some differences in the size of your Active Directory objects and replication traffic based on the number of attributes you fill out in each object, whether you include custom attributes, and whether these attributes are copied to the Global Catalog.

Table 7.2 Sizing Statistics

Component	Definition	Size
Security principal	User, Group, any object that can be granted rights to other objects	3600 bytes
Nonsecurity principal	Organizational Unit, Organization, any object that is not granted rights to other objects	1100 bytes
Attributes	Additional attributes added to support services on the network, such as DNS	100 bytes per attribute

Continued

Table 7.2 Continued

Component	Definition	Size
Intrasite replication of a single user	The average amount of replication traffic generated within a site when creating a new user account	13,000 bytes
Intrasite replication of a single attribute change	The average amount of replication traffic generated within a site when changing a single attribute on an AD object	4500 bytes
Intersite replication of a single user	The average amount of replication traffic generated between sites when creating a new user account	11,000 bytes
Intersite replication of a single attribute	The average amount of replication traffic generated between sites when changing a single attribute	4000 bytes

When you determine the size of your Active Directory storage needs, usually you can be assured that any standard hard drive will be able to house even the largest domain partitions. Use the following equation to estimate your storage needs:

(#Security Principals * 3600 bytes) +

(#Non-security principals * 1100 Bytes) =

Active Directory Size

To ensure that you have enough space for growth, multiply this result by at least 200 percent or more, depending on your company's growth over the last three years.

Active Directory Size * 200% = Minimum DC capacity required

If you have a domain with 200,000 users, 1000 organizational units, then you can safely estimate your AD database storage needs:

(200,000 * 3600)+(1000 * 1100)= 721100000 Bytes = 687 MB * 200% = 1374 MB = 1.2 GB

Table 7.2 shows that the size of the replication of new objects and changed attributes turns out to be more expensive than the incremental storage of that same data on a single DC hard disk. For example, if you have one DC storing all the objects in a single domain that is the only domain in its forest, then there is no replication traffic that will interrupt other network traffic on the wire. (However, you won't have any redundancy in case that DC fails, so always make certain to have two DCs per domain.) If you have two domain controllers, then you will have one time replication for each change on the Active Directory database. If you have three DCs, then replication will occur twice (from DC1 to DC2, then from DC2 to DC3) for each update on the Active Directory. Replication is simply the number of DCs (one, as shown in Figure 7.14). Since hard drive storage is cheap and bandwidth has a lot of competition for its use by applications on the network, it is cheaper from a network traffic standpoint to maintain fewer DCs!

Figure 7.14 Active Directory replication between four DCs.

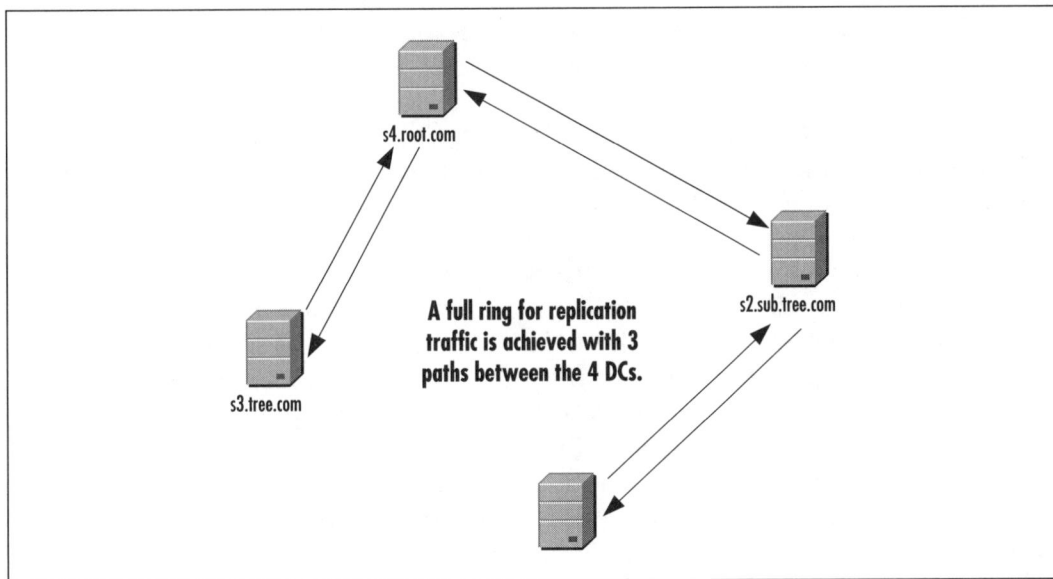

A DC's processor utilization increases as the number of users increases in a domain. Several factors contribute to this phenomenon. The main issue is not replication or storage, but happens to be the number of users that log on simultaneously or query the network for resources at the same time. The differences in processor types that are supported by Windows 2000 are widely varied. Not only are the manufacturers and processor models variables, but the speed of the processor (MHz) and the supported bus speed of the motherboard (also in MHz, but different from the processor speed) are also variables—and these can make all the difference in how your processor performs. You will need to test your processor in a lab environment to determine its maximum simultaneous processing capabilities. You can test these capabilities using Performance monitor and simulation

/benchmarking utilities. (You can find many simulation or benchmarking utilities on the Internet. One of the largest benchmarking software developers is ZDNet's Benchmark Operation, whose Web site is www.zdnet.com/zdbop/.) But just finding the maximum simultaneous capacity is not enough; you need to consider the likelihood of that maximum capacity. For example, if you have a processor that reaches 99 percent utilization with 1000 simultaneous logons, you will also want to consider how often 1000 users would log on simultaneously. If 1000 people were to arrive at work at the same time and log on, they would probably do so within the space of several minutes. If you give them five minutes, then you would be estimating that your server could support up to 5000 users in a network before it was maxed out.

Again, the maximum capacity is not the beginning capacity for your network; you want to make certain to include enough room for growth. One way to do this is to add domain controllers to the domain. Another way to do this is to load up on the hardware for your domain controller. If you think that one processor will just about be sufficient to support your network, two processors will be better, and four will give that domain controller room for growth for quite a while.

Once you specify how many DCs you need in each domain, compare that to how many domain controllers you will need to support your sites. From this comparison, select the number of DCs that is larger. For example, if you have three sites and intend to place a DC in each, and you have determined that only two DCs are needed to support the domain's users, then you will need three DCs in total. What is nice about this situation is that you know exactly where each DC will be placed. However, if you have three sites and you need five DCs to support the domain, then you must determine where to place the other two DCs. Look at the number of users in each site. If two of the sites have 200 users each, and the third site has 7000 users, then the two other DCs should be placed in the site with 7000 users. This method will ensure that the workload is balanced for those DCs.

Aside from balancing the workload, redundancy is another issue to consider when deciding the number of DCs per site. If a WAN link is untrustworthy (it fails often or is overutilized), you should ensure that the number of DCs in each site connected to that WAN link is at least two.

Global Catalog Servers

The Global Catalog is required to be available in each site *if the Active Directory forest consists of more than one domain.* The multidomain forest is an important factor. In a single-domain forest, there is no need for a Global

Catalog since all resources will be available in the domain partition of the Active Directory.

The Global Catalog is important for multidomain forests because:

- It is used during the logon process to determine memberships of universal groups. If unable to contact a GC server, logon is refused to ensure that the user had not been denied access to resources through a universal group membership.

- It is used for queries of resources that exist outside of a user's own domain.

If you have more than one domain, you will want to place at least one GC server in each site. This will probably not require any extra physical servers because a GC server is simply an enhanced domain controller, and will consume only a minor amount of storage and processing power. Although you will not need as many GC servers as you do DCs, wherever possible, you should try to ensure that workload is balanced among the GC servers in a site, and that redundant GC servers are placed in sites separated by untrustworthy WAN links.

DNS Servers

The Active Directory depends on DNS in order for

- DCs to contact each other for replication
- Users to contact DCs to log on to the network
- Users to contact GCs to execute a query

Without DNS, there is no communication—users can't log on, and the Active Directory cannot replicate updates. Because of DNS's importance, you should ensure that at least one DNS server exists in each site, and two should exist in any site that is separated from other DNS servers by untrustworthy WAN links.

You can install DNS services on the existing DCs in the forest. The DNS service will consume a minor amount of storage and processing power. It is recommended that you test the capacity of a DC with additional services loaded on it when you add DNS and the Global Catalog.

WINS Servers

Windows Internet Naming Service (WINS) is used to map NetBIOS names to IP addresses. WINS is not necessary to the working domain running in native mode. You may not need to plan for WINS servers at all, but for those networks that do need to provide WINS services for downlevel clients, they should be placed in a centrally available network location. You should have at least two WINS servers on the internetwork for redundancy.

FSMOs

There are five Flexible Single Masters of Operations (FSMOs) that you need to consider for placement on the network:

- RID master
- PDC emulator
- Domain naming master
- Infrastructure master
- Schema master

Relative ID (RID) Master

The RID master is a designated DC. It provides unique relative ID portions of the SID to other DCs. When those DCs assign SIDs to security principals (users, groups, or other objects that can be granted rights), the RID master ensures that the SID is unique. This is especially necessary when moving an object between domains.

When placing the RID master, you need to consider which DC is most easily accessible by other DCs in the domain. If you have a hub-and-spoke formation in your network where there is one main site and the rest of your sites all connect to it, it is fairly simple to select a DC in that site. If, however, you have a more complex internetwork with several major sites, you should still select the site that is most central to all other DCs.

In the case of a downed RID master, where the RID master is not recoverable, you will need to change the role to another DC on the internetwork. This means that you should select a DC to serve as the backup RID master. Remember that the RID master backup will not automatically happen by itself; you will need to change the role over manually:

1. Open the Active Directory Users and Computers console.
2. Right-click on the domain.
3. Select Connect to Domain Controller from the menu.
4. Select the DC which you are going to transfer the RID master role to.
5. Click OK.
6. Right-click on the domain.
7. Select Operations Master from the menu.

8. Click the Change button on the RID tab.

9. Click OK.

PDC Emulator

The PDC Emulator does more than act as a backward-compatible PDC in a mixed mode domain. It still exists in a native mode domain. Overall, the PDC emulator handles these important functions:

- Mixed mode PDC authority over Windows NT BDCs

- Native mode and mixed mode central repository for domain password changes

- Native mode and mixed mode central authority for time synchronization

When the domain is in mixed mode, the PDC Emulator is the PDC for any Windows NT BDCs in the same domain. The PDC Emulator cannot exist in a domain that has a Windows NT PDC in it, which is why a migration plan must upgrade the Windows NT PDC first, when retaining the same domain.

When the domain is in any mode, the PDC Emulator is contacted by each DC on which a password change has been made, and then stores that password change. If a user changes his or her password on one DC, and then attempts to authenticate to another DC that still holds the old password, the DC first contacts the PDC Emulator to check for a password change there. In this way, the user's logon can be accepted.

The PDC Emulator also takes on the role of the time authority for the domain. All other DCs will synchronize their clocks to the PDC Emulator, and then serve that time to the time clients in the domain.

The PDC Emulator needs to be highly available to the entire domain, especially to DCs in its own domain. You will want to place that PDC Emulator in a location that is central to other DCs and is highly available to them. Because of the PDC Emulator's critical nature for password changes, you will want to give that role to a DC that has fault tolerant hardware, such as a RAID array or cluster. You will also need to designate a potential backup PDC Emulator in case the original DC holding that role fails. To change the role of a DC to a PDC Emulator, follow a nearly identical process as that of changing the RID master role:

1. Open the Active Directory Users and Computers console.

2. Right-click on the domain.

3. Select Connect to Domain Controller from the menu.

4. Select the DC to which you are going to transfer the PDC Emulator role.

5. Click OK.

6. Right-click on the domain.

7. Select Operations Master from the menu.

8. Click the PDC tab.

9. Click the Change button.

10. Click OK.

Domain Naming Master

There is a single Domain Naming master per Active Directory forest. The first DC installed is granted this role by default. The Domain Naming master ensures that the domain namespace is unique within a forest, and is used each time a domain is added or removed from the forest. The Domain Naming master must be installed on a Global Catalog server.

When placing the Domain Naming master, you should select a DC within the root domain (although being a member of the root domain is not necessarily a requirement, it can enhance performance because of its Kerberos trust relationships) of the forest that is also a Global Catalog server. It must be available to each domain in the forest, so this Domain Naming master's site must be site-linked or site-link-bridged to every other site in the forest.

You can change the Domain Naming master through the Active Directory Domains and Trusts console:

1. Open the Active Directory Domains and Trusts console.

2. Right-click the root.

3. Select Connect to Domain Controller from the menu.

4. Type the name of the DC that will be the new Domain Naming master (make certain you select a Global Catalog server) and press Enter.

5. Right-click on the root again.

6. Select Operations Masters from the menu.

7. Click the Change button.

8. Click OK.

Infrastructure Master

There is a single Infrastructure master in each domain. It is used to maintain a reference to objects in other domains—specifically those objects that have been moved to other domains, or group members that belong to other domains.

The Infrastructure master should reside on a DC that is highly available to the rest of the DCs for that domain. Try to place the server in a central location for that domain. To change the Infrastructure master role:

1. Open the Active Directory Users and Computers console.
2. Right-click on the domain.
3. Select Connect to Domain Controller from the menu.
4. Select the DC that will be the new Infrastructure master.
5. Click OK.
6. Right-click the domain.
7. Select Operations Masters from the menu.
8. Click the Infrastructure tab.
9. Click the Change Button.
10. Click OK.

Schema Master

There is a single Schema master within an Active Directory forest. It is the only domain controller on which the schema can be changed. You can change the Schema master role from one DC to another.

TIP

To make any changes to the schema or the Schema master, you must install the Windows 2000 Administrative Tools. To do this, use the Add/Remove Programs icon in the Control Panel, select Windows 2000 Administrative Tools, and click Change. Then install all the administrative tools.

To start the Active Directory Schema snap-in, click Start and then Run. Type MMC and press Enter. Click the Console menu and select Add/Remove Snap-In. Click Add and select the Active Directory Schema. Click Add, then Close and OK to return to the console window.

Because the schema should not be changed often, and because only a very few persons should ever be granted access to change the schema, the placement of the Schema master will not affect Active Directory performance. You may wish to grant the Schema master role to a DC that is not easily accessible. To change the Schema master role:

1. Open the Active Directory Schema Manager console.

2. Right-click on the root.

3. Select Change Domain Controller from the menu.

4. Type the name of the new Schema master.

5. Click OK.

6. Right-click on the root.

7. Select Operations Master from the menu.

8. Click the Change button.

9. Click OK.

RAS Servers

Placing a RAS server for dial-up users on the network is a matter of bringing the server closer to the resources that users need to access. If you are placing a RAS server for a VPN, then bring the server closer to the WAN link, from which users will be connecting. In the best of worlds, you will be able to place that server close to the resources and move the WAN link or dial-up lines to where that server resides.

DHCP Servers

If you apply static IP addresses to both clients and servers currently, then you should look into adding DHCP to the network. DHCP will assign IP addresses to workstations and servers when they authenticate to the network. The addresses can be pooled so that they are efficiently handed out to workstations on an as-needed basis. If you are currently using DHCP, then you already know of the benefits that it can bring to your network.

DHCP is important for every network client and server that uses it. A workstation or a server would not be able to access the network without receiving an assigned IP address from a DHCP server or being able to contact the DHCP server to renew it.

When you consider the placement of the DHCP servers, you need to look at the:

- Number of sites
- Size of the sites
- Speed and reliability of the WAN links

You will want to place DHCP servers at your main sites, and then place DHCP servers at any site that is connected to the internetwork via slow or unreliable WAN links. This does not necessarily mean adding yet another server to the network; you can install the DHCP service on a Windows 2000 DC, or other Windows 2000 server.

Terminal Services

Terminal Services offer a thin-client solution for applications across the network. They also have an option of being installed to provide server management via remote control of the server console. The placement of the Terminal server depends on the role that the Terminal Service is playing.

If Terminal Services are being added to Windows 2000 servers and domain controllers in order to provide a method of server management, then it does not matter where those servers are placed. They should be placed solely in accordance with the other services that they are providing on the network.

For example, if Terminal Services are installed on a Windows 2000 server or domain controller in order to provide an application to thin-clients, then the server should be placed close to the application data source. You see, a Terminal server is the middle tier of a three-tier system, as shown in Figure 7.15. As the middle tier, the Terminal server acts as a client to network server applications. The application client must be installed on the Terminal server. Workstations are installed with a Terminal server client, with which they access the Terminal server, take remote control of a session, and then use the application client to access other network servers.

Figure 7.15 Terminal Services as the middle tier in a three-tier system.

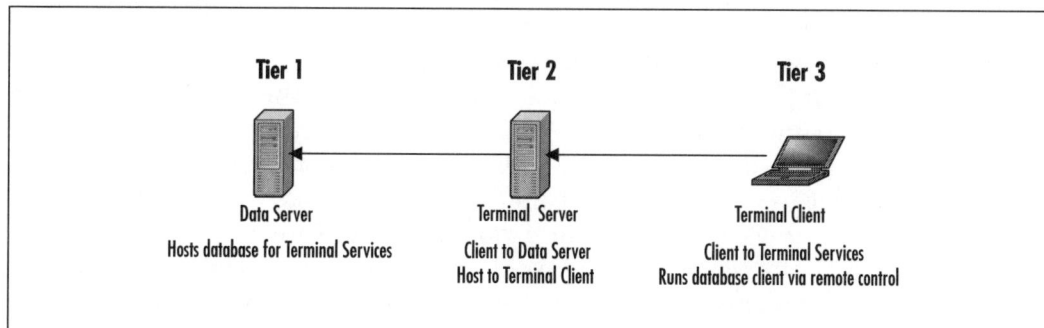

Tier 1	Tier 2	Tier 3
Data Server	Terminal Server	Terminal Client
Hosts database for Terminal Services	Client to Data Server Host to Terminal Client	Client to Terminal Services Runs database client via remote control

Terminal Services should be placed close to servers that provide data to the applications. For example, if a Terminal server was going to be used for access to a SQL application, then the Terminal server and the SQL server should both be placed on the same network segment, or two segments that are well connected. This rule does not prove true for the workstations since they use a thin-client application (which uses very little network bandwidth, for example) to take control of a Terminal server. Workstations can be placed anywhere on a network relative to the Terminal server.

When you size a Terminal server itself, you need to consider the number of simultaneous users. A single Pentium II processor generally can provide sessions for about 20 to 25 users. Therefore if you want to provide Terminal Services for 50 simultaneous users, you would need at least two or more processors. (Simultaneous users are not the total number of users that are allowed to use the server, but are the total number of users that would actually use the server at the exact same time.)

The number of simultaneous users also governs the amount of RAM. First, you would allocate about 256MB of RAM for the base operating system. Although Windows 2000 will operate with around 128MB of RAM, you will want to double it to 256MB to handle all the services that will run on the server. Then you will want to add 8MB RAM for each simultaneous user. This means that if you have 50 simultaneous users, you will add another 400MB RAM to your total. This gives us a total of 656MB RAM, but since no machine has that specific amount, you will round it up to the next level or more. So if the server supports RAM in 256MB increments, you would install 768MB or RAM of more. (More RAM cannot hurt your server's performance.)

Infrastructure Components

The infrastructure is everything that sits between a client workstation and a Windows 2000 server, including the wiring, hubs, switches, routers, and gateways. The Active Directory can be optimized to work well on many existing internetworks. Generally, it can use the existing infrastructure components. Even so, the internetwork may perform better if it is also optimized to work with the Active Directory in return.

The goal of sizing the infrastructure is to maximize the availability of services while minimizing the bandwidth that those same services consume. One of the challenges that businesses face today is an increasing use of the Internet to perform daily business procedures. This leads to competition for bandwidth from all end-points to the Internet connection (or connections) that exist on the internetwork. When reviewing infrastructure components, you need to take this growing bandwidth consumption into account and plan for managing it, whether through cache engines, proxies, or increased bandwidth availability.

Table 7.3 is a list of the components that you should review. If the questions that you ask reveal that any component currently is not sufficient or will not be sufficient in the future, then you should upgrade that component.

Table 7.3 Infrastructure Components

Component	Analysis
Cabling	Is the cabling stable, or does it perform with faults?
Cabling	Can the cabling support faster Physical/Data Link protocols?
WAN Links	Is there available bandwidth on the existing WAN links?
WAN Links	Are there redundant WAN links in case of a failure?
WAN Links	Will a WAN link support additional bandwidth consumption given an average of 5% compounded growth in consumption month over month over the next year?
LAN Links	Is the local LAN segment experiencing excessive delays or, in the case of Ethernet, excessive collisions?
LAN Links	Are hubs used for shared network segment access?
LAN Links	Are switches used with microsegmentation (each workstation receiving its own port) or do switches connect multiple shared access hubs?
Routers/Bridges	Does the infrastructure support all the protocols required—TCP/IP, DNS, Dynamic DNS, DHCP, Quality of Service (QoS), IPSec?
Routers/Bridges	Does the infrastructure support the needs for voice and video data?
Network Interface Cards (NICs)	Are all network interfaces compatible with Windows 2000?

WARNING

An administrator who creates a large number of objects over a short period of time can cause a denial of service for end users. What happens in this case is that massive replication occurs within the domain and throughout the Global Catalog for the forest—especially within a site where replication takes place upon demand rather than on a schedule. The replication within a site is not compressed and therefore can take up most of the network bandwidth. Then, when the replicated traffic reaches a Global Catalog server, it must use its processing power to handle the changes to its database. As a result, a user who accesses the network can be denied access because the network is busy transmitting replication traffic. Or a user who attempts to access a Global Catalog server at the time that it is processing these changes will be denied access to the Active Directory or to the server's resources.

Quality of Service

If you intend to deploy Quality of Service (QoS), you must ensure that the internetwork will support it. Many older versions of routers will not recognize a QoS packet. When this happens, the packet is handled just like any other packet, and if the header is stripped and rebuilt in order to pass that packet from one segment to another, then all remaining infrastructure components will treat that packet without any priority whatsoever. It is imperative for you to ensure that all infrastructure components support QoS in the path from a packet's source to its destination.

Monitoring the Infrastructure

The same tools used to measure replication traffic can be used to monitor the network infrastructure traffic. Monitoring the infrastructure is critical to managing an internetwork. The activity on the network impacts the performance of both the infrastructure components and the Windows 2000 servers.

The types of information to monitor can be subdivided into each layer of the OSI protocol reference model. By dividing the monitoring tasks this way, you can better trace a bottleneck to its source problem. Table 7.4 shows the types of data and the OSI Protocol model layers from which they originate.

Table 7.4 Monitoring Traffic through the OSI Layers

Layer Numbers	OSI Reference Model Layer	Application Data to Monitor
Layer 1 and Layer 2	Physical and Data Link	Most physical protocols also contain a data link portion. To monitor the Physical/Data Link traffic, monitor the Network Interface of each server.
Layer 3	Network	This protocol handles the routed data, which in turn requires addressing. You will need to monitor IP for the TCP/IP protocol, and NWLink for the IPX/SPX protocol.
Layer 4	Transport	The transport layer handles segmentation and provides sockets, or ports, for upper layers to use. You will need to monitor TCP and UDP for the TCP/IP protocol.
Layer 5	Session	The establishment and breakdown of end-to-end sessions are handled at this layer. NetBIOS is implemented as a Session layer API when it is used over TCP/IP. To monitor NetBIOS over TCP/IP, use the NBT Connection counters.
Layer 6 and Layer 7	Application and Presentation	The Application and Presentation layers are often grouped together. The Presentation layer manages the format of data, inclusive of encryption and compression, and the Application layer provides the user interface to the network. To monitor at these layers, look at the server and redirector counters.

For IT Professionals

Optimizing Windows 2000 TCP/IP Performance for Slow WAN Links

Windows 2000 is fairly self-optimizing. But if it is serving clients across a slow WAN link, it may benefit from some performance tuning. As it was for Windows NT, much of the Windows 2000 performance optimization can be done through editing the registry. To edit the registry, you need to execute the REGEDT32.EXE command.

Proceed with caution when you edit the registry! Whenever you edit the registry, your computer's operability is being risked. You should always test a registry edit on a test computer before using it on a production computer. In addition, you should always back up your production computer before editing its registry even if your tests were completely successful.

The HKEY_LOCAL_MACHINE hive contains the parameters for TCP/IP in HKLM\System\CurrentControlSet\Services\Tcpip\Parameters. These are not the only keys that can be changed, but for increased performance, you will definitely want to look at modifying the following keys:

MaxUserPort To increase throughput by allowing more sockets to be created, increase this parameter. It ranges from 0x400 to 0xFFFE. The default behavior of Windows 2000 is to grant TCP ports between the value of 1024 and 5000, which is generally sufficient. Changing this key to a higher value will enable more ports to be available. It will have a negative effect on the computer if its processor or memory is unable to handle the additional load.

MaxFreeTcbs To increase the number of available preallocated Transport Control Blocks (TCBs). TCBs are maintained for each TCP/IP connection. The range for this parameter is between 0 and 0xFFFFFFFF. The default value is 2000 TCBs for servers with more than 64MB RAM. You should increase this value only when you have a lot of available RAM because it will reduce the available RAM by setting aside a cache for more TCBs.

Continued

MaxHashTableSize To increase throughput (on a single processor computer) by creating a faster connection lookup, increase this parameter. It ranges from 0x40 to 0x10000. This parameter manages how fast a TCB can be found for a TCP connection. It should be increased only when you increase MaxFreeTcbs.

Network Monitor

Network monitor is intended to analyze network activity sent to or from a Windows 2000 computer on a local area network segment. Network monitor captures the frames that pass on the network segment. When using a switch between two devices, you will have difficulty tracking the data on the network because each switch port is a separate network segment. (A switch is simply a multiport bridge, and gains the higher throughput due to the segmentation of each port.)

To get around this issue temporarily, you can replace a switch with a hub, given that they are both using compatible media and physical/datalink network protocol and data rate. A switch can connect Ethernet 10BaseT over unshielded twisted pair with Ethernet 100BaseT over unshielded twisted pair. In more rare cases, switches can connect these with Ethernet 10BaseF over fiber or 10Base2 over thin-wire coaxial cable or 10Base5 over thick-wire coaxial cable. The multiple media types can become an issue if the switch is replaced with a single-media hub. Alternatively, if the switch supports it, you can connect to the switch's internal "mirror port." Some switches have a mirror port that is actually an internal channel through which all data between the ports passes.

IP frames include a header with the source address of the sending computer, the destination address of the computer that will receive the frame, other header information, and the actual data that is being sent. Not only does Network monitor look at frames, it also looks at bandwidth utilization and transmission rates in bytes per second or frames per second.

To use Network monitor, you must install it on the computer where you want to capture data. But you also install Network monitor on a Windows 2000 server to receive the data from multiple clients. Then you capture the data and review the results. You can also monitor for certain patterns within a frame and then execute a *trigger* such as stop capturing or executing a command line.

When you review data to solve a performance issue, you will want to look for repeated sequences of data transmissions or for lengthy delays in acknowledgements or replies. Retries indicate that the network is congested or that there is a breakdown in the path to the destination computer, or even that there is a problem with a higher layer protocol timing out. When there are lengthy delays, it could indicate that either the destination computer, or some router in the path to the destination, is performing poorly.

If you wish to test the ability of RPCs to travel across a link, you can use the RPC Ping utility. This consists of two components: one resides on a server, RPINGS.EXE, and the other is executed on the client, RPINGC32.EXE. To use this, load the server component, and then run the RPINGC32.EXE component on the other machine.

PathPing is a utility for tracing a path from one computer to another. What PathPing does is send a set of packets to each router along the way to a destination computer. Not only does PathPing trace the route between the two computers, it then shows which routers dropped packets along the way.

Case Studies

Preparing the infrastructure for Windows 2000 is more of an art than a science. The two case studies, ABC Chemical Company and West Coast Accounting, both will need to go through this exercise before installing Windows 2000 on the network.

ABC Chemical Company

The ABC Chemical Company first needs to review its site topology plan. ABC has three sites in its site topology plan: one represents the campus and the other two represent the warehouses in its production forest. (Since the e-commerce forest contains only a single site, we will only discuss the configuration of the production forest.)

Each warehouse is physically connected to the campus network via Frame Relay links, which are slow 56 Kbps network connections. The maximum amount of traffic can be estimated by considering how much it would take to replace each user account in the warehouse and upload those changes to the central site. Then, estimate how much time it would take to upload the changes based on the number of domain controllers that would be replicating from the remote site to the central site. (We assume only one domain controller will upload replication across the Frame Relay link because there are only 50 users there.)

1 ReplicationCycle * 50 users * 11000 Bytes = 4296 Kbits / 56 Kbps = 76 seconds for full upload + 10 seconds for overhead traffic = 86 seconds

Note that this is the *maximum* traffic that could possibly be expected to cross the link due to Active Directory. You would probably see 10 percent of this traffic or less at any time that replication occurs. That means that you would want to upgrade the WAN link if 430 Kbits (10 percent of the 4296) is too much traffic to occur once every hour, if you configure frequency of replication for 60 minutes.

Once you have the time it would take for the most traffic you expect to go across the WAN links, then you need to determine if this is tolerable, as well how often such a change would happen. Remember, ABC Chemical can adjust the frequency of replication and schedule if this is too much during high utilization hours, or upgrade the link speed. ABC Chemical Company decides that the replication traffic should not occur from 10:00 AM to 2:00 PM for either link. The site links are listed in Table 7.5 along with the site link bridge.

Table 7.5 ABC Chemical Company Site Links and Site Link Bridge

Site Link or Site Link Bridge	Cost	Frequency	Schedule
EastWarehouse-HQ	5	60 minutes	Available 12:00 AM to 10:00 AM, 2:00 PM to 11:59 PM
WestWarehouse-HQ	5	60 minutes	Available 12:00 AM to 10:00 AM, 2:00 PM to 11:59 PM
East-WestBridge	10	NA	Not configurable—follows the additive rules of the site links

The next step is to decide how many DCs are required for the domain. Given only 1100 users, a single DC can be used; however, that does not allow for redundancy. Since there are three separate sites, and each site should have a DC within it, there are three domain controllers required overall, one in each site.

Since there is only a single domain, ABC Chemical Company does not need Global Catalog servers available to all the users. ABC will place a Global Catalog server at the main HQ and install it on the existing DC there. The RID Master FSMO will be installed on that DC, as well as the PDC Emulator and the Domain Naming master. However, the Infrastructure master and the Schema master will each be placed on the DCs at the East and West sites, respectively.

DNS services must be available everywhere, so the server at the HQ site will contain the primary zone, and the East and West DCs will run DNS service with secondary zones to the HQ primary zone.

DHCP is required at each site, and because the Frame Relay links have been very stable, ABC Chemical decides to use a single DHCP server at the HQ site and forward DHCP requests to the warehouses. ABC decides to use a Windows 2000 member server, rather than a DC for this role.

ABC Chemical Company does not need RAS or Terminal Services, so there is no need to place them on the network.

Although the 1100 users for ABC Chemical Company will not tax even a small, single-processor server with a 2GB hard drive and 256MB of RAM, ABC Chemical makes the decision to use a clustered server for the main DC. The decision is made to place the single DHCP server on a clustered server as well. In addition, ABC Chemical installs three file and print servers at the HQ site. The final Windows 2000 infrastructure is depicted in Figure 7.16.

Figure 7.16 ABC Chemical Company's Windows 2000 infrastructure.

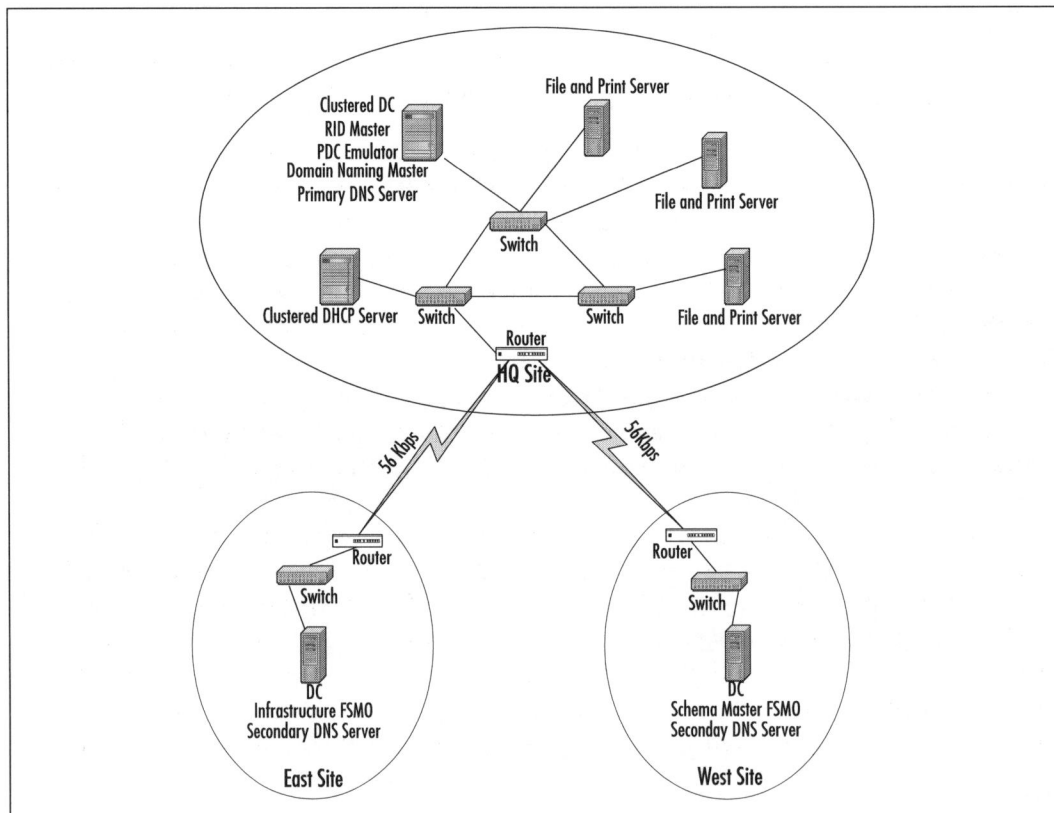

West Coast Accounting, L.L.C.

West Coast Accounting has two domains in its production forest—westcoast.com is the root domain and the e-commerce domain is wcacctg.com. All users will belong to westcoast.com, but only Web users belong to the wcacctg.com, and they are connected through San Francisco. West Coast Accounting has five relatively small sites:

- Seattle, with 50 users
- Los Angeles, with 50 users
- Portland, with 50 users
- Phoenix, with 50 users
- San Francisco, with 100 users

To calculate the maximum amount of traffic for West Coast Accounting, you can look at what would happen if each site updated all of its users at the same time. (We assume that there are four replication cycles because there are five DCs. And we use a T1 line at 1.544 Mbps for the speed of the WAN link.)

4 Replication Cycles * 300 users * 11000 Bytes = 100 Mbits / 1.544 Mbps = 65 seconds for upload + 10 seconds for overhead traffic = 75 seconds

Here, we've calculated the traffic for all the users in the entire domain to be updated at once across a T1 line. In reality, the traffic will be taking place across multiple lines for far less than this. It is likely that 56 Kbps Frame Relay links can withstand all the traffic that would be generated from each of the various sites because the amount of traffic from any site into San Francisco would constitute about one-sixtieth of this (one-sixth of 300 users = 50 users * 10% = one-sixtieth).

Because San Francisco and Los Angeles share several cases in California, they require updates to be more available to each site. West Coast Accounting has the site links and site link bridges as shown in Table 7.6.

There is no need for more than a single DC to support 300 users for the westcoast.com domain. However, since users are spread throughout the various sites, there should be at least one DC for westcoast.com in each site. The wcacctg.com domain will exist only in the San Francisco site. The IT Group intends to use anonymous Web users initially and to add the ability to support individual user accounts into the domain later on. For now, the decision is to place two DCs for wcacctg.com in the San Francisco site.

Table 7.6 West Coast Accounting Site Links and Site Link Bridge

Site Link or Site Link Bridge	Cost	Frequency	Schedule
Seattle-SanFran	5	60 minutes	Available all hours
LA-SanFran	1	30 minutes	Available all hours
Portland-SanFran	5	60 minutes	Available all hours
Phoenix-SanFran	5	60 minutes	Available all hours
AllSitesBridge	16	NA	Not configurable

Because of the multiple domains, there should be a Global Catalog server in each site. A Global Catalog will be installed on each DC for the westcoast.com domain. The PDC Emulator, the Domain Naming master, and the RID master will all be installed on a westcoast.com DC in the San Francisco site. The LA site will have the Infrastructure master and Schema master on its DC. wcacctg.com will have the Infrastructure master and RID master installed on one of its DCs, with the PDC Emulator on the other DC. (Since the Schema master and Domain Naming master exist only as one per forest, they do not need to exist in wcacctg.com.)

West Coast Accounting decides to install DNS on each DC, with Active Directory-integrated zones for each domain. In addition, West Coast needs to maintain WINS for backward compatibility for the remote workstations that end-users use to dial in to the network. West Coast Accounting places the WINS service on a member server that also serves as a RAS server. West Coast Accounting also installs DHCP on the RAS server.

West Coast Accounting installs Terminal Services on a member server in the westcoast.com domain. West Coast selects a four-way processor machine with 1GB RAM in anticipation of heavy use of the thin-client sessions.

West Coast installs Internet Information Services on a member server in the wcacctg.com domain to provide the e-commerce solution. The final West Coast Accounting infrastructure is depicted in Figure 7.17.

Figure 7.17 West Coast Accounting infrastructure for Windows 2000.

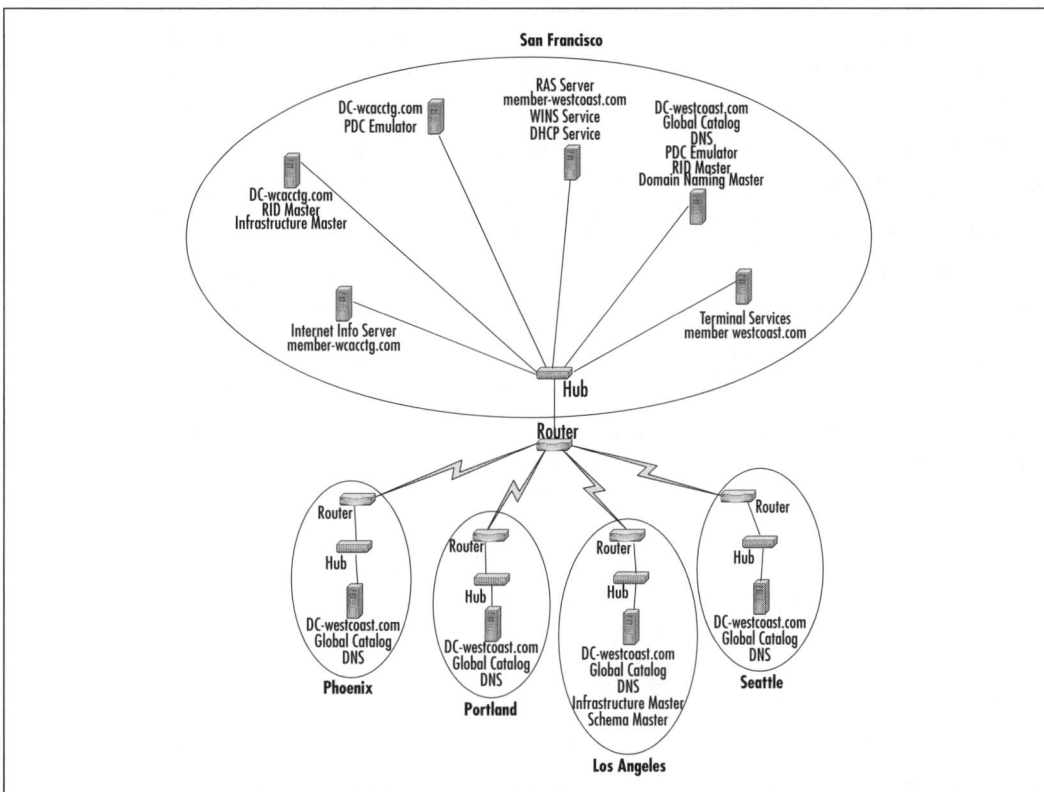

Summary

Windows 2000 Server depends on the infrastructure of the network to be able to communicate with clients. Because it is a network operating system, it was built to work on an internetwork. Windows 2000 is built on Windows NT technology. Active Directory is a new feature that has been added to Windows 2000. The Active Directory is a multimaster directory service that organizes domains and servers.

The infrastructure is affected by replication of the Active Directory updates between the various domain controllers on the internetwork. The replication is controlled by the site topology that the administrator configures. A site is a set of well-connected IP subnets, typically LANs, that are designated as sites in the Active Directory Sites and Services console.

Within the site, replication traffic uses RPCs over IP. It is uncompressed traffic that occurs, by default, every five minutes. A replication topology is generated automatically within a site by the Knowledge Consistency

Checker (KCC), in which there are no more than three hops (four servers) in a circle for replication to occur. This ensures that synchronization of all updates within a site can be completed within 15 minutes.

Between sites, replication traffic can use either RPCs over IP, or SMTP. This traffic is compressed, and is configured by an administrator to occur on a scheduled basis. Site links and site link bridges are created by administrators to create a conduit for replication traffic between sites. The intersite replication traffic can be scheduled to occur on a periodic basis, and the site link itself can be scheduled to be available during certain hours.

FRS, the file replication service, also follows the replication topology. FRS enables files to be replicated between Windows 2000 servers. Files that are updated are wholly replicated to other servers, rather than just updates that were made on the files.

There are four types of partitions in the Active Directory:

- Schema
- Configuration
- Domain(s)
- Global catalog

The schema and configuration partitions are rarely changed and do not cause much replication traffic. Each domain is a separate partition of the Active Directory. When a domain does not span a site, then less traffic crosses between the sites—only the Global Catalog, schema, and configuration would be transmitted.

Part of preparing a Windows 2000 infrastructure is knowing where each server will be placed on the internetwork, to which domains those servers belong, and what services they provide. The map of the internetwork and the number of users within each site will enable you to determine how much traffic to expect on your WAN links. Then you can determine whether to upgrade links or to optimize Windows 2000 Server.

Follow these general rules when determining your server placement:

- Each site should have at least one domain controller.
- If there are multiple domains in the forest, each site should have at least one Global Catalog server, installed on a domain controller.
- The RID master, Domain Naming master and PDC Emulator FSMOs should be placed in highly available sites. When using a hub and spoke configuration, they should always be located at the hub.

- The Schema master FSMO can be placed anywhere in the network.

- The Infrastructure master FSMO should be placed in a site that contains the root domain of the forest.

- DNS servers should be placed in every site that is separated by untrustworthy WAN links from the other sites.

- When using DHCP, the DHCP servers should be placed in every site that is separated by untrustworthy WAN links from the other sites.

- When using WINS, the WINS servers should be placed in a highly available site.

- RAS servers should be placed near the point of entry for remote users. If users are dialing in, RAS servers should be near the dial-up location. If users are entering the network via a VPN over the Internet, the RAS servers should be placed near the Internet connection.

- Terminal Services should be placed on the same link as the servers that host the application data source.

Infrastructure changes are expected since networks tend to grow and change over time. To optimize, an administrator can use the Performance monitor, Network monitor, and Replication monitor tools for Windows 2000.

FAQs

Q: When should I use bridgehead servers?

A: You should configure bridgehead servers (one in each site) between two sites so that you can control the flow of traffic between those sites. This is most effective when you have more than one domain controller in each site, and when there are multiple IP subnets in each site. You would probably want the traffic within a site to head toward the DC that is located closest to the site link. Then that DC, once configured as a bridgehead server, would be the sole sender of replication traffic to the other site. You should ascertain that there are always a pair of bridgehead servers configured, and that there are no connection objects for any other servers that cross the link in order to truly reduce the replication traffic on that link.

Q: I have two sites in the same domain and 12,000 users. We are going to implement video conferencing after we finish Windows 2000 deployment. The current link between the sites is 256 Kbps. Is this enough bandwidth?

A: No, the 256 Kbps is not enough bandwidth for the videoconferencing, never mind the overhead of the Active Directory replication traffic. If videoconferencing is going to be implemented for multiple users, you will want to investigate the traffic needs that it will require and then calculate the replication traffic overhead, or even consider scheduling replication to occur only during hours that videoconferences will not.

Q: With three sites that are spanned by two domains, can we use SMTP between the sites for replication traffic?

A: No. SMTP traffic will not replicate updates to domain partitions. It will replicate traffic only for the Global Catalog, schema, and configuration. As such, SMTP can be used only between sites that do not contain domain controllers from the same domain.

Chapter 8

Designing the Cisco Infrastructure

Solutions in this chapter:

- Getting started
- Applications and network services
- Server farm placement
- Secondary server placement
- WAN link considerations
- LAN switching considerations
- Redundancy and reliability design

Introduction

Networking is making two or more computers talk to each other; *internetworking* is making two or more networks talk to each other. It seems like such a simple concept when you see it in writing. If it were only that simple. Internetworks have grown with the advent of the Information Age, and with that growth has come a need to design fast, efficient, and cost-effective networks.

In this chapter we will be designing the infrastructure. This is where the network engineers are separated from the network administrators. If you design the network properly, no one will ever know your name, but if you design it poorly, your name will be on the tongues of all the users. Designing the network is a thankless job, and it is probably one of the hardest and most overlooked areas in networking. If I can impart any type of wisdom to you, it is this: Good designs react well to problems, and great designs would have prevented the problem. That said, there is no such thing as a perfect network, but this chapter shows how you go about trying to achieve one.

A great deal of detail focuses on site preparation alone. In this chapter there are some best practices on design and location of equipment; these are general guidelines and not a complete list, so if you are setting up a major data center, the designs in this chapter may not be large enough examples, since they are scaled to medium and large businesses.

Getting Started: The Design Process— Campus, WAN, and Remote

An internetwork requires many layers of thought and design, which encompasses everything from physical space to future network considerations. There are generally three components when designing a large internetwork—campus networks, wide area networks (WAN), and remote users:

- Campus networks generally are comprised of locally connected users in a building or set of buildings.

- Wide area networks are the connections between the campuses.

- Remote users are your mobile workforce; telecommuter traffic is mostly composed of any traffic that is not created within the campus site.

Designing the network is a challenging task. You must take into account that each of the three components has its own distinct requirements. For example, an internetwork that is composed of five meshed routers can create all sorts of unpredictable problems, so attempting to create an even larger series of intermeshed networks can be downright mind boggling.

In an age where equipment is getting faster and allowing more to be done with it, network design is becoming more difficult; campuses are moving toward more sophisticated environments that use multiple protocols and multiple media, and allowing connections to domains outside your area of influence.

Campus, WAN, and Remote Links Defined

Let's start defining our internetwork areas. The campus is a building or set of buildings that subscribe to the enterprise network. Most campuses consist of many smaller local area networks (LANs) joined to form the enterprise backbone. Campuses usually use LAN technologies such as Fiber Distributed Data Interface (FDDI), Token Ring, Ethernet, Fast Ethernet, Gigabit Ethernet, and Asynchronous Transfer Mode (ATM) to power their network.

Usually, in a campus environment, the wiring is installed and/or owned by the campus. This allows the ability to create local WAN links that span the campus area. When you cannot build your own wiring for a local WAN (that is, the building is across campus, but you cannot put in new wiring because of cost or zoning), a good practice is to optimize for the fastest functional architecture that is supported with existing cabling. When you use WAN technologies that are implemented over campus buildings that span a large geographical area, and the campus does not own the wiring, you must pay for bandwidth from a service provider.

Remote users can enter the network in various ways. The more common ways are remote access servers (RASs) and access through an Internet service provider (ISP).

NOTE

When using remote access, it is generally a good practice to implement a virtual private network (VPN) solution. This allows for security by allowing encryption and authentication services.

There are several companies that provide clients for these type networks. Be sure to research whether these clients will support the types of traffic that will be running over these connections; for example, AppleTalk, IPX/SPX, and Systems Network Architecture (SNA) bridging.

For Managers

End-to-End Network Services for a Campus Environment

Some of the challenges associated with creating an end-to-end campus solution are protecting mission-critical programs and applications, security, manageability, high availability, support for multimedia (voice and video), and scalability. Keep these issues in mind when asking for funding to build or expand your network. Remember that these add value to the company, so stress that whenever possible.

The Design Process—Getting down to Business

Let's start where all good designs start, with a pencil and paper (or if you are more inclined, feel free to use Visio or any other publishing software with which you are comfortable) and some brainstorming. This is a multiple-step process, and these designs may never be fully finished, as they should be updated as the network grows and changes. Remember, one of the most important features of network design is to be expandable.

NOTE

Diagramming is useful as a reference tool, and later as documentation. This will help when you bring in other people to support your network and to explain how and why your network functions the way it does, so you might not have to take that weekend call while you are on vacation when someone decides to "modify" or "streamline" the network. It is also a good recruiting tool for our highly competitive market.

The first step of this process is diagramming the design from the proverbial "30,000-foot view." Depending on the situation, the first drawing should be just the physical locations and possible future locations of your buildings if designing on a campus or WAN model. Add appropriate WAN connections as well as future circuit provisions (see Figure 8.1).

Figure 8.1 The 30,000-foot view.

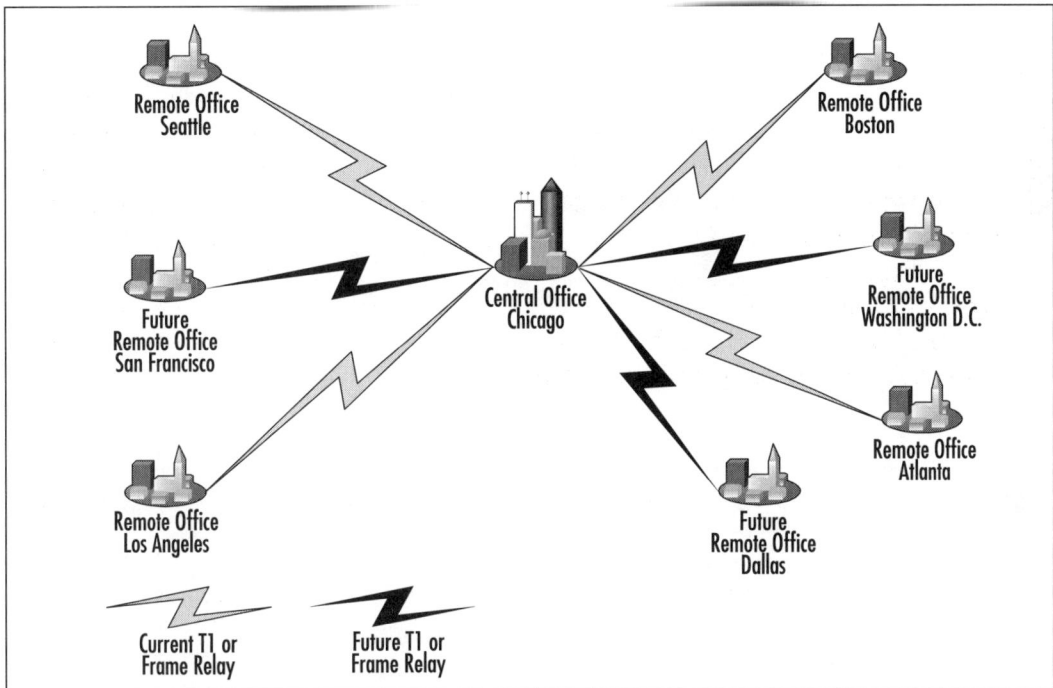

NOTE

Remember that provisioning bandwidth is an important issue; it should be covered in great detail. The design in Figure 8.1 might not be the most cost effective, but may be necessary due to network requirements. We will discuss that later in this chapter.

The second step is segmenting the drawing to contain floors (if there are multiple floors), departments, and the current and future users. This does not have to be very detailed; it is just a quick overview to make sure that you are including all users and potential sites. Many times, just by doing this, you will recall an area that previously had been left off the map (see Figure 8.2).

As we continue to move down these layers, we will drill down on each successive step with more and more detail. The next level may include the number of users at each location (site and department) and the possible growth that is expected. After that, a list of servers that should or would be

Figure 8.2 Site with floor and department.

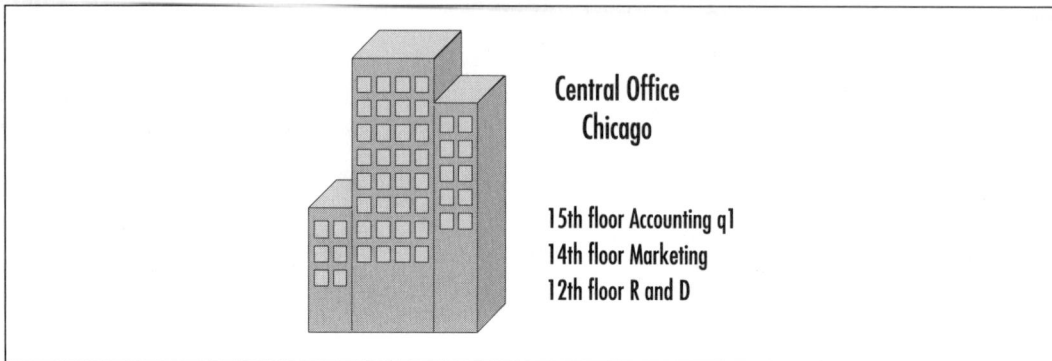

Central Office
Chicago

15th floor Accounting q1
14th floor Marketing
12th floor R and D

Figure 8.3 Department with suggested information.

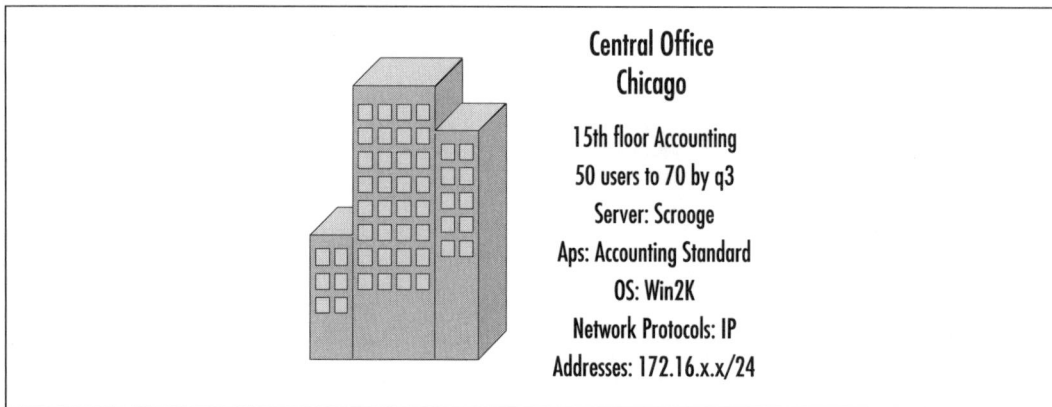

Central Office
Chicago

15th floor Accounting
50 users to 70 by q3
Server: Scrooge
Aps: Accounting Standard
OS: Win2K
Network Protocols: IP
Addresses: 172.16.x.x/24

in the vicinity of those users as well as what applications, network protocols, and network addresses might be necessary for those systems. This
can be accomplished on the main drawing, but it is usually better to partition the locations into individual drawings. This is so that when you are
adding to your drawing, you have to modify only one area, not affecting the
entire drawing (see Figure 8.3).

Notice that this is a very basic template, and at this level you can go
into more detail. Again, do what you feel comfortable with. The more detail
that you go into, the fewer surprises you'll have later.

Site Considerations

Now that we have a conceptual drawing, we can delve into site considerations. This is probably the area over which you have the least control, yet
it has a high impact on your design. The following sections provide the

basis of how to implement your design, while taking physical limitations into account.

Physical Space for Equipment

The next step in the design process is an analysis of the physical space. If there is insufficient space and/or resources (such as power, air-conditioning, etc.), there will be severe limitations on design and implementation. Most of the time, when you are building a new physical plant (otherwise known as the "wiring in the wall") for your company, you will find that there is either no space allocated or, as in most cases, you are given a pre-existing space that was formerly slotted for janitorial storage. If possible, work with the facilities manager and make sure that there is adequate space available for your needs, and that the space is sufficiently resourced (power and cabling, as well as security).

Here are some considerations for the physical plant implementation:

- Scope out the physical layout of the room; there should be sufficient space to place the equipment that will be installed.

- Find out whether the room has adequate fire protection, and if the room is climate controlled.

- Find out how secure the room is (combination lock, keyed, keyless entry).

- Decide on floor racks and/or cabinets for build-out purposes. Sometimes these issues are decided for you by outside factors, for example, if this is an existing build-out area (such as a closet) or if the cabling plant might be in one area of the room that will not reach your rack.

- Pay attention to weight, power, and environment concerns.

Weight, as expected, will vary according to equipment and cabling. Try to determine what type of equipment will go into each rack and where it will be placed. Depending on your wiring scheme, there might be an uneven distribution of weight, which might unbalance the racks you are installing. If at all possible get the weight requirements from the vendor and find a rack that is suitable to maintain what you are placing, plus approximately 20 percent of that weight for future equipment and swap-out. Also take into account whether the flooring can support the rack.

Power is also an easy component to scope out. Does the room have a dedicated power source? Does that source support the needs of the proposed equipment? Is there a backup power supply (an uninterruptible power supply)? Does the room have a circuit breaker and a master shutoff switch? These are important questions for current and future expandability. If you have any major questions, call an electrician.

Environmental concerns are always a little tricky, as this is the area with the most variance. You could write an entire book on this topic, but it probably would be only for civil engineers and architects. How is the room secured? How is the climate control and ventilation handled (heat, ventilation and air-conditioning)? Is the room sealed and is it set up for fire control? Does the flooring prevent static buildup? How is the cabling plant implemented?

First, let's deal with the security issue: since there will be a high cost associated in each room just from installing the equipment, you will want the room theft proof. The other security issue is that you don't want people just to come in and change the equipment on a whim, so you should allow only restricted access to authorized personnel.

Climate control encompasses many variables, such as temperature and humidity. If the room is too hot and the equipment overheats, it will not function properly; if it is too cold there is the possibility the equipment will freeze and crack. If the room is too humid, the equipment could short from the moisture; if it is too dry, then you run the risk of a short from static electricity. Recall that the equipment will give off its own heat, so even though the room may feel chilled while the equipment is off, once equipment is running, the temperature should average out. Make sure to check the BTU ratings of the equipment prior to designing your facility.

Fireproofing is more straightforward. In the average workspace, the walls only go up to the suspended ceiling. In a controlled room the walls go all the way to the roof to create an enclosed/sealed environment. The main reason for a sealed environment is that a Halon dispensation system or other viable fire deterrent system will smother the fire by displacing the oxygen in the room.

Preventing static buildup is usually accomplished by installing anti-static tile flooring. Do not use carpeting because it will actually increase the static buildup that is natural with movement. If you are building from scratch, consider raised flooring; this will also help with cable management.

For cable plant implementation and management, hire a company that can install and certify their work with a Registered Communication Distribution Designer (RCDD). This will make insuring the room and equipment somewhat easier. Also they can usually come up with a best practice for you and your location.

Network Equipment Basics

In this section we will discuss hardware and the layers they function on; as a refresher for the terminology introduced earlier in the book, here is an overview of hubs, bridges, switches, and routers.

- A hub (sometimes referred to as a *concentrator*) is used to connect multiple users to a single physical device that connects to the network. A hub also acts as a repeater, as it regenerates the signal as it passes traffic.

- A bridge is Layer 2 hardware that segments the network within the same network and is independent of higher layer protocols.

- A switch is Layer 2 hardware that provides network ports and separate collision domains. A switch is generally used in place of a hub in network designs. They offer higher speed, as they do not share bandwidth as a hub does.

- Routers are Layer 3 devices that are used to connect separate networks and pass traffic between subnets. Routers are protocol dependent.

Since most network designs center on switches and routers, we will focus on their roles (later in this chapter) within the network.

Capacity Planning

How many times have you come into an organization, and there just isn't a network drop, let alone an area for you to sit? This is usually an issue in companies that did not plan properly for explosive growth. A side-effect of this is that the network probably is struggling with the number of users that were added. In this section we will discuss some best practices for implementing a capacity plan.

Connection and Expansion

Capacity planning is an issue that you will have to deal with along with the design and implementation procedure. If you have a general idea of where you stand for the number of users and expected growth, you can use those as a baseline for the capacity of your network. The reason that I say "baseline" is that many things can happen in the business world over the course of six months that might cause your design to be underpowered and/or oversubscribed. Depending on the size of the current and expected network there should be a padding area of approximately 10 percent for unexpected growth.

Best Practices

One of the best practices for planning is to map out where the departments are located and what the headcount is going to be. Once these figures are worked out, decide if the users need only one data jack or multiple connections. The idea is to allocate the proper number of drops to a location for growth and also for your power users who may have multiple workstations that perform various tasks.

> **NOTE**
>
> If at all possible, try to avoid running local switches or hubs at user locations. Usually they only lead to network congestion, plus they make it harder to perform troubleshooting.

With the number of drops decided, you now need to plan on subscription and maximum bandwidth provisions of the network. Sounds impressive, huh? It really isn't that difficult. What you are doing is calculating the aggregate average bandwidth of the network devices located on the segment. With these calculations in place, you can plan whether the segment is powerful enough to support the users and resources on a given network.

So how do you calculate the aggregate average bandwidth? The calculations are based on network topology, users' traffic patterns, and network connections. Ask questions such as: What type of links should we use to connect the users to the backbone? What should the bandwidth requirement be for the backbone? You need to plan what type of link goes to each desktop so that it has the proper bandwidth, yet does not allow for the monopolization of a segment, and/or the complete shutdown of the network with oversubscription of a segment. Monopolization of a segment occurs when a user has the equal bandwidth of a resource (such as a server) and the application takes all of the available bandwidth and maintains the trunk. This will not allow other users to access the resource.

Oversubscription of a segment occurs when multiple users take up all of the resource's bandwidth, and therefore other users are unable to access the resource. Although these two symptoms result in the same conclusion, they are different because the segment in a monopolized environment runs consistently, whereas the segment that is oversubscribed may shut itself down because it cannot pass traffic due to multiple requests flooding the buffers on the switches and routers.

In general, follow industry standards and try to keep the cable runs from the wall jacks to the workstation less than five meters, from the switch to the wall jack at less than 90 meters, and from the router to the switch less than five meters (assuming that you are running Category 5 Ethernet). With all of this information, you should get an idea of the type and capacity of network equipment to be deployed at each location.

For Managers

Combining Voice and Data Jacks

There has been a recent increase in movement toward Internet Protocol (IP) telephones that combine the data and voice over one line. Voice-over IP (VoIP) allows for all-in-one voice and data solutions as long as there is a guaranteed Quality of Service (QoS).

Further concerns for planning capacity are based on factors such as the protocol you use, addressing schemes, geography, and how these things fit the topology of the network. Let's go over some considerations in the next section.

Protocol Addressing Planning

The following section discusses how to choose a protocol to best match your environment. With proper planning and implementation, any choice will work. By determining the physical layout of the network, you will be able to map out the correct topology and form a logical addressing scheme that will grow as your network grows.

Routing Protocols

Choosing routing protocols and their configuration is an important part of every network design. You must be prepared to spend a significant amount of time implementing your policies in order for the network to provide optimal performance. Routing protocols are a fundamental component of networking and creating a reachable network that can transfer data. If designed properly, the network will build routing tables and maps that can be used to see adjacent routers and their status, as well as to see network paths, congestion, and bandwidth of those links. This information helps in deciding on the optimal network paths.

The more complex routing protocols allow you to add secondary metrics. Some of those metrics include reliability, delay, load, and bandwidth. Using these metrics, the router can make these routing decisions dynamically.

The basic difference among the various routing protocols lies in the sophistication of their decision-making capabilities and metric support. This is one of the main factors to consider when choosing a protocol to match the characteristics of your network.

Generally, the simpler the network topology is, the simpler the routing protocol you can use. Simpler networks generally are also easier to configure, as they don't tax the router as heavily as more massive networks. Company networks are growing more complex, so the more sophisticated routing protocols will likely be used in your infrastructure.

There are two types of routing protocols, interior and exterior. Interior protocols are those that you would implement within your private network, and are controlled completely within that domain. Conversely, exterior protocols work with external domains, such as the Internet. These protocols are designed to protect your domain from external errors or misrepresentation. To read more about interior and exterior protocols, visit the Internet Engineering Task Force's site (www.ietf.org).

Interior Protocols

So how do you decide on which interior protocol to use? The following sections will explain some of the inherent differences that are implemented in each of the interior protocols. Some are self-explanatory, and some are just plain cryptic. Hopefully this section will clarify some of the terms and allow you to make reasonable, well thought-out decisions.

Let's discuss interior protocols first, since those are the ones that you have most control over and therefore the most need to cover. With the exception of Open Shortest Path First (OSPF) and Intermediate System-to-Intermediate System (IS-IS), the interior routing protocols described are all known as distance-vector protocols, and they use distance and next-hop data to make their routing and forwarding decisions. Some distance-vector protocols are very simplistic and don't scale well in larger environments. One example is Routing Information Protocol (RIP), which uses hops (the number of connections between it and its destination) as its determining factor. The largest hop count before it disregards the packet is 15, making it one of the least scalable protocols. Another drawback to RIP is that it does not take into account varying available bandwidth. If, for example, you had a packet that needed to get from network A to network D, RIP will take a path with one hop rather than a path with two hops but higher speed (see Figure 8.4).

Figure 8.4 RIP and routing decisions.

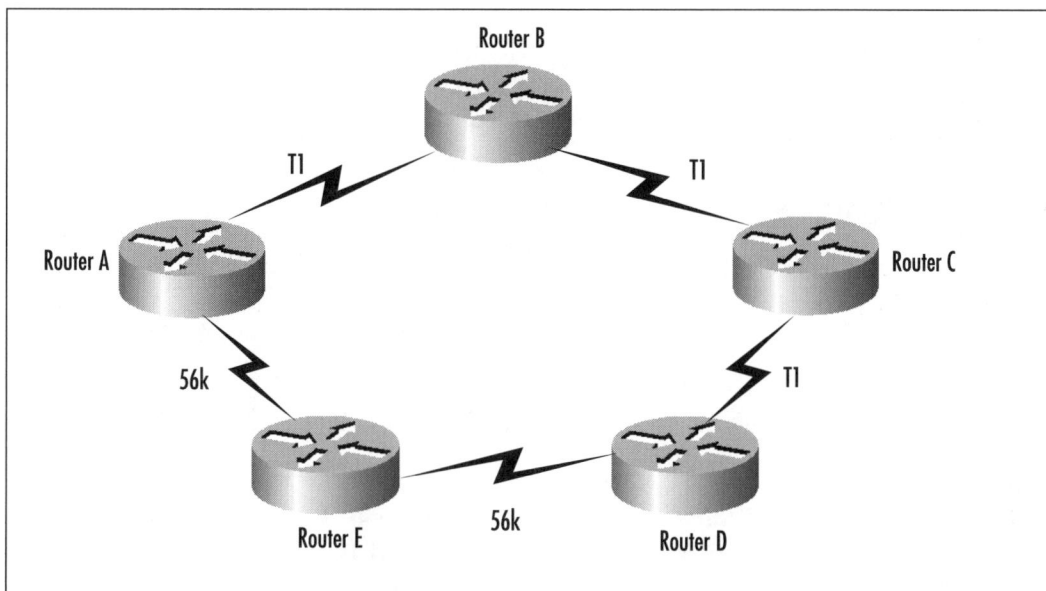

If your network is fairly simple in terms of the topology and the number of routers, a distance-vector protocol such as RIP or Interior Gateway Routing Protocol (IGRP, discussed later in this chapter) could work fine. If you're running a multivendor network, RIP, RIPv2, IS-IS, and OSPF are common protocols across many vendors' router implementations.

Now it is time to discuss the protocols available in most instances using Cisco equipment. I am going to list what is available for use in a semichronological order. I also listed some of the strengths and limitations for each protocol.

Routing Information Protocol (RIP)

This protocol was derived from Xerox Corporation's Xerox Network Systems (XNS) for IP networks. It supports IP networks. Its strengths are that it is still viable in networks that use a constant internal subnet; it is usable on most vendors' equipment, and it is a low-cost option (it's generally free from most vendors). Its weaknesses are that its scalability is minimal (15 hops maximum); its path is determined by hop count, and it may take best path; it broadcasts the full routing table frequently, wasting bandwidth; and it cannot handle variable-length subnet masks (VLSM).

Interior Gateway Routing Protocol (IGRP)

This protocol was created by Cisco and it supports Cisco IP and OSI networks. Its strengths are that it uses multiple metrics in decision-making, and it provides fast convergence. Its weaknesses are that it runs only on Cisco equipment, and it broadcasts the routing table frequently, wasting bandwidth.

Open Shortest Path First (OSPF)

This protocol was developed by the IETF for IP networks. Its strengths are that it is usable on most vendors' equipment, and it broadcasts the routing table only when changes are made. Its weaknesses are that it uses only bandwidth as a metric, and it restricts some topologies.

Intermediate System-to-Intermediate System (IS-IS)

This protocol was developed by IETF for OSI and IP networks. Its strengths are that it is usable on most vendors' equipment; it broadcasts the routing table only when changes are made; and it provides fast convergence. Its weaknesses are that it uses only bandwidth as a metric, and restricts some topologies.

RIPv2

This protocol was developed by the IETF for IP networks. Its strengths are added authentication and multicast ability to RIP, and it is usable on most vendors' equipment. Its weaknesses are that its scalability is minimal (15 hops maximum) and it only uses bandwidth as metric.

Enhanced IGRP

Designed by Cisco for multiprotocol Cisco networks, this protocol supports IP, IPX, and AppleTalk networks. Its strengths are its incremental updates to cut down on broadcast traffic; it supports VLSMs; it uses multiple metrics; it provides fast convergence; and it retains backward compatibility with IGRP. Its weakness is that it works only with Cisco equipment.

Convergence can be defined as such: When the topology of the network changes, the network must reroute the traffic quickly—when routers make a decision on which path they will use, they are said to have come to a convergence. Convergence is the time that it takes for the network to start using new routes. Routers must update the tables that are used to define the next hop. This allows routers to make their own routing decisions dynamically and, therefore, routing tables must be current. There are some drawbacks that are associated with convergence; for example, if the router is updating its routing table and there are additional changes implemented, there is a tendency toward instability. Three things must occur at the router when topologies change:

- Identify the change
- Choose a new route
- Broadcast the changed route information

Some changes are readily noticed, like when the fiber finder finds the local loop to your service provider. In this instance the serial line will fail and the router will detect loss of carrier. Sometimes the problem is a little harder to find, like when a point-to-point circuit becomes unstable. It might still be passing packets, and therefore there is no loss of carrier (but possibly a lot of collisions).

There are other concerns—some connections don't have carrier detect active on them. For example, if an Ethernet connection is lost when a router reboots, other routers might not detect it at that time. So you must remember that when something fails, detection for the lost connection is dependent on which routing protocol and media type are used.

When a failure has been detected, the routing protocol must calculate a new path. How it does this is protocol dependent. When that is complete, the routing protocol must then broadcast the changes to the rest of the network.

Choosing the Right Protocol

Using the previous references, which explained the differences that are inherent with the interior protocols, it is time to sit down and address which networking protocol will be best for your network. There are several considerations to take into account: you want the protocol to add functionality, you want it to be scalable, you want it to adapt easily to changes that will be implemented, you want it to be manageable, and you want it to be cost effective.

When you add a protocol, you are trying to add functionality to the network. If you didn't want enhanced functions, you would have left the network as it was. (If it ain't broke, don't fix it!) So what are you trying to achieve? Is there a benefit that is necessary for your network? Sometimes the answer really is not to implement more complex protocols, but usually they are truly necessary to maintain and enhance the network.

Scalability is an issue that will keep cropping up. You want your design to meet current and future growth. What happens if you decide to implement RIP and then exceed the hop count within your own network?

Preplanning will save you some massive restructuring headaches later in the development of the infrastructure.

Adaptability to new technologies is a must. With the world moving towards higher and higher bandwidth usage, you must take into account that what you design must be readily adaptable for future technologies (some examples are VoIP and video traffic) that may be implemented. This is an area where adding value to your network will save your company money in the long run.

Another key concern that should be noted is the manageability of the network. You are probably going to get into an area where there is more network traffic than bandwidth, and you are going to want to manage traffic and to some extent monitor the usage of the links that are on your network. With that criteria in mind, plan on protocols that will be more beneficial to you and the management of the network.

Finally, one of the toughest areas when choosing a routing protocol is cost effectiveness. Some of the protocols can be run only on Cisco equipment because they are proprietary; some require additional hardware to run effectively. Although RIP will run on all equipment (within reason) and is very cost efficient, the network would have to be scaled down so that it could be implemented properly. A protocol such as EIGRP would be fantastic in a larger scale environment, but it only works with Cisco equipment so you need to keep that in mind if you have legacy equipment you are working on phasing out.

Route Selection

So why are we talking about route selection? It seems kind of silly if there is only one route to the destination. The question is: What happens if that route should fail? What about using other routes to allow more traffic and less congestion? These reasons are why most networks are designed with multiple routes (redundancy and load balancing) so there is always an alternative connection in case of failure or to alleviate traffic issues. Routing protocols use metrics to select the best route based on weighted decisions, from groups of existing routes.

Metrics are values that can be assigned and weighted to make decisions on routing paths within a network. Metrics are assigned characteristics or a set of characteristics on each link/route of a network. When traffic is passed along a link, the network equipment makes a choice on how to route the traffic by calculating values of the metrics and assigning the traffic to the selected path.

Depending on the routing protocol, metrics are handled differently. Most of the routing protocols can use multiple paths if they are considered equal cost. Some protocols can use paths that have routes that are not cost equivalents. By implementing multiple paths, you can use load balancing to improve bandwidth allocation.

With a multiple path design, there are two widely used ways for packet distribution. These are *per-packet load balancing* and *per-destination load balancing*.

Per-packet load balancing uses all possible routes in proportion to the route metrics. What this means is that if all routes are equal cost, it will cycle through them in a "round robin" selection scheme, where one packet is sent to each possible path that is available. Routers default to this method when fast switching is disabled.

Per-destination load balancing uses routes based on what their destination is. Each destination is assigned an available route and maintains that route for future use. This way traffic tends to arrive in the proper order. Routers are defaulted to this method when fast switching is enabled.

NOTE

Transmission Control Protocol (TCP) can accommodate out-of-order packets, and there will always be some of this on multipath networks. Excessive out-of-order packets can cause performance issues so don't go overboard on the redundant load balancing. Make sure to have at least one extra path between segments and *no more* if redundancy is an issue.

Preplanning these rollouts will save aggravation and long nights of troubleshooting. Sometimes it is best to sit down and create a matrix with these considerations and cross-reference what will be best for your network. Try to use a single routing protocol for your network. Sometimes this is not possible, so in those instances, plan for the best protocol mesh and implement as cleanly as possible. The best advice that I can offer is to keep it simple. Complexity is not a good thing in the network design. You want a stable, simple network. Now onto the next decision-making process, *addressing*.

Addressing Considerations

The addressing scheme is dependent on several variables. Since most companies are now creating firewalls and implementing Network Address Translation (NAT) and/or Port Address Translation (PAT) to their public address space to conserve addresses, you have to figure out how to implement your addresses in a logical manner. Since Network Address Translation is so popular, private addressing is almost completely up to you. As specified in Request For Comments (RFC) 1918, the three private address spaces are:

- Class A: 10.0.0.0–10.255.255.255 (10/8 prefix)
- Class B: 172.16.0.0–172.31.255.255 (172.16/12 prefix)
- Class C: 192.168.0.0–192.168.255.255 (192.168/16 prefix)

Since these are private addresses, they cannot be routed on the Internet. Using subnet masks will allow you to configure network and host IDs to suit your needs. As an example, using our sample network in Figure 8.3, the fifteenth floor has an address of 172.16.x.x with a subnet of 255.255.255.0, which would allow us to set up multiple users and allow for subnets to differentiate the users if necessary. With this example, the design is with a class B address scheme and a class C subnet, giving us more network IDs and fewer host IDs. We could have used the 10-net addressing scheme, but I decided to maintain a smaller class of addresses due to the number of current and future users.

Since addressing is important and also time consuming, plan out allocation of addresses as neatly as possible so you have to readdress your network as little as possible. Plan on how you want to slice up the company, whether it is by site, location, department, telecommuter, etc. If you are using a public address scheme, conservation is key. If you are using a private addressing scheme, you should focus on layout. Deployment should be in a logical and readily understood manner for public and private addressing. You want to keep similar users as well as similar resources together.

Set aside address space for current and potential users (have I said this enough?). If you want to keep all of the servers in one address space, set aside enough for future growth. Generally, layout should be handled by grouping users with similar needs in similar locations (with the advent of virtual LANs, or VLANs, this is not quite as major a concern as it was in the past). As in Figure 8.3's example with the fifteenth floor, users in accounting can be separated by subnets if required. Remember that when you add subnets, there is the need to place routers between subnets that cannot speak to each other.

Since the network doesn't physically exist at this point in time, be sure to revise all of your ideas on paper. This will help during the actual implementation. Another way to help segment traffic and design your addressing scheme is by topology.

Topology

The topology of a network is defined by sets of routers and the networks to which they connect. Routing protocols also can establish a logical topology depending upon implementation. Some routing protocols use addressing to segment traffic and domains to create a logical topology. These networks are called flat networks, so no topology creation is required.

TCP/IP requires the creation of a hierarchical topology that establishes a core layer, a distribution layer, and an access layer. For example, OSPF and IS-IS protocols use a hierarchical design. The hierarchical topology takes precedence over any topology created through address segmentation. So if you choose a hierarchical routing protocol you should also create the addressing topology to reflect the hierarchy. If you decide to use a flat routing protocol, the addressing will create the topology.

There are two regularly accepted ways of assigning addresses in a hierarchical network. The easiest way is to assign all network areas (including the core) a unique network address. A more complex way is to assign ranges of addresses to each area. Areas should be composed of contiguous addresses for networks and hosts. Areas should also include all the router interfaces on any of the included networks. By doing so, each area maintains its own topology database because all interfaces run a separate copy of the basic routing algorithm.

Flat networks were originally campus networks that consisted of a single LAN to which new users were added. This LAN was a logical or physical cable into which the network devices connected. In the case of Ethernet, all the devices shared the half-duplex 10 Mbps available. The LAN was considered a collision domain, because all packets were visible to all devices on the LAN, and are therefore free to collide, given the carrier sense multiple access collision detect (CSMA/CD) scheme used by Ethernet.

When the collision domain of the LAN became congested, a bridge was inserted. This allowed a segmentation of traffic into several collision domains, because a bridge is a store-and-forward packet switch. With this ability to cut collision traffic, there were increases made to network throughput. The drawback is that bridges pass all traffic, including flood broadcasts, multicasts, and unknown unicasts to all segments. So all the bridged segments in the campus together form a single broadcast domain. The Spanning Tree Protocol (STP) was developed to prevent loops in the network and to route around failed connections.

NOTE

There are some issues with the STP broadcast domain. It has a high time threshold for convergence, typically 40 to 50 seconds. It allows for nonoptimized paths to exist. Redundant links carry no data as they are blocked. Broadcast storms affect the whole domain and each network host must process all traffic. Security is limited within the domain, and troubleshooting problems takes a lot of time.

Broadcast traffic sets a practical limit to the size of the broadcast domain. Managing and troubleshooting a bridged campus becomes increasingly difficult as the number of users increases, because it adds to the broadcast domain. One misconfigured or malfunctioning workstation can disable an entire broadcast domain for an extended period of time, as it is generally hard to locate.

When designing a flat, bridged campus, each bridged segment should correspond to a workgroup. The workgroup server was used as file server, logon server, and application server for the workgroup and was placed in the same segment as its clients, which allowed most of the traffic to be contained within the domain. This design principle is referred to as the 80/20 rule and refers to the goal of keeping at least 80 percent of the traffic contained within the local broadcast domain or segment.

NOTE

With the campus-wide VLAN model (discussed later in this chapter), the logical domains are dispersed across the campus, but still organized such that 80 percent of traffic is contained within the VLAN. The remaining 20 percent of traffic leaves the network or subnet through a router.

The 80/20 traffic rule has been steadily changing due to the rise of intranets and distributed applications. With new and existing applications moving toward a distributed applications and storage model, which are accessed though World Wide Web (WWW) retrieval, the traffic pattern is going toward the 20/80 model, where only 20 percent of traffic is local to the workgroup LAN and 80 percent of the traffic is destined for a nonlocal domain.

Meshed networks are generally flat networks where all the routers perform the same functions. Network expansion is usually handled in an ad hoc manner and will not support several of the routing protocols properly (for example, OSPF).

Hierarchical networks are organized in layers that have clearly defined specific functions. Whatever media you plan to use for your solution (Asynchronous Transfer Mode (ATM), Ethernet, and so on), the hierarchical model has many benefits. Due to the multilayer design being somewhat modular, troubleshooting as well as scaling the network is made easier. By implementing Layer 3 routing, you are able to create broadcast domains and keep traffic only on the network for which it was destined. Another benefit of Layer 3 routing is the ability to run routing protocols (discussed earlier in this chapter). With the proper protocol there is the ability to add redundancy and fast convergence. This is the three-tier model discussed in Chapter 3—the core layer, the distribution layer, and the access layer.

Application Services

Knowing the various network applications that will be on the wire is essential to the planning and design of your new network. You need to take into account all of the different types of protocols, ports, and bandwidth that will be utilized on the wire when running different programs. For instance, standard file and print traffic has *far* less overhead than database and backup applications. Each program behaves in its own way and you need to anticipate the behavior in order to design the network properly.

Make a list of the applications that will be running on the wire—be meticulous! Make sure that you take into account every possible traffic generator that you can think of, no matter how trivial, and add it into the pile of your bandwidth calculations. Make sure also to give each application its proper "weight" in your calculations. For instance, it is highly doubtful that people will be printing 100 percent of the time on the network, so make sure that you apply the proper percentage "time on the wire" in your calculations when you are working them out as to how much time you will see the traffic.

Although this seems like a tedious task, it is well worth the exercise—you will be blamed if the bandwidth is choked on Day One of the new network rollout. Try to overestimate the amount of bandwidth required at the worst times of traffic by about 20 percent of the time. That will always lead to a safe estimate of bandwidth.

Server Farm Placement

When designing the server farm, you should build the network as a modular building block using multilayer switching. This way you can segment the traffic so that it goes over specific bandwidths. For example, the Gigabit Ethernet trunk carries the server-to-server traffic and the Fast EtherChannel trunk carries the backbone traffic, so all server-to-server traffic is kept off the backbone, which has performance and security advantages. The server farms should have Hot Standby Router Protocol (HSRP) redundancy between the multilayer switches running, and access lists can control access policy to the server farm. With this setup, the core switches are separate from distribution switches, cutting down on broadcast domains and allowing for better throughput.

By placing servers in a server farm you avoid problems such as IP redirect and choosing the best gateway router when servers are attached directly to the backbone subnet.

Positioning Servers

Centralization of servers is becoming more and more popular. Generally, services are consolidated into a single server, but sometimes servers are grouped at a data center for security or administration purposes. It is also common for workgroups or individuals to publish Web pages locally and to make them accessible to the rest of the network (an intranet).

When servers are connected directly to the backbone, all traffic passes from a subnet in the access layer to a subnet in the core. Access lists applied at the distribution layer implement policy-based control of access to enterprise servers.

Servers that are attached directly to the core must use proxy Address Resolution Protocol (ARP), ICMP Router Discovery Protocol (IRDP), Gateway Discovery Protocol (GDP), or RIP snooping to populate their routing tables. HSRP should not be used at the core subnets, because in the distribution layer, switches connect to different parts of the site.

NOTE

In Cisco equipment, using HSRP can also add redundancy, and implementing Fast EtherChannel can scale bandwidth from Fast Ethernet, and from Gigabit Ethernet to Gigabit EtherChannel.

This area also will affect where you place your Dynamic Host Configuration Protocol (DHCP), Domain Name System (DNS) server, and Windows Internet Naming Service (WINS) servers. Remember that these services should be within the network firewall.

For IT Professionals

When Not to Use HSRP

Sometimes HSRP should not be used, for example where servers use proxy ARP, IRDP, GDP, or RIP to populate their routing tables. Be sure to take these items into account when deploying your redundant network designs.

Terminal Services Farms

One of the great benefits to Windows 2000 is the built-in capability to use Terminal Services on the network. Terminal Services is the Microsoft version of thin-client technology, which allows for the workstations to receive a video snapshot of a desktop being run on another machine and to control that machine remotely. The benefit of this is so that bandwidth-heavy applications such as databases and other query-based applications need not send the queries back and forth over the entire network on the slow WAN links; instead they have access to the client machine via high speed switched links, and the user, who is out there on the network, will be accessing the database applications as if they are right next to the database servers on the switch.

This technology has been increasingly popular over the last couple of years as bandwidth has become a premium on the WAN links. Microsoft has built this technology into Windows 2000 so that any Windows 2000 server can activate this remote control capability.

Make sure when you are designing your server farms to take into account how Terminal Services can aid you on your network infrastructure. It is built into the system, so try to find a way to utilize it!

LAN and Switching Considerations

Designing a network with multilayer switching allows you scalability, easy troubleshooting, and efficient utilization of bandwidth; the following sections discuss minimizing network traffic through the effective use of high-level routing protocols, IP multicast for video and voice applications, and the role of VLANs in creating the backbone topology for a manageable network.

Scaling Bandwidth

Bandwidth in the multilayer model can be scaled in many ways. Ethernet can be upgraded to Fast Ethernet, and Fast Ethernet can be combined into Fast EtherChannel or Gigabit Ethernet or Gigabit EtherChannel. Access switches can be partitioned into multiple VLANs with multiple trunks, and using Inter-Switch Link (ISL) in the VLAN to combine the different trunks. Fast EtherChannel provides more efficient utilization of bandwidth by multiplexing multiple VLANs over one trunk. By segmenting each VLAN so that it uses only one trunk, one trunk can be congested while another is unused. Otherwise, more ports will be required to get the same type of performance. To scale bandwidth within ATM backbones, you must add more OC-3 or OC-12 trunks. Routing provided by Private Network-to-Network Interface (PNNI) can handle load balancing and fast fail-over issues.

Scaling Considerations

The great thing about designing the network with multilayer switching is that is extremely scalable. Routing is able to scale because it is distributed and therefore it is easy to add pieces that point to other pieces. The backbone performance scales when you add more connections and/or switches.

Because the network is compartmentalized, it is also scalable from a management and administration perspective. When issues crop up in the network, you can pin the problem down to one of the layers and troubleshoot it down from there.

When designing your network, avoid creating STP loops in the backbone. STP takes 40 to 50 seconds to converge and does not allow for load balancing across multiple paths. When using ATM for your backbone, use PNNI to handle load balancing.

You should always try to use high-level routing protocols like OSPF and Enhanced IGRP, which allow for path determination and load balancing. OSPF operating costs at the core will rise linearly as the number of switches in the distribution layer grows. What happens is OSPF elects a router and a backup router, which will connect with all of the other routers in the distribution layer. If multiple VLANs or emulated LANs (ELANs) are created in the backbone, a primary and a backup router are elected for each. Remember that with OSPF routing traffic, CPU overhead increases as the number of VLANs or ELANs increases on the backbone. So try to keep the number of VLANs or ELANs to a minimum. The following are some suggestions for best practices:

- Remember to consider that OSPF needs summarization to allow it to scale. It is a common practice in large campuses to make each building an OSPF area and to make the routers area border routers (ABRs).

- Try to make all of the subnets in a building form a contiguous block of addresses. This will allow you to use a single summary advertisement on the ABRs. By doing so, you will reduce the amount of routing information traffic and increase the stability of the routing table.

- Enhanced IGRP can be configured in roughly the same way. There are some exceptions to the rule, though. Protocols such as Novell Service Advertising Protocol (SAP), RIP, and AppleTalk Routing Table Maintenance Protocol (RTMP) have an overhead that increases exponentially as you add connections.

NOTE

When routers (Layer 3) are used in a campus, the number of router hops from edge to edge is called the diameter. It is considered good practice to design for a consistent diameter within a campus.

IP Multicast

Applications that use IP multicast are a rapidly growing piece of company intranets. Applications such as Microsoft NetShow and NetMeeting are being used more commonly to do voice and video streaming. There are several considerations to using IP multicast:

- Protocol Independent Multicast (PIM) routing, in either dense mode or sparse mode

- Clients/servers join multicast groups with Internet Group Management Protocol (IGMP)
- Multicast tree pruning with Cisco Group Multicast Protocol (CGMP) or IGMP snooping
- Switch and router multicast performance
- Multicast policy

The most common routing protocol for multicast is PIM. PIM is broken up into two parts, PIM sparse mode and PIM dense mode. Sparse-mode operation is used with applications like NetMeeting, whereas dense-mode operation is used for an application like IP/TV. PIM is being used in the Internet as well as in corporate intranets. A strong point of PIM is that it works with various unicast routing protocols such as OSPF and Enhanced IGRP. PIM routers are also compatible with the Distance Vector Multicast Routing Protocol (DVMRP). DVMRP is an older multicast routing protocol that was used somewhat extensively on the Internet multicast backbone (MBONE). It is expected that DVMRP will replaced over time by PIM.

PIM works by building multicast trees that minimize traffic on the network. This is important for applications such as real-time video, which use large amounts of bandwidth. PIM is usually configured in sparse-dense mode and automatically uses either sparse or dense mode depending upon application. Multicast clients and servers that wish to join or advertise multicast groups use IGMP. The router in this type of environment makes multicast available on subnets with configured (open to receive) clients, but blocks the traffic if there are no clients open. CGMP allows multicast pruning on a Catalyst switch. A Cisco router sends out a CGMP message to advertise all Media Access Control (MAC) addresses that have joined the multicast group. Catalyst switches receive the CGMP message and forward traffic only to ports with those MAC address in the forwarding table. This blocks multicast traffic from ports that don't have members connected to them. The Catalyst 5000 series has an architecture that forwards multicast streams to one port, multiple ports, or all ports (there is no performance penalty). Catalyst switches can support many multicast groups concurrently. Multicast policy can be implemented by placing multicast servers in a server farm behind a Catalyst switch. The multilayer switch acts as a multicast firewall that controls access to multicast traffic. To segregate multicast traffic, create a separate multicast VLAN or subnet on the backbone. Also you have to create a PIM rendezvous point, which is the root of the multicast tree.

Virtual LANs and Emulated LANs

A technology that was developed to enable Layer 2 switching across the campus is called VLANs, or virtual LANs. A VLAN is a way to create an extended logical network that is independent of the physical network layout, and functions as a separate broadcast domain. A VLAN is similar to an extended bridged network. STP is generally implemented between the switches in a VLAN.

Another technology that was developed to enable campus-wide VLANs is called VLAN trunking. Trunking allows traffic from several logical Layer 2 networks to be multiplexed (combined). Creating a VLAN trunk between a Layer 2 switch and a router allows the router to connect to several networks with a single physical interface.

ISL, 802.10, and 802.1q are VLAN tagging protocols that were created for VLAN trunking. A VLAN tag is a number that is placed into the header of frames that go between two devices. The tag number value allows the data from different VLANs to be multiplexed and demultiplexed.

ATM LAN Emulation (LANE) is the technology that permits multiple logical LANs to exist over a single switched ATM network. ATM Emulated LANs (ELANs) use a similar tagging method as packet-based technologies, so ISL, 802.10, and 802.1q are compatible with Ethernet VLANs. LANE clients (LECs) connect Ethernet VLANs across the ATM backbone. To make ATM LANE work like Ethernet, you also need a LANE Configuration Server (LECS), LANE Server (LES), and Broadcast and Unknown Server (BUS). With these implemented, ATM LANE will emulate Ethernet broadcast protocol over ATM.

NOTE

Ethernet connected hosts and servers in one VLAN cannot talk to Ethernet connected hosts and servers in a different VLAN.

Policy in the Core

With routing done in the distribution layer, it is possible to implement the backbone as a single logical network or multiple logical networks. VLANs can be used to create separate logical networks that can be used for multiple purposes. For example, a VLAN could be created for traffic management. Policies could be implemented for each core VLAN and applied with access lists on the router.

You could partition the core by protocol. What you would need to do is create one VLAN for each server, based on the protocols that they use (for example, IP, IPX, etc.). These partitions can become complete physical separations on multiple core switches.

Try to keep the backbone topology simple. Keep the number of VLANs (or ELANs) small so that they are easily managed.

Comparing Campus Network Design Models

This section briefly compares several campus network designs using multilayer switching. I will use it to describe the hierarchal approach to network design, so that you can create an optimized network environment that is scalable, manageable, and fault tolerant.

The Hub and Router Model

In a hub and router model, the access layer devices are hubs that act as repeaters, the distribution layer consists of routers (or Layer 3 switches), and the core layer contains hubs or multilayer switches. Routers in the distribution layer provide broadcast control and segmentation. Several hubs can be bridged or cascaded together to form one logical subnet or network.

The hub and router model has the ability to implement routing protocols such as OSPF and Enhanced IGRP, so it is very scalable. Due to the fact that the network is segmented, it also simplifies troubleshooting and administration. This model is good because it supports protocols such as Novell IPX, AppleTalk, DECnet, and TCP/IP.

The hub and router model is easy to configure and maintain because it is very modular. Each router is configured with the same features. In fact, many of the configurations can be cut and pasted from router to router. Because each router is programmed the same way, it creates a predictable network, which makes troubleshooting easier.

This model can be upgraded as performance demands increase because of its modular nature. The access and core layer can be upgraded to Layer 2 switching, and the distribution layer can be upgraded to Layer 3 switching with multilayer switching. Upgrading hubs to switches does not change the network addressing, the design, or the configuration of the routers.

The Campus-wide VLAN Model

In the campus-wide VLAN model, Layer 2 switching is used in the access, distribution, and core layers. To connect the different VLANs, a router must be connected to all VLANs. Layer 3 switching is done at the router.

In this setup, the router is typically referred to as a "router-on-a-stick" or a "one-armed router." Other routers can be added to distribute the load, where each router attaches to several or all VLANs. With this method, traffic must traverse the campus from the source VLAN to a port on the gateway router, then back out into the destination VLAN.

The campus-wide VLAN model is highly dependent upon the 80/20 rule (discussed earlier in this chapter). If 80 percent of the traffic stays within a domain, then 80 percent of the packets are switched at Layer 2 from client to server. However, if 90 percent of the traffic goes outside of the local domain, then the one-armed router must switch 90 percent of the packets. The scalability and performance of the VLAN model are limited by the characteristics of STP (also discussed earlier). Each VLAN is equivalent to a flat-bridged network.

By installing a Catalyst series multilayer switch that supports either Route Switch Modules, or a Multilayer Switch Feature Card (MSFC), you can replace the one-armed router and do all of your routing on high-speed switch-routing blades in the switches. Enterprise servers in the server farm may be attached by Fast Ethernet or by Fast EtherChannel to increase the bandwidth.

The campus-wide VLAN model provides the flexibility to have statically configured connections move within the campus. Cisco's VLAN Membership Policy Server (VMPS) and the VLAN Trunking Protocol (VTP) were designed to make this possible. For example, a laptop user plugs a PC into a LAN port in another building, and the local switch sends a query to the VMPS to determine whether the user is allowed in the VLAN through access policies. The switch then adds the user's port to the appropriate VLAN.

Multiprotocol over ATM

Multiprotocol over ATM (MPOA) adds cut-through, Layer 3 switching to ATM LANE. The ATM design is the same as in ATM LANE; the LECS and the LES/BUS for each ELAN are configured in the same manner as before.

With MPOA, Multiprotocol Client (MPC) hardware and software need to be added on the access switches as well as the multiprotocol server (MPS), which is implemented in software installed on the router. When a client in the VLAN talks to an enterprise server in the server farm, the first packet goes from the MPC in the access switch to the MPS using LANE. The MPS forwards the packet to the destination MPC using LANE. Then the MPS tells the two MPCs to establish a switched virtual circuit (SVC) path.

Also with MPOA, IP unicast packets use the cut-through SVC. Multicast packets are sent to the BUS to be flooded in the originating ELAN. The router then copies the multicast to the BUS in every ELAN that needs to receive the packet, which was determined by multicast routing. Then, each BUS again floods the packet for each destination ELAN.

Protocols packets, other than IP, are processed from LANE to router to LANE, which does not establish a direct cut-through SVC. MPOA designs must take into account the amount of broadcast, multicast, and non-IP traffic and how they relate to the performance of the router. MPOA should be used in networks that are predominately IP unicast traffic and ATM trunks to the wiring closet switch.

For IT Professionals

The Cisco 3524

Cisco has marketed a power-enabled port design on the 3524 series that will power phones. This is a crucial design consideration when using IP phone sets that do not supply their own power.

WAN Link Considerations with Windows 2000

When creating a converged network (something with voice, data, video, etc.), the need for QoS comes into play. Any time there is a potential bottleneck in the network, queuing techniques should be applied so that delay- and drop-sensitive traffic such as voice and real-time video pass through with the least interference. This is typical at the WAN edge router, where all data traffic destined for other networks are aggregated into slower-speed links. Whatever the queuing mechanism you use, it will likely classify data, voice, and video packets so that they have been allowed proper throughput.

Low-speed links need special considerations. For example, if voice traffic has been sent out a connection, and a data packet to get sent at the same time, the data packet could possibly be in the order of 1500 bytes long. That size data packet will take more than 200 milliseconds to get clocked out a slow-speed interface. Cisco recommends that latency for voice links be kept below 214 milliseconds, so anything that could push the latency to this limit is bad. Fortunately both point-to-point and Frame Relay networks that use Cisco routers can support fragmentation techniques that will allow smaller packets and therefore keep latency low.

Using Access Control Lists (ACLs) will also allow the ability to keep certain types of traffic such as unnecessary routing protocol traffic off slow network links. Directory Enabled Network services allow for management of dynamic data that is required to utilize the full potential of network-aware applications and policy-based networking. Directories are ideal for storing and distributing user, network, and policy definitions, but these items must be evaluated for use in a dynamic network.

Active Directory, Cisco Networking Services for Active Directory (CNS/AD), is probably the first Directory Enabled Network service because it allows directory technology to link network users to network services. CNS/AD allows users control of network management applications; it uses Lightweight Directory Access Protocol (LDAP) to support network services and management.

Routing and Scalability

As I discussed earlier in the chapter, a router provides connectivity between networks and broadcast domains. Routers forward packets based on network addresses rather than MAC addresses (which is how Layer 2 works). Internetworks are generally more scalable than flat-bridged networks because routers summarize status by network number. Routers use protocols such as OSPF and Enhanced IGRP to exchange network status information.

NOTE

When compared with STP, routing protocols have improved on these issues: Convergence is achieved in a more acceptable time frame; it allows for more load balancing and optimization of links by implementing metrics; and it is more scalable because it maintains status and routing tables.

Planning for the Future Growth of the Company's Infrastructure

Okay, so you have secured funding with your stellar speech that made the CFO pull out the checkbook and hand you a blank check. Now what? A run for political office? A screen test in Hollywood? No, it's time to purchase networking equipment (and a small condo in the Swiss Alps).

If at all possible, err on the side of building out too much. Although this might be a cost concern, think about the loss of money that will be caused by downtime or insufficient resources. Also, there is the issue of future technologies that may be able to add value to the network. Bring these points up in allocation meetings and discuss why more, in these instances, is necessary.

Network Scalability

Okay, you designed this network and took into account that there would be more people added and more bandwidth being used for applications, so what happens when that is max'ed out? Can you expand on your existing design? Is your resume printed out and ready to go?

Here is where your design can be put to the test. Remember that scalability is dependent on what you have installed in the way of hardware, and on what you are using at the software level (routing protocols). Scalability is usually limited by two factors: technical issues and operational issues.

Technical issues with scaling are mainly about finding the right mix of routing protocols and network equipment. What you would like are protocols that scale well with the addition of more network equipment.

Operational issues on the other hand, are mainly concerned with large areas and protocols that aren't based on the hierarchical design.

Remember that when designing your network, choosing the right equipment is key. There are three resources that must be taken into account for your decisions: the CPU, memory, and bandwidth.

The CPU utilization is dependent on protocols. Some of the protocols use the speed of the processor in their routing metrics, so that they can choose the best path. Other protocols use the CPU to help with convergence (which is fairly processor intensive). It's helpful to keep areas small and use route summarization when using link-state protocols. This reduces the convergence issues by keeping the number of routes that need to be recalculated to a minimum.

Routing protocols use memory to store topology information and routing tables. Summarization eases the usage of memory for the same reasons as the CPU.

Finally there is bandwidth, which, believe it or not, is dependent upon the protocol. There are three bandwidth issues that you need to take into account:

- When the routing tables are sent
- What those routing tables are sending
- Where the information is being sent

Distance routing protocols such as RIP, IGRP, SAP, and RTMP broadcast their complete routing tables on a periodic schedule. These updates will occur whether or not there have been any changes to the network. These replications happen anywhere from every 10 seconds to every three minutes (sometimes this is dependent on what you set for the variable). These advertisements use up bandwidth, and if failures occur within the network, they may take a long time to come to convergence.

Link-state protocols like OSPF and IS-IS were designed to improve on the limitations of the distance vector routing protocols like slow convergence and unnecessary usage of bandwidth. There are caveats to running these protocols, though—they require more CPU and memory usage.

Enhanced IGRP is an advanced distance vector protocol that tries to be the best of both worlds. It does not suffer from standard distance vector issues, and only updates when there is a change in the network.

Layer 2 Switching

Layer 2 switching is hardware-based bridging. In particular, the frame forwarding is handled by hardware, usually application-specific integrated circuits (ASICs). As stated earlier in this chapter, Layer 2 switches are replacing hubs at the wiring closet in campus network designs.

The performance advantage of a Layer 2 switch compared with a shared hub is dramatic. In a workgroup with 100 users in a subnet sharing a single half-duplex Ethernet segment, the average available throughput per user is 10 Mbps divided by 100, or just 100 Kbps. By replacing the hub with a full-duplex Ethernet switch, the average available throughput per user is 10 Mbps times two, or 20 Mbps. The amount of network capacity available to the switched workgroup is 200 times greater than to the shared workgroup.

The limiting factor with this setup is the workgroup server, which is a 10-Mbps bottleneck. The high performance of Layer 2 switching has led to some network designs that increase the number of hosts per subnet. Increasing the hosts leads to a flatter design with fewer subnets or logical networks in the campus. However, for all its advantages, Layer 2 switching has all the same characteristics and limitations as bridging. Broadcast domains built with Layer 2 switches still experience the same scaling and performance issues as the large bridged networks; broadcasts interrupt all the end stations. The STP issues of slow convergence and blocked links still apply.

Layer 3 Switching

Layer 3 switching is hardware-based routing. The packet forwarding is handled by hardware, usually ASICs. Depending on the protocols, interfaces, and features supported, Layer 3 switches can be used in place of routers in a campus design (for this reason, I will sometimes refer to a router as a Layer 3 switch). Layer 3 switches that support standards-based packet header rewrite and time-to-live (TTL) decrement are called packet-by-packet Layer 3 switches.

High-performance packet-by-packet Layer 3 switching is achieved in different ways. The Cisco Gigabit Switch Router (GSR) series achieves wire-speed Layer 3 switching with a method called crossbar switch matrix. The Catalyst series of multilayer switches performs Layer 3 switching with ASICs that are located in the Supervisor Engine. Regardless of the underlying technology, Cisco's packet-by-packet Layer 3 switching works like a router to external networks.

Cisco's Layer 3 switching on the Catalyst series of switches combines multiprotocol routing with hardware-based Layer 3 switching. The Route Switch Module (RSM) is an IOS-based router with the same Reduced Instruction Set Computing (RISC) processor engine as the Cisco 7500 router family. The Layer 3 switching is also done with ASICs on the NetFlow feature module. The NetFlow feature module is a daughter-card upgrade to the Supervisor Engine on a Catalyst 5000 family multilayer switch.

Layer 4 Switching

Layer 4 switching is hardware-based routing that considers the application. Cisco routers have the ability to control traffic based on Layer 4 information using extended access lists and provide accounting using NetFlow switching. In Transmission Control Protocol (TCP) or User Datagram Protocol (UDP) traffic flow, a port number in the packet header is encoded as for each application.

The Catalyst series of switches can be configured to operate as a Layer 3 or Layer 4 switch. When operating as a Layer 3 switch, the NetFlow feature module caches flows based on destination IP address. When operating as a Layer 4 switch, the card caches flows based on source address, destination address, source port, and destination port. Because the NetFlow feature card performs Layer 3 or Layer 4 switching in hardware, there is no performance difference between the two modes. Choose Layer 4 switching if you want your policy to dictate control of traffic by application, or you require accounting of traffic by application.

ATM/LANE Backbone

When designing a network that requires guaranteed Quality of Service (QoS), ATM is a good choice. With the use of real-time voice and video applications, networks work well on ATM because of features such as per-flow queuing, which provides latency controls.

The Catalyst 5000 or 6000 series multilayer switch is a good choice to implement in your network because it is equipped with a LANE card, which acts as LEC so that the distribution layer switches can communicate. The LANE card has a redundant ATM OC-3 physical interface called dual-PHY. Routers and servers with ATM interfaces can attach directly to ATM ports in the core. The server farm can be attached to Catalyst 5000 switches. The servers should either be Fast Ethernet or Fast EtherChannel, to allow for higher throughput. These Catalyst 5000 or 6000 series switches can also act as LECs that connect Ethernet-based servers to the ATM ELAN in the backbone. The PNNI protocol handles load balancing and routing between the ATM switches.

Routing becomes increasingly important as the backbone scales up to multiple switches. STP is not used in the core. Routing protocols such as OSPF and Enhanced IGRP manage path determination and load balancing between routers. Cisco has created the Simple Server Redundancy Protocol (SSRP) to provide redundancy to the LECS and the LES/BUS. Depending on the size of the campus, SSRP can take a few seconds (for a small site) to a few minutes (for a large site).

NOTE

In large site designs, dual ELANs are used to provide fast convergence in case of an LES/BUS failure. This applies only to routed protocols.

Bridged Protocol Needs

The great thing about the multilayer design is that addressing and routers are not dependent on media. The principles are the same whether the implementation occurs on FDDI, Token Ring, Ethernet, or ATM. This is not always true in the case of bridged protocols such as NetBIOS and Systems Network Architecture (SNA), which depend on the media type.

Cisco has implemented data-link switching plus (DLSw+) in their systems, an updated version of standard DLSw. This allows SNA frames from native SNA clients, which are then encapsulated in TCP/IP by a router. A second router de-encapsulates the SNA traffic. Using DLSw+ will allow you to use multiple media types; for example, you can translate the traffic out to a Token Ring-attached front-end processor (FEP) at a centralized area on the network. Multilayer switches can be attached to different media types with Versatile Interface Processor (VIP) cards and port adapters (PA).

Bridging in the Multilayer Model

When using nonrouted protocols such as NetBIOS, bridging must be configured. Bridging between VLANs on the access layer and the core layer is handled by the RSM. Remember that when using access-layer VLANs and running spanning tree, the RSM cannot be configured with a bridge group. The reason is that by allowing bridging on the RSM, it collapses all the spanning trees from the VLANs into a single spanning tree and a single root bridge.

Security to Other Remote Sites

Security in the campus can be handled in several ways. A common security measure is to use Access Control Lists (ACLs). Multilayer switching supports ACLs with little to no performance degradation. The best place to implement the ACL is at the distribution layer, because at the core and access layers, you want high-speed switching, and also all traffic must pass through the distribution layer. The great thing about ACLs is that they can be used to control networks by restricting access to the switches themselves.

You could also implement additional security by using Terminal Access Controller Access Control System Plus (TACACS+) and Remote Authentication Dial-In User Service (RADIUS), which will provide centralized access control to switches. The Cisco software itself will also provide security as it can assign multiple levels of authorization by password. This is a lot like using root level or administrator level access where people who manage the network can be assigned a password that will allow them access to certain sets of commands.

Using Layer 2 switches at the access layer and in the server farms also has security benefits. When using bridges or other shared media networking equipment, all traffic is visible to all other connected clients on the local network. This could allow a user to capture clear-text passwords or files with a sniffer program. By implementing switches, packets are normally visible only to the sender and receiver. In the server farm, all server-to-server traffic is kept off the campus core.

Security on the WAN is usually taken care of with firewalls, like a Cisco PIX (formerly Centri) Firewall. A firewall is implemented in a demilitarized zone (DMZ), where routers are attached between outside connections and the firewall. The DMZ usually houses servers that need outside access to the Internet, such as Web servers. On the inside of the DMZ, a router is connected to the Firewall and to the internal network.

Redundancy and Reliability Design

Have you ever had a network connection just drop? This is usually due to either a hardware failure or the network connection going down. Any places that users could lose their connections to the backbone—for example in the event of a power failure or if links from a wiring closet switch to the distribution-layer switch become disconnected—are known as *points of failure*.

To deal with these points of failure, there are technologies designed to circumvent these issues. The two most common features that should be incorporated into most designs are redundancy and load balancing.

NOTE

There are instances where load balancing and redundancy are not necessary. There are also instances where it is not cost effective.

Some multilayer switches are able to provide redundant connectivity to the domain. Redundant links from access-layer switches connect to the distribution-layer switches. Redundancy in the core can be achieved by installing two or more Catalyst switches in the backbone. Redundant links from the distribution layer can provide fail over and load balancing over multiple paths across the core, depending on the routing.

If you can implement the redundant links that connect access-layer switches to a pair of Catalyst multilayer switches in the distribution layer, fail over at the router (or Layer 3) can be achieved with Cisco's HSRP. The distribution-layer switches provide HSRP gateway routers for all hosts on the domain. Fast fail over at Layer 2 is achieved by using Cisco's UplinkFast feature. With UplinkFast, fail over takes about three seconds for convergence from the primary link to the backup link, as opposed to conventional STP, where convergence would take 40 to 50 seconds.

> **NOTE**
>
> Cisco IOS software supports load balancing over up to six equal-cost paths for IP, and over many paths for other protocols.

Summary

With all these factors taken into consideration, you can probably understand why this area of networking is a science all to itself (there may be some dark arts involved in there as well). With a little planning and a lot of foresight, your networks should provide stability and efficiency for you and your company.

We started the chapter by drawing the network out at a conceptual level and trying to keep things at the 30,000-foot view to encompass future growth issues. Remember that the network must start out somewhere, and this is always a good place to begin. Consider the campus model, and how it should relate to the overall picture, and remember mobile users and the home workforce if you want to correctly build your network.

The physical design and layout of the network are impacted by environment, electricity, and weight concerns; these factors will affect the growth of the network, so positioning of the equipment is a very important area of design. Because some things cannot be planned for, think big, and plan your network accordingly. The chapter outlines some best practices that should be implemented on the network.

Routing protocols and how they relate to the network are a major concern to the network design; consider your choices in the selection of the interior protocols and how they are affected by convergence. This chapter also focused on redundancy and route selection and how it allows for bandwidth dedication.

The chapter discusses address considerations and how they can affect all areas of the network and topology to create stable, efficient, secure networks. The server farm placement section covered where server farms should be placed within the network. By preplanning the placement, you allow for added security and lower bandwidth consumption. The LAN switching section discussed scaling bandwidth and other considerations that can hinder the overall growth of the network. With the proper planning and layout of equipment you can alleviate many of the issues before the network goes into production.

IP Multicast is a growing part of the new network, and must be taken into account for design considerations. You need to be aware of the impact that the use of video and other corporate meeting software will have on the network's efficiency. VLANs, ELANs, and policy in the core are other ways to improve efficiency and stability, and to allow greater security by segmenting the network traffic.

This chapter touched on the router and hub model and where you would implement it, as well the campus-wide VLAN model and how it may be best utilized. Multiprotocol over ATM was also covered, as this can be an important topic in regards to fiber-based networks.

In the WAN link considerations section, we discussed QoS and how it affects the implementation of the WAN router and bandwidth provisioning.

Planning for future growth and network scalability can be accomplished through use of different layers of multilayer switching; security in the multilayer model can be handled in various ways, including access control lists, which help with security and bandwidth concerns. Reliability and redundancy were covered throughout the chapter; the last section of the chapter discusses where and when to deploy HSRP.

FAQs

Q: What happens if I have existing equipment that was not made by Cisco and I am running EIRGP on the new Cisco gear?

A: First, is the existing equipment using any routed protocols, such as IPX or AppleTalk? If so, it has the ability to create tunnels through many non-Cisco routers that can pass these routed protocols. If the network is not using these routed protocols, you might want to implement OSPF.

Q: I want to combine my infrastructure to handle the IP phones and computers on the same ports but I need to feed these phones power. What do I do for my older phones if they do not have the built-in power supplies that the new IP phones have?

A: Make sure to look into the Cisco switching lines that allow power to be fed to the far nodes over the wire at the switched ports. The new Cisco 3524 switches supply power to phones plugged into its switches.

Q: I have built out my infrastructure and now the boss says we need to add on another floor to our current offices. The problem is that I need to keep the new floor on the same logical segment as the other floor two stories down. What do I do?

A: Luckily, you have deployed the Cisco switching family, which is capable of using Campus Wide VLAN models. Just add the new wiring closets into the existing VLANs on the lower floors. The trick to this is to watch your uplink bandwidths and make sure you do not overrun them with inter-VLAN traffic.

Chapter 9

Implementing the Cisco Routers

Solutions in this chapter:

- Initial routing considerations
- Planning your routed architecture
- Protocol consolidation and performance
- Redundancy and reliability
- Security on the routed architecture
- Quality of Service on the LAN/WAN

Introduction

By now you should have an understanding of the various areas of Windows 2000 architecture design and a basic overview of infrastructure design. We have covered the following topics in the preceding chapters:

- How the servers, Active Directory, and DEN work
- How to lay out the Cisco infrastructure environment
- How to design a Cisco switched environment

It is now time to get down to the heart of the network environment: the routing infrastructure. On any network the routers are the core piece of equipment for handling any and all communications. As a matter of fact, unless your network is going to be completely isolated from the outside world with no e-mail, Internet, or outside resources you will always have to deploy routers in some shape or form to handle the communications.

In this chapter we will be covering the topics necessary to plan out and implement the Cisco routed architecture that will operate in conjunction with the Windows 2000 operating system. We will be able to produce a complete, robust, and reliable networking architecture from the applications level all the way down to the networking level.

This chapter is a comprehensive overview of what you will need to know in order to successfully implement your infrastructure. It is always a good idea when working with the routing equipment to consult with another professional who has experience with this type of design work; have them review your designs and make sure that all areas of concern have been covered prior to purchase of the equipment.

With that said, let's dive in and see how Cisco routers are the heart of any network design and how they interoperate with Windows 2000.

Initial Routing Considerations

To start handling routing issues, you need to understand the basics as to what routers are used for on the network, where they lie in the network topology, and what the various factors are when designing the network.

Different Types of Routers and Their Uses

Not all routers are alike, and not all routers perform the same function on the network. As a matter of fact, the types of routers you purchase depend on what their function will be on the network and how they will interact with the other routers. Remember, routers are used to control *all* traffic on the network so the proper analysis and planning is needed prior to designing your network.

Border Routers: Defining the Geographic Areas

The first thing to look at when designing a Cisco routing architecture is to review the overall topology of the business and see where routers are going to be needed in the design. A basic rule to follow: Look for points of access to autonomous areas of the network; in other words, look where two or more areas of your business are physically separated from each other for any reason—different buildings, different cities, or even different countries. These access points are easy identification points for the placement of *border* routers. Border routers are designed to handle communications between autonomous networks. Autonomous networks are systems that are not attached to each other.

Examples of border routers are Internet access routers, company-to-company communications routers, or *core* routers that handle the communications for extremely large companies. In Figure 9.1, we see a set of border routers that not only handle communications to the outside world for the company, but also join different geographic factions of the company together. The core router is a high-powered 7500 that can handle the high throughput and firepower needed to centrally control the WAN. The remote core router can be a little less robust, such as the 7200 or 3600 series.

Distribution Routers: Controlling the Flow of Traffic

The next type of router to be placed is internal to the company and helps define the integrated topology of the infrastructure. It controls how communications are handled to different parts of the internal network. One of the areas that switches cannot control completely is network congestion and traffic flow. Switches are designed to handle data transmissions within defined segments of the network. What switches do *not* do is define how to get from one segment of the network to the other and how to control traffic flow within the network. This is where the distribution router comes into play.

Think of it in terms of traffic in a city—the switches are the streets that the cars use to get from one part of the city to the other. What do you think would happen if there were no street name signs, traffic lights, one-way or yield signs? There would be utter chaos and gridlock in the city—all traffic would stop and the network of streets would come to a grinding

Figure 9.1 Border or core router placement.

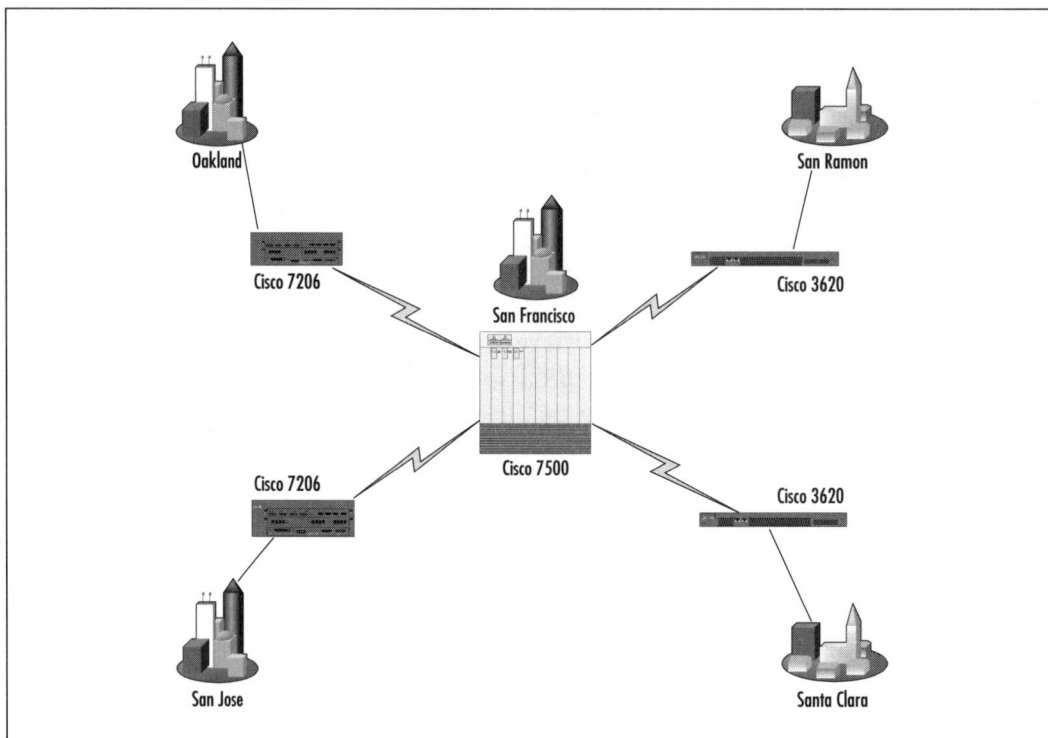

halt! Luckily those signs and traffic controls do exist to control the flow of traffic. That is exactly what routers are for—they handle the flow of traffic, give direction to packets on the network so that they have directions to find their destination, and make sure that traffic does not go the wrong way down a one-way street and arrive in a prohibited area. These types of routers are called *distribution* routers; Figure 9.2 shows an example of their deployment.

Access Routers: Controlling the Flow of Data on the Main Network

The last type of router that we need to place on the network will be the *access* router. These routers control access to the main pathways of a network and keep any traffic not destined for other areas in the network segment in which they originated. In the case of a packet needing to get to another area of the network, the access router will allow the packets

Figure 9.2 Deployment of distribution routers.

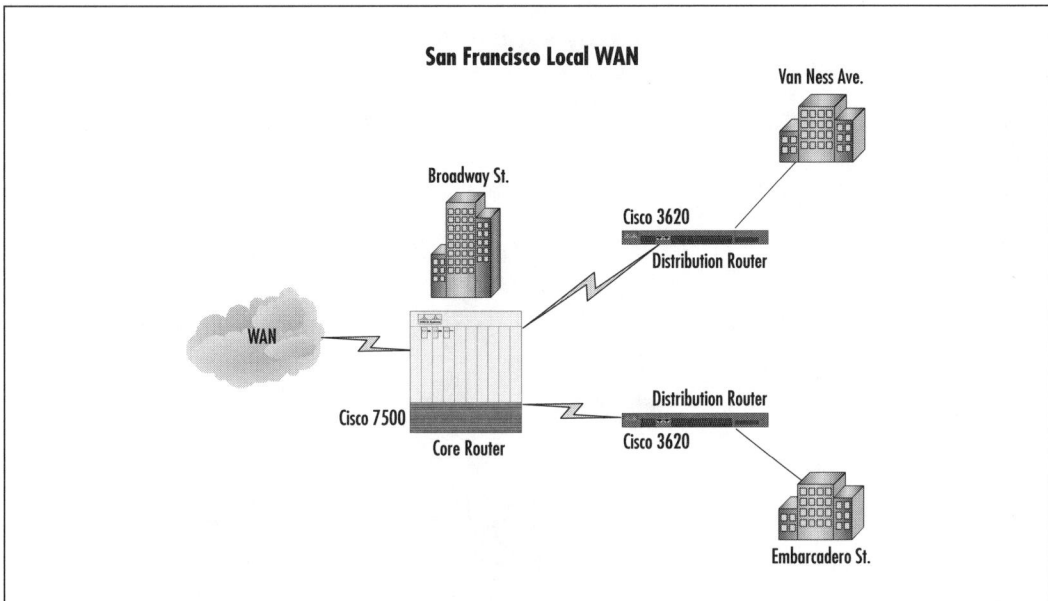

San Francisco Local WAN

Van Ness Ave.

Broadway St.

Cisco 3620
Distribution Router

WAN

Distribution Router

Cisco 7500
Core Router

Cisco 3620

Embarcadero St.

through based on criteria presented at the access port. An example of this, using our city traffic analogy, would be to look at the traffic at the local city airport.

The airport allows all kinds of traffic to go into and out of its network of roads and access points. Along with all kinds of regular passenger traffic there are also buses that go to and from the car rental areas, shuttles to other terminals, and security and other emergency vehicles. The regular passenger car traffic needs to be allowed in and out of the airport area, but all other types of traffic (especially the airplanes!) need to stay in the airport's own traffic system and never be allowed to leave that confined area. There are access points at the entrances to the airport to enforce these traffic rules. These access points allow particular traffic in and out of the main city traffic network—the passenger cars only. Access routers are akin to the same function of these access points—they allow only the appropriate traffic onto the main network of communications and keep all other types of traffic in their proper areas. Figure 9.3 shows an example of the deployment of access routers.

Figure 9.3 Placement of access routers.

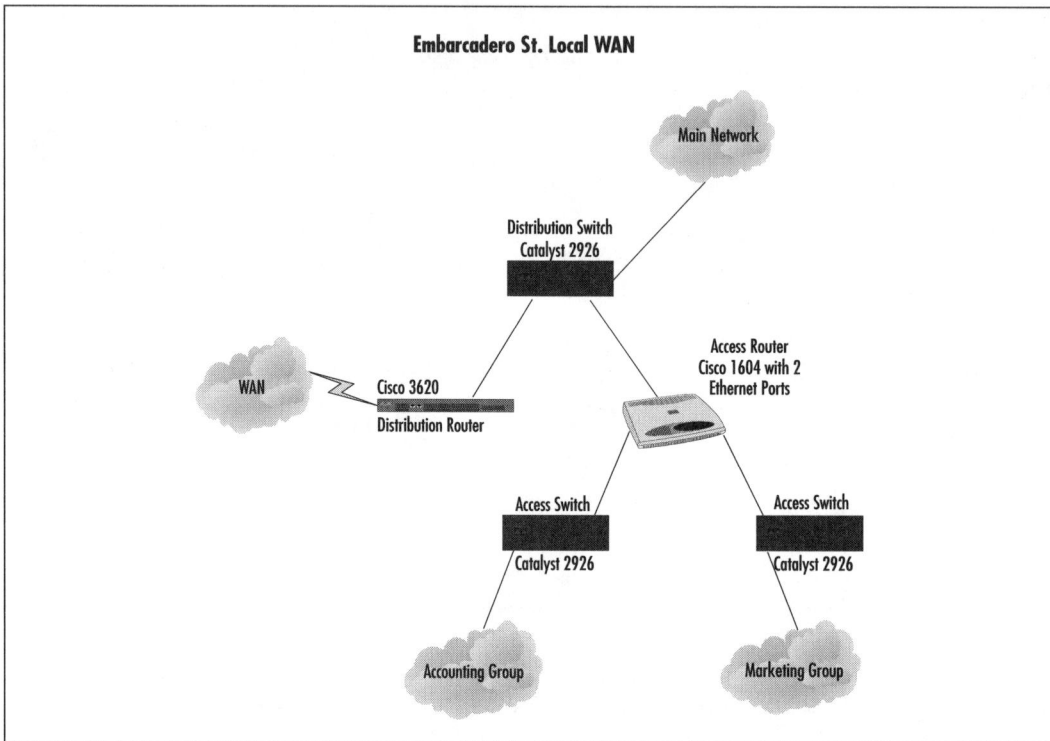

Segmentation and Why It Is Required

We have mentioned segmentation of the network already, but we need to make sure that concept of segmentation is correctly understood. Networks need to be designed with one main driving purpose in mind—to control the flow of traffic and manage the available bandwidth. Data traffic will attempt to use any and all available bandwidth to complete its transmissions. At the application layer of the network, the data has no idea how to get from one area of the network to the other unless it is given direction on how to do so. Segmentation is the method to isolate unwanted traffic from areas of the network that do not require its transmission.

Broadcast Storms

One of the most common side effects of poor traffic management is called the *broadcast storm*. Broadcasts are packets sent out by network nodes to the rest of the network if the originating network node does not have any information on how to direct its transmissions—it simply sends the information to everyone. Now, imagine not just one node doing this, but hundreds, and they are all doing it at Fast Ethernet speeds! To make the problem worse, the broadcast traffic will continue to increase in conjunction with the number of network nodes on the same wire. In other words, the more computers, the more broadcasts. When the broadcast traffic on a network becomes too much for the bandwidth to handle and thus causes normal traffic to begin to suffer, this is called a *broadcast storm*.

One of the main functions of routers is to stop the propagation of broadcast traffic; they simply will not forward any packets without a specific destination and thus will not forward broadcasts. In this way, they help keep the broadcasting of packets to the segmented area in which they originated, thus saving the rest of the network from broadcast storms.

Now for the obvious question: why use broadcasting as a communication method if it is that much of a problem? TCP/IP, and thus Windows 2000, needs to utilize the broadcast method for several of its functions: Address Resolution Protocol (ARP), Dynamic Host Control Protocol (DHCP), Reverse Address Resolution Protocol (RARP), and several others. It is a necessary evil in the networking world to deal with broadcasts. One of the main components to network design is to determine broadcast domains and figure out which nodes need to be in the same domains to communicate efficiently with each other over broadcasts.

When designing your company's network, keep the following issues in mind when designing your broadcast areas:

- Different departments and how they communicate
- Server farms and how they communicate (remember backup issues!)
- Remote offices and whether they need access to corporate resources

Figure 9.4 gives an example of how to define broadcast domains.

Notice that we define each department as a broadcast domain. Also notice that these domains lie within other larger broadcast areas that we define on geographic parameters—they may be in a different building or city. It does not make sense to have broadcast domains traversing geographically separated areas because you do not want storms propagating over your slow serial links, so make sure to keep that in mind when you are deciding who gets to sit where in your buildings. (Sure, the VP of Finance would like to have a thirtieth-story corner office, but if his servers and staff are in the two-story building across the street he will *not* have easy access to them on the network. Sometimes politics and status must suffer for good network design. Good luck in the next executive meeting trying to explain that one!)

Figure 9.4 Broadcast domains defined.

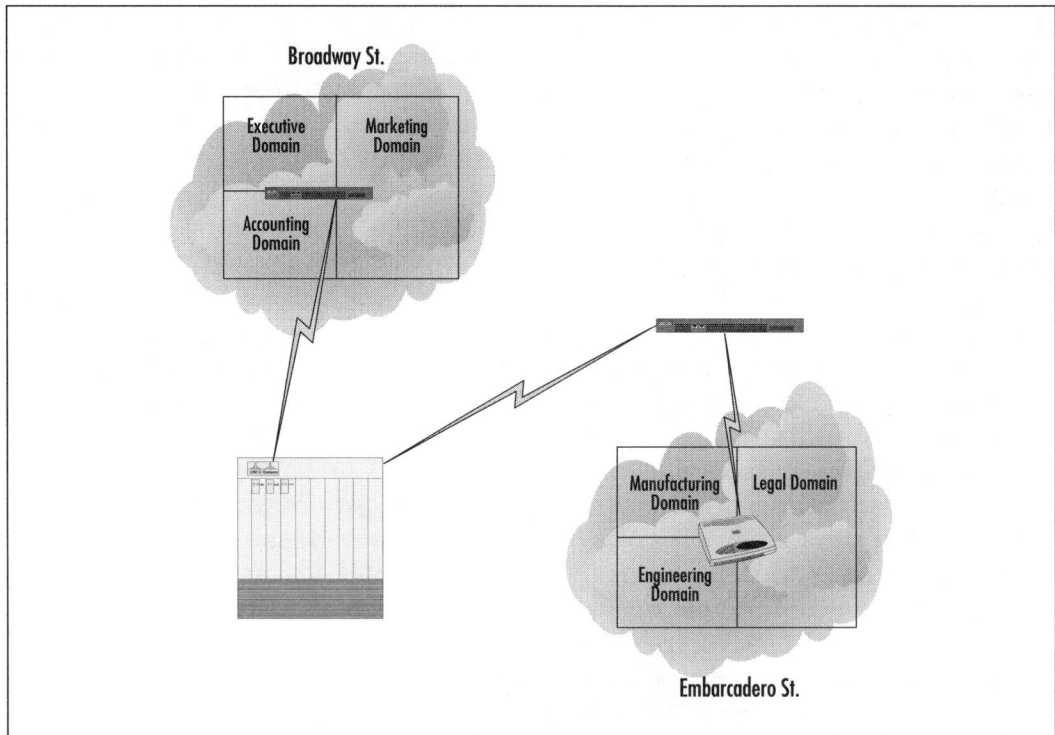

Protocol Traffic

The next task is to determine what protocols are going to be used to communicate on the network. Along with the vital TCP/IP protocol suite, there may be legacy protocols that need to be handled and routed on the network. It is often the case that any of the following protocols can easily be found on the network that will be upgraded to Windows 2000:

- IPX/SPX, from old Novell systems still in use

- SNA/APPN, from IBM mainframe environments

- AppleTalk, from Macintosh machines

- NetBEUI, from old Windows and some UNIX systems

These protocols are not uncommon in today's architectures and need to be considered if they exist in the environment. The first thing that needs to be determined is the reason why they are active—what application is requiring their use? Can it be upgraded or modified to use TCP/IP? The best course of action is always to try to consolidate the number of protocols on the wire. Each protocol present will take up a certain amount of the available bandwidth, and by reducing the number of protocols we conserve that bandwidth. Try to find ways to use TCP/IP applications only in the network, and if this is not possible, limit the number of systems accessing the other protocols.

If there are legacy applications that simply must use one of these protocols then we will have to incorporate the protocol into the routed architecture. If that is the case, make sure to analyze the broadcast domains while looking at each protocol separately. If one broadcast domain uses multiple protocols, then separate routing tables will need to be kept by the access router for the broadcast and routed to other areas. Some protocols, like NetBEUI, are not routable at all and *need* to broadcast everything they do. Protocols like NetBEUI should be utilized as little as possible, but in the extreme case where they are required we use a method called *bridging*. Bridging is *not* recommended because it will propagate broadcast traffic! For that reason, broadcast specific protocols like NetBEUI should be avoided.

Figure 9.5 shows how multiple protocol broadcast domains can exist on the same network segment.

Figure 9.5 Multiple protocol broadcast domains.

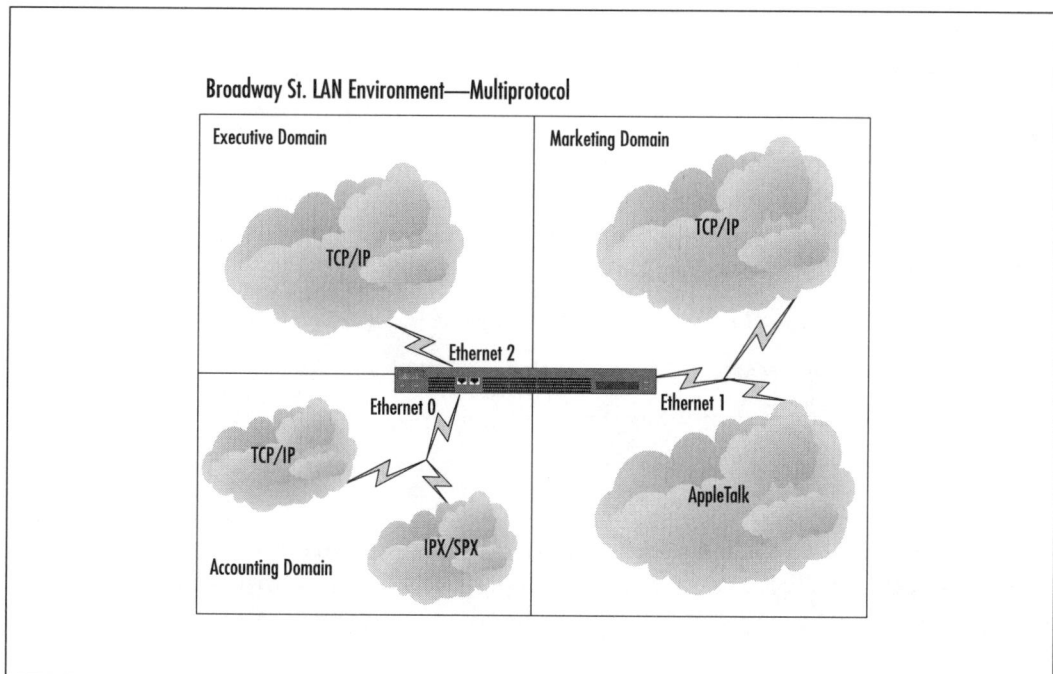

In this case, we need to apply instructions to the routers to handle *all* of the protocols; otherwise any protocol traffic not handled will be dropped at the router port. Here is an example of Router A's configurations so that both IPX and TCP/IP can be routed out of the network segment:

```
ip forward-protocol UDP
appletalk routing eigrp 25000
appletalk route-redistribution
ipx routing 0000.0b1c.2c3e

   !

   interface Ethernet 0
   description Accounting
   ip address 192.9.200.1 255.255.255.0
   ipx network B
   ipx type-20-propagation
     !

   interface Ethernet 1
   description Marketing
   ip address 192.9.201.1 255.255.255.0
   ip helper-address 192.9.200.10
   appletalk cable-range 3001-3010
   appletalk zone Manufacturing
     !
   interface Ethernet 2
   description Executive
   ip address 192.9.202.1 255.255.255.0

     !
```

As you can see, each Ethernet port has configurations to handle whatever protocols lie in its domain of control. The router maintains separate routing tables for all protocols that it needs to handle.

Networking Protocols and "Hidden" Traffic

The last logical protocol issue we need to look at before we start planning out the actual physical architecture is the issue of the "hidden" (otherwise known as *networking*) protocols. These special protocols are not the ones with which the average LAN administrator will concern him- or herself. They handle all of the router-to-router, router-to-switch, and switch-to-switch communications. Without these underlying protocols, there would be no way for the network to attain *convergence*.

Convergence: The Goal of Any Good Router

Convergence is the process of all of the routers in a network synchronizing with each other, to learn each other's routes, and get together to optimize the traffic on the network. It is the primary goal of any router when it comes online to converge with the rest of the network and then work with the other routers to propagate the best routes and optimize network performance.

   The more complicated the network, the more time it will take the network to converge and come to what is referred to as a *steady state*. To improve convergence times both when the network turns up and when changes are made to the network (either intentional or accidental) the routers will use one of two methods: *static routes* or *dynamic routing.*

Static Routes versus Dynamic Routing Protocols

Static routes are routes that are defined manually on the router by the network administrator and will not be changed without a manual change to the router configurations. These routes override dynamic routing controls and will not change no matter what happens on the network. Static routes are therefore unwieldy in the case of a rapidly changing or dynamic network. Although static routing allows for the most control over a router's routing tables and the most control over traffic flow for the network administrator, it also brings with it the most administrative overhead and the least amount of flexibility. Static routes should be used only in small networks that will not be changing over a long period of time. In the case of a network that has expansion, redundancy, and most importantly, a large amount of routed segments and locations, dynamic routing protocols are needed to handle convergence on a much larger, faster, and cleaner level.

   There are several types of dynamic routing protocols available on Cisco routers:

Routing Information Protocol (RIP) and RIP2 RIP and RIP2 are the most basic of dynamic protocols and take the least amount of administration and planning overhead. They are actually implemented by default on

Cisco routers running TCP/IP if no other networking protocol is specified. The problem with RIP and RIP2 is the overhead they cause on the network bandwidth. The way they operate is to send out a route update to all listeners (other routers running RIP) every 30 seconds whether there are changes or not. This causes a large amount of unneeded traffic on the wire and can have adverse effects on the performance of the network. It especially can cause problems for "slow" WAN links where bandwidth is at a premium.

Open Shortest Path First (OSPF) Commonly accepted by the router vendor community as the industry standard, OSPF is designed to have all routers in the *OSPF area* to update a *Designated Router* (DR), which is a central router controlling the area. All of the routing information that each router contains is sent to the DR, thus allowing the DR to compile the information and hand out an optimized routing table for everyone's use. The routing tables are recalculated and an update is sent only when a change in the network occurs, thus conserving bandwidth from unnecessary updates.

Interior Gateway Routing Protocol (IGRP) A Cisco proprietary networking protocol, IGRP is designed to take a combination of the qualities of both RIP and OSPF and combine them into a more streamlined process. In reality, IGRP is no longer commonly used, being replaced by its successor, EIGRP.

Enhanced Interior Routing Protocol (EIGRP) Also Cisco proprietary, EIGRP brings out the most robust options among the networking protocol options. If you have a completely Cisco-enabled infrastructure, then the best option is to enable and configure EIGRP to handle your network convergence and stability (if you do not have a complete Cisco network, then OSPF will be the most advanced networking protocol at your disposal). It also has the ability to *redistribute* other protocol information (such as RIP, OSPF, AppleTalk, or IPX) by encapsulating the information within EIGRP packets, thus allowing multiprotocol networks to have a way to cross-communicate over WAN links while conserving bandwidth and processor power. Consequentially, EIGRP is capable of controlling all routing updates, even updates provided by other protocols.

When planning out your network and bandwidth needs, your networking protocols need to be considered and planned out to ensure the proper programming and allocation of resources to handle them. In the instance of using BGP, for example, the routing tables can be potentially *huge* depending on the routes seeded to your Internet service provider's (ISP's) BGP routers. Therefore, Cisco recommends at least a 3640 router to handle the memory and processing power in order to handle a full BGP border router's needs. If you are unsure as to which router line will suit your needs, be sure to ask an experienced Cisco consultant which router will be right for the application in question. Not allocating the right routing equipment is an easy to way to cripple a network!

Planning Your Routed Architecture

Now that we have a basic understanding of the functions and protocols of the routing environment, we need to figure out where, why, and how the routers on your LAN and WAN are going to be needed and how to deploy them. To start, we will briefly discuss the differences between WAN and LAN routing, and then we will dive into some detail on how to define the router implementation methodologies.

There are going to be two different routing functions on your network: first, internal routing devices to separate internal subnets and departments, server farms, and/or resources; and second, external link routing devices that connect two physical geographic facilities over "slow" WAN links using methods like Frame Relay, Point-to-Point, or High-Level Data Link Control (HDLC). We will cover the WAN first since it usually affects the design and rollout of the internal routing architecture and address schemes. It is also the harder of the two to handle, because of the issues of bandwidth control and data translation, from LAN transport methods like Ethernet and Token Ring to WAN traffic mode using serial link technologies like Frame Relay and Point-to-Point.

Identifying Your Access Points

The first, and best, step in planning your routed architecture is to examine your physical facilities and see how many WAN access points you will need to interconnect your network. This is really pretty easy—just keep in mind that for every facility link, you need a router on each side of the link to translate the traffic from Ethernet to Serial and then from Serial back to Ethernet. By drawing out a simple map, you can quickly and easily determine the number and placement of routed links for your WAN. Refer to Figure 9.6 as an example.

In Figure 9.6 we have four cities that will house the company's personnel and offices. By analyzing the situation we can then apply a "first pass" at the routed WAN architecture, as seen in Figure 9.7. We place routers at each endpoint at each serial link to handle the slow serial connections.

Figure 9.6 Facilities layout—prerouting design.

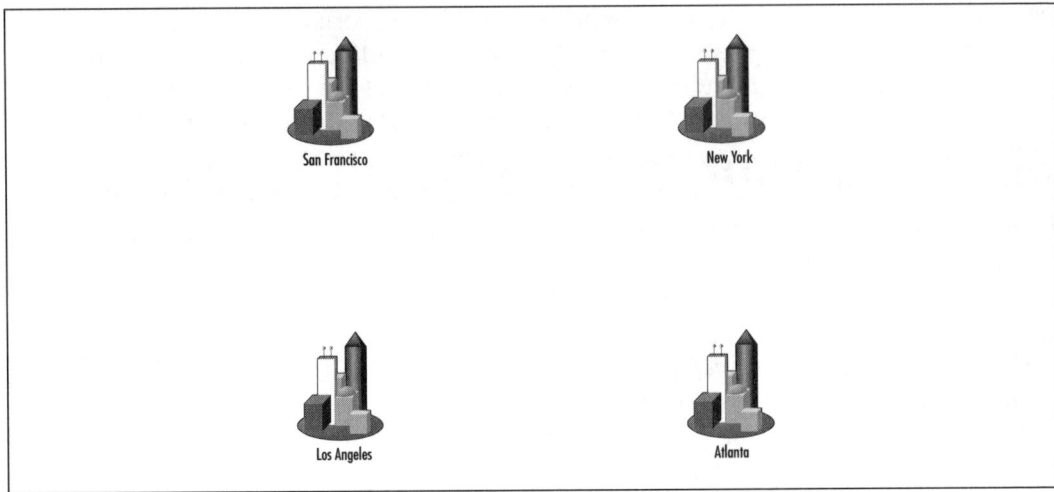

Figure 9.7 First pass—router placement.

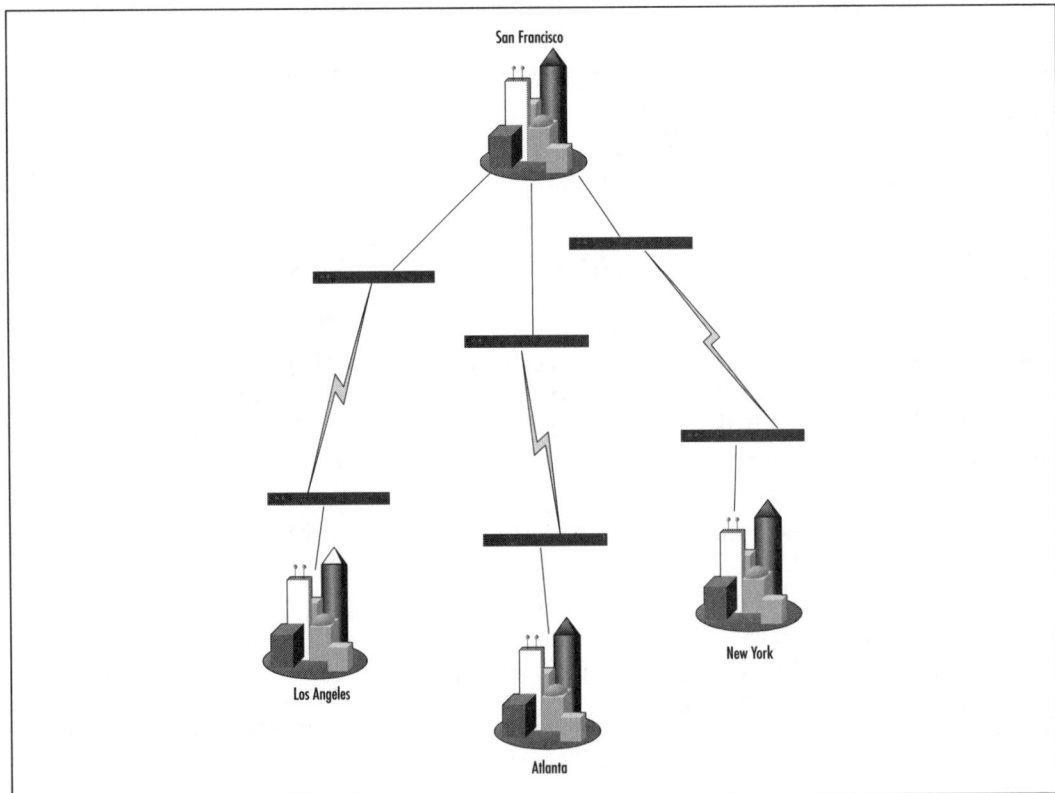

The next step is to consolidate the number of routers needed to truly complete the design. Most Cisco routers, from the 2600 line on up, come in a chassis design so that you can mix and match routing ports and access hardware like Ethernet ports and serial ports. So in the case of Figure 9.7, we can replace the three small routers at the main site with one large chassis router with multiple serial ports, thus consolidating equipment costs. This also reduces the overall "cost of ownership" by reducing the number of manageable routing devices. The consolidated design is displayed in Figure 9.8.

Figure 9.8 Consolidated routing design.

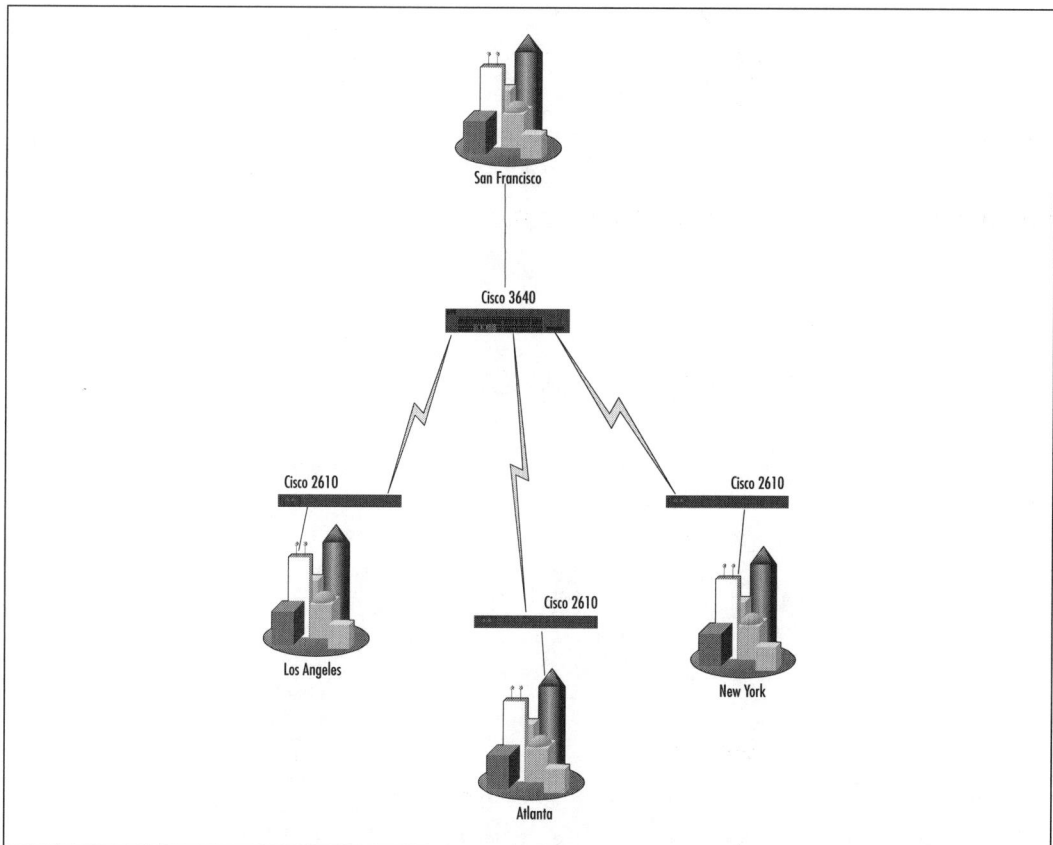

Adding the Internet Securely

Now that you have the company's WAN routed architecture in order as far as the facility-to-facility connectivity, you need to take one last step, and add access to the Internet. The easy answer would be just to link the Internet into the core router in San Francisco and just let everyone have access to it via a serial port on the 3640, right? Well, any good network administrator knows that this is just asking for trouble from a security standpoint; there needs to be an Internet firewall in place to secure the link to the outside world.

The problem then arises that in order to connect to your ISP you need a router, because that link will always be a serial link for the connection. The firewall can be accessed only via an Ethernet port. Figure 9.9 displays the problem in detail.

To alleviate this problem of firewall placement and ISP connectivity, use the basic design illustrated in Figure 9.10.

Figure 9.9 Firewall placement problem.

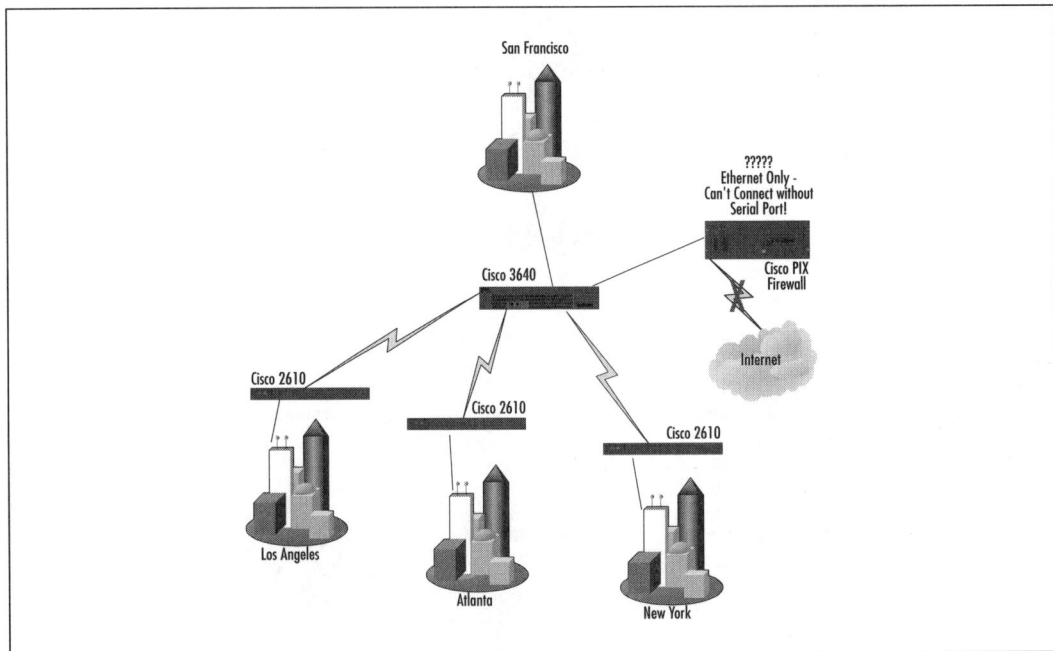

We have added another small router into the design on the outside of the firewall. The sole purpose of this router is to handle ISP serial connectivity. *No internal routing will be advertised to the Internet. Only static routes are used on this router.* The reason for this is that if an intruder tries to hack attack your business, the only access they will have will be to this external router—the rest of the routing architecture is safe from attack due to the firewall beyond. If the external router goes down, so be it, since at least the main LAN and WAN will still be safe and uncompromised.

Figure 9.10 ISP connectivity design.

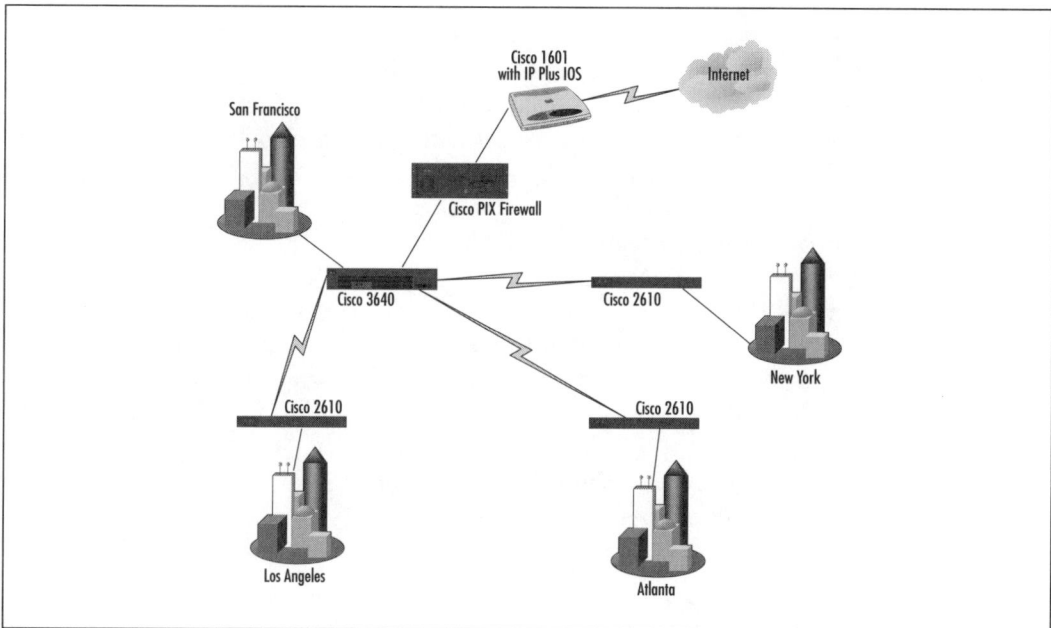

Continued

Autonomous System (AS) numbers. Each ISP has an AS number, and the company is assigned as well. All three autonomous systems are synchronized via BGP protocol so that load-balanced transmissions can occur between all three autonomous systems.

Note that the router used in this design is a 3640 instead of the 1601 used in the previous design. The 3640 is utilized so that a full BGP table can be held and processed by the router. The 1600 series would simply be overpowered by the implementation of BGP.

By its very nature, BGP will affect the routing of other people's companies and networks, so you should make sure to get the assistance of your ISP to help set up and control the BGP protocol. The concepts and configuring of BGP can be *very* complex; Cisco offers a week-long course solely on the topic of BGP deployment.

Figure 9.11 Internet router using BGP for load-balancing.

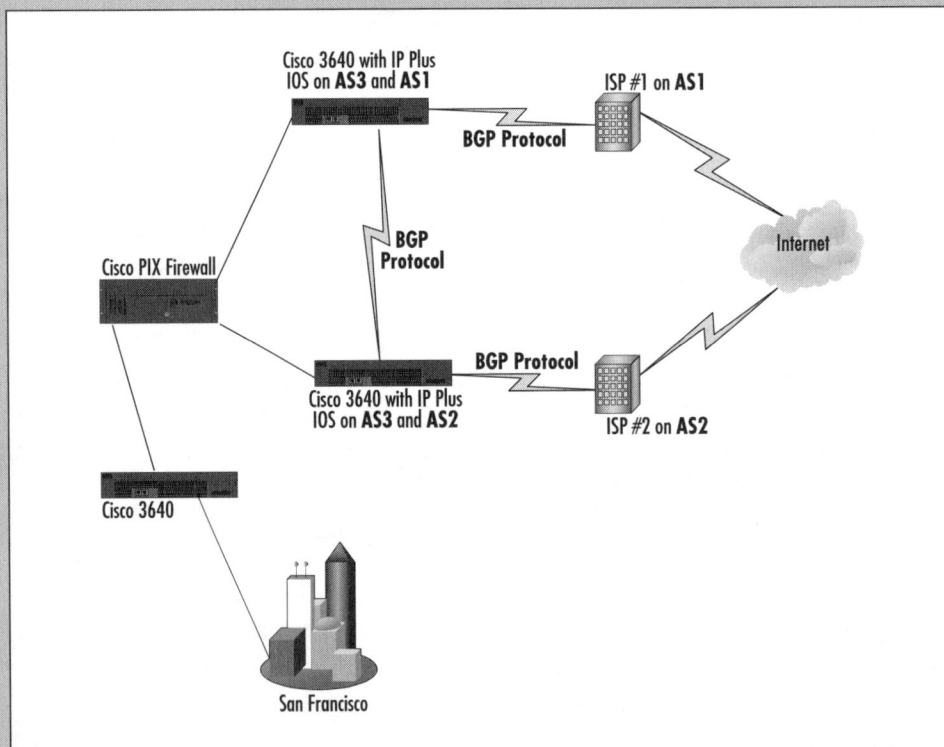

What Kind of Traffic Will Be Going across the WAN Link?

Now that we have determined where the WAN links are, we need to determine what kind of WAN links are needed to handle the traffic between the sites. The best way to start this process is to look at the types of traffic that will be traversing the links and then use the best transport method to handle that traffic. There are several factors that need to be taken into consideration:

Type of traffic Data, voice, video, and/or multimedia packets.

Types of protocols Are they chatty, reliable (like TCP), unreliable (like UDP), or time sensitive (TCP/IP will timeout if it does not get an acknowledgement packet)? Perhaps they are broadcast intensive (for instance, IPX has Service Advertising Packets (SAP) that will broadcast and eat up serial link bandwidth if not controlled). These issues need to be determined to control the routing of the protocols.

Types of services Applications and servers that need to be accessed between users and resources in other buildings and segments on the network.

Price and Redundancy Some transport types are much more expensive than others. For instance, Frame Relay usually costs less than a PPP link because PPP is dedicated bandwidth that is guaranteed all of the time. Frame Relay can have what is called a Committed Information Rate (CIR) that is less than the overall bandwidth. The CIR is a guaranteed level of service from the provider who will in turn give you the full bandwidth of the link if they have it available at any given time. By giving the provider the ability to "burst" at less busy times means added incentive for them to reduce the cost of the circuits. You must decide if you really need to spend the money on dedicated bandwidth or save some overall costs by reducing your full-time bandwidth needs.

Amount of Bandwidth Required You should do some analysis to determine the bandwidth needs of the company between sites. If you have the financial resources, it is always better to be proactive in bandwidth allocation, but if budgetary issues are a constraint on your designs, then you will need to control how much bandwidth you are willing to have between sites. You can use varied types of circuits between sites ranging from slow Frame Relay links with a CIR of 128Kbps guaranteed up to full DS3 multiple T1 links with a range of up to 45 Mbps. The cost can get exorbitant as the bit rates go up past T1 speeds, so try to be conservative in your estimates.

> **NOTE**
>
> When determining the bandwidth necessary for your design, always remember to account for the minimum bandwidth required for Windows 2000 to operate, and then adjust up from there.

Determining the Transport Method

We now have the various parameters identified for your routing design, so let's take a look at the different methods of serial communications. Given the benefits or caveats described next, determine the most appropriate methodology to use for your network.

Frame Relay Frame Relay is used when there are multiple sites over the WAN that are linked into a central site. Some of the benefits to using Frame Relay are that several sites can be linked in on the same main circuit using logical mappings known as permanent virtual circuits (PVCs). The ability to use lower guaranteed bandwidths to save on costs as described in the previous section is also a plus. The downfall is that the circuit can be run through several different access switches at the provider end and there is not a lot of control over how the bandwidth is controlled or how much will be available beyond the CIR for the user community. Still, Frame Relay is by far the most widely used serial communication method today.

ATM Asynchronous Transfer Mode is a high-speed broadband method of transport normally handled over fiber optic networks. Due to the fact that ATM uses what is called *cell* technology, it can attain speeds and bandwidth much higher than traditional packet-based technology. Cell technology employs the ability to have packets routed by hardware called Application Specific Integrated Circuits, or ASICs, which is a vast improvement over routing being handled by a processor dependent on software. The downfall to ATM is that it requires fiber (copper is also available, but is not widely used and not nearly as reliable), and a dedicated backbone of ATM specific equipment. In today's market, Gigabit Ethernet has mostly made ATM an exorbitant cost to implement given the prioritized equipment needed to run it.

HDLC HDLC is the standard method of serial communications and is the default setting for all Cisco serial ports. It has no overlay technology and simply gives a pure serial connection between two ports. There are no special abilities as in the case of Frame Relay and Point-to-Point. You will simply get two serial ports to transport to each other over HDLC—nothing more, and nothing less.

Wireless Wireless technologies are available for interconnection of buildings, but they are usable only with "line of sight" capability. In other words, there can be no obstructions, such as other buildings, in the way of the wireless connection. This makes wireless a less viable solution than others as far as versatility goes, but if it is possible to use it you will get a significant cost savings.

Point-to-Point (PPP) PPP technology is the most expensive of all because it allows for dedicated bandwidth and secure connections between sites over serial links. The technology uses an overlay that applies timing, sequencing, and security along with a predefined path of transmission, thus increasing secure and fast performance on the circuit. There is no sharing of bandwidth with other virtual circuits, so the circuit goes only from "one point to another" with no other arbitrary rerouting by the provider. This causes an overhead to the provider, hence the extra costs involved to the user.

Deciding which technology to use is simply a function of necessity (how much bandwidth), reliability (provider- vs user-controlled bandwidth), and of course, budget. It is most attractive to have all PPP circuits, but the cost of extra serial ports and circuits would be exorbitant for most businesses. The most common WAN serial connection is Frame Relay, due to the versatility and the cost savings on bandwidth and equipment to control it.

Placement of Routers in the Network

The final factor that needs to be determined is which type of router needs to be deployed at various access points on the network. Depending on the processor speeds, memory, and capabilities needed at each access point, you will use different levels of routing equipment.

High-end Chassis Routers

In general, when you need firepower and processing in addition to versatility and flexibility, you should look at chassis-based routers such as the 3600, 7200 or 7500 line. The 3600 lines of routers are the most common, since they give a wide range of capabilities and have plenty of firepower in the processor and memory department for the price.

The 7200 line is the midrange router of the higher end router lines. It can handle transmission connections like DS3 and above, which would be getting a bit beyond the 3600's capabilities.

For the most firepower, you should consider the 7500 router series. This is the "tough guy" of the Cisco routers and should be used only if it is in a core position of a company that has a *ton* of data flowing per second and the company needs a superpowered router. The 7500s need special power and environmental concerns addressed due to the different power supplies and the heat they produce, so be sure to look at the current specification sheets from Cisco to make sure that your server room can handle the load of power and environmental control.

Low-end Chassis Routers

To handle routing while conserving costs, space, and power in the server room, you can utilize the low-end router lines such as the 2600, 1700, and 1600 series. These routers have fewer slots to handle expansion modules and are not as versatile as the others listed earlier, but still handle a decent amount of transmission firepower. If you have a limited routing need (such as for a small remote office or home user), then these routers are well designed for your purposes. They are also very versatile as access routers. The 2600 and 1700 lines are even able to handle some Voice-over IP (VoIP) with the proper add-ins and Internetworking Operating System (IOS) upgrades—just be careful not to overload the processor capabilities of these smaller units.

For example, if you know you want to use an Internet router for serial transmission access to a firewall (as described in previous sections), your first choice would be either a 2600 or 1600 router. On the other hand, if you are planning on using BGP on the router, you will need to use at least a 3600 to handle the memory and processing power to accommodate the BGP functions. Always be sure not to underestimate the needs of your network; there are no second chances with your boss once the network fails due to poor design!

Determining How Much Processor and Memory Is Required on the Router

It is always tempting to say, "Well, why worry about it, just max out the memory and let's get on to bigger and better problems." However, router memory is often just as expensive as the router chassis and the cost can be huge! Memory upgrades are probably the most difficult decision to make in buying your company's routers. The best place to start when trying to determine how much flash memory to order for your equipment is with your Cisco consultant; figure out how much memory is needed for the IOS you need to run your network and buy the appropriate amount of flash memory to hold your IOS and configurations. The amount of DRAM, or dynamic random access memory, to use will depend on the amount of data the router will need to process per second. This can be a hard number to come up with and sometimes may require a network protocol analysis to get true numbers. The best method for figuring out the amount of memory can be determined by "guesstimation" of the memory usage based on the amount of application traffic beyond the norm that would be seen on your network over a standard business day. The standard memory that comes with the router can handle most basic network functions like file, print, and Internet. If you are going to use anything beyond the norm (like video, voice, and/or special highly routed applications like databasing or graphics design), buy the upgrade to DRAM so that you can be sure that the router can handle the load.

The amount of processor power that is required for the applications and protocols that you will be running is a hard one to call on your own. The decision on processor power is a subjective guess at best, but there are certain situations and utilities that require no less than a certain level of processor power. The best suggestion is to contact Cisco Technical Assistance Center (TAC) or your Cisco consultant to determine the proper amount of processor for your routed architecture.

Layer 3 Switching: RSM and MSFC Cards

We have been discussing external connectivity points for routing and have so far stayed away from company internal routing between internal subnets and address spaces. The reason for this is because so far we have been discussing routers as if they were separate devices from the switch architecture of the internal network. The fact is that you should design your internal LAN and architecture by utilizing the technology known as virtual local area networks (VLANs).

Using VLANs, you can make switches define and use broadcast domains and network segments based on logical configurations inside the switch. In effect, this makes the switch act as if it has separate routed segments on it! The trick is that you need to use Layer 3 switching devices in the switches to route between the VLANs that you have created. This is the same as using an external router for routing between the VLANs, but by using the Layer 3 switching devices on board the switches, routing can happen at wire speeds on the LAN.

The concept of VLANs can get very complex; in this chapter we will cover the devices that enable the switches to perform routing internally—the RSM and MFSC cards—and Chapter 10 presents more in-depth information on VLANs and Layer 3 switching.

The Route Switch Module (RSM) is designed to plug into the 5500 series switch. It enables the switch to handle on-board routing between VLANs at switching speeds. The Multi-Function Switch Card (MFSC) does the same job on the 6500 series switches. Essentially, both cards are the same as having a 7500 router on a blade in the switch. The only difference is that 7500 routers have physical interfaces for their network segments and the RSM and MFSC cards have virtual segments that align with the VLANs programmed on the switch. See Chapter 10 for more detail on the Layer 3 switching capabilities of Cisco products.

The point we want to make here is to use these switches and cards in strategic places on the LAN—central points that all other switches are uplinked into and also where the main core of actual routers are, thus allowing the best mode of convergence on the network between the routing and switching environments. Figure 9.12 shows how the Layer 3 devices can be placed on a switched LAN with routers to be used as distribution routing devices that operate at wire speed.

Figure 9.12 Placement of RSM or MFSC cards.

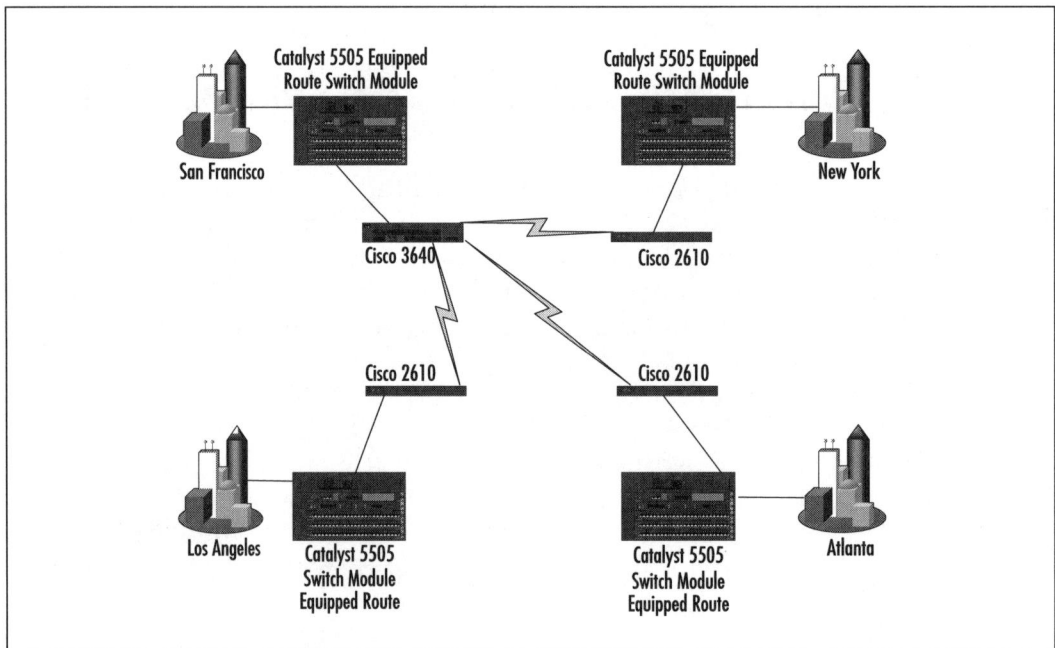

Protocol Consolidation and Performance

One of the jobs of routers is to handle the address routing and traffic management of the network. The way they do this is to control the traffic through the management of protocols that identify the placement of network resources. The more protocols that are running on the network, the more work the routers have to do to control the network. Therefore, it is always best to consolidate the number of protocols that are running to improve performance and efficiency.

Reducing the Number of Protocols on the Network

Now that we have all of the hardware for routing and networking devices that handle protocol management placed in the network, the physical part of our design is over. We now need to focus on the logical design of the network. The first places to look are at the applications running on the network and see what protocols are necessary to make the network operate efficiently and cleanly.

The general rule to follow is: the fewer protocol stacks to manage, the less routing tables and protocol translation the routing architecture has to do, and the more performance you will get out of the processor of the router. Think of it in terms of using your own computer on your desk. The fewer programs running, the faster the computer can operate. The more programs you turn on simultaneously, the slower the computer gets until it may even freeze up and stop processing altogether. Routers have essentially the same parameters to work with—the more you make them do, the less speed and processing you'll get out of them. The problem here is that if a computer slows down, you are only affecting the computer itself. If a router slows down, it potentially affects the *entire* network!

Reducing the number of protocols on the wire will conversely increase the performance of the routers, so the idea is to use as few protocols as possible in your overall network design. It is also best to stay away from "chatty" protocols as much as possible because they give the network more work to do.

For instance, NetBEUI is an extremely easy protocol to use since, by just turning it on, it basically does all of the work for you with little-to-no configuration on your part. On the other hand, the reason for that is because it runs by using broadcasting *constantly*. This is a tremendous overhead on the routers and switches, overhead that more robust protocols like TCP/IP don't have.

Most networks today can run solely on TCP/IP since almost all programs and operating systems use it today. The only time you should have multiple LAN protocols in a new infrastructure design is if there are legacy systems like old Novell and/or Macintosh systems on the line that use IPX/SPX or AppleTalk. (We don't even want to get into other protocols like SNA or VINES here. Cisco routers can handle all of them but if you encounter them, the best thing to do is find a way to get rid of them! The management overhead and problems on the user community of maintaining such protocols can be a massive strain on your IT staff.) Understand, Cisco routers can handle these and many other types of protocols on the system at the same time, but each added protocol adds more processing power and takes up more resources. The more processing power taken up, the slower the network will run, so be cautious and frugal on your use of protocols beyond TCP/IP if possible.

Network Addressing and Segmentation

Everyone will tell you that segmenting the network decreases broadcasting and improves efficiency to the network. This is true—to a point. The more segments you create, the more network addressing management you need to do. The more network addressing management that needs to be done, the harder the network routers need to work to keep the network converged and running. Also, the more routing that occurs, the longer it takes for all of the routers to converge and bring the network back up to peak performance when changes in the topology occur.

Segmentation design is the art of knowing which resources and nodes need high-speed access to each other, and which can handle some delay in reaching other areas of the network.

Segmentation design should be based on the following criteria:

The amount of addressable network nodes in a given geographic area. In other words, when using TCP/IP you cannot have more than 254 addressable nodes per Class C segment. If you know that you will be exceeding this number, either use Class B segmentation addressing for your *entire* network, or plan to use more than one Class C in a given area (by using VLSM, or variable-length subnet masks), or plan to break up the area into more than one address segment.

The amount of traffic that will be on the segment. For most user segments, the traffic will be limited to file and print with some server level access. For the general user population the level of traffic will be low. If a particular group is doing high bandwidth applications such as testing of software, graphics, and/or database applications, then you should plan to segment off that area from the rest of the LAN to improve performance for both the local segment and the rest of the network.

The type of protocol to be used on the segment. For instance, if you have an entire section of your LAN that will be the only segment using AppleTalk, you will want to isolate them to their own segment, thus keeping the AppleTalk packets off of the rest of the network. This situation comes up frequently with networks with graphics departments that need special Macintosh machines for their work.

Benefits and Caveats to Mixing and Matching Protocols

Sometimes there are actually some benefits to using multiple protocols on the network. There are situations, such as the one described earlier about the graphics department, where using another protocol besides TCP/IP can be beneficial, since the routers will not allow the protocol in question off of the segment it is on without specific instruction to do so. How is this a benefit? Well, by deploying this type of design you know with complete confidence now that the nodes on the segment with AppleTalk will *never* communicate with nodes on other segments—it simply isn't possible! Figure 9.13 is an example of a protocol segmented network.

Figure 9.13 Protocol segmented network.

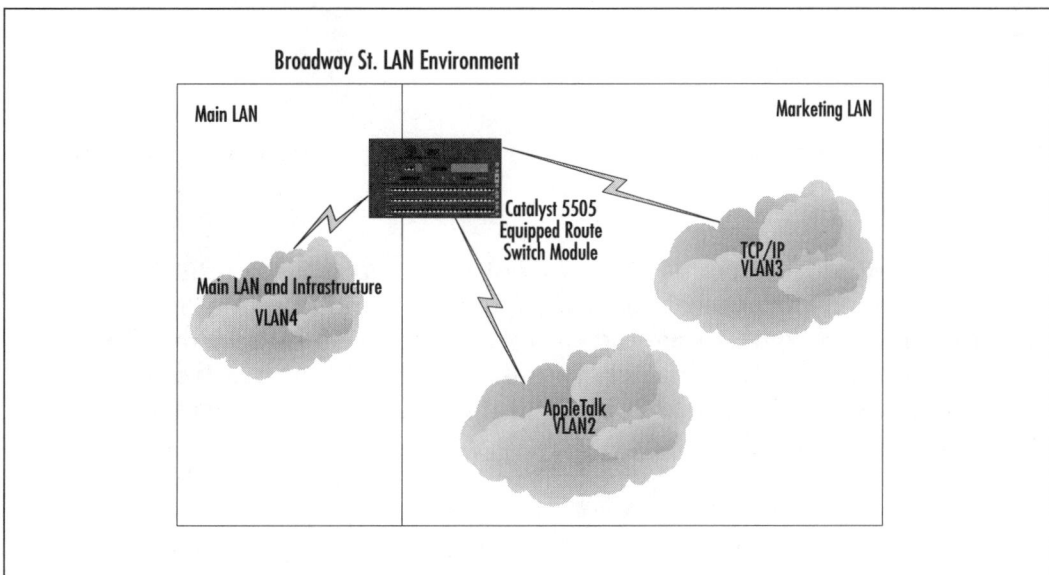

The downfall to using multiple protocols is that now somehow you have to perform protocol translation between segments. If one port on the router is getting AppleTalk or IPX, and another is getting TCP/IP, then protocol translation needs to occur somewhere on the local segment for communications to happen to other resources on the network not using the local protocol. Somewhere, somehow, some device must translate and route between nodes on the network to allow for communications. Following the previous example of the AppleTalk network, at least one of the nodes on the AppleTalk segment will need to convert and act as a proxy between the Macintosh nodes using AppleTalk and the rest of the network using TCP/IP. This causes an obvious bottleneck in communications, as shown in Figure 9.14.

Figure 9.14 Bottlenecks caused by proxy networking.

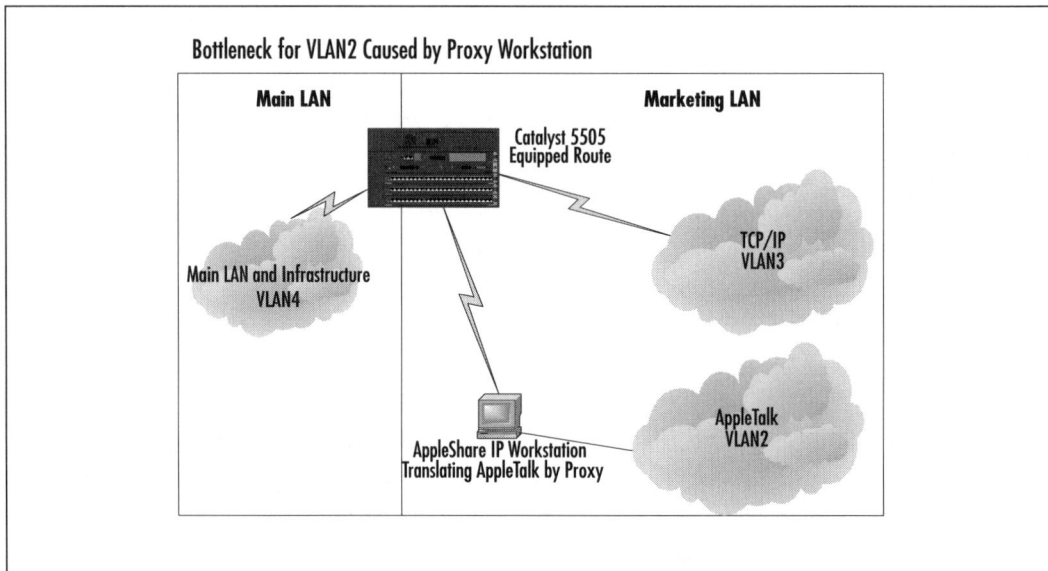

You will need to weigh whether or not it is a good idea to use protocols for segmentation purposes, but always keep in mind one final important fact: the more configurations and protocols on your architecture, the more administration and configuration you as an administrator will need to keep track of and maintain. Consolidation is the key to a happy network and administrator!

Redundancy and Reliability

We now have an understanding of where and how to place routers into the network and how they function. Also, we have a good idea of what the benefits and caveats are to using various protocols and techniques to logical design and how they are handled in the routed environment. Now it is time to get into the stuff that is beyond basic connectivity issues: redundancy and reliability on the routed architecture.

The deal is this: you know where your vital resources are going to be on your Windows 2000 network and you know how people will be accessing them through the infrastructure. Now we need to integrate Windows 2000's special features and tie-ins to the Cisco IOS to make one cohesive machine between the two systems.

We need to ensure, before we can even get the two systems interoperating on the levels that they are capable of, that there is no way that the communications between the vital resources of the network and the network user community are interrupted. This means that we have to design *redundancy* into the network. Once we have redundancy in the design, it will provide a level of *reliability* that takes out the risk inherent in losing connectivity on high performance operating systems like Windows 2000. Let's take the network from Figure 9.8 and see if we can enhance it to a level that has redundancy and reliability.

Circuitry Failover Design

As you can see, we have a consolidated router design here, but if one of the circuit links goes down we will lose connectivity to the site it services, or worse, if the central site router goes down, all facilities will lose their connections to the central server farm *and* each other. This is not a great situation if the company truly depends on its infrastructure and network to conduct business, so we will now develop a redundancy design to allow for some failover as needed in case of emergencies, as shown in Figure 9.15.

By deploying secondary Integrated Services Digital Network (ISDN) circuitry throughout the network, we are now able to ensure that at least connectivity and services will be available in the event that one of the primary circuit lines has a failure. Using a method from the Cisco IOS called DDR, or dial-on-demand routing, we can handle the failover issue. We set up DDR on the routers to have the ISDN port monitor the primary serial port. If the system detects that there is less than 25 percent bandwidth (or actually no bandwidth due to circuit failure) left available on the serial circuit, the ISDN port will activate and provide additional bandwidth to compensate.

Figure 9.15 Redundant circuits.

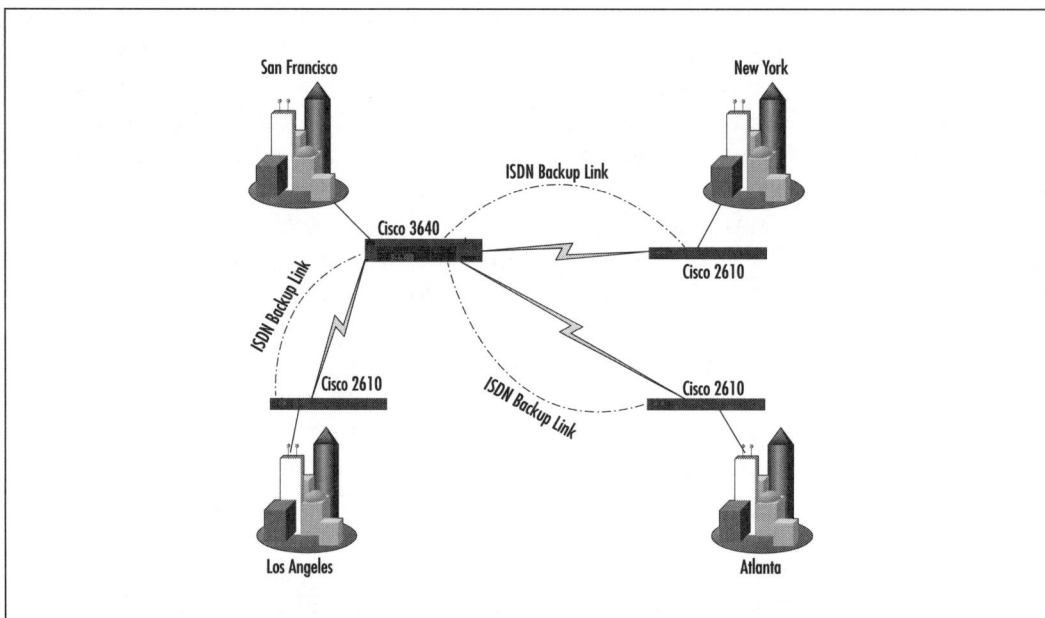

Hardware Failover Design

Now, from looking at Figure 9.15, an obvious question comes up—sure the circuits will failover, but what if we lose an actual router? Worse, what if we lose the main router at the main site? Well, it all comes down to price point vs redundancy when it comes to hardware. Routers are expensive enough—does it make sense to duplicate all of them throughout the network and run separate circuits to each redundant router? Usually not, but what we can do is give the core router some hardware failover capability and take a slightly different tack on the back-up circuitry to make this setup a bit more reliable while saving overall costs. Take a look at Figure 9.16.

In Figure 9.16, we can see that the ISDN lines have been rerouted to form a triangular configuration with other sites. The core router is also reworked so that it has a redundant counterpart as well. This configuration not only allows for circuitry failover but hardware failure as well. The difference is that instead of using DDR to make the failover work on the core routers we are using Hot Standby Router Protocol (HSRP) to handle the redundant links. HSRP monitors one of the ports, which is considered the primary, and if it fails, a secondary port on another piece of equipment will take over the link. The triangular design will then adjust everyone's

Figure 9.16 Redundancy redesign to accommodate hardware failure.

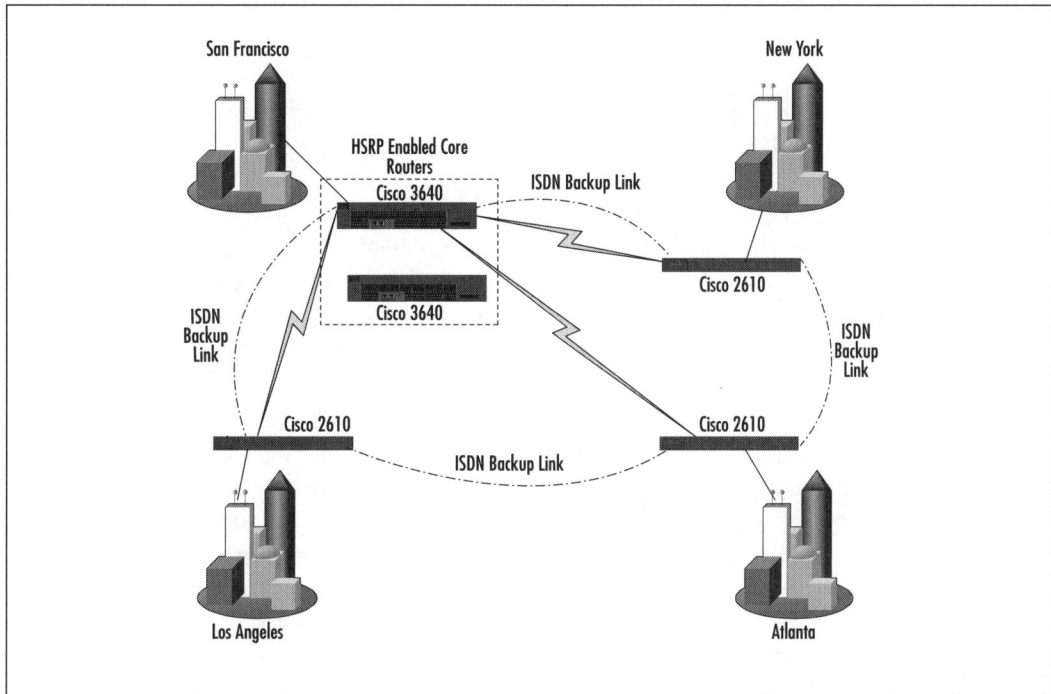

routing tables to use the new, secondary pathing created by the backup circuit.

The Financial Costs of Redundancy

Obviously, the cost of redundancy and reliability seems high and hard on the budget, and quite frankly, it is! There is simply no way to make a networking infrastructure redundant without doubling up on circuitry and/or hardware. The question you need to ask yourself is: Can my business stand an outage without losing money? If so, then for how long? To determine this, look at the core competencies of the business you are running and decide what it would cost the company if the network were down for a day. Would the company be able to function at all? For instance, if the network exists for simple file and print and some Internet access, and the core competency of the business is to run a day care center—do we really need to make it redundant?

On the other hand, it may be that your company would do just fine if the network were partially or fully down for a period of time and you have a window of repair that is acceptable to running the business. Remember that in most companies, the LAN/WAN exists to serve a higher purpose than just to exist for itself—businesses that don't exist for the IT purposes range from selling retail products to healthcare in hospitals. The network is normally not the business itself but a tool that supports it, so judge accordingly when you are deciding to increase your IT budget by 200 percent as to whether it is money well spent or just overkill.

How Do Redundancy and Reliability Affect the Windows 2000 Network?

Obviously, you do not want to lose connectivity to the network if it can be helped and for older networks it was not devastating to lose a WAN link. Now, think of the adverse effects that losing a link between domains can be to the Active Directory of Windows 2000. Having a segment pop on and off of the network several times an hour can cause havoc on the internal directory systems of Windows 2000 and could potentially cause corruption and/or inaccurate directory trees to be formed. Always make sure to apply as much infrastructure redundancy and reliability as possible into the network between main sites that have server replication and transmissions between them. That way, even if users have slow-downs between sites, at least the network will remain "stable" enough that the directory services will remain unscathed.

Security on the Routed Architecture

Obviously, you do not want the routers to blindly allow information to go all over the network to areas that either do not need it or that should not see it. For instance, most companies shield off the Human Resources segment of the network from outside access to hide personnel sensitive documentation.

Cisco handles security on the network through the use of access control lists (ACLs). The ACL system can be applied on each routed interface to give a list of allowed or disallowed traffic to any of the network segments. The ACLs can be configured to handle security on an address-based level at its basic configuration levels, or can filter traffic based on information as detailed as the protocol port of the transmissions coming through the packets on the routed ports.

The criteria for applying ACLs and how to program them can be very complex and is much too large a topic to cover here, but you can find detailed ACL configuration examples if you go to Cisco Connection Online (CCO), at www.cisco.com.

How Does Windows 2000 Help Manage ACLs?

Windows 2000 has add-in products provided by Cisco as third-party pieces of software that allow you to set company security policies and automatically have Windows 2000 create the ACL commands. The software add-ons will then apply them to the appropriate interfaces on the routers.

WARNING

ACLs can easily cut off access to complete segments of the network and take out all communications on the network if not handled properly.

One of the features of the Cisco add-ins is to allow you to see the commands for the routers before they are applied to the routed ports by Windows 2000. If you do not have a complete understanding of the network applications running over your routers, check these commands with a networking engineer *prior* to applying them. It is always good to err on the side of caution when it comes to routing-level security features like ACLs, because the end result may be the loss of communications to complete segments of the network if misapplied.

If you need to apply security to anything on the Windows 2000 architecture, try to accomplish it via the normal operating system's level of security before doing it on your routing infrastructure. This method is much more *predictable* and *fixable* in case something goes wrong. Remember, Windows 2000 offers a nice GUI interface that you can use to control ACLs, whereas Cisco will leave you with only the Cisco IOS to play with; if something goes wrong, you'll need to change things manually on the routers. Don't do anything on the Cisco architecture that you are *not* comfortable with. If you are not sure how the IOS commands generated by Windows 2000 affect the routers, check with your Cisco consultant first before allowing them to be applied.

Quality of Service on the LAN/WAN Using Windows 2000

And now, the real claim to fame between Cisco and Windows 2000: the ability to manage Quality of Service (QoS) based on the Active Directory and the login of the person in question at any point on the network. In short, Windows 2000 will allow certain users higher guaranteed bandwidth and access to services on the network based upon settings in the Active Directory and their account.

This is done dynamically using a QoS technique called Reservation Protocol (RSVP), tied into the Cisco IOS at the switch port level. RSVP, via the Active Directory, will be activated at the Cisco switch port level and a certain amount of priority will be given to that port's traffic on the wire by creating a *reservation tunnel* over the routed and switched infrastructure. When the user in question logs out of the system, the tunnel will be torn down, thus freeing up the bandwidth on the infrastructure again. This means that no matter where this user logs in, they will have a guaranteed bandwidth level on the network! The only way these features could be activated previously was to hard-code these settings on the switch and routers manually. Before the release of Windows 2000, the user could not activate this feature dynamically, which indicates the power of the Windows 2000 and Cisco systems when working together.

The Real Integration—Prioritizing Traffic on the LAN/WAN

These features and functionality seems pretty cool, huh? This means that you can make sure that the VP of Finance gets high bandwidth to the Internet no matter where he or she logs in on the network! What is not cool about this setup is that it can be *very* dangerous to the LAN administrator of the company.

"But if I can make sure that the main guys always have connectivity no matter where they log in, I am going to be a Golden Boy in their eyes, right?" Let us not forget, the LAN and WAN administrators are never noticed when the network is running well, but they are noticed when the network is having problems! It is a truism that we of the IT world need to work in a proactive mode on our networks; otherwise people may actually start calling our office! What you need to keep in mind is that *any* changes in QoS potentially can shut down bandwidth accidentally if not well planned. Dynamic allocation of QoS can be a very dangerous thing.

Dynamic QoS—Is This Really a Great Idea?

Applying QoS of any kind on the network can be dangerous—if you prioritize any kind of bandwidth or traffic, you are automatically *unprioritizing* all of the other traffic on the wire. Normally, when asked to apply QoS to any routers or switches, you would want to analyze all of the traffic prior to application, to make sure that none of it will suffer for prioritizing a particular type of data. Any good network engineer will only apply QoS out of necessity and only when he or she has made sure the rest of the traffic on the wire will not be adversely affected.

Now, imagine a user that can apply QoS settings and change the mode of traffic control on the network simply by arbitrarily logging in on any PC in the company. Does this sound like a great idea? How about if several people have a guaranteed bandwidth setting and they all log onto the same area on the network? What happens then? Remember, as the administrator you will have no control over where they log in, so *your* network can be affected at any time.

Be *extremely* cautious when using the QoS qualities incorporated in the Active Directory. Rampant QoS can cause serious repercussions if not properly planned and controlled.

When Should Another Method of QoS Be Used?

RSVP is used when you want to create QoS and prioritization *dynamically* on the network on the fly. A reservation request is created at the point of transmission origin, in this case the switch port, and a message is passed all the way through the network to each piece of network equipment; when the destination switch port is reached, a reservation tunnel is created, giving a guaranteed bandwidth level all along the path. The reservation request is identified using the Windows 2000 login and AD settings that are associated with that login.

In most cases, the infrastructure designer would not worry about user and application layer stuff; your head is down in the trenches of the infrastructure at the network and physical levels. You may want to apply QoS to an entire set of protocols, such as access to certain applications, or deter access by limiting the bandwidth of an entire protocol, such as HyperText Transfer Protocol, or HTTP, to limit Internet use during working hours at the company. To apply QoS at these levels, we use a technique called *queuing* to control the flow of traffic in and out of the network routers. There are several kinds of QoS techniques available on the Cisco routers:

First In, First Out (FIFO) The simplest technique of queuing—it does exactly what you think it would do. The first packet into the queue is the first packet out of the queue. There is no differentiation between different types of packets at all and therefore there isn't any QoS to speak of using FIFO.

Weighed Fair Queuing (WFQ) A technique that allows "smaller" streams of traffic a fair chance to get out of the buffers when "larger" streams are monopolizing the bandwidth. In FIFO, if a major File Transfer Protocol (FTP) file transfer is taking place, all other traffic must sit and wait for the data stream to finish before getting a chance to get out of the queue. With WFQ, smaller data streams are given a higher priority than the larger ones in the queue, thus allowing them through the buffers ahead of the larger data streams. This allows all data streams equal time on the outgoing ports.

Class Based Weighted Fair Queuing (CBWFQ) Works the same as WFQ, but it has the added feature of allowing the network administrator to place different types of traffic into a specific class, and then apply priority to the defined classes. Let's say that all traffic coming from the 172.16.2.x subnet, which is the server room, is placed in Class A, and then all HTTP traffic is placed in Class C. All other types of traffic are placed in Class B. Class A is given High priority, Class B is given Normal priority, and Class C is given Low priority. CBWFQ is then applied to the router ports. Now all server traffic will be the first through the routers, and Web traffic will be the last through the routers, but within the classes *everything still works on the WFQ algorithms.* Why is this point important? To answer that, let's look at the next category.

Priority Queuing Priority Queuing works much the same way as CBWFQ and is configured very similarly. The difference is that in Priority Queuing there is no WFQ factor to it—the priority traffic gets the bandwidth—that's it! There are the same level of classifications—High, Normal, and Low. The difference is that now "larger" data streams, if they are in the proper priority class, will have first crack at the output queues ahead of the "smaller" data streams. This negates the WFQ processes and potentially can cause connection outages for certain types of traffic if not well designed.

Custom Queuing Custom Queuing is by far the most difficult and complex to configure, but also allows the greatest range of possibilities for configuration. In Custom Queuing, you can actually set percentage levels on the different types of traffic coming through as to what percentage bandwidth they get. Unlike priority queuing, where you only have the few predefined classifications, you can have up to 16 different priority classes manually defined in the system.

IP Prioritization—Voice on the LAN Finally, there is one other basic prioritization method available for routers that have voice traffic enabled over the bandwidth—IP Prioritization. It works not on its own, but in conjunction with the other queuing techniques listed. By applying an IP priority to

Figure 9.17 ABC Chemical Company's routing infrastructure.

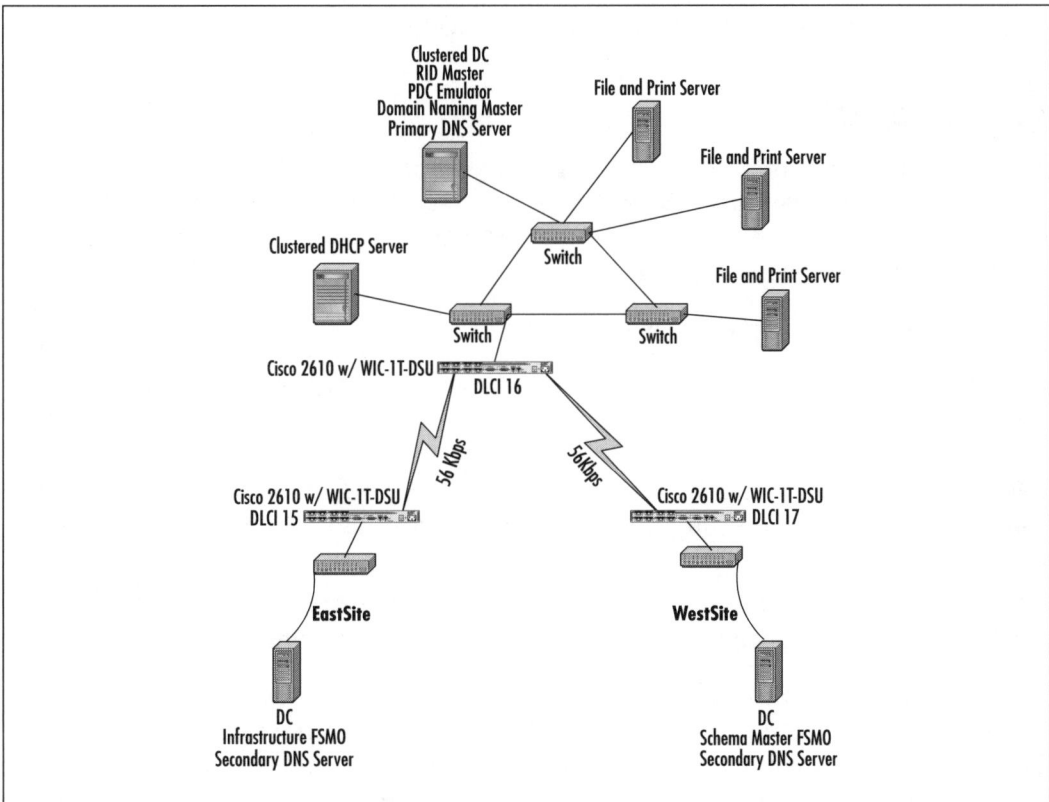

packets as they enter the voice ports, those packets are tagged as high priority by modifying their header information to be identified as voice traffic. The packets are then given complete priority to the system to allow for "real-time" traffic queuing.

Windows 2000 does not manage these methods; they are manually configured on the routers' configurations and cannot be changed dynamically like RSVP. Cisco is producing automated tools for the application of these queuing techniques that is not available to the general public as of yet, but the tools work in very much the same way as the automated tool to set ACLs—it will allow you to define QoS rules via a GUI interface in laymen's terms and then produce a set of QoS queuing commands to be propagated to routers specified on the network.

As in the case of the ACL automatic generator, *use caution* with these tools. QoS misapplied can cause huge detrimental affects on your network. Before using QoS, know your LAN, WAN, and the traffic on it well enough to know what adverse affects the application of QoS may have. Also, if possible, run the configurations by your Cisco consultant to ensure that they will not be damaging to the traffic on the network.

Case Studies

Now that we have an understanding of how router and serial links affect an infrastructure running Windows 2000, we will take the data produced from Chapter 7's case studies and add in the necessary routers to complete the Frame Relay designs.

ABC Chemical Company

Let's first go over the original requirements for ABC Chemical Company as laid out in Chapter 7:

Each warehouse is physically connected to the campus network via Frame Relay links, which are slow 56 Kbps network connections. The maximum amount of traffic has been estimated as follows (see Chapter 7 for full details):

1 ReplicationCycle * 50 users * 11000 Bytes = 4296 Kbits / 56 Kbps = 76 seconds for full upload + 10 seconds for overhead traffic = 86 seconds

The next step is to add the appropriate routing devices at the central location border switch to enable the Frame Relay connections to operate. Since these are basic Frame Relay connections with no special accommodations being made at this time for Voice-over IP and/or hard-coded QoS settings, the configurations can be kept at a minimum for the serial ports running Frame Relay. In Figure 9.17, we have modified the settings from Chapter 7 to include the appropriate routing devices to handle the job.

In the case of ABC, the network simply isn't that router-intensive and we do not need a large amount of firepower to accomplish the connection on the WAN. We can utilize Cisco 2610 routers using a WAN interface card, or WIC, to handle the serial connection. Specifically, the WIC to be used would be a WIC-1T-DSU, which is capable of handling a T1 circuit and has a DSU service module built into it. The DSU service module is the device that normally handles circuit termination at the local site. DSUs can be external or internal devices to the router, so we simplify the solution by having the DSU built into the port itself. The router at the main site would have a configuration as seen in the next section.

Main Router Configuration

```
!
ip subnet-zero
no ip domain-lookup
!
interface Ethernet0
 ip address 10.1.1.1 255.0.0.0
!
interface Serial0
 no ip address <*>
 encapsulation frame-relay
 frame-relay lmi-type ansi
!
interface Serial0.15 point-to-point
 description Frame Relay to EastSite
 ip unnumbered Ethernet0
 frame-relay interface-dlci 15 broadcast
!
interface Serial0.17 point-to-point
 description Frame Relay to WestSite
 ip unnumbered Ethernet0
 frame-relay interface-dlci 17 broadcast
!
```

Note that the data-link connection identifier (DLCI) numbers for the Frame Relay are directly related to the number of the subinterfaces on the serial ports. This is not vital to the configurations—you can use whatever numbers you want for the subinterface numbers, but it is always a best practice to use the DLCI numbers for reference so that you do not need to keep track of two sets of numbers on the Frame Relay configurations.

EastSite Router Configuration

```
!
ip subnet-zero
no ip domain-lookup
!
interface Ethernet0
 ip address 20.1.1.1 255.0.0.0
!
interface Serial0
 no ip address <*>
```

```
 encapsulation frame-relay
!
interface Serial0.16 point-to-point
 description Frame Relay to MainSite
ip unnumbered Ethernet0
 frame-relay interface-dlci 16 broadcast
!
```

WestSite Router Configuration

```
!
ip subnet-zero
no ip domain-lookup
!
interface Ethernet0
 ip address 30.1.1.1 255.0.0.0
!
interface Serial0
 no ip address <*>
 encapsulation frame-relay
 frame-relay lmi-type ansi
!
interface Serial0.16 point-to-point
 description Frame Relay to MainSite
 ip unnumbered Ethernet0
 frame-relay interface-dlci 16 broadcast
!
```

These configurations are basic but sufficient for the setup of the WAN network for ABC Chemical. There is no need for hard-coded QoS features like traffic shaping, since we are only sending data across the wire, and neither Voice-over X nor video signals are being deployed. We can simply use the DLCI numbers to map to the IP addresses on the far routers and let Frame Relay handle the rest of the communications.

West Coast Accounting, L.L.C.

West Coast Accounting has essentially the same routing requirements over Frame Relay as does ABC Chemical Company, only more interfaces are needed at the core site. To accommodate the amount of processing and caching power needed to handle the larger level of routed traffic, as well as provide for more expansion in the future to more satellite offices, we will deploy a Cisco 3640 router at the core site, as shown in Figure 9.18.

Figure 9.18 West Coast Accounting Cisco routing infrastructure.

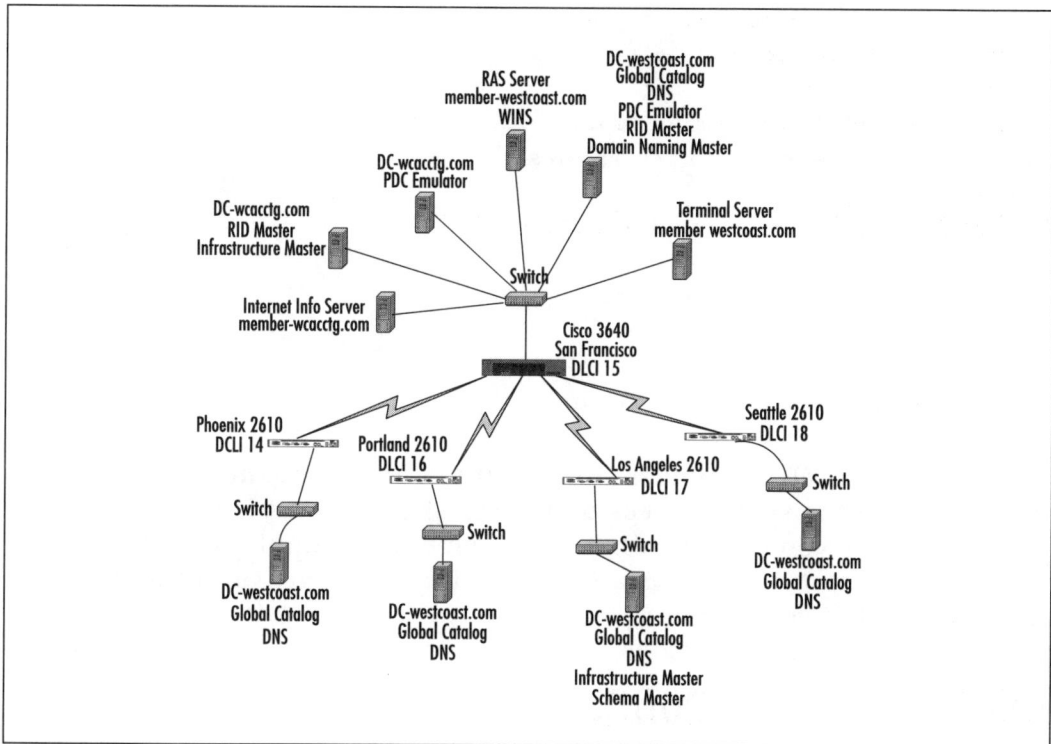

San Francisco Router Configuration

```
!
ip subnet-zero
no ip domain-lookup
!
interface Ethernet0
 ip address 10.1.1.1 255.0.0.0
!
interface Serial0/0
 no ip address <*>
 encapsulation frame-relay
 frame-relay lmi-type ansi
!
interface Serial0/0.14 point-to-point
 description Frame Relay to Phoenix
 ip unnumbered Ethernet0
 frame-relay interface-dlci 14 broadcast
!
```

```
interface Serial0/0.16 point-to-point
 description Frame Relay to Portland
 ip unnumbered Ethernet0
 frame-relay interface-dlci 16 broadcast
!
interface Serial0/0.17 point-to-point
 description Frame Relay to Los Angeles
 ip unnumbered Ethernet0
 frame-relay interface-dlci 17 broadcast
!
interface Serial0/0.18 point-to-point
 description Frame Relay to Seattle
 ip unnumbered Ethernet0
 frame-relay interface-dlci 18 broadcast
!
```

Note that the DLCI numbers for the Frame Relay are directly related to the number of the subinterfaces on the serial ports. This is not vital to the configurations—you can use whatever numbers you want for the subinterface numbers, but it is always a best practice to use the DLCI numbers for reference so that you do not need to keep track of two sets of numbers on the Frame Relay configurations.

Phoenix Router Configuration

```
!
ip subnet-zero
no ip domain-lookup
!
interface Ethernet0
 ip address 20.1.1.1 255.0.0.0
!
interface Serial0
 no ip address <*>
 encapsulation frame-relay
!
interface Serial0.16 point-to-point
 description Frame Relay to San Francisco
ip unnumbered Ethernet0
 frame-relay interface-dlci 16 broadcast
!
```

Portland Router Configuration

```
!
ip subnet-zero
no ip domain-lookup
!
interface Ethernet0
 ip address 30.1.1.1 255.0.0.0
!
interface Serial0
 no ip address <*>
 encapsulation frame-relay
 frame-relay lmi-type ansi
!
interface Serial0.16 point-to-point
 description Frame Relay to San Francisco
 ip unnumbered Ethernet0
 frame-relay interface-dlci 16 broadcast
!
```

Los Angeles Router Configuration

```
!
ip subnet-zero
no ip domain-lookup
!
interface Ethernet0
 ip address 40.1.1.1 255.0.0.0
!
interface Serial0
 no ip address <*>
 encapsulation frame-relay
 frame-relay lmi-type ansi
!
interface Serial0.16 point-to-point
 description Frame Relay to San Francisco
 ip unnumbered Ethernet0
 frame-relay interface-dlci 16 broadcast
!
```

Seattle Router Configuration

```
!
ip subnet-zero
no ip domain-lookup
!
interface Ethernet0
 ip address 50.1.1.1 255.0.0.0
!
interface Serial0
 no ip address <*>
 encapsulation frame-relay
 frame-relay lmi-type ansi
!
interface Serial0.16 point-to-point
 description Frame Relay to San Francisco
 ip unnumbered Ethernet0
 frame-relay interface-dlci 16 broadcast
!
```

Summary

To design and execute a successful router infrastructure for Windows 2000, you need to take a step-by-step approach to come up with the overall routed design, and then drill down deeper and deeper until you get all of the precise detail down for the complete infrastructure. The routed architecture is the heart and soul of the network—without it you cannot control or maintain the traffic management on your network.

The first task in creating any good design is to understand where your entry points onto your network are and then identify the appropriate routing resource to handle the traffic at that entry point. This chapter identified the different types of routers and classifications that they belong to: core, distribution, access, and central core routers. Also, in order to accomplish a good router design, you need to understand the core concerns that routers handle for the network infrastructure and traffic load. You need to understand the concepts of broadcast domains, broadcast storms, and various protocols and how they affect your bandwidth. Finally, you need to understand how the "hidden" protocols work—those protocols that operate solely between the routers and maintain the routing controls for the network such as RIP, RIP2, OSPF, and EIGRP.

In planning the architecture, you need to understand the different types of LAN protocols you are using on your network. Along with TCP/IP, which is the native protocol for Windows 2000 and Cisco, there are also other legacy protocols like IPX/SPX, SNA/APPN, NetBEUI, and AppleTalk that can affect the traffic and bandwidth out there on the LAN. When looking at serial communications between sites, you will need to decide upon which serial transport method to use: Frame Relay, HDLC, Point-to-Point, or even ATM in some cases.

You need to understand the different types of routers that are available and what level of Cisco router will be appropriate for the application and entry point in question, including switch routers such as the RSM or the MFSC cards for switches. Keep in mind the level of processor and memory needed to help the router perform the necessary functions.

Try to consolidate the protocols on the LAN and WAN to reduce the overhead on the routed architecture and understand how multiple protocols can bring benefits and caveats to any segmentation on your network.

Three key aspects of the routed architecture need to be considered and programmed when designing your routed architecture—redundancy, reliability, and security. These factors will determine how well your network infrastructure will hold up in the case of purposeful or accidental changes to the topology of the network.

Finally, Windows 2000 and Cisco routers truly come together when working with QoS settings and bandwidth controls. Windows 2000 uses RSVP in conjunction with Cisco IOS and the Active Directory to allow bandwidth control for key entities and users on the network. Be very cautious when applying QoS to a network; you can easily adversely affect the network's performance. We also went over the other queuing techniques supplied by the Cisco IOS that are not controlled by Windows 2000, and how they can assist in the control of the routed network infrastructure.

FAQs

Q: How can I find out more details about the kinds of Cisco routers available?

A: The best resource by far for information on the latest router equipment available is Cisco Connection Online (CCO) at www.cisco.com. You can find information on every kind of router, and CCO also has tools to help you determine which routers would be best for your concerns.

Q: Are there any special considerations when applying Firewall Feature Sets to my routers when I have to pass AD or DEN information between firewalled segments of my WAN/LAN?

A: Microsoft does pass AD and DEN information over specific IP ports on the network and you need to take these into account when setting up any firewall policies. Make sure to consult Microsoft's and Cisco's websites for the most current information on using firewalls on the Windows 2000/Cisco network to make sure that all conduits on the PIX conform to the basic requirements of Windows 2000 communications.

Q: I have heard that routers can act as firewalls for the Internet. Do I really need a firewall *and* a router to maintain security?

A: Absolutely. You should use an actual firewall in conjunction with your Internet router. Routers can have a special IOS applied that allows for a "Firewall Feature Set," but this IOS is best utilized to allow for IP Security Protocol (IPSec) and virtual private network (VPN) solutions as well as basic traffic denial. For true firewall capacity and versatility, use a Cisco PIX Firewall along with your router to maximize your Internet security.

Q: How do I determine how much memory I require for the IOS feature set I need to handle my routed protocols?

A: There are tools on CCO to help you determine the amount of memory you need to handle the IOS and functions on your router. The best way to determine it is to look up the IOS configuration tool; it will tell you how much DRAM and flash you need to run the feature set in question. Not everyone can access this tool (you need CCO login capability to get to it), so ask your Cisco consultant to help you on this one.

Q: I don't know a lot about my traffic levels and I haven't done protocol monitoring before. Must I use QoS on my network or can I just leave it off of the system?

A: No, you do not need to use QoS if you do not want to! As a matter of fact, if you do not know *everything* about the traffic flow on your network, avoid QoS entirely until you do! The best way to determine if QoS is needed is to have a professional sniffer analysis done on the key segments of your network. Have your Cisco consultant help you analyze the results and see where you can safely apply QoS as needed.

Q: Do I have to apply ACLs and/or QoS to have normal traffic control?

A: No, ACLs are an add on to arbitrarily restrict or allow certain traffic through network routed interfaces, and QoS controls the active bandwidth. Most networks can run perfectly fine without the use of either ACLs or QoS—they are simply tools to improve your performance once the base network is running.

Chapter 10

Implementing the Cisco Switches

Solutions in this chapter:

- Cisco IOS-based switching products
- Cisco set-based switching products
- Supervisor modules
- Route Switch Modules
- Multilayer Switch Modules

Introduction

This chapter focuses on the several models and features that make up the family of Cisco Catalyst switches. Cisco offers a complete line of switching products for all levels of the hierarchical and campus networking models: core, distribution, and access. By knowing the various features and models of Catalyst switches, you will be able to design and optimize scaleable, multilayer networks that can meet your business needs both now and in the future, as the need for bandwidth and access increases.

The Cisco Catalyst series is a large and diverse product line. Although Cisco uses virtually the same configuration and IOS across most of their router product line, each product in the Catalyst series can have its own configuration utilities. For example, the 1900 series uses a menu-driven command-line interface (CLI), and the Catalyst 5000 uses a CLI similar to a router. This is because Cisco has acquired much of the Catalyst line from third-party sources. Each manufacturer has (or had) their own way of configuring their particular line of switches. In most cases, Cisco has maintained the basic configuration feature set for each model with only a few modifications.

The Cisco family of Catalyst switches can be subdivided into models that function at the various layers of the hierarchical networking design. Depending upon your business needs, you may consider using larger/smaller switches for various layers. For example, if you are building a network for a small company of only 100+ employees, you could probably get by with only a couple of Catalyst 5000 switches or four or five 2900XLs in a cluster. It is important that you understand the current and future needs of any business where you are required to design and build a multi-layer switching network. Table 10.1 lists the switches you would most likely use for each layer of a distributed LAN.

Table 10.1 Switches for Each Layer of a Distributed LAN

Layer	Switch
Core layer (network backbone)	Catalyst 6000/8500/12000 series
Distribution layer (departmental/site connectivity)	Catalyst 4000/5000/6000 series
Access layer (workgroup/wiring closets)	Catalyst 1900/2820/2900XL/3500XL series Catalyst 5000 (large wiring closets)

Cisco IOS-based Switching Products

The Catalyst IOS-based series of products serve as a low-cost, scaleable solution for many companies today. This series can be used as a replacement for hubs and repeaters that are often found in backroom wiring closets. In many cases, these switches can also serve as the central switch for small companies or remote sites. The Cisco IOS-based switching products work at the second layer of the OSI model, called the data-link layer. These switches make their destination decisions based on the hardware (MAC, or media access control) address of the nodes on the switch. This is Layer 2 switching. These switches are called IOS-based because their CLI used for configuration is similar to that of a router IOS. The set-based products (in the next section) use the **set** command for much of their configuration.

The actual means of configuration for the IOS-based switches will vary depending upon the version of software running on the switch. For example, the 2900/3500 series will run the IOS-like CLI with the Standard edition of the switching software. On the other hand, all 1900/2820 switches come with a menu-based configuration utility in the Standard edition software that can support the needs of a small network or virtual local area network (VLAN). You would need an upgrade to the Enterprise edition software to get the CLI functionality on the 1900/2820 series. There is also a Web-based configuration utility—the Cisco Visual Switch Manager (CVSM)—for basic configuration and maintenance on all IOS-based switches.

Catalyst 1900/2820 Series

The 1900/2820 series is the access layer solution for small networks and workgroups. They share the same switching architecture, but have slightly different port configurations and modular features.

Hardware Features of the 1900 Series

The Catalyst 1900 switches offer a low-cost solution for small networks and VLANs. The 1900 series uses a 1-Gbps switching bus to connect up to 24 10BaseT RJ-45 ports together with two 100BaseT ports (either FX or TX). These products also feature one attachment unit interface (AUI) Ethernet port in the back. The 19xx Catalyst series is a "fixed configuration" product, which means that the hardware is not modular or upgradeable. You will need to select the right model of switch that allows you to scale your network with either 100BaseTX (100-Mbps Ethernet) or 100BaseFX (fiber optic) connections. For example, a 1924 series switch that is a stand-alone switch at a remote site or small company might use the two 100BaseTX ports as fast links to servers within the network that are running 100BaseTX Ethernet cards. On the other hand, if the 1924 switch is one of several in a large network, an administrator might use 100BaseFX ports to hook into a fiber optic backbone for high-speed access to the rest of the network. Table 10.2 lists the port configurations for the 1900 series of switches.

In addition to the ports listed in Table 10.2, all 19xx series switches have one Ethernet AUI port in the back and one console port for configuration. This can be used for Thinnet, Thicknet, Ethernet, or fiber-optic connections.

The 19xx series can store up to 1024 MAC addresses in the Cisco Access Manager (CAM) table. The entire architecture of the switch is linked together by a 1-Gbps bus. All the 19xx Catalyst switches also have a 3MB packet buffer for network surges. This reduces the chance that a switch will drop a packet if it gets busy. All 1900 switches have room for a redundant power supply for backup. For operational and status information, the front of the 1900 series includes LED readouts for status indicators and diagnostics.

Table 10.2 Port Configurations for the Catalyst 1900 Series

Ports	1912	1912C	1924	1924C	1924F
10BaseT	12	12	24	24	24
100BaseTX	2	1	2	1	0
100BaseFX	0	1	0	1	2

For IT Professionals

Troubleshooting 101: Basic Catalyst Issues

A green LED readout on a switch usually means everything is operational, amber means something may be interfering with a procedure, and red means bad news. The idea is to become familiar with whether an amber switch means something like an extra power supply, or if there really is an issue with the switch. Many network problems are discovered by a bright red light that you might notice while walking past your

Continued

switches on a day-to-day job. For example, one of my first networking duties involved going to three sites every morning with a checklist (to be signed) and checking the routers, switches, and CSU/DSUs in the wiring closets for red lights! However, when dealing with connectivity issues, a green LED on a 19xx series port (and practically any hub/switch, for that matter) is usually only an indication of Layer 2 (data link) connectivity. Likewise, red lights are a sign of issues or malfunctions. Amber lights can have various meanings, but usually refer to intermittent issues or standby situations, such as a backup power supply or a port that is being blocked by the Spanning Tree Protocol. Remember, when troubleshooting connectivity issues, Cisco wants you to start at the physical layer with the cable and switch, and work your way up.

There are several LEDs on the front of a 19xx/2820 series switch that can keep you updated on the status of the switch and any issues that might arise.

Hardware Features of the 2820 Series

The 2820 series consists of two models: the 2822 and 2828. However, the 2822 series has been discontinued by Cisco, so in the future, only the 2828 will be available. The 2820 series use the same 1-Gbps switching fabric as well as the 3MB shared buffer used by the 1900 series. There are really only two differences between the 2820 and 1900 series switches: modular expansion and address storage.

The 2820 series offers a modular solution to small networks. The design of the 2800 series consists of 24 10BaseT ports, one Ethernet AUI port, and two expansion slots for modules. The 2820 expansion slots can support the following modules:

- The dual attachement station (DAS) fiber distributed data interface (FDDI) Fiber module comes with two ports that use a ST Fiber-Optic Connector.

- The single attachement station (SAS) FDDI Fiber module has one port that uses the ST Fiber-Optic Connector (these come in medium and long-reach models).

- The SAS FDDI User Datagram Protocol (UDP) module supports one port with an RJ-45 connector.

- 100BaseTX modules come with either one switched or eight shared 100Base TX ports.

- Likewise, 100BaseFX modules have either one switched or four shared 100Base FX ports.

- The Asynchronous Transfer Mode (ATM) 155 multimode (MM) and single-mode (SM) Fiber Modules support one ATM interface using SC Fiber-Optic Connectors.

- The ATM 155 UDP module supports one ATM interface using the RJ-45 standard.

The other difference between the 1900 series and the 2820 series is the number of MAC addresses that can be stored in the CAM table. Whereas the 1900 series can store only 1024 MAC addresses, the 2822 can store up to 2048 MAC addresses, and the 2828 can store up to 8192 MAC addresses.

Software Features of the 1900/2820 Series

There are two editions of the Cisco Switching operating system: Standard and Enterprise. Some of the Standard edition IOS features for the 1900/2820 series are the following:

Cisco Visual Switch Manager A Web-based management system for basic configuration of Cisco switches. A preconfigured IP address and inline connection are required.

VLAN support Up to four VLANs can be configured per switch on the 1900/2820 series.

Network port A default port for the network (like a default gateway). It serves as a final point of departure for unknown MAC addresses.

CGMP Cisco Group Multicast Protocol; a protocol used to manage multicasts on Catalyst switches.

Spanning Tree Protocol For management of redundant paths and switching loops.

Three switching modes Cut-Through, Store-and-Forward, and FragmentFree.

Fast EtherChannel and Gigabit EtherChannel A means of clustering multiple links together to one source for faster performance than just one link.

Remote monitoring (RMON) This switch can store RMON data for collection and analysis. RMON is a Request for Comments (RFC) established protocol for network management and monitoring.

For larger networks, the Enterprise edition software offers advanced control, clustering, configuration, and authentication features required for large-scale networks:

Increased VLAN support The Enterprise edition will support 64 VLANs with Inter-Switch Link (ISL) and 802.1Q VLAN tagging. This edition also supports the VLAN Trunking Protocol.

Uplink Fast A port feature for Catalyst switches that can reduce the time taken for a port to upgrade from "blocking" to "forwarding" states.

TACACS+ (Terminal Access Controller Access Control System Plus) Authorization support for devices on the switch. Instead of simply logging in with a standard name and password on the switch, you can have the switch refer to a TACACS+ server for authentication. This will ensure that outside users won't simply be logging in and guessing the password; they would need an account on the TACACS+ server.

CLI An IOS-type configuration utility that can be used rather than the menu-configuration features of the 1900/2820 series. The CLI is also used for advanced configuration of the Enterprise edition features.

Catalyst 2900XL/3500XL

The 2900XL/3500XL series represents some of the newer access and distribution switches. These switches, developed by Cisco, take advantage of newer technology and features like clustering and gigabit modules to expand the speed and flexibility of desktop/enterprise switching.

NOTE

There are major differences between the 2900XL series (the 2912 and 2924) and the 2900G series that is based on the Catalyst 5000 switches (the 2948G and now discontinued 2926G)—make sure you understand the differences between the two models. This section will focus on the 2900XLs, and the 2900G series is covered with the Catalyst 5000s. There is also an older model 3xxx (3000–3200) series that is different from the 3500XL series. In short, you will be hard pressed to find any rhyme or reason for why some switches are named the way they are. One standard that Cisco has been using in creating its new line of gigabit switches is ending them with the "G" designation (3508G/2948G); modular switches usually end in "M," and fiber-optic switches usually end in "F."

Gigabit Interface Converters (GBICs)

The Gigabit Interface Converter (GBIC) is a new IEEE (Institute of Electrical and Electronics Engineers) technology that is designed to provide a higher speed link between switches. GBICs are installed into slots and work in a modular configuration. There are three types of GBIC modules available for GBIC slots. Depending on variables like range, speed, and usage in a cluster, they can transmit data at a range from 550 m to 100 km. (Performance will vary depending on physical factors like the quality of cable and the wavelength used.)

- 1000BaseSX (short wavelength) uses the multimode fiber-optic link for data transmission. Depending upon the wavelength and type of cable, data can be transmitted up to 550 meters.

- 1000BaseLX/LH is a single-mode fiber-optic link that can transmit up to 10 km.

- 1000BaseZX can transmit in single mode up to 100 km with a high-quality cable. Average quality will only transmit data about 70 km.

Cisco is designing new switches that use the GBIC standard for high-speed connections to distribution and core layer switches. The 3500XL and 4000 series Catalyst switches all have switches with integrated GBIC ports, and new modules bring GBIC compatibility to the Catalyst 5000. The new Catalyst 6000 and 8500 series came out with GBIC modules already designed and engineered for them. The older 1900 and 2820 series do not have the capability to use GBIC modules.

Switch Clustering

Switch *clustering* is a means of combining Catalyst stacks under one IP address and central control. Switch clustering is available on the 2900XL/3500XL series, and can be combined with 1900 and 2820 switches. Up to 16 switches can be connected under one cluster and managed under one IP address. (Only nine GBIC switches can be included in one cluster.)

All clusters start with a Command switch. This switch must be running Catalyst software version 12.0(5) or later to serve as a Master switch. Only the 2900XL and 3500XL series can serve as a Command switch. Higher-level switches, including the 4000 series and the 3xxx (non-XL), cannot function as a Command or Member switch. In addition to the IOS requirements, the switches must be running the Cisco Discovery Protocol (CDP), and the ports that are connected must belong to the same management

VLAN. Up to 16 switches, including 1900 and 2820s connected through EtherChannel, can be managed in this way.

NOTE

Just because a switch can run as a Member switch doesn't mean it will work as a Command switch. Pay close attention to the requirements of the Command switch. You can have a 2900XL switch enabled as a Command switch at the top of a Gigastack bus because it's running 12.0(5), and the switches below it could be running a lower version of the Catalyst software that wouldn't permit one of them to function as a Command switch, although they will work as Member switches provided they're running cluster member software.

3500 series switches can also be stacked in a *Gigastack*. This is a high-speed clustering of Gigabit-compatible switches linked together with GBIC technology, either to each other in a bus topology, or with a Master switch like the 3508G running the cluster in a hub-and-spoke topology. In this case, the GBIC cable can only run a maximum of one meter between each switch, and only nine switches can operate in a Gigastack. The actual speed varies depending on the type of Gigastack built.

- A bus Gigastack has each switch hooked in a line with the next one. Each GBIC's receive port is hooked up to the next GBIC's transmit port. The GBIC switch at the bottom hooks back up to the top. In this configuration, 1 Gbps is distributed in the bus among the entire stack. Because the switches are hooked in a loop, there is a redundant path that can be brought up if a cable or switch goes down.

- A hub-and-spoke Gigastack has each GBIC switch hooked up to a Master GBIC switch with several ports, such as a 3508G or the 4912G. In this case, the Master switch will deliver up to its maximum forwarded bandwidth within its internal switching fabric (up to 5 Gbps on a 3508G, for example) with a 2-Gbps full-duplex connection between each switch. Each GBIC's Receive and Transmit ports are cross-connected with the GBIC Receive and Transmit ports on the other switch. This design lacks the redundancy of the bus design, but is faster because each link is running in full-duplex mode.

The entire cluster is managed through the Cluster Manager, a component of the CVSM. However, you can also use the CLI for many configuration details. Devices are discovered and added to the cluster using the Cluster Builder, and managed using the CVSM Cluster Manager. From here, the cluster can be monitored, configured, or even upgraded—all at once if desired. This greatly expands an administrator's ability to maintain current software IOS images across the network.

Note that in some cases, a cluster topology will be established, such as the hub-and-spoke topology, but the switches will not be clustered together internally. This is referred to as *aggregation*, and is useful for pulling workgroups, stacks, and servers together under one switch. You can also establish multiple links using Gigabit EtherChannel, which uses multiple Gigabit Ethernet links to one destination for increased bandwidth.

Additional Network Management Features

In addition to the features just described, several other technologies (that are common to all Catalyst products mentioned hereafter) can be used for network analysis. Simple Network Management Protocol (SNMP) support is an early protocol designed for easy management of certain functions and statistics across network platforms. This has been replaced somewhat by remote monitoring (RMON), which can monitor various features using nine different types of statistics. However, most Cisco products only include four, with additional RMON support coming with expansion modules.

For duplication of traffic from the LAN to your PC for analysis, switched port analyzer (SPAN) technology is designed to mirror a VLAN or port to another port of your choosing. You can mirror all the traffic, or just a certain port. This can be for analysis of data, statistics, or just general traffic sniffing.

TIP

If you are going to be sniffing network traffic, you will want to route the traffic you are sniffing to a SPAN port. On a hub or repeater, all traffic is broadcast to all ports, so there would be no need. However, on a Catalyst switch, only broadcast traffic would be hitting your sniffer, as point-to-point traffic goes straight from port to port within the switch without hitting every port. Therefore, to pick up traffic specifically intended for a certain port, you would have to mirror that traffic with a SPAN port and then analyze it with a sniffer or some other analysis tool.

Hardware Features of the 2900XL Series

The 2900XL series is the "big brother" of the 1900/2820 series. The 2900XL series offers a 4MB shared buffer for all ports and a 3.2-Gbps switching bus. Currently, there are five different models from which to choose, depending on whether you need 10BaseT, 100BaseTX, or 100BaseFX. The 100BaseTX ports are autosensing (10/100) as well as autonegotiating (half/full duplex) for 10BaseT NICs or Cat. 3 wiring.

In general, the Modular 2900XL series (2924M and 2912MF) offers more features than the standard switches. The M switches come with two modular slots for additional options. The M series also stores more MAC addresses; they can hold up to 8192 addresses in its shared buffer, while the other three models (the XL and C) can hold up to 2048 addresses in their CAM tables. Otherwise, each model in the series has its own port configuration. Table 10.3 lists the possible port and module configurations for the 2900XL series.

Table 10.3 Port Configuration for the Catalyst 2900XL Series

Ports/Modules	2912XL	2924XL	2924M	2924C	2912MF
10BaseT	12	0	0	0	0
10/100BaseTX	0	24	24	22	0
100BaseFX	0	0	0	2	12
Module slots	0	0	2	0	2

In addition to the ports listed in Table 10.3, the following modules are available for the 2924M and 2912MF:

- 100BaseFX module with two or four switched ports using SC connectors.

- 10/100BaseTX module with four switched ports using RJ-45 connectors.

- Four different ATM OC-3 modules for Multimode, Single-Mode/Medium Range, and Single-Mode/Long Range fiber optic connections, as well as a separate UDP model.

- The 1000BaseX module for Gigabit Interface Converters (GBICs). Note that this is a newer module with a slot for the GBIC. This module is used for Gigastacking, connectivity, and compatibility with the Catalyst switches that are already using newer GBIC technology. This will require Catalyst software version 12.0(5)XU.

Hardware Features of the 3500XL Series

The 3500XL series is a recent addition to the Cisco line. With this product, the GBIC port is already integrated into the hardware. This new line of switches is designed to deliver the increased bandwidth down to the workgroup and desktop levels.

There are four models currently available in the 3500XL series. They all operate with a 10-Gbps switching fabric and a 4MB shared memory buffer for all the ports. Internally, the 3500XL series can forward up to 5.4 Gbps. All the ports on the 3500XL series are capable of full-duplex operation. This can be up to 200 Mbps for the 100BaseTX ports, and 2 Gbps for the GBIC ports. A 3500XL switch is capable of storing up to 8192 MAC addresses in its CAM table. Table 10.4 lists the models and port/slot configurations for the 3500XL series.

Table 10.4 Port Configuration for the Catalyst 3500XL Series

Port/Slot	3512XL	3524XL	3548XL	3508G
10/100BaseTX	12	24	48	0
GBIC ports	2	2	2	8

Software Features of the 2900XL/3500XL Series

In the past, there was a distinction between the Enterprise and Standard editions of the Catalyst IOS software for the 2900XL/3500XL series. As with the 1900/2820 series, Standard software came with limited VLAN support and the CVSM, and the Enterprise edition came with additional TACACS+, Uplink Fast, and other Enterprise features like those on the 2820 series. There were also various IOS packages for the 2900XL series that would make it capable of being a Member/Command switch for a cluster of switches. However, with release 12.0(5)XU, several new features are introduced, and both Standard and Enterprise editions are combined into one software feature set. Some of the new features included with this IOS release are the Hot Standby Router Protocol (HSRP), Virtual Terminal Protocol (VTP) pruning, SPAN port mirroring, and additional RMON support for the CLI and SNMP operation. From here on out, Cisco combines the Standard and Enterprise editions of Catalyst software on their switches, since no one would buy a 5000/6000/8500 and not intend it for an enterprise anyway.

The 2900XL series was recently upgraded to support the new 12.0(5)XU series. These are called the 8MB series, and the older models are referred to by Cisco as the 4MB series. The 4MB series cannot be upgraded to

12.0(5)XU. The 29xx M series (with modular support) and the 3500 series support up to 250 VLANs; the 2900XL series (2912XL/2924XL/2924C) supports only 64 VLANs.

Cisco Set-based Switching Products

The second group of switches we will be looking at are called *set-based* switching products. In these switches, the CLI is less like a router and takes on a distinctive form of its own. The commands **set** and **clear** are used most predominantly. Each series fills a niche in the hierarchical network design. From this point on, most of these switches will focus more on modular and flexibility, and less on fixed configurations. This is also the point where multilayer switching really becomes evident. The following switches make up the set-based switching product line.

- The Catalyst 4000 switches are a new line designed to put the flexibility of the 5000 series into a smaller package for wiring closets and clusters.

- The Catalyst 5000s (and their 2900 counterparts) are meant to serve at the backbone layer. These switches use older technology, but have new modules and Supervisor Engines that have been designed to bring them up to current Cisco technology levels. These switches are best used now in smaller networks that you may not want to upgrade to GBIC speeds, or a wiring closet where you require high port densities and ATM connectivity.

- The Catalyst 6000/6500 series is a new series for the distribution/core layers. These switches use GBIC, ATM, and 100BaseTX modules to provide enterprise connectivity with multilayer switching. These switches are built on Gigabit technology and are optimized for Gigabit speeds.

- The Catalyst 8500 series is the answer for campus-wide core routing and switching. In addition to using the newest technology for high-speed routing and switching, the 8500 series also maintains some backward compatibility with the Catalyst 5xxx switches in their hardware and modules, so that an investment in Catalyst 5000s can still be put to good use in an 8500 environment.

Catalyst 4000

The Catalyst 4000 series is designed to be the next-generation access/backbone switch for Gigabit technology. In addition to Layer 2 switching, the newest switches (as of January, 2000) incorporate Layer 3 switching engines on some modules and switches for an introduction to multilayer switching (we'll cover that in more depth in the next sections). At this time, these are the available models of the Catalyst 4000 series:

- The 4003 Catalyst switch offers three slots (two with a Supervisor Engine model I) for a small, high-density bandwidth solution.

- The 4912G switch is a fixed configuration 12-GBIC-port switch for when you don't need the added complexity and flexibility provided by modules and Supervisor Engines. In essence, it's like a 4003 that has 12 GBIC ports, but without the need of a Supervisor Engine or modular flexibility.

In addition to these two switches, Cisco introduced two new additions to the 4000 series in January of 2000 that offer Layer 3 connectivity.

- The 4006 Catalyst switch has six slots (five with Supervisor Engines) for a higher bandwidth and flexible solution. A module is available for this switch that permits Layer 3 switching.

- The 4908G offers the fixed Gigabit centralization of the 4912G, but with Layer 3 switching for multilayer campus designs. This switch has eight GBIC ports.

Hardware Features of the 4003/4006 Series

The Catalyst 4003 is a three-slot modular switch. A Supervisor Engine I module is required in slot 1. This Supervisor Engine has one Ethernet and one Console port for network connectivity, an 8MB memory buffer, and the Gigabit switching engine. Like most switches in the 4000 series, this switch is capable of storing 16,000 MAC addresses and 1024 VLANs. It is still a Layer 2 switch, and incapable of performing multilayer switching. However, with new modules, the 4006 series is capable of supporting a module with a Layer 3 switching engine, and future modifications to the Catalyst IOS may make this module backward-compatible with the 4003 series.

For the two empty slots, the Catalyst 4003 series is capable of providing 12 Gbps of full-duplex switching within the switch fabric. The two empty slots can be filled with the following hot swappable modules:

- A 48-port 10/100baseTX autosensing module using RJ-45 ports

- A 32-port 10/100baseTX autosensing module with two GBIC 1000baseX ports for uplink

- A 32-port 10/100baseTX autosensing module with a daughter card uplink (currently, the only card that is supported is a four-port MT-RJ uplink card)

- A six-port switched 1000BaseX GBIC module

- An 18-port Server-switched 1000baseX GBIC module (this module has the same bandwidth as the six-port version—there are two fully connected GBICs and 16 GBICs that share the remaining 4 Gbps of bandwidth in a 4:1 ratio)

The 4006 Catalyst switch is similar to the 4003. The 4006 switches have six slots instead of three, and run a Supervisor Engine II module that has two GBIC ports available for uplink. The Supervisor Engine for the 4006 has a 24MB shared memory buffer to ensure that increased data rates don't overwhelm the switch and cause it to drop packets. The other five slots can hold a number of modules, including several models that aren't yet supported on the 4003. The 4006 series has a 32-Gbps switching fabric (enough bandwidth for two built-in GBIC ports and five separate six-port GBIC modules), and is capable of storing 16,000 MAC addresses and 1024 VLANs.

In addition to running the same modules as the 4003, several new modules have come out for the 4006, improving flexibility and giving Layer 3 switching capabilities. These additional modules include:

- A 12-port 1000BaseTX (using RJ-45 connectors and shared bandwidth) with two GBIC ports for uplink

- A 32-port 10/100BaseTX module with two ports of Ethernet Routing through GBIC (this is a new module that should provide Layer 3 switching services for IP/IPX/ through the Switching Engine built into the module)

- A 48-port 10/100-based switching module that uses RJ-21 ports

- A 24-port 100BaseFX switching module

Hardware Features of the Catalyst 4912G Series

The 4912G series is a GBIC-dedicated solution for when you may not need the advanced features of a Supervisor Engine, but you still want the large bandwidth of a Gigabit backbone. The 4912G switches have the same 12-Gbps switching plane as the 4003. However, instead of offering modular slots, the 4912G switches come with 12 GBIC ports in a fixed configuration. As on most current switches, the GBIC ports are autosensing and capable of operating at half or full duplex. This switch is capable of supporting 1024 VLANs and 16,000 MAC addresses in the CAM table.

Software Features of the 4xxx Series

The switches in the 4xxx series all use the same Supervisor Engine software as the Catalyst 5000 series. (It's written for each switch, but the platform is consistent across all switches.) They can support RMON, SNMP, SPAN, CDP, Authentication with RADIUS, and ISL trunking. All switches in the 4xxx series support the prerequisite 1024 VLANs. They also support Fast EtherChannel and Gigabit EtherChannel bundling with store-and-forward technology.

Features of the Catalyst 4908G-L3

This switch is being set apart from the others in the 4000 series. The 4908G-L3 is a Layer 3 switching solution that supports the Cisco IOS and provides full routing and switching capabilities over a 22-Gbps switching fabric. When it is released, the 4908G-L3 will support routing protocols such as Enhanced Interior Gateway Routing Protocol (EIGRP) and Open Shortest Path First (OSPF), access lists, Quality of Service (QoS) and multi-protocol routing of Internet Protocol (IP) and Internetwork Packet Exchange (IPX), as well as IP Multicast. This new line of switches will use a multi-layer form of switching called Cisco Express Forwarding (CEF).

Catalyst 5000

This series of switches (both the 5000 and 5500) are the former heavy-weight champions of Catalyst switches. Although the 5000 series has lost some of its luster in the wake of new advances in Gigabit technology, it is still widely deployed in LAN enterprises all over the world. Cisco is protecting this investment by introducing new modules that can take advantage of Gigabit EtherChannel and the latest in multilayer switching (MLS).

TIP

You may not want to consider the Catalyst 5000 when designing a new network. Although Cisco has been updating the features of the 5000 series to support Gigabit speeds and new forms of multilayer switching for companies that have spent a lot of money on a Catalyst 5000 infrastructure, there are now better solutions that can take advantage of the newest switching features. High cost, limited scalability, and newer switches are all better reasons to look at your network and determine if one of Cisco's 4000/6000/8500 series wouldn't do a better job of meeting the needs of your enterprise. These days, Cisco recommends the Catalyst 5000 switch as a wiring closet solution, and other switches like the 6000/8500 as backbone and core switches.

One thing that hasn't changed much is the list of available models for the Catalyst 5000 series. Although the Supervisor Engines and operating systems have changed to meet the networks of today, the chassis of the 5000 series has remained pretty stable. These are the switches available in the Catalyst 5000 series. Remember that all of the switches in the 5000 series (except for the 2948G, which is a separate beast in itself) require a Supervisor Engine in slot 1. The remaining slots may be filled with inter-changeable modules depending on which switch you are using and what you need. This section will cover the basics of the Catalyst 5000 series; the brains (the Supervisor Engine) are covered later in the chapter. The following models are currently available for the Catalyst 5000 series:

- The Catalyst 2900 series is a separate group of products that fall under the Catalyst 5000 classification. Almost all other 29xx products (non-XL) have been retired in favor of the new 2948G. Newer 29xx models that maintain Catalyst 5000 functionality while expanding into Gigabit and Layer 3 switching are coming out later in the year 2000.

- The Catalyst 5000 is a five-slot chassis that has a 1.2-Gbps switching fabric.

- The Catalyst 5002 has only two slots (one of which must be taken by a Supervisor Engine), but supports virtually any 5000 series module in the second slot at 1.2-Gbps switching speed.

- The Catalyst 5505 is also a five-slot chassis, but can support 3.6 Gbps in its backplane (instead of the 1.2 Gbps that the 5000 has).

- The Catalyst 5509 supports nine slots on 3.6 Gbps; it's essentially a bigger 5505.

- The Catalyst 5500 is the 13-slot Catalyst chassis with the standard 3.6-Gbps backplane and a separate 5 Gbps that supports ATM switching. The last slot is reserved for an ATM engine card and cannot be used for any other purpose.

Hardware Features of the Catalyst 2900 Series

As stated earlier, most of the 2900 series has been phased out, but we will review the basics of the hardware just in case it comes up. The 2900 series is based on the Catalyst 5000 series. It is a fixed-configuration series of switches that have built-in Supervisor Engines based on the Catalyst 5000 Supervisor Engine. Most of these switches have been retired, but the 2948G-L3 is a new switch introduced by Cisco that can use multilayer switching. It supports 48 ports in a 10/100BaseTX configuration, and two

GBIC ports at 1000BaseT. Essentially, this switch is a poor man's Catalyst 5002 with fixed configurations of 12 and 24 10/100BaseTX ports. The 2900 series has become very popular in that respect—it can be used as a substitute for the Catalyst 5000, since it operates in the same manner using the same IOS, but without the swappable modules.

Hardware Features of the Catalyst 5000/5002 Series

Most of the functions in a Catalyst 500x series switch take place in the Supervisor Engine, so those will be covered in the Supervisor Engine section. For basic hardware purposes, the 5000 series has a 1.2-Gbps backplane, but within modules, switching can take place at Gigabit speeds if those modules are supported (note that any switch traffic that has to go through the backplane will drop to the speed of the backplane). The 5000 series holds one Supervisor Engine and one slot for any ATM, Ethernet, FDDI, GBIC, or Route Switch Module (RSM) module. The 5005 has five slots (one for the Supervisor Engine, and four slots for whatever port modules you want). Both the 5000 and 5002 have two power supplies (one for backup), but the 5002's power supplies are internal.

Hardware Features of the Catalyst 5500 Series

The Catalyst 5500 is the top model of the 5xxx series. These switches support additional features like redundant and specialized Supervisor Engines and a 3.6-Gbps backplane (although not all the switches use the backplane in the same way).

> **NOTE**
>
> When dealing with the 55xx series, the Supervisor Engine *always* goes in slot 1. The backup Supervisor Engine *always* goes in slot 2. Furthermore, if a Supervisor module is to be a redundant one, it must be of the same type (II G with a IIG, IIIF with a IIIF). Also if you're using a 5500, the LS1010 ATM Switch modules *always* go in slots 9–12, and the ASP module *always* goes in slot 13. This is due to the structure of the backplane.

The 5505 is a pumped-up version of the 5000 with the extra 5500 features. The 5509 is a newer switch that supports up to nine slots on its switching backplane. The 5500 is the 13-slot switch that runs the series. On this particular switch, the backplane is structured a bit differently.

There are three separate 1.2-Gbps backplanes that are linked together through the application-specific integrated circuit (ASIC), and certain slots can only service certain backplanes. To further complicate matters, four slots are reserved for LS1010 modules (an ATM switch that can share modules with the 5500), and these modules use the 10-Gbps ATM Cell. Table 10.5 lists the various slots and buses, and which modules are allowed to connect to them.

Table 10.5 Slot/Module Configurations for the Catalyst 5500

Slot Number	Buses Used	Modules Allowed
1	Ethernet A,B,C	Supervisor module
2	Ethernet A,B,C	Backup Supervisor module or Line module
3–5	Ethernet A,B,C	Line modules
6–8	Ethernet B	Line module
9	Ethernet B, ATM cell	Either a Line module or LS1010 module
10–12	ATM cell	LS1010 modules
13	None	ASP module (an ATM switching module

Modules for the Catalyst 5000

Several modules are available for the Catalyst 5000, which can come in various configurations. This list is more of a general summary than a specific listing of every module. Furthermore, new modules are coming out all the time. What you need to know is the types of connections and technologies supported by the modules.

- 10BaseT and 10/100BaseTX for RJ-45 and RJ-21 ports
- 10BaseFL and 100BaseFX using SC fiber-optic connections
- Fast EtherChannel with 10/100BaseTX and 100BaseFX connections
- Gigabit EtherChannel with three linked or nine shared interfaces
- FDDI/Copper Distributed Data Interface (CCDI) modules with one interface
- ATM modules (supported on the 5500 switch)

- Token Ring

- An ATM Switch Processor (ASP) module for 5500 ATM switching (this is a special module just for the 5500, not the ASP module from the LS1010 switch)

- A new Network monitoring module for traffic analysis, RMON, and monitoring

Software Features of the Catalyst 5xxx Series

All of the features available on the previously discussed models are available with the Catalyst 5000. This includes, but is not limited to, Fast Uplink, Spanning Tree, ISL, Trunking, VLAN support, CDP, Remote Authentication Dial-in User Service (RADIUS) and TACACS+, RMON2 and SNMP capabilities, SPAN port mirroring, and LAN emulation (LANE). These are available on the 5000 series through the Supervisor module. In addition to that, new features that can be added to the Supervisor Engine series will permit multilayer switching and QoS functionality.

Catalyst 6000

The Catalyst 6000 switches are a new type of switch introduced by Cisco to provide large-scale Gigabit speeds (up to 256 Gbps) to campus and network backbones. They are modular solutions with their own model of Supervisor Engine. There are two series, each with two slot configurations: 6006, 6009, 6506, and 6509. The last number in each model is equal to the number of slots the switch has in the chassis. Again, one slot is reserved for the Supervisor Engine.

Hardware Features of the Catalyst 6xxx Series

The two models in the Catalyst 6xxx series (6000 and 6500) are virtually identical; the major difference is in the switching fabric. The 6000 series has a 32-Gbps backbone available for six or nine modules. This is more for the medium-sized campus/network backbone. For higher performance and speed, the 6500 series is recommended. This series has a scalable backbone of up to 256 Gbps (compare that to the Catalyst 5000, which has a 3.6-Gbps backbone). The construction of the 6500 series also allows for redundant switching fabric links.

The 6006 and 6506 switches have six slots each, with a Supervisor Engine going in slot 1 and a redundant Supervisor Engine if desired in slot 2. The 6009 and 6509 have nine slots each, with the Supervisor module in slot 1 and the redundant one in slot 2. As far as port modules go, the 6xxx series has the usual range of modules from which to choose.

There are GBIC modules that support 8 and 16 fully switched ports. There are single-port ATM OC-12 modules, and for high-density port configurations, there is a choice of 10/100BaseTX (48 ports in RJ-45 or RJ-21), 100BaseFX (24 ports), and 10FL (24 ports) modules. There is also a Multilayer Switch Module (MSM) for those who want multilayer switching but didn't buy the cards necessary for the Supervisor Engine. The MSM is different from the Catalyst 5000 RSM; it will not work in the Catalyst 5000, and the RSM will not work in the Catalyst 6000.

One thing to remember about this switch (and the 5000 series) is that although it is called a "multilayer" switch, you still need to have the two cards in the Supervisor Engine (MSFC and PFC) to make it a multilayer switch. If you throw in a Supervisor Engine without those cards or the Multilayer Switch Module, you won't have Layer 3 switching functionality for the Catalyst 6000. Otherwise, this switch has the high speeds necessary to service large campus backbones, and is a good choice for new networks that don't require legacy equipment.

Software Features of the Catalyst 6000 Series

Like the Catalyst 5000 series, the 6000 series has the core software functions handled by the Supervisor Engine. All the standard features of the Catalyst switches such as RMON, SNMP, SPAN, Syslog support, CDP, VLAN, VTP, and Fast EtherChannel/Gigabit EtherChannel are supported here. By adding Layer 3 functionality, either with an MSM or the MSFC/PFC combo, you can provide multilayer and multicast switching, routing protocols like OSPF and EIGRP, and QoS to your Catalyst 6000 switch. New features come out with each new IOS release, so keep up to date on the current Catalyst IOS software, and be sure to check what has been added with each new update.

Catalyst 8500

The Catalyst 8500 switches are designed to be the core switch at the center of the large-scale LAN/WAN network. They offer a scalable multilayer solution that uses Cisco Express Forwarding to get superior performance out of Layer 3 switching. Unlike the 5000/6000 series, this switch was designed to perform Layer 3 switching and routing out of the box. For this reason, it is often referred to as a *switch/router*, since it performs virtually all the functions of a router, and almost treats Layer 2 switching as a secondary feature. The Catalyst 8500 also takes advantage of new multilayer technology that will become standard in many future switches and routers.

Hardware Features of the 85xx Series

The 8500 switches are divided into two categories: the 8510, which comes with five slots, and the 8540, which comes with 13. Furthermore, each model comes with one of two designated functions: the Campus Switch Router (CSR) or Multiservice ATM switch router (MSR). The CSR comes with native Ethernet support and is primarily for Ethernet backbones; the MSR is for ATM backbones and supports ATM as the primary media. It is still possible to get some ATM support in the CSR series and Ethernet support in the MSR series, but the primary configuration of the 8500 series is established by whether it's a CSR or MSR. That means that Cisco is selling four different products for the 8500 series: the 8510 CSR, 8510 MSR, 8540 CSR, and 8540 MSR.

The heart of the 8500 series is the Switch Route Processor (SRP). This module is similar in function to the Supervisor module in the Catalyst 5000. However, it runs the Cisco IOS, and uses a new technology called Cisco Express Forwarding (CEF). CEF uses the routing table on the switch to compile two databases: a Forwarding Information Base (FIB) and an Adjacency table. The FIB is compiled from the Routing table. This maps a Layer 3 IP or IPX address to a port. The Adjacency table then maintains a Layer 2 next-hop address for each FIB entry. All of this is done in the SRP under the CEF design. The result is a large-scale L2/L3 CAM table (although you wouldn't call it a CAM table) that compiles information from IP addresses and can make switching decisions further up the OSI model.

However, one of the best features of CEF is the way information is distributed and used within the 8500 series. Once the SRP gets this database of L2/L3 routing information, it forwards it to a CEF-enabled application-specific integrated circuit (ASIC) on each line module (called the CEFA). This enables each line module to make the switching and routing decisions without having to go back to the SRP for decision-making and path determination. This does require a more sophisticated line module, but the result is that switching performance and knowledge transfer is more distributed. CEF is a new Cisco technology that is being developed for Cisco routers starting with IOS version 12.0.

WARNING

Unlike the Catalyst 5000 series, the SRP doesn't go in the first slot. On the 8510, the SRP goes in the middle slot (slot 2). On the 8540 series, the middle five slots (5–9) are reserved for SRPs, fabric modules, and redundant units. The SRP goes into slot 5 on the 8540.

In addition, there are two types of SRPs. The standard SRP supports Fast Ethernet, GBIC, and ATM uplinks. The multiservice switch route processor (MSRP) supports the same features as the SRP, along with ATM switching interface cards and ATM circuit emulation modules. Both the 8510 and 8540 can use either SRP in their architecture, and that choice is made depending on whether you are getting a CSR or MSR. Obviously, the CSR doesn't require the extra ATM features of the MSRP, but it's nice to know you can get that if you suddenly need to make a possibly catastrophic change to the core of the network (Translation: Management wants it tomorrow).

The 8510 series supports up to four separate eight-port Ethernet modules for 32 ports of 10/100BaseTX or 100BaseFX, or a one-port GBIC module that can give you four ports on the switch. The 8540 series can use a 16-port 100Base module and a two-port GBIC module for a total of 128 100BaseTX/FX ports or 16 Gigabit Ethernet ports spread out over eight slots. These modules would be used primarily in an 8500 CSR switch. The ATM modules range from TI/E1 ATM (1.5 Mbps) to OC-12 (622 Mbps). These modules are used in the 8500 MSR series.

The one thing that's tricky is the module configuration for the 8540 series. Three modules are needed: one SRP and two switching module fabrics. The SRP goes in line 5 (with the redundant one going in slot 9), and the processor fabrics go in slots 6 and 8 (with a spare in slot 7). You need all three of these modules to get the 8540 up and running. This gives the 8540 a backplane of 40 Gbps. The 8510 series has an integrated switching fabric that can sustain 10 Gbps. That's why even though it has half the available slots of an 8540, it requires separate modules with only half the port densities. The switching fabric on the 8510 is only one-quarter that of the 8540.

Software Features of the 8500 Series

Because the Catalyst 8500 uses hardware to perform many of its switching functions, much of the software in an 8500 is dedicated to the Cisco IOS and routing information. The 8500 series supports IP, IPX, IP Multicast, and IOS routing protocols such as OSPF and EIGRP. It can also perform VLANs, SNMP, RMON, SPAN, CDP, and other routing functions such as Remote Access Security using TACACS+ and RADIUS.

Catalyst 12000 GSR Switches

The 12000 series is a full-sized solution for Gigabit switching. They are designed to take WAN technologies like Frame Relay, Cable, ATM, and so forth, and convert this traffic to the IP Gigabit switching fabric. There are three models: the 12008, 12012, and 12016.

The important thing to remember about these "switches" is that GSR stands for Gigabit Switching Router. Like the 8500, these Catalyst products are really designed to be routers that switch as a secondary feature. In fact, a check of Cisco's Web site will have them labeled primarily under the Router section. This appears to be a trend that Cisco will follow in the future as they seek to blend the technologies of routing and switching into common products.

Supervisor Modules

The Catalyst 4000/5000/6000 series rely on Supervisor modules (also called Supervisor Engines and the Supervisor II or III) to do their processing. The Supervisor module is the brain of a Catalyst 4000/5000/6000 switch, and you will need one for each switch you are using in your network. In the past, Supervisor Engines were simple devices that ran the switching software and functions. Now, more features and additional functionality are being added to them to increase support for multilayer switching. At the same time, Cisco is discontinuing some of the older models because prices are going down on the newer ones, and no one wants to buy an obsolete product.

Most Supervisor Engines have status, power supply, reset, and informational LEDs on the front of their display, as well as a Console port for Out-of-Band management. Each Supervisor module also has either uplink ports built into them, or a module slot that can support one of several uplink modules. Most devices use either the Supervisor Engine II or III, but some switches (like the 4003) use a Supervisor Engine I. However, the Supervisor modules are not the same from Catalyst platform to platform, and a Supervisor I in a Catalyst 5000 is not the same as a Supervisor I in a Catalyst 4000. It's confusing because they have the same name, but it is important to note that these modules are not interchangeable within families of Catalyst switches. For example, you could use a Supervisor II module in any 5500 switch, but don't swap it with the 4006's Supervisor II module.

The Supervisor module is responsible for the IOS, memory, routing, VLANs, configuration, and just about anything else that you can imagine on a Catalyst switch. For that reason, they are focused on separately from the switches, and several models of Supervisor Engines exist for each series depending upon your needs, budget, and previous investment.

Catalyst 5000 Supervisor Modules

The Catalyst 5000 was the first switch that introduced the concept of the Supervisor module for most people, so it seems fitting to start here. There are several models of the Supervisor module: I, II, and III. In addition, there are new enhanced Supervisor modules that can support multilayer switching using daughter cards that are installed on the Supervisor module.

The Supervisor I card is the original card. This module (along with the II series) can handle 16,000 MAC address and 1024 VLANs. It is only capable of performing Layer 2 switching and even then, it won't work correctly with the 5500 series. This engine was really only for the 5000 series. This card was discontinued in 1999, and although it has pretty much been retired, you may see one around. There is a Console port on the front for configuration, and there are models with 10/100BaseTX and 100BaseFX connections for uplinks. The Supervisor II supports the same features as the Supervisor I, but works with the 5500 switches—although it may not be able to use all the available bandwidth. It also has some built-in redundancy in the engine and clock. From a packet performance, however, the Supervisor II can switch three times the amount of packets as the Supervisor I, so there is a definite improvement in performance.

In an effort to provide multilayer switching capabilities to the Supervisor II series, Cisco came out with the Supervisor II G. This engine has most of the same features as the II, but comes with an onboard NetFlow Feature Card II (NFFC II), and can host a Route Switch Feature Card (RSFC). Cisco has also upgraded the processor from 25 MHz to a 37.5 Motorola processor. All these extra features allow the Supervisor II G to perform multilayer switching. The II G also features a modular uplink port instead of the fixed uplinks on the Supervisor I and II. Therefore, you can change and reconfigure your uplinks on the Supervisor II G without replacing the whole engine. It is important to note that Cisco has announced an end-of-life (EOL) for this product (meaning it will be retired and support will be discontinued within five years), and future switches will use the Supervisor III and III G.

The one thing to note about the Supervisor II series is that there are major issues using this module with Catalyst 5500 switches. The Supervisor II and II G can support only a 1.2-Gbps backplane, making this a wasteful investment for the 5500 switch that uses a 3.6-Gbps backplane. In these circumstances, you want to use the Supervisor III.

The Supervisor III series is the workhorse of the Supervisor Engines. It can support the NFCC, which with a Route Switch Module or external router can support Layer 3 switching. This engine also has the modular slot for the uplinks and has a processor that runs at 150 MHz. The Supervisor III can also support the full 3.6-Gbps backplane of the Catalyst 5500.

Cisco has released two cheaper versions of the Supervisor module: the Supervisor III F and the III G. The Supervisor III F isn't quite as fast as the III, but can still use a NFFC II card for multilayer switching. It has fixed GBIC uplinks instead of the modular slot, so if you know what you need before you buy the module, this may be a good economical choice.

The Supervisor III G was designed primarily for wiring closet applications, but has been designed with the latest in Cisco technology. For example, the NFFC II is already integrated into the card, and there is a slot available for the Route Switch Feature Card (RSFC). This same card is used for the Supervisor II G, and can provide the same router functionality as an RSM, but without using a module in the switch. This frees up an extra slot that might have been previously taken by a RSM module. Like the Supervisor III, this Engine has modular uplinks for flexibility, and performs at nearly the same level as the III F. This makes the Supervisor III G a better choice for most Catalyst 5000s.

Since there are more models of the Supervisor Engine for the 5000 series than any other switch, it's important to be familiar with all the features of all the Supervisor Engines.

Catalyst 4000 Supervisor Modules

The Catalyst 4003 and 4006 use a special form of Supervisor module designed for the 4000 series. The 4003 has a status light, Ethernet port, console port, reset button, and a load status LED display. It supports the 12-Gbps switching fabric required for the 4003. The 4006 is similar to the 4003, but also has two GBIC uplink ports and can support the 32 Gbps required for the 4006. These are sometimes called Supervisor Engine I (4003) and Supervisor Engine II (4006) in some documentation, but that can be confusing, as they aren't the same modules as the Catalyst 5000 Supervisor modules, so it's best just to know them as the 4003 and 4006 Supervisor modules.

Catalyst 6000 Supervisor Modules

The Catalyst 6000 series use a Supervisor Engine I, which is only for the Catalyst 6000 series. Again, don't confuse this module with the old and dated Supervisor Engine I for the Catalyst 5000. Unlike the Catalyst 4000 series, both the 6006 and 6009 can share the same Supervisor Engine between the two models. Like most Supervisor modules, the front of the module has the Console port, status LEDs, and a reset button. There is also a PCMCIA (Personal Computer Memory Card International Association) slot on the front of the Supervisor Engine that can take flash memory, and it can come with two fixed configuration GBIC slots for

Gigabit Ethernet uplinks. This Supervisor Engine can support the 32- to 256-Gbps backplane required for the Catalyst 6000 series. There is a subset of the Supervisor Engine I, called the I-A. This module comes with extras like a Policy Feature Card, Multiswitch Feature Card, or both, depending upon the model number.

Catalyst 8500 Supervisor Modules

Technically, the 8500 series doesn't use a Supervisor module; it actually requires the Switch Route Processor (SRP), but since that is similar to what the Supervisor modules do, we'll take a moment to review it. There is SRP for Ethernet and Gigabit switching in a Campus Switch Router like the 8510 CSR or 8540 CSR, and the multiservice ATM switch route processor (MSRP) for ATM switching in a 8510 MSR or 8540 MSR. These run the Cisco IOS and perform the routing functions of the router/switch, such as maintaining the routing table. The SRP/MSRP also uses Cisco Express Forwarding to compile the Forwarding Information Base and Adjacency tables. The SRP/MSRP then forwards this information to the CEF ASIC on the Line module.

Route-Switching Modules

Routing does several tasks that are different from switching. Routing actually involves breaking the network down into a hierarchical structure. It forms segments based on network addresses, and depending upon the destination, may rewrite the packet and ship from segment to segment. Switching is a Layer 2 function that usually performs a straight point-to-point connection based on the MAC address. This creates a flat network design that can become unwieldy. As a result, VLANs are used to separate the switched network into logical segments. Switching won't function between these points, so a routing solution is required to move these packets from segment to segment. Cisco has several solutions for packet routing, although most of these are now less favorable compared to the multilayer switching features of newer Cisco switches. This section will focus on some of the routing technologies used by Cisco in the Catalyst switches.

Router-on-a-Stick

This is a tongue-in-cheek term for a router that is attached to a Catalyst network and performs the routing functions for those switches. You attach a router to the network, and all the VLANs connect to the backbone that the router connects to. The packets then go to the router, are routed, and sent back down the backbone to whatever VLAN is receiving the packet. This is still done quite frequently, but it is less favorable than an integrated solution. You could use this solution with virtually any switched network that supports it, but since it requires a separate link to every VLAN, it's not very feasible for large networks. There are also router limitations. At this time, the router-on-a-stick only works with certain routers in the 4000 and 7000 series.

RSM

The RSM is the Route Switch Module. This module uses a slot within a switch and runs the Cisco IOS software. This puts the switching solution into the switch and integrates directly into the backplane, thus avoiding the congestion that may come from several separate interfaces or one trunked line. This solution is not Layer 3 switching, so instead of getting millions of packets per second, you may get only thousands. Still, it's a good solution for wiring closets and small/medium scale networks serviced by the Catalyst 5000. This solution can be used with a NetFlow Feature Card to perform multilayer routing.

NOTE

Remember that Layer 2 switching goes straight from source to destination address without rewriting the packet, but Layer 3 routing rewrites the source and destination address when sending a packet. Layer 3 switching is designed to rewrite these fields like a router does, while maintaining the switching functionality and speed of a Layer 2 switching solution.

RSFC/MSFC

These cards usually aren't used without their MLS counterparts, but if a Cisco IOS with routing functionality is required, the Route Switch Feature Card (Catalyst 5000) and Multilayer Switch Feature Card (Catalyst 6000) could supply routing functionality. If you spend the money for this, however, you might as well get the additional pieces required for MLS switching.

Available Switch Platforms

The RSM is available only for the Catalyst 5000 series. The router-on-a-stick technique can be performed with virtually any switch, although high-level routers like the Cisco 7500 are needed for some of the features. This technology is less important, as multilayer switching has become the standard over just routing packets.

Multilayer Switching Modules

Cisco has surpassed the RSM with the latest in multilayer switching. New daughter cards, modules, and integrated hardware combine the structured approach of Layer 3 routing with the speed of Layer 2 switching. Although there are many approaches and forms of implementation, you need to meet the two requirements of Layer 3 switching to call it multilayer:

Multilayer Switching Route Processor (MLS-RP) This component runs on the Cisco IOS software and controls all the routing features for the switch. This can include an RSM.

Multilayer Switching Switch Engine (MLS-SE) This component runs on hardware and performs the switching functions on the switch.

It's also important to remember that routing requires that changes be made to a packet that aren't made during switching. This can include the source and destination address. In a flat-switched network, the packet already heads straight from one to the other, but on a router, you have to rewrite the packet as it goes through default gateways and is forwarded. Multilayer switching can rewrite these packets, and this qualifies the process as multilayer switching.

NFFC/RSFC

The NetFlow Feature Card (NFFC) and the next-generation NFFC II are the solution for Catalyst 5000 switches that need the MLS-SE solution for their switches. The NFFC is able to identify, rewrite, and switch packets at the third layer of the OSI model. It is usually a daughter card that works on the Supervisor Engine of the Catalyst 5000. However, the new G series of the Catalyst Engine builds the NFFC straight into the Supervisor Engine. You still need something to serve as a route processor. This solution can include an RSM, router-on-a-stick, or the new Route Switch Feature Card.

The Route Switch Feature Card (RSFC) is a card that performs the same functions as a router or RSM. It can maintain routing tables, protocols, and access lists. Instead of running as a module, it runs in the daughter card slot of a Catalyst 5000 (which will be free on the G series because the NFFC is built into the card). When you want a tight, integrated solution, this is the card to buy. Otherwise, it is acceptable to use any of the router technologies as long as routing functions can take place.

MSM

The Multilayer Switch Module (MSM) is the module designed for all-in-one multilayer switching in the Catalyst 6000 series. This module works in any slot, and can be installed with a redundant backup if desired.

To perform multilayer switching, the MSM throws both the MLS-RP and MLS-SE on the module. The MSM is capable of IP/IPX/IP multicast routing and can use the OSPF/EIGRP/IGRP (Interior Gateway Routing Protocol) routing protocols. The MSM is also capable of handling several other IP protocols, such as IPX SAPs, Dynamic Host Configuration protocol (DHCP), and BOOTstrap Protocol (BOOTP). At the same time, the hardware-based ASICs run the switching engine and take the pressure off the IOS. This solution can provide wire-speed Layer 3 switching to the Catalyst 6000 series. It plugs straight into the backplane and can take full advantage of the switching fabric. However, if you really want or need that module space, then a second solution is needed: one that can take the routing decisions out of the module.

MSFC/PFC

The Multilayer Switch Feature Card (MSFC) is the card that does for the 6000 what the RSFC does for the Catalyst 5000. The MSFC runs a full-featured Cisco IOS on a coupled card that attaches to the Supervisor Engine of the Catalyst 6000. To really get multilayer switching, you also need the Policy Feature Card (PFC). This card holds the advanced features that rewrite a packet for Layer 3 switching. When these two cards are put together, you have a multilayer switching solution that binds directly to the Supervisor module and frees up another slot on the 6000 series for whatever module you need.

Route Switch Processor for the 8500

This is the RSP for the 8500 series. It was covered in the previous two sections. What's important to know here is that this is the only thing you need for the multilayer solution in the 8500 series; no special cards or modules are needed to add this function to the 8500. In fact, the 8500 is essentially a router with advanced switching built in. This multilayer switching solution will become the norm for many future Cisco products, as many customers will want multilayer capabilities already built in. Future switches like the 4908G-L3 are already starting to incorporate Layer 3 switching directly into the Catalyst IOS and hardware.

Available Switch Platforms

Multilayer switching technology is available for the Catalyst 5000, 6000, and 8500 series. In some new switches, it is available for the Catalyst 4000 series—specifically, the 4908G-L3. Each switching family has its own hardware requirements to bring the switch up to MLS standards.

On the Catalyst 4908G and the 8500 series, the IOS and hardware for multilayer switching are already built into the switch; no additional daughter cards or Supervisor modules are needed. In addition, the new features of Cisco Express Forwarding (CEF) ensure that traffic is passed quickly from port to port without having to consult the Supervisor Engine. With their integrated hardware and advanced switching technology, the 4908G and 8500 switches are among the fastest and most advanced switches in the Catalyst product line.

In the Catalyst 5000 series, the components for multilayer switching need to be added. The NetFlow Feature Card provides much of the switching engine component for multilayer switching. This card serves as the MLS-SE, providing the packet rewrite features and switching ASIC necessary to obtain faster speeds. To provide router functionality and the MLS-RP component, the 5000 series can use a Route Switch Module, a Route Switch Feature Card, or an external router to perform the routing duties and maintain the IOS information. The RSM attaches inside the Catalyst 5000, the RSFC works as a daughter card inside the Supervisor module, and the External router solution would be a Cisco router that hooks into the backbone and VLANs of the switched network.

In the Catalyst 6000 series, there are two solutions. One is the complete package that comes with the Multilayer Switch Module. This module provides both MLS components in one package. It will require one slot within the switch, so this may not be the best solution if you require high port densities. On the other hand, if what is needed is a fast and easy solution that can be implemented without pulling out the Supervisor Engine and loading it full of cards, then this is the solution. Otherwise, two cards can be added to the Catalyst 6000 Supervisor Engine to make it MLS compliant. The Multilayer Switch Feature Card (MSFC) will provide the MLS-RP, and the Policy Feature Card will provide the MLS-SE features.

Cisco Switches and Windows 2000

OK, so this is all great information and now we know all we need to know about the Cisco switching lines of equipment. The question now is: how does all this affect my Windows 2000 architecture? Well, the real answer is that in order to use all of the feature-rich QoS integration with Active Directory and all of the built-in security between Cisco and Microsoft technologies, you need to have one thing for each and every Windows-based machine on the network—each machine must have its own switched port.

The trick to choosing which switch is the right one for your needs on your Windows network is to ask the following questions:

1. How much port capacity do I need on the segment of the network in question?

2. How fast does that port have to be to accommodate the level of traffic that will be going to that node on the network?

3. Will I be using multiple VLANs on that segment?

4. Will I need to increase or decrease the number of ports on the segment any time in the future?

5. How much versatility does the segment need (fiber, copper, 100Mb, 10Mb, 1000Mb) from its ports?

6. Is this a core, distribution, or access switch, and how much backplane does the segment require?

By using the material throughout the chapter you can determine what is the best type of switch and the type of ports you need to connect all of the various nodes of the network. The important thing to remember is this: When it comes to Windows 2000 networks, all nodes need to be switched in order for Windows 2000 and Cisco devices to handle all of the integrated features. If the ports are on shared media (otherwise known as a hub) then the QoS and security features will cease to work for the nodes in question.

Always design your network with *only* switches in mind for node connectivity and you will be fine with Windows 2000. Active Directory works by allocating bandwidth right down to the port level—this can be done only with the use of switched ports. All of the features described in this chapter relate to Cisco interactions with other Cisco devices, and as long as you are in a completely switched environment there is nothing to worry about with Windows 2000 connectivity.

If you do happen to have some hubs out there, make sure that they are isolated from the rest of the network by using VLANs. That way, the shared media will not affect the switch caching of the overall network and thus will not slow down the network in any way. Keep in mind that the hub-based nodes will not be able to use QoS or security tie-ins with Active Directory—*do not* try to activate QoS on these nodes, as you will only cause administrative nightmares.

Case Studies

To complete our Cisco infrastructure we now need to add in the appropriate switches at the appropriate locations to finish off our high-speed networking designs.

ABC Chemical Company

At the main site of ABC Chemical Company, we have a clustered set of switches that allow for high-speed access to the server environments as well as connectivity to the local users. The servers will be allocated to their own VLANs to prevent the propagation of server communications and broadcast traffic to their own virtual segment. The user community can be spread out among other VLANs as appropriate, but for the sake of clarity (not to make a mess out of the case study) we will stick to the types of switches that would be deployed at the locations already defined.

ABC Chemical Company is using Cisco 6505 switches at the core in tri-angular configuration (see Figure 10.1). This provides for redundancy and reliability at the core. The central switch is also enabled with a MSFC card to allow for Layer 3 switching throughout the network using VLANs. Spanning Tree technology controls the possibility of redundant paths and potential network loops throughout the switched network.

At the remote sites we deploy 3500 series switches. This allows for the amount of capacity at each site while saving on overall costs.

West Coast Accounting, L.L.C.

West Coast Accounting has essentially the same switching requirements as ABC Chemical Company, only more interfaces and less redundancy are needed at the core site (see Figure 10.2). A Cisco 6505 with an MFSC card to allow for Layer 3 switching is used at the core site, which will accommodate all of the port capacity and needs of the server environment. The user community switches are not shown, because depending on the port capacity needs, these ports may just be VLANed off of the 6505s blades and isolated from the server traffic.

Cisco 3500-XL switches are utilized at the remote sites to allow for future expandability and added capacity.

Figure 10.1 ABC Chemical Company's switching and routing infrastructure.

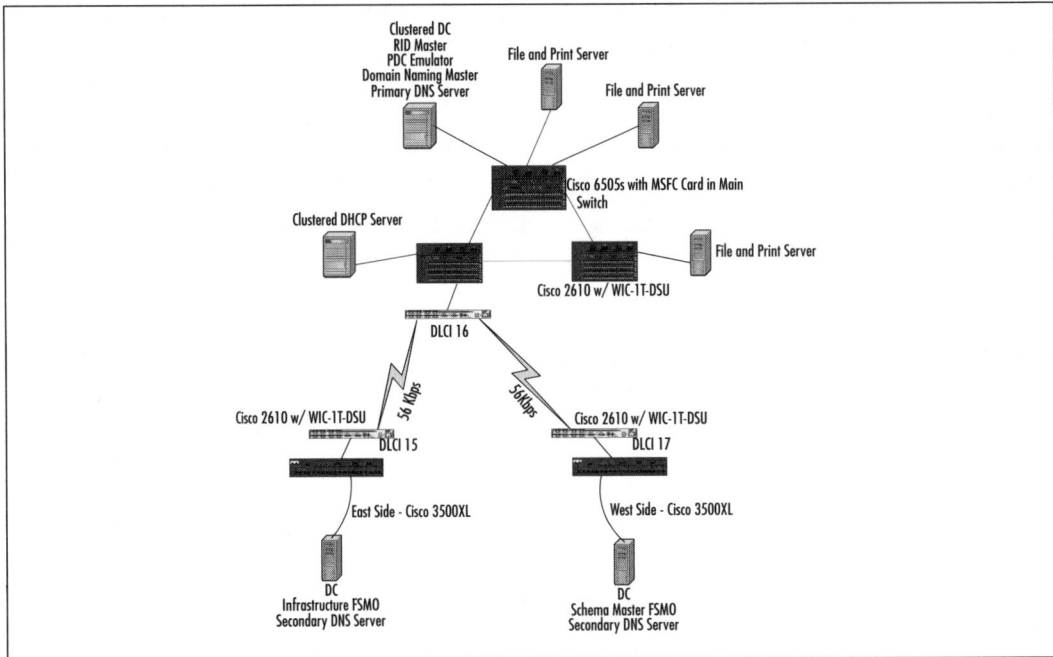

Figure 10.2 West Coast Accounting's switching and routing infrastructure.

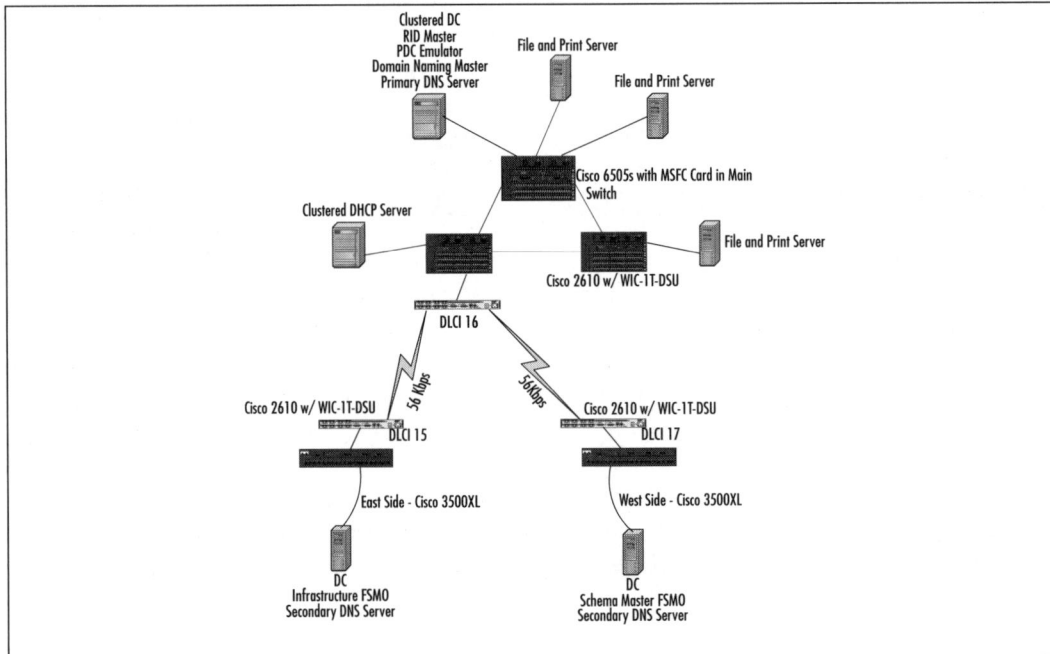

Summary

The center of the campus/corporate LAN is the switching network. Cisco offers many solutions to your switching requirements by offering several types of Catalyst switches for everything from the workgroup environment to the campus backbone. The 1900, 2820, 2900XL, and 3500XL series are designed for small wiring closets and workgroup situations where you need many ports in one location at the edge or end of a LAN. In the backbone, Cisco has Catalyst products like the 4000, 5000, and 6000 series. The Catalyst 5000 series is a standard workhorse for the backbone, but also works well in large-scale wiring closets where many ports are needed. At the same time, Cisco has implemented Gigabit Ethernet technology in the 4000 and 6000 series to get much higher speeds out of the LAN environment. At the core layer, Cisco has designed the 8500 series, a routing switch that can perform all the routing features of a Cisco router, while implementing a new form of multilayer switching called Cisco Express Forwarding.

Switches are separated into VLANs, and VLANs need to be able to direct packets in between them. Initially, Cisco came up with the RSM and router-on-a-stick. This would allow packets to be routed if necessary between networks and VLANs. The problem was that this resulted in slower performance, as it takes much longer to route and rewrite a packet at Layer 3 than it does to switch it. As a result, Cisco began working on multilayer switching, which could take control of a packet and switch it at the network layer. This results in much faster performance. Multilayer switching has two components: a card or feature that runs IOS and routing, called the Multilayer Switching Route Processor (MLS-RP), and another card/feature that does multilayer switching and packet rewriting at the hardware level, called the Multilayer Switching Switch Engine (MLS-SE). Switches like the 4000, 5000, and 6000 are capable of becoming multilayer switches, whereas models like the 8500 and the 4908G-L3 already come with MLS features designed in the hardware.

As networks become more bandwidth intensive and applications like multicast become more common, the traditional network design of switches that are separated by routers becomes less appealing. Instead, the new campus network design would use Layer 3 switches that can pass traffic much faster than before, yet are still capable of reading and writing at Layer 3.

Always use switches instead of hubs in a Windows 2000 network, otherwise you will lose all of the special functionality that Microsoft and Cisco have built into the systems to use QoS and security features together right down to the node level.

FAQs

Q: What commands are most appropriate for use on a Catalyst 5000?

A: Set Port duplex and **Show config**. The Catalyst 5000 series uses the set-based IOS configuration commands **set** and **show**.

Q: Are there any switching features that would interfere with Windows 2000 traffic and operations that I need to consider in my designs?

A: The most important feature to keep in mind, especially when working with redundant networks topologies, is Spanning Tree Protocol (STP). Make sure that you program the proper weighting factors to redundant ports on your Windows 2000 network to prevent STP "bouncing," which can wreak havoc on your Active Directory. This is a symptom of two ports having the same cost and going to the same redundant link, thus making STP bounce back and forth between them as the optimal route. By adding in the appropriate weighting parameters, you avoid bouncing conditions.

Q: Which Catalyst switches can be used in a switch cluster?

A: The Catalyst 3500XLs can be used as a Command switch and the Catalyst 1924s can be used as a Member switch.

Q: Which modules can I put in slot 2 of a Catalyst 5500 switch?

A: Either a redundant Supervisor Engine or line module can go in slot 2.

Q: What is the best way to ensure that my Catalyst 5000 doesn't go down in case of Supervisor Engine failure?

A: A redundant Supervisor Engine can be installed as a backup, but only in slot 2.

Q: What are the two components required for multilayer switching?

A: The two components of MLS are the Multilayer Switching-Route Processor (MLS-RP), and the Multilayer Switching-Switching Engine (MLS-SE).

Q: The Cisco 7500 router that my company uses for the entire network is being replaced. If we are to put in a switching/routing solution that could hook into an Ethernet backbone, what should we use?

A: The Catalyst 8500 CSR series can handle all the features and functions of a core router, and the CSR series is optimized for Ethernet backbones.

Q: Our fiber-optic backbone is acting up, and management wants to replace it with a high-speed Ethernet solution. What should I suggest?

A: The Catalyst 6000 series with Gigabit Ethernet and multilayer switching can serve as a replacement for backbone routers.

Chapter 11

Implementing the Windows 2000 Servers

Solutions in this chapter:

- **Understand the installation options for Windows 2000**

- **Installing Windows 2000 Active Directory**

- **Configuring services on Windows 2000 servers**

Introduction

Network infrastructure can be dissected into three layers:

- Backbone
- Shared systems or the security layer
- Workstation systems or the access layer

The infrastructure backbone is a high-speed freeway for data transmission. All network segments should be capable of accessing the network backbone, even if they are not directly attached to that backbone.

A backbone can exist within each building or campus of a global network, and then a connection to other buildings or campuses leads off of it. The backbone does not have computers directly attached to it. It should not connect directly to the Internet or any other public network. It should not have any extraneous applications or security filters preventing traffic from flowing speedily through it. Routers are the main backbone infrastructure components.

The shared systems area represents all the network segments that connect directly to the backbone. These segments have significant security placed upon them, with firewalls, access list filters, and login authentication required. Connections to public networks and the Internet should occur in this area. Servers are connected to these segments, as well as any secured resources. You will find routers and high-speed switches at this level.

The access layer of the internetwork represents each segment that includes workstations and workgroup printers. These segments are connected to the shared systems segments, making them two hops down from the backbone. You should find only hubs, switches, and bridges at this level.

So where does Windows 2000 fit into all of this? Windows 2000 (all versions) is a network operating system. It was designed to work on a network and to interact with other computers. This interaction—whether it is logging on, looking for resources, using a database, accessing a mainframe, reading e-mail, sending print jobs to a network printer, Web browsing, or downloading files from a server—consumes bandwidth by causing traffic on the network. You will need to implement your Windows 2000 servers while considering how Windows 2000 usage will affect your network. The design that you have started with will take shape, but you need to remain flexible enough to test that design and to ensure that the results meet your business requirements.

Installing Windows 2000

Windows 2000 installation is not a difficult process to undertake. In fact, it is fairly simple to install Windows 2000 directly from the installation program. If you intend to roll out multiple Windows 2000 Professional workstations, however, you should investigate unattended installation methods either using a script or disk duplication:

- Unattend.txt
- SYSPREP
- RIPREP

Automating Windows 2000 installation is one way to save costs. Automating the installation significantly reduces the time spent at each workstation or server, and only a minor amount of time is spent in a lab creating the automated setup. The method of installation should be selected according to your environment. When you have multiple types of hardware, a scripted installation probably will be best. If you have a few workstations, then a disk duplication method is best. For remote installation, you need to make certain that your workstations are equipped with the right network interface cards and you have a spare Windows 2000 server available.

Workstation installations can be automated either way; however, it is typical for servers to be installed in an attended mode. There are times when scripting a server installation makes sense:

- Server hardware is standardized
- Operating system configuration is standardized
- Many different people can install servers

When hardware or operating system configurations are standardized, then automating an installation of the operating system becomes a time saver. When several different people are installing your servers, then automation ensures a standard result, avoids errors, reduces the need for assistance, and saves time overall. (You can find in-depth coverage of installing Windows 2000 in the book *Deploying Windows 2000 with Support Tools* published by Syngress Media.)

Overview of a Scripted Installation

Windows 2000 inherits the same scripted capabilities that Windows NT included. An administrator can create a custom script to answer the Setup executable's questions so that there is no user input needed. A sample script called unattend.txt can be used for testing how scripts work. The script sometimes is called an *answer file* because it answers setup questions.

TIP
_____

> Many people use the name *unattend.txt* for their scripts, although they do not have to. As long as the correct script name is used in the setup command parameters, then the script will execute. If you roll out Windows 2000 on different types of hardware, it may be more useful to include some abbreviation for the hardware as part of the script name. For example, if you are installing Windows 2000 on HP Vectras, then you could have a vectra.txt script.

The unattend.txt script is typical of an installation script in that it contains various sections that supply information for the installation. Each section has a section heading *[section]* followed by parameters and their values in the form of *parameter=value*.

You can create a script using two different methods:

- Manually, where you edit a text file and type the various section headings and parameter/value pairs

- Using Setup Manager, where you use the Setup Manager application, found in the CD:\support\tools\deploy.cab file, to configure a script and output the text file

There are two ways of executing Windows 2000 setup. The executable that you select is entirely dependent on the operating system currently running on the machine. If using DOS, then the command is WINNT.EXE with the following parameters:

```
Winnt /S:PathToSourceFiles /T:TempDriveLetter /U:YourScriptFile
```

If you are using a 32-bit version of Windows (Windows 95, Windows 98, Windows NT), the command is WINNT32.EXE with the following parameters:

```
Winnt32 /s:PathToSourceFiles /tempdrive:TempDriveLetter /unattend:
YourScriptFile
```

There are additional parameters for both of these setup executables, described in Table 11.1.

Not only can the Windows 2000 installation be automated, it can prompt additional application installations. The administrator can add commands using cmdlines.txt, or the administrator can place a setup file (or batch file containing multiple setup files within it) in the [GuiRunOnce] section of the answer file. In addition, the administrator can run the Windows Installer Service for any compatible applications, or use a third-party tool that is intended to automate an application's installation.

Table 11.1 Windows 2000 Setup File Switches

Command	Parameter	Used For	Example
Winnt	/S	States the source location for the Windows 2000 installation files	/S:e:\i386
Winnt	/T	States the location for temporary files used during the installation process	/T:d
Winnt	/U	States the name of the script file	/U:e:\myscript.txt
Winnt	/R[x]	Identifies a directory to be created, or copied if using the "x" parameter	/R:c:\myfolder
Winnt	/E	Executes a command after Windows 2000 is installed	/E:e:\myfile.exe
Winnt32	/s	States the source location for the Windows 2000 installation files; up to 8 separate /s switches can be used to provide multiple source file locations	/s:e:\i386
Winnt32	/tempdrive	States the location for temporary files used during the installation process	/tempdrive:d

Continued

Table 11.1 Continued

Command	Parameter	Used For	Example
Winnt32	/unattend	States the name of the script file	/unattend:e:\ myscript.txt
Winnt32	/copydir	Copies a directory of files on the hard drive	/copydir:c:\myfolder
Winnt32	/copysource	States the source directory to be copied	/copysource:e:\myfold
Winnt32	/cmd	Executes a command after Windows 2000 is installed	/cmd:e:\myfile.exe
Winnt32	/debug	Runs the Windows 2000 installation in debug mode	/debug
Winnt32	/udf:[id]	Pulls the specific information related to the given id out of a file with multiple users' information	/udf:jmar,e:\udf.txt
Winnt32	/syspart	Creates the system partition on the stated drive letter	/syspart:d
Winnt32	/noreboot	Suppresses a PC from restarting	/noreboot
Winnt32	/makelocalsource	Copies source files to the local drive	/makelocalsource
Winnt32	/checkupgradeonly	Determines whether the given PC can be upgraded	/checkupgradeonly
Winnt32	/m	Copies replacement files from a different source location first and, if files are not present, uses files from the default location	/m:c:\folder

Overview of Disk Duplication Methods

You can use two different types of disk duplication methods for Windows 2000. Although they are nearly identical as far as the Windows 2000 setup method, the setup initialization is completely different. Disk duplication is a good choice for identically installed workstations—applications and settings included.

SYSPREP

SYSPREP is the short form of System Preparation, which refers to the process of preparing a Windows 2000 Professional system (SYSPREP does not work with the Server versions of Windows 2000) for duplication on multiple computers. SYSPREP disk duplication is a spectacularly shorter process than a scripted installation. Not only that, but it works in conjunction with third-party disk duplication applications. The process is straightforward:

1. Select a master computer that uses the same hardware (specifically, the same Hardware Access Layer (HAL), Advanced Configuration and Power Interface (ACPI), and storage controllers) as the system on which you will be duplicating Windows 2000. If you are using SYSPREP v1.1, it is not necessary to have identical storage controllers. Instead, you can specify storage controllers in the sysprep.inf file.

2. Install Windows 2000 on the master computer.

3. Install applications on the master computer that you will want on all the duplicated computers.

4. Configure desktop and system settings that should appear on each of the duplicated computers.

5. Remove data that you do not want to be copied to the target computers, such as temporary Internet files, log files, document histories, pagefile.sys (pagefile.sys can be deleted from the image only at a DOS prompt, not while the system is running and loaded into RAM), etc. Copy the sysrep.exe, sysprep.inf, and setupcl.exe files from the Windows 2000 CD:\Support\tools\deploy.cab file to C:\SYSPREP folder.

6. Verify that the Windows 2000 image is exactly what you want to appear on all duplicated computers.

7. Run SYSPREP on the master computer. SYSPREP can be run with three parameters: -quiet runs SYSPREP without user prompts. -nosidgen runs SYSPREP but doesn't keep the Security Identifiers (SIDs) that were on the master computer. -reboot runs SYSPREP

with an automatic restart when SYSPREP has completed. If you are running SYSPREP v1.1, you have an additional parameter, -pnp, which forces Plug and Play to discover new hardware on the next reboot.

8. Boot the computer from a floppy disk and connect to a server. Copy the contents of the master computer's hard drive to the server.

9. Connect to the server from the target computers and copy the image down to the hard drive.

10. Starting the target computers will run SETUPC1.EXE to generate new SIDs for the target computers and to start the mini-setup wizard. (The mini-setup wizard can be automated with the sysprep.inf. It prompts the user for the license agreement, regional settings, and other configuration information.)

TIP

Many of the tools needed to deploy Windows 2000 are not part of the Windows 2000 operating system. Some tools can be found on the Windows 2000 CD in the Support\Tools directory and are installed by running the setup file in that directory. Others can be found on Microsoft's Web site under Windows 2000 downloads. www.microsoft.com/windows2000/downloads/deployment/sysprep/ is the location for downloading the SYSPREP tool.

RIPREP

RIPREP is the executable associated with the Remote Operating System installation. This is a disk duplication method that uses a Pre-boot-Execution-Environment (PXE)-capable network interface card on the target computer, and a Remote Installation Service (RIS) running on a server. The RIS server can deliver an image to a workstation without anyone having to boot the target computer with a boot disk, as you would have to use with the SYSPREP method.

The same hardware limitations for SYSPREP apply to RIPREP—the HAL, ACPI, and storage controllers must be identical for the master and target computers. It is likely that many images will be needed for an enterprise that has multiple hardware types. In addition, if different users require different application sets, then multiple images will be required. RIS requires the service to be running on a Windows 2000 server. The RIS process is as follows:

1. The Remote Operating System Installation service is installed on a Windows 2000 server.

2. A master computer is selected, and Windows 2000 is installed on it. The master computer is the one that you will be duplicating on other computers.

3. Applications are installed on the master computer.

4. Settings and configuration changes are made to the master computer.

5. The image is validated.

6. RIPREP is run on the master computer to package the image for delivery.

7. The RIS server is configured to provide the image to target computers.

8. The client creates a RIS service request based on the Dynamic Host Configuration Protocol (DHCP) discovery process.

9. The RIS remote boot request is forwarded to both a DHCP and a RIS server, or the request will fail.

10. If passing through a router, the router must be configured to forward DHCP broadcasts (DHCP is based on User Datagram Protocol (UDP); and UDP packets typically are not forwarded).

11. Upon receiving the request, the RIS server checks the Active Directory for a computer account with a Globally Unique Identifier (GUID) matching the GUID in the service request. If the GUID exists and a RIS server has been configured for it, the response to the client includes the RIS server.

12. The configured RIS server answers the request and delivers the image.

WARNING

When you install Windows 2000 from a server share to multiple target computers, you create a huge traffic load for the network. The method that you use to install—whether SYSPREP, RIPREP, or scripted installation—is inconsequential to the resulting impact on the network. To counteract the impact, you should follow a few simple rules: Never install workstations during business hours. If the business is open 24 hours a day, 7 days a week, then you should never install workstations during busy hours. Also, never install workstations across slow, unreliable, or wide area network links. If at all possible, do install workstations on the same network segment to isolate the traffic. Limit the servers from which specific remote installation clients can download an image.

Configuring Remote Installation Services starts in the Control Panel by opening the Add Remove Programs icon and then selecting Add/Remove Windows Components. The option to Configure Remote Installation Services should be listed, or you will need to add the component. When you select this option, you will see the Welcome screen shown in Figure 11.1. Both a valid Domain Name System (DNS) and DHCP server are required, as well as the Windows 2000 Professional CD-ROM. (Like SYSPREP, RIPREP is intended to install only Windows 2000 Professional.)

Figure 11.1 RIS Welcome screen.

The next screen prompts you for the location of the RIS file structure. You should indicate a directory on the local file server but it cannot be the same drive as the server's operating system and it *must* be an NTFS formatted partition. After selecting your location and clicking Next, you are prompted for the response settings of your RIS server. You can select whether the RIS server will respond to client requests, and whether those requests must come from known clients. This screen is shown in Figure 11.2.

Next, you are prompted for the location of the Windows 2000 files. This can be copied from a network share or from the original CD-ROM. The default location will be the drive letter of your CD-ROM drive. After this, the RIS service copies the files into the new remote installation share. After completing the RIS Wizard, you are ready to begin RIPREP on your selected master computer.

Figure 11.2 Client support settings.

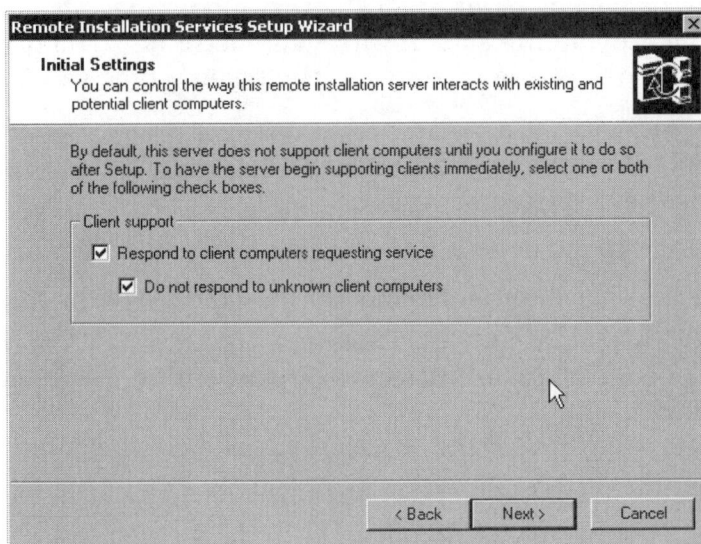

Windows 2000 Setup Phases

When you install Windows 2000, you will encounter three phases during setup:

- WINNT
- Text mode
- Graphical User Interface (GUI) mode (including SYSSETUP and OCMANAGER)

WINNT Phase

During this setup phase, the Winnt32.exe (or winnt.exe) executable file is in control of the processes running on the computer. The following processes are completed:

- Files that are listed in DOSNET.INF are copied to two directories: C:\$WIN_NT$.~BT and C:\$WIN_NT$.~LS

- A new boot sector is written to C:\WIN_NT.~BT\BOOTSEC.DAT

- An entry is placed in the BOOT.INI file to boot to BOOTSEC.DAT

Text Mode

After the WINNT phase is completed, the text mode phase begins. Text mode is indicated by a blue screen with white lettering. The primary purpose of the text mode phase is to install the basic Windows 2000 operating system. During this phase:

- The end-user license agreement (EULA) must be accepted by the end-user or scripted as agreed

- The HAL type is detected or selected by the installer and installed

- Power management is detected or selected by the installer and installed

- Storage controllers are detected or selected by the installer and installed

GUI Mode

Text mode ends with a reboot and leads into the GUI (Graphical User Interface) mode. There are two parts of GUI mode:

- SysSetup (System Setup) installs the remaining Windows 2000 operating system

- OCManager (Optional Component Manager) installs optional components

The optional components are installed in an orderly fashion. The list of the components that can be selected are found in SYSOC.INF. Security is set up, then Plug and Play (PNP) devices are installed. Regional settings are selected. Then the name of the user, the company, and the computer are added. Finally, licenses are added.

For IT Professionals

Network Monitor

Many times, Network Monitor is not installed as part of the base operating system. This is a unique tool since it requires both a driver and an application to be set up on a computer. To install Network Monitor after the server's installation is complete, make certain to have a copy of the Windows 2000 CD's i386 directory available in either the original installation location or another known location.

1. Click Start | Settings | Control Panel.
2. Double-click the Add/Remove Programs icon.
3. Double-click Add/Remove Windows Components.
4. Click Next.
5. Click Management and Monitoring Tools.
6. Click the Details button.
7. Check the Network Monitor Tools check box.
8. Click OK.
9. Click Next.
10. Click Finish and Close to exit, then exit out of Control Panel.

Both the network monitor and the network monitor tools are now installed on the computer. You can now use this tool to measure network traffic for the computer.

Installing the Active Directory

The Active Directory is installed on each and every domain controller. Those servers that do not need to be domain controllers are simply members of the Active Directory, dependent upon the domain controllers to provide them with Active Directory access, so they do not need to have it installed on them.

There are many decisions to be made about the Active Directory installation. You need to know which domain to install first. You need to know whether a domain needs to be upgraded, and which of the upgraded servers to migrate first and thereafter.

Which Domain First?

Regardless of whether you are upgrading an existing Windows NT network, or you are installing a fresh Windows 2000 network, you will need to decide which domain to install first. You should follow these rules in determining which domain to install, and in what order, for each forest:

- The root domain should always be installed or migrated first.

- If you are upgrading an existing domain to Windows 2000, you must migrate the PDC first. Then you should upgrade all the BDCs and add any new domain controllers before moving to the next domain.

- If there are any subdomains of the root domain, do those next. Follow the namespace down the tree from the root until it ends for all subdomains before installing the next namespace.

- If there are other namespaces in the forest, select one and begin with the root domain of that namespace.

- Follow that namespace until it ends for each subdomain, and until they are all migrated or installed.

- Repeat this process for each namespace until the forest is fully installed.

For example, imagine that you have a forest as shown in Figure 11.3. In this forest you will migrate the domain trunk.root.com and the second namespace, tree.com, from existing NT domains that are named TRUNK and TREE, respectively, with NetBIOS naming. In addition, you will install a new root.com domain and a domain called sub.tree.com with new domain controllers.

1. Install the new root.com domain, and ensure that the domain controllers are all installed within it.

2. Migrate the existing TRUNK NT domain to trunk.root.com. Ensure that the PDC and all BDCs are migrated before migrating the next domain.

3. Migrate the existing TREE NT domain to tree.com. Ensure that the PDC and all BDCs are migrated before going to the next domain in the forest.

4. Install a new sub.tree.com domain, and ensure that the domain controllers are all installed within it.

Figure 11.3 Migration and installation of a forest.

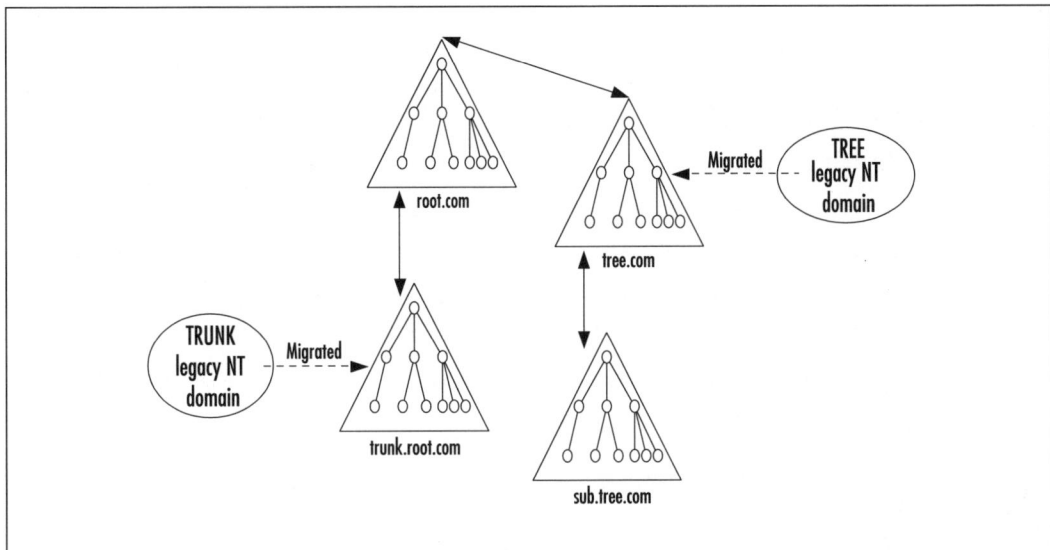

Which Server First?

Once you're ready to install the first server in a domain, you need to know which one to start with. The first server to install into a domain is a domain controller (DC). No matter what, the first DC in a domain will take on the five Flexible Single Master of Operations (FSMO) roles, and is a Global Catalog server.

If you are migrating a Windows NT domain, the first NT server to upgrade is the PDC. The PDC will become an Active Directory DC and take on the FSMO roles, including the PDC Emulator FSMO role. The NT domain user and machine account data will be migrated into the Active Directory, too.

Migrations require some preparation. Because the users, groups, and machine accounts are upgraded from the Windows NT domain Security Accounts Manager (SAM) database, the Active Directory domain will inherit any problem accounts that exist. Problem accounts can be those that do not have passwords, have not been used in a lengthy period of time, groups without members, and accounts that do not use the enterprise naming convention. Preparation steps include:

1. Review the existing user accounts and delete any that have not been used in over 90 days, and remove their associated home directories.

2. Review the existing group accounts and delete any empty ones. Also, consolidate any groups that can be consolidated.

3. Remove machine accounts that have not been used in over 90 days.

4. Back up the PDC twice.

5. Verify that the hardware is compatible with Windows 2000.

6. Verify that applications are compatible with Windows 2000.

7. Download any Beginning Input Output System (BIOS) updates from the BIOS manufacturer's or server vendor's Web site.

8. Download any Windows 2000 drivers required for legacy hardware.

9. Validate the domain security policies.

10. Simplify protocols to TCP/IP only, if possible.

11. Update existing Windows NT OS and the applications with service packs.

12. Convert the file system to NT File System (NTFS).

13. Delete any unnecessary files on the server, such as temporary Internet files, etc.

DCPromo

Installing the Active Directory is done through the DCPromo.exe application, also known as the Active Directory Wizard. The Active Directory Wizard will both promote a member server to a domain controller and demote a domain controller to a member server. If you've inadvertently installed a server into the wrong domain, you can uninstall the Active Directory with DCPROMO.EXE at any time—effectively demoting a domain controller to a member server—without having to reinstall the server completely. For those who are familiar with Windows NT, this is a major improvement!

The difference between a domain controller (DC) and a member server is that a DC carries a copy of the domain partition of the Active Directory locally, but a member server must contact a DC in order to access it.

When you run DCPROMO, you will need to know what role the DC will be playing in the Active Directory forest and other information.

- Is this the first DC in the domain?
- Is this the root domain for a domain namespace?
- Is this the first domain in the forest (e.g., the root domain)?

- Will this server be a DNS server?

- Is the server a DNS client?

- If a new domain, what is its DNS domain name?

- If a new domain, what will be the NetBIOS name?

- Where will the Active Directory files be located?

- Where will the system volume be located?

- Will security be relaxed for NT Remote Access Service (RAS) backward compatibility?

- What is the password to be used on this server to restore Active Directory?

The first screen that you reach when running DCPROMO, the Welcome screen, is shown in Figure 11.4. You can bypass this screen by clicking Next.

The second dialog lets you select whether this DC is the first in a new domain, or if it will be a new DC in an existing domain. From this screen forward, the answer you give to the question will determine what screen you will encounter next. For example, if this is the first DC that you install in the Active Directory forest and it will run the DNS service, you will come across the dialogs and answers in Table 11.2.

Figure 11.4 DCPromo Welcome screen.

Table 11.2 Active Directory Wizard

Dialog Screen	Options	Actions
Welcome Screen	None	Click Next.
Domain Controller Type	▪ First domain controller in a new domain. ▪ Domain controller in an existing domain.	Select First DC in New domain and click Next.
Create Tree or Child Domain	▪ First domain in a new domain tree. ▪ Child domain of an existing domain tree.	Select First domain in a domain tree and click Next.
Create or Join Forest	▪ Create a new forest. ▪ Place this domain tree in an existing forest.	Select Create a new forest and click Next.
DNS configuration	▪ Configure this computer as a DNS client. ▪ Install this server as a DNS server.	Select the option to install the server as a DNS server and click Next.
DNS domain name	▪ Enter the domain name in the DNS namespace format of domain.com.	Type in the domain name and click Next.
NetBIOS domain name	▪ Enter the NetBIOS domain name in the NET-BIOS format of DOMAIN. This will automatically default to the first 15 characters of the first section of the DNS domain name provided in the previous dialog.	If changing the name, type in the domain name and click Next.
Active Directory files location	▪ Enter the location for the database and logging files for Active Directory. This will default to the system partition within the WINNT directory. It is recommended that the database and logging files should exist on separate disks for recoverability.	If changing the location as recommended, type in the new path(s) and click Next.

Continued

Table 11.2 Continued

Dialog Screen	Options	Actions
System Volume	■ Enter the location for the system volume. This defaults to WINNT\SYSVOL. The system volume is replicated to all DCs. It will grow over time because it holds scripts, group policies, and other files that enable logon, so place the directory on a partition with room for growth.	If changing the location, type in the new path and click Next.
Security	■ Standard Windows 2000 security ■ Relaxed permissions for backwards compatibility with Windows NT 4 Remote Access Servers (RAS). Select this option only if planning to use Windows NT 4.0 RAS.	As a new Windows 2000 domain, there is no need for backward compatibility, so select the standard security and click Next.
Directory Services Restore Password	■ Enter and confirm the administrative password that will be used to restore the Active Directory on this DC.	Type in the password and verify it, then click Next.
Summary page	■ Provides a summary of the options selected during the Active Directory Installation.	Review the page and click Next.

Installing the Recovery Console

Windows 2000 Server provides a way to restore a domain controller without having to rely on reinstalling the server and restoring data from a tape backup—the Recovery Console. The Recovery Console is a command line console that you can use to

- Format a hard disk
- Manipulate files on an NTFS hard disk

- Reconfigure a service
- Start or stop a service

The Recovery Console is not installed by default. If you do not install the Recovery Console, you can still access it by booting the Windows 2000 Setup program from the Windows 2000 CD-ROM. When you install the Recovery Console, it is listed as an option in the boot menu. To install it:

1. Log on Windows 2000 Server as an administrator.
2. Open a command prompt window by clicking the Start menu, select the Run option, type **CMD** into the Run box, and press Enter.
3. From the Windows 2000 source files in the i386 directory, type **WINNT32 /CMDCONS**.
4. Follow the dialog screens until the command console is installed.

The Recovery Console will be available as an option in the boot menu the next time the server is started. To run it, simply select that option at startup.

Populating a Domain with Organizational Units (OUs) and Objects

Each domain has a number of default containers. These default containers are not intended to be the only containers in the domain, nor are they appropriate for placing your new users and groups. The default containers play the roles listed in Table 11.3.

Table 11.3 Default Containers for a Domain

Container Name	Role
Builtin	Contains backward-compatible (Windows NT) security groups.
Computers	Contains member computers of the domain after their domain is upgraded from Windows NT. Can contain new member computers, as needed.
Domain controllers	Contains all Active Directory DCs belonging to that domain.
ForeignSecurity Principals	Active Directory places objects representing security principals (usually just users and groups) from domains outside the forest that are trusted through a trust relationship.
Users	Contains the initial default users and group accounts. Upgraded user and group accounts are initially placed here.

Creating an OU

To create an OU, you start in the Active Directory User and Computers console. The first OU you will create should be at the top level of the domain.

1. Right-click the domain object at the top of the tree hierarchy.
2. Click New from the pop-up menu options.
3. Select Organizational Unit.
4. The New object dialog will appear, as shown in Figure 11.5.
5. Type a name in the box for the OU.
6. Click OK.

Figure 11.5 Creating a new OU.

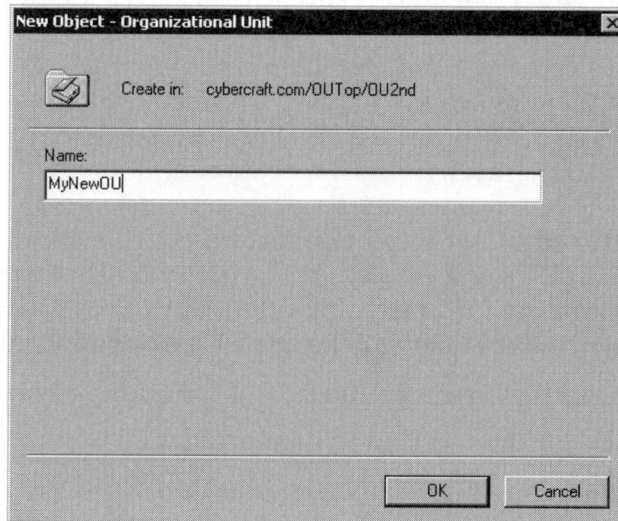

Create an OU for Hidden Objects

If you do not want objects to be seen by every user, you can use an OU to hide them. This can be useful if there are some highly secure objects (for example, objects containing confidential HR data) that no one should have access to except certain users. To hide objects in an OU:

1. Enable the Advanced Features of the Active Directory Users and Computers console by clicking the View menu and selecting Advanced Features.

2. In the Active Directory Users and Computers console, right-click the OU that will contain the hidden objects.

3. Select Properties.

4. Click on the Security tab.

5. Remove all permissions.

6. Click Advanced.

7. Clear the checkbox for Inherit permissions from parent.

8. Click OK.

9. You should be back in the Security dialog. Add the groups and users who need rights to the OU to see its contents.

Delegating Authority

Once you have an OU, you can delegate the authority to manage that OU and its contents to other users. Many legacy Windows NT domains were created in order to create boundaries between different administrative groups. This was the only way to achieve that separation without a third-party add-on. However, with the Active Directory, authority can be delegated within the OU hierarchy, and separation of domains is no longer required.

The Active Directory Users and Computers console contains a Delegation of Control Wizard, shown in Figure 11.6. This wizard simplifies the process of delegating authority, including both predefined roles and the ability to customize what is being delegated. To delegate control:

1. Start the Active Directory Users and Computers console.

2. Right-click on the OU that will be delegated.

3. Select Delegate Control from the pop-up menu.

4. At the Welcome dialog, click Next.

5. In the Group or User Selection dialog, click Add.

6. Select the group or user to whom you are granting authority.

7. You will be returned to the Group or User Selection dialog; click Next.

8. In the Predefined Delegations window, select the role that the group or user will play, or select Do customized delegation. Click Next.

9. If you are doing customized delegation, you can select the entire OU, or a specific list of objects within it. You will also be prompted to select which permissions are being granted.

10. When complete, click Finish at the Summary dialog.

Figure 11.6 Delegation of Control Wizard.

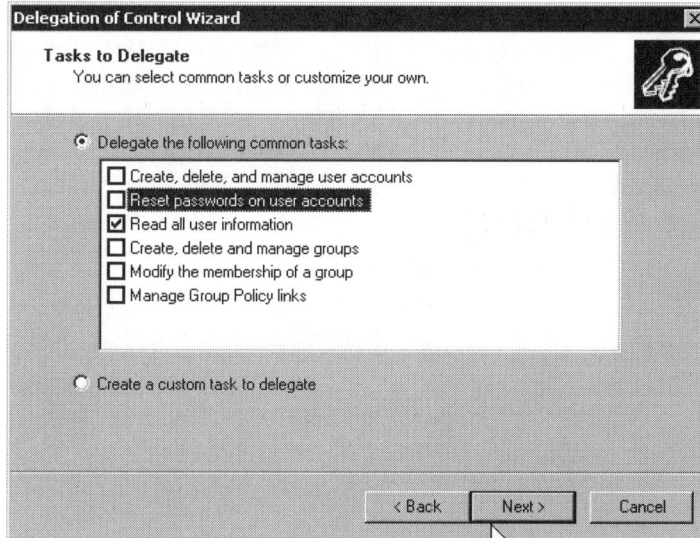

One type of permission is in high demand for large enterprises—resetting passwords. Why? Large enterprises require strict security because they have so many end users. They execute this security by requiring passwords on all their systems, by requiring frequent password changes, and by requiring lengthy passwords with odd characters. The end result is that users forget their long, odd-character-including, recently changed passwords—especially if they have more than one password to access more than one computer system. To become productive, those users need to log on to the network; so, the enterprise needs to provide a way for those users to get a new password to replace their forgotten one. It is not productive for the highest level administrators to change passwords, nor is it secure if everyone who is given the right to change passwords is also granted full administrative authority. This is where Delegation of Control Wizard comes in. One of the predefined roles is set for Reset Passwords. For all the Call Center, Help Desk, or other IT folks who need to reset passwords, simply create a group, grant that group the Reset Password predefined role, and then add those users to that group. If only the rest of IT were this easy.

Creating a User Account

For users to begin logging on, they need user accounts. If you have upgraded a Windows NT Primary Domain Controller (PDC) to Windows 2000 Active Directory DC, those users will be migrated into the Users container of the domain. Then move them into your OU hierarchy.

If you created a new Active Directory domain and want to migrate user accounts from a legacy Windows NT domain, then you need to use a tool such as the Active Directory Migration Tool (ADMT). ADMT provides a GUI interface and migration wizards for domain components; the user migration wizard, shown in Figure 11.7, is used to migrate objects from an existing NT domain to a Windows 2000 domain. This is helpful when merging domains. ADMT is downloadable from Microsoft's Web site at http://download.microsoft.com/download/win2000srv/Install/1.0/NT5/EN-US/ADMT.exe.

Figure 11.7 ADMT.

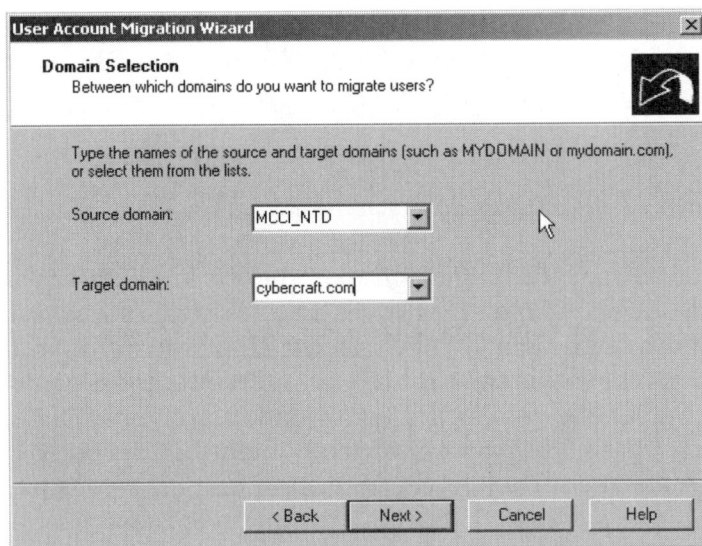

Once you install the Active Directory Migration Tool, you can select the components that you want to migrate using the wizards for those components. For example, to migrate member computers, select the Action menu and then the Computer Migration Wizard.

ClonePrincipal is another tool that you can use to migrate multiple user accounts. The ClonePrincipal tool uses a customizable Visual Basic script for migrating security principals from an existing domain to an Active Directory domain.

If you are adding a few users to the Active Directory, the best way to go about it is to create them manually in the Active Directory Users and Computers console. To create a new user account:

1. Right-click on the OU that will contain the new user.
2. Select New from the pop-up menu.
3. Select User from the sub-pop-up menu.
4. Type in the user's name—first, initial, last—and logon names in the dialog shown in Figure 11.8.
5. Click Next.
6. Type the user's password and verify it.
7. Select the user's password options in the dialog shown in Figure 11.9.
8. Click Next.
9. Review the summary and click Finish.
10. To configure the user's detailed properties, double-click the new user object and make any changes or additions to the dialog shown in Figure 11.10.

Figure 11.8 User creation dialog.

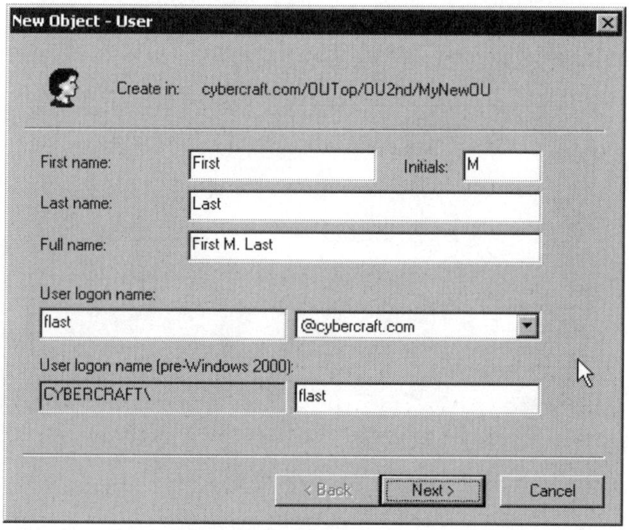

Figure 11.9 User password dialog.

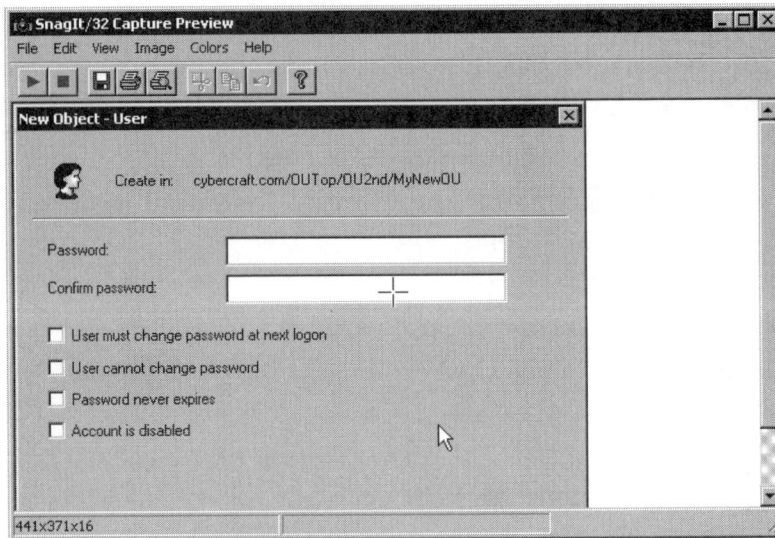

Figure 11.10 User properties dialog.

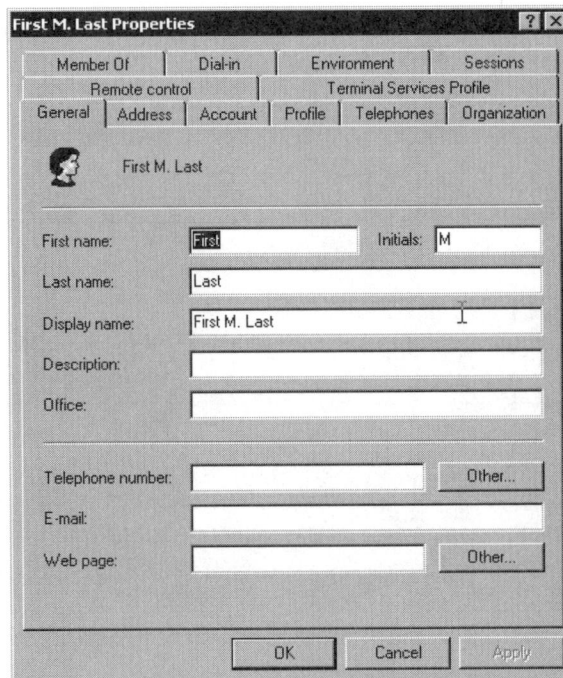

Creating Groups

When you create a group, you need to know whether your domain is in mixed mode or native mode. Mixed mode is the default state of a domain—it accepts Windows NT Backup Domain Controllers (BDCs) as part of the domain. A domain will remain in mixed mode even if all the servers are Windows 2000 servers until the network administrator switches it to native mode. Once a domain has been changed to native mode, it cannot be changed back to mixed mode. To switch a domain to native mode:

1. In the left pane of the Active Directory Users and Computers console, click on the domain.
2. Select the Action menu.
3. Select the Properties option.
4. Click the General Tab.
5. Click the Change Mode button.

If you intend to use nested groups—where groups are members of other groups—you must switch your domain to native mode. Nested groups are not applicable to NT domains, so they cannot be used in mixed mode. There are new types of groups available in the Active Directory domains, too:

Local groups These groups can be granted access to any resource on a particular server. They can contain members from anywhere in the forest or trusted domains. A local group in native mode can contain global groups and universal groups as members. Local groups work the same as they did in Windows NT when the domain is in mixed mode.

Domain local groups These groups can be granted access to any resource in a single domain. They can contain members from anywhere in the forest or trusted domains. A domain local group in native mode can contain global groups and universal groups as members.

Global groups These groups can be granted access to resources in any domain in the forest or a trusted domain. They can contain members only of the local domain. In native mode, a global group can contain other global groups or universal groups as members. Global groups have the same capabilities as they did in Windows NT when in mixed mode.

Universal groups These groups can be granted access to any resource in a trusted domain that is in native mode. A universal group can contain members of any domain within the forest.

To create a group:

1. In the Active Directory Users and Computers console, right-click the OU where the group will reside.

2. Select New.

3. Select Group from the pop-up menu.

4. Specify the type of group you want. To assign permissions to a group, do not select Distribution as the Group Type. Specify the name of the group. The group dialog is shown in Figure 11.11.

5. Click OK.

To nest a group, you simply make one group a member of another group. This is done through the members tab when you view a group's properties. As you can see from Figure 11.11, a group is defined through its scope and its type. The scope refers to whether the group is a domain local, global, or universal group. (Local groups are available on member servers and workstations, and the rest are available on DCs in the Active Directory.) The type refers to whether a group is a security group (it will be granted permissions to resources) or a distribution group used for e-mail lists. Since you will most likely be using your groups for resource access, select Security. If you want to use the universal group, switch your domain to native mode first.

Figure 11.11 New Group dialog box.

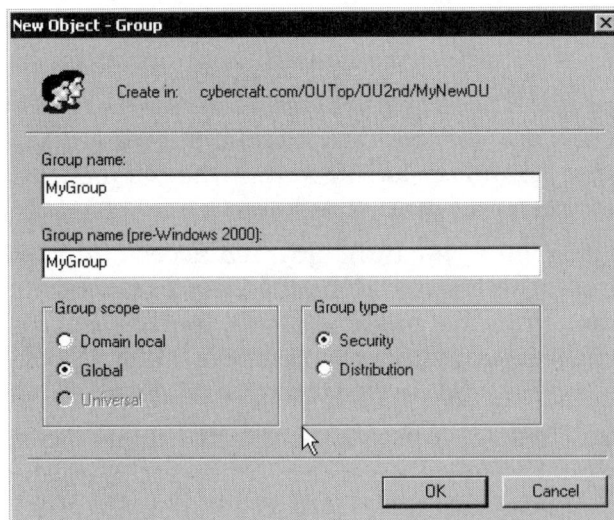

Publishing Printers

Printers are published in the Active Directory, by default, through the Add Printer Wizard. Publishing a printer enables it to be searched for using an Active Directory executed query. If the printer is not published in the Active Directory, follow this procedure:

1. On the server from where the printer is shared, open the printers folder.
2. Right-click on the printer object.
3. Select Properties.
4. Click the Sharing tab.
5. Check the box for List in Directory shown in Figure 11.12.

Figure 11.12 Publishing a printer in the Active Directory.

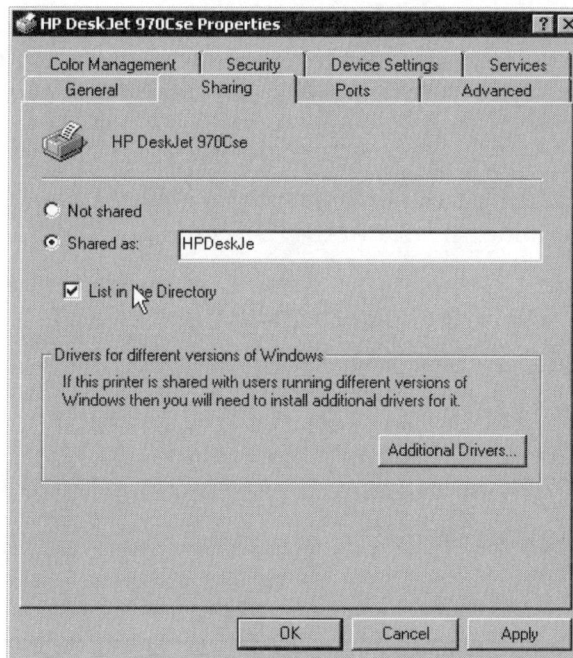

After a printer has been published, a user can query the directory and look for certain characteristics for that printer. These include duplex printing, color, location in the network, and so on. The user's query will look similar to Figure 11.13.

Figure 11.13 Querying the directory for printers.

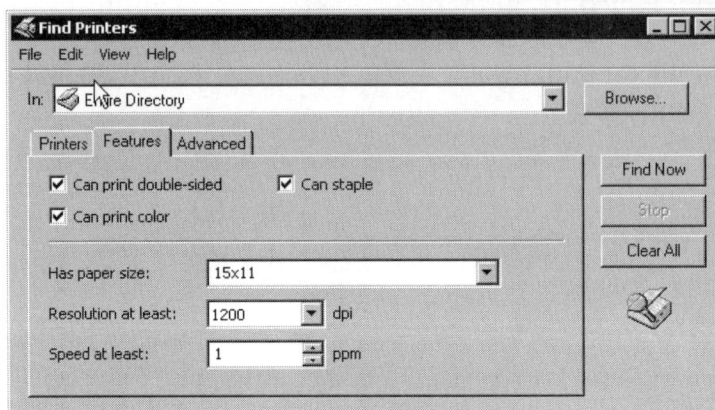

Publishing Folders

Unlike printers, folders are not published in the Active Directory by default. Once a folder is published in the Active Directory, users can search for it in the Active Directory through queries or even browsing. To publish a folder, it must first be shared. Sharing folders is a simple matter of right-clicking the folder in the Windows Explorer and selecting the Sharing tab, then setting the permissions for specific users and groups. To further publish the folder in the Active Directory:

1. In the Active Directory Users and Computers console, right-click on the OU where the folder will be published.

2. Select New.

3. Select Shared Folder.

4. Type the Universal Naming Convention (UNC) for the share—it's in the format of \\server\share, as shown in Figure 11.14.

5. Click OK.

TIP

If you want to publish folders that are not online, you can go ahead and do so. The Active Directory does not check for the folder when it publishes. This is helpful for offline publishing, but it can also be an issue if you have a typo. Make certain to double check that you've typed the published folder name correctly if it is offline. If the folder is available online, then verify that it was published correctly by browsing for it in the Active Directory and expanding it.

Figure 11.14 Published folder dialog.

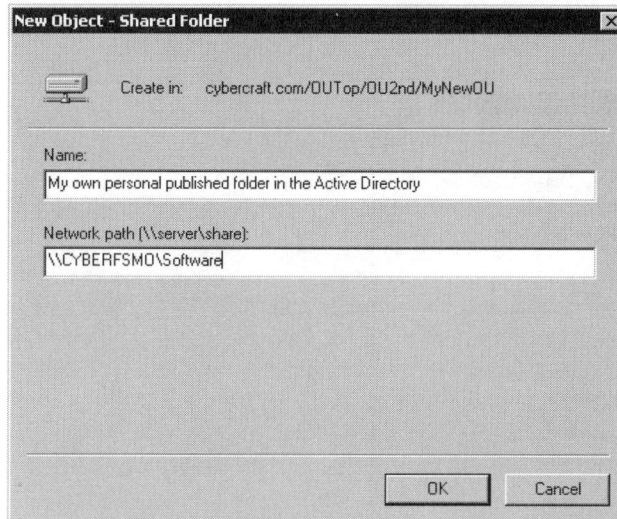

Applying a Group Policy

Group policies can be applied to a domain, a site, or an OU. If you've created an OU hierarchy that is functionally designed for a nested group
policy application, then you will most likely and most often apply group
policies to OUs. To create a group policy:

1. Right-click the OU in the Active Directory Users and Computers
   console. (Alternatively, you can right-click the domain or site in the
   Active Directory Sites and Services console and follow this same
   sequence to create a Group Policy.)

2. Select Properties.

3. Click the Group Policy tab.

4. Click New.

5. Name the policy.

6. Click Edit.

7. The Group Policy Editor will start as shown in Figure 11.15.
   Configure the policy options for this Group Policy.

8. Exit the Group Policy Editor after you have configured all the
   options you require. You return to the Group Policy tab for the OU.

9. Click Close.

Figure 11.15 Group Policy Editor.

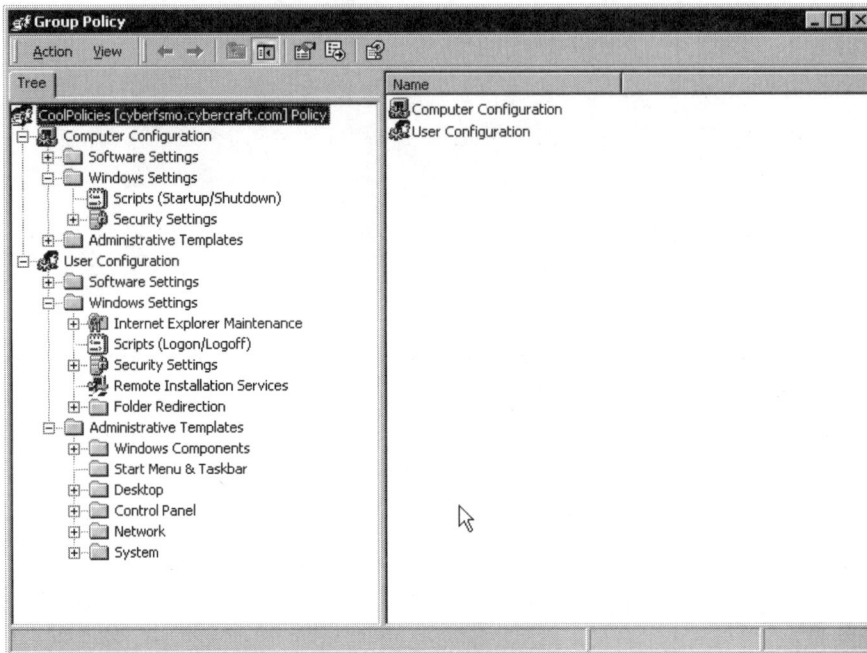

Setting Up Sites

IP subnets can be assigned to sites immediately following the installation of the first DC. The value in doing this step first is realized when further Windows 2000 computers are installed. Each Windows 2000 computer contacts the Active Directory to find a DC that is within its own site for authentication purposes. When the Active Directory is installed, it automatically will install the DC into the site that is associated with the server's own IP subnet. If a site is not identified with the server's IP subnet, then the server is placed within the default site. For a company with a site in Florence, Italy and another in Sydney, Australia, a DC installed into the wrong site could cause logon delays and excessive wide area network bandwidth consumption. It is best to ensure that all DCs are placed into the appropriate sites at the earliest opportunity. To associate IP subnets with a site, you first need to create the sites and then create the IP subnets within each one.

1. In the Active Directory Sites and Services console, right-click on Sites.

2. Select New Site.

3. Type the name for the site.

4. Select a site link (you can change this later, if you need to).

5. Click OK.

6. Right-click on Subnets.

7. Select New Subnet.

8. Type the IP subnet address and subnet mask.

9. Click OK.

When you have multiple sites, you need to create site links, site link bridges, and connection objects to enable them to transfer information. To create the site link:

1. In the Active Directory Sites and Services console, navigate below the Sites container to the Inter-Site Transports.

2. There are two transports listed—IP and SMTP. Right-click on the transport you will use. Most often, you will only use IP.

3. Select New Site Link from the pop-up menu.

4. In the New Site Link dialog, select the sites that will participate in this site link and type the name of the site, as shown in Figure 11.16. You must place at least two sites in each site link.

5. Click OK.

Figure 11.16 New site link.

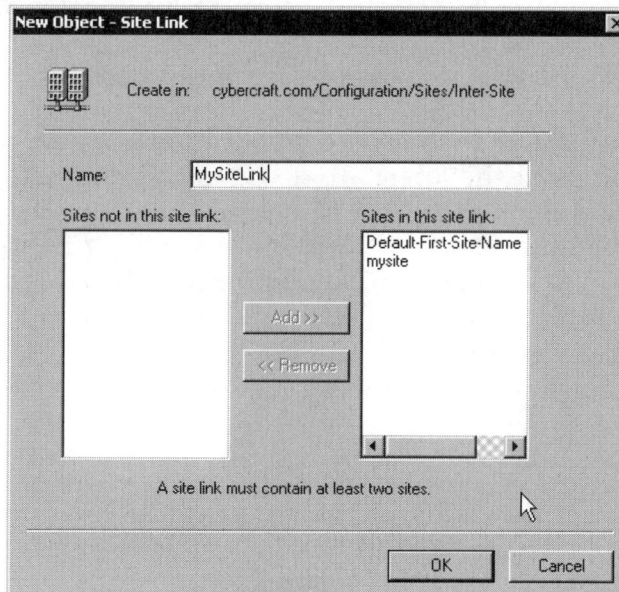

For IT Professionals

Connection Object Management

Even though you have created site links, your DCs will need to have connection objects in order to synchronize updates across the site link. Think of a site link like a road for traffic, but without any cars. The connection objects are like the cars that carry traffic across the road.

It is easy to ignore connection object management because objects are generated automatically by the Knowledge Consistency Checker (KCC) within any particular site. They are *not* generated automatically across sites.

Be careful when you move servers from one site to another! If you move a server from one site to another, the connection objects that were created by the KCC will move with it and never be changed thereafter. These connection objects may not be desirable if you want to manage traffic over that site link with bridgehead servers or by reducing the number of intersite connections.

If you are creating bridgehead servers, you will need to check each server in each site to ensure that there are no connection objects created between nonbridgehead servers in the different sites. You will also need to make sure that there is only one connection object in the bridgehead server's NTDS Settings object pointing from the other site's bridgehead server. NTDS stands for NT Directory Service. Each domain controller has an NTDS Settings object.

An administrator may wish to force replication to make recent changes synchronize throughout the forest. To do this, the administrator can use the Active Directory Sites and Services console to access the Replicate Now option, shown in Figure 11.17. Replication is forced by right-clicking the connection object below the NTDS Site Settings of the server that you want to have synchronized.

Figure 11.17 Replicate Now.

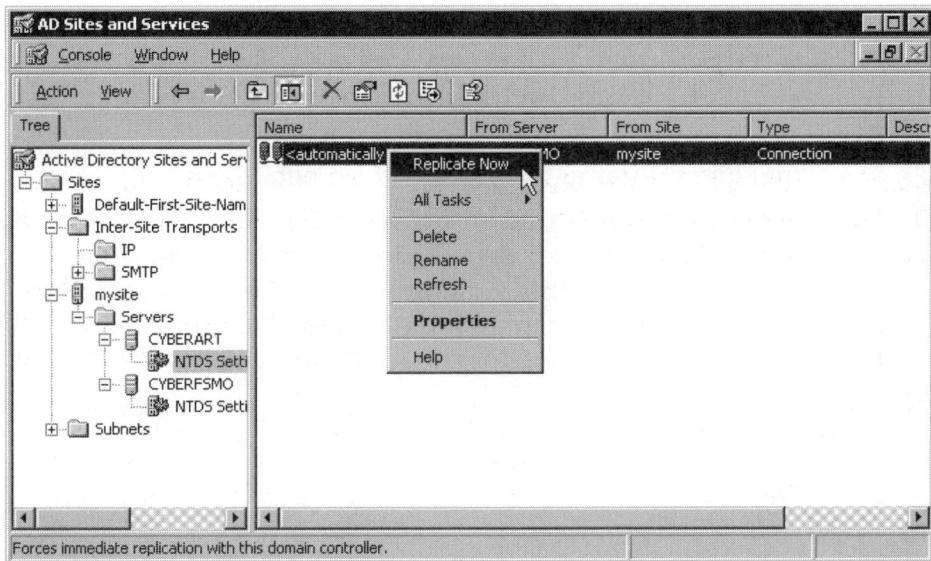

Installing and Configuring Windows 2000 Components

Once the Active Directory is installed on the Domain Controllers, your work is still not done. You will need to install or configure other Windows 2000 services such as the Domain Name System, Remote Access Services, and Terminal Services.

Configuring DNS

To start configuring DNS, you will want to start the DNS Manager, located in the Administrative Tools menu.

1. In the DNS Manager, shown in Figure 11.18, select the server that will be configured for DNS.

2. Click the Action menu.

3. Select Configure the server.

4. The Configure DNS Server wizard will start. Click Next at the Welcome dialog.

5. Select whether the server is the first DNS server on the network or not. Click Next.

6. Create a Forward Lookup Zone. This is the domain name of the zone that the server will manage.

7. Select whether this zone is Active Directory Integrated, Standard Primary, or Secondary. If the server is not a DC, you will see that the first option, Active Directory Integrated, is grayed out. Click Next.

8. State the domain name for the zone and click Next.

9. You are then prompted to create a reverse lookup zone. For DNS experts, this is an In.Addr.Arpa zone, which can look up an IP address and find the domain name—the reverse of a standard zone. It is not necessary to create a reverse lookup zone for Windows 2000 Active Directory to function correctly.

10. The Configure DNS Server wizard completes with a summary page. Click Finish.

Figure 11.18 DNS Manager.

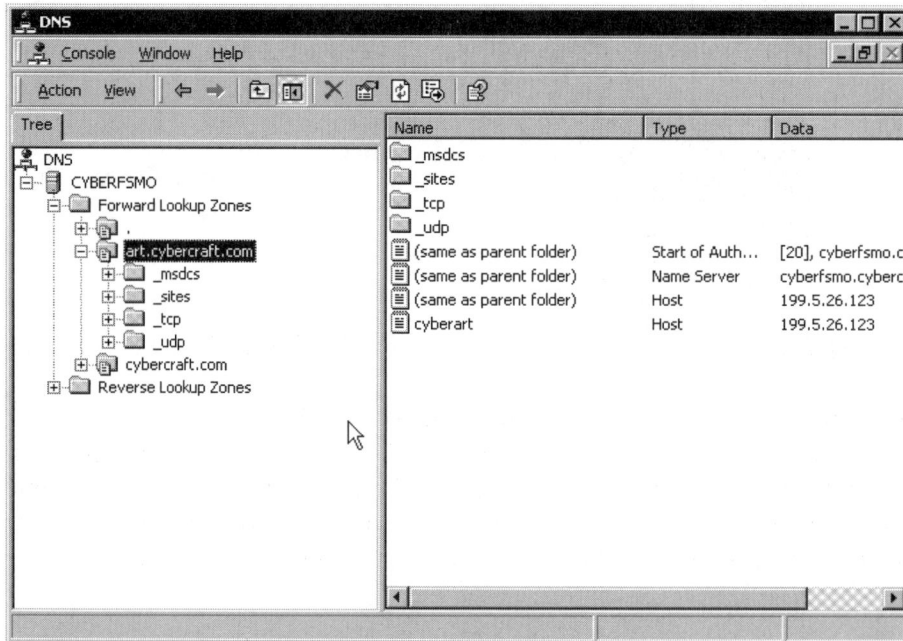

Configuring the Distributed File System

The Distributed file system (Dfs) can be configured in two ways—as an Active Directory stored system, or as a standalone system. To create the Dfs root, start the Distributed file system console from the Administrative Tools menu. When you start the configuration wizard, you will be prompted for the type of system. To store the Dfs topology in the Active Directory, select the Create a Domain Dfs Root option. You will be prompted for the domain that will host Dfs, the server to host Dfs, a shared folder for the Dfs root, and a name for the Dfs root. The summary page of the wizard is shown in Figure 11.19.

Figure 11.19 Dfs Configuration wizard.

Dfs creates a full mesh topology between all the replicas. Each new replica and every other member of the replica set will share a link. This can create a lot of traffic on the network. To optimize Dfs, you can delete the connections that you don't really need in the Active Directory Users and Computers console. Otherwise, Dfs is managed in the Distributed file system console shown in Figure 11.20.

Figure 11.20 Dfs MMC.

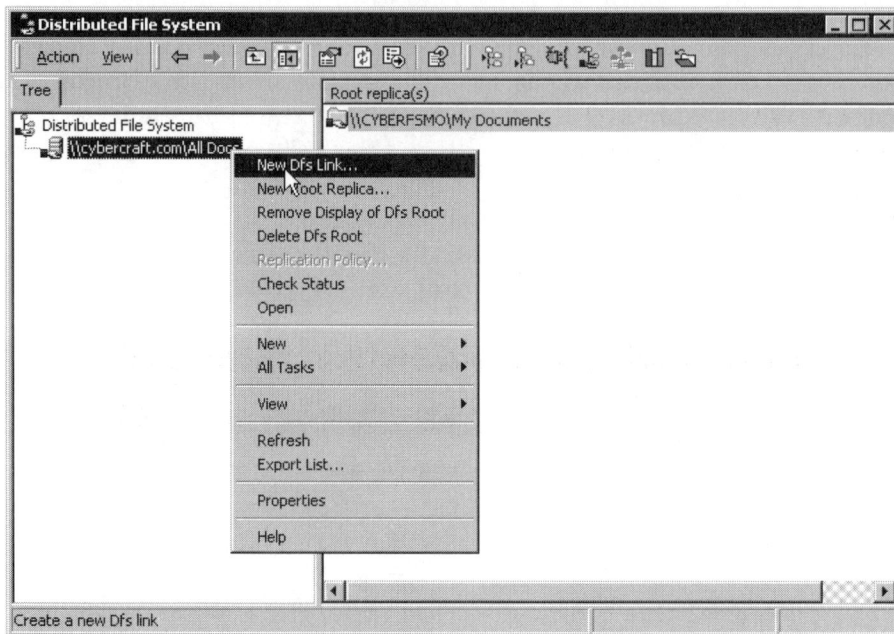

Public Key Infrastructure

The Public Key Infrastructure (PKI) is an authentication method based on digital certificates and certification authority (CA) servers. Windows 2000 provides CA services natively. Once you install a server with CA services, you will not be able to change the role of the server, or the domain to which it belongs. The implementation process of PKI is:

1. Install one or more root CAs in the top-level domains of each Windows 2000 domain tree in the forest. The root CA is placed at the top of a CA hierarchy and is self-signed. It should be configured to issue only subordinate CA certificates. When you install the CA server, you will not be able to rename the server or change its domain membership (whether it is a DC or member server, or which domain it belongs to). You are given four choices for installing the server at the CA services installation, depicted in Figure 11.21.

2. Install subordinate CA servers in the child domains to implement certificate policy. Subordinate CAs are issued their certificates from the root CA. These CA servers request a certificate from the root CA. When you install a CA on a subdomain, then the Enterprise Root CA option is grayed out.

3. Configure the CA servers to issue certificates for users. Issuing CA servers should be configured to issue appropriate certificates such as user certificates or session certificates.

4. Configure certificate revocation lists.

5. Configure Group Policy.

6. Configure certificate renewal and enrollment.

7. Issue certificates.

Figure 11.21 Creating a CA server.

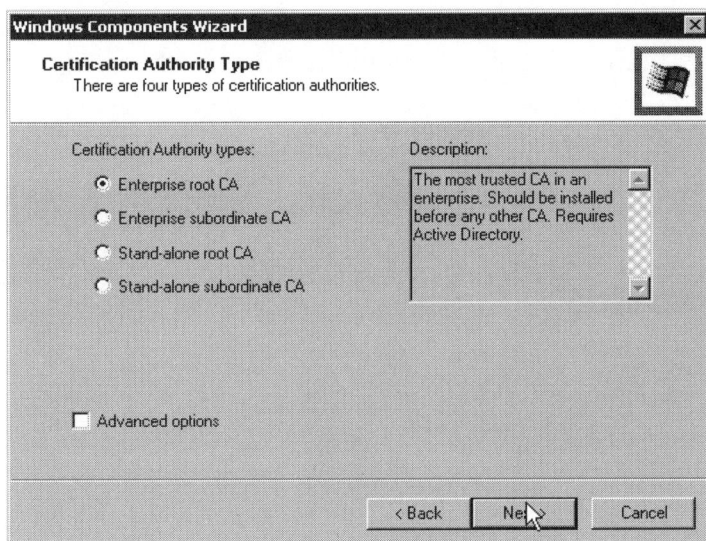

To create a CA on a Windows 2000 server:

1. Open the Control Panel.

2. Double-click Add/Remove Programs.

3. Select Add/Remove Windows Components.

4. Add Certificate Services.

5. Install an enterprise root CA.

6. You can optionally select Advanced options to specify whether the server is going to be a Cryptographic Service Provider (CSP)—which is responsible for creating and destroying keys and performing cryptographic operations. You can also change the hash algorithm, which detects modifications in message data. You can choose to

use existing public and private keys, and set the key length. When you complete your selections, click Next.

7. Type the name of the CA server and its detailed information and click Next.

8. Specify the Validity Duration for the server. This value states when the CA expires, so carefully consider how long this server will remain in service. Click Next.

9. State the location for the CA database and log files and shared folder. Click Next.

10. If you have IIS running, you will be prompted to stop it. Click OK.

The CA server is managed using the Certification Authority console that is found in the Administrative Tools menu and shown in Figure 11.22.

Figure 11.22 Certificates management.

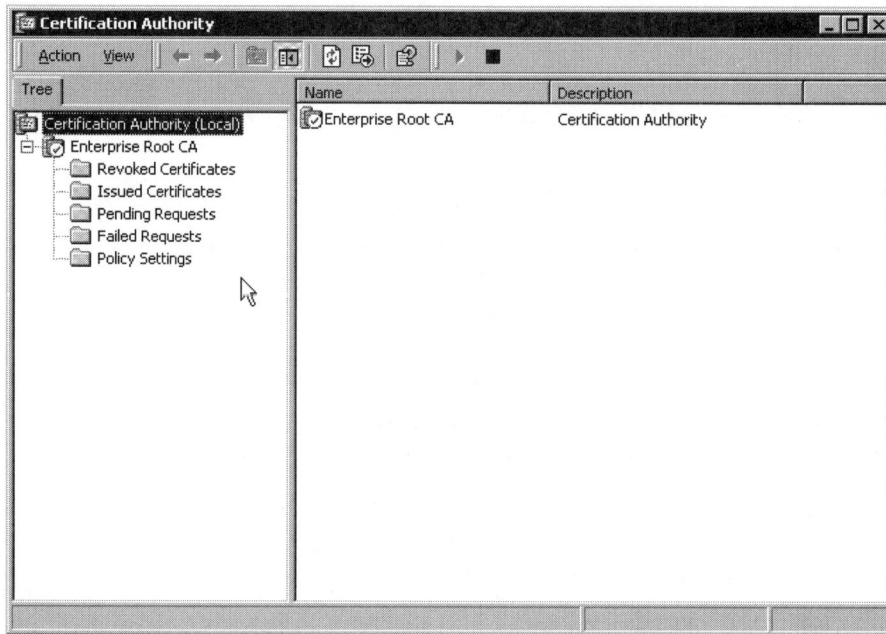

PKI policies can be established through Group Policy. These policies are located in the Computer Configuration group policy under Windows Settings\Security Settings\Public Key Policies. This group policy section is illustrated in Figure 11.23.

Figure 11.23 PKI group policies.

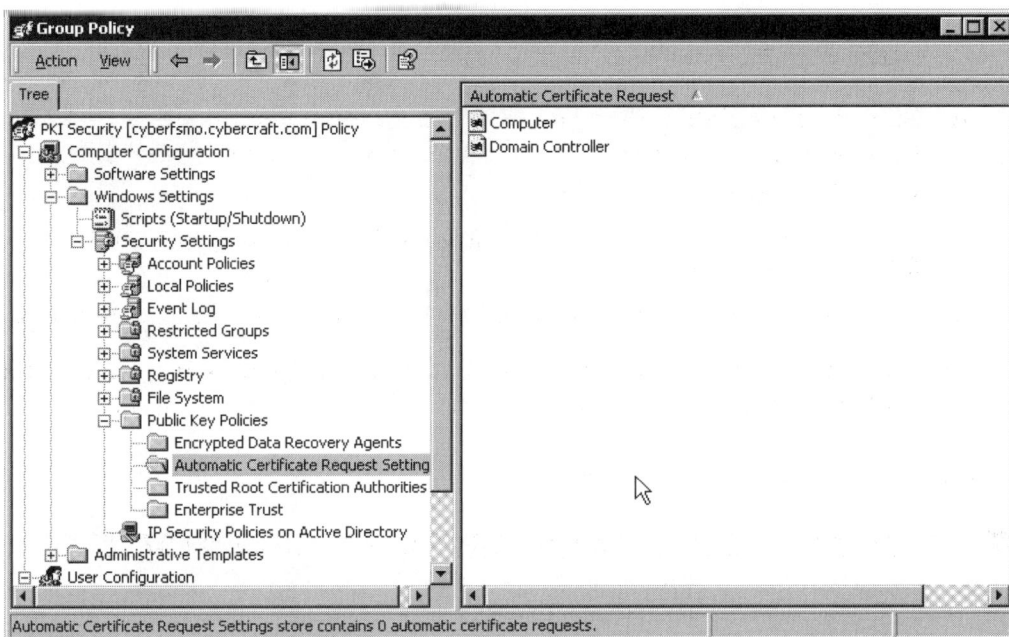

Internet Information Services

Internet Information Services (IIS) is installed by default on every Windows 2000 server, but must be installed as an option on Windows 2000 Professional workstations. To add IIS to a machine that does not have it, use the Add/Remove Programs icon in the Control Panel.

When it is used to serve files to the Web, IIS can create a tremendous load on a server. You can optimize IIS by selecting one of the application protection options for IIS processing of your directory:

- High (Isolated) means that the application runs in a separate process.

- Medium (Pooled) means that many applications share the same process, thus improving reliability (the default option).

- Low (IIS Process) means that the HTML application runs in the same process as IIS. Selecting this can cause IIS to fail if the HTML application fails.

To configure this option for the Web, open the IIS console, shown in Figure 11.24. Select the Properties for the Web site.

Click on the Home Directory tab and select the Application Protection drop-down box shown in Figure 11.25.

Figure 11.24 Internet Services Manager.

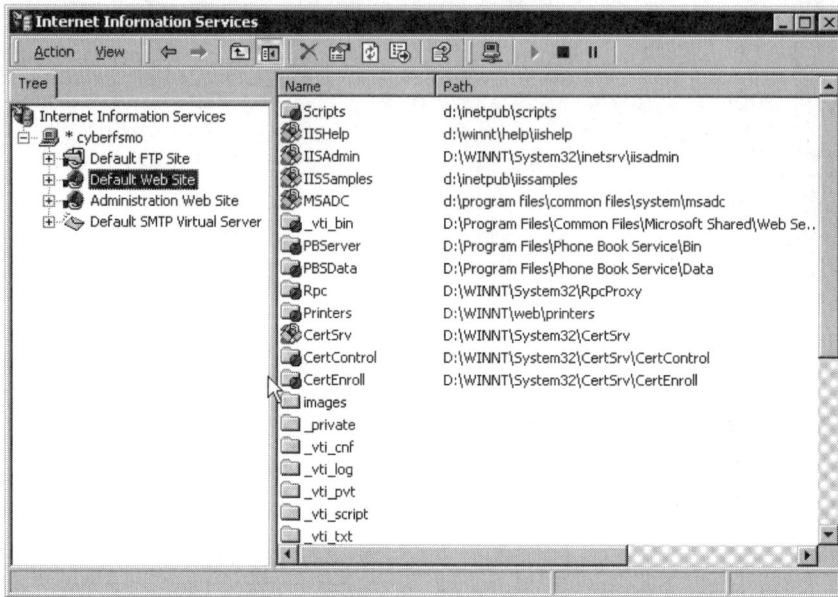

Figure 11.25 Configuring IIS bandwidth throttling.

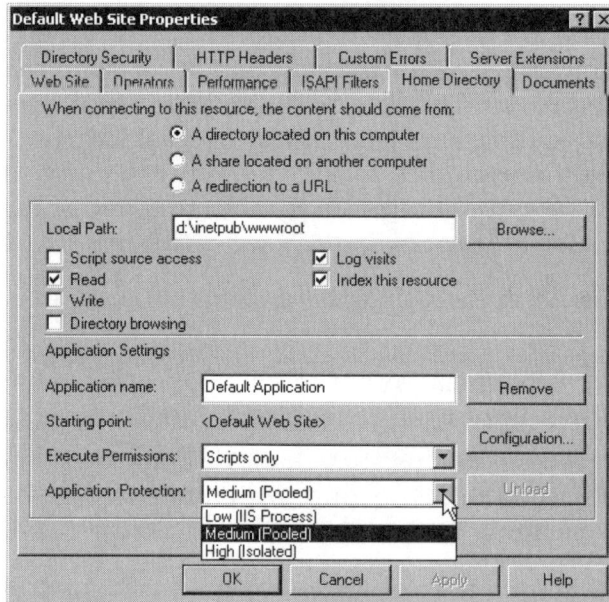

Asynchronous Transfer Mode

Asynchronous Transfer Mode (ATM) is a protocol that is based on cell switching. Cells are small frames, in this case 53 bytes in length. Cell switching is faster than standard packet switching because the small cells do not need to be written to disk as they are being switched throughout an internetwork. Instead, they can stay in random access memory (RAM). ATM typically is implemented as a wide area network backbone technology, but it is slowly permeating local area networks as well.

Windows 2000 supports ATM natively. You can install ATM from the backbone to the workstation. To enable IP over ATM:

1. Open the Control Panel.
2. Double-click Network and Dial-up Connections.
3. Select the Properties tab of the Network Connections dialog box.
4. Double-click the ATM adapter.
5. Select the TCP/IP Protocol and click Enable.

If you are connecting directly to an ATM permanent virtual circuit (PVC), you must configure the Asynchronous Transfer Mode Address Resolution Protocol (ATMARP) client:

1. Open the Control Panel.
2. Double-click Network and Dial-up Connections.
3. Right-click ATM Connection.
4. Choose the Properties tab.
5. Select ATM Call Manager and then its Properties tab.
6. Click Add.
7. Enter the PVC name and Virtual Channel Identifier (VCI) number.
8. Change the Application Type to Default ATMARP.

Terminal Services

Terminal Services are an optional Windows 2000 Server component. In Windows NT 4.0, there was a special *Terminal Server Edition* that was required to run this application service. Now, all Windows 2000 Server editions—Server, Advanced Server, and DataCenter Server—are equipped with an option to run Terminal Services. You can install Terminal Services from the Control Panel using the Add/Remove Programs icon and selecting the Add/Remove Windows Components option.

You should install Terminal Services with one of two situations in mind:

Remote administration Enables servers to be managed remotely from any Terminal Services client over TCP/IP connections. Two Terminal Services connections are included without any licensing requirements or configuration needed.

Application services Enables applications to be available over TCP/IP connections. Terminal Services connections must be configured and licensed in order to be available to users.

The effect of Terminal Services being enabled on a server for remote administration is minimal. However, providing applications to users can create a processing load that increases incrementally for each simultaneously attached terminal services client. Reasons for using the application services can be simply to provide a specific application, to provide a line of business applications to remote offices, or even to create a full desktop of applications for all users to access. You will need to configure the items listed in Table 11.4 depending on which way you deploy Terminal Services.

Table 11.4 Terminal Services Configuration Requirements

Configured Option	Remote Administration	Application Services
Terminal Services Licensing	Not required	Required
Terminal Licenses Server	Not required	Required
User security	Required for administrators only	Required for all application users
Connections	Not required	Required
Application installation	Not required	Required for each application

To begin, you must install the Terminal Services License Server. If you have the Active Directory installed, you must install the license server on a DC. Otherwise, it can be installed on any Windows 2000 server. To install and configure the Terminal Services License Server:

1. In the Control Panel, open the Add/Remove Programs icon.
2. Select Add/Remove Windows Components.
3. Check the box for Terminal Services Licensing.
4. Select your entire enterprise.

5. Click Next.

6. Click Finish.

7. When complete, you can configure licensing by executing the Terminal Services Licensing console from the Administrative Tools menu.

8. Terminal Services Licensing will locate all Terminal Services servers and list them in its window, shown in Figure 11.26.

9. To activate a server, right-click on the server and select Activate from the pop-up menu.

10. You can change licensing options by right-clicking on a server and selecting Properties from the pop-up menu, illustrated in Figure 11.27.

Figure 11.26 Terminal Services Licensing.

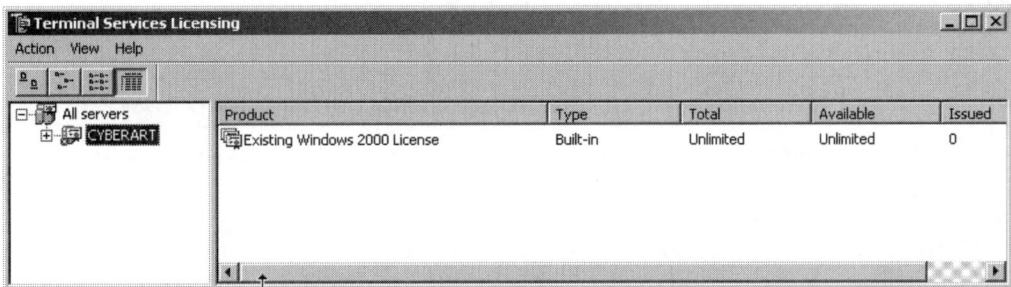

Figure 11.27 Server licensing properties.

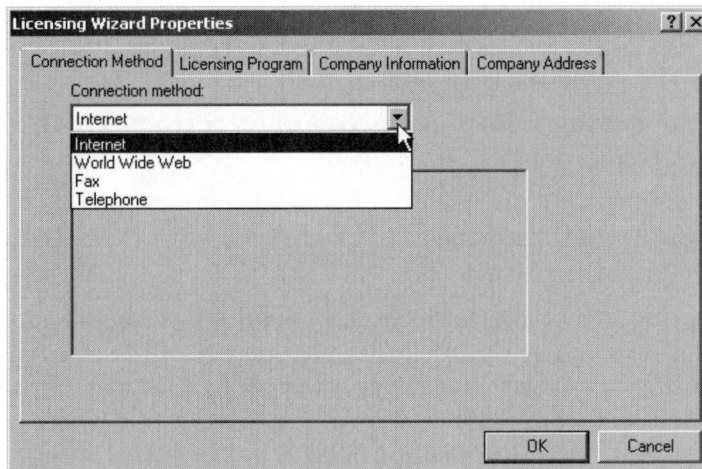

Next you must configure routers and firewalls. Configuration may not be necessary, however, unless the existing configuration would block the passage of Terminal Services traffic. You should ensure that the Remote Desktop Protocol (RDP) port is not blocked on any routers and firewalls that are placed between the Terminal Servers, the Terminal Services License Server and the Terminal Services clients. RDP uses TCP port 3389. In addition, you must ensure that the IP addresses of your servers and clients are not blocked on any routers or firewalls either. If you have an application layer firewall, you should make certain that there is a filter defined for RDP.

Then, install the Terminal Service on the Windows 2000 Servers that will provide remote administration or application services. This can be executed during the server's installation, or afterward using the Control Panel. To install Terminal Services:

1. In the Control Panel, open the Add/Remove Programs icon.

2. Select Add/Remove Windows Components.

3. Check the box for Terminal Services.

4. Click Next.

5. Select the mode—Remote administration or Application server.

6. Click Next.

7. Click Finish.

Connections are configured in the Terminal Services Configuration console found in the Administrative Tools menu. You must add connections for each simultaneous user. To add a connection, select the Action menu and then the Create New Connection option. The Terminal Services Connection Wizard will start. Select the following during the wizard:

Connection type RDP 5.0.

Encryption level Medium is default.

Remote control settings for shadowing user actions on this connection The default is to depend on each user's settings for shadowing the connection.

Transport type Type the connection name and select the Transport type for TCP.

Network adapter Select the adapter that users can use to access this connection and how many connections can be established over that adapter. If you have a server that is connected to the Internet as well as an internal network, you may wish only internal users to access the server. In this case, select only the adapter connected to the internal network.

You can change a connection's properties after initial creation by right-clicking the connection and selecting Properties. The Properties dialog is illustrated in Figure 11.28.

Figure 11.28 Connection properties.

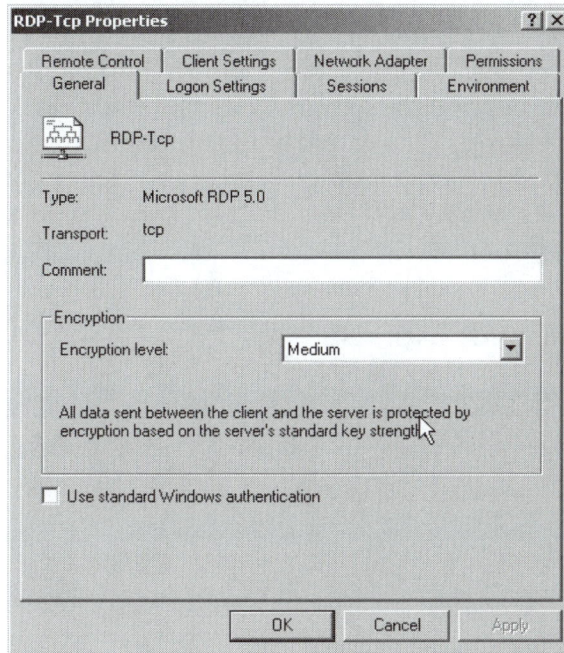

User Security is configured through the Active Directory Users and Computers console for domain-participating Terminal Servers. To change a user's Terminal Services properties, right-click the user account and select Properties. The three tabs that directly affect how a user's terminal connection works are Sessions, Remote Control, and Terminal Services Profile.

- Sessions, shown in Figure 11.29, allows you to manage how a connection will work for the user. This includes whether to disconnect or end a session. Disconnected sessions can be connected later, so an application can be left open at a certain point even if there is an error in transmission between the client and the server. An ended session, on the other hand, goes away completely.

- Remote Control allows you to configure whether the user's session can be shadowed by another user. For example, if you configured Terminal Services for a classroom, you would enable remote control without user's permission but with interaction for all students, but disable remote control for all teachers. This would enable a teacher to look at what a student was doing remotely, and then demonstrate how to execute some function within the application.

- Terminal Services Profile allows you to configure a different profile for terminal connections than would be used on a standard Windows desktop. This is particularly helpful when you provide a standard desktop environment through application services, but you want to enable each user to maintain a different profile on their own computer.

Figure 11.29 Configuring user sessions.

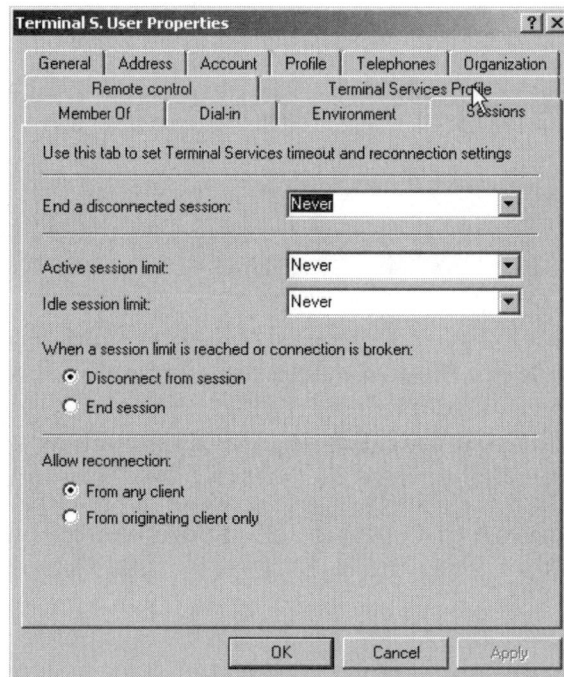

Installing applications on the server requires the server's mode to be changed. In a case such as Office 2000, there may be a special scripted installation specifically meant for Terminal Servers. Applications are installed differently on a Terminal Services server than they are on a standard server in order to place user files in multiple user locations rather than a single multiple-access directory. In this way, users can have separate preferences for their applications. To install an application:

1. Open a command prompt by clicking Start | Run, typing **cmd**, and then pressing Enter.

2. Change to the directory from which you will install.

3. Type **change user/install** and press Enter.

4. Install the application.

5. When the installation is complete, type **change user/execute** and press Enter to change back to the standard mode. If the application requires the server to reboot, or at any time, you can check the mode that the server is in at reboot by typing **change user/query** at a command prompt. The **change user** command is illustrated in Figure 11.30.

Figure 11.30 Change user command for application installation.

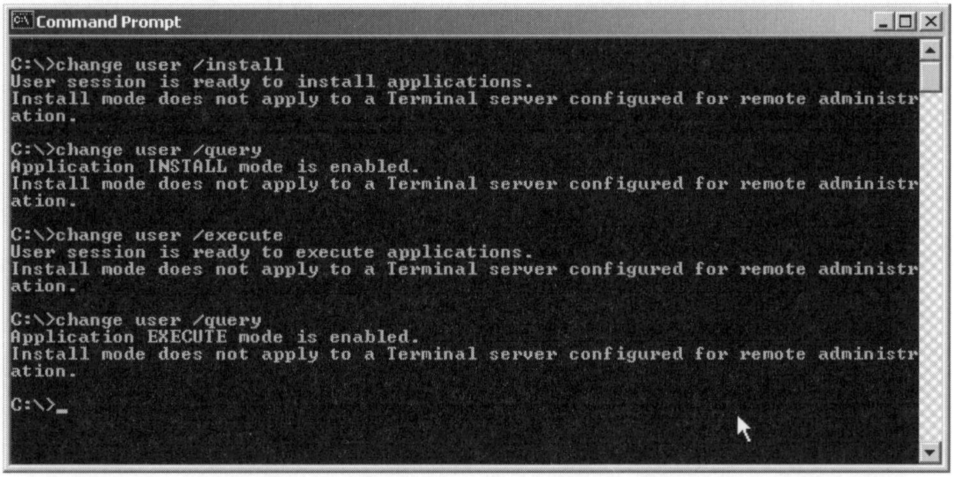

Creating Terminal Services clients is the final step in the Terminal Services deployment. There is a utility in the Administrative Tools menu of each Terminal Services server called Terminal Services Client Creator. This utility will create diskettes for deploying the Terminal Server client to either 16-bit Windows workstations, or to 32-bit Windows workstations, as shown in Figure 11.31. You can use the Setup executable on the diskette to install the client on workstations so that they can access the Terminal Services server.

Figure 11.31 Terminal Services Client Creator.

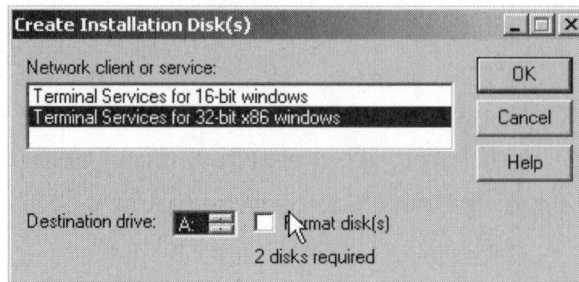

Configuring Routing and Remote Access Services

Routing and remote access is configured through the Routing and Remote Access console available in the Administrative Tools menu. You must configure routing and remote access when you use a server to provide routing between network segments, to provide remote access services to dial-up users, or to provide virtual private network (VPN) services to Internet users. To configure a server:

1. Start the Routing and Remote Access Server (RRAS) console on the Windows 2000 Server.

2. Right-click on the server in the left-hand pane.

3. Select Configure and Enable Routing and Remote Access from the pop-up menu.

4. The RRAS Setup Wizard will start. Click Next.

5. Select the type of services that the server will provide. To provide custom settings, select the Manually configured server option. Otherwise, select the settings that match the role for your new server.

6. Depending on which option you select, the wizard will walk you through the requirements for that option. For example, if you select Remote access server, the next screen allows you to select the remote access protocols, shows how to assign IP addresses (as shown in Figure 11.32), and asks whether you will use Remote Authentication Dial-In User Service (RADIUS) for central remote access authentication.

7. After you make your selections, click Finish. The service will start and the RRAS console will show configurable options below your new RRAS server.

Figure 11.32 Remote Access Services IP address assignment.

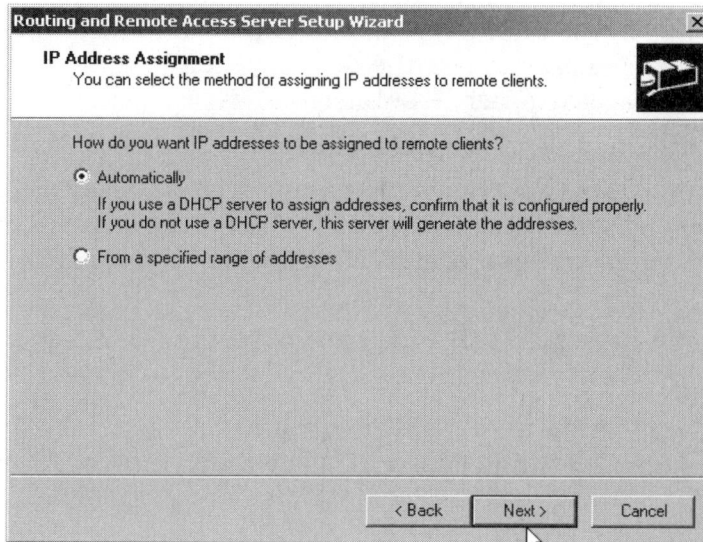

DHCP

You can configure Dynamic Host Configuration Protocol (DHCP) scopes on any Windows 2000 Server through the DHCP console in the Administrative Tools menu. This console is shown in Figure 11.33. There are two steps to this process:

1. Create a DHCP scope of IP addresses to be assigned to computers requesting a dynamic address.

2. Authorize the DHCP server as a security precaution to ensure that it can run on the Windows 2000 network.

To create a DHCP scope:

1. In the DHCP console, right-click the server.

2. Select New Scope.

3. The New Scope Wizard will start. Click Next.

4. Type a name and description for the scope and click Next.

5. Type the IP address range for this scope and the subnet mask. Click Next.

6. If you have statically assigned IP addresses that should be excluded from the scope, add them in at the next wizard dialog. Click Next.

7. Specify the duration for the DHCP lease. Click Next.

8. Select the option to configure the DHCP options and click Next. Options are the additional address information that is passed on to DHCP clients, such as the default gateway that enables the clients to access other IP subnets.

9. Type the address of the Default gateway and click Next.

10. Type the DNS name of the domain to which these DHCP clients will belong, and then provide the DNS server names and IP addresses to contact, and in which order to contact them. Click Next.

11. Type the names and IP addresses of all the WINS servers on the network, if any. Click Next.

12. Select Yes to activate the scope. Click Next.

13. Click Finish to complete the DHCP wizard.

Figure 11.33 DHCP console.

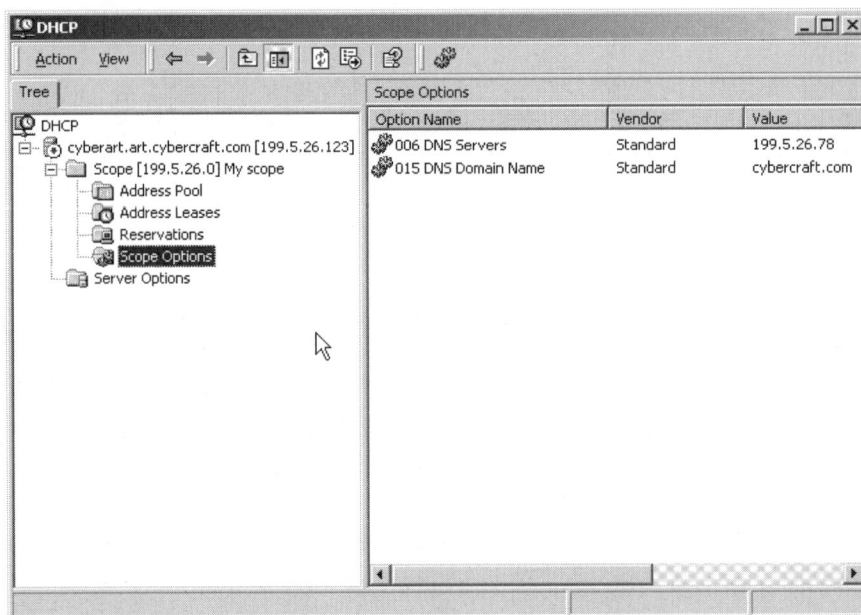

To authorize the new DHCP server:

1. Click the Action menu in the DHCP console.

2. Select Authorize.

WINS

Windows Internet Naming Service (WINS) is a leftover from Windows NT. If you have member servers or clients that require WINS, you will want to maintain at least two WINS servers on your network. To configure WINS, simply start the WINS console and add a server using the Action menu. Then configure replication partners for each WINS server.

Case Studies

Both ABC Chemical and West Coast Accounting need to install different types of servers throughout their enterprises. We're going to walk through the installation and configuration of a selected server for ABC Chemical Company first and then follow with West Coast Accounting's installation.

ABC Chemical Company

In the ABC Chemical Company, there are three sites—one for the main campus and one for each warehouse. We will walk through the installation for the domain controller located in the WestSite, which is a Windows 2000 server. This will be a secondary DNS server, as well as a DC for the ABCChem.com that serves as a Global Catalog server and as the Schema FSMO. This will be an upgraded server from Windows NT 4.0.

Before the server is installed, the site structure should be created. This will be done from the first DC installed using the Active Directory Sites and Services console. The first DC will be installed into the Default-First-Site-Name. The three sites that need to be created are HQ, EastWarehouse, and WestWarehouse.

1. Instead of creating a new site for HQ, rename Default-First-Site-Name. Just right-click on the Default-First-Site-Name, select Rename from the pop-up menu, and type the new name **HQ**.

2. Create the two other sites by right-clicking on the sites' containers and selecting New Site from the pop-up menu. Type the EastWarehouse site name and select the DefaultIPSiteLink to create the site. Repeat this to create the WestWarehouse site.

3. Create two site links, WestWarehouse-HQ and EastWarehouse-HQ, and one site link bridge, East-WestBridge. Because the sites each belong to the same domain, they require IP site links. To generate the site links, right-click on the IP container below Inter-Site Transports and select New Site Link. Type the name of the site link—**EastWarehouse-HQ**—and select the two sites, EastWarehouse and HQ, to participate in the link.

4. Double-click the site link to display its properties, change the Cost to 5, the frequency to 60 minutes, and set the schedule so that the link is not available between 10 AM to 2 PM Monday through Friday.

5. To create a site link bridge, right-click on the IP container and select New Site Link Bridge.

6. Type the name for the bridge, **East-WestBridge**, and select the two site links to participate in the bridge.

7. To add the correct IP subnets to each site, right-click the Subnets container and select New Subnet from the pop-up menu.

8. Type the address and subnet mask for a subnet in the EastWarehouse site, select the EastWarehouse site from the Site Name box, and click OK. Repeat this for each IP subnet in each site.

Now it's time to upgrade your NT server. Begin by placing the CD-ROM into the computer and executing the command **D:\I386\WINNT32 /CHECKUPGRADEONLY** (where D: represents the letter of your CD-ROM drive) to determine whether the server can be upgraded. Once this is acceptable, you can run the D:\I386\WINNT32 command. Using the information that you have for the server hardware, you can easily run the upgrade. After the upgrade is complete, the Active Directory must be installed. Since the NT Server was a Windows NT 4 BDC, the DCPROMO application will start automatically. Configure the DC to belong to an existing domain in an existing forest, placing the log files and the database files on separate hard disks. When complete, the server will prompt to be rebooted.

The new DC requires that DNS be configured with a secondary zone. On the server, start the DNS console. Select the Action menu and the option to Configure this server. When the configuration wizard starts, select the creation of a forward lookup zone and then select Secondary for the type and ABCChem.com as the zone name. After the zone is installed, right-click it and select Properties, then click Yes to Allow Dynamic Updates.

The new DC will need to be changed to a Global Catalog server. Open the Active Directory Sites and Services console. Expand the Sites container, the EastWarehouse site, and then the server object within that. Right-click on the NTDS Settings object and select Properties from the pop-up menu. On the General tab, check the box for Global Catalog.

This server must also be designated as the Schema Master FSMO. First, the Schema Manager must be enabled on the server with the REGSRVR command. Then, open the Schema Manager console, right-click on the root, and select Operations Master. Click the Change button and select the new DC. Select the Schema May be Modified on this server.

West Coast Accounting

In the West Coast Accounting offices, the administrator decides to install Windows 2000 Professional on workstations using a scripted installation method. In this way, the West Coast Accounting administrator can send a few things to a remote office's administrator and ensure that all desktop clients are installed in a consistent manner. These things include:

- The script, or answer file
- An installation batch file
- Source files for Windows 2000 Professional on CD-ROM
- Instructions

The West Coast Accounting administrator can drastically reduce the work involved if the image is identical for each workstation, as well as if the hardware involved is identical. The administrator creates a script that looks like the following:

```
[Data]
Unattendedinstall = Yes
Msdosinitiated = "0"
AutoPartition = 1


[Unattended]
UnattendMode = FullUnattended
OemPreinstall = Yes
TargetPath = Winpro
FileSystem = LeaveAlone
OemSkipEula = Yes


[GuiUnattended]
TimeZone = "004"
AdminPassword = xx3rILacc88
AutoLogon = Yes
AutoLogonCount = 1
OemSkipWelcome = 1
OemSkipRegional = 1
```

```
[UserData]
FullName = "West Coast Accounting"
OrgName = "West Coast Accounting, LLC"
ComputerName = "WCA001"
ProductId = "askjf-sajio-ajkl3-1233j-jakls"


[Display]
BitsPerPel = 8
XResolution = 800
YResolution = 600
VRefresh = 60


[Networking]
InstallDefaultComponents = Yes


[Identification]
JoinDomain = wcacctg.com
DomainAdmin = Administrator
DomainAdminPassword = ask88abc
```

In addition to the script, the administrator creates a batch file that consists of essentially one command to install Windows 2000 from a computer booted with a DOS-formatted diskette. This command is:

```
WINNT /S:d:\i386 /T:c: /U:a:\unattend.txt /E:a:\setupapp.bat
```

Summary

Implementing Windows 2000 involves more than just throwing a CD into a CD-ROM drive and running SETUP. In fact, there is no traditional setup.exe file; instead, there's your choice of winnt.exe and winnt32.exe, which execute either for DOS or 32-bit Windows, respectively.

WINNT (and WINNT32) can be executed with a script to automate an installation. Organizations benefit from automating the installation of an operating system since identical operating systems will have a smaller range of problems with applications than those installed with different options. Unattend.txt is the default name for a script file. It typically is used in migrating workstations to Windows 2000 Professional, but can also be used for Windows 2000 servers.

Disk duplication is available with two methods—System Preparation (SYSPREP) and Remote Installation Services (RIPREP).

Disk duplication is limited to rolling out Windows 2000 Professional. The difference between SYSPREP and RIPREP is that SYSPREP requires a manual way (usually a boot disk) to access the image on the network, whereas RIPREP can be delivered automatically using a Remote Installation Server to Preboot-Execution-Environment (PXE)-capable network adapters.

There are three phases of the Windows setup process. It begins with the WINNT phase, which begins copying necessary files to the hard drive, and then moves to a Text mode portion. Text mode gathers information about the hardware access layer (HAL), power, and storage, and begins the basic operating system installation. GUI mode occurs next and completes the installation with specific information and optional component installation.

When installing a new Windows 2000 network or upgrading an existing NT network, you need to decide which domain to begin with, and then which server within that domain. The rules are simple:

1. Start with the root domain—if it is a new domain, begin installing its first new domain controller. If it is an upgraded domain, begin by upgrading its PDC.

2. Move onto any child domains of the root domain namespace. If your root domain is root.com, then you would install or migrate sub.root.com before installing or migrating tree.com.

3. Complete the root domain tree until all the root namespace domains are migrated before beginning a new namespace.

4. Migrate each additional namespace within the forest starting with the top of the namespace and installing each subdomain in order.

When you upgrade an NT domain controller, the Active Directory installation wizard begins automatically. However, when you install a new server and wish to make it a domain controller, you must run the Active Directory installation wizard using the DCPROMO.EXE file. If you have an existing DC that you wish to transform into a member or standalone server, then you can also run DCPROMO to demote it.

After the Active Directory is installed in each domain, you create the Organizational Unit hierarchy, and then populate it with users and groups.

These tasks are all completed using the Active Directory Users and Computers console.

Before installing or migrating all domains and servers to Windows 2000, you should establish the sites structure, creating

- Sites
- Connection objects
- Site links
- Site link bridges
- IP subnets

After installing the remaining domains and DCs, you can create bridge-head servers between the sites to manage the traffic traveling across site links.

Just installing and configuring the Active Directory does not complete the installation of a Windows 2000 server. There are other components to install and configure, depending on the role that your server will play in the internetwork, as shown in Table 11.5.

Table 11.5 Configuration of Various Windows 2000 Server Roles

Server Role	Component	Configuration Method
DNS Server	DNS	Configure the server using the DNS console in the Administrative Tools menu. Configure a forward lookup zone and enable dynamic updates.
File Server	Windows 2000	Right-click a folder in the Windows Explorer and select the Sharing tab. Assign rights and permissions appropriate to the share.
Print Server	Windows 2000	Use the Printers icon in the Control Panel to start the Add Printer wizard. Right-click the printer after creation to change the rights and permissions assigned to it. Select the List in Directory option to publish the printer in the Active Directory.
Dfs root	Dfs	Configure a shared folder to be the root. Then add a root on a DC using the Distributed file system console in the Administrative Tools menu, indicating the shared folder that you created.

Continued

Table 11.5 Continued

Server Role	Component	Configuration Method
Certificate Authority	PKI	Create a hierarchy of CA servers on the internet-work. Start by installing the root CA, adding the sub-CA, and finally the issuing CA server. Install CA services using the Add/Remove Program icon in the Control Panel from the Add/Remove Windows Components option. Configure the CA services using the Certificate Authority console to create certificates and issue them. Further configure Group Policies for CA services using the Group Policy tab in the Active Directory properties for OUs, domains, or sites.
Web Server	IIS	IIS is installed by default. Configure the server using the Internet Services Manager in the Administrative Tools menu.
Terminal Services License server	Terminal Services Licensing	Install Terminal Services Licensing using the Add/Remove Programs icon in the Control Panel and selecting the Add/Remove Windows Components option. Configure the licenses using the Terminal Services Licensing console in the Administrative Tools menu.
Terminal Server	Terminal Services	Install Terminal Services using the Add/Remove Programs icon in the Control Panel and selecting the Add/Remove Windows Components option. Configure connections using the Terminal Services Configuration console in the Administrative Tools menu. Create client diskettes using the Terminal Services Client Creator in the Administrative Tools menu and install those on workstations. Configure users individual sessions using the Sessions, Remote Control, and Terminal Services Profile tabs in the Active Directory properties for each user object. Manage active connections using the Terminal Services Manager once Terminal Services are up and running.
Remote Access Server	Routing and Remote Access	Configure remote access using the Routing and Remote Access console in the Administrative Tools menu. Select a Remote Access Server to access the most common remote access needs.

Continued

Table 11.5 Continued

Server Role	Component	Configuration Method
VPN Server	Routing and Remote Access	Configure VPN using the Routing and Remote Access console in the Administrative Tools menu. Select VPN Server to access the most common VPN needs during the configuration wizard.
Router	Routing and Remote Access	Configure a Windows 2000 Server to act as a router using the Routing and Remote Access console in the Administrative Tools menu. Select Router to access the most common routing needs during the configuration wizard.
DHCP Server	DHCP	Configure DHCP using the DHCP console in the Administrative Tools menu. Create a scope of IP addresses to be assigned dynamically to clients, identify the IP addresses that should be excluded from the scope, and provide the additional IP addressing information to be delivered to the DHCP clients when they request an IP address, such as default gateway and DNS server information.
WINS Server	WINS	Configure WINS using the WINS console in the Administrative Tools menu. Add a WINS Server and any WINS Replication partners.

FAQs

Q: Can I use disk duplication to copy one server to other servers on my network? I want to make sure that the installation does not veer from the company standards.

A: Disk duplication is not supported by Windows 2000 Server, Advanced Server, or DataCenter Server. You cannot use SYSPREP or RIPREP to deploy the server version of Windows 2000. You can use an unattend.txt file to script the installation of a Windows 2000 Server. This will reduce the time it takes and will manage the installation to reduce operator input errors.

Q: I'm going to have a mixed domain of Windows NT 4 and Windows 2000 DCs for at least a year, and I don't plan to upgrade my Windows 98 or Windows NT 4 clients until two years after that. I am currently not using WINS because we deployed NWLink (IPX compatible) protocols on the network. Do I need to deploy WINS in my network?

A: Since you will need to upgrade all your clients and servers to TCP/IP in order to participate with the Windows 2000 DCs, and since the older versions of Windows depend on NetBIOS naming, you should deploy WINS. WINS will map the new IP addresses to the NetBIOS names of the computers on the network.

Q: I want to install DHCP for a group of workstations, but I want to statically assign the server IP addresses. I may be adding new servers in the future to the same subnet, too. These are all on the same IP subnet. How do I make certain that the DHCP server doesn't give out one of the servers' IP addresses?

A: When you configure the DHCP scope, you can specify which IP addresses are excluded from the scope during the DHCP Configuration wizard. An excluded set of IP addresses will not be handed out to a DHCP client. If you install a new server and you need to reserve an IP address that was previously part of the DHCP scope, you can do so by right-clicking on the Address Pool object under the Scope container and selecting New Exclusion Range from the pop-up menu. Then you can specify the IP address(es) that you want to exclude from the scope.

Chapter 12

Fast Track

Solutions in this chapter:

- Directory Enabled Networks (DEN)
- Cisco Networking Services (CNS)
- Microsoft's Windows 2000
- Cisco's Internetwork Operating System (IOS)

Introduction

Technology evolves at an incredibly fast pace. Each new development builds upon some element of a past technology, but also includes some innovative way of processing information. Microsoft and Cisco are two manufacturers that are at the crest of the latest technology developments. They have been successful in the marketplace, and many businesses use both Microsoft and Cisco technologies in their networks. When businesses change their business requirements, their networks change to accommodate them. This brings about the need to update Cisco hardware and the Cisco IOS, as well as the Microsoft operating systems' configurations and versions. It also means implementing emerging technologies such as Cisco Networking Services (CNS).

Directory-Enabled Networks

Cisco and Microsoft collaborated on Directory Enabled Networks (DEN), and then jointly launched that initiative through the Distributed Management Task Force (DMTF). What DEN entails is an information model composed of the participating network hosts, user accounts, applications, services, protocols, and the relationships between these elements. DMTF's Common Information Model (CIM) forms the basis of DEN, along with a mapping of CIM to Lightweight Directory Access Protocol (LDAP).

DEN stipulates a directory service with a common schema. A schema is a set of classes that define the types of objects in the directory and their properties or attributes. The directory service's objects correspond to nework elements such as user accounts, hosts, and services. One other directory service component is a policy, or rule, that manages how these objects interoperate.

DEN transforms a wide area network (WAN) into an intelligent internetwork. Intelligence is gained from the use of policies to control the network and its distributed resources in a logically centralized repository. A policy can define:

- Access control
- Resource usage
- Consumption control for resources, applications, and services
- Interaction of directory service elements

The result of using a DEN-compliant directory service is the ability to provide end-to-end services on the network. The application of policies is independent of a user's location, since the directory service can manage a dynamic environment. A DEN model is illustrated in Figure 12.1.

Figure 12.1 Directory Enabled Networks model.

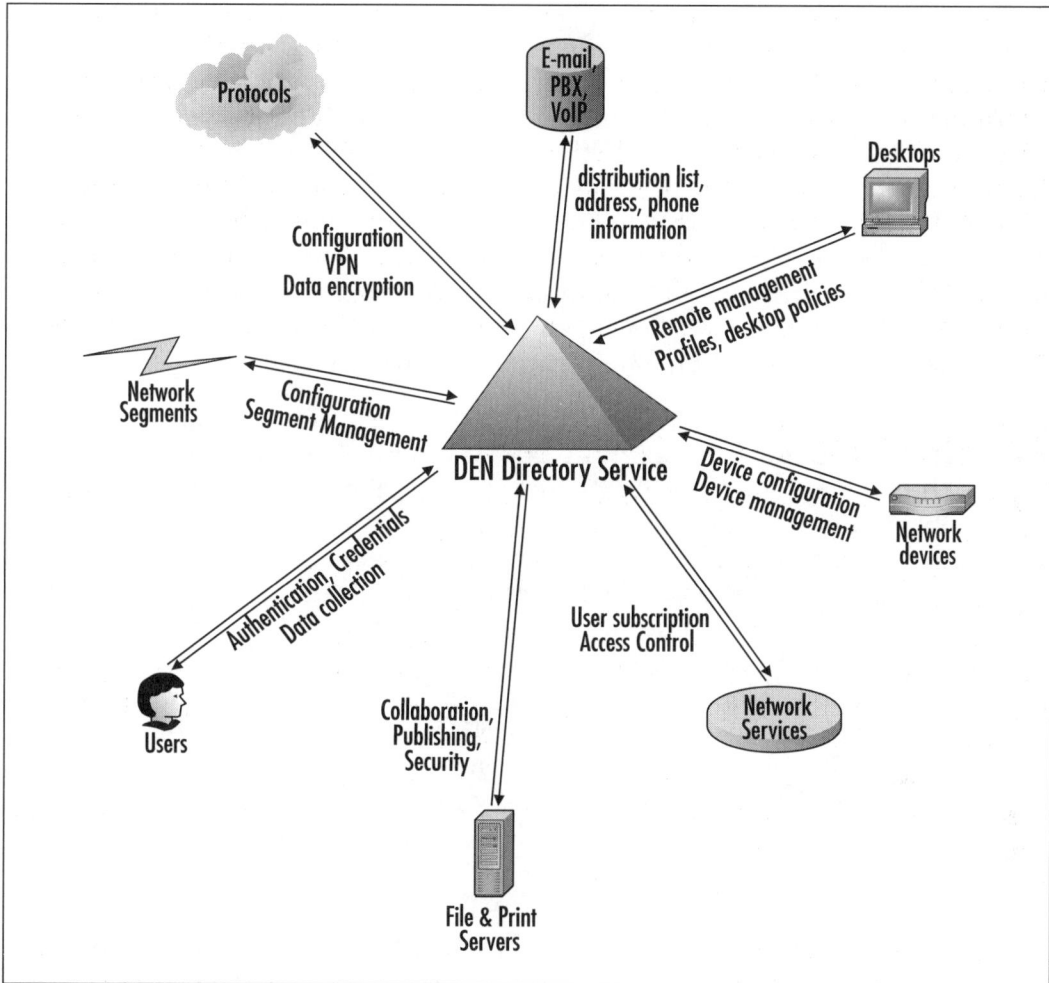

The IP Protocol Stack

The IP protocol stack is the basis for Internet standards, including DEN. Transmission Control Protocol/Internet Protocol (TCP/IP) is the protocol stack used on the Internet, enabling network hosts around the globe to communicate with each other. It is nearly universal in its usage on private networks as well, because of the popularity and growth of Internet usage both privately and within businesses. There are four layers within the stack:

Physical Access Layer Specifies physical media, frame formats, and media access.

Network Layer Specifies network addressing and routing. There is only one protocol at this layer—Internet Protocol (IP).

Transport Layer Specifies connection-oriented or connectionless connectivity from end-to-end. There are two protocols at this layer—Transmission Control Protocol (TCP) provides connection-oriented connectivity, and User Datagram Protocol (UDP) provides connectionless connectivity.

Application Layer Specifies the user access to the network. Multiple protocols function at this layer, including (but not limited to) File Transfer Protocol (FTP), HyperText Transfer Protocol (HTTP), Network News Transfer Protocol (NNTP), and Simple Mail Transfer Protocol (SMTP).

Each network node is given a 32-bit IP address that is typically written in dotted decimal notation, such as 10.12.38.252. Network nodes are given names that are much easier for people to remember. To be able to use the names instead of IP addresses, there must be some form of mapping system between the IP address and the name. The Domain Name System (DNS) provides this mapping mechanism. Although not required for strict IP connectivity, DNS is a must for the Active Directory to function. The Active Directory uses DNS—in particular, service locator resource records (SRV RRs) to enable domain controllers to locate each other and for clients to discover servers for authentication. DNS lookups work in a hierarchical structure. A DNS server, if it cannot service a request for an IP address, will pass it up the hierarchy to eventually reach a server that can handle the request. Windows 2000 can provide DNS services, and Cisco provides a DNS server application too.

Dynamic Host Configuration Protocol (DHCP) assigns IP addresses to network nodes. This replaces the individual configuration of a network node's IP address by an administrator, which reduces the time and effort spent on IP address management as well as increases the availability of IP addresses to a group of network nodes. DHCP uses a scope, or pool of IP addresses that can be assigned to network nodes. When a node requests an address, the DHCP will first check to see if there is a reserved IP address and then will assign it; otherwise, it will assign one within the pool of available IP addresses on that subnet. Windows 2000 includes a native DHCP client on all versions, and Windows 2000 Server has a DHCP service that can be installed. Cisco also provides a DHCP server application.

Cisco Networking Services

Cisco Networking Services (CNS) is a unique technology development that integrates a directory service (Microsoft's Active Directory) and infrastructure components (Cisco's routers and switches). CNS is the culmination of Microsoft and Cisco technologies and the DEN initiative.

The basis of CNS is found in DEN and its Common Information Model (CIM) standards. The goal of CNS is to manage network components and network services in a seamlessly integrated model, such that an entire network can be managed from a single seat, even as that network scales up in size. This in turn reduces the time it takes to deliver interoperable services.

To examine the benefits of CNS, you must first understand the traditional network and how it is managed. Take an example network—ACME has 14 Cisco routers, 22 Cisco switches, 7 Frame Relay links, 3 T3 Leased lines, 4 Asynchronous Transfer Mode (ATM) switches, 3 Token Ring MultiStation Access Units (MSAUs), 12 Windows 2000 Servers, 3 Linux Web servers, 4 Novell NetWare servers, 1 IBM AS/400 minicomputer, 3000 Windows 2000 Professional desktops, 1000 Apple Macintoshes, and 250 Sun UNIX machines.

With this type of network, you will find a division of network management from the application standpoint: each different type of equipment and operating system uses a different application to manage it. You will also find a division of network management from the administrative standpoint: each different type of connection, operating system, and equipment requires a different skill set to use the various applications. Typically, administrators for LAN/WAN links are separate from those who handle network servers, and each of those groups is separate from those who support the desktop workstations. Within the LAN/WAN group, you will find further division between the administrators for each link type, so in this example, there might be a Frame Relay administrator, leased line administrator, and an ATM administrator; or perhaps a WAN administrator and a LAN administrator. Within the server administrator group, you will find Windows 2000 administrators, Linux administrators, IBM AS/400 administrators, and NetWare administrators. And the desktop group might be divided into Windows 2000 administrators, UNIX administrators, and Macintosh administrators. This type of "silo" management is illustrated in Figure 12.2.

If a service such as videoconferencing were to be deployed on this example network, each administrator must configure his or her own portion of the network and try to ensure that each component interacts seamlessly with each other. In videoconferencing for example, a file transfer from a NetWare server should be configured to take a backseat to the video

Figure 12.2 Management silos in a network environment.

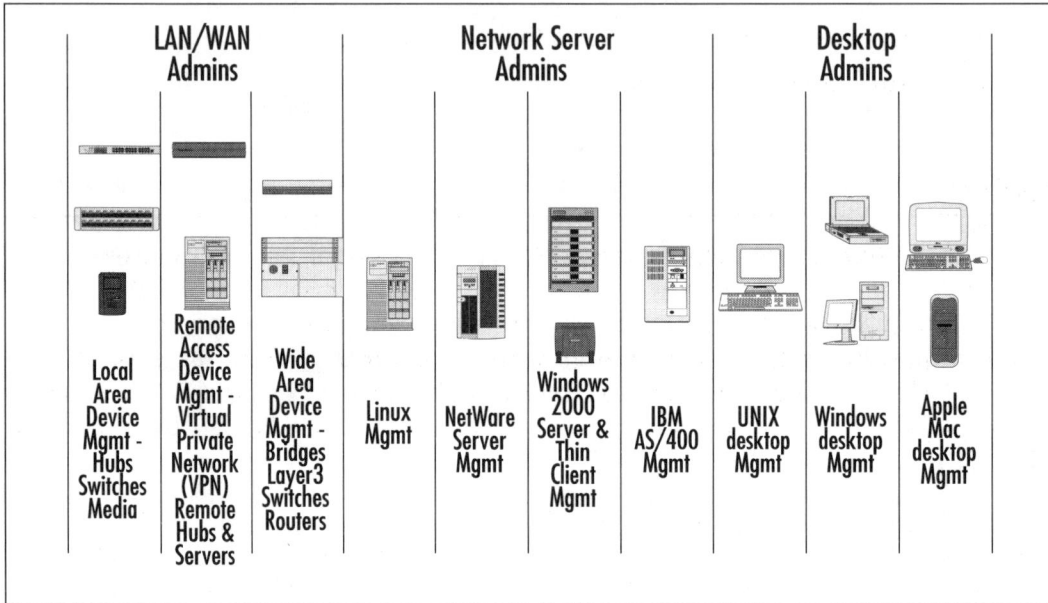

data traversing the network from the videoconferencing server, regardless of which router it travels through or on which desktops the videoconference runs. In addition, because the network addresses don't necessarily know which user they are attached to, a mobile workforce will stress the limits of the administrators while they create rules on systems throughout the network to follow those mobile users.

To minimize administrative intervention, you need an application that "glues" all of these systems together and can manage them as a cohesive group. In an internetwork with redundant links and mobile users, data can travel through any combination of hosts (routers, servers, switches) on a path between two network hosts. Each host on the path must be able to understand how to treat the data, whether that includes giving it priority over other data or maintaining a certain data format such as encryption.

CNS was created to address these issues. It provides for intelligent network services using the Active Directory and LDAP client services. CNS extends the Active Directory to incorporate new objects and attributes that represent Cisco hardware and IOS services. If you had a Cisco 3640 router on the network, you could add the router as an object in the Active Directory. The router object would have appropriate attributes such as:

- Passwords

- Protocols

- Slot configuration with network modules

- Connectivity information

NOTE

CNS version 1.0 is being released to Cisco's independent software vendors, partners, and systems integrators. Future directory-enabled products will be capable of integrating with these provider networks, bringing benefits directly to end-users. In addition, future releases of CNS should be widely available to the full spectrum of Cisco customers.

To integrate the hardware and IOS services into the rest of the network, LDAP is employed for communication with the directory service. When the hardware is booted up, it uses LDAP to check the Active Directory for any policies that will influence how traffic is handled as it passes through it. Thereafter, the hardware uses LDAP to continue to communicate with the Active Directory to validate or update these policies.

The Active Directory policies are extended with CNS to include Cisco hardware and IOS-specific information. They are also integrated with the existing objects within the Active Directory. For example, prior to CNS, Quality of Service (QoS) was managed by establishing rules that stated certain traffic types traveling from certain IP addresses would be granted priority over other types of traffic. This can be a cumbersome administrative problem when IP addresses are distributed through DHCP or when users travel from site to site. In both cases, an IP address is not static and needs to be changed any time that the user's IP address changes. With CNS, the Active Directory lets the QoS policy be applied to a user. The user's logon will update the Active Directory information with the user's IP address. When a Cisco router communicates with the Active Directory, it determines the user's IP address from the Active Directory information and then can provide QoS to that IP address. The policy can be established regardless of which IP address a user is granted. In addition to that, the same policy can be applied to any router (or all the routers) on the network. This greatly reduces the administrative overhead of configuring multiple routers. CNS provides the tools to manage:

- QoS—inclusive of Resource Reservation Protocol (RSVP) and DiffServ

- Basic configuration

- Automated service deployment

The use of a central repository (in this case, the Active Directory) solves the separation of administration issues, too. When a policy for QoS is placed in the Active Directory, it can be applied to the users, their workstations, the servers, the routers, and the switches. This ensures that the policies are cohesive. Furthermore, there is only a single place where the policy needs to be applied. In contrast, the former method of applying a QoS policy required that each separate administrative application for each separate network host had to be configured—and a separate administrative group would have performed that task for each type of host.

Many businesses find that a centralized administrative group reduces their costs. Others find the opposite because their business requirements are considerably dissimilar. However, a distributed administrative structure can still take advantage of the Active Directory and CNS because of the ability to delegate administrative duties in the Active Directory. By using CNS, distributed administrators can still apply policies that will manage traffic network-wide for those users that the distributed administrators manage. This common information model ensures that the entire network functions in a cohesive manner, regardless of who applies the policies.

CNS consists of several components, some of which have already been discussed:

Events Network Management traditionally is dependent upon protocols such as Simple Network Management Protocol (SNMP), but effective management is limited due to the lack of scalability. Events in CNS are provided as a publish/subscribe event service based on TIBCO Rendezvous. This means that events can be published and subscribed using the TIBCO 6.1 Application Programming Interface (API) as an event bus by CNS event gateways, which then pass event messages between the event bus Cisco IOS clients. This architecture scales globally, if need be.

Schema A common information model applied to the Active Directory, whose schema is extended to incorporate Cisco hardware and IOS services. The schema package provides for systems, applications, devices, physical, network, and core, applied as the standard DMTF CIM 2.2 model. The schema package also provides for the core policy and QoS data model in accordance with the Internet Engineering Task Force (IETF) schema.

Concurrency control service (CCS) Dynamic data reflecting Cisco device or service status. As the state of the device varies over time, applications can utilize CCS to access and share dynamic data. Because CCS is used, the directory service information store does not need to bear constant updates.

Clients CNS clients are based on the LDAP version 3.0 standard. The client services include Kerberos simple bind security and directory service location via DNS SRV RR lookup. The client supports IP Security (IPSec) virtual private networking (VPN) in an agent form, a provisioning agent for Cisco device event services, and a change notification agent.

These components integrate with the Active Directory, and other network services integrate with the Active Directory in a hub-and-spoke fashion, as shown in Figure 12.3.

The hub-and-spoke interaction enables a centralized administration of the internetwork. An administrator can establish a policy or set of policies that creates end-to-end service management. The benefits of this type of management will reduce costs by removing management silos, reducing errors through centralization, and by ensuring a consistent policy application.

Microsoft's Windows 2000

Microsoft released Windows 2000 as a set of four operating systems. Like its predecessor, Windows NT, one of the operating systems for Windows 2000 is meant to be used on a desktop workstation—it is called Windows 2000 Professional. The remaining versions are all meant to be used on servers that scale up in size and capabilities. Windows 2000 Server supports workgroup-size servers and is considered the upgrade version of Windows NT Server 4.0. Windows 2000 Advanced Server supports enterprise-size servers and is considered the upgrade for Windows NT Server 4.0 Enterprise Edition. Windows 2000 DataCenter Server is released only on high-performance server equipment by the Original Equipment Manufacturer (OEM).

There are several new features within Windows 2000. All of the server versions support the Active Directory, which is the new domain-based directory service. Each server can become a domain controller, or remain a standalone outside the Active Directory or member server of one of the domains within the Active Directory. The Active Directory provides a hierarchical management of the participating network hosts, user accounts, and services. It is the central repository for directory information as specified by the DEN model, and is required for CNS to function.

Figure 12.3 Interaction between Active Directory and participating services.

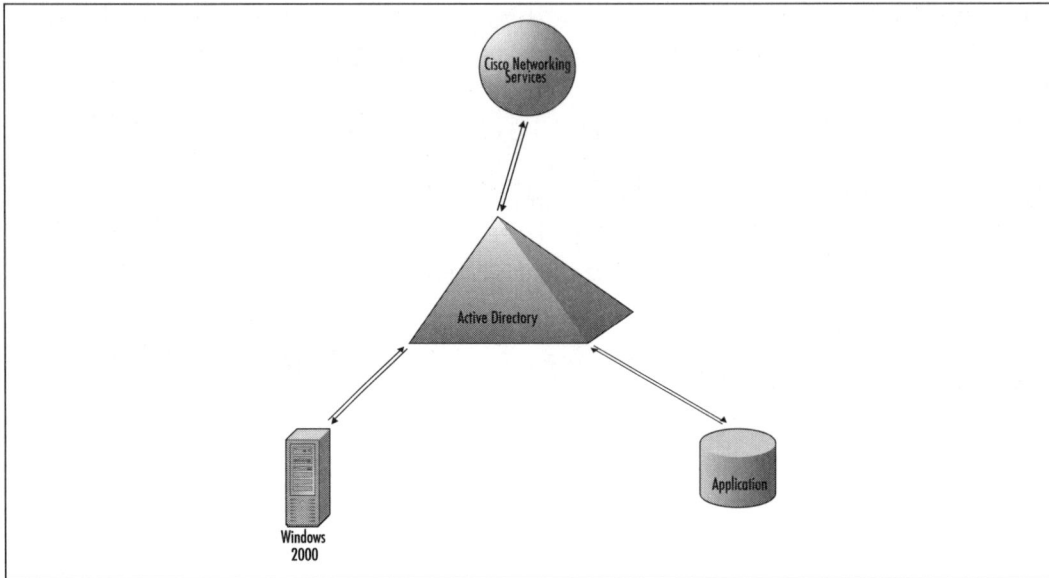

Installation

One of the problems faced by businesses when they prepare to install an operating system on an enterprise-wide basis is the ability to quickly install an operating system with a standard configuration. Windows 2000 has several options for installation on an unattended basis.

Scripting A file is used to script the options that the Windows 2000 installation program will take. Each computer that runs the script runs the installation program, but with little or no user intervention. Additional files are provided that can kick off scripts for applications, but those scripts are dependent upon whether the application includes its own scripting method.

Disk duplication A program called SYSPREP is used to copy the configuration and files of an already-installed computer so that the operating system can be copied directly onto another computer. This method requires that the hardware for each of the copied computers is identical, or nearly identical, to that of the computer used to create the original configuration file set. It is not easily used in an environment with a wide variety of hardware types.

Remote Installation Services (RIS) A program called RIPREP is used to copy the configuration and files of an already-installed computer so that the operating system can be copied onto another computer. This method requires a Windows 2000 Server to provide remote installation services—network interface cards using Pre-boot Execution Environment (PXE) so that remote computers can access the available operating system configurations. Like the SYSPREP disk duplication method, this method is not easily used in an environment with a wide variety of hardware types. Unlike SYSPREP, this method can be used without a person visiting the computer to boot its installation.

The installation of a Windows 2000 machine is executed with the WINNT command, if beginning from DOS. If executing the installation from a Windows 95, Windows 98, or Windows NT machine, use WINNT32.

Although the scripted or disk duplication methods can automate the installation of various Windows 2000 features, you may find that manually installing these features later is preferable. To install these features, use the Control Panel Add/Remove Programs icon. After installation of some services, such as the Routing and Remote Access Service or the Internet Information Service, you will still need to configure the service so that it can be used.

Security

Security has been updated in Windows 2000. Additions to the operating system include support for virtual private networking (VPN) using Layer 2 Tunneling Protocol (L2TP). L2TP is a protocol based on Cisco's Layer 2 Forwarding (L2F) protocol and Microsoft's Point-to-Point Tunneling Protocol (PPTP). L2TP is somewhat more secure than PPTP, which has suffered a few security holes. L2TP is implemented over IP Security (IPSec) tunnels.

Another security innovation in Windows 2000 is the use of Kerberos. Kerberos authentication is provided within the Active Directory. Kerberos defines the trust relationships between Active Directory domains. These trust relationships are both transitive and bidirectional within a forest. For example, in Figure 12.4, Domain A trusts Domain B and Domain B trusts Domain C. Since the trust relationship is transitive, that means that Domain A trusts Domain C. Kerberos trusts are bidirectional, so that when Domain A trusts Domain B, Domain B trusts Domain A in return.

Under Windows NT, trust relationships were nontransitive and unidirectional. A trust relationship can be created between an Active Directory domain and a Kerberos realm. A trust can be established between Windows NT domains and Active Directory domains, or between Active Directory domains in two separate forests. Each of these types of trusts is unidirectional and nontransitive.

Figure 12.4 Kerberos transitive trusts.

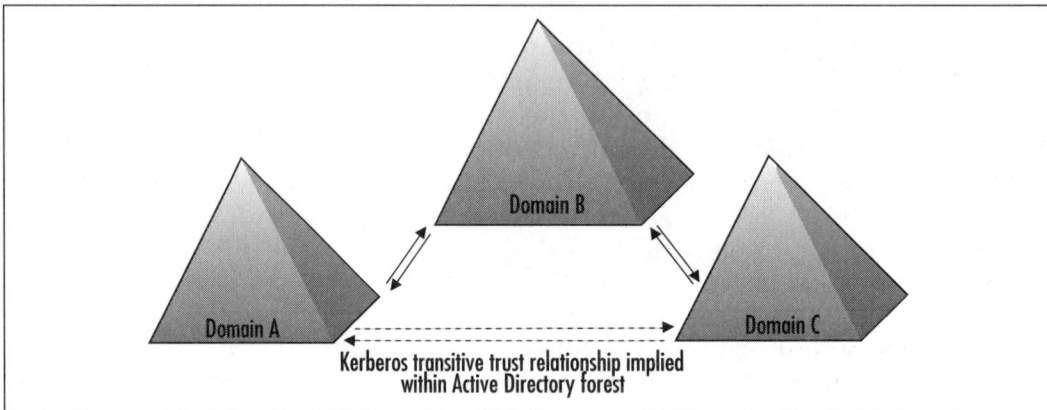

Services

Windows 2000 Server provides Routing and Remote Access Service (RRAS). This means that a Windows 2000 Server can perform routing functions when it has two or more interfaces to the network, and that Windows 2000 can provide native dialup services to remote computers. Remote users are able to logon to the network, share data, and run applications in much the same way as they could if they were connected locally to the network.

Every Windows 2000 computer provides the Internet Information Service (IIS). IIS consists of World Wide Web (WWW) publishing services, File Transfer Protocol (FTP) publishing services, Simple Mail Transport Protocol (SMTP) services, and Network News Transport Protocol (NNTP) services. A Windows 2000 server can act as a native Internet or intranet server.

One of the advantages of using Windows 2000 Server is Terminal Services, which provide thin-client remote control of a Windows 2000 Server for multiple, simultaneous users. Thin-client services are provided using the Remote Data Protocol (RDP) v5. The client is considered "thin" because it consumes a very small portion of network bandwidth. Applications can be managed centrally, much like those installed on mainframes, but their graphical nature does not impede their centralization. Remote control is established using an application that is similar to terminal emulation. The low-bandwidth utilization properties make Windows 2000 Terminal Services ideal as an application server for remote users.

Active Directory

When you execute a Windows 2000 Server installation project on a network, you must first decide whether you will use the Active Directory for managing user accounts and network resources. Your alternate choice is to deploy each server as though it were a standalone server with its own set of user accounts and resources—a system that can add a tremendous amount of administrative overhead to your network. Because of this, Active Directory is nearly always deployed!

Planning your Windows 2000 project begins with your design. You will first need your business requirements established for the project and then you will need to examine how to implement those requirements with the Active Directory. For example, you can design an Active Directory that is highly secure, or one that is much less so. Some factors you should look at when you design are:

- Directory service availability and fault tolerance
- Bandwidth consumption by domain controllers and clients
- Scalability of the directory with expected growth of the company

You should develop four basic plans when you design the Active Directory:

1. Forest Plan
2. DNS/Domain Plan
3. Organizational Unit Plan
4. Site Plan

A Forest plan consists of the number of forests that you plan to deploy on the internetwork. Each forest should be given a designated root domain. You can have one or more domains in each forest, but only a single root domain.

The DNS/Domain plan lists your namespace designations, the domains within the Active Directory forest, their hierarchical organization, and the functions designated for each domain. Since Kerberos provides bidirectional, transitive trust relationships, there is no need to specify the trusts between domains within the forest—they are created automatically. However, if there are trusts outside the forest to domains that exist in other forests or Windows NT domains, they should be designated in this plan. Since these trusts are nontransitive and unidirectional, each trust should be specified and the direction to which the trust points.

The Organizational Unit (OU) plan should determine the hierarchy of the containers within each domain in the forest. It should designate the top administrative containers, hidden object containers, and remaining organizational and group policy containers. The OU plan can contain a description of group policies required and the inheritance in each domain, as well as any blocked inheritance. The OU plan can also contain the access control security designations for users and groups.

The site plan should detail the topology for the sites. This includes the number of sites, their locations, and the site links and site link bridges that need to be established for each link. If there are site links that require SMTP instead of Remote Procedure Calls (RPCs), then those site links should be specified. The site plan should designate the location of Global Catalog servers and Flexible Single Master Operations (FSMO) servers.

Replication

The Active Directory is an extensible storage engine (ESE) database. It is distributed among multiple domain controllers (DCs). Unlike the Windows NT domain architecture where there is a primary domain controller (PDC), there is no single master for the domain updates in Windows 2000. Each DC in the Windows 2000 Active Directory architecture is a master, which means that updates can be made on any DC. The multiple master DCs must synchronize through a process called replication in order for the updates to be propagated throughout the rest of the DCs.

Replication is controlled by the site topology detailed in the Site plan. Each site is considered a set of well-connected IP subnets. Well-connected is defined as a reliable network connection with significant available bandwidth. That definition can be stretched to fit many different types of links, but you should consider any LAN link to be part of a site. WAN links, however, can be part of either a site or separate sites, depending on the number of users existing on each side of that WAN link and the bandwidth available to the link, and whether or not a domain controller will exist at either location. Site topology is easy to reconfigure at any point in time. This lets the administrator scale the site topology with the growth and changes experienced by the business network.

RPCs over IP are used for replication traffic within each site. This is uncompressed traffic periodically transmitted each five minutes by default. The Knowledge Consistency Checker (KCC) automatically generates replication topology. The KCC makes certain that there are no more than three hops between servers in a replication circle. This ensures that the Active Directory can be synchronized within a maximum of 15 minutes after any update inside a particular site.

Replication is somewhat different when it occurs between sites. First, you can use either RPCs or SMTP to transmit replication traffic between sites instead of just RPCs. SMTP is actually used in special cases only. You should use it if you cannot establish an RPC connection between the sites *and* if the two sites that are linked by SMTP are *not* spanned by a domain. Intersite replication is compressed automatically. It is scheduled by an administrator to occur on a regular basis and the site links can be made unavailable during high-traffic times so that replication does not interrupt production business traffic. There is nothing automatically configured by the KCC between sites. Instead, an administrator must configure a site link for each two directly connected sites and a site link bridge for sites that share a site in common. Connection objects must also be created to direct the replication traffic.

The data that is replicated from the Active Directory is segregated into four partitions:

1. Schema
2. Configuration
3. Domain
4. Global Catalogue

The schema is replicated only when it has been extended. This is a rare occurrence and should not affect replication much. The configuration partition contains the Active Directory site topology and other configuration information. This, too, seldom needs to be replicated. Most of the changes that will need to be replicated occur in the domain partitions and the global catalogue. Each domain is a separate partition of the Active Directory. When two DCs are members of the same domain, they will each contain a copy of that domain partition. However, when they are members of different domains, they will not need to replicate domain updates to each other.

The File Replication Service (FRS) is the method by which files are replicated between DCs. Login scripts are one of the types of files necessary to replicate to all domain controllers. However, FRS can replicate any files that need to be distributed enterprise-wide. FRS uses the same replication topology as the Active Directory, so it is not necessary to generate a second topology. When a file is changed, it is fully replicated to the other DCs. If you have a large file and make small changes to it on a consistent basis, FRS could stress the network with excessive traffic.

You should consider several rules when you establish your site topology:

1. Try to place a DC in each site.
2. When there are multiple domains in your Active Directory forest, try to place a Global Catalogue server in each site.

3. Place FSMOs in central, highly available sites.

4. Try to place a DNS server in each site, especially when it is separated from other sites by unreliable links.

Cisco's Internetwork Operating System

Cisco manufactures internetworking equipment such as routers and switches. To operate this equipment, Cisco has developed the Internetwork Operating System (IOS). IOS equipment can scale from a small workgroup LAN to a global internetwork. Cisco also creates applications such as CNS to assist in network functionality.

Hierarchical Design Model

Cisco uses a hierarchical design model in segmenting an internetwork. This model consists of three levels, as shown in Figure 12.5.

Core Layer Provides backbone service for the internetwork. Its primary function is to provide speed of data transmission.

Distribution Layer Provides a boundary between end-user access and backbone services. Its primary function is to secure data by distributing it appropriately to end-users; therefore it does utilize filtering of packets.

Access Layer Provides the access point for end-users onto the network. Its primary function is to enable data access.

Using this model, you can make decisions about the locations and functions of routers and switches on the internetwork.

Cisco Switches

Cisco provides several series of switches. Each series is intended for a slightly different use on an internetwork.

Catalyst 2900 Provides 12- or 24-port stackable switching. Intended for use in microsegmentation at the access layer.

Catalyst 3500 Provides modular stacking for use in scalable switching; for example, Ethernet, Fast Ethernet, and Gigabit Ethernet switching. Intended for use in the distribution and access layers.

Catalyst 5000 Provides Ethernet, Fast Ethernet, Gigabit Ethernet, Token Ring, Fiber Distributed Data Interface (FDDI), Asynchronous Transfer Mode (ATM), and Ethernet over Fiber (10BaseFL) network interfaces for high-speed switching. Intended for use in any layer, from segmenting backbones at the core layer to microsegmentation at the access layer.

Figure 12.5 The hierarchical design model for networks.

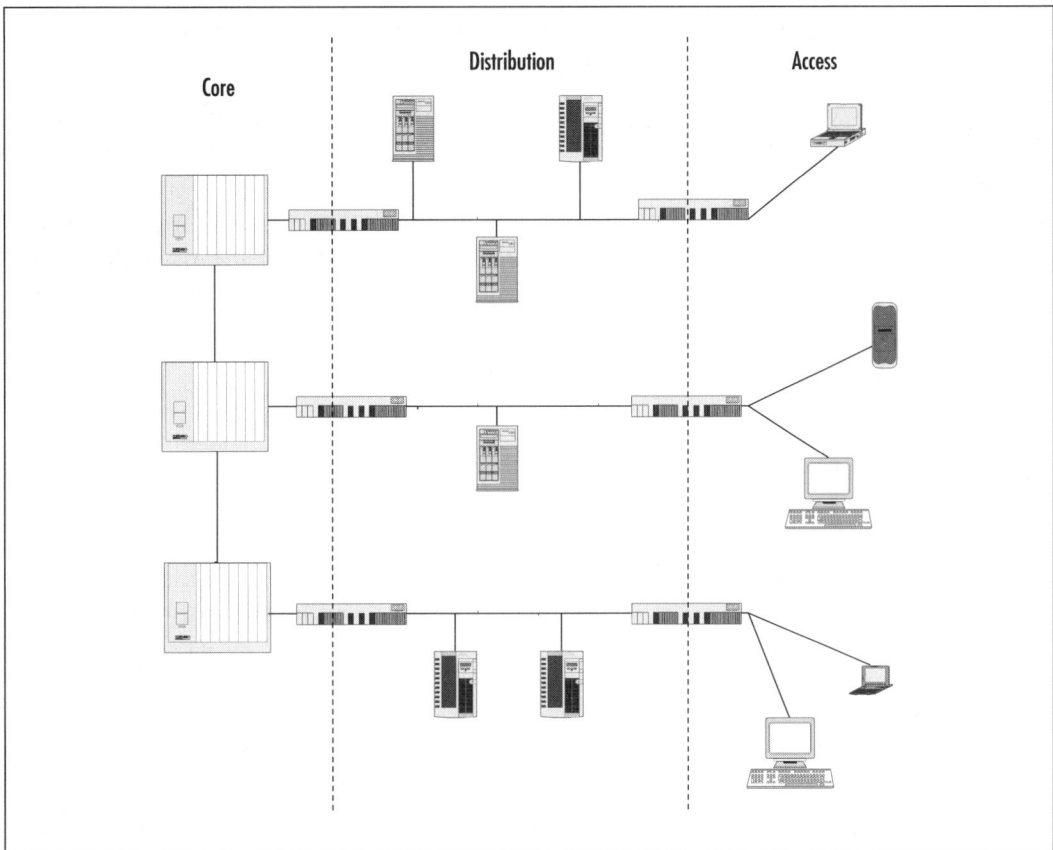

Catalyst 6500 Provides 150 Mbps switching capacity as a multilayer switch. Intended for use in backbones at the core layer, or within the distribution layer.

Cisco Routers

Cisco developed routers with the same scalability in mind. Each series of routers is intended to be used in a certain size network, or to provide functions at a certain layer in the hierarchical design model.

800 series This router series has multiple models, all intended for the small-office home office (SOHO) in connecting to a larger internetwork. Depending on the usage, it can route at the access layer or distribution layer.

1600 series This router series is intended for small offices, for use at the access layer or the distribution layer in a small to medium-sized business.

1700 series This is a router intended for small, remote offices at the distribution layer in small or medium-sized businesses.

3600 series This is a midlevel platform for routing data, voice, and video. Intended for use in small or medium-sized offices at the backbone or distribution layer.

7200 series This series of routers' small physical form belies its high-end capabilities for routing of data, voice, and video. Intended for use on backbones, especially those connected to remote offices.

7500 series High-end platform for data, voice, and video. Intended for use in backbones at the core layer.

Routing and Remote Access

The function of routing is nearly identical to the function of remote access. In a routed environment, data is passed through a router from one network interface to another. In a remote access server, data is passed from a remote interface, typically some form of modem or wide area network interface, to a local area network interface, usually some form of Ethernet. This is illustrated in Figure 12.6. As a result, many routers perform the functions of remote access servers and vice versa. This is true for both Microsoft's Windows 2000 Routing and Remote Access Service and many of Cisco's routers and remote access server equipment.

Modems use highly available plain old telephone service (POTS) analog lines. A remote user will dial up to a remote access server using the modem and either a Serial Line Internet Protocol (SLIP) or Point-to-Point Protocol (PPP). SLIP is an older protocol and used mainly for UNIX servers or clients. PPP is not only newer, but provides some additional enhancements such as the ability to encrypt or compress data. Although modems were the original method used to dial up from remote locations to networks, there are new methods of remote access:

- Integrated Services Digital Network (ISDN)
- Digital Subscriber Line (DSL)

Both of these methods are digital access over copper telephone wires. ISDN is more widely implemented in Europe than in the United States. ISDN offers identical upload and download speeds on the wire. There are two offerings:

Basic Rate Interface (BRI)   128 Kbps bandwidth using two bearer (B) channels of 64 Kbps, and one data (D) channel at 16 Kbps. The D channel handles bandwidth overhead traffic, and the B channels can carry voice and data. BRI runs over standard telephone wires.

Primary Rate Interface (PRI)   1.472 Mbps bandwidth using 23 B channels of 64 Kbps and one D channel of 64 Kbps. PRI cannot use standard telephone wire; it must run across a T1 line.

There are several types of DSL, but the one most commonly provided is Asymmetric Digital Subscriber Line (ADSL). ADSL provides a much slower upload rate than a download rate, hence the name "asymmetric." ADSL's upload and download rates are variable because they depend on the length of the wire from the local office to the endpoint. Download rates can be as high as 9 Mbps, and upload rates are available up to 640 Kbps.

Figure 12.6 Routing and remote access services are identical in nature.

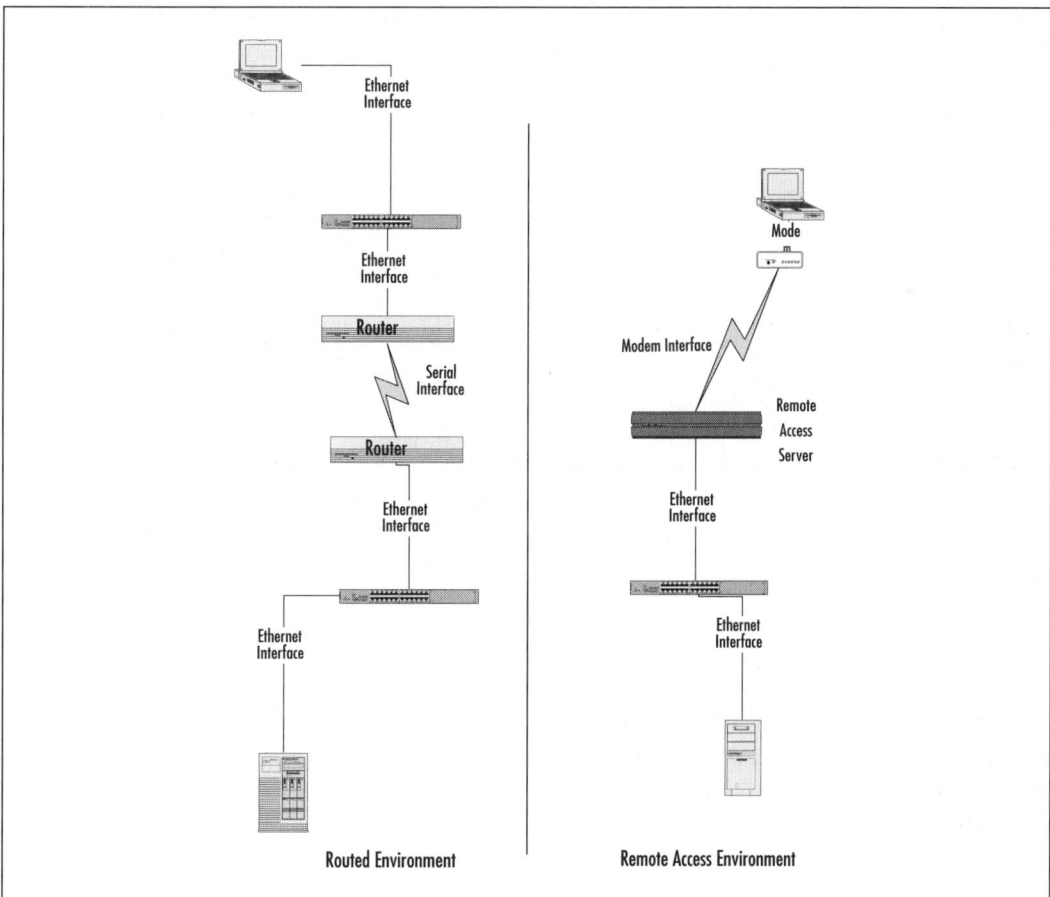

Routing Protocols

Routing protocols are somewhat of a misnomer. Routing protocols do not move data from one network segment to another, as the name implies; they dynamically discover and maintain routes in a router's routing information table. You can route data without using a routing protocol simply by creating and maintaining the appropriate routing tables on each router on your network. Doing so, however, is a tremendous amount of extra work if your network is large or changes often. Routing protocols can replace a manual process of route table maintenance.

Distance vector routing protocols use two factors for routes—the distance, in number of hops or routers that are crossed, to the destination network; and the vector, or direction of the interface, for that destination. This routing table is broadcast periodically from each router to its neighbors. When the table is large, this can be cumbersome.

Another issue with distance vector protocols is the susceptibility to routing loops. A routing loop occurs when a router's broadcast of a route is returned to itself by a neighboring router as if it were a new route. The router would then update its routing table and rebroadcast the route, and essentially the network would become flooded with multiple routers rebroadcasting the updates until the route reached an assumed unreachable distance (typically 16 hops). This network flood can cause a denial-of-service condition. Split horizon is a method used to counteract routing loops. Split horizon ensures that a router will not broadcast a route back to a neighboring router from which the route was learned. Poison reverse is a variation of the split horizon theme. In poison reverse, the router goes ahead and broadcasts the route back to the neighbor from where it learned the route, but it marks the route with an unreachable destination number of hops, so that the neighbor discards the route from its routing table.

One of the most common distance vector protocols used in the TCP/IP protocol stack is the Routing Information Protocol (RIP). RIP-2 is a newer version of RIP and is most often the version that is implemented. Both are referred to as RIP, however, so you really have to examine which version has been deployed.

Cisco's IOS supports the Interior Gateway Routing Protocol (IGRP) and the Enhanced Interior Gateway Routing Protocol (EIGRP) for routing IP traffic across an internetwork. To implement either of these protocols, the router at both ends of the network connection must understand and use IGRP or EIGRP. If you route between a Cisco router and a Windows 2000 server that is using RRAS, you will not be able to use either of these protocols.

Link-state routing protocols were developed to overcome some of the issues that distance vector protocols have. For example, a distance vector protocol is not easily scalable because of the fact that entire routing tables usually are transferred between neighboring routers. As a network grows, the routing table can become very cumbersome. In addition, though poison reverse and split horizon can combat some routing loops, distance vector protocols are still susceptible to them when there are slow links or redundant links in the internetwork because of the secondhand information exchanged between routers. Link-state protocols are scalable because they use a Link-State Update packet to advertise route changes on the internetwork. This means that only firsthand information is exchanged between routers, and only route changes are exchanged on a frequent basis rather than entire routing table transmissions between neighbors.

The link state protocol used in the TCP/IP protocol stack is Open Shortest Path First (OSPF). Both Cisco's IOS and Windows 2000 RRAS can implement OSPF.

Network Design

When designing a network, you need to consider the existing network, growth, and future network configuration. For example, if you have five offices in different cities where two are connected via WAN links and three are completely disconnected from the main office, you need to determine when and if those three offices need to be connected to the main office, what services they will need, and what type of link is appropriate for them. You should also discover whether you have existing remote users and if there is a need for future remote users. This process should result in a high-level overview of your network, similar to Figure 12.7.

The next step is to drill down into the physical layout of the various buildings. You should detail the floors and general map of buildings that will be connected. For each level, you should document

- Users
- Groups
- Applications
- Equipment needs
- Services
- Network protocols
- Network addressing
- Power
- Climate control
- Security

Figure 12.7 High-level WAN design.

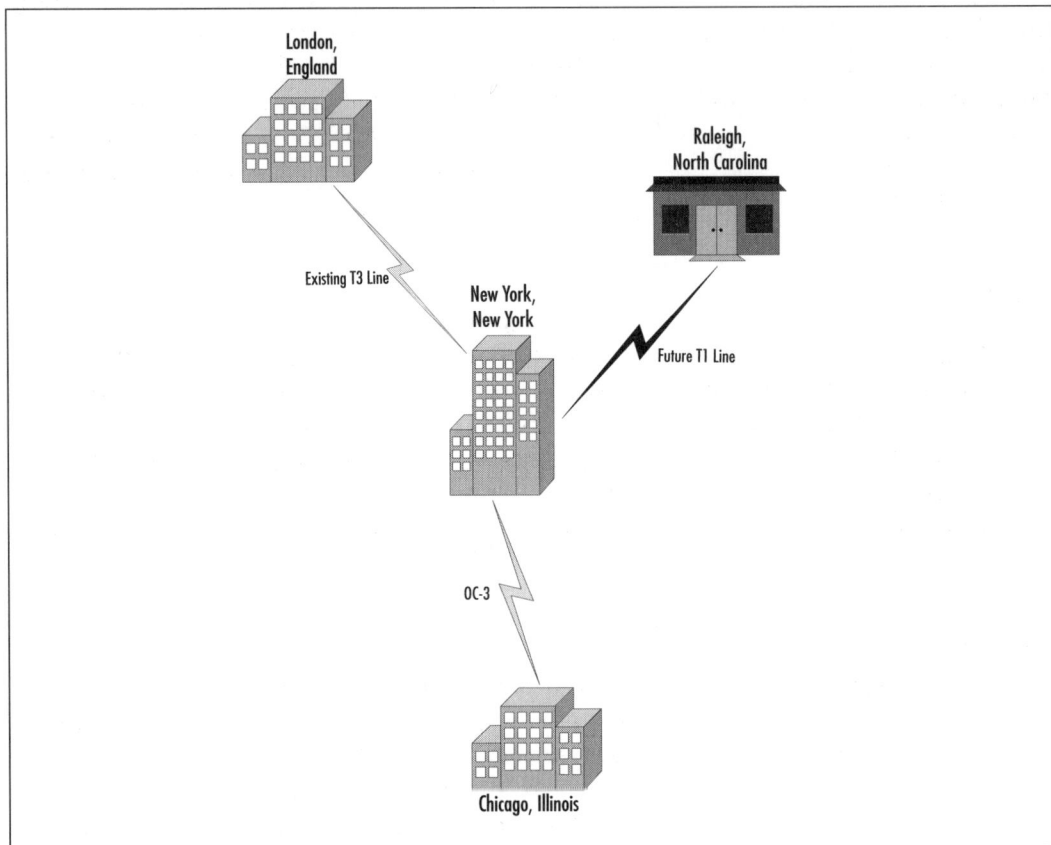

Then, you need to establish a baseline for bandwidth needs within each location and between each location. You should consider the growth of the business in each location when considering the needs for bandwidth.

The location of backbone or core layer routers should be decided as part of the design. In addition, the interfaces for each of the routers should be specified. Then, the location of distribution layer servers should be specified and switches and routers should be placed to separate that layer from the access layer where end-users will access the network. If there are workgroups in buildings or campuses that are not grouped together physically, you should consider establishing virtual local area networks (VLANs) and select appropriate switches to support them.

Your next task is selecting the routing protocol to be used by the routers in the network. You may decide to use a different routing protocol on the backbone at the core layer than you do for the distribution and access layers.

Segmentation

Designing an internetwork should be done with the intention of controlling the flow of traffic. A design for managing traffic flow should secondarily enable you to control the bandwidth consumption. At the access layer, there is no need for some data to be broadcast to some users. This is where segmentation comes into play. You can manage traffic flow, control bandwidth consumption, and direct traffic to where it must be received by segmenting the network.

NOTE

Segmentation avoids broadcast storms. A broadcast storm is a situation in which a network node transmits data packets to each network node in the broadcast domain simply because it does not have information about the destination network node. If the broadcast domain is set too large, the storm can interrupt the normal network traffic.

Redundancy and Failover

When you first begin to design, your goal is to reduce the amount of traffic that flows around the internetwork to the minimal amount that must be sent. When you finalize your design, your last task is to add redundancy and failover mechanisms to the network. This is counterintuitive, since up to now you've been reducing expenses (in terms of bandwidth consumption) and now you are adding them.

When you have your design in front of you, you need to look it over and start considering the effects of router loss. If you have a hub and spoke design for your network links, what happens if your central router fails? Will all remote sites lose connectivity to the network? If so, you should definitely place a backup router into your design. In many cases, however, you will simply need to consider a backup dialup link—placing appropriate serial interfaces on the routers that need this backup link.

When you use redundant routers, you should establish the Hot Standby Router Protocol (HSRP) to be used in case of failure. This will ensure that the failure of a router will automatically switch to the backup router and the network will continue functioning, seemingly without interruption to most end-users.

Summary

Computing technology is an ever-evolving phenomenon. Some people are obsessed with the latest and greatest technology innovations, whereas others use it as an enabler—to make their lives and businesses work better and faster than they would without that technology. It seems nearly impossible to keep up with the pace of technology changes, so when selecting technology you should do so with your business requirements in mind.

One of the business requirements that many people have is reducing the administrative overhead of a network. A network that "runs by itself," will cost far less than one that constantly requires a person to care for it. A homogenous environment, one in which the same type of technology—hardware and software—is deployed across the entire network, requires the least amount of administrative overhead because the number of problems encountered is reduced and the number of skill sets required is reduced.

Many businesses have implemented networks using both Cisco and Microsoft technologies. Because Cisco and Microsoft technologies are complementary as far as the duties that they perform on the network, they can be used in building a fairly homogenous environment.

These two companies jointly have developed and introduced the Directory Enabled Networks (DEN) initiative, launching it through the Distributed Management Task Force. DEN has fueled the development of Microsoft's Active Directory as well as Cisco's Network Services. Although still in the early stages of creating a directory-enabled homogenous environment, these technologies are beginning to provide us with a glimpse of future possibilities for networking!

FAQs

Q: Can anyone implement CNS today?

A: No. Cisco has introduced a controlled release of the first version of CNS. It is available to their partners, systems integrators, and independent software vendors. Future versions and future directory-enabled applications will be available to all customers.

Q: When is it appropriate to use a Windows 2000 Server as a router instead of using a Cisco router?

A: From the network design perspective, you should use highest-performing routers at the core layer of your network, so you would limit that to Cisco routers. Between the distribution and access layers, and for a small-office home office implementation, you might wish to use a Windows 2000 Server as your router. But if you are also using that server as a file and print server, a domain controller, or for other services, you would find that the performance will suffer on both sides. An 800 series Cisco router is far more functional and appropriate for this situation. In most cases, I wouldn't recommend it, but you really have to look at the requirements and your resources to make a qualified decision.

Q: Does CNS work with Novell's Directory Services or any other directory services?

A: At this writing, CNS only works with Microsoft's Active Directory.

Appendix

Sample FastStep Configuration File

The following file was produced using the Cisco FastStep application for an 800 series router. More about FastStep is discussed in Chapter 1.

```
[PC to Router Connection]
ConnectionType=2


[DHCP Server in Router]
SetRouterAsDHCPServerOnE0=0


[DHCP Relay Settings]
SetDHCPRelay=0
RemoteDHCPServerAddress=


[PC Settings]
UsePCGatewayAsRouterLANIP=0
SetAutomaticChangeIPStackWhenNeededByFastStep=1
SetChangeIPStackOnConsole=0
SetForceStaticAddressOnPCAlways=0
ForceStaticIPAddress=
ForceStaticIPMask=
UseRouterLANIPAsPCGateway=0
SetAdjustPCStackSettings=1


[Belle Systems]
SetBelleSystemSupport=0
RebootCount=-1
ISPSetupURL=http://www.cisco.com/go/faststep
ISPLocalURL=http://www.cisco.com
UniqueID=4


[Service Selection]
ShowTestConnectionButton=1
ShowTechSupportInfoButton=1
ISPSuccessText1=
```

```
ISPSuccessText2=

ISPSuccessText3=

ISPSuccessText4=

UniqueID=5


[Local LAN Ethernet0 Settings]

LANIPAddressE0=111.222.33.9

LANIPSubnetMaskE0=255.255.255.0


[Router Security]

RouterName=FastStepRtr

ReadonlyPassword=HELPME

EnablePassword=HELPME


[Setup Type]

SetRouterToDefaultConfig=1

SetSkipTesting=0

SetRunMonitorNow=0


[ISDN Settings]

EnableAOCTimeout=0

AOCShortHoldTimeOut=120

IdleTimeoutISP=300

LoadThresholdISP=10

HoldQueueISP=10


[Remote Phone]

RemotePhoneNumberISP1=

RemotePhoneNumberISP2=


[PPP Settings]

HideCentralRouternameISP=0

UserNameISP=

PasswordISP=
```

```
CentralRouterISP=

[NAT Settings]
HidePAT=0
HideAddressRange=0
HideNetworkAddress=0
FirstAddress=10.10.10.5
LastAddress=10.10.10.32
NetworkSubnetMask=255.255.255.192

[Remote Network Interface Settings]
WANIPAddressISP=10.10.10.33
WANIPSubnetMaskISP=255.255.255.192
AutomaticWANIPAddressDiscoverISP=3

[Local Internet Servers]
LocalWebServerAddress=111.222.33.4
ISPWebServerAddress=10.10.10.2
LocalMailServerAddress=111.222.33.5
ISPMailServerAddress=10.10.10.3
LocalFTPServerAddress=111.222.33.6
ISPFTPServerAddress=10.10.10.4

[Serial Settings]
HideProtocolNotSure=0

[Skipped Dialogs]
SkipToSetupandTest=0
PCToRouterConnection=0
ReviewSettings=0
SaveFileAs=0
StartMonitoring=0
TestingInterfaceConnectionISP=0
```

```
InternetServersEnableDMZ=0

InternetServerTypeSelection=0

InternetServersIPAddressGivenbyISP=0

RemoteConnectionType=0

SelectEncapsulationForSerialConn=0

PPPUserNameAndPasswordISP=0

InternetServersIPAddressRangeGivenByYourISP=0

WANIPAddressAndMaskISP=0

LanIPAddressAndMaskForEthernet0=0

UniqueID=6


[TechSupportInfoDetail]

Title=

PhoneDescription1=

PhoneDescription2=

PhoneDescription3=

PhoneDescription4=

Phone1=

Phone2=

Phone3=

Phone4=

EmailAddress=

ServiceProviderURL=


[Additional IOS Commands]

cmd1=


; ******************************************************************

; The flags below this line are private to Cisco Fast Step. Please do
not modify them.

; ******************************************************************


[RouterData]

SupportedService=10
```

```
ServiceSupportedMember(0)=9

ServiceSupportedMember(1)=21

ServiceSupportedMember(2)=23

ServiceSupportedMember(3)=20

ServiceSupportedMember(4)=16

ServiceSupportedMember(5)=5

ServiceSupportedMember(6)=15

ServiceSupportedMember(7)=13

ServiceSupportedMember(8)=14

ServiceSupportedMember(9)=7

RouterModel=C805

IOSVersion=

UserName=

UniqueIDCounter=65

SkipAllTests=1

FirewallGenned=1

InterfaceCount=2

InterfaceListItem(0)=Ethernet interface(0)

InterfaceListItem(1)=Serial interface(1)

LineListCount=2

LineListItem(0)=LINE_CONSOLE(0)

LineListItem(1)=LINE_VTY(1)

ServiceCount=10

ServiceListItem(0)=SERVICE_IPROUTING(0)

ServiceListItem(1)=SERVICE_FIREWALL(1)

ServiceListItem(2)=SERVICE_USER_LIST(2)

ServiceListItem(3)=SERVICE_DHCPSERVER(3)

ServiceListItem(4)=SERVICE_DNS(4)

ServiceListItem(5)=SERVICE_NAT(5)

ServiceListItem(6)=SERVICE_INETSERVER(6)

ServiceListItem(7)=SERVICE_IPACCESSLIST(7)

ServiceListItem(8)=SERVICE_IPACCESSLIST(8)

ServiceListItem(9)=SERVICE_IPACCESSLIST(9)

RouterMessageCount=0
```

```
GUISettingCount=2
GUISettingListItem(0)=CGUISetting(0)
GUISettingListItem(1)=CGUISetting(1)


[Router-M-Board]
CPU 5 Seconds=-1
CPU 1 Minute=-1
CPU 5 Minutes=-1
Memory Total=-1
Memory Free=-1
Memory Used=-1
UniqueID=2


[HVD]
UniqueID=1


[CurrentConnection]
UniqueID=0


[Ethernet interface(0)]
Type=4
InterfaceNumber=0
SlotNumber=-1
ShutdownFlag=0
SkipTestFlag=0
KeepAliveFlag=0
ProtectedFlag=0
Layer2NodeListCount=1
Layer2NodeListItem(0)=LAYER_2_ETHERNET(0)Ethernet interface(0)
UniqueID=10


[LAYER_2_ETHERNET(0)Ethernet interface(0)]
MACAddress=
BackupID=0
```

```
ParentID=10

Type=5

Destination Name=

Delay Backup Down=60

Delay Backup Up=5

Sub Interface Number=-1

Destination Type=1

RCN Type=3

Node Number=-1

SkipTest=0

Layer2Valid=1

Dunno Encaps=0

Layer 3 Node List Count=1

Layer 3 Node List Item(0)=IP Node(0)LAYER_2_ETHERNET(0)Ethernet interface(0)

UniqueID=19


[IP Node(0)LAYER_2_ETHERNET(0)Ethernet interface(0)]

IPUnnumberedInterfaceType=2

IPUnnumberedInterfaceNumber=-1

IPPoolEnabled=0

AddressSource=3

Type=2

UniqueID=20


[Serial interface(1)]

Type=7

InterfaceNumber=0

SlotNumber=-1

ShutdownFlag=0

SkipTestFlag=0

KeepAliveFlag=0

ProtectedFlag=0

Layer2NodeListCount=1

Layer2NodeListItem(0)=LAYER_2_PPP(0)Serial interface(1)
```

```
UniqueID=11

[LAYER_2_PPP(0)Serial interface(1)]
AuthenticationType=1
MultiLink=0
Callin=1
BackupID=0
ParentID=11
Type=2
Destination Name=
Delay Backup Down=60
Delay Backup Up=5
Sub Interface Number=-1
Destination Type=2
RCN Type=3
Node Number=-1
SkipTest=0
Layer2Valid=1
Dunno Encaps=0
Layer 3 Node List Count=1
Layer 3 Node List Item(0)=IP Node(0)LAYER_2_PPP(0)Serial interface(1)
UniqueID=17

[IP Node(0)LAYER_2_PPP(0)Serial interface(1)]
IPUnnumberedInterfaceType=2
IPUnnumberedInterfaceNumber=-1
IPPoolEnabled=0
DHCPServerEnabled=0
Type=2
UniqueID=18

[LINE_CONSOLE(0)]
Type=3
StartNumber=0
```

```
EndNumber=0
LoginType=-1
ExecTimeout=120
LoginPassword=
UniqueID=8


[LINE_VTY(1)]
Type=5
StartNumber=0
EndNumber=4
LoginType=3
ExecTimeout=0
LoginPassword=
UniqueID=9


[SERVICE_IPROUTING(0)]
DefaultGatewayID=11
DefaultGateway=
RoutingType=2
AutonomousSystem=-1
Area=-1
ProcessID=-1
IPRouterCache=1
IPProxyARP=0
IPClassless=1
RoutingLayer2NodeListCnt=2
RoutingInterfaceMember(0)=10
RoutingLayer2NodeMember(0)=19
RoutingInterfaceMember(1)=11
RoutingLayer2NodeMember(1)=17
StaticRouteListCnt=0
Type=9
SkipTestFlag=0
ServiceEnabled=1
```

```
UniqueID=12

[SERVICE_FIREWALL(1)]
sFirewallName=firewall
nTCPIdleTime=-1
nUDPIdleTime=-1
nNDNSTimeout=-1
InspectedProtocolListCnt=13
InspectedProtocolListCnt(0)=FirewallProtocol(0)SERVICE_FIREWALL(1)
InspectedProtocolListCnt(1)=FirewallProtocol(1)SERVICE_FIREWALL(1)
InspectedProtocolListCnt(2)=FirewallProtocol(2)SERVICE_FIREWALL(1)
InspectedProtocolListCnt(3)=FirewallProtocol(3)SERVICE_FIREWALL(1)
InspectedProtocolListCnt(4)=FirewallProtocol(4)SERVICE_FIREWALL(1)
InspectedProtocolListCnt(5)=FirewallProtocol(5)SERVICE_FIREWALL(1)
InspectedProtocolListCnt(6)=FirewallProtocol(6)SERVICE_FIREWALL(1)
InspectedProtocolListCnt(7)=FirewallProtocol(7)SERVICE_FIREWALL(1)
InspectedProtocolListCnt(8)=FirewallProtocol(8)SERVICE_FIREWALL(1)
InspectedProtocolListCnt(9)=FirewallProtocol(9)SERVICE_FIREWALL(1)
InspectedProtocolListCnt(10)=FirewallProtocol(10)SERVICE_FIREWALL(1)
InspectedProtocolListCnt(11)=FirewallProtocol(11)SERVICE_FIREWALL(1)
InspectedProtocolListCnt(12)=FirewallProtocol(12)SERVICE_FIREWALL(1)
InsideLayer2NodeListCnt=1
InsideInterfaceMember(0)=10
InsideLayer2NodeMember(0)=19
OutsideLayer2NodeListCnt=0
Type=15
SkipTestFlag=0
ServiceEnabled=1
UniqueID=13

[FirewallProtocol(0)SERVICE_FIREWALL(1)]
ProtocolType=4
TimeOut=-1
Maximum=-1
```

```
WaitTime=-1

ProgNum=-1

JavaList=-1

UniqueID=29


[FirewallProtocol(1)SERVICE_FIREWALL(1)]

ProtocolType=19

TimeOut=-1

Maximum=-1

WaitTime=-1

ProgNum=-1

JavaList=-1

UniqueID=30


[FirewallProtocol(2)SERVICE_FIREWALL(1)]

ProtocolType=5

TimeOut=-1

Maximum=-1

WaitTime=-1

ProgNum=-1

JavaList=-1

UniqueID=31


[FirewallProtocol(3)SERVICE_FIREWALL(1)]

ProtocolType=6

TimeOut=-1

Maximum=-1

WaitTime=-1

ProgNum=-1

JavaList=-1

UniqueID=32


[FirewallProtocol(4)SERVICE_FIREWALL(1)]

ProtocolType=7
```

```
TimeOut=-1

Maximum=-1

WaitTime=-1

ProgNum=-1

JavaList=-1

UniqueID=33


[FirewallProtocol(5)SERVICE_FIREWALL(1)]

ProtocolType=9

TimeOut=-1

Maximum=-1

WaitTime=-1

ProgNum=-1

JavaList=-1

UniqueID=34


[FirewallProtocol(6)SERVICE_FIREWALL(1)]

ProtocolType=11

TimeOut=-1

Maximum=-1

WaitTime=-1

ProgNum=-1

JavaList=-1

UniqueID=35


[FirewallProtocol(7)SERVICE_FIREWALL(1)]

ProtocolType=12

TimeOut=-1

Maximum=-1

WaitTime=-1

ProgNum=-1

JavaList=-1

UniqueID=36
```

```
[FirewallProtocol(8)SERVICE_FIREWALL(1)]
ProtocolType=13
TimeOut=-1
Maximum=-1
WaitTime=-1
ProgNum=-1
JavaList=-1
UniqueID=37


[FirewallProtocol(9)SERVICE_FIREWALL(1)]
ProtocolType=14
TimeOut=-1
Maximum=-1
WaitTime=-1
ProgNum=-1
JavaList=-1
UniqueID=38


[FirewallProtocol(10)SERVICE_FIREWALL(1)]
ProtocolType=15
TimeOut=-1
Maximum=-1
WaitTime=-1
ProgNum=-1
JavaList=-1
UniqueID=39


[FirewallProtocol(11)SERVICE_FIREWALL(1)]
ProtocolType=2
TimeOut=-1
Maximum=-1
WaitTime=-1
ProgNum=-1
JavaList=-1
```

```
UniqueID=40


[FirewallProtocol(12)SERVICE_FIREWALL(1)]

ProtocolType=3

TimeOut=-1

Maximum=-1

WaitTime=-1

ProgNum=-1

JavaList=-1

UniqueID=41


[SERVICE_USER_LIST(2)]

Type=16

SkipTestFlag=0

ServiceEnabled=1

UniqueID=14


[SERVICE_DHCPSERVER(3)]

DHCPPoolListCnt=0

ExcludedAddressRangeListCnt=0

Type=7

SkipTestFlag=0

ServiceEnabled=1

UniqueID=15


[SERVICE_DNS(4)]

DNSServerCnt=0

DNSTestTarget=www.cisco.com

Type=5

SkipTestFlag=0

ServiceEnabled=0

UniqueID=16


[SERVICE_NAT(5)]
```

```
Pool Name=ISPNATPool
nOutsideLayer2NodeID=17
Overloaded Flag=0
StaticTranslationListCount=3
StaticTranslationListItem(0)=StaticTranslation(0)SERVICE_NAT(5)
StaticTranslationListItem(1)=StaticTranslation(1)SERVICE_NAT(5)
StaticTranslationListItem(2)=StaticTranslation(2)SERVICE_NAT(5)
NatPoolListCount=1
NatPoolListItem(0)=NAT Pool(0)SERVICE_NAT(5)
InsideLayer2NodeListCnt=1
InsideLayer2NodeMember(0)=19
Type=13
SkipTestFlag=0
ServiceEnabled=1
UniqueID=22


[StaticTranslation(0)SERVICE_NAT(5)]
InsideIPAddress=111.222.33.4
OutsideIPAddress=10.10.10.2
InsidePort=80
OutsidePort=80
UniqueID=58


[StaticTranslation(1)SERVICE_NAT(5)]
InsideIPAddress=111.222.33.5
OutsideIPAddress=10.10.10.3
InsidePort=25
OutsidePort=25
UniqueID=59


[StaticTranslation(2)SERVICE_NAT(5)]
InsideIPAddress=111.222.33.6
OutsideIPAddress=10.10.10.4
InsidePort=21
```

```
OutsidePort=21
UniqueID=60


[NAT Pool(0)SERVICE_NAT(5)]
Pool Name=ISPNATPool
UniqueID=61


[SERVICE_INETSERVER(6)]
DMZ=0
ServerListCnt=3
ServerMember(0)=InetServer(0)SERVICE_INETSERVER(6)
ServerMember(1)=InetServer(1)SERVICE_INETSERVER(6)
ServerMember(2)=InetServer(2)SERVICE_INETSERVER(6)
Type=20
SkipTestFlag=0
ServiceEnabled=1
UniqueID=25


[InetServer(0)SERVICE_INETSERVER(6)]
ProtocolType=6
InsidePort=80
OutsidePort=80
InterfaceID=10
UniqueID=26


[InetServer(1)SERVICE_INETSERVER(6)]
ProtocolType=11
InsidePort=25
OutsidePort=25
InterfaceID=10
UniqueID=27


[InetServer(2)SERVICE_INETSERVER(6)]
ProtocolType=5
```

```
InsidePort=21
OutsidePort=21
InterfaceID=10
UniqueID=28


[SERVICE_IPACCESSLIST(7)]
ProtocolListCnt=1
ProtocolMember(0)=IPAccessListProtocol(0)SERVICE_IPACCESSLIST(7)
InsideLayer2NodeListCnt=1
InsideInterfaceMember(0)=10
InsideLayer2NodeMember(0)=19
OutsideLayer2NodeListCnt=0
Type=21
SkipTestFlag=0
ServiceEnabled=1
UniqueID=42


[IPAccessListProtocol(0)SERVICE_IPACCESSLIST(7)]
Source=111.222.33.0
SourceMask=0.0.0.255
Destination=0.0.0.0
DestinationMask=255.255.255.255
PermitOrDeny=2
Protocol=18
ICMPMessage=-1
SourcePort=-1
DestinationPort=-1
UniqueID=43


[SERVICE_IPACCESSLIST(8)]
ProtocolListCnt=10
ProtocolMember(0)=IPAccessListProtocol(0)SERVICE_IPACCESSLIST(8)
ProtocolMember(1)=IPAccessListProtocol(1)SERVICE_IPACCESSLIST(8)
ProtocolMember(2)=IPAccessListProtocol(2)SERVICE_IPACCESSLIST(8)
```

```
ProtocolMember(3)=IPAccessListProtocol(3)SERVICE_IPACCESSLIST(8)

ProtocolMember(4)=IPAccessListProtocol(4)SERVICE_IPACCESSLIST(8)

ProtocolMember(5)=IPAccessListProtocol(5)SERVICE_IPACCESSLIST(8)

ProtocolMember(6)=IPAccessListProtocol(6)SERVICE_IPACCESSLIST(8)

ProtocolMember(7)=IPAccessListProtocol(7)SERVICE_IPACCESSLIST(8)

ProtocolMember(8)=IPAccessListProtocol(8)SERVICE_IPACCESSLIST(8)

ProtocolMember(9)=IPAccessListProtocol(9)SERVICE_IPACCESSLIST(8)

InsideLayer2NodeListCnt=0

OutsideLayer2NodeListCnt=1

OutsideInterfaceMember(0)=10

OutsideLayer2NodeMember(0)=19

Type=21

SkipTestFlag=0

ServiceEnabled=1

UniqueID=44


[IPAccessListProtocol(0)SERVICE_IPACCESSLIST(8)]

Source=0.0.0.0

SourceMask=255.255.255.255

Destination=0.0.0.0

DestinationMask=255.255.255.255

PermitOrDeny=2

Protocol=17

ICMPMessage=1

SourcePort=-1

DestinationPort=-1

UniqueID=45


[IPAccessListProtocol(1)SERVICE_IPACCESSLIST(8)]

Source=0.0.0.0

SourceMask=255.255.255.255

Destination=0.0.0.0

DestinationMask=255.255.255.255

PermitOrDeny=2
```

```
Protocol=17

ICMPMessage=2

SourcePort=-1

DestinationPort=-1

UniqueID=46


[IPAccessListProtocol(2)SERVICE_IPACCESSLIST(8)]

Source=0.0.0.0

SourceMask=255.255.255.255

Destination=0.0.0.0

DestinationMask=255.255.255.255

PermitOrDeny=2

Protocol=17

ICMPMessage=3

SourcePort=-1

DestinationPort=-1

UniqueID=47


[IPAccessListProtocol(3)SERVICE_IPACCESSLIST(8)]

Source=0.0.0.0

SourceMask=255.255.255.255

Destination=0.0.0.0

DestinationMask=255.255.255.255

PermitOrDeny=2

Protocol=17

ICMPMessage=4

SourcePort=-1

DestinationPort=-1

UniqueID=48


[IPAccessListProtocol(4)SERVICE_IPACCESSLIST(8)]

Source=0.0.0.0

SourceMask=255.255.255.255

Destination=0.0.0.0
```

```
DestinationMask=255.255.255.255

PermitOrDeny=2

Protocol=17

ICMPMessage=5

SourcePort=-1

DestinationPort=-1

UniqueID=49


[IPAccessListProtocol(5)SERVICE_IPACCESSLIST(8)]

Source=0.0.0.0

SourceMask=255.255.255.255

Destination=0.0.0.0

DestinationMask=255.255.255.255

PermitOrDeny=2

Protocol=17

ICMPMessage=6

SourcePort=-1

DestinationPort=-1

UniqueID=50


[IPAccessListProtocol(6)SERVICE_IPACCESSLIST(8)]

Source=0.0.0.0

SourceMask=255.255.255.255

Destination=0.0.0.0

DestinationMask=255.255.255.255

PermitOrDeny=2

Protocol=17

ICMPMessage=7

SourcePort=-1

DestinationPort=-1

UniqueID=51


[IPAccessListProtocol(7)SERVICE_IPACCESSLIST(8)]

Source=0.0.0.0
```

```
SourceMask=255.255.255.255
Destination=111.222.33.4
DestinationMask=0.0.0.0
PermitOrDeny=2
Protocol=6
ICMPMessage=-1
SourcePort=0
DestinationPort=80
UniqueID=52


[IPAccessListProtocol(8)SERVICE_IPACCESSLIST(8)]
Source=0.0.0.0
SourceMask=255.255.255.255
Destination=111.222.33.5
DestinationMask=0.0.0.0
PermitOrDeny=2
Protocol=11
ICMPMessage=-1
SourcePort=0
DestinationPort=25
UniqueID=53


[IPAccessListProtocol(9)SERVICE_IPACCESSLIST(8)]
Source=0.0.0.0
SourceMask=255.255.255.255
Destination=111.222.33.6
DestinationMask=0.0.0.0
PermitOrDeny=2
Protocol=5
ICMPMessage=-1
SourcePort=0
DestinationPort=21
UniqueID=54
```

```
[SERVICE_IPACCESSLIST(9)]

ProtocolListCnt=2

ProtocolMember(0)=IPAccessListProtocol(0)SERVICE_IPACCESSLIST(9)

ProtocolMember(1)=IPAccessListProtocol(1)SERVICE_IPACCESSLIST(9)

InsideLayer2NodeListCnt=1

InsideInterfaceMember(0)=11

InsideLayer2NodeMember(0)=17

OutsideLayer2NodeListCnt=0

Type=21

SkipTestFlag=0

ServiceEnabled=1

UniqueID=55


[IPAccessListProtocol(0)SERVICE_IPACCESSLIST(9)]

Source=111.222.33.0

SourceMask=0.0.0.255

Destination=0.0.0.0

DestinationMask=255.255.255.255

PermitOrDeny=3

Protocol=18

ICMPMessage=-1

SourcePort=-1

DestinationPort=-1

UniqueID=56


[IPAccessListProtocol(1)SERVICE_IPACCESSLIST(9)]

Source=0.0.0.0

SourceMask=255.255.255.255

Destination=0.0.0.0

DestinationMask=255.255.255.255

PermitOrDeny=2

Protocol=18

ICMPMessage=-1

SourcePort=-1
```

```
DestinationPort=-1
UniqueID=57

[CGUISetting(0)]
Key=InstalledInterfaceCard
Value=
UniqueID=7

[CGUISetting(1)]
Key=ISP Range Type Key
Value=Using Range
UniqueID=21
```

Index

The Global Knowledge Advantage

Global Knowledge has a global delivery system for its products and services. The company has 28 subsidiaries, and offers its programs through a total of 60+ locations. No other vendor can provide consistent services across a geographic area this large. Global Knowledge is the largest independent information technology education provider, offering programs on a variety of platforms. This enables our multi-platform and multi-national customers to obtain all of their programs from a single vendor. The company has developed the unique CompetusTM Framework software tool and methodology which can quickly reconfigure courseware to the proficiency level of a student on an interactive basis. Combined with self-paced and on-line programs, this technology can reduce the time required for training by prescribing content in only the deficient skills areas. The company has fully automated every aspect of the education process, from registration and follow-up, to "just-in-time" production of courseware. Global Knowledge through its Enterprise Services Consultancy, can customize programs and products to suit the needs of an individual customer.

Global Knowledge Classroom Education Programs

The backbone of our delivery options is classroom-based education. Our modern, well-equipped facilities staffed with the finest instructors offer programs in a wide variety of information technology topics, many of which lead to professional certifications.

Custom Learning Solutions

This delivery option has been created for companies and governments that value customized learning solutions. For them, our consultancy-based approach of developing targeted education solutions is most effective at helping them meet specific objectives.

Self-Paced and Multimedia Products

This delivery option offers self-paced program titles in interactive CD-ROM, videotape and audio tape programs. In addition, we offer custom development of interactive multimedia courseware to customers and partners. Call us at 1-888-427-4228.

Electronic Delivery of Training

Our network-based training service delivers efficient competency-based, interactive training via the World Wide Web and organizational intranets. This leading-edge delivery option provides a custom learning path and "just-in-time" training for maximum convenience to students.

Global Knowledge Courses Available

Microsoft
- Windows 2000 Deployment Strategies
- Introduction to Directory Services
- Windows 2000 Client Administration
- Windows 2000 Server
- Windows 2000 Update
- MCSE Bootcamp
- Microsoft Networking Essentials
- Windows NT 4.0 Workstation
- Windows NT 4.0 Server
- Windows NT Troubleshooting
- Windows NT 4.0 Security
- Windows 2000 Security
- Introduction to Microsoft Web Tools

Management Skills
- Project Management for IT Professionals
- Microsoft Project Workshop
- Management Skills for IT Professionals

Network Fundamentals
- Understanding Computer Networks
- Telecommunications Fundamentals I
- Telecommunications Fundamentals II
- Understanding Networking Fundamentals
- Upgrading and Repairing PCs
- DOS/Windows A+ Preparation
- Network Cabling Systems

WAN Networking and Telephony
- Building Broadband Networks
- Frame Relay Internetworking
- Converging Voice and Data Networks
- Introduction to Voice Over IP
- Understanding Digital Subscriber Line (xDSL)

Internetworking
- ATM Essentials
- ATM Internetworking
- ATM Troubleshooting
- Understanding Networking Protocols
- Internetworking Routers and Switches
- Network Troubleshooting
- Internetworking with TCP/IP
- Troubleshooting TCP/IP Networks
- Network Management
- Network Security Administration
- Virtual Private Networks
- Storage Area Networks
- Cisco OSPF Design and Configuration
- Cisco Border Gateway Protocol (BGP) Configuration

Web Site Management and Development
- Advanced Web Site Design
- Introduction to XML
- Building a Web Site
- Introduction to JavaScript
- Web Development Fundamentals
- Introduction to Web Databases

PERL, UNIX, and Linux
- PERL Scripting
- PERL with CGI for the Web
- UNIX Level I
- UNIX Level II
- Introduction to Linux for New Users
- Linux Installation, Configuration, and Maintenance

Authorized Vendor Training
Red Hat
- Introduction to Red Hat Linux
- Red Hat Linux Systems Administration
- Red Hat Linux Network and Security Administration
- RHCE Rapid Track Certification

Cisco Systems
- Interconnecting Cisco Network Devices
- Advanced Cisco Router Configuration
- Installation and Maintenance of Cisco Routers
- Cisco Internetwork Troubleshooting
- Designing Cisco Networks
- Cisco Internetwork Design
- Configuring Cisco Catalyst Switches
- Cisco Campus ATM Solutions
- Cisco Voice Over Frame Relay, ATM, and IP
- Configuring for Selsius IP Phones
- Building Cisco Remote Access Networks
- Managing Cisco Network Security
- Cisco Enterprise Management Solutions

Nortel Networks
- Nortel Networks Accelerated Router Configuration
- Nortel Networks Advanced IP Routing
- Nortel Networks WAN Protocols
- Nortel Networks Frame Switching
- Nortel Networks Accelar 1000
- Comprehensive Configuration
- Nortel Networks Centillion Switching
- Network Management with Optivity for Windows

Oracle Training
- Introduction to Oracle8 and PL/SQL
- Oracle8 Database Administration

Custom Corporate Network Training

Train on Cutting Edge Technology
We can bring the best in skill-based training to your facility to create a real-world hands-on training experience. Global Knowledge has invested millions of dollars in network hardware and software to train our students on the same equipment they will work with on the job. Our relationships with vendors allow us to incorporate the latest equipment and platforms into your on-site labs.

Maximize Your Training Budget
Global Knowledge provides experienced instructors, comprehensive course materials, and all the networking equipment needed to deliver high quality training. You provide the students; we provide the knowledge.

Avoid Travel Expenses
On-site courses allow you to schedule technical training at your convenience, saving time, expense, and the opportunity cost of travel away from the workplace.

Discuss Confidential Topics
Private on-site training permits the open discussion of sensitive issues such as security, access, and network design. We can work with your existing network's proprietary files while demonstrating the latest technologies.

Customize Course Content
Global Knowledge can tailor your courses to include the technologies and the topics which have the greatest impact on your business. We can complement your internal training efforts or provide a total solution to your training needs.

Corporate Pass
The Corporate Pass Discount Program rewards our best network training customers with preferred pricing on public courses, discounts on multimedia training packages, and an array of career planning services.

Global Knowledge Training Lifecycle
Supporting the Dynamic and Specialized Training Requirements of Information Technology Professionals

- Define Profile
- Assess Skills
- Design Training
- Deliver Training
- Test Knowledge
- Update Profile
- Use New Skills

Global Knowledge

Global Knowledge programs are developed and presented by industry professionals with "real-world" experience. Designed to help professionals meet today's interconnectivity and interoperability challenges, most of our programs feature hands-on labs that incorporate state-of-the-art communication components and equipment.

ON-SITE TEAM TRAINING

Bring Global Knowledge's powerful training programs to your company. At Global Knowledge, we will custom design courses to meet your specific network requirements. Call (919)-461-8686 for more information.

YOUR GUARANTEE

Global Knowledge believes its courses offer the best possible training in this field. If during the first day you are not satisfied and wish to withdraw from the course, simply notify the instructor, return all course materials and receive a 100% refund.

REGISTRATION INFORMATION

In the US:
call: (888) 762–4442
fax: (919) 469–7070
visit our website:
www.globalknowledge.com

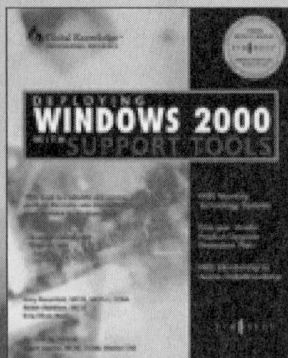